C++ Primer
Fourth Edition

C++ *Primer*
Fourth Edition

Stanley B. Lippman
Josée Lajoie
Barbara E. Moo

♦▾Addison-Wesley

Upper Saddle River, NJ • Boston • Indianapolis • San Francisco
New York • Toronto • Montreal • London • Munich • Paris • Madrid
Capetown • Sidney • Tokyo • Singapore • Mexico City

The publisher offers excellent discounts on this book when ordered in quantity for bulk purchases or special sales, which may include electronic versions and/or custom covers and content particular to your business, training goals, marketing focus, and branding interests. For more information, please contact:

U. S. Corporate and Government Sales
(800) 382-3419
corpsales@pearsontechgroup.com

For sales outside the U. S., please contact:

International Sales
international@pearsoned.com

Visit us on the Web: www.awprofessional.com

Library of Congress Cataloging-in-Publication Data

Lippman, Stanley B.
  C++ primer / Stanley B. Lippman, Josée Lajoie, Barbara E. Moo. — 4th ed.
    p.   cm.
  Includes index.
  ISBN 0-201-72148-1 (pbk. : alk. paper)
  1. C++ (Computer program language) I. Lajoie, Josée. II. Moo, Barbara E. III. Title.

QA76.73.C153L57697 2005
005.13'3–dc22   2004029301

ISBN 0-201-72148-1
Text printed in the United States on recycled paper at Courier in Stoughton, Massachusetts.
First printing, February 2005

To Beth,
who makes this,
and all things,
possible.

———

To Daniel and Anna,
who contain
virtually
all possiblities.
—SBL

To Mark and Mom,
for their
unconditional love and support.
—JL

To Andy,
who taught me
to program
and so much more.
—BEM

Contents

Preface

C++ Primer, Fourth Edition, provides a comprehensive introduction to the C++ language. As a primer, it provides a clear tutorial approach to the language, enhanced by numerous examples and other learning aids. Unlike most primers, it also provides a detailed description of the language, with particular emphasis on current and effective programming techniques.

Countless programmers have used previous editions of *C++ Primer* to learn C++. In that time C++ has matured greatly. Over the years, the focus of the language—and of C++ programmers—has grown beyond a concentration on run-time efficiency to focus on ways of making *programmers* more efficient. With the widespread availability of the standard library, it is possible to use and learn C++ more effectively than in the past. This revision of the *C++ Primer* reflects these new possiblities.

Changes to the Fourth Edition

In this edition, we have completely reorganized and rewritten the *C++ Primer* to highlight modern styles of C++ programming. This edition gives center stage to using the standard library while deemphasizing techniques for low-level programming. We introduce the standard library much earlier in the text and have reformulated the examples to take advantage of library facilities. We have also streamlined and reordered the presentation of language topics.

In addition to restructuring the text, we have incorporated several new elements to enhance the reader's understanding. Each chapter concludes with a Chapter Summary and glossary of Defined Terms, which recap the chapter's most important points. Readers should use these sections as a personal checklist: If you do not understand a term, restudy the corresponding part of the chapter.

We've also incorporated a number of other learning aids in the body of the text:

- Important terms are indicated in **bold**; important terms that we assume are already familiar to the reader are indicated in ***bold italics***. Each term appears in the chapter's Defined Terms section.

- Throughout the book, we highlight parts of the text to call attention to important aspects of the language, warn about common pitfalls, suggest good programming practices, and provide general usage tips. We hope that these notes will help readers more quickly digest important concepts and avoid common pitfalls.

- To make it easier to follow the relationships among features and concepts, we provide extensive forward and backward cross-references.

- We have provided sidebar discussions that focus on important concepts and supply additional explanations for topics that programmers new to C++ often find most difficult.

- Learning any programming language requires writing programs. To that end, the primer provides extensive examples throughout the text. Source code for the extended examples is available on the Web at the following URL:

      http://www.awprofessional.com/cpp_primer

What hasn't changed from earlier versions is that the book remains a comprehensive tutorial introduction to C++. Our intent is to provide a clear, complete and correct guide to the language. We teach the language by presenting a series of examples, which, in addition to explaining language features, show how to make the best use of C++. Although knowledge of C (the language on which C++ was originally based) is not assumed, we do assume the reader has programmed in a modern block-structured language.

Structure of This Book

C++ Primer provides an introduction to the International Standard on C++, covering both the language proper and the extensive library that is part of that standard. Much of the power of C++ comes from its support for programming with abstractions. Learning to program effectively in C++ requires more than learning new syntax and semantics. Our focus is on how to use the features of C++ to write programs that are safe, that can be built quickly, and yet offer performance comparable to the sorts of low-level programs often written in C.

C++ is a large language and can be daunting to new users. Modern C++ can be thought of as comprising three parts:

- The low-level language, largely inherited from C

- More advanced language features that allow us to define our own data types and to organize large-scale programs and systems

- The standard library, which uses these advanced features to provide a set of useful data structures and algorithms

Most texts present C++ in this same order: They start by covering the low-level details and then introduce the the more advanced language features. They explain the standard library only after having covered the entire language. The result, all too often, is that readers get bogged down in issues of low-level programming or the complexities of writing type definitions and never really understand the power of programming in a more abstract way. Needless to say, readers also often do not learn enough to build their own abstractions.

In this edition we take a completely different tack. We start by covering the basics of the language and the library together. Doing so allows you, the reader, to write significant programs. Only after a thorough grounding in using the library—and writing the kinds of abstract programs that the libary allows—do we move on to those features of C++ that will enable you to write your own abstractions.

Parts I and II cover the basic language and library facilities. The focus of these parts is to learn how to write C++ programs and how to use the abstractions from the library. Most C++ programmers need to know essentially everything covered in this portion of the book.

In addition to teaching the basics of C++, the material in Parts I and II serves another important purpose. The library facilities are themselves abstract data types written in C++. The library can be defined using the same class-construction features that are available to any C++ programmer. Our experience in teaching C++ is that by first using well-designed abstract types, readers find it easier to understand how to build their own types.

Parts III through V focus on how we can write our own types. Part III introduces the heart of C++: its support for classes. The class mechanism provides the basis for writing our own abstractions. Classes are also the foundation for object-oriented and generic programming, which we cover in Part IV. The *Primer* concludes with Part V, which covers advanced features that are of most use in structuring large, complex systems.

Acknowledgments

As in previous editions of this *Primer*, we'd like to extend our thanks to Bjarne Stroustrup for his tireless work on C++ and for his friendship to these authors throughout most of that time. We'd also like to thank Alex Stepanov for his original insights that led to the containers and algorithms that form the core of the standard library. Finally, our thanks go to the C++ Standards committee members for their hard work in clarifying, refining, and improving C++ over many years.

We also extend our deep-felt thanks to our reviewers, whose helpful comments on multiple drafts led us to make improvements great and small throughout the book: Paul Abrahams, Michael Ball, Mary Dageforde, Paul DuBois, Matt Greenwood, Matthew P. Johnson, Andrew Koenig, Nevin Liber, Bill Locke, Robert Murray, Phil Romanik, Justin Shaw, Victor Shtern, Clovis Tondo, Daveed Vandevoorde, and Steve Vinoski.

This book was typeset using LATEX and the many packages that accompany the LATEX distribution. Our well-justified thanks go to the members of the LATEX community, who have made available such powerful typesetting tools.

The examples in this book have been compiled on the GNU and Microsoft compilers. Our thanks to their developers, and to those who have developed all the other C++ compilers, thereby making C++ a reality.

Finally, we thank the fine folks at Addison-Wesley who have shepherded this edition through the publishing process: Debbie Lafferty, our original editor, who initiated this edition and who had been with the *Primer* from its very first edition; Peter Gordon, our new editor, whose insistence on updating and streamlining the text have, we hope, greatly improved the presentation; Kim Boedigheimer, who keeps us all on schedule; and Tyrrell Albaugh, Jim Markham, Elizabeth Ryan, and John Fuller, who saw us through the design and production process.

CHAPTER 1

GETTING STARTED

CONTENTS

This chapter introduces most of the basic elements of C++: built-in, library, and class types; variables; expressions; statements; and functions. Along the way, we'll briefly explain how to compile and execute a program.

Having read this chapter and worked through the exercises, the reader should be able to write, compile, and execute simple programs. Subsequent chapters will explain in more detail the topics introduced here.

1

Learning a new programming language requires writing programs. In this chapter, we'll write a program to solve a simple problem that represents a common data-processing task: A bookstore keeps a file of transactions, each of which records the sale of a given book. Each transaction contains an ISBN (International Standard Book Number, a unique identifier assigned to most books published throughout the world), the number of copies sold, and the price at which each copy was sold. Each transaction looks like

```
0-201-70353-X 4 24.99
```

where the first element is the ISBN, the second is the number of books sold, and the last is the sales price. Periodically the bookstore owner reads this file and computes the number of copies of each title sold, the total revenue from that book, and the average sales price. We want to supply a program do these computations.

Before we can write this program we need to know some basic features of C++. At a minimum we'll need to know how to write, compile, and execute a simple program. What must this program do? Although we have not yet designed our solution, we know that the program must

- Define variables

- Do input and output

- Define a data structure to hold the data we're managing

- Test whether two records have the same ISBN

- Write a loop that will process every record in the transaction file

We'll start by reviewing these parts of C++ and then write a solution to our bookstore problem.

1.1 Writing a Simple C++ Program

Every C++ program contains one or more *functions*, one of which must be named **main**. A function consists of a sequence of *statements* that perform the work of the function. The operating system executes a program by calling the function named `main`. That function executes its constituent statements and returns a value to the operating system.

Here is a simple version of `main` does nothing but return a value:

```
int main()
{
    return 0;
}
```

The operating system uses the value returned by `main` to determine whether the program succeeded or failed. A return value of 0 indicates success.

The `main` function is special in various ways, the most important of which are that the function must exist in every C++ program and it is the (only) function that the operating system explicitly calls.

We define `main` the same way we define other functions. A function definition specifies four elements: the ***return type***, the ***function name***, a (possibly empty) ***parameter list*** enclosed in parentheses, and the ***function body***. The `main` function may have only a restricted set of parameters. As defined here, the parameter list is empty; Section 7.2.6 (p. 243) will cover the other parameters that can be defined for `main`.

The `main` function is required to have a return type of `int`, which is the type that represents integers. The `int` type is a **built-in type**, which means that the type is defined by the language.

The final part of a function definition, the function body, is a ***block*** of statements starting with an open **curly brace** and ending with a close curly:

```
{
    return 0;
}
```

The only statement in our program is a `return`, which is a statement that terminates a function.

Note the semicolon at the end of the `return` statement. Semicolons mark the end of most statements in C++. They are easy to overlook, but when forgotten can lead to mysterious compiler error messages.

When the `return` includes a value such as `0`, that value is the return value of the function. The value returned must have the same type as the return type of the function or be a type that can be converted to that type. In the case of `main` the return type must be `int`, and the value `0` is an `int`.

On most systems, the return value from `main` is a status indicator. A return value of `0` indicates the successful completion of `main`. Any other return value has a meaning that is defined by the operating system. Usually a nonzero return indicates that an error occurred. Each operating system has its own way of telling the user what `main` returned.

1.1.1 Compiling and Executing Our Program

Having written the program, we need to compile it. How you compile a program depends on your operating system and compiler. For details on how your particular compiler works, you'll need to check the reference manual or ask a knowledgeable colleague.

Many PC-based compilers are run from an integrated development environment (IDE) that bundles the compiler with associated build and analysis tools. These environments can be a great asset in developing complex programs but require a fair bit of time to learn how to use effectively. Most of these environments include a point-and-click interface that allows the programmer to write a program and use various menus to compile and execute the program. Learning how to use such environments is well beyond the scope of this book.

Most compilers, including those that come with an IDE, provide a command-line interface. Unless you are already familiar with using your compiler's IDE, it can be easier to start by using the simpler, command-line interface. Using the command-line interface lets you avoid the overhead of learning the IDE before learning the language.

Program Source File Naming Convention

Whether we are using a command-line interface or an IDE, most compilers expect that the program we want to compile will be stored in a file. Program files are referred to as **source files**. On most systems, a source file has a name that consists of two parts: a file name—for example, `prog1`—and a file suffix. By convention, the suffix indicates that the file is a program. The suffix often also indicates what language the program is written in and selects which compiler to run. The system that we used to compile the examples in this book treats a file with a suffix of `.cc` as a C++ program and so we stored this program as

        prog1.cc

The suffix for C++ program files depends on which compiler you're running. Other conventions include

        prog1.cxx
        prog1.cpp
        prog1.cp
        prog1.C

INVOKING THE GNU OR MICROSOFT COMPILERS

The command used to invoke the C++ compiler varies across compilers and operating systems. The most common compilers are the GNU compiler and the Microsoft Visual Studio compilers. By default the command to invoke the GNU compiler is g++:

        $ g++ prog1.cc -o prog1

where $ is the system prompt. This command generates an executable file named `prog1` or `prog1.exe`, depending on the operating system. On UNIX, executable files have no suffix; on Windows, the suffix is `.exe`. The `-o prog1` is an argument to the compiler and names the file in which to put the executable file. If the `-o prog1` is omitted, then the compiler generates an executable named `a.out` on UNIX systems and `a.exe` on Windows.

The Microsoft compilers are invoked using the command `cl`:

        C:\directory> cl -GX prog1.cpp

where `C:directory>` is the system prompt and `directory` is the name of the current directory. The command to invoke the compiler is `cl`, and `-GX` is an option that is required for programs compiled using the command-line interface. The Microsoft compiler automatically generates an executable with a name that corresponds to the source file name. The executable has the suffix `.exe` and the same name as the source file name. In this case, the executable is named `prog1.exe`.

For further information consult your compiler's user's guide.

Running the Compiler from the Command Line

If we are using a command-line interface, we will typically compile a program in a console window (such as a shell window on a UNIX system or a Command Prompt window on Windows). Assuming that our `main` program is in a file named `prog1.cc`, we might compile it by using a command such as:

```
$ CC prog1.cc
```

where `CC` names the compiler and `$` represents the system prompt. The output of the compiler is an executable file that we invoke by naming it. On our system, the compiler generates the executable in a file named `a.exe`. UNIX compilers tend to put their executables in a file named `a.out`. To run an executable we supply that name at the command-line prompt:

```
$ a.exe
```

executes the program we compiled. On UNIX systems you sometimes must also specify which directory the file is in, even if it is in the current directory. In such cases, we would write

```
$ ./a.exe
```

The "`.`" followed by a slash indicates that the file is in the current directory.

The value returned from `main` is accessed in a system-dependent manner. On both UNIX and Windows systems, after executing the program, you must issue an appropriate `echo` command. On UNIX systems, we obtain the status by writing

```
$ echo $?
```

To see the status on a Windows system, we write

```
C:\directory> echo %ERRORLEVEL%
```

EXERCISES SECTION 1.1.1

Exercise 1.1: Review the documentation for your compiler and determine what file naming convention it uses. Compile and run the `main` program from page 2.

Exercise 1.2: Change the program to return `-1`. A return value of `-1` is often treated as an indicator that the program failed. However, systems vary as to how (or even whether) they report a failure from `main`. Recompile and rerun your program to see how your system treats a failure indicator from `main`.

1.2   A First Look at Input/Output

C++ does not directly define any statements to do input or output (IO). Instead, IO is provided by the **standard library**. The IO library provides an extensive set of facilities. However, for many purposes, including the examples in this book, one needs to know only a few basic concepts and operations.

Most of the examples in this book use the **iostream library**, which handles formatted input and output. Fundamental to the iostream library are two types named **istream** and **ostream**, which represent input and output streams, respectively. A stream is a sequence of characters intended to be read from or written to an IO device of some kind. The term "stream" is intended to suggest that the characters are generated, or consumed, sequentially over time.

1.2.1   Standard Input and Output Objects

The library defines four IO objects. To handle input, we use an object of type istream named **cin** (pronounced "see-in"). This object is also referred to as the **standard input**. For output, we use an ostream object named **cout** (pronounced "see-out"). It is often referred to as the **standard output**. The library also defines two other ostream objects, named **cerr** and **clog** (pronounced "see-err" and "see-log," respectively). The cerr object, referred to as the **standard error**, is typically used to generate warning and error messages to users of our programs. The clog object is used for general information about the execution of the program.

Ordinarily, the system associates each of these objects with the window in which the program is executed. So, when we read from cin, data is read from the window in which the program is executing, and when we write to cout, cerr, or clog, the output is written to the same window. Most operating systems give us a way of redirecting the input or output streams when we run a program. Using redirection we can associate these streams with files of our choosing.

1.2.2   A Program that Uses the IO Library

So far, we have seen how to compile and execute a simple program, although that program did no work. In our overall problem, we'll have several records that refer to the same ISBN. We'll need to consolidate those records into a single total, implying that we'll need to know how to add the quantities of books sold.

To see how to solve part of that problem, let's start by looking at how we might add two numbers. Using the IO library, we can extend our main program to ask the user to give us two numbers and then print their sum:

```
#include <iostream>
int main()
{
    std::cout << "Enter two numbers:" << std::endl;
    int v1, v2;
    std::cin >> v1 >> v2;
    std::cout << "The sum of " << v1 << " and " << v2
              << " is " << v1 + v2 << std::endl;
    return 0;
}
```

This program starts by printing

```
Enter two numbers:
```

on the user's screen and then waits for input from the user. If the user enters

```
3 7
```

followed by a newline, then the program produces the following output:

```
The sum of 3 and 7 is 10
```

The first line of our program is a **preprocessor directive**:

```
#include <iostream>
```

which tells the compiler that we want to use the `iostream` library. The name inside angle brackets is a **header**. Every program that uses a library facility must include its associated header. The `#include` directive must be written on a single line—the name of the header and the `#include` must appear on the same line. In general, `#include` directives should appear outside any function. Typically, all the `#include` directives for a program appear at the beginning of the file.

Writing to a Stream

The first statement in the body of `main` executes an **expression**. In C++ an expression is composed of one or more operands and (usually) an operator. The expressions in this statement use the **output operator** (the `<<` operator) to print the prompt on the standard output:

```
std::cout << "Enter two numbers:" << std::endl;
```

This statement uses the output operator twice. Each instance of the output operator takes two operands: The left-hand operand must be an `ostream` object; the right-hand operand is a value to print. The operator writes its right-hand operand to the `ostream` that is its left-hand operand.

In C++ every expression produces a result, which typically is the value generated by applying an operator to its operands. In the case of the output operator, the result is the value of its left-hand operand. That is, the value returned by an output operation is the output stream itself.

The fact that the operator returns its left-hand operand allows us to chain together output requests. The statement that prints our prompt is equivalent to

```
(std::cout << "Enter two numbers:") << std::endl;
```

Because `(std::cout << "Enter two numbers:")` returns its left operand, `std::cout`, this statement is equivalent to

```
std::cout << "Enter two numbers:";
std::cout << std::endl;
```

endl is a special value, called a **manipulator**, that when written to an output stream has the effect of writing a newline to the output and flushing the *buffer* associated with that device. By flushing the buffer, we ensure that the user will see the output written to the stream immediately.

Programmers often insert print statements during debugging. Such statements should always flush the stream. Forgetting to do so may cause output to be left in the buffer if the program crashes, leading to incorrect inferences about where the program crashed.

Using Names from the Standard Library

Careful readers will note that this program uses std::cout and std::endl rather than just cout and endl. The prefix std:: indicates that the names cout and endl are defined inside the **namespace** named **std**. Namespaces allow programmers to avoid inadvertent collisions with the same names defined by a library. Because the names that the standard library defines are defined in a namespace, we can use the same names for our own purposes.

One side effect of the library's use of a namespace is that when we use a name from the library, we must say explicitly that we want to use the name from the std namespace. Writing std::cout uses the **scope operator** (the :: operator) to say that we want to use the name cout that is defined in the namespace std. We'll see in Section 3.1 (p. 78) a way that programs often use to avoid this verbose syntax.

Reading From a Stream

Having written our prompt, we next want to read what the user writes. We start by defining two *variables* named v1 and v2 to hold the input:

```
int v1, v2;
```

We define these variables as type int, which is the built-in type representing integral values. These variables are *uninitialized*, meaning that we gave them no initial value. Our first use of these variables will be to read a value into them, so the fact that they have no initial value is okay.

The next statement

```
std::cin >> v1 >> v2;
```

reads the input. The **input operator** (the >> operator) behaves analogously to the output operator. It takes an istream as its left-hand operand and an object as its right-hand operand. It reads from its istream operand and stores the value it read in its right-hand operand. Like the output operator, the input operator returns its left-hand operand as its result. Because the operator returns its left-hand operand, we can combine a sequence of input requests into a single statement. In other words, this input operation is equivalent to

```
std::cin >> v1;
std::cin >> v2;
```

The effect of our input operation is to read two values from the standard input, storing the first in v1 and the second in v2.

Completing the Program

What remains is to print our result:

```
std::cout << "The sum of " << v1 << " and " << v2
          << " is " << v1 + v2 << std::endl;
```

This statement, although it is longer than the statement that printed the prompt, is conceptually no different. It prints each of its operands to the standard output. What is interesting is that the operands are not all the same kinds of values. Some operands are **string literals**, such as

```
"The sum of "
```

and others are various int values, such as v1, v2, and the result of evaluating the arithmetic expression:

```
v1 + v2
```

The iostream library defines versions of the input and output operators that accept all of the built-in types.

When writing a C++ program, in most places that a space appears we could instead use a newline. One exception to this rule is that spaces inside a string literal cannot be replaced by a newline. Another exception is that spaces are not allowed inside preprocessor directives.

KEY CONCEPT: INITIALIZED AND UNINITIALIZED VARIABLES

Initialization is an important concept in C++ and one to which we will return throughout this book.

Initialized variables are those that are given a value when they are defined. Uninitialized variables are not given an initial value:

```
int val1 = 0;      // initialized
int val2;          // uninitialized
```

It is almost always right to give a variable an initial value, but we are not required to do so. When we are certain that the first use of a variable gives it a new value, then there is no need to invent an initial value. For example, our first nontrivial program on page 6 defined uninitialized variables into which we immediately read values.

When we define a variable, we should give it an initial value unless we are *certain* that the initial value will be overwritten before the variable is used for any other purpose. If we cannot guarantee that the variable will be reset before being read, we should initialize it.

EXERCISES SECTION 1.2.2

Exercise 1.3: Write a program to print "Hello, World" on the standard output.

Exercise 1.4: Our program used the built-in addition operator, +, to generate the sum of two numbers. Write a program that uses the multiplication operator, *, to generate the product of two numbers.

Exercise 1.5: We wrote the output in one large statement. Rewrite the program to use a separate statement to print each operand.

Exercise 1.6: Explain what the following program fragment does:

```
std::cout << "The sum of " << v1;
          << " and " << v2;
          << " is " << v1 + v2
          << std::endl;
```

Is this code legal? If so, why? If not, why not?

1.3 A Word About Comments

Before our programs get much more complicated, we should see how C++ handles *comments*. Comments help the human readers of our programs. They are typically used to summarize an algorithm, identify the purpose of a variable, or clarify an otherwise obscure segment of code. Comments do not increase the size of the executable program. The compiler ignores all comments.

 In this book, we italicize comments to make them stand out from the normal program text. In actual programs, whether comment text is distinguished from the text used for program code depends on the sophistication of the programming environment.

There are two kinds of comments in C++: single-line and paired. A single-line comment starts with a double slash (//). Everything to the right of the slashes on the current line is a comment and ignored by the compiler.

The other delimiter, the comment pair (/* */), is inherited from the C language. Such comments begin with a /* and end with the next */. The compiler treats everything that falls between the /* and */ as part of the comment:

```
#include <iostream>
/* Simple main function: Read two numbers and write their sum   */
int main()
{
    // prompt user to enter two numbers
    std::cout << "Enter two numbers:" << std::endl;
    int v1, v2;             // uninitialized
    std::cin >> v1 >> v2; // read input
    return 0;
}
```

A comment pair can be placed anywhere a tab, space, or newline is permitted. Comment pairs can span multiple lines of a program but are not required to do so. When a comment pair does span multiple lines, it is often a good idea to indicate visually that the inner lines are part of a multi-line comment. Our style is to begin each line in the comment with an asterisk, thus indicating that the entire range is part of a multi-line comment.

Programs typically contain a mixture of both comment forms. Comment pairs generally are used for multi-line explanations, whereas double slash comments tend to be used for half-line and single-line remarks.

Too many comments intermixed with the program code can obscure the code. It is usually best to place a comment block above the code it explains.

Comments should be kept up to date as the code itself changes. Programmers expect comments to remain accurate and so believe them, even when other forms of system documentation are known to be out of date. An incorrect comment is worse than no comment at all because it may mislead a subsequent reader.

Comment Pairs Do Not Nest

A comment that begins with /* always ends with the next */. As a result, one comment pair cannot occur within another. The compiler error message(s) that result from this kind of program mistake can be mysterious and confusing. As an example, compile the following program on your system:

```
#include <iostream>
/*
 * comment pairs /*   */ cannot nest.
 * "cannot nest" is considered source code,
 * as is the rest of the program
 */
int main()
{
    return 0;
}
```

When commenting out a large section of a program, it can seem easiest to put a comment pair around a region that you want to omit temporarily. The trouble is that if that code already has a comment pair, then the newly inserted comment will terminate prematurely. A better way to temporarily ignore a section of code is to use your editor to insert single-line comment at the beginning of each line of code you want to ignore. That way, you need not worry about whether the code you are commenting out already contains a comment pair.

1.4 Control Structures

Statements execute sequentially: The first statement in a function is executed first, followed by the second, and so on. Of course, few programs—including the one we'll need to write to solve our bookstore problem—can be written using only sequential execution. Instead, programming languages provide various control

Exercise 1.7: Compile a program that has incorrectly nested comments.

Exercise 1.8: Indicate which, if any, of the following output statements, are legal.

```
std::cout << "/*";
std::cout << "*/";
std::cout << /* "*/" */;
```

After you've predicted what will happen, test your answer by compiling a program with these three statements. Correct any errors you encounter.

structures that allow for more complicated execution paths. This section will take a brief look at some of the control structures provided by C++. Chapter 6 covers statements in detail.

1.4.1   The `while` Statement

A **`while` statement** provides for iterative execution. We could use a `while` to write a program to sum the numbers from 1 through 10 inclusive as follows:

```
#include <iostream>
int main()
{
    int sum = 0, val = 1;
    // keep executing the while until val is greater than 10
    while (val <= 10) {
        sum += val;   // assigns sum + val to sum
        ++val;        // add 1 to val
    }
    std::cout << "Sum of 1 to 10 inclusive is "
              << sum << std::endl;
    return 0;
}
```

This program when compiled and executed will print:

```
Sum of 1 to 10 inclusive is 55
```

As before, we begin by including the `iostream` header and define a `main` function. Inside `main` we define two `int` variables: `sum`, which will hold our summation, and `val`, which will represent each of the values from 1 through 10. We give `sum` an initial value of zero and start `val` off with the value one.

The important part is the `while` statement. A `while` has the form

```
while (condition) while_body_statement;
```

A `while` executes by (repeatedly) testing the *condition* and executing the associated *while_body_statement* until the *condition* is false.

A **condition** is an expression that is evaluated so that its result can be tested. If the resulting value is nonzero, then the condition is true; if the value is zero then the condition is false.

If the *condition* is true (the expression evaluates to a value other than zero) then *while_body_statement* is executed. After executing *while_body_statement*, the *condition* is tested again. If *condition* remains true, then the *while_body_statement* is again executed. The `while` continues, alternatively testing the *condition* and executing *while_body_statement* until the *condition* is false.

In this program, the `while` statement is:

```
//  keep executing the while until val is greater than 10
while (val <= 10) {
    sum += val;   //  assigns sum + val to sum
    ++val;        //  add 1 to val
}
```

The condition in the `while` uses the **less-than-or-equal operator** (the `<=` operator) to compare the current value of `val` and `10`. As long as `val` is less than or equal to 10, we execute the body of the `while`. In this case, the body of the `while` is a **block** containing two statements:

```
{
    sum += val;   //  assigns sum + val to sum
    ++val;        //  add 1 to val
}
```

A block is a sequence of statements enclosed by curly braces. In C++, a block may be used wherever a statement is expected. The first statement in the block uses the **compound assignment operator**, (the `+=` operator). This operator adds its right-hand operand to its left-hand operand. It has the same effect as writing an addition and an **assignment**:

```
sum = sum + val;   //  assign sum + val to sum
```

Thus, the first statement adds the value of `val` to the current value of `sum` and stores the result back into `sum`.

The next statement

```
++val;        //  add 1 to val
```

uses the **prefix increment operator** (the `++` operator). The increment operator adds one to its operand. Writing `++val` is the same as writing `val = val + 1`.

After executing the `while` body we again execute the condition in the `while`. If the (now incremented) value of `val` is still less than or equal to 10, then the body of the `while` is executed again. The loop continues, testing the condition and executing the body, until `val` is no longer less than or equal to 10.

Once `val` is greater than 10, we fall out of the `while` loop and execute the statement following the `while`. In this case, that statement prints our output, followed by the `return`, which completes our `main` program.

KEY CONCEPT: INDENTATION AND FORMATTING OF C++ PROGRAMS

C++ programs are largely free-format, meaning that the positioning of curly braces, indentation, comments, and newlines usually has no effect on the meaning of our programs. For example, the curly brace that denotes the beginning of the body of main could be on the same line as main, positioned as we have done, at the beginning of the next line, or placed anywhere we'd like. The only requirement is that it be the first nonblank, noncomment character that the compiler sees after the close parenthesis that concludes main's parameter list.

Although we are largely free to format programs as we wish, the choices we make affect the readability of our programs. We could, for example, have written main on a single, long line. Such a definition, although legal, would be hard to read.

Endless debates occur as to the right way to format C or C++ programs. Our belief is that there is no single correct style but that there is value in consistency. We tend to put the curly braces that delimit functions on their own lines. We tend to indent compound input or output expressions so that the operators line up, as we did with the statement that wrote the output in the main function on page 6. Other indentation conventions will become clear as our programs become more complex.

The important thing to keep in mind is that other ways to format programs are possible. When choosing a formatting style, think about how it affects readability and comprehension. Once you've chosen a style, use it consistently.

1.4.2   The for Statement

In our while loop, we used the variable val to control how many times we iterated through the loop. On each pass through the while, the value of val was tested and then in the body the value of val was incremented.

The use of a variable like val to control a loop happens so often that the language defines a second control structure, called a **for statement**, that abbreviates the code that manages the loop variable. We could rewrite the program to sum the numbers from 1 through 10 using a for loop as follows:

```
#include <iostream>
int main()
{
    int sum = 0;
    // sum values from 1 up to 10 inclusive
    for (int val = 1; val <= 10; ++val)
        sum += val;   // equivalent to sum = sum + val

    std::cout << "Sum of 1 to 10 inclusive is "
              << sum << std::endl;
    return 0;
}
```

Prior to the for loop, we define sum, which we set to zero. The variable val is used only inside the iteration and is defined as part of the for statement itself. The for statement

```
for (int val = 1; val <= 10; ++val)
    sum += val;  // equivalent to sum = sum + val
```

has two parts: the `for` header and the `for` body. The header controls how often the body is executed. The header itself consists of three parts: an *init-statement*, a *condition*, and an *expression*. In this case, the *init-statement*

```
int val = 1;
```

defines an `int` object named `val` and gives it an initial value of one. The *init-statement* is performed only once, on entry to the `for`. The *condition*

```
val <= 10
```

which compares the current value in `val` to 10, is tested each time through the loop. As long as `val` is less than or equal to 10, we execute the `for` body. Only after executing the body is the *expression* executed. In this `for`, the expression uses the prefix increment operator, which as we know adds one to the value of `val`. After executing the *expression*, the `for` retests the *condition*. If the new value of `val` is still less than or equal to `10`, then the `for` loop body is executed and `val` is incremented again. Execution continues until the *condition* fails.

In this loop, the `for` body performs the summation

```
sum += val;  // equivalent to sum = sum + val
```

The body uses the compound assignment operator to add the current value of `val` to `sum`, storing the result back into `sum`.

To recap, the overall execution flow of this `for` is:

1. Create `val` and initialize it to `1`.

2. Test whether `val` is less than or equal to `10`.

3. If `val` is less than or equal to 10, execute the `for` body, which adds `val` to `sum`. If `val` is not less than or equal to 10, then break out of the loop and continue execution with the first statement following the `for` body.

4. Increment `val`.

5. Repeat the test in step 2, continuing with the remaining steps as long as the condition is true.

Beware

When we exit the `for` loop, the variable `val` is no longer accessible. It is not possible to use `val` after this loop terminates. However, not all compilers enforce this requirement.

In pre-Standard C++ names defined in a `for` header *were* accessible outside the `for` itself. This change in the language definition can surprise people accustomed to using an older compiler when they instead use a compiler that adheres to the standard.

COMPILATION REVISITED

Part of the compiler's job is to look for errors in the program text. A compiler cannot detect whether the meaning of a program is correct, but it can detect errors in the *form* of the program. The following are the most common kinds of errors a compiler will detect.

1. Syntax errors. The programmer has made a grammatical error in the C++ language. The following program illustrates common syntax errors; each comment describes the error on the following line:

```
                          // error: missing ')' in parameter list for main
    int main ( {
                          // error: used colon, not a semicolon after endl
        std::cout << "Read each file." << std::endl:
                          // error: missing quotes around string literal
        std::cout << Update master. << std::endl;
                          // ok: no errors on this line
        std::cout << "Write new master." << std::endl;
                          // error: missing ';' on return statement
        return 0
    }
```

2. Type errors. Each item of data in C++ has an associated type. The value 10, for example, is an integer. The word "hello" surrounded by double quotation marks is a string literal. One example of a type error is passing a string literal to a function that expects an integer argument.

3. Declaration errors. Every name used in a C++ program must be declared before it is used. Failure to declare a name usually results in an error message. The two most common declaration errors are to forget to use `std::` when accessing a name from the library or to inadvertently misspell the name of an identifier:

```
    #include <iostream>
    int main()
    {
        int v1, v2;
        std::cin >> v >> v2;   // error: uses "v" not "v1"
        // cout not defined, should be std::cout
        cout << v1 + v2 << std::endl;
        return 0;
    }
```

An error message contains a line number and a brief description of what the compiler believes we have done wrong. It is a good practice to correct errors in the sequence they are reported. Often a single error can have a cascading effect and cause a compiler to report more errors than actually are present. It is also a good idea to recompile the code after each fix—or after making at most a small number of obvious fixes. This cycle is known as *edit-compile-debug*.

Exercise 1.9: What does the following `for` loop do? What is the final value of `sum`?

```
int sum = 0;
for (int i = -100; i <= 100; ++i)
    sum += i;
```

Exercise 1.10: Write a program that uses a `for` loop to sum the numbers from 50 to 100. Now rewrite the program using a `while`.

Exercise 1.11: Write a program using a `while` loop to print the numbers from 10 down to 0. Now rewrite the program using a `for`.

Exercise 1.12: Compare and contrast the loops you wrote in the previous two exercises. Are there advantages or disadvantages to using either form?

Exercise 1.13: Compilers vary as to how easy it is to understand their diagnostics. Write programs that contain the common errors discussed in the box on 16. Study the messages the compiler generates so that these messages will be familiar when you encounter them while compiling more complex programs.

1.4.3 The `if` Statement

A logical extension of summing the values between 1 and 10 is to sum the values between two numbers our user supplies. We might use the numbers directly in our `for` loop, using the first input as the lower bound for the range and the second as the upper bound. However, if the user gives us the higher number first, that strategy would fail: Our program would exit the `for` loop immediately. Instead, we should adjust the range so that the larger number is the upper bound and the smaller is the lower. To do so, we need a way to see which number is larger.

Like most languages, C++ provides an **if statement** that supports conditional execution. We can use an `if` to write our revised sum program:

```
#include <iostream>
int main()
{
    std::cout << "Enter two numbers:" << std::endl;
    int v1, v2;
    std::cin >> v1 >> v2; //  read input
    //  use smaller number as lower bound for summation
    //  and larger number as upper bound
    int lower, upper;
    if (v1 <= v2) {
        lower = v1;
        upper = v2;
    } else {
        lower = v2;
        upper = v1;
    }
```

```
int sum = 0;
// sum values from lower up to and including upper
for (int val = lower; val <= upper; ++val)
    sum += val;  // sum = sum + val

std::cout << "Sum of " << lower
          << " to " << upper
          << " inclusive is "
          << sum << std::endl;

return 0;
}
```

If we compile and execute this program and give it as input the numbers 7 and 3, then the output of our program will be

Sum of 3 to 7 inclusive is 25

Most of the code in this program should already be familiar from our earlier examples. The program starts by writing a prompt to the user and defines four `int` variables. It then reads from the standard input into `v1` and `v2`. The only new code is the `if` statement

```
// use smaller number as lower bound for summation
// and larger number as upper bound
int lower, upper;
if (v1 <= v2) {
    lower = v1;
    upper = v2;
} else {
    lower = v2;
    upper = v1;
}
```

The effect of this code is to set `upper` and `lower` appropriately. The `if` condition tests whether `v1` is less than or equal to `v2`. If so, we perform the block that immediately follows the condition. This block contains two statements, each of which does an assignment. The first statement assigns `v1` to `lower` and the second assigns `v2` to `upper`.

If the condition is false—that is, if `v1` is larger than `v2`—then we execute the statement following the `else`. Again, this statement is a block consisting of two assignments. We assign `v2` to `lower` and `v1` to `upper`.

1.4.4   Reading an Unknown Number of Inputs

Another change we might make to our summation program on page 12 would be to allow the user to specify a set of numbers to sum. In this case we can't know how many numbers we'll be asked to add. Instead, we want to keep reading numbers until the program reaches the end of the input. When the input is finished, the program writes the total to the standard output:

EXERCISES SECTION 1.4.3

Exercise 1.14: What happens in the program presented in this section if the input values are equal?

Exercise 1.15: Compile and run the program from this section with two equal values as input. Compare the output to what you predicted in the previous exercise. Explain any discrepancy between what happened and what you predicted.

Exercise 1.16: Write a program to print the larger of two inputs supplied by the user.

Exercise 1.17: Write a program to ask the user to enter a series of numbers. Print a message saying how many of the numbers are negative numbers.

```
#include <iostream>
int main()
{
    int sum = 0, value;
    //  read till end-of-file, calculating a running total of all values read
    while (std::cin >> value)
        sum += value; //  equivalent to sum = sum + value
    std::cout << "Sum is: " << sum << std::endl;
    return 0;
}
```

If we give this program the input

    3 4 5 6

then our output will be

    Sum is: 18

As usual, we begin by including the necessary headers. The first line inside `main` defines two `int` variables, named `sum` and `value`. We'll use `value` to hold each number we read, which we do inside the condition in the `while`:

    while (std::cin >> value)

What happens here is that to evaluate the condition, the input operation

    std::cin >> value

is executed, which has the effect of reading the next number from the standard input, storing what was read in `value`. The input operator (Section 1.2.2, p. 8) returns its left operand. The condition tests that result, meaning it tests `std::cin`.

When we use an `istream` as a condition, the effect is to test the state of the stream. If the stream is valid—that is, if it is still possible to read another input—then the test succeeds. An `istream` becomes invalid when we hit *end-of-file* or encounter an invalid input, such as reading a value that is not an integer. An `istream` that is in an invalid state will cause the condition to fail.

Until we do encounter end-of-file (or some other input error), the test will succeed and we'll execute the body of the `while`. That body is a single statement that uses the compound assignment operator. This operator adds its right-hand operand into the left hand operand.

ENTERING AN END-OF-FILE FROM THE KEYBOARD

Operating systems use different values for end-of-file. On Windows systems we enter an end-of-file by typing a control-z—simultaneously type the "ctrl" key and a "z." On UNIX systems, including Mac OS-X machines, it is usually control-d.

Once the test fails, the `while` terminates and we fall through and execute the statement following the `while`. That statement prints `sum` followed by `endl`, which prints a newline and flushes the buffer associated with `cout`. Finally, we execute the `return`, which as usual returns zero to indicate success.

EXERCISES SECTION 1.4.4

Exercise 1.18: Write a program that prompts the user for two numbers and writes each number in the range specified by the two numbers to the standard output.

Exercise 1.19: What happens if you give the numbers 1000 and 2000 to the program written for the previous exercise? Revise the program so that it never prints more than 10 numbers per line.

Exercise 1.20: Write a program to sum the numbers in a user-specified range, omitting the `if` test that sets the upper and lower bounds. Predict what happens if the input is the numbers 7 and 3, in that order. Now run the program giving it the numbers 7 and 3, and see if the results match your expectation. If not, restudy the discussion on the `for` and `while` loop until you understand what happened.

1.5   Introducing Classes

The only remaining feature we need to understand before solving our bookstore problem is how to write a *data structure* to represent our transaction data. In C++ we define our own data structure by defining a **class**. The class mechanism is one of the most important features in C++. In fact, a primary focus of the design of C++ is to make it possible to define **class types** that behave as naturally as the built-in types themselves. The library types that we've seen already, such as `istream` and `ostream`, are all defined as classes—that is, they are not strictly speaking part of the language.

Complete understanding of the class mechanism requires mastering a lot of information. Fortunately, it is possible to use a class that someone else has written without knowing how to define a class ourselves. In this section, we'll describe a simple class that we can use in solving our bookstore problem. We'll implement this class in the subsequent chapters as we learn more about types, expressions, statements, and functions—all of which are used in defining classes.

To use a class we need to know three things:

1. What is its name?

2. Where is it defined?

3. What operations does it support?

For our bookstore problem, we'll assume that the class is named `Sales_item` and that it is defined in a header named `Sales_item.h`.

1.5.1 The `Sales_item` Class

The purpose of the `Sales_item` class is to store an ISBN and keep track of the number of copies sold, the revenue, and average sales price for that book. How these data are stored or computed is not our concern. To use a class, we need not know anything about how it is implemented. Instead, what we need to know is what operations the class provides.

As we've seen, when we use library facilities such as IO, we must include the associated headers. Similarly, for our own classes, we must make the definitions associated with the class available to the compiler. We do so in much the same way. Typically, we put the class definition into a file. Any program that wants to use our class must include that file.

Conventionally, class types are stored in a file with a name that, like the name of a program source file, has two parts: a file name and a file suffix. Usually the file name is the same as the class defined in the header. The suffix usually is `.h`, but some programmers use `.H`, `.hpp`, or `.hxx`. Compilers usually aren't picky about header file names, but IDEs sometimes are. We'll assume that our class is defined in a file named `Sales_item.h`.

Operations on `Sales_item` Objects

Every class defines a type. The type name is the same as the name of the class. Hence, our `Sales_item` class defines a type named `Sales_item`. As with the built-in types, we can define a variable of a class type. When we write

```
Sales_item item;
```

we are saying that `item` is an object of type `Sales_item`. We often contract the phrase "an object of type `Sales_item`" to "a `Sales_item` object" or even more simply to "a `Sales_item`."

In addition to being able to define variables of type `Sales_item`, we can perform the following operations on `Sales_item` objects:

• Use the addition operator, +, to add two `Sales_items`

• Use the input operator, >>, to read a `Sales_item` object

- Use the output operator, `<<`, to write a `Sales_item` object

- Use the assignment operator, `=`, to assign one `Sales_item` object to another

- Call the `same_isbn` function to determine if two `Sales_items` refer to the same book

Reading and Writing `Sales_items`

Now that we know the operations that the class provides, we can write some simple programs to use this class. For example, the following program reads data from the standard input, uses that data to build a `Sales_item` object, and writes that `Sales_item` object back onto the standard output:

```
#include <iostream>
#include "Sales_item.h"
int main()
{
    Sales_item book;
    //  read ISBN, number of copies sold, and sales price
    std::cin >> book;
    //  write ISBN, number of copies sold, total revenue, and average price
    std::cout << book << std::endl;
    return 0;
}
```

If the input to this program is

```
0-201-70353-X 4 24.99
```

then the output will be

```
0-201-70353-X 4 99.96 24.99
```

Our input said that we sold four copies of the book at $24.99 each, and the output indicates that the total sold was four, the total revenue was $99.96, and the average price per book was $24.99.

This program starts with two `#include` directives, one of which uses a new form. The `iostream` header is defined by the standard library; the `Sales_item` header is not. `Sales_item` is a type that we ourselves have defined. When we use our own headers, we use quotation marks (`"  "`) to surround the header name.

 Headers for the standard library are enclosed in angle brackets (`<  >`). Nonstandard headers are enclosed in double quotes (`"  "`).

Inside `main` we start by defining an object, named `book`, which we'll use to hold the data that we read from the standard input. The next statement reads into that object, and the third statement prints it to the standard output followed as usual by printing `endl` to flush the buffer.

> ## KEY CONCEPT: CLASSES DEFINE BEHAVIOR
>
> As we go through these programs that use `Sales_items`, the important thing to keep in mind is that the author of the `Sales_item` class defined *all* the actions that can be performed by objects of this class. That is, the author of the `Sales_item` data structure defines what happens when a `Sales_item` object is created and what happens when the addition or the input and output operators are applied to `Sales_item` objects, and so on.
>
> In general, only the operations defined by a class can be used on objects of the class type. For now, the only operations we know we can peeform on `Sales_item` objects are the ones listed on page 21.
>
> We'll see how these operations are defined in Sections 7.7.3 and 14.2.

Adding `Sales_items`

A slightly more interesting example adds two `Sales_item` objects:

```cpp
#include <iostream>
#include "Sales_item.h"
int main()
{
    Sales_item item1, item2;
    std::cin >> item1 >> item2;    // read a pair of transactions
    std::cout << item1 + item2 << std::endl; // print their sum
    return 0;
}
```

If we give this program the following input

```
0-201-78345-X 3 20.00
0-201-78345-X 2 25.00
```

our output is

```
0-201-78345-X 5 110 22
```

This program starts by including the `Sales_item` and `iostream` headers. Next we define two `Sales_item` objects to hold the two transactions that we wish to sum. The output expression does the addition and prints the result. We know from the list of operations on page 21 that adding two `Sales_items` together creates a new object whose ISBN is that of its operands and whose number sold and revenue reflect the sum of the corresponding values in its operands. We also know that the items we add must represent the same ISBN.

It's worth noting how similar this program looks to the one on page 6: We read two inputs and write their sum. What makes it interesting is that instead of reading and printing the sum of two integers, we're reading and printing the sum of two `Sales_item` objects. Moreover, the whole idea of "sum" is different. In the case of `int`s we are generating a conventional sum—the result of adding two numeric values. In the case of `Sales_item` objects we use a conceptually new meaning for sum—the result of adding the components of two `Sales_item` objects.

Exercise 1.21: The Web site (http://www.awprofessional.com/cpp_primer) contains a copy of Sales_item.h in the Chapter 1 code directory. Copy that file to your working directory. Write a program that loops through a set of book sales trans-actions, reading each transaction and writing that transaction to the standard output.

Exercise 1.22: Write a program that reads two Sales_item objects that have the same ISBN and produces their sum.

Exercise 1.23: Write a program that reads several transactions for the same ISBN. Write the sum of all the transactions that were read.

1.5.2   A First Look at Member Functions

Unfortunately, there is a problem with the program that adds Sales_items. What should happen if the input referred to two different ISBNs? It doesn't make sense to add the data for two different ISBNs together. To solve this problem, we'll first check whether the Sales_item operands refer to the same ISBNs:

```
#include <iostream>
#include "Sales_item.h"
int main()
{
    Sales_item item1, item2;
    std::cin >> item1 >> item2;
    // first check that item1 and item2 represent the same book
    if (item1.same_isbn(item2)) {
        std::cout << item1 + item2 << std::endl;
        return 0;    // indicate success
    } else {
        std::cerr << "Data must refer to same ISBN"
                  << std::endl;
        return -1;   // indicate failure
    }
}
```

The difference between this program and the previous one is the if test and its associated else branch. Before explaining the if condition, we know that what this program does depends on the condition in the if. If the test succeeds, then we write the same output as the previous program and return 0 indicating success. If the test fails, we execute the block following the else, which prints a message and returns an error indicator.

What Is a Member Function?

The if condition

```
    // first check that item1 and item2 represent the same book
    if (item1.same_isbn(item2)) {
```

calls a **member function** of the Sales_item object named item1. A member function is a function that is defined by a class. Member functions are sometimes referred to as the **methods** of the class.

Member functions are defined once for the class but are treated as members of each object. We refer to these operations as member functions because they (usually) operate on a specific object. In this sense, they are members of the object, even though a single definition is shared by all objects of the same type.

When we call a member function, we (usually) specify the object on which the function will operate. This syntax uses the **dot operator** (the "." operator):

        item1.same_isbn

means "the same_isbn member of the object named item1." The dot operator fetches its right-hand operand from its left. The dot operator applies only to objects of class type: The left-hand operand must be an object of class type; the right-hand operand must name a member of that type.

> Unlike most other operators, the right operand of the dot (".") operator is not an object or value; it is the name of a member.

When we use a member function as the right-hand operand of the dot operator, we usually do so to call that function. We execute a member function in much the same way as we do any function: To call a function, we follow the function name by the **call operator** (the "()" operator). The call operator is a pair of parentheses that encloses a (possibly empty) list of *arguments* that we pass to the function.

The same_isbn function takes a single argument, and that argument is another Sales_item object. The call

        item1.same_isbn(item2)

passes item2 as an argument to the function named same_isbn that is a member of the object named item1. This function compares the ISBN part of its argument, item2, to the ISBN in item1, the object on which same_isbn is called. Thus, the effect is to test whether the two objects refer to the same ISBN.

If the objects refer to the same ISBN, we execute the statement following the if, which prints the result of adding the two Sales_item objects together. Otherwise, if they refer to different ISBNs, we execute the else branch, which is a block of statements. The block prints an appropriate error message and exits the program, returning -1. Recall that the return from main is treated as a status indicator. In this case, we return a nonzero value to indicate that the program failed to produce the expected result.

1.6 The C++ Program

Now we are ready to solve our original bookstore problem: We need to read a file of sales transactions and produce a report that shows for each book the total revenue, average sales price, and the number of copies sold.

Exercise 1.24: Write a program that reads several transactions. For each new transaction that you read, determine if it is the same ISBN as the previous transaction, keeping a count of how many transactions there are for each ISBN. Test the program by giving multiple transactions. These transactions should represent multiple ISBNs but the records for each ISBN should be grouped together.

We'll assume that all of the transactions for a given ISBN appear together. Our program will combine the data for each ISBN in a `Sales_item` object named `total`. Each transaction we read from the standard input will be stored in a second `Sales_item` object named `trans`. Each time we read a new transaction we'll compare it to the `Sales_item` object in `total`. If the objects refer to the same ISBN, we'll update `total`. Otherwise we'll print the value in `total` and reset it using the transaction we just read.

```cpp
#include <iostream>
#include "Sales_item.h"
int main()
{
    //  declare variables to hold running sum and data for the next record
    Sales_item total, trans;
    //  is there data to process?
    if (std::cin >> total) {
        //  if so, read the transaction records
        while (std::cin >> trans)
            if (total.same_isbn(trans))
                //  match: update the running total
                total = total + trans;
            else {
                //  no match: print & assign to total
                std::cout << total << std::endl;
                total = trans;
            }
        //  remember to print last record
        std::cout << total << std::endl;
    } else {
        //  no input!, warn the user
        std::cout << "No data?!" << std::endl;
        return -1;   //  indicate failure
    }
    return 0;
}
```

This program is the most complicated one we've seen so far, but it uses only facilities that we have already encountered. As usual, we begin by including the headers that we use: `iostream` from the library and `Sales_item.h`, which is our own header.

Inside `main` we define the objects we need: `total`, which we'll use to sum the data for a given ISBN, and `trans`, which will hold our transactions as we read them. We start by reading a transaction into `total` and testing whether the read was successful. If the read fails, then there are no records and we fall through to the outermost `else` branch, which prints a message to warn the user that there was no input.

Assuming we have successfully read a record, we execute the code in the `if` branch. The first statement is a `while` that will loop through all the remaining records. Just as we did in the program on page 18, our `while` condition reads a value from the standard input and then tests that valid data was actually read. In this case, we read a `Sales_item` object into `trans`. As long as the read succeeds, we execute the body of the `while`.

The body of the `while` is a single `if` statement. We test whether the ISBNs are equal, and if so we add the two objects and store the result in `total`. If the ISBNs are not equal, we print the value stored in `total` and reset `total` by assigning `trans` to it. After execution of the `if`, we return to the condition in the `while`, reading the next transaction and so on until we run out of records.

Once the `while` completes, we still must write the data associated with the last ISBN. When the `while` terminates, `total` contains the data for the last ISBN in the file, but we had no chance to print it. We do so in the last statement of the block that concludes the outermost `if` statement.

EXERCISES SECTION 1.6

Exercise 1.25: Using the `Sales_item.h` header from the Web site, compile and execute the bookstore program presented in this section.

Exercise 1.26: In the bookstore program we used the addition operator and not the compound assignment operator to add `trans` to `total`. Why didn't we use the compound assignment operator?

Chapter Summary

This chapter introduced enough of C++ to let the reader compile and execute simple C++ programs. We saw how to define a main function, which is the function that is executed first in any C++ program. We also saw how to define variables, how to do input and output, and how to write if, for, and while statements. The chapter closed by introducing the most fundamental facility in C++: the class. In this chapter we saw how to create and use objects of a given class. Later chapters show how to define our own classes.

Defined Terms

argument A value passed to a function when it is called.

block Sequence of statements enclosed in curly braces.

buffer A region of storage used to hold data. IO facilities often store input (or output) in a buffer and read or write the buffer independently of actions in the program. Output buffers usually must be explicitly flushed to force the buffer to be written. By default, reading cin flushes cout; cout is also flushed when the program ends normally.

built-in type A type, such as int, defined by the language.

cerr ostream object tied to the standard error, which is often the same stream as the standard output. By default, writes to cerr are not buffered. Usually used for error messages or other output that is not part of the normal logic of the program.

cin istream object used to read from the standard input.

class C++ mechanism for defining our own data structures. The class is one of the most fundamental features in C++. Library types, such as istream and ostream, are classes.

class type A type defined by a class. The name of the type is the class name.

clog ostream object tied to the standard error. By default, writes to clog are buffered. Usually used to report information about program execution to a log file.

comments Program text that is ignored by the compiler. C++ has two kinds of comments: single-line and paired. Single-line comments start with a //. Everything from the // to the end of the line is a comment. Paired comments begin with a /* and include all text up to the next */.

condition An expression that is evaluated as true or false. An arithmetic expression that evaluates to zero is false; any other value yields true.

cout ostream object used to write to the standard output. Ordinarily used to write the output of a program.

curly brace Curly braces delimit blocks. An open curly ({) starts a block; a close curly (}) ends one.

data structure A logical grouping of data and operations on that data.

edit-compile-debug The process of getting a program to execute properly.

end-of-file System-specific marker in a file that indicates that there is no more input in the file.

expression The smallest unit of computation. An expression consists of one or more operands and usually an operator. Expressions are evaluated to produce a result. For example, assuming i and j are ints, then i + j is an arithmetic addition expression and yields the sum of the two int values. Expressions are covered in more detail in Chapter 5.

for statement Control statement that provides iterative execution. Often used to step through a data structure or to repeat a calculation a fixed number of times.

function A named unit of computation.

function body Statement block that defines the actions performed by a function.

function name Name by which a function is known and can be called.

header A mechanism whereby the definitions of a class or other names may be made available to multiple programs. A header is included in a program through a #include directive.

if statement Conditional execution based on the value of a specified condition. If the condition is true, the if body is executed. If not, control flows to the statement following the else if there is one or to the statement following the if if there is no else.

iostream library type providing stream-oriented input and output.

istream Library type providing stream-oriented input.

library type A type, such as istream, defined by the standard library.

main function Function called by the operating system when executing a C++ program. Each program must have one and only one function named main.

manipulator Object, such as std::endl, that when read or written "manipulates" the stream itself. Section A.3.1 (p. 825) covers manipulators in more detail.

member function Operation defined by a class. Member functions ordinarily are called to operate on a specific object.

method Synonym for member function.

namespace Mechanism for putting names defined by a library into a single place. Namespaces help avoid inadvertent name clashes. The names defined by the C++ library are in the namespace std.

ostream Library type providing stream-oriented output.

parameter list Part of the definition of a function. Possibly empty list that specifies what arguments can be used to call the function.

preprocessor directive An instruction to the C++ preprocessor. #include is a preprocessor directive. Preprocessor directives must appear on a single line. We'll learn more about the preprocessor in Section 2.9.2.

return type Type of the value returned by a function.

source file Term used to describe a file that contains a C++ program.

standard error An output stream intended for use for error reporting. Ordinarily, on a windowing operating system, the standard output and the standard error are tied to the window in which the program is executed.

standard input The input stream that ordinarily is associated by the operating system with the window in which the program executes.

standard library Collection of types and functions that every C++ compiler must support. The library provides a rich set of capabilities including the types that support IO. C++ programmers tend to talk about "the library," meaning the entire standard library or about particular parts of the library by referring to a library type. For example, programmers also refer to the "iostream library," meaning the part of the standard library defined by the iostream classes.

standard output The output stream that ordinarily is associated by the operating system with the window in which the program executes.

statement The smallest independent unit in a C++ program. It is analogous to a sentence in a natural language. Statements in C++ generally end in semicolons.

std Name of the namespace used by the standard library. `std::cout` indicates that we're using the name `cout` defined in the `std` namespace.

string literal Sequence of characters enclosed in double quotes.

uninitialized variable Variable that has no initial value specified. There are no uninitialized variables of class type. Variables of class type for which no initial value is specified are initialized as specified by the class definition. You must give a value to an uninitialized variable before attempting to use the variable's value. *Uninitialized variables can be a rich source of bugs.*

variable A named object.

while statement An iterative control statement that executes the statement that is the `while` body as long as a specified condition is true. The body is executed zero or more times, depending on the truth value of the condition.

() operator The call operator: A pair of parentheses "`()`" following a function name. The operator causes a function to be invoked. Arguments to the function may be passed inside the parentheses.

++ operator Increment operator. Adds one to the operand; `++i` is equivalent to `i = i + 1`.

+= operator A compound assignment operator. Adds right-hand operand to the left and stores the result back into the left-hand operand; `a += b` is equivalent to `a = a + b`.

. operator Dot operator. Takes two operands: the left-hand operand is an object and the right is the name of a member of that object. The operator fetches that member from the named object.

:: operator Scope operator. We'll see more about scope in Chapter 2. Among other uses, the scope operator is used to access names in a namespace. For example, `std::cout` says to use the name `cout` from the namespace `std`.

= operator Assigns the value of the right-hand operand to the object denoted by the left-hand operand.

<< operator Output operator. Writes the right-hand operand to the output stream indicated by the left-hand operand: `cout << "hi"` writes `hi` to the standard output. Output operations can be chained together: `cout << "hi << "bye"` writes `hibye`.

>> operator Input operator. Reads from the input stream specified by the left-hand operand into the right-hand operand: `cin >> i` reads the next value on the standard input into `i`. Input operations can be chained together: `cin >> i >> j` reads first into `i` and then into `j`.

== operator The equality operator. Tests whether the left-hand operand is equal to the right-hand.

!= operator Assignment operator. Tests whether the left-hand operand is not equal to the right-hand.

<= operator The less-than-or-equal operator. Tests whether the left-hand operand is less than or equal to the right-hand.

< operator The less-than operator. Tests whether the left-hand operand is less than the right-hand.

>= operator Greater-than-or-equal operator. Tests whether the left-hand operand is greater than or equal to the right-hand.

> operator Greater-than operator. Tests whether the left-hand operand is greater than the right-hand.

P A R T I

THE BASICS

CONTENTS

Programming languages have distinctive features that determine the kinds of applications for which they are well suited. They also share many fundamental attributes. Essentially all languages provide:

- Built-in data types such as integers, characters, and so forth

- Expressions and statements to manipulate values of these types

- Variables, which let us give names to the objects we use

- Control structures, such as `if` or `while`, that allow us to conditionally execute or repeat a set of actions

- Functions that let us abstract actions into callable units of computation

Most modern programming languages supplement this basic set of features in two ways: They let programmers extend the language by defining their own data types, and they provide a set of library routines that define useful functions and data types not otherwise built into the language.

In C++, as in most programming languages, the type of an object determines what operations can be performed on it. Depending on the type of the objects involved, a statement might or might not be legal. Some languages, notably Smalltalk and Python, check the types involved in expressions at run time. In contrast, C++ is a statically typed language; type-checking is done at compile time. As a consequence, the compiler must be told the type of every name used in the program before that name can be used.

C++ provides a set of built-in data types, operators to manipulate those types, and a small set of statements for program flow control. These elements form an alphabet with which many large, complex real-world systems can and have been written. At this basic level, C++ is a simple language. Its expressive power arises from its support for mechanisms that allow the programmer to define new data structures.

Perhaps the most important feature in C++ is the class, which allows programmers to define their own data types. In C++ such types are sometimes called "class types" to distinguish them from the types that are built into the language. Some languages let programmers define data types that specify only what data make up the type. Others, like C++, allow programmers to define types that include operations as well as data. One of the primary design goals of C++ is to let programmers define their own types that are as easy to use as the built-in types. The Standard C++ library uses these features to implement a rich library of class types and associated functions.

The first step in mastering C++—learning the basics of the language and library—is the topic of Part I. Chapter 2 covers the built-in data types and looks briefly at the mechanisms for defining our own new types. Chapter 3 introduces two of the most fundamental library types: `string` and `vector`. Arrays, which are covered in Chapter 4, are a lower-level data structure built into C++ and many other languages. Arrays are similar to `vector`s but harder to use. Chapters 5 through 7 cover expressions, statements, and functions. This part concludes in Chapter 8, which covers the most important facilities from the IO library.

C H A P T E R   2

VARIABLES AND BASIC TYPES

CONTENTS

Types are fundamental to any program. They tell us what our data mean and what operations we can perform on our data.

C++ defines several primitive types: characters, integers, floating-point numbers, and so on. The language also provides mechanisms that let us define our own data types. The library uses these mechanisms to define more complex types such as variable-length character `strings`, `vectors`, and so on. Finally, we can modify existing types to form compound types. This chapter covers the built-in types and begins our coverage of how C++ supports more complicated types.

Types determine what the data and operations in our programs mean. As we saw in Chapter 1, the same statement

```
i = i + j;
```

can mean different things depending on the types of `i` and `j`. If `i` and `j` are integers, then this statement has the ordinary, arithmetic meaning of +. However, if `i` and `j` are `Sales_item` objects, then this statement adds the components of these two objects.

In C++ the support for types is extensive: The language itself defines a set of primitive types and ways in which we can modify existing types. It also provides a set of features that allow us to define our own types. This chapter begins our exploration of types in C++ by covering the built-in types and showing how we associate a type with an object. It also introduces ways we can both modify types and can build our own types.

2.1   Primitive Built-in Types

C++ defines a set of **arithmetic types**, which represent integers, floating-point numbers, and individual characters and boolean values. In addition, there is a special type named **void**. The void type has no associated values and can be used in only a limited set of circumstances. The void type is most often used as the return type for a function that has no return value.

The size of the arithmetic types varies across machines. By size, we mean the number of bits used to represent the type. The standard guarantees a minimum size for each of the arithmetic types, but it does not prevent compilers from using larger sizes. Indeed, almost all compilers use a larger size for int than is strictly required. Table 2.1 (p. 36) lists the built-in arithmetic types and the associated minimum sizes.

 Because the number of bits varies, the maximum (or minimum) values that these types can represent also vary by machine.

2.1.1   Integral Types

The arithmetic types that represent integers, characters, and boolean values are collectively referred to as the **integral types**.

There are two character types: `char` and `wchar_t`. The `char` type is guaranteed to be big enough to hold numeric values that correspond to any character in the machine's basic character set. As a result, `char`s are usually a single machine byte. The `wchar_t` type is used for extended character sets, such as those used for Chinese and Japanese, in which some characters cannot be represented within a single `char`.

The types `short`, `int`, and `long` represent integer values of potentially different sizes. Typically, `short`s are represented in half a machine word, `int`s in a

---

MACHINE-LEVEL REPRESENTATION OF THE BUILT-IN TYPES

The C++ built-in types are closely tied to their representation in the computer's memory. Computers store data as a sequence of bits, each of which holds either 0 or 1. A segment of memory might hold

```
00011011011100010110010000111011 ...
```

At the bit level, memory has no structure and no meaning.

The most primitive way we impose structure on memory is by processing it in chunks. Most computers deal with memory as chunks of bits of particular sizes, usually powers of 2. They usually make it easy to process 8, 16, or 32 bits at a time, and chunks of 64 and 128 bits are becoming more common. Although the exact sizes can vary from one machine to another, we usually refer to a chunk of 8 bits as a "byte" and 32 bits, or 4 bytes, as a "word."

Most computers associate a number—called an address—with each byte in memory. Given a machine that has 8-bit bytes and 32-bit words, we might represent a word of memory as follows:

736424	0	0	0	1	1	0	1	1
736425	0	1	1	1	0	0	0	1
736426	0	1	1	0	0	1	0	0
736427	0	0	1	1	1	0	1	1

In this illustration, each byte's address is shown on the left, with the 8 bits of the byte following the address.

We can use an address to refer to any of several variously sized collections of bits starting at that address. It is possible to speak of the word at address 736424 or the byte at address 736426. We can say, for example, that the byte at address 736425 is not equal to the byte at address 736427.

To give meaning to the byte at address 736425, we must know the type of the value stored there. Once we know the type, we know how many bits are needed to represent a value of that type and how to interpret those bits.

If we know that the byte at location 736425 has type "unsigned 8-bit integer," then we know that the byte represents the number 112. On the other hand, if that byte is a character in the ISO-Latin-1 character set, then it represents the lower-case letter q. The bits are the same in both cases, but by ascribing different types to them, we interpret them differently.

---

machine word, and `longs` in either one or two machine words (on 32-bit machines, `ints` and `longs` are usually the same size).

The type `bool` represents the truth values, `true` and `false`. We can assign any of the arithmetic types to a `bool`. An arithmetic type with value 0 yields a `bool` that holds `false`. Any nonzero value is treated as `true`.

Signed and Unsigned Types

The integral types, except the boolean type, may be either **signed** or **unsigned**. As its name suggests, a signed type can represent both negative and positive numbers

Table 2.1: C++: Arithmetic Types		
Type	**Meaning**	**Minimum Size**
bool	boolean	NA
char	character	8 bits
wchar_t	wide character	16 bits
short	short integer	16 bits
int	integer	16 bits
long	long integer	32 bits
float	single-precision floating-point	6 significant digits
double	double-precision floating-point	10 significant digits
long double	extended-precision floating-point	10 significant digits

(including zero), whereas an unsigned type represents only values greater than or equal to zero.

The integers, int, short, and long, are all signed by default. To get an unsigned type, the type must be specified as unsigned, such as unsigned long. The unsigned int type may be abbreviated as unsigned. That is, unsigned with no other type implies unsigned int.

Unlike the other integral types, there are three distinct types for char: plain char, signed char, and unsigned char. Although there are three distinct types, there are only two ways a char can be represented. The char type is respresented using either the signed char or unsigned char version. Which representation is used for char varies by compiler.

How Integral Values Are Represented

In an unsigned type, all the bits represent the value. If a type is defined for a particular machine to use 8 bits, then the unsigned version of this type could hold the values 0 through 255.

The C++ standard does not define how signed types are represented at the bit level. Instead, each compiler is free to decide how it will represent signed types. These representations can affect the range of values that a signed type can hold. We are guaranteed that an 8-bit signed type will hold at least the values from −127 through 127; many implementations allow values from −128 through 127.

Under the most common strategy for representing signed integral types, we can view one of the bits as a sign bit. Whenever the sign bit is 1, the value is negative; when it is 0, the value is either 0 or a positive number. An 8-bit integral signed type represented using a sign-bit can hold values from −128 through 127.

Assignment to Integral Types

The type of an object determines the values that the object can hold. This fact raises the question of what happens when one tries to assign a value outside the allowable range to an object of a given type. The answer depends on whether the type is signed or unsigned.

For unsigned types, the compiler *must* adjust the out-of-range value so that it will fit. The compiler does so by taking the remainder of the value modulo the number of distinct values the unsigned target type can hold. An object that is an 8-bit unsigned char, for example, can hold values from 0 through 255 inclusive. If we assign a value outside this range, the compiler actually assigns the remainder of the value modulo 256. For example, we might attempt to assign the value 336 to an 8-bit signed char. If we try to store 336 in our 8-bit unsigned char, the actual value assigned will be 80, because 80 is equal to 336 modulo 256.

For the unsigned types, a negative value is always out of range. An object of unsigned type may never hold a negative value. Some languages make it illegal to assign a negative value to an unsigned type, but C++ does not.

> In C++ it is perfectly legal to assign a negative number to an object with unsigned type. The result is the negative value modulo the size of the type. So, if we assign –1 to an 8-bit unsigned char, the resulting value will be 255, which is –1 modulo 256.

When assigning an out-of-range value to a signed type, it is up to the compiler to decide what value to assign. In practice, many compilers treat signed types similarly to how they are required to treat unsigned types. That is, they do the assignment as the remainder modulo the size of the type. However, we are not guaranteed that the compiler will do so for the signed types.

2.1.2   Floating-Point Types

The types float, double, and long double represent floating-point single-, double-, and extended-precision values. Typically, floats are represented in one word (32 bits), doubles in two words (64 bits), and long double in either three or four words (96 or 128 bits). The size of the type determines the number of significant digits a floating-point value might contain.

> The float type is usually not precise enough for real programs—float is guaranteed to offer only 6 significant digits. The double type guarantees at least 10 significant digits, which is sufficient for most calculations.

2.2   Literal Constants

A value, such as 42, in a program is known as a **literal constant**: literal because we can speak of it only in terms of its value; constant because its value cannot be changed. Every literal has an associated type. For example, 0 is an int and 3.14159 is a double. Literals exist only for the built-in types. There are no literals of class types. Hence, there are no literals of any of the library types.

ADVICE: USING THE BUILT-IN ARITHMETIC TYPES

The number of integral types in C++ can be bewildering. C++, like C, is designed to let programs get close to the hardware when necessary, and the integral types are defined to cater to the peculiarities of various kinds of hardware. Most programmers can (and should) ignore these complexities by restricting the types they actually use.

In practice, many uses of integers involve counting. For example, programs often count the number of elements in a data structure such as a vector or an array. We'll see in Chapters 3 and 4 that the library defines a set of types to use when dealing with the size of an object. When counting such elements it is always right to use the library-defined type intended for this purpose. When counting in other circumstances, it is usually right to use an unsigned value. Doing so avoids the possibility that a value that is too large to fit results in a (seemingly) negative result.

When performing integer arithmetic, it is rarely right to use shorts. In most programs, using shorts leads to mysterious bugs when a value is assigned to a short that is bigger than the largest number it can hold. What happens depends on the machine, but typically the value "wraps around" so that a number too large to fit turns into a large negative number. For the same reason, even though char is an integral type, the char type should be used to hold characters and not for computation. The fact that char is signed on some implementations and unsigned on others makes it problematic to use it as a computational type.

On most machines, integer calculations can safely use int. Technically speaking, an int can be as small as 16 bits—too small for most purposes. In practice, almost all general-purpose machines use 32-bits for ints, which is often the same size used for long. The difficulty in deciding whether to use int or long occurs on machines that have 32-bit ints and 64-bit longs. On such machines, the *run-time* cost of doing arithmetic with longs can be considerably greater than doing the same calculation using a 32-bit int. Deciding whether to use int or long requires detailed understanding of the program and the actual run-time performance cost of using long versus int.

Determining which floating-point type to use is easier: It is almost always right to use double. The loss of precision implicit in float is significant, whereas the cost of double precision calculations versus single precision is negligible. In fact, on some machines, double precision is faster than single. The precision offered by long double usually is unnecessary and often entails considerable extra run-time cost.

Rules for Integer Literals

We can write a literal integer constant using one of three notations: decimal, octal, or hexadecimal. These notations, of course, do not change the bit representation of the value, which is always binary. For example, we can write the value 20 in any of the following three ways:

```
20      // decimal
024     // octal
0x14    // hexadecimal
```

Literal integer constants that begin with a leading 0 (zero) are interpreted as octal; those that begin with either 0x or 0X are interpreted as hexadecimal.

By default, the type of a literal integer constant is either int or long. The precise type depends on the value of the literal—values that fit in an int are type

> ## EXERCISES SECTION 2.1.2
>
> **Exercise 2.1:** What is the difference between an int, a long, and a short value?
>
> **Exercise 2.2:** What is the difference between an unsigned and a signed type?
>
> **Exercise 2.3:** If a short on a given machine has 16 bits then what is the largest number that can be assigned to a short? To an unsigned short?
>
> **Exercise 2.4:** What value is assigned if we assign 100,000 to a 16-bit unsigned short? What value is assigned if we assign 100,000 to a plain 16-bit short?
>
> **Exercise 2.5:** What is the difference between a float and a double?
>
> **Exercise 2.6:** To calculate a mortgage payment, what types would you use for the rate, principal, and payment? Explain why you selected each type.

int and larger values are type long. By adding a suffix, we can force the type of a literal integer constant to be type long or unsigned or unsigned long. We specify that a constant is a long by immediately following the value with either L or l (the letter "ell" in either uppercase or lowercase).

When specifying a long, use the uppercase L: the lowercase letter l is too easily mistaken for the digit 1.

In a similar manner, we can specify unsigned by following the literal with either U or u. We can obtain an unsigned long literal constant by following the value by both L and U. The suffix must appear with no intervening space:

```
128u    /* unsigned */        1024UL   /* unsigned long */
1L      /* long */            8Lu      /* unsigned long */
```

There are no literals of type short.

Rules for Floating-Point Literals

We can use either common decimal notation or scientific notation to write floating-point literal constants. Using scientific notation, the exponent is indicated either by E or e. By default, floating-point literals are type double. We indicate single precision by following the value with either F or f. Similarly, we specify extended precision by following the value with either L or l (again, use of the lowercase l is discouraged). Each pair of literals below denote the same underlying value:

```
3.14159F        .001f        12.345L        0.
3.14159E0f      1E-3F        1.2345E1L      0e0
```

Boolean and Character Literals

The words true and false are literals of type bool:

```
bool test = false;
```

Printable character literals are written by enclosing the character within single quotation marks:

```
'a'          '2'          ','          ' ' // blank
```

Such literals are of type `char`. We can obtain a wide-character literal of type `wchar_t` by immediately preceding the character literal with an `L`, as in

```
L'a'
```

Escape Sequences for Nonprintable Characters

Some characters are **nonprintable**. A nonprintable character is a character for which there is no visible image, such as backspace or a control character. Other characters have special meaning in the language, such as the single and double quotation marks, and the backslash. Nonprintable characters and special characters are written using an **escape sequence**. An escape sequence begins with a backslash. The language defines the following escape sequences:

newline	`\n`	horizontal tab	`\t`
vertical tab	`\v`	backspace	`\b`
carriage return	`\r`	formfeed	`\f`
alert (bell)	`\a`	backslash	`\\`
question mark	`\?`	single quote	`\'`
double quote	`\"`		

We can write any character as a generalized escape sequence of the form

```
\ooo
```

where ooo represents a sequence of as many as three octal digits. The value of the octal digits represents the numerical value of the character. The following examples are representations of literal constants using the ASCII character set:

```
\7 (bell)     \12 (newline)     \40 (blank)
\0 (null)     \062 ('2')        \115 ('M')
```

The character represented by '`\0`' is often called a "null character," and has special significance, as we shall soon see.

We can also write a character using a hexadecimal escape sequence

```
\xddd
```

consisting of a backslash, an `x`, and one or more hexadecimal digits.

Character String Literals

All of the literals we've seen so far have primitive built-in types. There is one additional literal—string literal—that is more complicated. String literals are *arrays* of constant characters, a type that we'll discuss in more detail in Section 4.3 (p. 130).

String literal constants are written as zero or more characters enclosed in double quotation marks. Nonprintable characters are represented by their underlying escape sequence.

```
"Hello World!"                  //  simple string literal
""                              //  empty string literal
"\nCC\toptions\tfile.[cC]\n"    //  string literal using newlines and tabs
```

For compatibility with C, string literals in C++ have one character in addition to those typed in by the programmer. Every string literal ends with a null character added by the compiler. A character literal

```
'A'    // single quote: character literal
```

represents the single character A, whereas

```
"A"      // double quote: character string literal
```

represents an array of two characters: the letter A and the null character.

Just as there is a wide character literal, such as

```
L'a'
```

there is a wide string literal, again preceded by L, such as

```
L"a wide string literal"
```

The type of a wide string literal is an array of constant wide characters. It is also terminated by a wide null character.

Concatenated String Literals

Two string literals (or two wide string literals) that appear adjacent to one another and separated only by spaces, tabs, or newlines are concatenated into a single new string literal. This usage makes it easy to write long literals across separate lines:

```
// concatenated long string literal
std::cout << "a multi-line "
             "string literal "
             "using concatenation"
          << std::endl;
```

When executed this statement would print:

a multi-line string literal using concatenation

What happens if you attempt to concatenate a string literal and a wide string literal? For example:

```
// Concatenating plain and wide character strings is undefined
std::cout << "multi-line " L"literal " << std::endl;
```

The result is **undefined**—that is, there is no standard behavior defined for concatenating the two different types. The program might appear to work, but it also might crash or produce garbage values. Moreover, the program might behave differently under one compiler than under another.

ADVICE: DON'T RELY ON UNDEFINED BEHAVIOR

Programs that use undefined behavior are in error. If they work, it is only by coincidence. Undefined behavior results from a program error that the compiler cannot detect or from an error that would be too much trouble to detect.

Unfortunately, programs that contain undefined behavior can appear to execute correctly in some circumstances and/or on one compiler. There is no guarantee that the same program, compiled under a different compiler or even a subsequent release of the current compiler, will continue to run correctly. Nor is there any guarantee that what works with one set of inputs will work with another.

Programs should not (knowingly) rely on undefined behavior.

Similarly, programs usually should not rely on machine-dependent behavior, such as assuming that the size of an int is a fixed and known value. Such programs are said to be *nonportable*. When the program is moved to another machine, any code that relies on machine-dependent behavior may have to be found and corrected. Tracking down these sorts of problems in previously working programs is, mildly put, a profoundly unpleasant task.

Multi-Line Literals

There is a more primitive (and less useful) way to handle long strings that depends on an infrequently used program formatting feature: Putting a backslash as the last character on a line causes that line and the next to be treated as a single line.

As noted on page 14, C++ programs are largely free-format. In particular, there are only a few places that we may not insert whitespace. One of these is in the middle of a word. In particular, we may not break a line in the middle of a word. We can circumvent this rule by using a backslash:

```
//  ok: A \ before a newline ignores the line break
std::cou\
t << "Hi" << st\
d::endl;
```

is equivalent to

```
std::cout << "Hi" << std::endl;
```

We could use this feature to write a long string literal:

```
//  multiline string literal
    std::cout << "a multi-line \
string literal \
using a backslash"
            << std::endl;
    return 0;
}
```

Note that the backslash must be the last thing on the line—no comments or trailing blanks are allowed. Also, any leading spaces or tabs on the subsequent lines are part of the literal. For this reason, the continuation lines of the long literal do not have the normal indentation.

Exercise 2.7: Explain the difference between the following sets of literal constants:

(a) `'a', L'a', "a", L"a"`
(b) `10, 10u, 10L, 10uL, 012, 0xC`
(c) `3.14, 3.14f, 3.14L`

Exercise 2.8: Determine the type of each of these literal constants:

    (a) `-10`   (b) `-10u`   (c) `-10.`   (d) `-10e-2`

Exercise 2.9: Which, if any, of the following are illegal?

    (a) `"Who goes with F\145rgus?\012"`
    (b) `3.14e1L`   (c) `"two" L"some"`
    (d) `1024f`   (e) `3.14UL`
    (f) `"multiple line`
        `comment"`

Exercise 2.10: Using escape sequences, write a program to print `2M` followed by a newline. Modify the program to print `2`, then a tab, then an `M`, followed by a newline.

2.3 Variables

Imagine that we are given the problem of computing 2 to the power of 10. Our first attempt might be something like

```
#include <iostream>
int main()
{
    //  a first, not very good, solution
    std::cout << "2 raised to the power of 10: ";
    std::cout << 2*2*2*2*2*2*2*2*2*2;
    std::cout << std::endl;
    return 0;
}
```

This program solves the problem, although we might double- or triple-check to make sure that exactly 10 literal instances of 2 are being multiplied. Otherwise, we're satisfied. Our program correctly generates the answer 1,024.

We're next asked to compute 2 raised to the power of 17 and then to the power of 23. Changing our program each time is a nuisance. Worse, it proves to be remarkably error-prone. Too often, the modified program produces an answer with one too few or too many instances of 2.

An alternative to the explicit brute force power-of-2 computation is twofold:

1. Use named objects to perform and print each computation.

2. Use flow-of-control constructs to provide for the repeated execution of a sequence of program statements while a condition is true.

Here, then, is an alternative way to compute 2 raised to the power of 10:

```
#include <iostream>
int main()
{
    // local objects of type int
    int value = 2;
    int pow = 10;
    int result = 1;
    // repeat calculation of result until cnt is equal to pow
    for (int cnt = 0; cnt != pow; ++cnt)
        result *= value;    // result = result * value;
    std::cout << value
             << " raised to the power of "
             << pow << ": \t"
             << result << std::endl;
    return 0;
}
```

`value`, `pow`, `result`, and `cnt` are variables that allow for the storage, modification, and retrieval of values. The `for` loop allows for the repeated execution of our calculation until it's been executed `pow` times.

EXERCISES SECTION 2.3

Exercise 2.11: Write a program that prompts the user to input two numbers, the base and exponent. Print the result of raising the base to the power of the exponent.

KEY CONCEPT: STRONG STATIC TYPING

C++ is a statically typed language, which means that types are checked at compile time. The process by which types are checked is referred to as type-checking.

In most languages, the type of an object constrains the operations that the object can perform. If the type does not support a given operation, then an object of that type cannot perform that operation.

In C++, whether an operation is legal or not is checked at compile time. When we write an expression, the compiler checks that the objects used in the expression are used in ways that are defined by the type of the objects. If not, the compiler generates an error message; an executable file is not produced.

As our programs, and the types we use, get more complicated, we'll see that static type checking helps find bugs in our programs earlier. A consequence of static checking is that the type of every entity used in our programs must be known to the compiler. Hence, we must define the type of a variable before we can use that variable in our programs.

2.3.1 What Is a Variable?

A variable provides us with named storage that our programs can manipulate. Each variable in C++ has a specific type, which determines the size and layout of the variable's memory; the range of values that can be stored within that memory; and the set of operations that can be applied to the variable. C++ programmers tend to refer to variables as "variables" or as "objects" interchangeably.

Lvalues and Rvalues

We'll have more to say about expressions in Chapter 5, but for now it is useful to know that there are two kinds of expressions in C++:

1. **lvalue** (pronounced "ell-value"): An expression that is an lvalue may appear as either the left-hand or right-hand side of an assignment.

2. **rvalue** (pronounced "are-value"): An expression that is an rvalue may appear on the right- but not left-hand side of an assignment.

Variables are lvalues and so may appear on the left-hand side of an assignment. Numeric literals are rvalues and so may not be assigned. Given the variables:

```
int units_sold = 0;
double sales_price = 0, total_revenue = 0;
```

it is a compile-time error to write either of the following:

```
//  error: arithmetic expression is not an lvalue
units_sold * sales_price = total_revenue;
//  error: literal constant is not an lvalue
0 = 1;
```

Some operators, such as assignment, require that one of their operands be an lvalue. As a result, lvalues can be used in more contexts than can rvalues. The context in which an lvalue appears determines how it is used. For example, in the expression

```
units_sold = units_sold + 1;
```

the variable units_sold is used as the operand to two different operators. The + operator cares only about the values of its operands. The value of a variable is the value currently stored in the memory associated with that variable. The effect of the addition is to fetch that value and add one to it.

The variable units_sold is also used as the left-hand side of the = operator. The = operator reads its right-hand side and writes to its left-hand side. In this expression, the result of the addition is stored in the storage associated with units_sold; the previous value in units_sold is overwritten.

In the course of the text, we'll see a number of situations in which the use of an rvalue or lvalue impacts the behavior and/or the performance of our programs—in particular when passing and returning values from a function.

EXERCISES SECTION 2.3.1

Exercise 2.12: Distinguish between an lvalue and an rvalue; show examples of each.

Exercise 2.13: Name one case where an lvalue is required.

TERMINOLOGY: WHAT IS AN OBJECT?

C++ programmers tend to be cavalier in their use of the term *object*. Most generally, an object is a region of memory that has a type. More specifically, evaluating an expression that is an lvalue yields an object.

Strictly speaking, some might reserve the term *object* to describe only variables or values of class types. Others might distinguish between named and unnamed objects, always referring to variables when discussing named objects. Still others distinguish between objects and values, using the term *object* for data that can be changed by the program and using the term *value* for those that are read-only.

In this book, we'll follow the more colloquial usage that an object is a region of memory that has a type. We will freely use *object* to refer to most of the data manipulated by our programs regardless of whether those data have built-in or class type, are named or unnamed, or are data that can be read or written.

2.3.2 The Name of a Variable

The name of a variable, its **identifier**, can be composed of letters, digits, and the underscore character. It must begin with either a letter or an underscore. Upper- and lowercase letters are distinct: Identifiers in C++ are case-sensitive. The following defines four distinct identifiers:

```
// declares four different int variables
int somename, someName, SomeName, SOMENAME;
```

 There is no language-imposed limit on the permissible length of a name, but out of consideration for others that will read and/or modify our code, it should not be too long.

For example,

```
gosh_this_is_an_impossibly_long_name_to_type
```

is a really bad identifier name.

C++ Keywords

C++ reserves a set of words for use within the language as keywords. Keywords may not be used as program identifiers. Table 2.2 on the next page lists the complete set of C++ keywords.

C++ also reserves a number of words that can be used as alternative names for various operators. These alternative names are provided to support character sets

Table 2.2: C++ Keywords				
asm	do	if	return	try
auto	double	inline	short	typedef
bool	dynamic_cast	int	signed	typeid
break	else	long	sizeof	typename
case	enum	mutable	static	union
catch	explicit	namespace	static_cast	unsigned
char	export	new	struct	using
class	extern	operator	switch	virtual
const	false	private	template	void
const_cast	float	protected	this	volatile
continue	for	public	throw	wchar_t
default	friend	register	true	while
delete	goto	reinterpret_cast		

that do not support the standard set of C++ operator symbols. These names, listed in Table 2.3, also may not be used as identifiers:

Table 2.3: C++ Operator Alternative Names					
and	bitand	compl	not_eq	or_eq	xor_eq
and_eq	bitor	not	or	xor	

In addition to the keywords, the standard also reserves a set of identifiers for use in the library. Identifiers cannot contain two consecutive underscores, nor can an identifier begin with an underscore followed immediately by an upper-case letter. Certain identifiers—those that are defined outside a function—may not begin with an underscore.

Conventions for Variable Names

There are a number of generally accepted conventions for naming variables. Following these conventions can improve the readability of a program.

- A variable name is normally written in lowercase letters. For example, one writes index, not Index or INDEX.

- An identifier is given a mnemonic name—that is, a name that gives some indication of its use in a program, such as on_loan or salary.

- An identifier containing multiple words is written either with an underscore between each word or by capitalizing the first letter of each embedded word. For example, one generally writes student_loan or studentLoan, not studentloan.

Best Practices The most important aspect of a naming convention is that it be applied consistently.

EXERCISES SECTION 2.3.2

Exercise 2.14: Which, if any, of the following names are invalid? Correct each identified invalid name.

```
(a) int double = 3.14159;        (b) char _;
(c) bool catch-22;               (d) char 1_or_2 = '1';
(e) float Float = 3.14f;
```

2.3.3 Defining Objects

The following statements define five variables:

```
int units_sold;
double sales_price, avg_price;
std::string title;
Sales_item  curr_book;
```

Each definition starts with a **type specifier**, followed by a comma-separated list of one or more names. A semicolon terminates the definition. The type specifier names the type associated with the object: `int`, `double`, `std::string`, and `Sales_item` are all names of types. The types `int` and `double` are built-in types, `std::string` is a type defined by the library, and `Sales_item` is a type that we used in Section 1.5 (p. 20) and will define in subsequent chapters. The type determines the amount of storage that is allocated for the variable and the set of operations that can be performed on it.

Multiple variables may be defined in a single statement:

```
double salary, wage;      // defines two variables of type double
int month,
    day, year;            // defines three variables of type int
std::string address;      // defines one variable of type std::string
```

Initialization

A definition specifies a variable's type and identifier. A definition may also provide an initial value for the object. An object defined with a specified first value is spoken of as **initialized**. C++ supports two forms of variable initialization: **copy-initialization** and **direct-initialization**. The copy-initialization syntax uses the equal (=) symbol; direct-initialization places the initializer in parentheses:

```
int ival(1024);    // direct-initialization
int ival = 1024;   // copy-initialization
```

In both cases, `ival` is initialized to `1024`.

> Although, at this point in the book, it may seem obscure to the reader, in C++ it is essential to understand that initialization is not assignment. Initialization happens when a variable is created and gives that variable its initial value. Assignment involves obliterating an object's current value and replacing that value with a new one.

Many new C++ programmers are confused by the use of the = symbol to initialize a variable. It is tempting to think of initialization as a form of assignment. But initialization and assignment are different operations in C++. This concept is particularly confusing because in many other languages the distinction is irrelevant and can be ignored. Moreover, even in C++ the distinction rarely matters until one attempts to write fairly complex classes. Nonetheless, it is a crucial concept and one that we will reiterate throughout the text.

> There are subtle differences between copy- and direct-initialization when initializing objects of a class type. We won't completely explain these differences until Chapter 13. For now, it's worth knowing that the direct syntax is more flexible and can be slightly more efficient.

Using Multiple Initializers

When we initialize an object of a built-in type, there is only one way to do so: We supply a value, and that value is copied into the newly defined object. For built-in types, there is little difference between the direct and the copy forms of initialization.

For objects of a class type, there are initializations that can be done only using direct-initialization. To understand why, we need to know a bit about how classes control initialization.

Each class may define one or more special member functions (Section 1.5.2, p. 24) that say how we can initialize variables of the class type. The member functions that define how initialization works are known as **constructors**. Like any function, a constructor can take multiple arguments. A class may define several constructors, each of which must take a different number or type of arguments.

As an example, we'll look a bit at the `string` class, which we'll cover in more detail in Chapter 3. The `string` type is defined by the library and holds character strings of varying sizes. To use `strings`, we must include the `string` header. Like the IO types, `string` is defined in the `std` namespace.

The `string` class defines several constructors, giving us various ways to initialize a `string`. One way we can initialize a `string` is as a copy of a character string literal:

```
#include <string>
// alternative ways to initialize string from a character string literal
std::string titleA = "C++ Primer, 4th Ed.";
std::string titleB("C++ Primer, 4th Ed.");
```

In this case, either initialization form can be used. Both definitions create a `string` object whose initial value is a copy of the specified string literal.

However, we can also initialize a `string` from a count and a character. Doing so creates a `string` containing the specified character repeated as many times as indicated by the count:

```
std::string all_nines(10, '9');   // all_nines = "9999999999"
```

In this case, the only way to initialize `all_nines` is by using the direct form of initialization. It is not possible to use copy-initialization with multiple initializers.

Initializing Multiple Variables

When a definition defines two or more variables, each variable may have its own initializer. The name of an object becomes visible immediately, and so it is possible to initialize a subsequent variable to the value of one defined earlier in the same definition. Initialized and uninitialized variables may be defined in the same definition. Both forms of initialization syntax may be intermixed:

```
#include <string>
// ok: salary defined and initialized before it is used to initialize wage
double salary = 9999.99,
       wage(salary + 0.01);
// ok: mix of initialized and uninitialized
int interval,
    month = 8, day = 7, year = 1955;
// ok: both forms of initialization syntax used
std::string title("C++ Primer, 4th Ed."),
            publisher = "A-W";
```

An object can be initialized with an arbitrarily complex expression, including the return value of a function:

```
double price = 109.99, discount = 0.16;
double sale_price = apply_discount(price, discount);
```

In this example, `apply_discount` is a function that takes two values of type `double` and returns a value of type `double`. We pass the variables `price` and `discount` to that function and use its return value to initialize `sale_price`.

2.3.4 Variable Initialization Rules

When we define a variable without an initializer, the system sometimes initializes the variable for us. What value, if any, is supplied depends on the type of the variable and may depend on where it is defined.

Initialization of Variables of Built-in Type

Whether a variable of built-in type is automatically initialized depends on where it is defined. Variables defined outside any function body are initialized to zero.

EXERCISES SECTION 2.3.3

Exercise 2.15: What, if any, are the differences between the following definitions:

```
int month = 9, day = 7;

int month = 09, day = 07;
```

If either definition contains an error, how might you correct the problem?

Exercise 2.16: Assuming `calc` is a function that returns a `double`, which, if any, of the following are illegal definitions? Correct any that are identified as illegal.

(a) `int car = 1024, auto = 2048;`
(b) `int ival = ival;`
(c) `std::cin >> int input_value;`
(d) `double salary = wage = 9999.99;`
(e) `double calc = calc();`

Variables of built-in type defined inside the body of a function are **uninitialized**. Using an uninitialized variable for anything other than as the left-hand operand of an assignment is undefined. Bugs due to uninitialized variables can be hard to find. As we cautioned on page 42, you should never rely on undefined behavior.

Best Practices

We recommend that every object of built-in type be initialized. It is not always necessary to initialize such variables, but it is easier and safer to do so until you can be certain it is safe to omit an initializer.

CAUTION: UNINITIALIZED VARIABLES CAUSE RUN-TIME PROBLEMS

Using an uninitialized object is a common program error, and one that is often difficult to uncover. The compiler is not required to detect a use of an uninitialized variable, although many will warn about at least some uses of uninitialized variables. However, no compiler can detect all uses of uninitialized variables.

Sometimes, we're lucky and using an uninitialized variable results in an immediate crash at run time. Once we track down the location of the crash, it is usually pretty easy to see that the variable was not properly initialized.

Other times, the program completes but produces erroneous results. Even worse, the results can appear correct when we run our program on one machine but fail on another. Adding code to the program in an unrelated location can cause what we thought was a correct program to suddenly start to produce incorrect results.

The problem is that uninitialized variables actually do have a value. The compiler puts the variable somewhere in memory and treats whatever bit pattern was in that memory as the variable's initial state. When interpreted as an integral value, any bit pattern is a legitimate value—although the value is unlikely to be one that the programmer intended. Because the value is legal, using it is unlikely to lead to a crash. What it is likely to do is lead to incorrect execution and/or incorrect calculation.

Initialization of Variables of Class Type

Each class defines how objects of its type can be initialized. Classes control object initialization by defining one or more constructors (Section 2.3.3, p. 49). As an example, we know that the `string` class provides at least two constructors. One of these constructors lets us initialize a `string` from a character string literal and another lets us initialize a `string` from a character and a count.

Each class may also define what happens if a variable of the type is defined but an initializer is not provided. A class does so by defining a special constructor, known as the **default constructor**. This constructor is called the default constructor because it is run "by default;" if there is no initializer, then this constructor is used. The default constructor is used regardless of where a variable is defined.

Most classes provide a default constructor. If the class has a default constructor, then we can define variables of that class without explicitly initializing them. For example, the `string` type defines its default constructor to initialize the `string` as an empty string—that is, a string with no characters:

```
std::string empty;   // empty is the empty string; empty = ""
```

Some class types do not have a default constructor. For these types, every definition must provide explicit initializer(s). It is not possible to define variables of such types without giving an initial value.

EXERCISES SECTION 2.3.4

Exercise 2.17: What are the initial values, if any, of each of the following variables?

```
std::string global_str;
int global_int;
int main()
{
    int local_int;
    std::string local_str;
    // ...
    return 0;
}
```

2.3.5   Declarations and Definitions

As we'll see in Section 2.9 (p. 67), C++ programs typically are composed of many files. In order for multiple files to access the same variable, C++ distinguishes between declarations and definitions.

A **definition** of a variable allocates storage for the variable and may also specify an initial value for the variable. There must be one and only one definition of a variable in a program.

A **declaration** makes known the type and name of the variable to the program. A definition is also a declaration: When we define a variable, we declare its name and type. We can declare a name without defining it by using the `extern` key-word. A declaration that is not also a definition consists of the object's name and its type preceded by the keyword `extern`:

```
extern int i;    // declares but does not define i
int i;           // declares and defines i
```

An `extern` declaration is *not* a definition and does not allocate storage. In effect, it claims that a definition of the variable exists elsewhere in the program. A variable can be declared multiple times in a program, but it must be defined only once.

A declaration may have an initializer only if it is also a definition because only a definition allocates storage. The initializer must have storage to initialize. If an initializer is present, the declaration is treated as a definition even if the declaration is labeled `extern`:

```
extern double pi = 3.1416; // definition
```

Despite the use of `extern`, this statement defines `pi`. Storage is allocated and initialized. An `extern` declaration may include an initializer only if it appears outside a function.

Because an `extern` that is initialized is treated as a definition, any subseqent definition of that variable is an error:

```
extern double pi = 3.1416; // definition
double pi;                 // error: redefinition of pi
```

Similarly, a subsequent `extern` declaration that has an initializer is also an error:

```
extern double pi = 3.1416; // definition
extern double pi;          // ok: declaration not definition
extern double pi = 3.1416; // error: redefinition of pi
```

The distinction between a declaration and a definition may seem pedantic but in fact is quite important.

 In C++ a variable must be defined exactly once and must be defined or declared before it is used.

Any variable that is used in more than one file requires declarations that are separate from the variable's definition. In such cases, one file will contain the definition for the variable. Other files that use that same variable will contain declarations for—but not a definition of—that same variable.

EXERCISES SECTION 2.3.5

Exercise 2.18: Explain the meaning of each of these instances of name:

```
extern std::string name;
std::string name("exercise 3.5a");
extern std::string name("exercise 3.5a");
```

2.3.6 Scope of a Name

Every name in a C++ program must refer to a unique entity (such as a variable, function, type, etc.). Despite this requirement, names can be used more than once in a program: A name can be reused as long as it is used in different contexts, from which the different meanings of the name can be distinguished. The context used to distinguish the meanings of names is a **scope**. A scope is a region of the program. A name can refer to different entities in different scopes.

Most scopes in C++ are delimited by curly braces. Generally, names are visible from their point of declaration until the end the scope in which the declaration appears. As an example, consider this program, which we first encountered in Section 1.4.2 (p. 14):

```
#include <iostream>
int main()
{
    int sum = 0;
    // sum values from 1 up to 10 inclusive
    for (int val = 1; val <= 10; ++val)
        sum += val;   // equivalent to sum = sum + val

    std::cout << "Sum of 1 to 10 inclusive is "
              << sum << std::endl;
    return 0;
}
```

This program defines three names and uses two names from the standard library. It defines a function named `main` and two variables named `sum` and `val`. The name `main` is defined outside any curly braces and is visible throughout the program. Names defined outside any function have **global scope**; they are accessible from anywhere in the program. The name `sum` is defined within the scope of the `main` function. It is accessible throughout the `main` function but not outside of it. The variable `sum` has **local scope**. The name `val` is more interesting. It is defined in the scope of the `for` statement (Section 1.4.2, p. 14). It can be used in that statement but not elsewhere in `main`. It has **statement scope**.

Scopes in C++ Nest

Names defined in the global scope can be used in a local scope; global names and those defined local to a function can be used inside a statement scope, and so on. Names can also be redefined in an inner scope. Understanding what entity a name refers to requires unwinding the scopes in which the names are defined:

```
#include <iostream>
#include <string>
/* Program for illustration purposes only:
 * It is bad style for a function to use a global variable and then
 * define a local variable with the same name
 */
```

```
std::string s1 = "hello";  // s1 has global scope
int main()
{
    std::string s2 = "world"; // s2 has local scope
    // uses global s1; prints "hello world"
    std::cout << s1 << " " << s2 << std::endl;
    int s1 = 42; // s1 is local and hides global s1
    // uses local s1; prints "42 world"
    std::cout << s1 << " " <<  s2 << std::endl;
    return 0;
}
```

This program defines three variables: a global `string` named `s1`, a local `string` named `s2`, and a local `int` named `s1`. The definition of the local `s1` *hides* the global `s1`.

Variables are visible from their point of declaration. Thus, the local definition of `s1` is not visible when the first output is performed. The name `s1` in that output expression refers to the global `s1`. The output printed is `hello world`. The second statement that does output follows the local definition of `s1`. The local `s1` is now in scope. The second output uses the local rather than the global `s1`. It writes `42 world`.

> Programs such as the preceeding are likely to be confusing. It is almost always a bad idea to define a local variable with the same name as a global variable that the function uses or might use. It is much better to use a distinct name for the local.

We'll have more to say about local and global scope in Chapter 7 and about statement scope in Chapter 6. C++ has two other levels of scope: **class scope**, which we'll cover in Chapter 12 and **namespace scope**, which we'll see in Section 17.2.

2.3.7 Define Variables Where They Are Used

In general, variable definitions or declarations can be placed anywhere within the program that a statement is allowed. A variable must be declared or defined before it is used.

> It is usually a good idea to define an object near the point at which the object is first used.

Defining an object where the object is first used improves readability. The reader does not have to go back to the beginning of a section of code to find the definition of a particular variable. Moreover, it is often easier to give the variable a useful initial value when the variable is defined close to where it is first used.

One constraint on placing declarations is that variables are accessible from the point of their definition until the end of the enclosing block. A variable must be defined in or before the outermost scope in which the variable will be used.

EXERCISES SECTION 2.3.6

Exercise 2.19: What is the value of j in the following program?

```
int i = 42;
int main()
{
    int i = 100;
    int j = i;
    // ...
}
```

Exercise 2.20: Given the following program fragment, what values are printed?

```
int i = 100, sum = 0;
for (int i = 0; i != 10; ++i)
    sum += i;
std::cout << i << " " << sum << std::endl;
```

Exercise 2.21: Is the following program legal?

```
int sum = 0;
for (int i = 0; i != 10; ++i)
    sum += i;
std::cout << "Sum from 0 to " << i
          << " is " << sum << std::endl;
```

2.4   const Qualifier

There are two problems with the following for loop, both concerning the use of 512 as an upper bound.

```
for (int index = 0; index != 512; ++index) {
    // ...
}
```

The first problem is readability. What does it mean to compare index with 512? What is the loop doing—that is, what makes 512 matter? (In this example, 512 is known as a **magic number**, one whose significance is not evident within the context of its use. It is as if the number had been plucked by magic from thin air.)

The second problem is maintainability. Imagine that we have a large program in which the number 512 occurs 100 times. Let's further assume that 80 of these references use 512 to indicate the size of a particular buffer but the other 20 use 512 for different purposes. Now we discover that we need to increase the buffer size to 1024. To make this change, we must examine every one of the places that the number 512 appears. We must determine—correctly in every case—which of those uses of 512 refer to the buffer size and which do not. Getting even one instance wrong breaks the program and requires us to go back and reexamine each use.

The solution to both problems is to use an object initialized to 512:

```
int bufSize = 512;      // input buffer size
```

```
for (int index = 0; index != bufSize; ++index) {
    // ...
}
```

By choosing a mnemonic name, such as bufSize, we make the program more readable. The test is now against the object rather than the literal constant:

```
index != bufSize
```

If we need to change this size, the 80 occurrences no longer need to be found and corrected. Rather, only the one line that initializes bufSize requires change. Not only does this approach require significantly less work, but also the likelihood of making a mistake is greatly reduced.

Defining a const Object

There is still a serious problem with defining a variable to represent a constant value. The problem is that bufSize is modifiable. It is possible for bufSize to be changed—accidentally or otherwise. The const type qualifier provides a solution: It transforms an object into a constant.

```
const int bufSize = 512;     // input buffer size
```

defines bufSize to be a constant initialized with the value 512. The variable bufSize is still an lvalue (Section 2.3.1, p. 45), but now the lvalue is unmodifiable. Any attempt to write to bufSize results in a compile-time error.

```
bufSize = 0; // error: attempt to write to const object
```

Because we cannot subsequently change the value of an object declared to be const, we must initialize it when it is defined:

```
const std::string hi = "hello!"; // ok: initialized
const int i, j = 0;  // error: i is uninitialized const
```

const Objects Are Local to a File By Default

When we define a nonconst variable at global scope (Section 2.3.6, p. 54), it is accessible throughout the program. We can define a nonconst variable in one file and—assuming an appropriate declaration has been made—can use that variable in another file:

```
// file_1.cc
int counter;  // definition
// file_2.cc
extern int counter; // uses counter from file_1
++counter;          // increments counter defined in file_1
```

Unlike other variables, unless otherwise specified, const variables declared at global scope are local to the file in which the object is defined. The variable exists in that file only and cannot be accessed by other files.

We can make a const object accessible throughout the program by specifying that it is extern:

```
// file_1.cc
// defines and initializes a const that is accessible to other files
extern const int bufSize = fcn();

// file_2.cc
extern const int bufSize; // uses bufSize from file_1

// uses bufSize defined in file_1
for (int index = 0; index != bufSize; ++index)
    // ...
```

In this program, `file_1.cc` defines and initializes `bufSize` to the result returned from calling the function named `fcn`. The definition of `bufSize` is `extern`, meaning that `bufSize` can be used in other files. The declaration in `file_2.cc` is also made `extern`. In this case, the `extern` signifies that `bufSize` is a declaration and hence no initializer is provided.

We'll see in Section 2.9.1 (p. 69) why `const` objects are made local to a file.

> Nonconst variables are `extern` by default. To make a `const` variable accessible to other files we must explicitly specify that it is `extern`.

EXERCISES SECTION 2.4

Exercise 2.22: The following program fragment, while legal, is an example of poor style. What problem(s) does it contain? How would you improve it?

```
for (int i = 0; i < 100; ++i)
    // process i
```

Exercise 2.23: Which of the following are legal? For those usages that are illegal, explain why.

```
(a) const int buf;
(b) int cnt = 0;
    const int sz = cnt;
(c) cnt++; sz++;
```

2.5 References

A **reference** serves as an alternative name for an object. In real-world programs, references are primarily used as formal parameters to functions. We'll have more to say about reference parameters in Section 7.2.2 (p. 232). In this section we introduce and illustrate the use of references as independent objects.

A reference is a **compound type** that is defined by preceding a variable name by the & symbol. A compound type is a type that is defined in terms of another type. In the case of references, each reference type "refers to" some other type. We cannot define a reference to a reference type, but can make a reference to any other data type.

A reference *must* be initialized using an object of the same type as the reference:

```
int ival = 1024;
int &refVal = ival; // ok: refVal refers to ival
int &refVal2;         // error: a reference must be initialized
int &refVal3 = 10;   // error: initializer must be an object
```

A Reference Is an Alias

Because a reference is just another name for the object to which it is bound, *all* operations on a reference are actually operations on the underlying object to which the reference is bound:

```
refVal += 2;
```

adds 2 to `ival`, the object referred to by `refVal`. Similarly,

```
int ii = refVal;
```

assigns to `ii` the value currently associated with `ival`.

 When a reference is initialized, it remains bound to that object as long as the reference exists. There is no way to rebind a reference to a different object.

The important concept to understand is that a reference is *just another name for an object*. Effectively, we can access `ival` either through its actual name or through its alias, `refVal`. Assignment is just another operation, so that when we write

```
refVal = 5;
```

the effect is to change the value of `ival` to 5. A consequence of this rule is that you must initialize a reference when you define it; initialization is the only way to say to which object a reference refers.

Defining Multiple References

We can define multiple references in a single type definition. Each identifier that is a reference must be preceded by the `&` symbol:

```
int i = 1024, i2 = 2048;
int &r = i, r2 = i2;       // r is a reference, r2 is an int
int i3 = 1024, &ri = i3;   // defines one object, and one reference
int &r3 = i3, &r4 = i2;    // defines two references
```

const References

A **const reference** is a reference that may refer to a `const` object:

```
const int ival = 1024;
const int &refVal = ival; // ok: both reference and object are const
int &ref2 = ival;            // error: nonconst reference to a const object
```

We can read from but not write to `refVal`. Thus, any assignment to `refVal` is illegal. This restriction should make sense: We cannot assign directly to `ival` and so it should not be possible to use `refVal` to change `ival`.

For the same reason, the initialization of `ref2` by `ival` is an error: `ref2` is a plain, **nonconst reference** and so could be used to change the value of the object to which `ref2` refers. Assigning to `ival` through `ref2` would result in changing the value of a `const` object. To prevent such changes, it is illegal to bind a plain reference to a `const` object.

TERMINOLOGY: CONST REFERENCE IS A REFERENCE TO CONST

C++ programmers tend to be cavalier in their use of the term `const` reference. Strictly speaking, what is meant by "const reference" is "reference to const." Similarly, programmers use the term "nonconst reference" when speaking of reference to a nonconst type. This usage is so common that we will follow it in this book as well.

A `const` reference can be initialized to an object of a different type or to an rvalue (Section 2.3.1, p. 45), such as a literal constant:

```
int i = 42;
//   legal for const references only
const int &r = 42;
const int &r2 = r + i;
```

The same initializations are not legal for nonconst references. Rather, they result in compile-time errors. The reason is subtle and warrants an explanation.

This behavior is easiest to understand when we look at what happens when we bind a reference to an object of a different type. If we write

```
double dval = 3.14;
const int &ri = dval;
```

the compiler transforms this code into something like this:

```
int temp = dval;        //   create temporary int from the double
const int &ri = temp;   //   bind ri to that temporary
```

If `ri` were not `const`, then we could assign a new value to `ri`. Doing so would not change `dval` but would instead change `temp`. To the programmer expecting that assignments to `ri` would change `dval`, it would appear that the change did not work. Allowing only `const` references to be bound to values requiring temporaries avoids the problem entirely because a `const` reference is read-only.

A nonconst reference may be attached only to an object of the same type as the reference itself.

A `const` reference may be bound to an object of a different but related type or to an rvalue.

EXERCISES SECTION 2.5

Exercise 2.24: Which of the following definitions, if any, are invalid? Why? How would you correct them?

```
(a) int ival = 1.01;      (b) int &rval1 = 1.01;
(c) int &rval2 = ival;    (d) const int &rval3 = 1;
```

Exercise 2.25: Given the preceeding definitions, which, if any, of the following assignments are invalid? If they are valid, explain what they do.

```
(a) rval2 = 3.14159;      (b) rval2 = rval3;
(c) ival = rval3;         (d) rval3 = ival;
```

Exercise 2.26: What are the differences among the definitions in (a) and the assignments in (b)? Which, if any, are illegal?

```
(a) int ival = 0;             (b) ival = ri;
    const int &ri = 0;            ri = ival;
```

Exercise 2.27: What does the following code print?

```
int i, &ri = i;
i = 5; ri = 10;
std::cout << i << " " << ri << std::endl;
```

2.6 Typedef Names

A **typedef** lets us define a synonym for a type:

```
typedef double wages;        // wages is a synonym for double
typedef int exam_score;      // exam_score is a synonym for int
typedef wages salary;        // indirect synonym for double
```

A typedef name can be used as a type specifier:

```
wages hourly, weekly;     // double hourly, weekly;
exam_score test_result;   // int test_result;
```

A typedef definition begins with the keyword `typedef`, followed by the data type and identifier. The identifier, or typedef name, does not introduce a new type but rather a synonym for the existing data type. A typedef name can appear anywhere in a program that a type name can appear.

Typedefs are commonly used for one of three purposes:

- To hide the implementation of a given type and emphasize instead the purpose for which the type is used

- To streamline complex type definitions, making them easier to understand

- To allow a single type to be used for more than one purpose while making the purpose clear each time the type is used

2.7   Enumerations

Often we need to define a set of alternative values for some attribute. A file, for example, might be open in one of three states: input, output, and append. One way to keep track of these state values might be to associate a unique constant number with each. We might write the following:

```
const int input = 0;
const int output = 1;
const int append = 2;
```

Although this approach works, it has a significant weakness: There is no indication that these values are related in any way. **Enumerations** provide an alternative method of not only defining but also grouping sets of integral constants.

Defining and Initializing Enumerations

An enumeration is defined using the enum keyword, followed by an optional enumeration name, and a comma-separated list of **enumerators** enclosed in braces.

```
//  input is 0, output is 1, and append is 2
enum open_modes {input, output, append};
```

By default, the first enumerator is assigned the value zero. Each subsequent enumerator is assigned a value one greater than the value of the enumerator that immediately precedes it.

Enumerators Are const Values

We may supply an initial value for one or more enumerators. The value used to initialize an enumerator must be a **constant expression**. A constant expression is an expression of integral type that the compiler can evaluate at compile time. An integral literal constant is a constant expression, as is a const object (Section 2.4, p. 56) that is itself initialized from a constant expression.

For example, we might define the following enumeration:

```
//  shape is 1, sphere is 2, cylinder is 3, polygon is 4
enum Forms {shape = 1, sphere, cylinder, polygon};
```

In the enum Forms we explicitly assigned shape the value 1. The other enumerators are implicitly initialized: sphere is initialized to 2, cylinder to 3, and polygon to 4.

An enumerator value need not be unique.

```
//  point2d is 2, point2w is 3, point3d is 3, point3w is 4
enum Points { point2d = 2, point2w,
              point3d = 3, point3w };
```

In this example, the enumerator point2d is explicitly initialized to 2. The next enumerator, point2w, is initialized by default, meaning that its value is one more than the value of the previous enumerator. Thus, point2w is initialized to 3. The enumerator `point3d` is explicitly initialized to `3`, and `point3w`, again is initialized by default, in this case to `4`.

It is not possible to change the value of an enumerator. As a consequence an enumerator is itself a constant expression and so can be used where a constant expression is required.

Each **enum** Defines a Unique Type

Each `enum` defines a new type. As with any type, we can define and initialize objects of type `Points` and can use those objects in various ways. An object of enumeration type may be initialized or assigned only by one of its enumerators or by another object of the same enumeration type:

```
Points pt3d = point3d;   //  ok: point3d is a Points enumerator
Points pt2w = 3;         //  error: pt2w initialized with int
pt2w = polygon;          //  error: polygon is not a Points enumerator
pt2w = pt3d;             //  ok: both are objects of Points enum type
```

Note that it is illegal to assign the value `3` to a `Points` object even though `3` is a value associated with one of the `Points` enumerators.

2.8   Class Types

In C++ we define our own data types by defining a **class**. A class defines the data that an object of its type contains and the operations that can be executed by objects of that type. The library types `string`, `istream`, and `ostream` are all defined as classes.

C++ support for classes is extensive—in fact, defining classes is so important that we shall devote Parts III through V to describing C++ support for classes and operations using class types.

In Chapter 1 we used the `Sales_item` type to solve our bookstore problem. We used objects of type `Sales_item` to keep track of sales data associated with a particular ISBN. In this section, we'll take a first look at how a simple class, such as `Sales_item`, might be defined.

Class Design Starts with the Operations

Each class defines an **interface** and **implementation**. The interface consists of the operations that we expect code that uses the class to execute. The implementation typically includes the data needed by the class. The implementation also includes any functions needed to define the class but that are not intended for general use.

When we define a class, we usually begin by defining its interface—the operations that the class will provide. From those operations we can then determine what data the class will require to accomplish its tasks and whether it will need to define any functions to support the implementation.

The operations our type will support are the operations we used in Chapter 1. These operations were outlined in Section 1.5.1 (p. 21):

- The addition operator to add two `Sales_items`

- The input and output operators to read and write `Sales_item` objects

- The assignment operator to assign one `Sales_item` object to another

- The `same_isbn` function to determine if two objects refer to the same book

We'll see how to define these operations in Chapters 7 and 14 after we learn how to define functions and operators. Even though we can't yet implement these functions, we can figure out what data they'll need by thinking a bit about what these operations must do. Our `Sales_item` class must

1. Keep track of how many copies of a particular book were sold

2. Report the total revenue for that book

3. Calculate the average sales price for that book

Looking at this list of tasks, we can see that we'll need an `unsigned` to keep track of how many books are sold and a `double` to keep track of the total revenue. From these data we can calculate the average sales price as total revenue divided by number sold. Because we also want to know which book we're reporting on, we'll also need a `string` to keep track of the ISBN.

Defining the `Sales_item` Class

Evidently what we need is the ability to define a data type that will have these three data elements and the operations we used in Chapter 1. In C++, the way we define such a data type is to define a class:

```
class Sales_item {
public:
    // operations on Sales_item objects will go here
private:
    std::string isbn;
    unsigned units_sold;
    double revenue;
};
```

A class definition starts with the keyword `class` followed by an identifier that names the class. The body of the class appears inside curly braces. The close curly must be followed by a semicolon.

> It is a common mistake among new programmers to forget the semicolon at the end of a class definition.

The class body, which can be empty, defines the data and operations that make up the type. The operations and data that are part of a class are referred to as its **members**. The operations are referred to as the member functions (Section 1.5.2, p. 24) and the data as **data members**.

The class also may contain zero or more `public` or `private` **access labels**. An access label controls whether a member is accessible outside the class. Code that uses the class may access only the `public` members.

When we define a class, we define a new type. The class name is the name of that type. By naming our class `Sales_item` we are saying that `Sales_item` is a new type and that programs may define variables of this type.

Each class defines its own scope (Section 2.3.6, p. 54). That is, the names given to the data and operations inside the class body must be unique within the class but can reuse names defined outside the class.

Class Data Members

The data members of a class are defined in somewhat the same way that normal variables are defined. We specify a type and give the member a name just as we do when defining a simple variable:

```
std::string isbn;
unsigned units_sold;
double revenue;
```

Our class has three data members: a member of type `string` named `isbn`, an `unsigned` member named `units_sold`, and a member of type `double` named `revenue`. The data members of a class define the contents of the objects of that class type. When we define objects of type `Sales_item`, those objects will contain a `string`, an `unsigned`, and a `double`.

There is one crucially important difference between how we define variables and class data members: We ordinarily cannot initialize the members of a class as part of their definition. When we define the data members, we can only name them and say what types they have. Rather than initializing data members when they are defined inside the class definition, classes control initialization through special member functions called constructors (Section 2.3.3, p. 49). We will define the `Sales_item` constructors in Section 7.7.3 (p. 262).

Access Labels

Access labels control whether code that uses the class may use a given member. Member functions of the class may use any member of their own class, regardless of the access level. The access labels, `public` and `private`, may appear multiple times in a class definition. A given label applies until the next access label is seen.

The **public** section of a class defines members that can be accessed by any part of the program. Ordinarily we put the operations in the `public` section so that any code in the program may execute these operations.

Code that is not part of the class does not have access to the **private** members. By making the `Sales_item` data members `private`, we ensure that code that operates on `Sales_item` objects cannot directly manipulate the data members. Programs, such as the one we wrote in Chapter 1, may not access the `private` members of the class. Objects of type `Sales_item` may execute the operations but not change the data directly.

Using the `struct` Keyword

C++ supports a second keyword, **struct**, that can be used to define class types. The `struct` keyword is inherited from C.

If we define a class using the `class` keyword, then any members defined before the first access label are implicitly `private`; if we use the `struct` keyword, then those members are `public`. Whether we define a class using the `class` keyword or the `struct` keyword affects only the default initial access level.

We could have defined our `Sales_item` equivalently by writing

```
struct Sales_item {
    // no need for public label, members are public by default
    // operations on Sales_item objects
private:
    std::string isbn;
    unsigned units_sold;
    double revenue;
};
```

There are only two differences between this class definition and our initial class definition: Here we use the `struct` keyword, and we eliminate the use of `public` keyword immediately following the opening curly brace. Members of a `struct` are public, unless otherwise specified, so there is no need for the `public` label.

> The only difference between a class defined with the `class` keyword or the `struct` keyword is the default access level: By default, members in a `struct` are `public`; those in a `class` are `private`.

EXERCISES SECTION 2.8

Exercise 2.28: Compile the following program to determine whether your compiler warns about a missing semicolon after a class definition:

```
class Foo {
    // empty
} // Note: no semicolon
int main()
{
    return 0;
}
```

If the diagnostic is confusing, remember the message for future reference.

Exercise 2.29: Distinguish between the `public` and `private` sections of a class.

Exercise 2.30: Define the data members of classes to represent the following types:
(a) a phone number   (b) an address
(c) an employee or a company   (d) a student at a university

2.9 Writing Our Own Header Files

We know from Section 1.5 (p. 20) that ordinarily class definitions go into a **header file**. In this section we'll see how to define a header file for the `Sales_item` class.

In fact, C++ programs use headers to contain more than class definitions. Recall that every name must be declared or defined before it is used. The programs we've written so far handle this requirement by putting all their code into a single file. As long as each entity precedes the code that uses it, this strategy works. However, few programs are so simple that they can be written in a single file. Programs made up of multiple files need a way to link the use of a name and its declaration. In C++ that is done through header files.

To allow programs to be broken up into logical parts, C++ supports what is commonly known as *separate compilation*. Separate compilation lets us compose a program from several files. To support separate compilation, we'll put the definition of `Sales_item` in a header file. The member functions for `Sales_item`, which we'll define in Section 7.7 (p. 258), will go in a separate source file. Functions such as `main` that use `Sales_item` objects are in other source files. Each of the source files that use `Sales_item` must include our `Sales_item.h` header file.

2.9.1 Designing Our Own Headers

A header provides a centralized location for related declarations. Headers normally contain class definitions, `extern` variable declarations, and function declarations, about which we'll learn in Section 7.4 (p. 251). Files that use or define these entities include the appropriate header(s).

Proper use of header files can provide two benefits: All files are guaranteed to use the same declaration for a given entity; and should a declaration require change, only the header needs to be updated.

Some care should be taken in designing headers. The declarations in a header should logically belong together. A header takes time to compile. If it is too large programmers may be reluctant to incur the compile-time cost of including it.

 To reduce the compile time needed to process headers, some C++ implementations support precompiled header files. For more details, consult the reference manual of your C++ implementation.

Headers Are for Declarations, Not Definitions

When designing a header it is essential to remember the difference between definitions, which may only occur once, and declarations, which may occur multiple times (Section 2.3.5, p. 52). The following statements are definitions and therefore should not appear in a header:

```
extern int ival = 10;      //  initializer, so it's a definition
double fica_rate;          //  no extern, so it's a definition
```

Although `ival` is declared `extern`, it has an initializer, which means this statement is a definition. Similarly, the declaration of `fica_rate`, although it does not

COMPILING AND LINKING MULTIPLE SOURCE FILES

To produce an executable file, we must tell the compiler not only where to find our main function but also where to find the definition of the member functions defined by the `Sales_item` class. Let's assume that we have two files: `main.cc`, which contains the definition of main, and `Sales_item.cc`, which contains the `Sales_item` member functions. We might compile these files as follows:

```
$ CC -c main.cc Sales_item.cc # by default generates a.exe
                              # some compilers generate a.out


# puts the executable in main.exe
$ CC -c main.cc Sales_item.cc -o main
```

where `$` is our system prompt and `#` begins a command-line comment. We can now run the executable file, which will run our main program.

If we have only changed one of our `.cc` source files, it is more efficient to recompile only the file that actually changed. Most compilers provide a way to separately compile each file. This process usually yields a `.o` file, where the `.o` extension implies that the file contains object code.

The compiler lets us *link* object files together to form an executable. On the system we use, in which the compiler is invoked by a command named `CC`, we would compile our program as follows:

```
$ CC -c main.cc           # generates main.o
$ CC -c Sales_item.cc     # generates Sales_item.o
$ CC main.o Sales_item.o  # by default generates a.exe;
                          # some compilers generate a.out


# puts the executable in main.exe
$ CC main.o Sales_item.o -o main
```

You'll need to check with your compiler's user's guide to understand how to compile and execute programs made up of multiple source files.

 Many compilers offer an option to enhance the error detection of the compiler. Check your compiler's user's guide to see what additional checks are available.

have an initializer, is a definition because the `extern` keyword is absent. Including either of these definitions in two or more files of the same program will result in a linker error complaining about multiple definitions.

 Because headers are included in multiple source files, they should not contain definitions of variables or functions.

There are three exceptions to the rule that headers should not contain definitions: classes, `const` objects whose value is known at compile time, and `inline` functions (Section 7.6 (p. 256) covers `inline` functions) are all defined in headers.

These entities may be defined in more than one source file as long as the definitions in each file are exactly the same.

These entities are defined in headers because the compiler needs their definitions (not just declarations) to generate code. For example, to generate code that defines or uses objects of a class type, the compiler needs to know what data members make up that type. It also needs to know what operations can be performed on these objects. The class definition provides the needed information. That `const` objects are defined in a header may require a bit more explanation.

Some `const` Objects Are Defined in Headers

Recall that by default a `const` variable (Section 2.4, p. 57) is local to the file in which it is defined. As we shall now see, the reason for this default is to allow `const` variables to be defined in header files.

In C++ there are places where constant expression (Section 2.7, p. 62) is required. For example, the initializer of an enumerator must be a constant expression. We'll see other cases that require constant expressions in later chapters.

Generally speaking, a constant expression is an expression that the compiler can evaluate at compile-time. A `const` variable of integral type may be a constant expression when it is itself initialized from a constant expression. However, for the `const` to be a constant expression, the initializer must be visible to the compiler. To allow multiple files to use the same constant value, the `const` and its initializer must be visible in each file. To make the initializer visible, we normally define such `const`s inside a header file. That way the compiler can see the initializer whenever the `const` is used.

However, there can be only one definition (Section 2.3.5, p. 52) for any variable in a C++ program. A definition allocates storage; all uses of the variable must refer to the same storage. Because, by default, `const` objects are local to the file in which they are defined, it is legal to put their definition in a header file.

There is one important implication of this behavior. When we define a `const` in a header file, every source file that includes that header has its own `const` variable with the same name and value.

When the `const` is initialized by a constant expression, then we are guaranteed that all the variables will have the same value. Moreover, in practice, most compilers will replace any use of such `const` variables by their corresponding constant expression at compile time. So, in practice, there won't be any storage used to hold `const` variables that are initialized by constant expressions.

When a `const` is initialized by a value that is not a constant expression, then it should not be defined in header file. Instead, as with any other variable, the `const` should be defined and initialized in a source file. An `extern` declaration for that `const` should be made in the header, enabling multiple files to share that variable.

2.9.2   A Brief Introduction to the Preprocessor

Now that we know what we want to put in our headers, our next problem is to actually write a header. We know that to use a header we have to `#include` it in our

---

Exercise 2.31: Identify which of the following statements are declarations and which ones are definitions. Explain why they are declarations or definitions.

```
(a) extern int ix = 1024;
(b) int iy;
(c) extern int iz;
(d) extern const int &ri;
```

Exercise 2.32: Which of the following declarations and definitions would you put in a header? In a source file? Explain why.

```
(a) int var;
(b) const double pi = 3.1416;
(c) extern int total = 255;
(d) const double sq2 = sqrt(2.0);
```

Exercise 2.33: Determine what options your compiler offers for increasing the warning level. Recompile selected earlier programs using this option to see whether additional problems are reported.

---

source file. In order to write our own headers, we need to understand a bit more about how a #include directive works. The #include facility is a part of the C++ **preprocessor**. The preprocessor manipulates the source text of our programs and runs before the compiler. C++ inherits a fairly elaborate preprocessor from C. Modern C++ programs use the preprocessor in a very restricted fashion.

A #include directive takes a single argument: the name of a header. The preprocessor replaces each #include by the contents of the specified header. Our own headers are stored in files. System headers may be stored in a compiler-specific format that is more efficient. Regardless of the form in which a header is stored, it ordinarily contains class definitions and declarations of the variables and functions needed to support separate compilation.

Headers Often Need Other Headers

Headers often #include other headers. The entities that a header defines often use facilities from other headers. For example, the header that defines our Sales_item class must include the string library. The Sales_item class has a string data member and so must have access to the string header.

Including other headers is so common that it is not unusual for a header to be included more than once in the same source file. For example, a program that used the Sales_item header might also use the string library. That program wouldn't—indeed shouldn't—know that our Sales_item header uses the string library. In this case, the string header would be included twice: once by the program itself and once as a side-effect of including our Sales_item header.

Accordingly, it is important to design header files so that they can be included more than once in a single source file. We must ensure that including a header file more than once does not cause multiple definitions of the classes and objects that the header file defines. A common way to make headers safe uses the preprocessor to define a **header guard**. The guard is used to avoid reprocessing the contents of a header file if the header has already been seen.

Avoiding Multiple Inclusions

Before we write our own header, we need to introduce some additional preprocessor facilities. The preprocessor lets us define our own variables.

 Names used for preprocessor variables must be unique within the program. Any uses of a name that matches a preprocessor variable is assumed to refer to the preprocessor variable.

To help avoid name clashes, preprocessor variables usually are written in all uppercase letters.

A preprocessor variable has two states: defined or not yet defined. Various preprocessor directives define and test the state of preprocessor variables. The #define directive takes a name and defines that name as a preprocessor variable. The #ifndef directive tests whether the specified preprocessor variable has not yet been defined. If it hasn't, then everything following the #ifndef is processed up to the next #endif.

We can use these facilities to guard against including a header more than once:

```
#ifndef SALESITEM_H
#define SALESITEM_H
// Definition of Sales_item class and related functions goes here
#endif
```

The conditional directive

```
#ifndef SALESITEM_H
```

tests whether the SALESITEM_H preprocessor variable has *not* been defined. If SALESITEM_H has not been defined, the #ifndef succeeds and all the lines following #ifndef until the #endif is found are processed. Conversely, if the variable SALESITEM_H has been defined, then the #ifndef directive is false. The lines between it and the #endif directive are ignored.

To guarantee that the header is processed only once in a given source file, we start by testing the #ifndef. The first time the header is processed, this test will succeed, because SALESITEM_H will not yet have been defined. The next statement defines SALESITEM_H. That way, if the file we are compiling happens to include this header a second time, the #ifndef directive will discover that SALESITEM_H is defined and skip the rest of the header file.

 Headers should have guards, even if they aren't included by another header. Header guards are trivial to write and can avoid mysterious compiler errors if the header subsequently is included more than once.

This strategy works well provided that no two headers define and use a pre-processor constant with the same name. We can avoid problems with duplicate preprocessor variables by naming them for an entity, such as a class, that is defined inside the header. A program can have only one class named `Sales_item`. By using the class name to compose the name of the header file and the preprocessor variable, we make it pretty likely that only one file will use this preprocessor variable.

Using Our Own Headers

The `#include` directive takes one of two forms:

```
#include <standard_header>
#include "my_file.h"
```

If the header name is enclosed by angle brackets (< >), it is presumed to be a standard header. The compiler will look for it in a predefined set of locations, which can be modified by setting a search path environment variable or through a command line option. The search methods used vary significantly across compilers. We recommend you ask a colleague or consult your compiler's user's guide for further information. If the header name is enclosed by a pair of quotation marks, the header is presumed to be a nonsystem header. The search for nonsystem headers usually begins in the directory in which the source file is located.

CHAPTER SUMMARY

Types are fundamental to all programming in C++.

Each type defines the storage requirements and the operations that may be performed on all objects of that type. The language provides a set of fundamental built-in types such as `int` and `char`. These types are closely tied to their representation on the machine's hardware.

Types can be nonconst or `const`; a `const` object must be initialized and its value may not be changed. In addition, we can define compound types, such as references. A reference provides another name for an object. A compound type is a type that is defined in terms of another type.

The language lets us define our own types by defining a class. The library uses the class facility to provide a set of higher-level abstractions such as the IO and `string` types.

C++ is a statically typed language: Variables and functions must be declared before they are used. A variable can be declared many times but defined only once. It is almost always a good idea to initialize variables when you define them.

DEFINED TERMS

access labels Members in a class may be defined to be `private`, which protects them from access from code that uses the type. Members may also be defined as `public`, which makes them accessible code throughout the program.

address Number by which a byte in memory can be found.

arithmetic types The arithmetic types represent numbers: integers and floating point. There are three types of floating point values: `long double`, `double`, and `float`. These represent extended, double, and single precision values. It is almost always right to use `double`. In particular, `float` is guaranteed only six significant digits—too small for most calculations. The integral types include `bool`, `char`, `wchar_t`, `short`, `int`, and `long`. Integer types can be signed or unsigned. It is almost always right to avoid `short` and `char` for arithmetic. Use `unsigned` for counting. The `bool` type may hold only two values: `true` or `false`. The `whcar_t` type is intended for characters from an extended character set; `char` type is used for characters that fit in 8 bits, such as Latin-1 or ASCII.

array Data structure that holds a collection of unnamed objects that can be accessed by an index. This chapter introduced the use of character arrays to hold string literals. Chapter 4 will discuss arrays in much more detail.

byte Typically the smallest addressable unit of memory. On most machines a byte is 8 bits.

class C++ mechanism for defining data types. Classes are defined using either the `class` or `struct` keyword. Classes may have data and function members. Members may be `public` or `private`. Ordinarily, function members that define the operations on the type are made `public`; data members and functions used in the implementation of the class are made `private`. By default, members in a class defined using the `class` keyword are private; members in a class defined using the `struct` keyword are public.

class member A part of a class. Members are either data or operations.

compound type A type, such as a reference, that is defined in terms of another type. Chapter 4 covers two additional compound types: pointers and arrays.

const reference A reference that may be bound to a const object, a nonconst object, or to an rvalue. A const reference may not change the object to which it refers.

constant expression An integral expression whose value can be evaluated at compile-time.

constructor Special member function that is used to initialize newly created objects. The job of a constructor is to ensure that the data members of an object have safe, sensible initial values.

copy-initialization Form of initialization that uses the = symbol to indicate that variable should be initialized as a copy of the initializer.

data member The data elements that constitute an object. Data members ordinarily should be private.

declaration Asserts the existence of a variable, function, or type defined elsewhere in the program. Some declarations are also definitions; only definitions allocate storage for variables. A variable may be declared by preceeding its type with the keyword extern. Names may not be used until they are defined or declared.

default constructor The constructor that is used when no explicit values are given for an initializer of a class type object. For example, the default constructor for string initializes the new string as the empty string. Other string constructors initialize the string with characters specified when the string is created.

definition Allocates storage for a variable of a specified type and optionally initializes the variable. Names may not be used until they are defined or declared.

direct-initialization Form of initialization that places a comma-separated list of initializers inside a pair of parentheses.

enumeration A type that groups a set of named integral constants.

enumerator The named members of an enumeration. Each enumerator is initialized to an integral value and the value of the enumerator is const. Enumerators may be used where integral constant expressions are required, such as the dimension of an array definition.

escape sequence Alternative mechanism for representing characters. Usually used to represent nonprintable characters such as newline or tab. An escape sequence is a backslash followed by a character, a three-digit octal number, or a hexadecimal number. The escape sequences defined by the language are listed on page 40. Escape sequences can be used as a literal character (enclosed in single quotes) or as part of a literal string (enclosed in double quotes).

global scope Scope that is outside all other scopes.

header A mechanism for making class definitions and other declarations available in multiple source files. User-defined headers are stored as files. System headers may be stored as files or in some other system-specific format.

header guard The preprocessor variable defined to prevent a header from being included more than once in a single source file.

identifier A name. Each identifier is a nonempty sequence of letters, digits, and underscores that must not begin with a digit. Identifiers are case-sensitive: Upper- and lowercase letters are distinct. Identifiers may not use C++ keywords. Identifiers may not contain two adjacent underscores nor may they begin with an underscore followed by a uppercase letter.

implementation The (usually private) members of a class that define the data and any operations that are not intended for use by code that uses the type. The istream and ostream classes, for example, manage an IO buffer that is part of their implementation and not directly accessible to users of those classes.

initialized A variable that has an initial value. An initial value may be specified when defining a variable. Variables usually should be initialized.

integral types See arithmetic type.

interface The operations supported by a type. Well-designed classes separate their interface and implementation, defining the interface in the `public` part of the class and the implementation in the `private` parts. Data members ordinarily are part of the implementation. Function members are part of the interface (and hence `public`) when they are operations that users of the type are expected to use and part of the implementation when they perform operations needed by the class but not defined for general use.

link Compilation step in which multiple object files are put together to form an executable program. The link step resolves interfile dependencies, such as linking a function call in one file to a function definition contained in a second file.

literal constant A value such as a number, a character, or a string of characters. The value cannot be changed. Literal characters are enclosed in single quotes, literal strings in double quotes.

local scope Term used to describe function scope and the scopes nested inside a function.

lvalue A value that may appear on the left-hand of an assignment. A `nonconst` lvalue may be read and written.

magic number A literal number in a program whose meaning is important but not obvious. It appears as if by magic.

nonconst reference A reference that may be bound only to a `nonconst` lvalue of the same type as the reference. A `nonconst` reference may change the value of the underlying object to which it refers.

nonprintable character A character with no visible representation, such as a control character, a backspace, newline, and so on.

object A region of memory that has a type. A variable is an object that has a name.

preprocessor The preprocessor is a program that runs as part of compilation of a C++ program. The preprocessor is inherited from C, and its uses are largely obviated by features in C++. One essential use of the preprocessor remains: the `#include` facility, which is used to incorporate headers into a program.

private member Member that is inaccessible to code that uses the class.

public member Member of a class that can be used by any part of the program.

reference An alias for another object. Defined as follows:

```
type &id = object;
```

Defines *id* to be another name for *object*. Any operation on *id* is translated as an operation on *object*.

run time Refers to the time during which the program is executing.

rvalue A value that can be used as the right-hand, but not left-hand side of an assignment. An rvalue may be read but not written.

scope A portion of a program in which names have meaning. C++ has several levels of scope:

> **global**—names defined outside any other scope.
>
> **class**—names defined by a class.
>
> **namespace**—names defined within a namespace.
>
> **local**—names defined within a function.

block—names defined within a block of statements, that is, within a pair of curly braces.

statement—names defined within the condition of a statement, such as an `if`, `for`, or `while`.

Scopes nest. For example, names declared at global scope are accessible in function and statement scope.

separate compilation Ability to split a program into multiple separate source files.

signed Integer type that holds negative or positive numbers, including zero.

statically typed Term used to refer to languages such as C++ that do compile-time type checking. C++ verifies at compile-time that the types used in expressions are capable of performing the operations required by the expression.

struct Keyword that can be used to define a class. By default, members of a `struct` are public until specified otherwise.

type-checking Term used to describe the process by which the compiler verifies that the way objects of a given type are used is consistent with the definition of that type.

type specifier The part of a definition or declaration that names the type of the variables that follow.

typedef Introduces a synonym for some other type. Form:

```
typedef type synonym;
```

defines *synonym* as another name for the type named *type*.

undefined behavior A usage for which the language does not specify a meaning. The compiler is free to do whatever it wants. Knowingly or unknowingly relying on undefined behavior is a great source of hard-to-track run-time errors and portability problems.

uninitialized Variable with no specified initial value. An uninitialized variable is not zero or "empty;" instead, it holds whatever bits happen to be in the memory in which it was allocated. Uninitialized variables are a great source of bugs.

unsigned Integer type that holds values greater than or equal to zero.

variable initialization Term used to describe the rules for initializing variables and array elements when no explicit initializer is given. For class types, objects are initialized by running the class's default constructor. If there is no default constructor, then there is a compile-time error: The object must be given an explicit initializer. For built-in types, initialization depends on scope. Objects defined at global scope are initialized to 0; those defined at local scope are uninitialized and have undefined values.

void type Special-purpose type that has no operations and no value. It is not possible to define a variable of type `void`. Most commonly used as the return type of a function that does not return a result.

word The natural unit of integer computation on a given machine. Usually a word is large enough to hold an address. Typically on a 32-bit machine machine a word is 4 bytes.

C H A P T E R 3

LIBRARY TYPES

In addition to the primitive types covered in Chapter 2, C++ defines a
rich library of abstract data types. Among the most important library
types are string and vector, which define variable-sized character strings and collections, respectively. Associated with string and
vector are companion types known as iterators, which are used to
access the characters in a string or the elements in a vector. These
library types are abstractions of more primitive types—arrays and
pointers—that are part of the language.

Another library type, bitset, provides an abstract way to manipulate a collection of bits. This class provides a more convenient
way of dealing with bits than is offered by the built-in bitwise operators on values of integral type.

This chapter introduces the library vector, string, and bitset
types. The next chapter covers arrays and pointers, and Chapter 5
looks at built-in bitwise operators.

The types that we covered in Chapter 2 are all low-level types: They represent abstractions such as numbers or characters and are defined in terms of how they are represented on the machine.

In addition to the types defined in the language, the standard library defines a number of higher level **abstract data types**. These library types are higher-level in that they mirror more complex concepts. They are abstract because when we use them we don't need to care about how the types are represented. We need to know only what operations they support.

Two of the most important library types are `string` and `vector`. The `string` type supports variable-length character strings. The `vector` type holds a sequence of objects of a specified type. These types are important because they offer improvements over more primitive types defined by the language. Chapter 4 looks at the language-level constructs that are similar to, but less flexible and more error-prone than, the library `string` and `vector` types.

Another library type that offers a more convenient and reasonably efficient abstraction of a language level facility is the `bitset` class. This class lets us treat a value as a collection of bits. It provides a more direct way of operating on bits than do the bitwise operators that we cover in Section 5.3 (p. 154).

Before continuing our exploration of the library types, we'll look at a mechanism for simplifying access to the names defined in the library.

3.1   Namespace `using` Declarations

The programs we've seen so far have referred to names from the library by explicitly noting that the name comes from the `std` namespace. For example, when we want to read from the standard input, we write `std::cin`. Such names use the `::` operator, which is the scope operator (Section 1.2.2, p. 8). This operator says that we should look for the name of the right-hand operand in the scope of the left-hand operand. Thus, `std::cin` says that we want the name `cin` that is defined in the namespace `std`. Referring to library names through this notation can be cumbersome.

Fortunately, there are easier ways to use namespace members. In this section we'll cover the safest mechanism: **using declarations**. We will see other ways to simplify the use of names from a namespace in Section 17.2 (p. 712).

A `using` declaration allows us to access a name from a namespace without the prefix `namespace_name::`. A `using` declaration has the following form:

```
using namespace::name;
```

Once the `using` declaration has been made, we can access *name* directly without reference to its namespace:

```
#include <string>
#include <iostream>
// using declarations states our intent to use these names from the namespace std
using std::cin;
using std::string;
```

```
int main()
{
    string s;        // ok: string is now a synonym for std::string
    cin >> s;        // ok: cin is now a synonym for std::cin
    cout << s;       // error: no using declaration; we must use full name
    std::cout << s;  // ok: explicitly use cout from namepsace std
}
```

Using the unqualified version of a namespace name without a using declaration is an error, although some compilers may fail to detect this error.

A Separate Using Declaration Is Required for Each Name

A using declaration introduces only one namespace member at a time. It allows us to be very specific regarding which names are used in our programs. If we want to use several names from std—or any other namespace—then we must issue a using declaration for each name that we intend to use. For example, we could rewrite the addition program from page 6 as follows:

```
#include <iostream>
//   using declarations for names from the standard library
using std::cin;
using std::cout;
using std::endl;
int main()
{
    cout << "Enter two numbers:" << endl;
    int v1, v2;
    cin >> v1 >> v2;
    cout << "The sum of " << v1
         << " and " << v2
         << " is " << v1 + v2 << endl;
    return 0;
}
```

The using declarations for cin, cout, and endl mean that we can use those names without the std:: prefix, making the code easier to read.

From this point on, our examples will assume that using declarations have been provided for the names we use from the standard library. Thus, we will refer to cin, not std::cin, in the text and in code examples. To keep the code examples short, we won't show the using declarations that are needed to compile the examples. Similarly, our code examples will not show the necessary #include directives. Table A.1 (p. 810) in Appendix A lists the library names and corresponding headers for standard-library names we use in this primer.

Beware

Readers should be aware that they must add appropriate #include and using declarations to our examples before compiling them.

Class Definitions that Use Standard Library Types

There is one case in which we should *always* use the fully qualified library names: inside header files. The reason is that the contents of a header are copied into our program text by the preprocessor. When we #include a file, it is as if the exact text of the header is part of our file. If we place a using declaration within a header, it is equivalent to placing the same using declaration in every program that includes the header *whether that program wants the using declaration or not.*

 Best Practices In general, it is good practice for headers to define only what is strictly necessary.

EXERCISES SECTION 3.1

Exercise 3.1: Rewrite the program from Section 2.3 (p. 43) that calculated the result of raising a given number to a given power to use appropriate using declarations rather than accessing library names through a std:: prefix.

3.2 Library `string` Type

The string type supports variable-length character strings. The library takes care of managing the memory associated with storing the characters and provides various useful operations. The library string type is intended to be efficient enough for general use.

As with any library type, programs that use strings must first include the associated header. Our programs will be shorter if we also provide an appropriate using declaration:

```
#include <string>
using std::string;
```

3.2.1 Defining and Initializing `strings`

Table 3.1: Ways to Initialize a `string`	
string s1;	Default constructor; s1 is the empty string
string s2(s1);	Initialize s2 as a copy of s1
string s3("value");	Initialize s3 as a copy of the string literal
string s4(n, 'c');	Initialize s4 with n copies of the character 'c'

The string library provides several constructors (Section 2.3.3, p. 49). A constructor is a special member function that defines how objects of that type can be initialized. Table 3.1 on the facing page lists the most commonly used `string` constructors. The default constructor (Section 2.3.4, p. 52) is used "by default" when no initializer is specified.

CAUTION: LIBRARY `string` TYPE AND STRING LITERALS

For historical reasons, and for compatibility with C, character string literals are *not* the same type as the standard library `string` type. This fact can cause confusion and is important to keep in mind when using a string literal or the `string` data type.

EXERCISES SECTION 3.2.1

Exercise 3.2: What is a default constructor?

Exercise 3.3: Name the three ways to initialize a `string`.

Exercise 3.4: What are the values of s and s2?

```
string s;
int main() {
    string s2;
}
```

3.2.2 Reading and Writing `strings`

As we saw in Chapter 1, we use the `iostream` library to read and write values of built-in types such as `int`, `double`, and so on. Similarly, we can use the `iostream` and `string` libraries to allow us to read and write `strings` using the standard input and output operators:

```
// Note: #include and using declarations must be added to compile this code
int main()
{
    string s;              // empty string
    cin >> s;              // read whitespace-separated string into s
    cout << s << endl;     // write s to the output
    return 0;
}
```

This program begins by defining a `string` named s. The next line,

```
cin >> s;                 // read whitespace-separated string into s
```

reads the standard input storing what is read into s. The `string` input operator:

- Reads and discards any leading whitespace (e.g., spaces, newlines, tabs)

- It then reads characters until the next whitespace character is encountered

So, if the input to this program is " **Hello World!** ", (note leading and trailing spaces) then the output will be "**Hello**" with no extra spaces.

The input and output operations behave similarly to the operators on the built-in types. In particular, the operators return their left-hand operand as their result. Thus, we can chain together multiple reads or writes:

```
string s1, s2;
cin >> s1 >> s2; // read first input into s1, second into s2
cout << s1 << s2 << endl; // write both strings
```

If we give this version of the program the same input as in the previous paragraph, our output would be

```
HelloWorld!
```

To compile this program, you must add #include directives for both the iostream and string libraries and must issue using declarations for all the names used from the library: string, cin, cout, and endl.
The programs presented from this point on will assume that the needed #include and using declarations have been made.

Reading an Unknown Number of strings

Like the input operators that read built-in types, the string input operator returns the stream from which it read. Therefore, we can use a string input operation as a condition, just as we did when reading ints in the program on page 18. The following program reads a set of strings from the standard input and writes what it has read, one string per line, to the standard output:

```
int main()
{
    string word;
    //  read until end-of-file, writing each word to a new line
    while (cin >> word)
        cout << word << endl;
    return 0;

}
```

In this case, we read into a string using the input operator. That operator returns the istream from which it read, and the while condition tests the stream after the read completes. If the stream is valid—it hasn't hit end-of-file or encountered an invalid input—then the body of the while is executed and the value we read is printed to the standard output. Once we hit end-of-file, we fall out of the while.

Using getline to Read an Entire Line

There is an additional useful string IO operation: **getline**. This is a function that takes both an input stream and a string. The getline function reads the next line of input from the stream and stores what it read, *not including* the newline, in its string argument. Unlike the input operator, getline does not ignore leading newlines. Whenever getline encounters a newline, even if it is the first character in the input, it stops reading the input and returns. The effect of encountering a newline as the first character in the input is that the string argument is set to the empty string.

The getline function returns its istream argument so that, like the input operator, it can be used as a condition. For example, we could rewrite the previous program that wrote one word per line to write a line at a time instead:

```
int main()
{
    string line;
    //  read line at time until end-of-file
    while (getline(cin, line))
        cout << line << endl;
    return 0;
}
```

Because line does not contain a newline, we must write our own if we want the strings written one to a line. As usual, we use endl to write a newline and flush the output buffer.

The newline that causes getline to return is discarded; it does *not* get stored in the string.

EXERCISES SECTION 3.2.2

Exercise 3.5: Write a program to read the standard input a line at a time. Modify your program to read a word at a time.

Exercise 3.6: Explain how whitespace characters are handled in the string input operator and in the getline function.

3.2.3 Operations on strings

Table 3.2 on the next page lists the most commonly used string operations.

The string size and empty Operations

The length of a string is the number of characters in the string. It is returned by the size operation:

```
int main()
{
    string st("The expense of spirit\n");
```

Table 3.2: **string** Operations	
`s.empty()`	Returns `true` if `s` is empty; otherwise returns `false`
`s.size()`	Returns number of characters in `s`
`s[n]`	Returns the character at position n in `s`; positions start at 0.
`s1 + s2`	Returns a `string` equal to the concatenation of `s1` and `s2`
`s1 = s2`	Replaces characters in `s1` by a copy of `s2`
`v1 == v2`	Returns `true` if `v1` and `v2` are equal; `false` otherwise
`!=, <, <=,` `>, and >=`	Have their normal meanings

```
    cout << "The size of " << st << "is " << st.size()
        << " characters, including the newline" << endl;
    return 0;
}
```

If we compile and execute this program it yields

```
The size of The expense of spirit
is 22 characters, including the newline
```

Often it is useful to know whether a `string` is empty. One way we could do so would be to compare `size` with 0:

```
if (st.size() == 0)
    // ok: empty
```

In this case, we don't really need to know how many characters are in the `string`; we are only interested in whether the `size` is zero. We can more directly answer this question by using the `empty` member:

```
if (st.empty())
    // ok: empty
```

The `empty` function returns the `bool` (Section 2.1, p. 34) value `true` if the `string` contains no characters; otherwise, it returns `false`.

`string::size_type`

It might be logical to expect that `size` returns an `int`, or, thinking back to the note on page 38, an `unsigned`. Instead, the `size` operation returns a value of type `string::size_type`. This type requires a bit of explanation.

The `string` class—and many other library types—defines several companion types. These companion types make it possible to use the library types in a machine-independent manner. The type **size_type** is one of these companion types. It is defined as a synonym for an `unsigned` type—either `unsigned int` or `unsigned long`—that is guaranteed to be big enough to hold the size of any `string`. To use the `size_type` defined by `string`, we use the scope operator to say that the name `size_type` is defined in the `string` class.

 Best Practices Any variable used to store the result from the `string size` operation ought to be of type `string::size_type`. It is particularly important *not* to assign the return from `size` to an `int`.

Although we don't know the precise type of `string::size_type`, we do know that it is an `unsigned` type (Section 2.1.1, p. 34). We also know that for a given type, the `unsigned` version can hold a positive value twice as large as the corresponding `signed` type can hold. This fact implies that the largest `string` could be twice as large as the size an `int` can hold.

Another problem with using an `int` is that on some machines the size of an `int` is too small to hold the size of even plausibly large `strings`. For example, if a machine has 16-bit `ints`, then the largest `string` an `int` could represent would have 32,767 characters. A `string` that held the contents of a file could easily exceed this size. The safest way to hold the `size` of a `string` is to use the type the library defines for this purpose, which is `string::size_type`.

The `string` Relational Operators

The `string` class defines several operators that compare two `string` values. Each of these operators works by comparing the characters from each `string`.

 Note `string` comparisons are case-sensitive—the upper- and lowercase versions of a letter are different characters. On most computers, the uppercase letters come first: Every uppercase letter is less than any lowercase letter.

The equality operator compares two `strings`, returning `true` if they are equal. Two `strings` are equal if they are the same length and contain the same characters. The library also defines `!=` to test whether two `strings` are unequal.

The relational operators `<`, `<=`, `>`, `>=` test whether one `string` is less than, less than or equal, greater than, or greater than or equal to another:

```
string big = "big", small = "small";
string s1 = big;      // s1 is a copy of big
if (big == small)     // false
    // ...
if (big <= s1)        // true, they're equal, so big is less than or equal to s1
    // ...
```

The relational operators compare `strings` using the same strategy as in a (case-sensitive) dictionary:

- If two `strings` have different lengths and if every character in the shorter `string` is equal to the corresponding character of the longer `string`, then the shorter `string` is less than the longer one.

- If the characters in two `strings` differ, then we compare them by comparing the first character at which the `strings` differ.

As an example, given the `strings`

```
string substr = "Hello";
string phrase = "Hello World";
string slang  = "Hiya";
```

then `substr` is less than `phrase`, and `slang` is greater than either `substr` or `phrase`.

Assignment for `strings`

In general the library types strive to make it as easy to use a library type as it is to use a built-in type. To this end, most of the library types support assignment. In the case of `strings`, we can assign one `string` object to another:

```
// st1 is an empty string, st2 is a copy of the literal
string st1, st2 = "The expense of spirit";
st1 = st2; // replace st1 by a copy of st2
```

After the assignment, `st1` contains a copy of the characters in `st2`.

Most `string` library implementations go to some trouble to provide efficient implementations of operations such as assignment, but it is worth noting that conceptually, assignment requires a fair bit of work. It must delete the storage containing the characters associated with `st1`, allocate the storage needed to contain a copy of the characters associated with `st2`, and then copy those characters from `st2` into this new storage.

Adding Two `strings`

Addition on `strings` is defined as concatenation. That is, it is possible to concatenate two or more `strings` through the use of either the plus operator (+) or the compound assignment operator (+=) (Section 1.4.1, p. 13). Given the two `strings`

```
string s1("hello, ");
string s2("world\n");
```

we can concatenate the two `strings` to create a third `string` as follows:

```
string s3 = s1 + s2;    // s3 is hello, world\n
```

If we wanted to append `s2` to `s1` directly, then we would use +=:

```
s1 += s2;    // equivalent to s1 = s1 + s2
```

Adding Character String Literals and `strings`

The `strings` `s1` and `s2` included punctuation directly. We could achieve the same result by mixing `string` objects and string literals as follows:

```
string s1("hello");
string s2("world");
string s3 = s1 + ", " + s2 + "\n";
```

When mixing strings and string literals, at least one operand to each + operator must be of string type:

```
string s1 = "hello";       //  no punctuation
string s2 = "world";
string s3 = s1 + ", ";              //  ok: adding a string and a literal
string s4 = "hello" + ", ";         //  error: no string operand
string s5 = s1 + ", " + "world";    //  ok: each + has string operand
string s6 = "hello" + ", " + s2;    //  error: can't add string literals
```

The initializations of s3 and s4 involve only a single operation. In these cases, it is easy to determine that the initialization of s3 is legal: We initialize s3 by adding a string and a string literal. The initialization of s4 attempts to add two string literals and is illegal.

The initialization of s5 may appear surprising, but it works in much the same way as when we chain together input or output expressions (Section 1.2, p. 5). In this case, the string library defines addition to return a string. Thus, when we initialize s5, the subexpression s1 + ", " returns a string, which can be concatenated with the literal "world\n". It is as if we had written

```
string tmp = s1 + ", ";  //  ok: + has a string operand
s5 = tmp + "world";      //  ok: + has a string operand
```

On the other hand, the initialization of s6 is illegal. Looking at each subexpression in turn, we see that the first subexpression adds two string literals. There is no way to do so, and so the statement is in error.

Fetching a Character from a string

The string type uses the **subscript** ([ ]) operator to access the individual characters in the string. The subscript operator takes a size_type value that denotes the character position we wish to fetch. The value in the subscript is often called "the subscript" or "an **index**."

Subscripts for strings start at zero; if s is a string, then if s isn't empty, s[0] is the first character in the string, s[1] is the second if there is one, and the last character is in s[s.size() - 1].
It is an error to use an index outside this range.

We could use the subscript operator to print each character in a string on a separate line:

```
string str("some string");
for (string::size_type ix = 0; ix != str.size(); ++ix)
    cout << str[ix] << endl;
```

On each trip through the loop we fetch the next character from str, printing it followed by a newline.

Subscripting Yields an Lvalue

Recall that a variable is an lvalue (Section 2.3.1, p. 45), and that the left-hand side of an assignment must be an lvalue. Like a variable, the value returned by the subscript operator is an lvalue. Hence, a subscript can be used on either side of an assignment. The following loop sets each character in `str` to an asterisk:

```
for (string::size_type ix = 0; ix != str.size(); ++ix)
    str[ix] = '*';
```

Computing Subscript Values

Any expression that results in an integral value can be used as the index to the subscript operator. For example, assuming `someval` and `someotherval` are integral objects, we could write

```
str[someotherval * someval] = someval;
```

Although any integral type can be used as an index, the actual type of the index is `string::size_type`, which is an `unsigned` type.

> The same reasons to use `string::size_type` as the type for a variable that holds the return from `size` apply when defining a variable to serve as an index. A variable used to index a `string` should have type `string::size_type`.

When we subscript a `string`, we are responsible for ensuring that the index is "in range." By in range, we mean that the index is a number that, when assigned to a `size_type`, is a value in the range from 0 through the size of the `string` minus one. By using a `string::size_type` or another `unsigned` type as the index, we ensure that the subscript cannot be less than zero. As long as our index is an `unsigned` type, we need only check that it is less than the size of the `string`.

> The library is not required to check the value of the index. Using an index that is out of range is undefined and usually results in a serious run-time error.

3.2.4 Dealing with the Characters of a `string`

Often we want to process the individual characters of a `string`. For example, we might want to know if a particular character is a whitespace character or whether the character is alphabetic or numeric. Table 3.3 on the facing page lists the functions that can be used on the characters in a `string` (or on any other `char` value). These functions are defined in the **cctype header**.

These functions mostly test the given character and return an `int`, which acts as a truth value. Each function returns zero if the test fails; otherwise, they return a (meaningless) nonzero value indicating that the character is of the requested kind.

For these functions, a printable character is a character with a visible representation; whitespace is one of space, tab, vertical tab, return, newline, and formfeed;

Table 3.3: cctype Functions	
isalnum(c)	true if c is a letter or a digit.
isalpha(c)	true if c is a letter.
iscntrl(c)	true if c is a control character.
isdigit(c)	true if c is a digit.
isgraph(c)	true if c is not a space but is printable.
islower(c)	true if c is a lowercase letter.
isprint(c)	true if c is a printable character.
ispunct(c)	true if c is a punctuation character.
isspace(c)	true if c is whitespace.
isupper(c)	true if c is an uppercase letter.
isxdigit(c)	true if c is a hexadecimal digit.
tolower(c)	If c is an uppercase letter, returns its lowercase equivalent; otherwise returns c unchanged.
toupper(c)	If c is a lowercase letter, returns its uppercase equivalent; otherwise returns c unchanged.

and punctuation is a printable character that is not a digit, a letter, or (printable) whitespace character such as space.

As an example, we could use these functions to print the number of punctuation characters in a given string:

```
string s("Hello World!!!");
string::size_type punct_cnt = 0;
// count number of punctuation characters in s
for (string::size_type index = 0; index != s.size(); ++index)
    if (ispunct(s[index]))
        ++punct_cnt;
cout << punct_cnt
     << " punctuation characters in " << s << endl;
```

The output of this program is

3 punctuation characters in Hello World!!!

Rather than returning a truth value, the tolower and toupper functions return a character—either the argument unchanged or the lower- or uppercase version of the character. We could use tolower to change s to lowercase as follows:

```
// convert s to lowercase
for (string::size_type index = 0; index != s.size(); ++index)
    s[index] = tolower(s[index]);
cout << s << endl;
```

which generates

hello world!!!

EXERCISES SECTION 3.2.4

Exercise 3.7: Write a program to read two strings and report whether the strings are equal. If not, report which of the two is the larger. Now, change the program to report whether the strings have the same length and if not report which is longer.

Exercise 3.8: Write a program to read strings from the standard input, concatenating what is read into one large string. Print the concatenated string. Next, change the program to separate adjacent input strings by a space.

Exercise 3.9: What does the following program do? Is it valid? If not, why not?

```
string s;
cout << s[0] << endl;
```

Exercise 3.10: Write a program to strip the punctuation from a string. The input to the program should be a string of characters including punctuation; the output should be a string in which the punctuation is removed.

3.3 Library vector Type

A vector is a collection of objects of a single type, each of which has an associated integer index. As with strings, the library takes care of managing the memory associated with storing the elements. We speak of a vector as a **container** because it contains other objects. All of the objects in a container must have the same type. We'll have much more to say about containers in Chapter 9.

To use a vector, we must include the appropriate header. In our examples, we also assume an appropriate using declaration is made:

```
#include <vector>
using std::vector;
```

A vector is a **class template**. Templates let us write a single class or function definition that can be used on a variety of types. Thus, we can define a vector that holds `strings`, or a `vector` to hold `ints`, or one to hold objects of our own class types, such as `Sales_items`. We'll see how to define our own class templates in Chapter 16. Fortunately, we need to know very little about how templates are defined in order to use them.

To declare objects of a type generated from a class template, we must supply additional information. The nature of this information depends on the template. In the case of `vector`, we must say what type of objects the `vector` will contain. We specify the type by putting it between a pair of angle brackets following the template's name:

```
vector<int> ivec;            //  ivec holds objects of type int
vector<Sales_item> Sales_vec; //  holds Sales_items
```

As in any variable definition, we specify a type and a list of one or more variables. In the first of these definitions, the type is `vector<int>`, which is a `vector` that holds objects of type `int`. The name of the variable is `ivec`. In the second, we define `Sales_vec` to hold `Sales_item` objects.

> `vector` is not a type; it is a template that we can use to define any number of types. Each of `vector` type specifies an element type. Hence, `vector<int>` and `vector<string>` are types.

3.3.1 Defining and Initializing `vectors`

The `vector` class defines several constructors (Section 2.3.3, p. 49), which we use to define and initialize `vector` objects. The constructors are listed in Table 3.4.

Table 3.4: Ways to Initialize a `vector`	
`vector<T> v1;`	`vector` that holds objects of type T; Default constructor v1 is empty
`vector<T> v2(v1);`	v2 is a copy of v1
`vector<T> v3(n, i);`	v3 has n elements with value i
`vector<T> v4(n);`	v4 has n copies of a value-initialized object

Creating a Specified Number of Elements

When we create a `vector` that is not empty, we must supply value(s) to use to initialize the elements. When we copy one `vector` to another, each element in the new `vector` is initialized as a copy of the corresponding element in the original `vector`. The two `vectors` must hold the same element type:

```
vector<int> ivec1;             //  ivec1 holds objects of type int
vector<int> ivec2(ivec1);      //  ok: copy elements of ivec1 into ivec2
vector<string> svec(ivec1);    //  error: svec holds strings, not ints
```

We can initialize a `vector` from a count and an element value. The constructor uses the count to determine how many elements the `vector` should have and uses the value to specify the value each of those elements will have:

```
vector<int> ivec4(10, -1);        //  10 elements, each initialized to -1
vector<string> svec(10, "hi!");  //  10 strings, each initialized to "hi!"
```

KEY CONCEPT: VECTORS GROW DYNAMICALLY

KEY CONCEPT: VECTORS GROW DYNAMICALLY

A central property of `vectors` (and the other library containers) is that they are required to be implemented so that it is efficient to add elements to them at run time. Because `vectors` grow efficiently, it is usually best to let the `vector` grow by adding elements to it dynamically as the element values are known.

As we'll see in Chapter 4, this behavior is distinctly different from that of built-in arrays in C and for that matter in most other languages. In particular, readers accustomed to using C or Java might expect that because `vector` elements are stored contiguously, it would be best to preallocate the `vector` at its expected size. In fact, the contrary is the case, for reasons we'll explore in Chapter 9.

Although we can preallocate a given number of elements in a `vector`, it is usually more efficient to define an empty `vector` and add elements to it (as we'll learn how to do shortly).

Value Initialization

When we do not specify an element initializer, then the library creates a **value initialized** element initializer for us. This library-generated value is used to initialize each element in the container. The value of the element initializer depends on the type of the elements stored in the `vector`.

If the `vector` holds elements of a built-in type, such as `int`, then the library creates an element initializer with a value of 0:

```
vector<string> fvec(10);   //  10 elements, each initialized to 0
```

If the `vector` holds elements of a class type, such as `string`, that defines its own constructors, then the library uses the value type's default constructor to create the element initializer:

```
vector<string> svec(10);   //  10 elements, each an empty string
```

As we'll see in Chapter 12, some classes that define their own constructors do not define a default constructor. We cannot initialize a `vector` of such a type by specifying only a size; we must also specify an initial element value.

There is a third possibility: The element type might be of a class type that does not define any constructors. In this case, the library still creates a value-initialized object. It does so by value-initializing each member of that object.

EXERCISES SECTION 3.3.1

Exercise 3.11: Which, if any, of the following vector definitions are in error?

```
(a) vector< vector<int> > ivec;
(b) vector<string> svec = ivec;
(c) vector<string> svec(10, "null");
```

Exercise 3.12: How many elements are there in each of the following vectors? What are the values of the elements?

```
(a) vector<int> ivec1;
(b) vector<int> ivec2(10);
(c) vector<int> ivec3(10, 42);
(d) vector<string> svec1;
(e) vector<string> svec2(10);
(f) vector<string> svec3(10, "hello");
```

3.3.2 Operations on vectors

The vector library provides various operations, many of which are similar to operations on strings. Table 3.5 lists the most important vector operations.

Table 3.5: vector Operations	
v.empty()	Returns true if v is empty; otherwise returns false
v.size()	Returns number of elements in v
v.push_back(t)	Adds element with value t to end of v
v[n]	Returns element at position n in v
v1 = v2	Replaces elements in v1 by a copy of elements in v2
v1 == v2	Returns true if v1 and v2 are equal
!=, <, <=, >, and >=	Have their normal meanings

The size of a vector

The empty and size operations are similar to the corresponding string operations (Section 3.2.3, p. 83). The size member returns a value of the size_type defined by the corresponding vector type.

To use size_type, we must name the type in which it is defined. A vector type *always* includes the element type of the vector:

```
vector<int>::size_type // ok
vector::size_type      // error
```

Adding Elements to a `vector`

The **push_back** operation takes an element value and adds that value as a new element at the back of a `vector`. In effect it "pushes" an element onto the "back" of the `vector`:

```
// read words from the standard input and store them as elements in a vector
string word;
vector<string> text;       // empty vector
while (cin >> word) {
    text.push_back(word);  // append word to text
}
```

This loop reads a sequence of `string`s from the standard input, appending them one at a time onto the back of the `vector`. We start by defining `text` as an initially empty `vector`. Each trip through the loop adds a new element to the `vector` and gives that element the value of whatever word was read from the input. When the loop completes, `text` will have as many elements as were read.

Subscripting a `vector`

Objects in the `vector` are not named. Instead, they can be accessed by their position in the `vector`. We can fetch an element using the subscript operator. Subscripting a `vector` is similar to subscripting a `string` (Section 3.2.3, p. 87).

The `vector` subscript operator takes a value and returns the element at that position in the `vector`. Elements in a `vector` are numbered beginning with 0. The following example uses a `for` loop to reset each element in the `vector` to 0:

```
// reset the elements in the vector to zero
for (vector<int>::size_type ix = 0; ix != ivec.size(); ++ix)
    ivec[ix] = 0;
```

Like the `string` subscript operator, the `vector` subscript yields an lvalue so that we may write to it, which we do in the body of the loop. Also, as we do for `string`s, we use the `size_type` of the `vector` as the type for the subscript.

Even if `ivec` is empty, this `for` loop executes correctly. If `ivec` is empty, the call to `size` returns 0 and the test in the `for` compares `ix` to 0. Because `ix` is itself 0 on the first trip, the test would fail and the loop body would not be executed even once.

Subscripting Does Not Add Elements

Programmers new to C++ sometimes think that subscripting a `vector` adds elements; it does not:

```
vector<int> ivec;   // empty vector
for (vector<int>::size_type ix = 0; ix != 10; ++ix)
    ivec[ix] = ix;  // disaster: ivec has no elements
```

KEY CONCEPT: SAFE, GENERIC PROGRAMMING

Programmers coming to C++ from C or Java might be surprised that our loop used != rather than < to test the index against the `size` of the `vector`. C programmers are probably also suprised that we call the `size` member in the `for` rather than calling it once before the loop and remembering its value.

C++ programmers tend to write loops using != in preference to < as a matter of habit. In this case, there is no particular reason to choose one operator or the other. We'll understand the rationale for this habit once we cover generic programming in Part II.

Calling `size` rather than remembering its value is similarly unnecessary in this case but again reflects a good habit. In C++, data structures such as `vector` can grow dynamically. Our loop only reads elements; it does not add them. However, a loop could easily add new elements. If the loop did add elements, then testing a saved value of `size` would fail—our loop would not account for the newly added elements. Because a loop might add elements, we tend to write our loops to test the current `size` on each pass rather than store a copy of what the `size` was when we entered the loop.

As we'll see in Chapter 7, in C++ functions can be declared to be `inline`. When it can do so, the compiler will expand the code for an `inline` function directly rather than actually making a function call. Tiny library functions such as `size` are almost surely defined to be `inline`, so we expect that there is little run-time cost in making this call on each trip through the loop.

This code intended to insert new 10 elements into `ivec`, giving the elements the values from 0 through 9. However, `ivec` is an empty `vector` and subscripts can only be used to fetch existing elements.

The right way to write this loop would be

```
for (vector<int>::size_type ix = 0; ix != 10; ++ix)
    ivec.push_back(ix);   // ok: adds new element with value ix
```

An element must exist in order to subscript it; elements are *not* added when we assign through a subscript.

3.4 Introducing Iterators

While we can use subscripts to access the elements in a `vector`, the library also gives us another way to examine elements: We can use an **iterator**. An iterator is a type that lets us examine the elements in a container and navigate from one element to another.

The library defines an iterator type for each of the standard containers, including `vector`. Iterators are more general than subscripts: All of the library containers define iterator types, but only a few of them support subscripting. Because iterators are common to all containers, modern C++ programs tend to use iterators

---

CAUTION: ONLY SUBSCRIPT ELEMENTS THAT ARE KNOWN TO EXIST!

It is crucially important to understand that we may use the subscript operator, (the **[]**
operator), to fetch only elements that actually exist. For example,

```
vector<int> ivec;        // empty vector
cout << ivec[0];         // Error: ivec has no elements!

vector<int> ivec2(10);   // vector with 10 elements
cout << ivec[10];        // Error: ivec has elements 0...9
```

Attempting to fetch an element that doesn't exist is a run-time error. As with most
such errors, there is no assurance that the implementation will detect it. The result
of executing the program is uncertain. The effect of fetching a nonexisting element is
undefined—what happens will vary by implementation, but the program will almost
surely fail in some interesting way at run time.

This caution applies any time we use a subscript, such as when subscripting a
string and, as we'll see shortly, when subscripting a built-in array.

Attempting to subscript elements that do not exist is, unfortunately, an extremely
common and pernicious programming error. So-called "buffer overflow" errors are
the result of subscripting elements that don't exist. Such bugs are the most common
cause of security problems in PC and other applications.

EXERCISES SECTION 3.3.2

Exercise 3.13: Read a set of integers into a **vector**. Calculate and print the sum of
each pair of adjacent elements in the **vector**. If there is an odd number, tell the user
and print the value of the last element without summing it. Now change your program
so that it prints the sum of the first and last elements, followed by the sum of the second
and second-to-last and so on.

Exercise 3.14: Read some text into a **vector**, storing each word in the input as an
element in the **vector**. Transform each word into uppercase letters. Print the transformed elements from the **vector**, printing eight words to a line.

Exercise 3.15: Is the following program legal? If not, how might you fix it?

```
vector<int> ivec;
ivec[0] = 42;
```

Exercise 3.16: List three ways to define a **vector** and give it 10 elements, each with
the value 42. Indicate whether there is a preferred way to do so and why.

rather than subscripts to access container elements, even on types such as `vector` that support subscripting.

The details of how iterators work are discussed in Chapter 11, but we can use them without understanding them in their full complexity.

Container `iterator` Type

Each of the container types, such as `vector`, defines its own iterator type:

```
vector<int>::iterator iter;
```

This statement defines a variable named `iter`, whose type is the type named `iterator` defined by `vector<int>`. Each of the library container types defines a member named `iterator` that is a synonym for the actual type of its iterator.

TERMINOLOGY: ITERATORS AND ITERATOR TYPES

When first encountered, the nomenclature around iterators can be confusing. In part the confusion arises because the same term, *iterator*, is used to refer to two things. We speak generally of the concept of an iterator, and we speak specifically of a concrete `iterator` type defined by a container, such as `vector<int>`.

What's important to understand is that there is a collection of types that serve as iterators. These types are related conceptually. We refer to a type as an iterator if it supports a certain set of actions. Those actions let us navigate among the elements of a container and let us access the value of those elements.

Each container class defines its own `iterator` type that can be used to access the elements in the container. That is, each container defines a type named `iterator`, and that type supports the actions of an (conceptual) iterator.

The `begin` and `end` Operations

Each container defines a pair of functions named `begin` and `end` that return iterators. The iterator returned by `begin` refers to the first element, if any, in the container:

```
vector<int>::iterator iter = ivec.begin();
```

This statement initializes `iter` to the value returned by the `vector` operation named `begin`. Assuming the `vector` is not empty, after this initialization, `iter` refers to the same element as `ivec[0]`.

The iterator returned by the `end` operation is an iterator positioned "one past the end" of the `vector`. It is often referred to as the **off-the-end iterator** indicating that it refers to a nonexistent element "off the end" of the `vector`. If the `vector` is empty, the iterator returned by `begin` is the same as the iterator returned by `end`.

 The iterator returned by the `end` operation does not denote an actual element in the `vector`. Instead, it is used as a **sentinel** indicating when we have processed all the elements in the `vector`.

Dereference and Increment on `vector` Iterators

The operations on iterator types let us retrieve the element to which an iterator refers and let us move an iterator from one element to another.

Iterator types use the **dereference operator** (the * operator) to access the element to which the iterator refers:

```
*iter = 0;
```

The dereference operator returns the element that the iterator currently denotes. Assuming `iter` refers to the first element of the `vector`, then `*iter` is the same element as `ivec[0]`. The effect of this statement is to assign 0 to that element.

Iterators use the increment operator (++) (Section 1.4.1, p. 13) to advance an iterator to the next element in the container. Incrementing an iterator is a logically similar operation to the increment operator when applied to `int` objects. In the case of `int`s, the effect is to "add one" to the `int`'s value. In the case of iterators, the effect is to "advance the iterator by one position" in the container. So, if `iter` refers to the first element, then `++iter` denotes the second element.

Because the iterator returned from end does not denote an element, it may not be incremented or dereferenced.

Other Iterator Operations

Another pair of useful operations that we can perform on iterators is comparison: Two iterators can be compared using either `==` or `!=`. Iterators are equal if they refer to the same element; they are unequal otherwise.

A Program that Uses Iterators

Assume we had a `vector<int>` named `ivec` and we wanted to reset each of its elements to zero. We might do so by using a subscript:

```
// reset all the elements in ivec to 0
for (vector<int>::size_type ix = 0; ix != ivec.size(); ++ix)
        ivec[ix] = 0;
```

This program uses a `for` loop to iterate through the elements in `ivec`. The `for` defines an index, which it increments on each iteration. The body of the `for` sets each element in `ivec` to zero.

A more typical way to write this loop would use iterators:

```
// equivalent loop using iterators to reset all the elements in ivec to 0
for (vector<int>::iterator iter = ivec.begin();
                          iter != ivec.end(); ++iter)
     *iter = 0;   // set element to which iter refers to 0
```

The `for` loop starts by defining `iter` and initializing it to refer to the first element in `ivec`. The condition in the `for` tests whether `iter` is unequal to the iterator returned by the end operation. Each iteration increments `iter`. The effect of this `for` is to start with the first element in `ivec` and process in sequence each element in the `vector`. Eventually, `iter` will refer to the last element in `ivec`. After we process the last element and increment `iter`, it will become equal to the value returned by `end`. At that point, the loop stops.

The statement in the `for` body uses the dereference operator to access the value of the current element. As with the subscript operator, the value returned by the dereference operator is an lvalue. We can assign to this element to change its value. The effect of this loop is to assign the value zero to each element in `ivec`.

Having walked through the code in detail, we can see that this program has exactly the same effect as the version that used subscripts: We start at the first element in the `vector` and set each element in the `vector` to zero.

> This program, like the one on page 94, is safe if the `vector` is empty. If `ivec` is empty, then the iterator returned from `begin` does not denote any element; it can't, because there are no elements. In this case, the iterator returned from `begin` is the same as the one returned from `end`, so the test in the `for` fails immediately.

`const_iterator`

The previous program used a `vector::iterator` to change the values in the `vector`. Each container type also defines a type named `const_iterator`, which should be used when reading, but not writing to, the container elements.

When we dereference a plain `iterator`, we get a nonconst reference (Section 2.5, p. 59) to the element. When we dereference a `const_iterator`, the value returned is a reference to a `const` (Section 2.4, p. 56) object. Just as with any `const` variable, we may not write to the value of this element.

For example, if `text` is a `vector<string>`, we might want to traverse it, printing each element. We could do so as follows:

```
// use const_iterator because we won't change the elements
for (vector<string>::const_iterator iter = text.begin();
                          iter != text.end(); ++iter)
      cout << *iter << endl; // print each element in text
```

This loop is similar to the previous one, except that we are reading the value from the iterator, not assigning to it. Because we read, but do not write, through the iterator, we define `iter` to be a `const_iterator`. When we dereference a `const_iterator`, the value returned is `const`. We may not assign to an element using a `const_iterator`:

```
for (vector<string>::const_iterator iter = text.begin();
                          iter != text.end(); ++ iter)
      *iter = " ";    // error: *iter is const
```

When we use the `const_iterator` type, we get an iterator whose own value can be changed but that cannot be used to change the underlying element value. We can increment the iterator and use the dereference operator to read a value but not to assign to that value.

A `const_iterator` should not be confused with an `iterator` that is `const`. When we declare an iterator as `const` we must initialize the iterator. Once it is initialized, we may not change its value:

```
vector<int> nums(10);   // nums is nonconst
const vector<int>::iterator cit = nums.begin();

*cit = 1;               // ok: cit can change its underlying element
++cit;                  // error: can't change the value of cit
```

A `const_iterator` may be used with either a `const` or nonconst `vector`, because it cannot write an element. An iterator that is `const` is largely useless: Once it is initialized, we can use it to write the element it refers to, but cannot make it refer to any other element.

```
const vector<int> nines(10, 9);   // cannot change elements in nines
// error: cit2 could change the element it refers to and nines is const
const vector<int>::iterator cit2 = nines.begin();
// ok: it can't change an element value, so it can be used with a const vector<int>
vector<int>::const_iterator it = nines.begin();

*it = 10; // error: *it is const
++it;     // ok: it isn't const so we can change its value
```

> ```
> // an iterator that cannot write elements
> vector<int>::const_iterator
> // an iterator whose value cannot change
> const vector<int>::iterator
> ```

EXERCISES SECTION 3.4

Exercise 3.17: Redo the exercises from Section 3.3.2 (p. 96), using iterators rather than subscripts to access the elements in the `vector`.

Exercise 3.18: Write a program to create a `vector` with 10 elements. Using an iterator, assign each element a value that is twice its current value.

Exercise 3.19: Test your previous program by printing the `vector`.

Exercise 3.20: Explain which iterator you used in the previous programs, and why.

Exercise 3.21: When would you use an iterator that is `const`? When would you use a `const_iterator`. Explain the difference between them.

3.4.1 Iterator Arithmetic

In addition to the increment operator, which moves an iterator one element at a time, `vector` iterators (but few of the other library container iterators) also support other arithmetic operations. These operations are referred to as **iterator arithmetic**, and include:

- `iter + n`
  `iter - n`
  We can add or subtract an integral value to an iterator. Doing so yields a new iterator positioned n elements ahead of (addition) or behind (subtraction) the element to which `iter` refers. The result of the addition or subtraction must refer to an element in the `vector` to which `iter` refers or to one past the end of that `vector`. The type of the value added or subtracted ought ordinarily to be the `vector`'s `size_type` or `difference_type` (see below).

- `iter1 - iter2`
  Computes the difference between two iterators as a value of a `signed` integral type named **`difference_type`**, which, like `size_type`, is defined by `vector`. The type is `signed` because subtraction might have a negative result. This type is guaranteed to be large enough to hold the distance between any two iterators. Both `iter1` and `iter2` must refer to elements in the same `vector` or the element one past the end of that `vector`.

We can use iterator arithmetic to move an iterator to an element directly. For example, we could locate the middle of a `vector` as follows:

```
vector<int>::iterator mid = vi.begin() + vi.size() / 2;
```

This code initializes `mid` to refer to the element nearest to the middle of `ivec`. It is more efficient to calculate this iterator directly than to write an equivalent program that increments the iterator one by one until it reaches the middle element.

Any operation that changes the size of a `vector` makes existing iterators invalid. For example, after calling `push_back`, you should not rely on the value of an iterator into the `vector`.

EXERCISES SECTION 3.4.1

Exercise 3.22: What happens if we compute `mid` as follows:
```
vector<int>::iterator mid = (vi.begin() + vi.end()) / 2;
```

3.5 Library `bitset` Type

Some programs deal with ordered collections of bits. Each bit can contain either a 0 (off) or a 1 (on) value. Using bits is a compact way to keep yes/no information (sometimes called flags) about a set of items or conditions. The standard library makes it easy to deal with bits through the **`bitset`** class. To use a `bitset` we must include its associated header file. In our examples, we also assume an appropriate `using` declaration for `std::bitset` is made:

```
#include <bitset>
using std::bitset;
```

3.5.1 Defining and Initializing `bitsets`

Table 3.6 lists the constructors for `bitset`. Like `vector`, the `bitset` class is a class template. Unlike `vector`, objects of type `bitset` differ by size rather than by type. When we define a `bitset`, we say how many bits the `bitset` will contain, which we do by specifying the size between a pair of angle brackets.

```
bitset<32> bitvec; //  32 bits, all zero
```

The size must be a constant expression (Section 2.7, p. 62). It might be defined, as we did here, using an integral literal constant or using a `const` object of integral type that is initialized from a constant.

This statement defines `bitvec` as a `bitset` that holds 32 bits. Just as with the elements of a `vector`, the bits in a `bitset` are not named. Instead, we refer to them positionally. The bits are numbered starting at 0. Thus, `bitvec` has bits numbered 0 through 31. The bits starting at 0 are referred to as the **low-order** bits, and those ending at 31 are referred to as **high-order** bits.

Table 3.6: Ways to Initialize a `bitset`	
`bitset<n> b;`	b has n bits, each bit is 0
`bitset<n> b(u);`	b is a copy of the unsigned long value u
`bitset<n> b(s);`	b is a copy of the bits contained in string s
`bitset<n> b(s, pos, n);`	b is a copy of the bits in n characters from s starting from position pos

Initializing a `bitset` from an `unsigned` Value

When we use an `unsigned long` value as an initializer for a `bitset`, that value is treated as a bit pattern. The bits in the `bitset` are a copy of that pattern. If the size of the `bitset` is greater than the number of bits in an `unsigned long`, then the remaining high-order bits are set to zero. If the size of the `bitset` is less than that number of bits, then only the low-order bits from the `unsigned` value are used; the high-order bits beyond the size of the `bitset` object are discarded.

On a machine with 32-bit `unsigned longs`, the hexadecimal value `0xffff` is represented in bits as a sequence of 16 ones followed by 16 zeroes. (Each `0xf` digit is represented as `1111`.) We can initialize a `bitset` from `0xffff`:

```
//  bitvec1 is smaller than the initializer
bitset<16> bitvec1(0xffff);  //  bits 0 ... 15 are set to 1
//  bitvec2 same size as initializer
bitset<32> bitvec2(0xffff);  //  bits 0 ... 15 are set to 1; 16 ... 31 are 0
//  on a 32-bit machine, bits 0 to 31 initialized from 0xffff
bitset<128> bitvec3(0xffff); //  bits 32 through 127 initialized to zero
```

In all three cases, the bits 0 to 15 are set to one. For `bitvec1`, the high-order bits in the initializer are discarded; `bitvec1` has fewer bits than an `unsigned` long. bitvec2 is the same size as an unsigned long, so all the bits are used to initialize that object. bitvec3 is larger than an unsigned long, so its high-order bits above 31 are initialized to zero.

Initializing a bitset from a string

When we initialize a bitset from a string, the string represents the bit pattern directly. The bits are read from the string *from right to left*:

```
string strval("1100");
bitset<32> bitvec4(strval);
```

The bit pattern in bitvec4 has bit positions 2 and 3 set to 1, while the remaining bit positions are 0. If the string contains fewer characters than the size of the bitset, the high-order bits are set to zero.

> The numbering conventions of strings and bitsets are inversely related: The rightmost character in the string—the one with the highest subscript—is used to initialize the low-order bit in the bitset—the bit with subscript 0. When initializing a bitset from a string, it is essential to remember this difference.

We need not use the entire string as the initial value for the bitset. Instead, we can use a substring as the initializer:

```
string str("1111111000000011001101");
bitset<32> bitvec5(str, 5, 4); //  4 bits starting at str[5], 1100
bitset<32> bitvec6(str, str.size() - 4); //  use last 4 characters
```

Here bitvec5 is initialized by a substring of str starting at str[5] and continuing for four positions. As usual, we start at the rightmost end of this substring when initializing the bitset, meaning that bitvec5 is initialized with bit positions 0 through 3 set to 1100 while its remaining bit positions are set to 0. Leaving off the third parameter says to use characters from the starting position to the end of the string. In this case, the characters starting four from the end of str are used to initialize the lower four bits of bitvec6. The remainder of the bits in bitvec6 are initialized to zero. We can view these initializations as

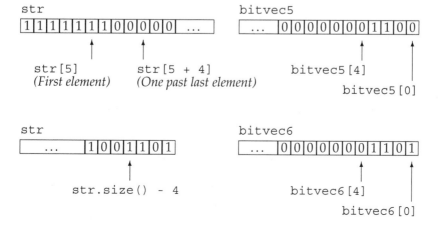

3.5.2   Operations on `bitset`

The `bitset` operations (Table 3.7) define various operations to test or set one or more bits in the `bitset`.

Table 3.7: `bitset` Operations	
`b.any()`	Is any bit in b on?
`b.none()`	Are no bits in b on?
`b.count()`	Number of bits in b that are on
`b.size()`	Number of bits in b
`b[pos]`	Access bit in b at position pos
`b.test(pos)`	Is bit in b in position pos on?
`b.set()`	Turn on all bits in b
`b.set(pos)`	Turn on the bit in b at position pos
`b.reset()`	Turn off all bits in b
`b.reset(pos)`	Turn off the bit in b at position pos
`b.flip()`	Change the state of each bit in b
`b.flip(pos)`	Reverse value of the bit in b in position pos
`b.to_ulong()`	Returns an unsigned `long` with the same bits as in b
`os << b`	Prints the bits in b to the stream os

Testing the Entire `bitset`

The any operation returns `true` if one or more bits of the `bitset` object are turned on—that is, are equal to 1. Conversely, the operation none returns `true` if all the bits of the object are set to zero.

```
bitset<32> bitvec; // 32 bits, all zero
bool is_set = bitvec.any();      // false, all bits are zero
bool is_not_set = bitvec.none(); // true, all bits are zero
```

If we need to know how many bits are set, we can use the `count` operation, which returns the number of bits that are set:

```
size_t bits_set = bitvec.count();   // returns number of bits that are on
```

The return type of the `count` operation is a library type named **`size_t`**. The `size_t` type is defined in the `cstddef` header, which is the C++ version of the `stddef.h` header from the C library. It is a machine-specific *unsigned* type that is guaranteed to be large enough to hold the size of an object in memory.

The `size` operation, like the one in `vector` and `string`, returns the total number of bits in the `bitset`. The value returned has type `size_t`:

```
size_t sz = bitvec.size();  // returns 32
```

Accessing the Bits in a `bitset`

The subscript operator lets us read or write the bit at the indexed position. As such, we can use it to test the value of a given bit or to set that value:

```
//  assign 1 to even numbered bits
for (int index = 0; index != 32; index += 2)
            bitvec[index] = 1;
```

This loop turns on the even-numbered bits of `bitvec`.

As with the subscript operator, we can use the `set`, `test`, and `reset` operations to test or set a given bit value:

```
//  equivalent loop using set operation
for (int index = 0; index != 32; index += 2)
            bitvec.set(index);
```

To test whether a bit is on, we can use the `test` operation or test the value returned from the subscript operator:

```
if (bitvec.test(i))
        //  bitvec[i] is on
//  equivalent test using subscript
if (bitvec[i])
        //  bitvec[i] is on
```

The result of testing the value returned from a subscript is `true` if the bit is 1 or `false` if the bit is 0.

Setting the Entire `bitset`

The `set` and `reset` operations can also be used to turn on or turn off the entire `bitset` object, respectively:

```
bitvec.reset(); //  set all the bits to 0.
bitvec.set();   //  set all the bits to 1
```

The `flip` operation reverses the value of an individual bit or the entire `bitset`:

```
bitvec.flip(0);     //  reverses value of first bit
bitvec[0].flip();   //  also reverses the first bit
bitvec.flip();      //  reverses value of all bits
```

Retrieving the Value of a `bitset`

The `to_ulong` operation returns an `unsigned long` that holds the same bit pattern as the `bitset` object. We can use this operation only if the size of the `bitset` is less than or equal to the size of an `unsigned long`:

```
unsigned long ulong = bitvec3.to_ulong();
cout << "ulong = " << ulong << endl;
```

The `to_ulong` operation is intended to be used when we need to pass a `bitset` to a C or pre-Standard C++ program. If the `bitset` contains more bits than the size of an `unsigned long`, a run-time exception is signaled. We'll introduce exceptions in Section 6.13 (p. 215) and look at them in more detail in Section 17.1 (p. 688).

Printing the Bits

We can use the output operator to print the bit pattern in a `bitset` object:

```
bitset<32> bitvec2(0xffff);   // bits 0 ... 15 are set to 1; 16 ... 31 are 0
cout << "bitvec2: " << bitvec2 << endl;
```

will print

```
bitvec2: 00000000000000001111111111111111
```

Using the Bitwise Operators

The `bitset` class also supports the built-in bitwise operators. As defined by the language, these operators apply to integral operands. They perform operations similar to the `bitset` operations described in this section. Section 5.3 (p. 154) describes these operators.

EXERCISES SECTION 3.5.2

Exercise 3.23: Explain the bit pattern each of the following `bitset` objects contains:

```
(a) bitset<64> bitvec(32);
(b) bitset<32> bv(1010101);
(c) string bstr; cin >> bstr; bitset<8>bv(bstr);
```

Exercise 3.24: Consider the sequence 1,2,3,5,8,13,21. Initialize a `bitset<32>` object that has a one bit in each position corresponding to a number in this sequence. Alternatively, given an empty `bitset`, write a small program to turn on each of the appropriate bits.

CHAPTER SUMMARY

The library defines several higher-level abstract data types, including strings and vectors. The string class provides variable-length character strings, and the vector type manages a collection of objects of a single type.

Iterators allow indirect access to objects stored in a container. Iterators are used to access and navigate between the elements in strings and vectors.

In the next chapter we'll cover arrays and pointers, which are types built into the language. These types provide low-level analogs to the vector and string libraries. In general, the library classes should be used in preference to low-level array and pointer alternatives built into the language.

DEFINED TERMS

abstract data type A type whose representation is hidden. To use an abstract type, we need know only what operations the type supports.

bitset Standard library class that holds a collection of bits and provides operations to test and set the bits in the collection.

cctype header Header inherited from C that contains routines to test character values. See page 88 for a listing of the most common routines.

class template A blueprint from which many potential class types can be created. To use a class template, we must specify what actual type(s) or value(s) to use. For example, a vector is a template that holds objects of a given type. When we create a vector, we must say what type *this* vector will hold. vector<int> holds ints, vector<string> holds strings, and so on.

container A type whose objects hold a collection of objects of a given type.

difference_type A signed integral type defined by vector that is capable of holding the distance between any two iterators.

empty Function defined by the string and vector types. empty returns a bool indicating whether the string has any characters or whether the vector has any

elements. Returns true if size is zero; false otherwise.

getline Function defined in the string header that takes an istream and a string. The function reads the stream up to the next newline, storing what it read into the string, and returns the istream. The newline is read and discarded.

high-order Bits in a bitset with the largest indices.

index Value used in the subscript operator to denote the element to retrieve from a string or vector.

iterator A type that can be used to examine the elements of a container and to navigate between them.

iterator arithmetic The arithmetic operations that can be applied to some, but not all, iterator types. An integral type can be added to or subtracted from an iterator, resulting in an iterator positioned that many elements ahead of or behind the original iterator. Two iterators can be subtracted, yielding the distance between the iterators. Iterator arithmetic is valid only on iterators that refer to elements in the same container or the off-the-end iterator of the container.

low-order Bits in a bitset with the lowest indices.

off-the-end iterator The iterator returned by end. It is an iterator that refers to a nonexistent element one past the end of a container.

push_back Function defined by `vector` that appends elements to the back of a `vector`.

sentinel Programming technique that uses a value as a guard to control processing. In this chapter, we showed the use of the iterator returned by `end` as a guard to stop processing elements in a `vector` once we had processed every element in the `vector`.

size Function defined by the library types `string`, `vector`, and `bitset` that returns the number of characters, elements, or bits respectively. The `string` and `vector` functions return a value of the `size_type` for the type. For example, `size` of a `string` returns a `string::size_type`. The `bitset` operation returns a value of type `size_t`.

size_t Machine-dependent unsigned integral type defined in `cstddef` header that is large enough to hold the size of the largest possible array.

size_type Type defined by the `string` and `vector` classes that is capable of containing the size of any `string` or `vector`, respectively. Library classes that define `size_type` define it as an `unsigned` type.

using declarations Make a name from a namespace accessible directly.

```
using namespace::name;
```

makes *name* accessible without the *namespace*`::` prefix.

value initialization Initialization that happens for container elements when the container size is specified but there is no explicit element initializer. The elements are initialized as a copy of a compiler-generated value. If the container holds built-in types, then the value copied into the elements is zero. For class types, the value is generated by running the class's default constructor. Container elements that are of class type can be value-initialized only if the class has a default constructor.

++ operator The iterator types define the increment operator to "add one" by moving the iterator to refer to the next element.

:: operator The scope operator. It finds the name of its right-hand operand in the scope of its left-hand operand. Used to access names in a namespace, such as `std::cout`, which represents the name `cout` from the namespace `std`. Similarly, used to obtain names from a class, such as `string::size_type`, which is the `size_type` defined by the `string` class.

[ ] operator An overloaded operator defined by the `string`, `vector`, and `bitset` types. It takes two operands: The left-hand operand is the name of the object and the right-hand operand is an index. It fetches the element whose position matches the index. Indices count from zero—the first element is element `0` and the last is element indexed by `obj.size() - 1`. Subscript returns an lvalue, so we may use a subscript as the left-hand operand of an assignment. Assigning to the result of a subscript assigns a new value to the indexed element.

* operator The iterator types define the dereference operator to return the object to which the iterator refers. Dereference returns an lvalue, so we may use a dereference operator as the left-hand operand of an assignment. Assigning to the result of a dereference assigns a new value to the indexed element.

<< operator The `string` and `bitset` library types define an output operator. The `string` operator prints the characters in a `string`. The `bitset` operator prints the bit pattern in the `bitset`.

>> operator The `string` and `bitset` library types define an input operator. The `string` operator reads whitespace delimited chunks of characters, storing what is read into the right-hand (`string`) operand. The `bitset` operator reads a bit sequence into its `bitset` operand.

C H A P T E R 4

ARRAYS AND POINTERS

The language defines two lower-level compound types—arrays and pointers—that are similar to `vectors` and iterators. Like a `vector`, an array holds a collection of objects of some type. Unlike `vectors`, arrays are fixed size; once an array is created, new elements cannot be added. Like iterators, pointers can be used to navigate among and examine the elements in an array.

Modern C++ programs should almost always use `vectors` and iterators in preference to the lower-level arrays and pointers. Well-designed programs use arrays and pointers only in the internals of class implementations where speed is essential.

Arrays are data structures that are similar to library `vector`s but are built into the language. Like a `vector`, an array is a container of objects of a single data type. The individual objects are not named; rather, each one is accessed by its position in the array.

Arrays have significant drawbacks compared to `vector`s: They are fixed size, and they offer no help to the programmer in keeping track of how big a given array is. There is no `size` operation on arrays. Similarly, there is no `push_back` to automatically add elements. If the array size needs to change, then the programmer must allocate a new, larger array and copy the elements into that new space.

Programs that rely on built-in arrays rather than using the standard `vector` are more error-prone and harder to debug.

Prior to the advent of the standard library, C++ programs made heavy use of arrays to hold collections of objects. Modern C++ programs should almost always use `vector`s instead of arrays. Arrays should be restricted to the internals of programs and used only where performance testing indicates that `vector`s cannot provide the necessary speed. However, there will be a large body of existing C++ code that relies on arrays for some time to come. Hence, all C++ programmers must know a bit about how arrays work.

4.1 Arrays

An array is a compound type (Section 2.5, p. 58) that consists of a type specifier, an identifier, and a *dimension*. The type specifier indicates what type the elements stored in the array will have. The dimension specifies how many elements the array will contain.

The type specifier can denote a built-in data or class type. With the exception of references, the element type can also be any compound type. There are no arrays of references.

4.1.1 Defining and Initializing Arrays

The dimension must be a constant expression (Section 2.7, p. 62) whose value is greater than or equal to one. A constant expression is any expression that involves *only* integral literal constants, enumerators (Section 2.7, p. 62), or `const` objects of integral type that are themselves initialized from constant expressions. A nonconst variable, or a `const` variable whose value is not known until run time, cannot be used to specify the dimension of an array.

The dimension is specified inside a [ ] bracket pair:

```
// both buf_size and max_files are const
const unsigned buf_size = 512, max_files = 20;
int staff_size = 27;            // nonconst
```

```
const unsigned sz = get_size();  // const value not known until run time
char input_buffer[buf_size];        // ok: const variable
string fileTable[max_files + 1]; // ok: constant expression

double salaries[staff_size];        // error: nonconst variable
int test_scores[get_size()];        // error: nonconst expression
int vals[sz];                        // error: size not known until run time
```

Although `staff_size` is initialized with a literal constant, `staff_size` itself is a nonconst object. Its value can be known only at run time, so it is illegal as an array dimension. Even though `size` is a `const` object, its value is not known until `get_size` is called at run time. Therefore, it may not be used as a dimension. On the other hand, the expression

```
max_files + 1
```

is a constant expression because `max_files` is a `const` variable. The expression can be and is evaluated at compile time to a value of 21.

Explicitly Initializing Array Elements

When we define an array, we can provide a comma-separated list of initializers for its elements. The initializer list must be enclosed in braces:

```
const unsigned array_size = 3;
int ia[array_size] = {0, 1, 2};
```

If we do not supply element initializers, then the elements are initialized in the same way that variables are initialized (Section 2.3.4, p. 50).

- Elements of an array of built-in type defined outside the body of a function are initialized to zero.

- Elements of an array of built-in type defined inside the body of a function are uninitialized.

- Regardless of where the array is defined, if it holds elements of a class type, then the elements are initialized by the default constructor for that class if it has one. If the class does not have a default constructor, then the elements must be explicitly initialized.

 Unless we explicitly supply element initializers, the elements of a local array of built-in type are uninitialized. Using these elements for any purpose other than to assign a new value is undefined.

An explicitly initialized array need not specify a dimension value. The compiler will infer the array size from the number of elements listed:

```
int ia[] = {0, 1, 2};  // an array of dimension 3
```

If the dimension size is specified, the number of elements provided must not exceed that size. If the dimension size is greater than the number of listed elements, the initializers are used for the first elements. The remaining elements are initialized to zero if the elements are of built-in type or by running the default constructor if they are of class type:

```
const unsigned array_size = 5;
// Equivalent to ia = {0, 1, 2, 0, 0}
// ia[3] and ia[4] default initialized to 0
int ia[array_size] = {0, 1, 2};
// Equivalent to str_arr = {"hi", "bye", "", "", ""}
// str_arr[2] through str_arr[4] default initialized to the empty string
string str_arr[array_size] = {"hi", "bye"};
```

Character Arrays Are Special

A character array can be initialized with either a list of comma-separated character literals enclosed in braces or a string literal. Note, however, that the two forms are not equivalent. Recall that a string literal (Section 2.2, p. 40) contains an additional terminating null character. When we create a character array from a string literal, the null is also inserted into the array:

```
char ca1[] = {'C', '+', '+'};        // no null
char ca2[] = {'C', '+', '+', '\0'};  // explicit null
char ca3[] = "C++";       // null terminator added automatically
```

The dimension of ca1 is 3; the dimension of ca2 and ca3 is 4. It is important to remember the null-terminator when initializing an array of characters to a literal. For example, the following is a compile-time error:

```
const char ch3[6] = "Daniel"; // error: Daniel is 7 elements
```

While the literal contains only six explicit characters, the required array size is seven—six to hold the literal and one for the null.

No Array Copy or Assignment

Unlike a vector, it is not possible to initialize an array as a copy of another array. Nor is it legal to assign one array to another:

```
int ia[] = {0, 1, 2}; // ok: array of ints
int ia2[](ia);         // error: cannot initialize one array with another
int main()
{
    const unsigned array_size = 3;
    int ia3[array_size]; // ok: but elements are uninitialized!

    ia3 = ia;            // error: cannot assign one array to another
    return 0;
}
```

Some compilers allow array assignment as a **compiler extension**. If you intend to run a given program on more than one compiler, it is usually a good idea to avoid using nonstandard compiler-specific features such as array assignment.

CAUTION: ARRAYS ARE FIXED SIZE
_____

Unlike the `vector` type, there is no `push_back` or other operation to add elements to the array. Once we define an array, we cannot add elements to it.

If we must add elements to the array, then we must manage the memory ourselves. We have to ask the system for new storage to hold the larger array and copy the existing elements into that new storage. We'll see how to do so in Section 4.3.1 (p. 134).

EXERCISES SECTION 4.1.1

Exercise 4.1: Assuming `get_size` is a function that takes no arguments and returns an `int` value, which of the following definitions are illegal? Explain why.

```
unsigned buf_size = 1024;

(a)  int ia[buf_size];
(b)  int ia[get_size()];
(c)  int ia[4 * 7 - 14];
(d)  char st[11] = "fundamental";
```

Exercise 4.2: What are the values in the following arrays?

```
string sa[10];
int ia[10];
int main() {
     string sa2[10];
     int    ia2[10];
}
```

Exercise 4.3: Which, if any, of the following definitions are in error?

```
(a)  int ia[7] = { 0, 1, 1, 2, 3, 5, 8 };
(b)  vector<int> ivec = { 0, 1, 1, 2, 3, 5, 8 };
(c)  int ia2[ ] = ia1;
(d)  int ia3[ ] = ivec;
```

Exercise 4.4: How can you initialize some or all the elements of an array?

Exercise 4.5: List some of the drawbacks of using an array instead of a `vector`.

4.1.2 Operations on Arrays

Array elements, like `vector` elements, may be accessed using the subscript operator (Section 3.3.2, p. 94). Like the elements of a `vector`, the elements of an array are numbered beginning with 0. For an array of ten elements, the correct index values are 0 through 9, not 1 through 10.

When we subscript a `vector`, we use `vector::size_type` as the type for the index. When we subscript an array, the right type to use for the index is `size_t` (Section 3.5.2, p. 104).

In the following example, a `for` loop steps through the 10 elements of an array, assigning to each the value of its index:

```
int main()
{
    const size_t array_size = 10;
    int ia[array_size]; //   10 ints, elements are uninitialized

    //   loop through array, assigning value of its index to each element
    for (size_t ix = 0; ix != array_size; ++ix)
        ia[ix] = ix;
    return 0;
}
```

Using a similar loop, we can copy one array into another:

```
int main()
{
    const size_t array_size = 7;
    int ia1[] = { 0, 1, 2, 3, 4, 5, 6 };
    int ia2[array_size]; //   local array, elements uninitialized

    //   copy elements from ia1 into ia2
    for (size_t ix = 0; ix != array_size; ++ix)
        ia2[ix] = ia1[ix];
    return 0;
}
```

Checking Subscript Values

As with both `strings` and `vectors`, the programmer must guarantee that the subscript value is in range—that the array has an element at the index value.

Nothing stops a programmer from stepping across an array boundary except attention to detail and thorough testing of the code. It is not inconceivable for a program to compile and execute and still be fatally wrong.

By far, the most common causes of security problems are so-called "buffer overflow" bugs. These bugs occur when a subscript is not checked and reference is made to an element outside the bounds of an array or other similar data structure.

4.2   Introducing Pointers

Just as we can traverse a `vector` either by using a subscript or an iterator, we can also traverse an array by using either a subscript or a **pointer**. A pointer is a compound type; a pointer points to an object of some other type. Pointers are iterators for arrays: A pointer can point to an element in an array. The dereference and increment operators, when applied to a pointer that points to an array element, have similar behavior as when applied to an iterator. When we dereference a pointer,

---

Exercise 4.6: This code fragment intends to assign the value of its index to each array element. It contains a number of indexing errors. Identify them.

```
const size_t array_size = 10;
int ia[array_size];

for (size_t ix = 1; ix <= array_size; ++ix)
        ia[ix] = ix;
```

Exercise 4.7: Write the code necessary to assign one array to another. Now, change the code to use vectors. How might you assign one vector to another?

Exercise 4.8: Write a program to compare two arrays for equality. Write a similar program to compare two vectors.

Exercise 4.9: Write a program to define an array of 10 ints. Give each element the same value as its position in the array.

---

we obtain the object to which the pointer points. When we increment a pointer, we advance the pointer to denote the next element in the array. Before we write programs using pointers, we need to know a bit more about them.

4.2.1 What Is a Pointer?

For newcomers, pointers are often hard to understand. Debugging problems due to pointer errors bedevil even experienced programmers. However, pointers are an important part of most C programs and to a much lesser extent remain important in many C++ programs.

Conceptually, pointers are simple: A pointer points at an object. Like an iterator, a pointer offers indirect access to the object to which it points. However, pointers are a much more general construct. Unlike iterators, pointers can be used to point at single objects. Iterators are used only to access elements in a container.

Specifically, a pointer holds the address of another object:

```
string s("hello world");
string *sp = &s;    // sp holds the address of s
```

The second statement defines sp as a pointer to string and initializes sp to point to the string object named s. The * in *sp indicates that sp is a pointer. The & operator in &s is the **address-of** operator. It returns a value that when dereferenced yields the original object. The address-of operator may be applied only to an lvalue (Section 2.3.1, p. 45). Because a variable is an lvalue, we may take its address. Similarly, the subscript and dereference operators, when applied to a vector, string, or built-in array, yield lvalues. Because these operators yield lvalues, we may apply the address-of to the result of the subscript or dereference operator. Doing so gives us the address of a particular element.

> **ADVICE: AVOID POINTERS AND ARRAYS**
>
> Pointers and arrays are surprisingly error-prone. Part of the problem is conceptual: Pointers are used for low-level manipulations and it is easy to make bookkeeping mistakes. Other problems arise because of the syntax, particularly the declaration syntax used with pointers.
>
> Many useful programs can be written without needing to use arrays or pointers. Instead, modern C++ programs should use `vectors` and iterators to replace general arrays and `strings` to replace C-style array-based character strings.

4.2.2   Defining and Initializing Pointers

Every pointer has an associated type. The type of a pointer determines the type of the objects to which the pointer may point. A pointer to `int`, for example, may only point to an object of type `int`.

Defining Pointer Variables

We use the `*` symbol in a declaration to indicate that an identifier is a pointer:

```
vector<int>   *pvec;        // pvec can point to a vector<int>
int           *ip1, *ip2;   // ip1 and ip2 can point to an int
string        *pstring;     // pstring can point to a string
double        *dp;          // dp can point to a double
```

 When attempting to understand pointer declarations, read them from right to left.

Reading the definition of `pstring` from right to left, we see that

```
string *pstring;
```

defines `pstring` as a pointer that can point to `string` objects. Similarly,

```
int *ip1, *ip2; // ip1 and ip2 can point to an int
```

defines `ip2` as a pointer and `ip1` as a pointer. Both pointers point to `int`s.
    The `*` can come anywhere in a list of objects of a given type:

```
double dp, *dp2;   // dp2 is a ponter, dp is an object: both type double
```

defines `dp2` as a pointer and `dp` as an object, both of type `double`.

A Different Pointer Declaration Style

The `*` symbol may be separated from its identifier by a space. It is legal to write:

```
string* ps;     // legal but can be misleading
```

which says that `ps` is a pointer to `string`.
    We say that this definition can be misleading because it encourages the belief that `string*` is the type and any variable defined in the same definition is a pointer to `string`. However,

```
string* ps1, ps2; // ps1 is a pointer to string, ps2 is a string
```

defines `ps1` as a pointer, but `ps2` is a plain `string`. If we want to define two pointers in a single definition, we must repeat the `*` on each identifier:

```
string* ps1, *ps2;  // both ps1 and ps2 are pointers to string
```

Multiple Pointer Declarations Can Be Confusing

There are two common styles for declaring multiple pointers of the same type. One style requires that a declaration introduce only a single name. In this style, the `*` is placed with the type to emphasize that the declaration is declaring a pointer:

```
string* ps1;
string* ps2;
```

The other style permits multiple declarations in a single statement but places the `*` adjacent to the identifier. This style emphasizes that the object is a pointer:

```
string *ps1, *ps2;
```

 As with all questions of style, there is no single right way to declare pointers. The important thing is to choose a style and stick with it.

In this book we use the second style and place the `*` with the pointer variable name.

Possible Pointer Values

A valid pointer has one of three states: It can hold the address of a specific object, it can point one past the end of an object, or it can be zero. A zero-valued pointer points to no object. An uninitialized pointer is invalid until it is assigned a value. The following definitions and assignments are all legal:

```
int ival = 1024;
int *pi = 0;      // pi initialized to address no object
int *pi2 = &ival; // pi2 initialized to address of ival
int *pi3;         // ok, but dangerous, pi3 is uninitialized
pi = pi2;         // pi and pi2 address the same object, e.g. ival
pi2 = 0;          // pi2 now addresses no object
```

Avoid Uninitialized Pointers

 Uninitialized pointers are a common source of run-time errors.

As with any other uninitialized variable, what happens when we use an uninitialized pointer is undefined. Using an uninitialized pointer almost always results in a run-time crash. However, the fact that the crash results from using an uninitialized pointer can be quite hard to track down.

Under most compilers, if we use an uninitialized pointer the effect will be to use whatever bits are in the memory in which the pointer resides as if it were an address. Using an uninitialized pointer uses this supposed address to manipulate the underlying data at that supposed location. Doing so usually leads to a crash as soon as we attempt to dereference the uninitialized pointer.

It is not possible to detect whether a pointer is uninitialized. There is no way to distinguish a valid address from an address formed from the bits that are in the memory in which the pointer was allocated. Our recommendation to initialize all variables is particularly important for pointers.

Best Practices

If possible, do not define a pointer until the object to which it should point has been defined. That way, there is no need to define an uninitialized pointer.

If you must define a pointer separately from pointing it at an object, then initialize the pointer to zero. The reason is that a zero-valued pointer can be tested and the program can detect that the pointer does not point to an object.

Constraints on Initialization of and Assignment to Pointers

There are only four kinds of values that may be used to initialize or assign to a pointer:

1. A constant expression (Section 2.7, p. 62) with value 0 (e.g., a `const` integral object whose value is zero at compile time or a literal constant 0)

2. An address of an object of an appropriate type

3. The address one past the end of another object

4. Another valid pointer of the same type

It is illegal to assign an `int` to a pointer, even if the value of the `int` happens to be 0. It is okay to assign the literal 0 or a `const` whose value is known to be 0 at compile time:

```
int ival;
int zero = 0;
const int c_ival = 0;

int *pi = ival;  // error: pi initialized from int value of ival
pi = zero;       // error: pi assigned int value of zero
pi = c_ival;     // ok: c_ival is a const with compile-time value of 0
pi = 0;          // ok: directly initialize to literal constant 0
```

In addition to using a literal 0 or a `const` with a compile-time value of 0, we can also use a facility that C++ inherits from C. The `cstdlib` header defines a preprocessor variable (Section 2.9.2, p. 69) named `NULL`, which is defined as 0. When we use a preprocessor variable in our code, it is automatically replaced by its value. Hence, initializing a pointer to `NULL` is equivalent to initializing it to 0:

```
//  cstdlib #defines NULL to 0
int *pi = NULL; //  ok: equivalent to int *pi = 0;
```

As with any preprocessor variable (Section 2.9.2, p. 71) we should not use the name NULL for our own variables.

 Preprocessor variables are not defined in the std namespace and hence the name is NULL, not std::NULL.

With two exceptions, which we cover in Sections 4.2.5 and 15.3, we may only initialize or assign a pointer from an address or another pointer that has the same type as the target pointer:

```
double dval;
double *pd = &dval;   //  ok: initializer is address of a double
double *pd2 = pd;     //  ok: initializer is a pointer to double

int *pi = pd;   //  error: types of pi and pd differ
pi = &dval;     //  error: attempt to assign address of a double to int *
```

The reason the types must match is that the type of the pointer is used to determine the type of the object that it addresses. Pointers are used to indirectly access an object. The operations that the pointer can perform are based on the type of the pointer: A pointer to int treats the underlying object as if it were an int. If that pointer actually addressed an object of some other type, such as double, then any operations performed by the pointer would be in error.

void* Pointers

The type **void*** is a special pointer type that can hold an address of any object:

```
double obj = 3.14;
double *pd = &obj;
//  ok: void* can hold the address value of any data pointer type
void *pv = &obj;   //  obj can be an object of any type
pv = pd;           //  pd can be a pointer to any type
```

A void* indicates that the associated value is an address but that the type of the object at that address is unknown.

There are only a limited number of actions we can perform on a void* pointer: We can compare it to another pointer, we can pass or return it from a function, and we can assign it to another void* pointer. We cannot use the pointer to operate on the object it addresses. We'll see in Section 5.12.4 (p. 183) how we can retrieve the address stored in a void* pointer.

4.2.3 Operations on Pointers

Pointers allow indirect manipulation of the object to which the pointer points. We can access the object by dereferencing the pointer. Dereferencing a pointer is similar to dereferencing an iterator (Section 3.4, p. 98). The * operator (the dereference operator) returns the object to which the pointer points:

Exercise 4.10: Explain the rationale for preferring the first form of pointer declaration:

```
int *ip;   // good practice
int* ip;   // legal but misleading
```

Exercise 4.11: Explain each of the following definitions. Indicate whether any are illegal and if so why.

```
(a) int* ip;
(b) string s, *sp = 0;
(c) int i; double* dp = &i;
(d) int* ip, ip2;
(e) const int i = 0, *p = i;
(f) string *p = NULL;
```

Exercise 4.12: Given a pointer, p, can you determine whether p points to a valid object? If so, how? If not, why not?

Exercise 4.13: Why is the first pointer initialization legal and the second illegal?

```
int i = 42;
void *p = &i;
long *lp = &i;
```

```
string s("hello world");
string *sp = &s;   // sp holds the address of s
cout << *sp;       // prints hello world
```

When we dereference sp, we fetch the value of s. We hand that value to the output operator. The last statement, therefore, prints the contents of s—that is, hello world.

Dereference Yields an Lvalue

The dereference operator returns the lvalue of the underlying object, so we can use it to change the value of the object to which the pointer points:

```
*sp = "goodbye";   // contents of s now changed
```

Because we assign to *sp, this statement leaves sp pointing to s and changes the value of s.

We can also assign a new value to sp itself. Assigning to sp causes sp to point to a different object:

```
string s2 = "some value";
sp = &s2;   // sp now points to s2
```

We change the value of a pointer by assigning to it directly—without dereferencing the pointer.

KEY CONCEPT: ASSIGNING *TO* OR *THROUGH* A POINTER

When first using pointers, the difference in whether an assignment is to the pointer or through the pointer to the value pointed to can be confusing. The important thing to keep in mind is that if the left-hand operand is dereferenced, then the value pointed to is changed. If there is no dereference, then the pointer itself is being changed. A picture can sometimes help:

```
string s1("some value");
string *sp1 = &s1;
```

```
string s2("another");
string *sp2 = &s2;
```

```
// assign through sp1
// value in s1 changed
*sp1 = "a new value";
```

```
// assign to sp1
// sp1 points to a different object
sp1 = sp2;
```

Comparing Pointers and References

While both references and pointers are used to indirectly access another value, there are two important differences between references and pointers. The first is that a reference always refers to an object: It is an error to define a reference without initializing it. The behavior of assignment is the second important difference: Assigning to a reference changes the object to which the reference is bound; it does not rebind the reference to another object. Once initialized, a reference *always* refers to the same underlying object.

Consider these two program fragments. In the first, we assign one pointer to another:

```
int ival = 1024, ival2 = 2048;
int *pi = &ival, *pi2 = &ival2;
pi = pi2;      // pi now points to ival2
```

After the assignment, `ival`, the object addressed by `pi` remains unchanged. The assignment changes the value of `pi`, making it point to a different object. Now consider a similar program that assigns two references:

```
int &ri = ival, &ri2 = ival2;
ri = ri2;      // assigns ival2 to ival
```

This assignment changes `ival`, the value referenced by `ri`, and not the reference itself. After the assignment, the two references still refer to their original objects, and the value of those objects is now the same as well.

Pointers to Pointers

Pointers are themselves objects in memory. They, therefore, have addresses that we can store in a pointer:

```
int ival = 1024;
int *pi = &ival;    //  pi points to an int
int **ppi = &pi;    //  ppi points to a pointer to int
```

which yields a pointer to a pointer. We designate a pointer to a pointer by using `**`. We might represent these objects as

As usual, dereferencing `ppi` yields the object to which `ppi` points. In this case, that object is a pointer to an `int`:

```
int *pi2 = *ppi;   //  ppi points to a pointer
```

To actually access `ival`, we need to dereference `ppi` twice:

```
cout << "The value of ival\n"
     << "direct value: " << ival << "\n"
     << "indirect value: " << *pi << "\n"
     << "doubly indirect value: " << **ppi
     << endl;
```

This program prints the value of `ival` three different ways. First, by direct reference to the variable. Then, through the pointer to `int` in `pi`, and finally, by dereferencing `ppi` twice to get to the underlying value in `ival`.

EXERCISES SECTION 4.2.3

Exercise 4.14: Write code to change the value of a pointer. Write code to change the value to which the pointer points.

Exercise 4.15: Explain the key differences between pointers and references.

Exercise 4.16: What does the following program do?

```
int i = 42, j = 1024;
int *p1 = &i, *p2 = &j;
*p2 = *p1 * *p2;
*p1 *= *p1;
```

4.2.4   Using Pointers to Access Array Elements

Pointers and arrays are closely intertwined in C++. In particular, when we use the name of an array in an expression, that name is automatically converted into a pointer to the first element of the array:

```
int ia[] = {0,2,4,6,8};
int *ip = ia;  //  ip points to ia[0]
```

If we want to point to another element in the array, we could do so by using the subscript operator to locate the element and then applying the address-of operator to find its location:

```
ip = &ia[4];   //  ip points to last element in ia
```

Pointer Arithmetic

Rather than taking the address of the value returned by subscripting, we could use **pointer arithmetic**. Pointer arithmetic works the same way (and has the same constraints) as iterator arithmetic (Section 3.4.1, p. 100). Using pointer arithmetic, we can compute a pointer to an element by adding (or subtracting) an integral value to (or from) a pointer to another element in the array:

```
ip = ia;             //  ok: ip points to ia[0]
int *ip2 = ip + 4;   //  ok: ip2 points to ia[4], the last element in ia
```

When we add 4 to the pointer ip, we are computing a new pointer. That new pointer points to the element four elements further on in the array from the one to which ip currently points.

More generally, when we add (or subtract) an integral value to a pointer, the effect is to compute a new pointer. The new pointer points to the element as many elements as that integral value ahead of (or behind) the original pointer.

Pointer arithmetic is legal only if the original pointer and the newly calculated pointer address elements of the same array or an element one past the end of that array. If we have a pointer to an object, we can also compute a pointer that points just after that object by adding one to the pointer.

Given that ia has 4 elements, adding 10 to ia would be an error:

```
//  error: ia has only 4 elements, ia + 10 is an invalid address
int *ip3 = ia + 10;
```

We can also subtract two pointers as long as they point into the same array or to an element one past the end of the array:

```
ptrdiff_t n = ip2 - ip; //  ok: distance between the pointers
```

The result is four, the distance between the two pointers, measured in objects. The result of subtracting two pointers is a library type named **ptrdiff_t**. Like size_t, the ptrdiff_t type is a machine-specific type and is defined in the cstddef header. The size_t type is an unsigned type, whereas ptrdiff_t is a signed integral type.

The difference in type reflects how these two types are used: size_t is used to hold the size of an array, which must be a positive value. The ptrdiff_t type is guaranteed to be large enough to hold the difference between any two pointers into the same array, which might be a negative value. For example, had we subtracted `ip2` from `ip`, the result would be `-4`.

It is always possible to add or subtract zero to a pointer, which leaves the pointer unchanged. More interestingly, given a pointer that has a value of zero, it is also legal to add zero to that pointer. The result is another zero-valued pointer. We can also subtract two pointers that have a value of zero. The result of subtracting two zero-valued pointers is zero.

Interaction between Dereference and Pointer Arithmetic

The result of adding an integral value to a pointer is itself a pointer. We can dereference the resulting pointer directly without first assigning it to another pointer:

```
int last = *(ia + 4);   // ok: initializes last to 8, the value of ia[4]
```

This expression calculates the address four elements past `ia` and dereferences that pointer. It is equivalent to writing `ia[4]`.

> The parentheses around the addition are essential. Writing
>
> ```
> last = *ia + 4;    // ok: last = 4, equivalent to ia[0] + 4
> ```
>
> means dereference `ia` and add four to the dereferenced value.

The parentheses are required due to the **precedence** of the addition and dereference operators. We'll learn more about precedence in Section 5.10.1 (p. 168). Simply put, precedence stipulates how operands are grouped in expressions with multiple operators. The dereference operator has a higher precedence than the addition operator.

The operands to operators with higher precedence are grouped more tightly than those of lower precedence. Without the parentheses, the dereference operator would use `ia` as its operand. The expression would be evaluated by dereferencing `ia` and adding four to the value of the element at the beginning of `ia`.

By parenthesizing the expression, we override the normal precedence rules and effectively treat `(ia + 4)` as a single operand. That operand is an address of an element four past the one to which `ia` points. That new address is dereferenced.

Subscripts and Pointers

We have already seen that when we use an array name in an expression, we are actually using a pointer to the first element in the array. This fact has a number of implications, which we shall point out as they arise.

One important implication is that when we subscript an array, we are really subscripting a pointer:

```
int ia[] = {0,2,4,6,8};
int i = ia[0];   // ia points to the first element in ia
```

When we write `ia[0]`, that is an expression that uses the name of an array. When we subscript an array, we are really subscripting a pointer to an element in that array. We can use the subscript operator on any pointer, as long as that pointer points to an element in an array:

```
int *p = &ia[2];    // ok: p points to the element indexed by 2
int j = p[1];       // ok: p[1] equivalent to *(p + 1),
                    //     p[1] is the same element as ia[3]
int k = p[-2];      // ok: p[-2] is the same element as ia[0]
```

Computing an Off-the-End Pointer

When we use a `vector`, the `end` operation returns an iterator that refers just past the end of the `vector`. We often use this iterator as a sentinel to control loops that process the elements in the `vector`. Similarly, we can compute an off-the-end pointer value:

```
const size_t arr_size = 5;
int arr[arr_size] = {1,2,3,4,5};
int *p = arr;               // ok: p points to arr[0]
int *p2 = p + arr_size;     // ok: p2 points one past the end of arr
                            //     use caution -- do not dereference!
```

In this case, we set p to point to the first element in `arr`. We then calculate a pointer one past the end of `arr` by adding the size of `arr` to the pointer value in p. When we add 5 to p, the effect is to calculate the address of that is five `int`s away from p—in other words, p + 5 points just past the end of `arr`.

It is legal to compute an address one past the end of an array or object. It is not legal to dereference a pointer that holds such an address. Nor is it legal to compute an address more than one past the end of an array or an address before the beginning of an array.

The address we calculated and stored in p2 acts much like the iterator returned from the `end` operation on `vector`s. The iterator we obtain from `end` denotes "one past the end" of the `vector`. We may not dereference that iterator, but we may compare it to another iterator value to see whether we have processed all the elements in the `vector`. Similarly, the value we calculated for p2 can be used *only* to compare to another pointer value or as an operand in a pointer arithmetic expression. If we attempt to dereference p2, the most likely result is that it would yield some garbage value. Most compilers, would treat the result of dereferencing p2 as an `int`, using whatever bits happened to be in memory at the location just after the last element in `arr`.

Printing the Elements of an Array

Now we are ready to write a program that uses pointers:

```
const size_t arr_sz = 5;
int int_arr[arr_sz] = { 0, 1, 2, 3, 4 };
// pbegin points to first element, pend points just after the last
for (int *pbegin = int_arr, *pend = int_arr + arr_sz;
        pbegin != pend; ++pbegin)
    cout << *pbegin << ' '; // print the current element
```

This program uses a feature of the `for` loop that we have not yet used: We may define multiple variables inside the *init-statement* (Section 1.4.2, p. 14) of a `for` as long as the variables are defined using the same type. In this case, we're defining two `int` pointers named `pbegin` and `pend`.

We use these pointers to traverse the array. Like other built-in types, arrays have no member functions. Hence, there are no `begin` and `end` operations on arrays. Instead, we must position pointers to denote the first and one past the last elements ourselves. We do so in the initialization of our two pointers. We initialize `pbegin` to address the first element of `int_arr` and `pend` to one past the last element in the array:

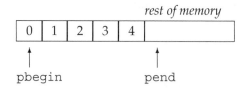

The pointer `pend` serves as a sentinel, allowing the `for` loop to know when to stop. Each iteration of the `for` loop increments `pbegin` to address the next element. On the first trip through the loop, `pbegin` denotes the first element, on the second iteration, the second element, and so on. After processing the last element in the array, `pbegin` will be incremented once more and will then equal `pend`. At that point we know that we have iterated across the entire array.

Pointers Are Iterators for Arrays

Astute readers will note that this program is remarkably similar to the program on page 99, which traversed and printed the contents of a `vector` of `string`s. The loop in that program

```
// equivalent loop using iterators to reset all the elements in ivec to 0
for (vector<int>::iterator iter = ivec.begin();
                           iter != ivec.end(); ++iter)
        *iter = 0;   // set element to which iter refers to 0
```

used iterators in much the same way that pointers are used in the program to print the contents of the array. This similarity is not a coincidence. In fact, the built-in array type has many of the properties of a library container, and pointers, when we use them in conjunction with arrays, are themselves iterators. We'll have much more to say about containers and iterators in Part II.

4.2.5   Pointers and the `const` Qualifier

There are two kinds of interactions between pointers and the `const` qualifier discussed in Section 2.4 (p. 56): We can have pointers to `const` objects and pointers that are themselves `const`. This section discusses both kinds of pointers.

Pointers to `const` Objects

The pointers we've seen so far can be used to change the value of the objects to which they point. But if we have a pointer to a `const` object, we do not want to

EXERCISES SECTION 4.2.4

Exercise 4.17: Given that p1 and p2 point to elements in the same array, what does the following statement do?

```
p1 += p2 - p1;
```

Are there any values of p1 or p2 that could make this code illegal?

Exercise 4.18: Write a program that uses pointers to set the elements in an array of ints to zero.

allow that pointer to change the underlying, const value. The language enforces this property by requiring that pointers to const objects must take the constness of their target into account:

```
const double *cptr;   // cptr may point to a double that is const
```

Here cptr is a pointer to an object of type const double. The const qualifies the type of the object to which cptr points, not cptr itself. That is, cptr itself is not const. We need not initialize it and can assign a new value to it if we so desire. What we cannot do is use cptr to change the value to which it points:

```
*cptr = 42; //  error: *cptr might be const
```

It is also a compile-time error to assign the address of a const object to a plain, nonconst pointer:

```
const double pi = 3.14;
double *ptr = &pi;        //  error: ptr is a plain pointer
const double *cptr = &pi; //  ok: cptr is a pointer to const
```

We cannot use a void* pointer (Section 4.2.2, p. 119) to hold the address of a const object. Instead, we must use the type **const void*** to hold the address of a const object:

```
const int universe = 42;
const void *cpv = &universe;   //  ok: cpv is const
void *pv = &universe;          //  error: universe is const
```

A pointer to a const object can be assigned the address of a nonconst object, such as

```
double dval = 3.14;    //  dval is a double; its value can be changed
cptr = &dval;          //  ok: but can't change dval through cptr
```

Although dval is not a const, any attempt to modify its value through cptr results in a compile-time error. When we declared cptr, we said that it would not change the value to which it points. The fact that it happens to point to a nonconst object is irrelevant.

We cannot use a pointer to const to change the underlying object. However, if the pointer addresses a nonconst object, it is possible that some other action will change the object to which the pointer points.

The fact that values to which a const pointer points can be changed is subtle and can be confusing. Consider:

```
dval = 3.14159;       //  dval is not const
*cptr = 3.14159;      //  error: cptr is a pointer to const
double *ptr = &dval;  //  ok: ptr points at non-const double
*ptr = 2.72;          //  ok: ptr is plain pointer
cout << *cptr;        //  ok: prints 2.72
```

In this case, cptr is defined as a pointer to const but it actually points at a nonconst object. Even though the object to which it points is nonconst, we cannot use cptr to change the object's value. Essentially, there is no way for cptr to know whether the object it points to is const, and so it treats all objects to which it might point as const.

When a pointer to const does point to a nonconst, it is possible that the value of the object might change: After all, that value is not const. We could either assign to it directly or, as here, indirectly through another, plain nonconst pointer. It is important to remember that there is no guarantee that an object pointed to by a pointer to const won't change.

It may be helpful to think of pointers to const as "pointers that *think* they point to const."

In real-world programs, pointers to const occur most often as formal parameters of functions. Defining a parameter as a pointer to const serves as a contract guaranteeing that the actual object being passed into the function will not be modified through that parameter.

const Pointers

In addition to pointers to const, we can also have const pointers—that is, pointers whose own value we may not change:

```
int errNumb = 0;
int *const curErr = &errNumb;   //  curErr is a constant pointer
```

Reading this definition from right to left, we see that "curErr is a constant pointer to an object of type int." As with any const, we may not change the value of the pointer—that is, we may not make it point to any other object. Any attempt to assign to a constant pointer—even assigning the same value back to curErr—is flagged as an error during compilation:

```
curErr = curErr; //  error: curErr is const
```

As with any const, we must initialize a const pointer when we create it.

The fact that a pointer is itself `const` says nothing about whether we can use the pointer to change the value to which it points. Whether we can change the value pointed to depends entirely on the type to which the pointer points. For example, `curErr` addresses a plain, nonconst `int`. We can use `curErr` to change the value of `errNumb`:

```
if (*curErr) {
    errorHandler();
    *curErr = 0;  //  ok: reset value of the object to which curErr is bound
}
```

`const` Pointer to a `const` Object

We can also define a constant pointer to a constant object as follows:

```
const double pi = 3.14159;
//  pi_ptr is const and points to a const object
const double *const pi_ptr = &pi;
```

In this case, neither the value of the object addressed by `pi_ptr` nor the address itself can be changed. We can read its definition from right to left as "`pi_ptr` is a constant pointer to an object of type `double` defined as `const`."

Pointers and Typedefs

The use of pointers in typedefs (Section 2.6, p. 61) often leads to surprising results. Here is a question almost everyone answers incorrectly at least once. Given the following,

```
typedef string *pstring;
const pstring cstr;
```

what is the type of `cstr`? The simple answer is that it is a pointer to `const` `pstring`. The deeper question is: what underlying type does a pointer to `const` `pstring` represent? Many think that the actual type is

```
const string *cstr;   //  wrong interpretation of const pstring cstr
```

That is, that a `const` `pstring` would be a pointer to a constant `string`. But that is incorrect.

The mistake is in thinking of a typedef as a textual expansion. When we declare a `const` `pstring`, the `const` modifies the type of `pstring`, which is a pointer. Therefore, this definition declares `cstr` to be a `const` pointer to `string`. The definition is equivalent to

```
//  cstr is a const pointer to string
string *const cstr;   //  equivalent to const pstring cstr
```

Part of the problem in reading `const` declarations arises because the `const` can go either before or after the type:

```
string const s1;    //  s1 and s2 have same type,
const string s2;    //  they're both strings that are const
```

When writing `const` definitions using typedefs, the fact that the `const` can precede the type can lead to confusion as to the actual type being defined:

```
string s;
typedef string *pstring;

const pstring cstr1 = &s;   //  written this way the type is obscured
pstring const cstr2 = &s;   //  all three decreations are the same type
string *const cstr3 = &s;   //  they're all const pointers to string
```

Putting the `const` after `pstring` and reading the declaration from right to left makes it clearer that `cstr2` is a `const pstring`, which in turn is a `const` pointer to `string`.

Unfortunately, most readers of C++ programs expect to see the `const` before the type. As a result, it is probably a good idea to put the `const` first, respecting common practice. But it can be helpful in understanding declarations to rewrite them to put the `const` after the type.

4.3   C-Style Character Strings

Although C++ supports C-style strings, they should not be used by C++ programs. C-style strings are a surprisingly rich source of bugs and are the root cause of many, many security problems.

In Section 2.2 (p. 40) we first used string literals and learned that the type of a string literal is array of constant characters. We can now be more explicit and note that the type of a string literal is an array of `const char`. A string literal is an instance of a more general construct that C++ inherits from C: **C-style character strings**. C-style strings are not actually a type in either C or C++. Instead, C-style strings are null-terminated arrays of characters:

```
char ca1[] = {'C', '+', '+'};        //  no null, not C-style string
char ca2[] = {'C', '+', '+', '\0'};  //  explicit null
char ca3[] = "C++";        //  null terminator added automatically
const char *cp = "C++";    //  null terminator added automatically
char *cp1 = ca1;     //  points to first element of a array, but not C-style string
char *cp2 = ca2;     //  points to first element of a null-terminated char array
```

Neither `ca1` nor `cp1` are C-style strings: `ca1` is a character array, but the array is not null-terminated. `cp1`, which points to `ca1`, therefore, does not point to a null-terminated array. The other declarations are all C-style strings, remembering that the name of an array is treated as a pointer to the first element of the array. Thus, `ca2` and `ca3` are pointers to the first elements of their respective arrays.

EXERCISES SECTION 4.3

Exercise 4.19: Explain the meaning of the following five definitions. Identify any illegal definitions.

```
(a) int i;
(b) const int ic;
(c) const int *pic;
(d) int *const cpi;
(e) const int *const cpic;
```

Exercise 4.20: Which of the following initializations are legal? Explain why.

```
(a) int i = -1;
(b) const int ic = i;
(c) const int *pic = &ic;
(d) int *const cpi = &ic;
(e) const int *const cpic = &ic;
```

Exercise 4.21: Based on the definitions in the previous exercise, which of the following assignments are legal? Explain why.

```
(a) i = ic;                    (d) pic = cpic;
(b) pic = &ic;                 (e) cpic = &ic;
(c) cpi = pic;                 (f) ic = *cpic;
```

Using C-style Strings

C-style strings are manipulated through (const) char* pointers. One frequent usage pattern uses pointer arithmetic to traverse the C-style string. The traversal tests and increments the pointer until we reach the terminating null character:

```
const char *cp = "some value";
while (*cp) {
    //  do something to *cp
    ++cp;
}
```

The condition in the while dereferences the const char* pointer cp and the resulting character is tested for its true or false value. A true value is any character other than the null. So, the loop continues until it encounters the null character that terminates the array to which cp points. The body of the while does whatever processing is needed and concludes by incrementing cp to advance the pointer to address the next character in the array.

This loop will fail if the array that cp addresses is not null-terminated. If this case, the loop is apt to read characters starting at cp until it encounters a null character somewhere in memory.

Beware

C Library String Functions

The Standard C library provides a set of functions, listed in Table 4.1, that operate on C-style strings. To use these functions, we must include the associated C header file

```
#include <cstring>
```

which is the C++ version of the `string.h` header from the C library.

> These functions do no checking on their string parameters.

The pointer(s) passed to these routines must be nonzero and each pointer must point to the initial character in a null-terminated array. Some of these functions write to a string they are passed. These functions assume that the array to which they write is large enough to hold whatever characters the function generates. It is up to the programmer to ensure that the target string is big enough.

Table 4.1: C-Style Character String Functions	
`strlen(s)`	Returns the length of s, not counting the null.
`strcmp(s1, s2)`	Compares s1 and s2 for equality. Returns 0 if s1 `==` s2, positive value if s1 `>` s2, negative value if s1 `<` s2.
`strcat(s1, s2)`	Appends s2 to s1. Returns s1.
`strcpy(s1, s2)`	Copies s2 into s1. Returns s1.
`strncat(s1, s2,n)`	Appends n characters from s2 onto s1. Returns s1.
`strncpy(s1, s2, n)`	Copies n characters from s2 into s1. Returns s1.

When we compare library `strings`, we do so using the normal relational operators. We can use these operators to compare pointers to C-style strings, but the effect is quite different; what we're actually comparing is the pointer values, not the strings to which they point:

```
if (cp1 < cp2)   // compares addresses, not the values pointed to
```

Assuming `cp1` and `cp2` point to elements in the same array (or one past that array), then the effect of this comparison is to compare the address in `cp1` with the address in `cp2`. If the pointers do not address the same array, then the comparison is undefined.

To compare the strings, we must use `strcmp` and interpret the result:

```
const char *cp1 = "A string example";
const char *cp2 = "A different string";
int i = strcmp(cp1, cp2);    //  i is positive
i = strcmp(cp2, cp1);        //  i is negative
i = strcmp(cp1, cp1);        //  i is zero
```

The `strcmp` function returns three possible values: 0 if the strings are equal; or a positive or negative value, depending on whether the first string is larger or smaller than the second.

Never Forget About the Null-Terminator

When using the C library string functions it is essential to remember the strings must be null-terminated:

```
char ca[] = {'C', '+', '+'};   // not null-terminated
cout << strlen(ca) << endl;    // disaster: ca isn't null-terminated
```

In this case, `ca` is an array of characters but is not null-terminated. What happens is undefined. The `strlen` function assumes that it can rely on finding a null character at the end of its argument. The most likely effect of this call is that `strlen` will keep looking through the memory that follows wherever `ca` happens to reside until it encounters a null character. In any event, the return from `strlen` will not be the correct value.

Caller Is Responsible for Size of a Destination String

The array that we pass as the first argument to `strcat` and `strcpy` *must* be large enough to hold the generated string. The code we show here, although a common usage pattern, is frought with the potential for serious error:

```
// Dangerous: What happens if we miscalculate the size of largeStr?
char largeStr[16 + 18 + 2];  // will hold cp1 a space and cp2
strcpy(largeStr, cp1);       // copies cp1 into largeStr
strcat(largeStr, " ");       // adds a space at end of largeStr
strcat(largeStr, cp2);       // concatenates cp2 to largeStr
// prints A string example A different string
cout << largeStr << endl;
```

The problem is that we could easily miscalculate the size needed in `largeStr`. Similarly, if we later change the sizes of the strings to which either `cp1` or `cp2` point, then the calculated size of `largeStr` will be wrong. Unfortunately, programs similar to this code are widely distributed. Programs with such code are error-prone and often lead to serious security leaks.

When Using C-Style Strings, Use the `strn` Functions

If you must use C-style strings, it is usually safer to use the `strncat` and `strncpy` functions instead of `strcat` and `strcpy`:

```
char largeStr[16 + 18 + 2]; // to hold cp1 a space and cp2
strncpy(largeStr, cp1, 17); // size to copy includes the null
strncat(largeStr, " ", 2);  // pedantic, but a good habit
strncat(largeStr, cp2, 19); // adds at most 18 characters, plus a null
```

The trick to using these versions is to properly calculate the value to control how many characters get copied. In particular, we must *always* remember to account for the null when copying or concatenating characters. We must allocate space for the null because that is the character that terminates `largeStr` after each call. Let's walk through these calls in detail:

- On the call to `strncpy`, we ask to copy 17 characters: all the characters in `cp1` plus the null. Leaving room for the null is necessary so that `largeStr` is properly terminated. After the `strncpy` call, `largeStr` has a `strlen` value of 16. Remember, `strlen` counts the characters in a C-style string, not including the null.

- When we call `strncat`, we ask to copy two characters: the space and the null that terminates the string literal. After this call, `largeStr` has a `strlen` of 17. The null that had ended `largeStr` is overwritten by the space that we appended. A new null is written after that space.

- When we append `cp2` in the second call, we again ask to copy all the characters from `cp2`, *including* the null. After this call, the `strlen` of `largeStr` would be 35: 16 characters from `cp1`, 18 from `cp2`, and 1 for the space that separates the two strings.

The array size of `largeStr` remains 36 throughout.

These operations are safer than the simpler versions that do not take a size argument as long as we calculate the size argument correctly. If we ask to copy or concatenate more characters than the size of the target array, we will still overrun that array. If the string we're copying from or concatenating is bigger than the requested size, then we'll inadvertently truncate the new version. Truncating is safer than overrunning the array, but it is still an error.

Whenever Possible, Use Library `strings`

None of these issues matter if we use C++ library `strings`:

```
string largeStr = cp1; // initialize largeStr as a copy of cp1
largeStr += " ";       // add space at end of largeStr
largeStr += cp2;       // concatenate cp2 onto end of largeStr
```

Now the library handles all memory management, and we need no longer worry if the size of either string changes.

 For most applications, in addition to being safer, it is also more efficient to use library `strings` rather than C-style strings.

4.3.1 Dynamically Allocating Arrays

A variable of array type has three important limitations: Its size is fixed, the size must be known at compile time, and the array exists only until the end of the block in which it was defined. Real-world programs usually cannot live with these restrictions—they need a way to allocate an array **dynamically** at run time. Although all arrays have fixed size, the size of a dynamically allocated array need

EXERCISES SECTION 4.3

Exercise 4.22: Explain the difference between the following two `while` loops:

```
const char *cp = "hello";
int cnt;
while (cp) { ++cnt; ++cp; }
while (*cp) { ++cnt; ++cp; }
```

Exercise 4.23: What does the following program do?

```
const char ca[] = {'h', 'e', 'l', 'l', 'o'};
const char *cp = ca;
while (*cp) {
    cout << *cp << endl;
    ++cp;
}
```

Exercise 4.24: Explain the differences between `strcpy` and `strncpy`. What are the advantages of each? The disadvantages?

Exercise 4.25: Write a program to compare two `strings`. Now write a program to compare the value of two C-style character strings.

Exercise 4.26: Write a program to read a `string` from the standard input. How might you write a program to read from the standard input into a C-style character string?

not be fixed at compile time. It can be (and usually is) determined at run time. Unlike an array variable, a dynamically allocated array continues to exist until it is explicitly freed by the program.

Every program has a pool of available memory it can use during program execution to hold dynamically allocated objects. This pool of available memory is referred to as the program's **free store** or **heap**. C programs use a pair of functions named `malloc` and `free` to allocate space from the free store. In C++ we use **new** and **delete** expressions.

Defining a Dynamic Array

When we define an array variable, we specify a type, a name, and a dimension. When we dynamically allocate an array, we specify the type and size but do not name the object. Instead, the `new` expression returns a pointer to the first element in the newly allocated array:

```
int *pia = new int[10]; // array of 10 uninitialized ints
```

This `new` expression allocates an array of ten `int`s and returns a pointer to the first element in that array, which we use to initialize `pia`.

A `new` expression takes a type and optionally an array dimension specified inside a bracket-pair. The dimension can be an arbitrarily complex expression. When we allocate an array, `new` returns a pointer to the first element in the array.

Objects allocated on the free store are unnamed. We use objects on the heap only indirectly through their address.

Initializing a Dynamically Allocated Array

When we allocate an array of objects of a class type, then that type's default constructor (Section 2.3.4, p. 50) is used to initialize each element. If the array holds elements of built-in type, then the elements are uninitialized:

```
string *psa = new string[10]; // array of 10 empty strings
int *pia = new int[10];        // array of 10 uninitialized ints
```

Each of these `new` expressions allocates an array of ten objects. In the first case, those objects are `strings`. After allocating memory to hold the objects, the default `string` constructor is run on each element of the array in turn. In the second case, the objects are a built-in type; memory to hold ten `ints` is allocated, but the elements are uninitialized.

Alternatively, we can value-initialize (Section 3.3.1, p. 92) the elements by following the array size by an empty pair of parentheses:

```
int *pia2 = new int[10]();     // array of 10 uninitialized ints
```

The parentheses are effectively a request to the compiler to value-initialize the array, which in this case sets its elements to 0.

The elements of a dynamically allocated array can be initialized only to the default value of the element type. The elements cannot be initialized to separate values as can be done for elements of an array variable.

Dynamic Arrays of `const` Objects

If we create an array of `const` objects of built-in type on the free store, we must initialize that array: The elements are `const`, there is no way to assign values to the elements. The only way to initialize the elements is to value-initialize the array:

```
// error: uninitialized const array
const int *pci_bad = new const int[100];
// ok: value-initialized const array
const int *pci_ok = new const int[100]();
```

It is possible to have a `const` array of elements of a class type that provides a default constructor:

```
// ok: array of 100 empty strings
const string *pcs = new const string[100];
```

In this case, the default constructor is used to initialize the elements of the array.

Of course, once the elements are created, they may not be changed—which means that such arrays usually are not very useful.

It Is Legal to Dynamically Allocate an Empty Array

When we dynamically allocate an array, we often do so because we don't know the size of the array at compile time. We might write code such as

```
size_t n = get_size(); // get_size returns number of elements needed
int* p = new int[n];
for (int* q = p; q != p + n; ++q)
    /* process the array */ ;
```

to figure out the size of the array and then allocate and process the array.

An interesting question is: What happens if `get_size` returns 0? The answer is that our code works fine. The language specifies that a call to `new` to create an array of size zero is legal. It is legal even though we could not create an array variable of size 0:

```
char arr[0];                // error: cannot define zero-length array
char *cp = new char[0];    // ok: but cp can't be dereferenced
```

When we use `new` to allocate an array of zero size, `new` returns a valid, nonzero pointer. This pointer will be distinct from any other pointer returned by `new`. The pointer cannot be dereferenced—after all, it points to no element. The pointer can be compared and so can be used in a loop such as the preceeding one. It is also legal to add (or subtract) zero to such a pointer and to subtract the pointer from itself, yielding zero.

In our hypothetical loop, if the call to `get_size` returned 0, then the call to `new` would still succeed. However, `p` would not address any element; the array is empty. Because n is zero, the `for` loop effectively compares q to p. These pointers are equal; q was initialized to p, so the condition in the `for` fails and the loop body is not executed.

Freeing Dynamic Memory

When we allocate memory, we must eventually free it. Otherwise, memory is gradually used up and may be exhausted. When we no longer need the array, we must *explicitly* return its memory to the free store. We do so by applying the `delete []` expression to a pointer that addresses the array we want to release:

```
delete [] pia;
```

deallocates the array pointed to by `pia`, returning the associated memory to the free store. The empty bracket pair between the `delete` keyword and the pointer is necessary: It indicates to the compiler that the pointer addresses an array of elements on the free store and not simply a single object.

If the empty bracket pair is omitted, it is an error, but an error that the compiler is unlikely to catch; the program may fail at run time.

The least serious run-time consequence of omitting brackets when freeing an array is that too little memory will be freed, leading to a memory leak. On some systems and/or for some element types, more serious run-time problems are possible. It is essential to remember the bracket-pair when deleting pointers to arrays.

CONTRASTING C-STYLE STRINGS AND C++ LIBRARY STRINGS

The following two programs illustrate the differences in using C-style character strings versus using the C++ library `string` type. The `string` version is shorter, easier to understand, and less error-prone:

```
// C-style character string implementation
const char *pc = "a very long literal string";
const size_t  len = strlen(pc +1);        // space to allocate

// performance test on string allocation and copy
for (size_t ix = 0; ix != 1000000; ++ix) {
    char *pc2 = new char[len + 1];  // allocate the space
    strcpy(pc2, pc);                //  do the copy
    if (strcmp(pc2, pc))            //  use the new string
        ;   // do nothing
    delete [] pc2;                  // free the memory
}
```

```
// string implementation
string str("a very long literal string");

// performance test on string allocation and copy
for (int ix = 0; ix != 1000000; ++ix) {
    string str2 = str;  // do the copy, automatically allocated
    if (str != str2)            // use the new string
        ;   // do nothing
}                       // str2 is automatically freed
```

These programs are further explored in the exercises to Section 4.3.1 (p. 139).

Using Dynamically Allocated Arrays

A common reason to allocate an array dynamically is if its dimension cannot be known at compile time. For example, `char*` pointers are often used to refer to multiple C-style strings during the execution of a program. The memory used to hold the various strings typically is allocated dynamically during program execution based on the length of the string to be stored. This technique is considerably safer than allocating a fixed-size array. Assuming we correctly calculate the size needed at run time, we no longer need to worry that a given string will overflow the fixed size of an array variable.

Suppose we have the following C-style strings:

```
const char *noerr = "success";
// ...
const char *err189 = "Error: a function declaration must "
                     "specify a function return type!";
```

We might want to copy one or the other of these strings at run time to a new character array. We could calculate the dimension at run time, as follows:

```
const char *errorTxt;
if (errorFound)
    errorTxt = err189;
else
    errorTxt = noerr;
// remember the 1 for the terminating null
int dimension = strlen(errorTxt) + 1;
char *errMsg = new char[dimension];
// copy the text for the error into errMsg
strncpy(errMsg, errorTxt, dimension);
```

Recall that `strlen` returns the length of the string *not* including the null. It is essential to remember to add 1 to the length returned from `strlen` to accommodate the trailing null.

EXERCISES SECTION 4.3.1

Exercise 4.27: Given the following new expression, how would you `delete pa`?

```
int *pa = new int[10];
```

Exercise 4.28: Write a program to read the standard input and build a `vector` of `int`s from values that are read. Allocate an array of the same size as the `vector` and copy the elements from the `vector` into the array.

Exercise 4.29: Given the two program fragments in the highlighted box on page 138,

(a) Explain what the programs do.

(b) As it happens, on average, the `string` class implementation executes considerably faster than the C-style string functions. The relative average execution times on our more than five-year-old PC are as follows:

```
user        0.47    # string class
user        2.55    # C-style character string
```

Did you expect that? How would you account for it?

Exercise 4.30: Write a program to concatenate two C-style string literals, putting the result in a C-style string. Write a program to concatenate two library `string`s that have the same value as the literals used in the first program.

4.3.2 Interfacing to Older Code

Many C++ programs exist that predate the standard library and so do not yet use the `string` and `vector` types. Moreover, many C++ programs interface to existing C programs that cannot use the C++ library. Hence, it is not infrequent to encounter situations where a program written in modern C++ must interface to code that uses arrays and/or C-style character strings. The library offers facilities to make the interface easier to manage.

Mixing Library `strings` and C-Style Strings

As we saw on page 80 we can initialize a `string` from a string literal:

```
string st3("Hello World");  // st3 holds Hello World
```

More generally, because a C-style string has the same type as a string literal and is null-terminated in the same way, we can use a C-style string anywhere that a string literal can be used:

- We can initialize or assign to a `string` from a C-style string.

- We can use a C-style string as one of the two operands to the `string` addition or as the right-hand operand to the compound assignment operators.

The reverse functionality is not provided: there is no direct way to use a library `string` when a C-style string is required. For example, there is no way to initialize a character pointer from a `string`:

```
char *str = st2; // compile-time type error
```

There is, however, a `string` member function named `c_str` that we can often use to accomplish what we want: .

```
char *str = st2.c_str(); // almost ok, but not quite
```

The name `c_str` indicates that the function returns a C-style character string. Literally, it says, "Get me the C-style string representation"—that is, a pointer to the beginning of a null-terminated character array that holds the same data as the characters in the `string`.

This initialization fails because `c_str` returns a pointer to an array of `const char`. It does so to prevent changes to the array. The correct initialization is:

```
const char *str = st2.c_str(); // ok
```

> The array returned by `c_str` is not guaranteed to be valid indefinitely. Any subsequent use of `st2` that might change the value of `st2` can invalidate the array. If a program needs continuing access to the data, then the program must copy the array returned by `c_str`.

Using an Array to Initialize a `vector`

On page 112 we noted that it is not possible to initialize an array from another array. Instead, we have to create the array and then explicitly copy the elements from one array into the other. It turns out that we can use an array to initialize a `vector`, although the form of the initialization may seem strange at first. To initialize a `vector` from an array, we specify the address of the first element and one past the last element that we wish to use as initializers:

```
const size_t arr_size = 6;
int int_arr[arr_size] = {0, 1, 2, 3, 4, 5};
// ivec has 6 elements: each a copy of the corresponding element in int_arr
vector<int> ivec(int_arr, int_arr + arr_size);
```

The two pointers passed to `ivec` mark the range of values with which to initialize the `vector`. The second pointer points one past the last element to be copied. The range of elements marked can also represent a subset of the array:

```
// copies 3 elements: int_arr[1], int_arr[2], int_arr[3]
vector<int> ivec(int_arr + 1, int_arr + 4);
```

This initialization creates `ivec` with three elements. The values of these elements are copies of the values in `int_arr[1]` through `int_arr[3]`.

EXERCISES SECTION 4.3.2

Exercise 4.31: Write a program that reads a string into a character array from the standard input. Describe how your program handles varying size inputs. Test your program by giving it a string of data that is longer than the array size you've allocated.

Exercise 4.32: Write a program to initialize a `vector` from an array of `int`s.

Exercise 4.33: Write a program to copy a `vector` of `int`s into an array of `int`s.

Exercise 4.34: Write a program to read `string`s into a `vector`. Now, copy that `vector` into an array of character pointers. For each element in the `vector`, allocate a new character array and copy the data from the `vector` element into that character array. Then insert a pointer to the character array into the array of character pointers.

Exercise 4.35: Print the contents of the `vector` and the array created in the previous exercise. After printing the array, remember to delete the character arrays.

4.4 Multidimensioned Arrays

Strictly speaking, there are no multidimensioned arrays in C++. What is commonly referred to as a multidimensioned array is actually an array of arrays:

```
// array of size 3, each element is an array of ints of size 4
int ia[3][4];
```

It can be helpful to keep this fact in mind when using what appears to be a multidimensioned array.

An array whose elements are an array is said to have two dimensions. Each dimension is referred to by its own subscript:

`ia[2][3]` *// fetches last element from the array in the last row*

The first dimension is often referred to as the row and the second as the column. In C++ there is no limit on how many subscripts are used. That is, we could have an array whose elements are arrays of elements that are arrays, and so on.

Initializing the Elements of a Multidimensioned Array

As with any array, we can initialize the elements by providing a bracketed list of initializers. Multidimensioned arrays may be initialized by specifying bracketed values for each row:

```
int ia[3][4] = {        /*  3 elements, each element is an array of size 4  */
    {0, 1, 2, 3} ,      /*  initializers for row indexed by 0  */
    {4, 5, 6, 7} ,      /*  initializers for row indexed by 1  */
    {8, 9, 10, 11}      /*  initializers for row indexed by 2  */
};
```

The nested braces, which indicate the intended row, are optional. The following initialization is equivalent, although considerably less clear.

```
//  equivalent initialization without the optional nested braces for each row
int ia[3][4] = {0,1,2,3,4,5,6,7,8,9,10,11};
```

As is the case for single-dimension arrays, elements may be left out of the initializer list. We could initialize only the first element of each row as follows:

```
//  explicitly initialize only element 0 in each row
int ia[3][4] = {{ 0 } , { 4 } , { 8 } };
```

The values of the remaining elements depend on the element type and follow the rules descibed on page 112.

If the nested braces were omitted, the results would be very different:

```
//  explicitly initialize row 0
int ia[3][4] = {0, 3, 6, 9};
```

initializes the elements of the first row. The remaining elements are initialized to 0.

Subscripting a Multidimensioned Array

Indexing a multidimensioned array requires a subscript for each dimension. As an example, the following pair of nested `for` loops initializes a two-dimensional array:

```
const size_t rowSize = 3;
const size_t colSize = 4;
int ia[rowSize][colSize];     //  12 uninitialized elements
//  for each row
for (size_t i = 0; i != rowSize; ++i)
    //  for each column within the row
    for (size_t j = 0; j != colSize; ++j)
        //  initialize to its positional index
        ia[i][j] = i * colSize + j;
```

When we want to access a particular element of the array, we must supply both a row and column index. The row index specifies which of the inner arrays we intend to access. The column index selects an element from that inner array. Remembering this fact can help in calculating proper subscript values and in understanding how multidimensioned arrays are initialized.

If an expression provides only a single index, then the result is the inner-array element at that row index. Thus, ia[2] fetches the array that is the last row in ia. It does not fetch any element from that array; it fetches the array itself.

4.4.1 Pointers and Multidimensioned Arrays

As with any array, when we use the name of a multidimensioned array, it is automatically converted to a pointer to the first element in the array.

 When defining a pointer to a multidimensioned array, it is essential to remember that what we refer to as a multidimensioned array is really an array of arrays.

Because a multidimensioned array is really an array of arrays, the pointer type to which the array converts is a pointer to the first inner array. Although conceptually straightforward, the syntax for declaring such a pointer can be confusing:

```
int ia[3][4];        // array of size 3, each element is an array of ints of size 4
int (*ip)[4] = ia;  // ip points to an array of 4 ints
ip = &ia[2];         // ia[2] is an array of 4 ints
```

We define a pointer to an array similarly to how we would define the array itself: We start by declaring the element type followed by a name and a dimension. The trick is that the name is a pointer, so we must prepend * to the name. We can read the definition of ip from the inside out as saying that *ip has type int[4] —that is, ip is a pointer to an int array of four elements.

 The parentheses in this declaration are essential:

```
int *ip[4];   // array of pointers to int
int (*ip)[4]; // pointer to an array of 4 ints
```

Typedefs Simplify Pointers to Multidimensioned Arrays

Typedefs (Section 2.6, p. 61) can help make pointers to elements in multidimensioned arrays easier to write, read, and understand. We might write a typedef for the element type of ia as

```
typedef int int_array[4];
int_array *ip = ia;
```

We might use this typedef to print the elements of ia:

```
for (int_array *p = ia; p != ia + 3; ++p)
    for (int *q = *p; q != *p + 4; ++q)
        cout << *q << endl;
```

The outer `for` loop starts by initializing p to point to the first array in `ia`. That loop continues until we've processed all three rows in `ia`. The increment, `++p`, has the effect of moving p to point to the next row (e.g., the next element) in `ia`.

The inner `for` loop actually fetches the `int` values stored in the inner arrays. It starts by making q point to the first element in the array to which p points. When we dereference p, we get an array of four `int`s. As usual, when we use an array, it is converted automatically to a pointer to its first element. In this case, that first element is an `int`, and we point q at that `int`. The inner `for` loop runs until we've processed every element in the inner array. To obtain a pointer just off the end of the inner array, we again dereference p to get a pointer to the first element in that array. We then add 4 to that pointer to process the four elements in each inner array.

EXERCISES SECTION 4.4.1

Exercise 4.36: Rewrite the program to print the contents of the array `ia` without using a typedef for the type of the pointer in the outer loop.

CHAPTER SUMMARY

This chapter covered arrays and pointers. These facilities provide functionality similar to that provided by the library `vector` and `string` types and their companion iterators. The `vector` type can be thought of as a more flexible, easier to manage array. Similarly, `string`s are a great improvement on C-style strings that are implemented as null-terminated character arrays.

Iterators and pointers allow indirect access to objects. Iterators are used to examine elements and navigate between the elements in `vector`s. Pointers provide similar access to array elements. Although conceptually simple, pointers are notoriously hard to use in practice.

Pointers and arrays can be necessary for certain low-level tasks, but they should be avoided because they are error-prone and hard to debug. In general, the library abstractions should be used in preference to low-level array and pointer alternatives built into the language. This advice is especially applicable to using `string`s instead of C-style null-terminated character arrays. Modern C++ programs should not use C-style strings.

DEFINED TERMS

C-style strings C programs treat pointers to null-terminated character arrays as strings. In C++, string literals are C-style strings. The C library defines a set of functions that operate on such strings, which C++ makes available in the `cstring` header. C++ programs should use C++ library strings in preference to C-style strings, which are inherently error-prone. A sizeable majority of security holes in networked programs are due to bugs related to using C-style strings and arrays.

compiler extension Feature that is added to the language by a particular compiler. Programs that rely on compiler extensions cannot be moved easily to other compilers.

compound type Type that is defined in terms of another type. Arrays, pointers, and references are compound types.

const void* A pointer type that can point to any `const` type. See `void*`.

delete expression A `delete` expression frees memory that was allocated by `new`:

```
delete [] p;
```

where `p` must be a pointer to the first element in a dynamically allocated array. The bracket pair is essential: It indicates to the compiler that the pointer points at an array, not at a single object. In C++ programs, `delete` replaces the use of the C library `free` function.

dimension The size of an array.

dynamically allocated An object that is allocated on the program's free store. Objects allocated on the free store exist until they are explicitly deleted.

free store Memory pool available to a program to hold dynamically allocated objects.

heap Synonym for free store.

new expression Allocates dynamic memory. We allocate an array of n elements as follows:

```
new type[n];
```

The array holds elements of the indicated *type*. `new` returns a pointer to the first element in the array. C++ programs use `new` in place of the C library `malloc` function.

pointer An object that holds the address of an object.

pointer arithmetic The arithmetic operations that can be applied to pointers. An integral type can be added to or subtracted from a pointer, resulting in a pointer positioned that many elements ahead or behind the original pointer. Two pointers can be subtracted, yielding the difference between the pointers. Pointer arithmetic is valid only on pointers that denote elements in the same array or an element one past the end of that array.

precedence Defines the order in which operands are grouped with operators in a compound expression.

ptrdiff_t Machine-dependent signed integral type defined in `cstddef` header that is large enough to hold the difference between two pointers into the largest possible array.

size_t Machine-dependent unsigned integral type defined in `cstddef` header that is large enough to hold the size of the largest possible array.

* operator Dereferencing a pointer yields the object to which the pointer points. The dereference operator returns an lvalue; we may assign to the value returned from the dereference operator, which has the effect of assigning a new value to the underlying element.

++ operator When used with a pointer, the increment operator "adds one" by moving the pointer to refer to the next element in an array.

[ ] operator The subscript operator takes two operands: a pointer to an element of an array and an index. Its result is the element that is offset from the pointer by the index. Indices count from zero—the first element in an array is element 0, and the last is element size of the array minus 1. The subscript operator returns an lvalue; we may use a subscript as the left-hand operand of an assignment, which has the effect of assigning a new value to the indexed element.

& operator The address-of operator. Takes a single argument that must be an lvalue. Yields the address in memory of that object.

void* A pointer type that can point to any `nonconst` type. Only limited operations are permitted on `void*` pointers. They can be passed or returned from functions and they can be compared with other pointers. They may not be dereferenced.

C H A P T E R 5

E X P R E S S I O N S

C++ provides a rich set of operators and defines what these operators do when applied to operands of built-in type. It also allows us to define meanings for the operators when applied to class types. This facility, known as operator overloading, is used by the library to define the operators that apply to the library types.

In this chapter our focus is on the operators as defined in the language and applied to operands of built-in type. We will also look at some of the operators defined by the library. Chapter 14 shows how we can define our own overloaded operators.

An expression is composed of one or more **operands** that are combined by **operators**. The simplest form of an **expression** consists of a single literal constant or variable. More complicated expressions are formed from an operator and one or more operands.

Every expression yields a **result**. In the case of an expression with no operator, the result is the operand itself, e.g., a literal constant or a variable. When an object is used in a context that requires a value, then the object is evaluated by fetching the object's value. For example, assuming `ival` is an `int` object,

```
if (ival)                        // evaluate ival as a condition
    // ....
```

we could use `ival` as an expression in the condition of an `if`. The condition succeeds if the value of `ival` is not zero and fails otherwise.

The result of expressions that involve operators is determined by applying each operator to its operand(s). Except when noted otherwise, the result of an expression is an rvalue (Section 2.3.1, p. 45). We can read the result but cannot assign to it.

> The meaning of an operator—what operation is performed and the type of the result—depends on the types of its operands.

Until one knows the type of the operand(s), it is not possible to know what a particular expression means. The expression

```
i + j
```

might mean integer addition, concatenation of `strings`, floating-point addition, or something else entirely. How the expression is evaluated depends on the types of `i` and `j`.

There are both *unary* operators and *binary* operators. Unary operators, such as address-of (`&`) and dereference (`*`), act on one operand. Binary operators, such as addition (`+`) and subtraction (`-`), act on two operands. There is also one ternary operator that takes three operands. We'll look at this operator in Section 5.7 (p. 165).

Some *symbols*, such as `*`, are used to represent both a unary and a binary operator. The `*` symbol is used as the (unary) dereference operator and as the (binary) multiplication operator. The uses of the symbol are independent; it can be helpful to think of them as two different symbols. The context in which an operator symbol is used always determines whether the symbol represents a unary or binary operator.

Operators impose requirements on the type(s) of their operand(s). The language defines the type requirements for the operators when applied to built-in or compound types. For example, the dereference operator, when applied to an object of built-in type, requires that its operand be a pointer type. Attempting to dereference an object of any other built-in or compound type is an error.

The binary operators, when applied to operands of built-in or compound type, usually require that the operands be the same type, or types that can be converted to a common type. We'll look at conversions in Section 5.12 (p. 178). Although the rules can be complex, for the most part conversions happen in expected ways.

For example, we can convert an integer to floating-point, and vice versa, but we cannot convert a pointer type to floating-point.

Understanding expressions with multiple operators requires understanding operator *precedence, associativity*, and the *order of evaluation* of the operands. For example, the expression

```
5 + 10 * 20/2;
```

uses addition, multiplication, and division. The result of this expression depends on how the operands are grouped to the operators. For example, the operands to the * operator could be 10 and 20, or 10 and 20/2, or 15 and 20 or 15 and 20/2. Associativity and precedence rules specify the grouping of operators and their operands. In C++ this expression evaluates to 105, which is the result of multiplying 10 and 20, dividing that result by 2, and then adding 5.

Knowing how operands and operators are grouped is not always sufficient to determine the result. It may also be necessary to know in what order the operands to each operator are evaluated. Each operator controls what assumptions, if any, can be made as to the order in which the operands will be evaluated—that is, whether we can assume that the left-hand operand is always evaluated before the right or not. Most operators do not guarantee a particular order of evaluation. We will cover these topics in Section 5.10 (p. 168).

5.1 Arithmetic Operators

Table 5.1: Arithmetic Operators		
Operator	**Function**	**Use**
+	unary plus	+ expr
-	unary minus	- expr
*	multiplication	expr * expr
/	division	expr / expr
%	remainder	expr % expr
+	addition	expr + expr
-	subtraction	expr - expr

Unless noted otherwise, these operators may be applied to any of the arithmetic types (Section 2.1, p. 34), or any type that can be converted to an arithmetic type.

The table groups the operators by their precedence—the unary operators have the highest precedence, then the multiplication and division operators, and then the binary addition and subtraction operators. Operators of higher precedence group more tightly than do operators with lower precedence. These operators are all left associative, meaning that they group left to right when the precedence levels are the same.

Applying precedence and associativity to the previous expression:

```
5 + 10 * 20/2;
```

we can see that the operands to the multiplication operator (*) are 10 and 20. The result of that expression and 2 are the operands to the division operator (/). The result of that division and 5 are the operands to the addition operator (+).

The unary minus operator has the obvious meaning. It negates its operand:

```
int i = 1024;
int k = -i;  // negates the value of its operand
```

Unary plus returns the operand itself. It makes no change to its operand.

CAUTION: OVERFLOW AND OTHER ARITHMETIC EXCEPTIONS

The result of evaluating some arithmetic expressions is undefined. Some expressions are undefined due to the nature of mathematics—for example, division by zero. Others are undefined due to the nature of computers—such as overflow, in which a value is computed that is too large for its type.

Consider a machine on which **shorts** are 16 bits. In that case, the maximum **short** is 32767. Given only 16 bits, the following compound assignment overflows:

```
// max value if shorts are 8 bits
short short_value = 32767;
short ival = 1;

// this calculation overflows
short_value += ival;
cout << "short_value: " << short_value << endl;
```

Representing a signed value of 32768 requires 17 bits, but only 16 are available. On many systems, there is *no* compile-time or run-time warning when an overflow might occur. The actual value put into **short_value** varies across different machines. On our system the program completes and writes

```
short_value: -32768
```

The value "wrapped around:" The sign bit, which had been 0, was set to 1, resulting in a negative value. Because the arithmetic types have limited size, it is always possible for some calculations to overflow. Adhering to the recommendations from the "Advice" box on page 38 can help avoid such problems.

The binary + and - operators may also be applied to pointer values. The use of these operators with pointers was described in Section 4.2.4 (p. 123).

The arithmetic operators, +, -, *, and / have their obvious meanings: addition, subtraction, multiplication, and division. Division between integers results in an integer. If the quotient contains a fractional part, it is truncated:

```
int ival1 = 21/6;  // integral result obtained by truncating the remainder
int ival2 = 21/7;  // no remainder, result is an integral value
```

Both ival1 and ival2 are initialized with a value of 3.

The % operator is known as the "remainder" or the "modulus" operator. It computes the remainder of dividing the left-hand operand by the right-hand operand. This operator can be applied only to operands of the integral types: bool, char, short, int, long, and their associated unsigned types:

```
int ival = 42;
double dval = 3.14;

ival % 12;    // ok: returns 6
ival % dval;  // error: floating point operand
```

For both division (/) and modulus (%), when both operands are positive, the result is positive (or zero). If both operands are negative, the result of division is positive (or zero) and the result of modulus is negative (or zero). If only one operand is negative, then the value of the result is machine-dependent for both operators. The sign is also machine-dependent for modulus; the sign is negative (or zero) for division:

```
21 % 6;    // ok: result is 3
21 % 7;    // ok: result is 0
-21 % -8;  // ok: result is -5
21 % -5;   // machine-dependent: result is 1 or -4

21 / 6;    // ok: result is 3
21 / 7;    // ok: result is 3
-21 / -8;  // ok: result is 2
21 / -5;   // machine-dependent: result -4 or -5
```

When only one operand is negative, the sign and value of the result for the modulus operator can follow either the sign of the numerator or of the denominator. On a machine where modulus follows the sign of the numerator then the value of division truncates toward zero. If modulus matches the sign of the denominator, then the result of division truncates toward minus infinity.

EXERCISES SECTION 5.1

Exercise 5.1: Parenthesize the following expression to indicate how it is evaluated. Test your answer by compiling the expression and printing its result.

```
12 / 3 * 4 + 5 * 15 + 24 % 4 / 2
```

Exercise 5.2: Determine the result of the following expressions and indicate which results, if any, are machine-dependent.

```
-30 * 3 + 21 / 5
-30 + 3 * 21 / 5
30 / 3 * 21 % 5
-30 / 3 * 21 % 4
```

Exercise 5.3: Write an expression to determine whether an int value is even or odd.

Exercise 5.4: Define the term overflow. Show three expressions that will overflow.

5.2 Relational and Logical Operators

Table 5.2: Relational and Logical Operators		
Each of these operators yields `bool`		
Operator	**Function**	**Use**
`!`	logical NOT	`!expr`
`<`	less than	`expr < expr`
`<=`	less than or equal	`expr <= expr`
`>`	greater than	`expr > expr`
`>=`	greater than or equal	`expr >= expr`
`==`	equality	`expr == expr`
`!=`	inequality	`expr != expr`
`&&`	logical AND	`expr && expr`
`||`	logical OR	`expr || expr`

The relational and logical operators take operands of arithmetic or pointer type and return values of type `bool`.

Logical AND and OR Operators

The logical operators treat their operands as conditions (Section 1.4.1, p. 12). The operand is evaluated; if the result is zero the condition is `false`, otherwise it is `true`. The overall result of the AND operator is `true` if and only if both its operands evaluate to `true`. The logical OR (`||`) operator evaluates to `true` if either of its operands evaluates to `true`. Given the forms

```
expr1 && expr2   // logical AND
expr1 || expr2   // logical OR
```

expr2 is evaluated if and only if *expr1* does not by itself determine the result. In other words, we're guaranteed that *expr2* will be evaluated if and only if

- In a logical AND expression, *expr1* evaluates to `true`. If *expr1* is `false`, then the expression will be `false` regardless of the value of *expr2*. When *expr1* is `true`, it is possible for the expression to be `true` if *expr2* is also `true`.

- In a logical OR expression, *expr1* evaluates to `false`; if *expr1* is `false`, then the expression depends on whether *expr2* is `true`.

The logical AND and OR operators always evaluate their left operand before the right. The right operand is evaluated only if the left operand does not determine the result. This evaluation strategy is often referred to as "short-circuit evaluation."

A valuable use of the logical AND operator is to have *expr1* evaluate to false in the presence of a boundary condition that would make the evaluation of *expr2* dangerous. As an example, we might have a `string` that contains the characters in a sentence and we might want to make the first word in the sentence all uppercase. We could do so as follows:

```
string s("Expressions in C++ are composed...");
string::iterator it = s.begin();
// convert first word in s to uppercase
while (it != s.end() && !isspace(*it)) {
    *it = toupper(*it);   // toupper covered in section 3.2.4 (p. 88)
    ++it;
}
```

In this case, we combine our two tests in the condition in the `while`. First we test whether `it` has reached the end of the `string`. If not, `it` refers to a character in s. Only if that test succeeds is the right-hand operand evaluated. We're guaranteed that `it` refers to an actual character before we test to see whether the character is a space or not. The loop ends either when a space is encountered or, if there are no spaces in s, when we reach the end of s.

Logical NOT Operator

The logical NOT operator (`!`) treats its operand as a condition. It yields a result that has the opposite truth value from its operand. If the operand evaluates as nonzero, then `!` returns `false`. For example, we might determine that a `vector` has elements by applying the logical NOT operator to the value returned by `empty`:

```
// assign value of first element in vec to x if there is one
int x = 0;
if (!vec.empty())
    x = *vec.begin();
```

The subexpression

```
!vec.empty()
```

evaluates to `true` if the call to `empty` returns `false`.

The Relational Operators Do Not Chain Together

The relational operators (`<`, `<=`, `>`, `<=`) are left associative. The fact that they are left associative is rarely of any use because the relational operators return `bool` results. If we do chain these operators together, the result is likely to be surprising:

```
// oops! this condition does not determine if the 3 values are unequal
if (i < j < k) { /* ... */ }
```

As written, this expression will evaluate as `true` if k is greater than one! The reason is that the left operand of the second less-than operator is the `true`/`false` result of the first—that is, the condition compares k to the integer values of 0 or 1. To accomplish the test we intended, we must rewrite the expression as follows:

```
if (i < j && j < k) { /* ... */ }
```

Equality Tests and the `bool` Literals

As we'll see in Section 5.12.2 (p. 180) a `bool` can be converted to any arithmetic type—the `bool` value `false` converts to zero and `true` converts to one.

> Because `bool` converts to one, is almost never right to write an equality test that tests against the `bool` literal `true`:
>
>   if (val == true) { /* ... */ }

Either `val` is itself a `bool` or it is a type to which a `bool` can be converted. If `val` is a `bool`, then this test is equivalent to writing

        if (val) { /* ... */ }

which is shorter and more direct (although admittedly when first learning the language this kind of abbreviation can be perplexing).

More importantly, if `val` is not a `bool`, then comparing `val` with `true` is equivalent to writing

        if (val == 1) { /* ... */ }

which is very different from

        // condition succeeds if val is any nonzero value
        if (val) { /* ... */ }

in which any nonzero value in `val` is true. If we write the comparison explicitly, then we are saying that the condition will succeed only for the specific value 1.

EXERCISES SECTION 5.2

Exercise 5.5: Explain when operands are evaluated in the logical AND operator, logical OR operator, and equality operator.

Exercise 5.6: Explain the behavior of the following `while` condition:

    char *cp = "Hello World";
    while (cp && *cp)

Exercise 5.7: Write the condition for a `while` loop that would read `int`s from the standard input and stop when the value read is equal to `42`.

Exercise 5.8: Write an expression that tests four values, a, b, c, and d, and ensures that a is greater than b, which is greater than c, which is greater than d.

5.3   The Bitwise Operators

The bitwise operators take operands of integral type. These operators treat their integral operands as a collection of bits, providing operations to test and set individual bits. In addition, these operators may be applied to `bitset` (Section 3.5, p. 101) operands with the behavior as described here for integral operands.

Table 5.3: Bitwise Operators		
Operator	**Function**	**Use**
~	bitwise NOT	`~expr`
<<	left shift	`expr1 << expr2`
>>	right shift	`expr1 >> expr2`
&	bitwise AND	`expr1 & expr2`
^	bitwise XOR	`expr1 ^ expr2`
|	bitwise OR	`expr1 | expr2`

The type of an integer manipulated by the bitwise operators can be either signed or unsigned. If the value is negative, then the way that the "sign bit" is handled in a number of the bitwise operations is machine-dependent. It is, therefore, likely to differ across implementations; programs that work under one implementation may fail under another.

 Best Practices Because there are no guarantees for how the sign bit is handled, we strongly recommend using an `unsigned` type when using an integral value with the bitwise operators.

In the following examples we assume that an `unsigned char` has 8 bits.

The bitwise NOT operator (~) is similar in behavior to the `bitset flip` (Section 3.5.2, p. 105) operation: It generates a new value with the bits of its operand inverted. Each 1 bit is set to 0; each 0 bit is set to 1:

```
unsigned char bits = 0227;
```
`1 0 0 1 0 1 1 1`
```
bits = ~bits;
```
`0 1 1 0 1 0 0 0`

The <<, >> operators are the bitwise shift operators. These operators use their right-hand operand to indicate by how many bits to shift. They yield a value that is a copy of the left-hand operand with the bits shifted as directed by the right-hand operand. The bits are shifted left (<<) or right (>>), discarding the bits that are shifted off the end.

```
unsigned char bits = 1;
```
`1 0 0 1 1 0 1 1`
```
bits << 1;  // left shift
```
`0 0 1 1 0 1 1 0`
```
bits << 2;  // left shift
```
`0 1 1 0 1 1 0 0`
```
bits >> 3;  // right shift
```
`0 0 0 1 0 0 1 1`

The left shift operator (<<) inserts 0-valued bits in from the right. The right shift operator (>>) inserts 0-valued bits in from the left if the operand is unsigned.

If the operand is signed, it can either insert copies of the sign bit or insert 0-valued bits; which one it uses is implementation defined. The right-hand operand must not be negative and must be a value that is strictly less than the number of bits in the left-hand operand. Otherwise, the effect of the operation is undefined.

The bitwise AND operator (&) takes two integral operands. For each bit position, the result is 1 if both operands contain 1; otherwise, the result is 0.

> It is a common error to confuse the bitwise AND operator (&) with the logical AND operator (&&) (Section 5.2, p. 152). Similarly, it is common to confuse the bitwise OR operator (|) and the logical OR operator(||).

Here we illustrate the result of bitwise AND of two unsigned char values, each of which is initialized by an octal literal:

```
unsigned char b1 = 0145;
```
| 0 | 1 | 1 | 0 | 0 | 1 | 0 | 1 |

```
unsigned char b2 = 0257;
```
| 1 | 0 | 1 | 0 | 1 | 1 | 1 | 1 |

```
unsigned char result = b1 & b2;
```
| 0 | 0 | 1 | 0 | 0 | 1 | 0 | 1 |

The bitwise XOR (exclusive or) operator (^) also takes two integral operands. For each bit position, the result is 1 if either but not both operands contain 1; otherwise, the result is 0.

```
result = b1 ^ b2;
```
| 1 | 1 | 0 | 0 | 1 | 0 | 1 | 0 |

The bitwise OR (inclusive or) operator (|) takes two integral operands. For each bit position, the result is 1 if either or both operands contain 1; otherwise, the result is 0.

```
result = b1 | b2;
```
| 1 | 1 | 1 | 0 | 1 | 1 | 1 | 1 |

5.3.1 Using `bitset` Objects or Integral Values

We said that the `bitset` class was easier to use than the lower-level bitwise operations on integral values. Let's look at a simple example and show how we might solve a problem using either a `bitset` or the bitwise operators. Assume that a teacher has 30 students in a class. Each week the class is given a pass/fail quiz. We'll track the results of each quiz using one bit per student to represent the pass or fail grade on a given test. We might represent each quiz in either a `bitset` or as an integral value:

```
bitset<30> bitset_quiz1;        // bitset solution
unsigned long int_quiz1 = 0;    // simulated collection of bits
```

In the `bitset` case we can define `bitset_quiz1` to be exactly the size we need. By default each of the bits is set to zero. In the case where we use a built-in type to hold our quiz results, we define `int_quiz1` as an `unsigned long`, meaning that it will have at least 32 bits on any machine. Finally, we explicitly initialize `int_quiz1` to ensure that the bits start out with well-defined values.

The teacher must be able to set and test individual bits. For example, assuming that the student represented by position 27 passed, we'd like to be able to set that bit appropriately:

```
bitset_quiz1.set(27);    // indicate student number 27 passed
int_quiz1 |= 1UL<<27;    // indicate student number 27 passed
```

In the `bitset` case we do so directly by passing the bit we want turned on to `set`. The `unsigned long` case will take a bit more explanation. The way we'll set a specific bit is to OR our quiz data with another integer that has only one bit—the one we want—turned on. That is, we need an `unsigned long` where bit 27 is a one and all the other bits are zero. We can obtain such a value by using the left shift operator and the integer constant 1:

```
1UL << 27;    // generate a value with only bit number 27 set
```

Now when we bitwise OR this value with `int_quiz1`, all the bits except bit 27 will remain unchanged. That bit will be turned on. We use a compound assignment (Section 1.4.1, p. 13) to OR this value into `int_quiz1`. This operator, `|=`, executes in the same way that `+=` does. It is equivalent to the more verbose:

```
// following assignment is equivalent to int_quiz1 |= 1UL << 27;
int_quiz1 = int_quiz1 | 1UL << 27;
```

Imagine that the teacher reexamined the quiz and discovered that student 27 actually had failed the test. The teacher must now turn off bit 27:

```
bitset_quiz1.reset(27);    // student number 27 failed
int_quiz1 &= ~(1UL<<27);   // student number 27 failed
```

Again, the `bitset` version is direct. We `reset` the indicated bit. For the simulated case, we need to do the inverse of what we did to set the bit: This time we'll need an integer that has bit 27 turned off and all the other bits turned on. We'll bitwise AND this value with our quiz data to turn off just that bit. We can obtain a value with all but bit 27 turned on by inverting our previous value. Applying the bitwise NOT to the previous integer will turn on every bit except the 27th. When we bitwise AND this value with `int_quiz1`, all except bit 27 will remain unchanged.

Finally, we might want to know how the student at position 27 fared. To do so, we could write

```
bool status;
status = bitset_quiz1[27];        // how did student number 27 do?
status = int_quiz1 & (1UL<<27);  // how did student number 27 do?
```

In the `bitset` case we can fetch the value directly to determine how that student did. In the `unsigned long` case, the first step is to set the 27th bit of an integer to 1. The bitwise AND of this value with `int_quiz1` evaluates to nonzero if bit 27 of `int_quiz1` is also on; otherwise, it evaluates to zero.

Best Practices

In general, the library `bitset` operations are more direct, easier to read, easier to write, and more likely to be used correctly. Moreover, the size of a `bitset` is not limited by the number of bits in an `unsigned`. Ordinarily `bitset` should be used in preference to lower-level direct bit manipulation of integral values.

EXERCISES SECTION 5.3.1

Exercise 5.9: Assume the following two definitions:

```
unsigned long ul1 = 3, ul2 = 7;
```

What is the result of each of the following expressions?

(a) `ul1 & ul2`   (c) `ul1 | ul2`
(b) `ul1 && ul2`   (d) `ul1 || ul2`

Exercise 5.10: Rewrite the `bitset` expressions that set and reset the quiz results using a subscript operator.

5.3.2 Using the Shift Operators for IO

The IO library redefines the bitwise `>>` and `<<` operators to do input and output. Even though many programmers never need to use the bitwise operators directly, most programs do make extensive use of the overloaded versions of these operators for IO. When we use an overloaded operator, it has the same precedence and associativity as is defined for the built-in version of the operator. Therefore, programmers need to understand the precedence and associativity of these operators even if they never use them with their built-in meaning as the shift operators.

The IO Operators Are Left Associative

Like the other binary operators, the shift operators are left associative. These operators group from left to right, which accounts for the fact that we can concatenate input and output operations into a single statement:

```
cout << "hi" << " there" << endl;
```

executes as:

```
( (cout << "hi") << " there" ) << endl;
```

In this statement, the operand `"hi"` is grouped with the first `<<` symbol. Its result is grouped with the second, and then that result is grouped to the third.

The shift operators have midlevel precedence: lower precedence than the arithmetic operators but higher than the relational, assignment, or conditional operators. These relative precedence levels affect how we write IO expressions involving operands that use operators with lower precedence. We often need to use parentheses to force the right grouping:

```
cout << 42 + 10;      // ok, + has higher precedence, so the sum is printed
cout << (10 < 42);  // ok: parentheses force intended grouping; prints 1
cout << 10 < 42;      // error: attempt to compare cout to 42!
```

The second cout is interpreted as

```
(cout << 10) < 42;
```

this expression says to "write 10 onto cout and then compare the result of that operation (e.g., cout) to 42."

5.4 Assignment Operators

The left-hand operand of an assignment operator must be a nonconst lvalue. Each of these assignments is illegal:

```
int i, j, ival;
const int ci = i; // ok: initialization not assignment
1024 = ival;        // error: literals are rvalues
i + j = ival;       // error: arithmetic expressions are rvalues
ci = ival;          // error: can't write to ci
```

Array names are nonmodifiable lvalues: An array cannot be the target of an assignment. Both the subscript and dereference operators return lvalues. The result of dereference or subscript, when applied to a nonconst array, can be the left-hand operand of an assignment:

```
int ia[10];
ia[0] = 0;     // ok: subscript is an lvalue
*ia = 0;       // ok: dereference also is an lvalue
```

The result of an assignment is the left-hand operand; the type of the result is the type of the left-hand operand.

The value assigned to the left-hand operand ordinarily is the value that is in the right-hand operand. However, assignments where the types of the left and right operands differ may require conversions that might change the value being assigned. In such cases, the value stored in the left-hand operand might differ from the value of the right-hand operand:

```
ival = 0;         // result: type int value 0
ival = 3.14159;  // result: type int value 3
```

Both these assignments yield values of type int. In the first case the value stored in ival is the same value as in its right-hand operand. In the second case the value stored in ival is different from the right-hand operand.

5.4.1   Assignment Is Right Associative

Like the subscript and dereference operators, assignment returns an lvalue. As such, we can perform multiple assignments in a single expression, provided that each of the operands being assigned is of the same general type:

```
int ival, jval;
ival = jval = 0; // ok: each assigned 0
```

Unlike the other binary operators, the assignment operators are right associative. We group an expression with multiple assignment operators from right to left. In this expression, the result of the rightmost assignment (i.e., jval) is assigned to ival. The types of the objects in a multiple assignment either must be the same type or of types that can be converted (Section 5.12, p. 178) to one another:

```
int ival; int *pval;
ival = pval = 0; // error: cannot assign the value of a pointer to an int
string s1, s2;
s1 = s2 = "OK";  // ok: "OK" converted to string
```

The first assignment is illegal because ival and pval are objects of different types. It is illegal even though zero happens to be a value that could be assigned to either object. The problem is that the result of the assignment to pval is a value of type int*, which cannot be assigned to an object of type int. On the other hand, the second assignment is fine. The string literal is converted to string, and that string is assigned to s2. The result of that assignment is s2, which is then assigned to s1.

5.4.2   Assignment Has Low Precedence

Inside a condition is another common place where assignment is used as a part of a larger expression. Writing an assignment in a condition can shorten programs and clarify the programmer's intent. For example, the following loop uses a function named get_value, which we assume returns int values. We can test those values until we obtain some desired value—say, 42:

```
int i = get_value(); // get_value returns an int
while (i != 42) {
    // do something ...
    i = get_value();
}
```

The program begins by getting the first value and storing it in i. Then it establishes the loop, which tests whether i is 42, and if not, does some processing. The last statement in the loop gets a value from get_value(), and the loop repeats. We can write this loop more succinctly as

```
int i;
while ((i = get_value()) != 42) {
    // do something ...
}
```

The condition now more clearly expresses our intent: We want to continue until get_value returns 42. The condition executes by assigning the result returned by get_value to i and then comparing the result of that assignment with 42.

 The additional parentheses around the assignment are necessary because assignment has lower precedence than inequality.

Without the parentheses, the operands to != would be the value returned from calling get_value and 42. The true or false result of that test would be assigned to i—clearly not what we intended!

Beware of Confusing Equality and Assignment Operators

The fact that we can use assignment in a condition can have surprising effects:

```
if (i = 42)
```

This code is legal: What happens is that 42 is assigned to i and then the result of the assignment is tested. In this case, 42 is nonzero, which is interpreted as a true value. The author of this code almost surely intended to test whether i was 42:

```
if (i == 42)
```

Bugs of this sort are notoriously difficult to find. Some, but not all, compilers are kind enough to warn about code such as this example.

EXERCISES SECTION 5.4.2

Exercise 5.11: What are the values of i and d after the each assignment:

```
int i;    double d;
d = i = 3.5;
i = d = 3.5;
```

Exercise 5.12: Explain what happens in each of the if tests:

```
if (42 = i)    // . . .
if (i = 42)    // . . .
```

5.4.3 Compound Assignment Operators

We often apply an operator to an object and then reassign the result to that same object. As an example, consider the sum program from page 14:

```
int sum = 0;
// sum values from 1 up to 10 inclusive
for (int val = 1; val <= 10; ++val)
    sum += val;  // equivalent to sum = sum + val
```

This kind of operation is common not just for addition but for the other arithmetic operators and the bitwise operators. There are compound assignments for each of these operators. The general syntactic form of a compound assignment operator is

```
a op= b;
```

where *op=* may be one of the following ten operators:

```
+=      -=      *=      /=      %=        //  arithmetic operators
<<=     >>=     &=      ^=      |=        //  bitwise operators
```

Each compound operator is essentially equivalent to

```
a = a op b;
```

There is one important difference: When we use the compound assignment, the left-hand operand is evaluated only once. If we write the similar longer version, that operand is evaluated twice: once as the right-hand operand and again as the left. In many, perhaps most, contexts this difference is immaterial aside from possible performance consequences.

EXERCISES SECTION 5.4.3

Exercise 5.13: The following assignment is illegal. Why? How would you correct it?
```
double dval; int ival; int *pi;
dval = ival = pi = 0;
```

Exercise 5.14: Although the following are legal, they probably do not behave as the programmer expects. Why? Rewrite the expressions as you think they should be.
```
(a) if (ptr = retrieve_pointer() != 0)
(b) if (ival = 1024)
(c) ival += ival + 1;
```

5.5   Increment and Decrement Operators

The increment (++) and decrement (--) operators provide a convenient notational shorthand for adding or subtracting 1 from an object. There are two forms of these operators: prefix and postfix. So far, we have used only the prefix increment, which increments its operand and yields the *changed* value as its result. The prefix decrement operates similarly, except that it decrements its operand. The postfix versions of these operators increment (or decrement) the operand but yield a copy of the original, *unchanged* value as its result:

```
int i = 0, j;
j = ++i; //  j = 1, i = 1: prefix yields incremented value
j = i++; //  j = 1, i = 2: postfix yields unincremented value
```

Because the prefix version returns the incremented value, it returns the object itself as an lvalue. The postfix versions return an rvalue.

ADVICE: USE POSTFIX OPERATORS ONLY WHEN NECESSARY

Readers from a C background might be surprised that we use the prefix increment in the programs we've written. The reason is simple: The prefix version does less work. It increments the value and returns the incremented version. The postfix operator must store the original value so that it can return the unincremented value as its result. For ints and pointers, the compiler can optimize away this extra work. For more complex iterator types, this extra work potentially could be more costly. By habitually favoring the use of the prefix versions, we do not have to worry if the performance difference matters.

Postfix Operators Return the Unincremented Value

The postfix version of ++ and -- is used most often when we want to use the current value of a variable and increment it in a single compound expression:

```
vector<int> ivec;                  // empty vector
int cnt = 10;
// add elements 10...1 to ivec
while (cnt > 0)
    ivec.push_back(cnt--);         // int postfix decrement
```

This program uses the postfix version of -- to decrement cnt. We want to assign the value of cnt to the next element in the vector and then decrement cnt before the next iteration. Had the loop used the prefix version, then the decremented value of cnt would be used when creating the elements in ivec and the effect would be to add elements from 9 down to 0.

Combining Dereference and Increment in a Single Expression

The following program, which prints the contents of ivec, represents a very common C++ programming pattern:

```
vector<int>::iterator iter = ivec.begin();
// prints 10 9 8 ... 1
while (iter != ivec.end())
    cout << *iter++ << endl; // iterator postfix increment
```

The expression *iter++ is usually very confusing to programmers new to both C++ and C.

The precedence of postfix increment is higher than that of the dereference operator, so *iter++ is equivalent to *(iter++). The subexpression iter++ increments iter and yields a copy of the previous value of iter as its result. Accordingly, the operand of * is a copy of the unincremented value of iter.

This usage relies on the fact that postfix increment returns a copy of its original, unincremented operand. If it returned the incremented value, we'd dereference the incremented value, with disastrous results: The first element of ivec would not get written. Worse, we'd attempt to dereference one too many elements!

EXERCISES SECTION 5.5

Exercise 5.15: Explain the difference between prefix and postfix increment.

Exercise 5.16: Why do you think C++ wasn't named ++C?

Exercise 5.17: What would happen if the while loop that prints the contents of a vector used the prefix increment operator?

5.6 The Arrow Operator

The arrow operator (->) provides a synonym for expressions involving the dot and dereference operators. The dot operator (Section 1.5.2, p. 25) fetches an element from an object of class type:

```
item1.same_isbn(item2);   // run the same_isbn member of item1
```

If we had a pointer (or iterator) to a Sales_item, we would have to dereference the pointer (or iterator) before applying the dot operator:

```
Sales_item *sp = &item1;
(*sp).same_isbn(item2);   // run same_isbn on object to which sp points
```

Here we dereference sp to get the underlying Sales_item. Then we use the dot operator to run same_isbn on that object. We must parenthesize the dereference because dereference has a lower precedence than dot. If we omit the parentheses, this code means something quite different:

```
// run the same_isbn member of sp then dereference the result!
*sp.same_isbn(item2);      // error: sp has no member named same_isbn
```

This expression attempts to fetch the `same_isbn` member of the object `sp`. It is equivalent to

```
*(sp.same_isbn(item2));   // equivalent to *sp.same_isbn(item2);
```

However, `sp` is a pointer, which has no members; this code will not compile.

Because it is easy to forget the parentheses and because this kind of code is a common usage, the language defines the arrow operator as a synonym for a dereference followed by the dot operator. Given a pointer (or iterator) to an object of class type, the following expressions are equivalent:

```
(*p).foo;   // dereference p to get an object and fetch its member named foo
p->foo;     // equivalent way to fetch the foo from the object to which p points
```

More concretely, we can rewrite the call to `same_isbn` as

```
sp->same_isbn(item2);     // equivalent to (*sp).same_isbn(item2)
```

EXERCISES SECTION 5.6

Exercise 5.18: Write a program that defines a `vector` of pointers to `strings`. Read the `vector`, printing each `string` and its corresponding size.

Exercise 5.19: Assuming that `iter` is a `vector<string>::iterator`, indicate which, if any, of the following expressions is legal. Explain the behavior of the legal expressions.

(a) `*iter++;`	(b) `(*iter)++;`
(c) `*iter.empty()`	(d) `iter->empty();`
(e) `++*iter;`	(f) `iter++->empty();`

5.7 The Conditional Operator

The **conditional operator** is the only ternary operator in C++. It allows us to embed simple if-else tests inside an expression. The conditional operator has the following syntactic form

```
cond ? expr1 : expr2;
```

where *cond* is an expression that is used as a condition (Section 1.4.1, p. 12). The operator executes by evaluating *cond*. If *cond* evaluates to 0, then the condition is `false`; any other value is `true`. *cond* is always evaluated. If it is `true`, then *expr1* is evaluated; otherwise, *expr2* is evaluated. Like the logical AND and OR (`&&` and `||`) operators, the conditional operator guarantees this order of evaluation for its operands. Only one of *expr1* or *expr2* is evaluated. The following program illustrates use of the conditional operator:

```
int i = 10, j = 20, k = 30;
// if i > j then maxVal = i else maxVal = j
int maxVal = i > j ? i : j;
```

Avoid Deep Nesting of the Conditional Operator

We could use a set of nested conditional expressions to set `max` to the largest of three variables:

```
int max = i > j
               ? i > k ? i : k
               : j > k ? j : k;
```

We could do the equivalent comparison in the following longer but simpler way:

```
int max = i;
if (j > max)
    max = j;
if (k > max)
    max = k;
```

Using a Conditional Operator in an Output Expression

The conditional operator has fairly low precedence. When we embed a conditional expression in a larger expression, we usually must parenthesize the conditional subexpression. For example, the conditional operator is often used to print one or another value, depending on the result of a condition. Incompletely parenthesized uses of the conditional operator in an output expression can have surprising results:

```
cout << (i < j ? i : j);   //  ok: prints larger of i and j
cout << (i < j) ? i : j;   //  prints 1 or 0!
cout << i < j ? i : j;     //  error: compares cout to int
```

The second expression is the most interesting: It treats the comparison between `i` and `j` as the operand to the `<<` operator. The value 1 or 0 is printed, depending on whether `i < j` is true or false. The `<<` operator returns `cout`, which is tested as the condition for the conditional operator. That is, the second expression is equivalent to

```
cout << (i < j); //  prints 1 or 0
cout ? i : j;    //  test cout and then evaluate i or j
                 //  depending on whether cout evaluates to true or false
```

EXERCISES SECTION 5.7

Exercise 5.20: Write a program to prompt the user for a pair of numbers and report which is smaller.

Exercise 5.21: Write a program to process the elements of a `vector<int>`. Replace each element with an odd value by twice that value.

5.8 The `sizeof` Operator

The `sizeof` operator returns a value of type `size_t` (Section 3.5.2, p. 104) that is the size, in bytes (Section 2.1, p. 35), of an object or type name. The result of `sizeof` expression is a compile-time constant. The `sizeof` operator takes one of the following forms:

```
sizeof (type name);
sizeof (expr);
sizeof expr;
```

Applying `sizeof` to an *expr* returns the size of the result type of that expression:

```
Sales_item item, *p;
// three ways to obtain size required to hold an object of type Sales_item
sizeof(Sales_item); // size required to hold an object of type Sales_item
sizeof item; // size of item's type, e.g., sizeof(Sales_item)
sizeof *p;    // size of type to which p points, e.g., sizeof(Sales_item)
```

Evaluating `sizeof` *expr* does not evaluate the expression. In particular, in `sizeof *p`, the pointer p may hold an invalid address, because p is not dereferenced.

The result of applying `sizeof` depends in part on the type involved:

- `sizeof char` or an expression of type `char` is guaranteed to be 1

- `sizeof` a reference type returns the size of the memory necessary to contain an object of the referenced type

- `sizeof` a pointer returns the size needed hold a pointer; to obtain the size of the object to which the pointer points, the pointer must be dereferenced

- `sizeof` an array is equivalent to taking the `sizeof` the element type times the number of elements in the array

Because `sizeof` returns the size of the entire array, we can determine the number of elements by dividing the `sizeof` the array by the `sizeof` an element:

```
// sizeof(ia)/sizeof(*ia) returns the number of elements in ia
int sz = sizeof(ia)/sizeof(*ia);
```

EXERCISES SECTION 5.8

Exercise 5.22: Write a program to print the size of each of the built-in types.

Exercise 5.23: Predict the output of the following program and explain your reasoning. Now run the program. Is the output what you expected? If not, figure out why.

```
int x[10];    int *p = x;

cout << sizeof(x)/sizeof(*x) << endl;
cout << sizeof(p)/sizeof(*p) << endl;
```

5.9   Comma Operator

A **comma expression** is a series of expressions separated by commas. The expressions are evaluated from left to right. The result of a comma expression is the value of the rightmost expression. The result is an lvalue if the rightmost operand is an lvalue. One common use for the comma operator is in a `for` loop.

```
int cnt = ivec.size();
//  add elements from size...1 to ivec
for(vector<int>::size_type ix = 0;
                ix != ivec.size(); ++ix, --cnt)
    ivec[ix] = cnt;
```

This loop increments `ix` and decrements `cnt` in the expression in the `for` header. Both `ix` and `cnt` are changed on each trip through the loop. As long as the test of `ix` succeeds, we reset the next element to the current value of `cnt`.

> **EXERCISES SECTION 5.9**
>
> **Exercise 5.24:**   The program in this section is similar to the program on page 163 that added elements to a `vector`. Both programs decremented a counter to generate the element values. In this program we used the prefix decrement and the earlier one used postfix. Explain why we used prefix in one and postfix in the other.

5.10   Evaluating Compound Expressions

An expression with two or more operators is a **compound expression**. In a compound expression, the way in which the operands are grouped to the operators may determine the result of the overall expression. If the operands group in one way, the result differs from what it would be if they grouped another way.

Precedence and associativity determine how the operands are grouped. That is, precedence and associativity determine which part of the expression is the operand for each of the operators in the expression. Programmers can override these rules by parenthesizing compound expressions to force a particular grouping.

 Precedence specifies how the operands are grouped. It says nothing about the order in which the operands are evaluated. In most cases, operands may be evaluated in whatever order is convenient.

5.10.1   Precedence

The value of an expression depends on how the subexpressions are grouped. For example, in the following expression, a purely left-to-right evaluation yields 20:

```
6 + 3 * 4 / 2 + 2;
```

Other imaginable results include 9, 14, and 36. In C++, the result is 14.

Multiplication and division have higher precedence than addition. Their operands are bound to the operator in preference to the operands to addition. Multiplication and division have the same precedence as each other. Operators also have associativity, which determines how operators at the same precedence level are grouped. The arithmetic operators are left associative, which means they group left to right. We now can see that our expression is equivalent to

```
int temp = 3 * 4;          // 12
int temp2 = temp / 2;      // 6
int temp3 = temp2 + 6;     // 12
int result = temp3 + 2;    // 14
```

Parentheses Override Precedence

We can override precedence with parentheses. Parenthesized expressions are evaluated by treating each parenthesized subexpression as a unit and otherwise applying the normal precedence rules. For example, we can use parentheses on our initial expression to force the evaluation to result in any of the four possible values:

```
// parentheses on this expression match default precedence/associativity
cout << ((6 + ((3 * 4) / 2)) + 2) << endl; // prints 14

// parentheses result in alternative groupings
cout << (6 + 3) * (4 / 2 + 2) << endl;     // prints 36
cout << ((6 + 3) * 4) / 2 + 2 << endl;     // prints 20
cout << 6 + 3 * 4 / (2 + 2) << endl;       // prints 9
```

We have already seen examples where precedence rules affect the correctness of our programs. For example, consider the expression described in the "Advice" box on page 164:

```
*iter++;
```

Precedence says that ++ has higher precedence than *. That means that iter++ is grouped first. The operand of *, therefore, is the result of applying the increment operator to iter. If we wanted to increment the value that iter denotes, we'd have to use parentheses to force our intention:

```
(*iter)++;   // increment value to which iter refers and yield unincremented value
```

The parentheses specify that the operand of * is iter. The expression now uses *iter as the operand to ++.

As another example, recall the condition in the while on page 161:

```
while ((i = get_value()) != 42) {
```

The parentheses around the assignment were necessary to implement the desired operation, which was to assign to i the value returned from get_value and then test that value to see whether it was 42. Had we failed to parenthesize the assignment, the effect would be to test the return value to see whether it was 42. The true or false value of that test would then be assigned to i, meaning that i would either be 1 or 0.

5.10.2 Associativity

Associativity specifies how to group operators at the same precedence level. We have also seen cases where associativity matters. As one example, the assignment operator is right associative. This fact allows concatenated assignments:

```
ival = jval = kval = lval        // right associative
(ival = (jval = (kval = lval))) // equivalent, parenthesized version
```

This expression first assigns `lval` to `kval`, then the result of that to `jval`, and finally the result of that to `ival`.

The arithmetic operators, on the other hand, are left associative. The expression

```
ival * jval / kval * lval        // left associative
(((ival * jval) / kval) * lval) // equivalent, parenthesized version
```

multiplies `ival` and `jval`, then divides that result by `kval`, and finally multiplies the result of the division by `lval`.

Table 5.4 presents the full set of operators ordered by precedence. The table is organized into segments separated by double lines. Operators in each segment have the same precedence, and have higher precedence than operators in subsequent segments. For example, the prefix increment and dereference operators share the same precedence and have higher precedence than the arithmetic or relational operators. We have seen most of these operators, although a few will not be defined until later chapters.

Table 5.4: Operator Precedence

Associativity and Operator		Function	Use	See Page
L	`::`	global scope	`::name`	p. 450
L	`::`	class scope	`class::name`	p. 85
L	`::`	namespace scope	`namespace::name`	p. 78
L	`.`	member selectors	`object.member`	p. 25
L	`->`	member selectors	`pointer->member`	p. 164
L	`[]`	subscript	`variable [ expr ]`	p. 113
L	`()`	function call	`name (expr_list)`	p. 25
L	`()`	type construction	`type (expr_list)`	p. 460
R	`++`	postfix increment	`lvalue++`	p. 162
R	`--`	postfix decrement	`lvalue--`	p. 162
R	`typeid`	type ID	`typeid(type)`	p. 775
R	`typeid`	run-time type ID	`typeid(expr)`	p. 775
R	explicit cast	type conversion	*cast_name*<type>(expr)	p. 183
R	`sizeof`	size of object	`sizeof expr`	p. 167
R	`sizeof`	size of type	`sizeof( type )`	p. 167
R	`++`	prefix increment	`++lvalue`	p. 162
R	`--`	prefix decrement	`--lvalue`	p. 162

Table 5.4: Operator Precedence
(continued)

Associativity and Operator		Function	Use	See Page
R	~	bitwise NOT	~expr	p. 154
R	!	logical NOT	!expr	p. 152
R	-	unary minus	-expr	p. 150
R	+	unary plus	+expr	p. 150
R	*	dereference	*expr	p. 119
R	&	address-of	&expr	p. 115
R	()	type conversion	(type) expr	p. 186
R	new	allocate object	new type	p. 174
R	delete	deallocate object	delete expr	p. 176
R	delete[]	deallocate array	delete[] expr	p. 137
L	->*	ptr to member select	ptr->*ptr_to_member	p. 783
L	.*	ptr to member select	obj.*ptr_to_member	p. 783
L	*	multiply	expr * expr	p. 149
L	/	divide	expr / expr	p. 149
L	%	modulo (remainder)	expr % expr	p. 149
L	+	add	expr + expr	p. 149
L	-	subtract	expr - expr	p. 149
L	<<	bitwise shift left	expr << expr	p. 154
L	>>	bitwise shift right	expr >> expr	p. 154
L	<	less than	expr < expr	p. 152
L	<=	less than or equal	expr <= expr	p. 152
L	>	greater than	expr > expr	p. 152
L	>=	greater than or equal	expr >= expr	p. 152
L	==	equality	expr == expr	p. 152
L	!=	inequality	expr != expr	p. 152
L	&	bitwise AND	expr & expr	p. 154
L	^	bitwise XOR	expr ^ expr	p. 154
L	|	bitwise OR	expr | expr	p. 154
L	&&	logical AND	expr && expr	p. 152
L	||	logical OR	expr || expr	p. 152
R	?:	conditional	expr ? expr : expr	p. 165
R	=	assignment	lvalue = expr	p. 159
R	*=, /=, %=,	compound assign	lvalue += expr, etc.	p. 159
R	+=, -=,			p. 159
R	<<=, >>=,			p. 159
R	&=, |=, ^=			p. 159
R	throw	throw exception	throw expr	p. 216
L	,	comma	expr , expr	p. 168

EXERCISES SECTION 5.10.2

Exercise 5.25: Using Table 5.4 (p. 170), parenthesize the following expressions to indicate the order in which the operands are grouped:

```
(a)   ! ptr == ptr->next
(b)   ch = buf[ bp++ ] != '\n'
```

Exercise 5.26: The expressions in the previous exercise evaluate in an order that is likely to be surprising. Parenthesize these expressions to evaluate in an order you imagine is intended.

Exercise 5.27: The following expression fails to compile due to operator precedence. Using Table 5.4 (p. 170), explain why it fails. How would you fix it?

```
string s = "word";
// add an 's' to the end, if the word doesn't already end in 's'
string pl = s + s[s.size() - 1] == 's' ? "" : "s" ;
```

5.10.3   Order of Evaluation

In Section 5.2 (p. 152) we saw that the && and || operators specify the order in which their operands are evaluated: In both cases the right-hand operand is evaluated if and only if doing so might affect the truth value of the overall expression. Because we can rely on this property, we can write code such as

```
// iter only dereferenced if it isn't at end
while (iter != vec.end() && *iter != some_val)
```

The only other operators that guarantee the order in which operands are evaluated are the conditional (? :) and comma operators. In all other cases, the order is unspecified.

For example, in the expression

```
f1() * f2();
```

we know that both f1 and f2 must be called before the multiplication can be done. After all, their results are what is multiplied. However, we have no way to know whether f1 will be called before f2 or vice versa.

 The order of operand evaluation often, perhaps even usually, doesn't matter. It can matter greatly, though, if the operands refer to *and change* the same objects.

The order of operand evaluation matters if one subexpression changes the value of an operand used in another subexpression:

```
// oops! language does not define order of evaluation
if (ia[index++] < ia[index])
```

The behavior of this expression is undefined. The problem is that the left- and right-hand operands to the < both use the variable `index`. However, the left-hand operand involves changing the value of that variable. Assuming `index` is zero, the compiler might evaluate this expression in one of the following two ways:

```
if (ia[0] < ia[0])    // execution if rhs is evaluated first
if (ia[0] < ia[1])    // execution if lhs is evaluated first
```

We can guess that the programmer intended that the left operand be evaluated, thereby incrementing `index`. If so, the comparison would be between `ia[0]` and `ia[1]`. The language, however, does not guarantee a left-to-right evaluation order. In fact, an expression like this is undefined. An implementation might evaluate the right-hand operand first, in which case `ia[0]` is compared to itself. Or the implementation might do something else entirely.

ADVICE: MANAGING COMPOUND EXPRESSIONS

Beginning C and C++ programmers often have difficulties understanding order of evaluation and the rules of precedence and associativity. Misunderstanding how expressions and operands are evaluated is a rich source of bugs. Moreover, the resulting bugs are difficult to find because reading the program does not reveal the error unless the programmer already understands the rules.

Two rules of thumb can be helpful:

1. When in doubt, parenthesize expressions to force the grouping that the logic of your program requires.

2. If you change the value of an operand, don't use that operand elsewhere in the same statement. If you need to use the changed value, then break the expression up into separate statements in which the operand is changed in one statement and then used in a subsequent statement.

An important exception to the second rule is that subexpressions that use the result of the subexpression that changes the operand are safe. For example, in `*++iter` the increment changes the value of `iter`, and the (changed) value of `iter` is then used as the operand to `*`. In this, and similar, expressions, order of evaluation of the operand isn't an issue. To evaluate the larger expression, the subexpression that changes the operand must first be evaluated. Such usage poses no problems and is quite common.

Do not use an increment or decrement operator on the same object in more than two subexpressions of the same expression.

One safe and machine-independent way to rewrite the previous comparison of two array elements is

```
if (ia[index] < ia[index + 1]) {
    // do whatever
}
++index;
```

Now neither operand can affect the value of the other.

EXERCISES SECTION 5.10.3

Exercise 5.28: With the exception of the logical AND and OR, the order of evaluation of the binary operators is left undefined to permit the compiler freedom to provide an optimal implementation. The trade-off is between an efficient implementation and a potential pitfall in the use of the language by the programmer. Do you consider that an acceptable trade-off? Why or why not?

Exercise 5.29: Given that `ptr` points to a class with an `int` member named `ival`, `vec` is a `vector` holding `int`s, and that `ival`, `jval`, and `kval` are also `int`s, explain the behavior of each of these expressions. Which, if any, are likely to be incorrect? Why? How might each be corrected?

```
(a) ptr->ival != 0            (b) ival != jval < kval
(c) ptr != 0 && *ptr++        (d) ival++ && ival
(e) vec[ival++] <= vec[ival]
```

5.11 The `new` and `delete` Expressions

In Section 4.3.1 (p. 134) we saw how to use `new` and `delete` expressions to dynamically allocate and free arrays. We can also use `new` and `delete` to dynamically allocate and free single objects.

When we define a variable, we specify a type and a name. When we dynamically allocate an object, we specify a type but do not name the object. Instead, the `new` expression returns a pointer to the newly allocated object; we use that pointer to access the object:

```
int i;              //  named, uninitialized int variable
int *pi = new int;  //  pi points to dynamically allocated,
                    //  unnamed, uninitialized int
```

This `new` expression allocates one object of type `int` from the free store and returns the address of that object. We use that address to initialize the pointer `pi`.

Initializing Dynamically Allocated Objects

Dynamically allocated objects may be initialized, in much the same way as we initialize variables:

```
int i(1024);                //  value of i is 1024
int *pi = new int(1024);    //  object to which pi points is 1024

string s(10, '9');              //  value of s is "9999999999"
string *ps = new string(10, '9');   //  *ps is "9999999999"
```

We must use the direct-initialization syntax (Section 2.3.3, p. 48) to initialize dynamically allocated objects. When an initializer is present, the `new` expression allocates the required memory and initializes that memory using the given initializer(s). In the case of `pi`, the newly allocated object is initialized to 1024. The object pointed to by `ps` is initialized to a string of 10 nines.

Default Initialization of Dynamically Allocated Objects

If we do not explicitly state an initializer, then a dynamically allocated object is initialized in the same way as is a variable that is defined inside a function. (Section 2.3.4, p. 50) If the object is of class type, it is initialized using the default constructor for the type; if it is of built-in type, it is uninitialized.

```
string *ps = new string;    // initialized to empty string
int *pi = new int;          // pi points to an uninitialized int
```

As usual, it is undefined to use the value associated with an uninitialized object in any way other than to assign a good value to it.

Best Practices Just as we (almost) always initialize the objects we define as variables, it is (almost) always a good idea to initialize dynamically allocated objects.

We can also value-initialize (Section 3.3.1, p. 92) a dynamically allocated object:

```
string *ps = new string(); // initialized to empty string
int *pi = new int();       // pi points to an int value-initialized to 0
cls *pc = new cls();       // pc points to a value-initialized object of type cls
```

We indicate that we want to value-initialize the newly allocated object by following the type name by a pair of empty parentheses. The empty parentheses signal that we want initialization but are not supplying a specific initial value. In the case of class types (such as string) that define their own constructors, requesting value-initialization is of no consequence: The object is initialized by running the default constructor whether we leave it apparently uninitialized or ask for value-initialization. In the case of built-in types or types that do not define any constructors, the difference is significant:

```
int *pi = new int;      // pi points to an uninitialized int
int *pi = new int();    // pi points to an int value-initialized to 0
```

In the first case, the int is uninitialized; in the second case, the int is initialized to zero.

Beware The () syntax for value initialization must follow a type name, not a variable. As we'll see in Section 7.4 (p. 251)

```
int x(); // does not value initialize x
```

declares a function named x with no arguments that returns an int.

Memory Exhaustion

Although modern machines tend to have huge memory capacity, it is always possible that the free store will be exhausted. If the program uses all of available memory, then it is possible for a new expression to fail. If the new expression cannot acquire the requested memory, it throws an exception named bad_alloc. We'll look at how exceptions are thrown in Section 6.13 (p. 215).

Destroying Dynamically Allocated Objects

When our use of the object is complete, we must *explicitly* return the object's memory to the free store. We do so by applying the `delete` expression to a pointer that addresses the object we want to release.

```
delete pi;
```

frees the memory associated with the `int` object addressed by `pi`.

 It is illegal to apply `delete` to a pointer that addresses memory that was not allocated by `new`.

The effect of deleting a pointer that addresses memory that was not allocated by new is undefined. The following are examples of safe and unsafe delete expressions:

```
int i;
int *pi = &i;
string str = "dwarves";
double *pd = new double(33);

delete str;  //  error: str is not a dynamic object
delete pi;   //  error: pi refers to a local
delete pd;   //  ok
```

It is worth noting that the compiler might refuse to compile the delete of `str`. The compiler knows that `str` is not a pointer and so can detect this error at compile-time. The second error is more insidious: In general, compilers cannot tell what kind of object a pointer addresses. Most compilers will accept this code, even though it is in error.

`delete` of a Zero-Valued Pointer

It is legal to `delete` a pointer whose value is zero; doing so has no effect:

```
int *ip = 0;
delete ip;   //  ok: always ok to delete a pointer that is equal to 0
```

The language guarantees that deleting a pointer that is equal to zero is safe.

Resetting the Value of a Pointer after a `delete`

When we write

```
delete p;
```

p becomes undefined. Although p is undefined, on many machines, p still contains the address of the object to which it pointed. However, the memory to which p points was freed, so p is no longer valid.

After deleting a pointer, the pointer becomes what is referred to as a **dangling pointer**. A dangling pointer is one that refers to memory that once held an object but does so no longer. A dangling pointer can be the source of program errors that are difficult to detect.

Best Practices Setting the pointer to 0 after the object it refers to has been deleted makes it clear that the pointer points to no object.

Dynamic Allocation and Deallocation of const Objects

It is legal to dynamically create const objects:

```
// allocate and initialize a const object
const int *pci = new const int(1024);
```

Like any const, a dynamically created const must be initialized when it is created and once initialized cannot be changed. The value returned from this new expression is a pointer to const int. Like the address of any other const object, the return from a new that allocates a const object may only be assigned to a pointer to const.

A const dynamic object of a class type that defines a default constructor may be initialized implicitly:

```
// allocate default initialized const empty string
const string *pcs = new const string;
```

This new expression does not explicitly initialize the object pointed to by pcs. Instead, the object to which pcs points is implicitly initialized to the empty string. Objects of built-in type or of a class type that does not provide a default constructor must be explicitly initialized.

CAUTION: MANAGING DYNAMIC MEMORY IS ERROR-PRONE

The following three common program errors are associated with dynamic memory allocation:

1. Failing to delete a pointer to dynamically allocated memory, thus preventing the memory from being returned to the free store. Failure to delete dynamically allocated memory is spoken of as a "memory leak." Testing for memory leaks is difficult because they often do not appear until the application is run for a test period long enough to actually exhaust memory.

2. Reading or writing to the object after it has been deleted. This error can sometimes be detected by setting the pointer to 0 after deleting the object to which the pointer had pointed.

3. Applying a delete expression to the same memory location twice. This error can happen when two pointers address the same dynamically allocated object. If delete is applied to one of the pointers, then the object's memory is returned to the free store. If we subsequently delete the second pointer, then the free store may be corrupted.

These kinds of errors in manipulating dynamically allocated memory are considerably easier to make than they are to track down and fix.

Deleting a `const` Object

Although the value of a `const` object cannot be modified, the object itself can be destroyed. As with any other dynamic object, a `const` dynamic object is freed by deleting a pointer that points to it:

```
delete pci;   // ok: deletes a const object
```

Even though the operand of the delete expression is a pointer to `const int`, the delete expression is valid and causes the memory to which `pci` refers to be deallocated.

EXERCISES SECTION 5.11

Exercise 5.30:   Which of the following, if any, are illegal or in error?

```
(a) vector<string> svec(10);
(b) vector<string> *pvec1 = new vector<string>(10);
(c) vector<string> **pvec2 = new vector<string>[10];
(d) vector<string> *pv1 = &svec;
(e) vector<string> *pv2 = pvec1;

(f) delete svec;
(g) delete pvec1;
(h) delete [] pvec2;
(i) delete pv1;
(j) delete pv2;
```

5.12   Type Conversions

The type of the operand(s) determine whether an expression is legal and, if the expression is legal, determines the meaning of the expression. However, in C++ some types are related to one another. When two types are related, we can use an object or value of one type where an operand of the related type is expected. Two types are related if there is a **conversion** between them.

As an example, consider

```
int ival = 0;
ival = 3.541 + 3;  // typically compiles with a warning
```

which assigns 6 to `ival`.

The operands to the addition operator are values of two different types: `3.541` is a literal of type `double`, and `3` is a literal of type `int`. Rather than attempt to add values of the two different types, C++ defines a set of conversions to transform the operands to a common type before performing the arithmetic. These conversions are carried out automatically by the compiler without programmer intervention— and sometimes without programmer knowledge. For that reason, they are referred to as **implicit type conversions**.

The built-in conversions among the arithmetic types are defined to preserve precision, if possible. Most often, if an expression has both integral and floating-point values, the integer is converted to floating-point. In this addition, the integer value 3 is converted to `double`. Floating-point addition is performed and the result, 6.541, is of type `double`.

The next step is to assign that `double` value to `ival`, which is an `int`. In the case of assignment, the type of the left-hand operand dominates, because it is not possible to change the type of the object on the left-hand side. When the left- and right-hand types of an assignment differ, the right-hand side is converted to the type of the left-hand side. Here the `double` is converted to `int`. Converting a `double` to an `int` truncates the value; the decimal portion is discarded. 6.541 becomes 6, which is the value assigned to `ival`. Because the conversion of a `double` to `int` may result in a loss of precision, most compilers issue a warning. For example, the compiler we used to check the examples in this book warns us:

```
warning: assignment to 'int' from 'double'
```

To understand implicit conversions, we need to know when they occur and what conversions are possible.

5.12.1 When Implicit Type Conversions Occur

The compiler applies conversions for both built-in and class type objects as necessary. Implicit type conversions take place in the following situations:

- In expressions with operands of mixed types, the types are converted to a common type:

```
int ival;
double dval;
ival >= dval    // ival converted to double
```

- An expression used as a condition is converted to `bool`:

```
int ival;
if (ival)       // ival converted to bool
while (cin)     // cin converted to bool
```

Conditions occur as the first operand of the conditional (? :) operator and as the operand(s) to the logical NOT (!), logical AND (&&), and logical OR (||) operators. Conditions also appear in the `if`, `while`, `for`, and `do while` statements. (We cover the `do while` in Chapter 6)

- An expression used to initialize or assign to a variable is converted to the type of the variable:

```
int ival = 3.14; // 3.14 converted to int
int *ip;
ip = 0;     // the int 0 converted to a null pointer of type int *
```

In addition, as we'll see in Chapter 7, implicit conversions also occur during function calls.

5.12.2 The Arithmetic Conversions

The language defines a set of conversions among the built-in types. Among these, the most common are the **arithmetic conversions**, which ensure that the two operands of a binary operator, such as an arithmetic or logical operator, are converted to a common type before the operator is evaluated. That common type is also the result type of the expression.

The rules define a hierarchy of type conversions in which operands are converted to the widest type in the expression. The conversion rules are defined so as to preserve the precision of the values involved in a multitype expression. For example, if one operand is of type `long double`, then the other is converted to type `long double` regardless of what the second type is.

The simplest kinds of conversion are **integral promotions**. Each of the integral types that are smaller than `int`—`char`, `signed char`, `unsigned char`, `short`, and `unsigned short`—is promoted to `int` if all possible values of that type fit in an `int`. Otherwise, the value is promoted to `unsigned int`. When `bool` values are promoted to `int`, a `false` value promotes to zero and `true` to one.

Conversions between Signed and Unsigned Types

When an `unsigned` value is involved in an expression, the conversion rules are defined to preserve the value of the operands. Conversions involving `unsigned` operands depend on the relative sizes of the integral types on the machine. Hence, such conversions are inherently machine dependent.

In expressions involving `short`s and `int`s, values of type `short` are converted to `int`. Expressions involving `unsigned short` are converted to `int` if the `int` type is large enough to represent all the values of an `unsigned short`. Otherwise, both operands are converted to `unsigned int`. For example, if `short`s are a half word and `int`s a word, then any `unsigned` value will fit inside an `int`. On such a machine, `unsigned short`s are converted to `int`.

The same conversion happens among operands of type `long` and `unsigned int`. The `unsigned int` operand is converted to `long` if type `long` on the machine is large enough to represent all the values of the `unsigned int`. Otherwise, both operands are converted to `unsigned long`.

On a 32-bit machine, `long` and `int` are typically represented in a word. On such machines, expressions involving `unsigned int`s and `long`s are converted to `unsigned long`.

Conversions for expressions involving signed and `unsigned int` can be surprising. In these expressions the signed value is converted to `unsigned`. For example, if we compare a plain `int` and an `unsigned int`, the `int` is first converted to `unsigned`. If the `int` happens to hold a negative value, the result will be converted as described in Section 2.1.1 (p. 36), with all the attendant problems discussed there.

Understanding the Arithmetic Conversions

The best way to understand the arithmetic conversions is to study lots of examples. In most of the following examples, either the operands are converted to the largest type involved in the expression or, in the case of assignment expressions, the right-hand operand is converted to the type of the left-hand operand:

```
bool     flag;        char              cval;
short    sval;        unsigned short usval;
int      ival;        unsigned int   uival;
long     lval;        unsigned long  ulval;
float    fval;        double            dval;
3.14159L + 'a';  // promote 'a' to int, then convert to long double

dval + ival;     //  ival converted to double

dval + fval;     //  fval converted to double

ival = dval;     //  dval converted (by truncation) to int

flag = dval;     //  if dval is 0, then flag is false, otherwise true

cval + fval;     //  cval promoted to int, that int converted to float

sval + cval;     //  sval and cval promoted to int

cval + lval;     //  cval converted to long

ival + ulval;    //  ival converted to unsigned long

usval + ival;    //  promotion depends on size of unsigned short and int

uival + lval;    //  conversion depends on size of unsigned int and long
```

In the first addition, the character constant lowercase 'a' has type char, which as we know from Section 2.1.1 (p. 34) is a numeric value. The numeric value that 'a' represents depends on the machine's character set. On our ASCII machine, 'a' represents the number 97. When we add 'a' to a long double, the char value is promoted to int and then that int value is converted to a long double. That converted value is added to the long double literal. The other interesting cases are the last two expressions involving unsigned values.

5.12.3 Other Implicit Conversions

Pointer Conversions

In most cases when we use an array, the array is automatically converted to a pointer to the first element:

```
int ia[10];     //  array of 10 ints
int* ip = ia;   //  convert ia to pointer to first element
```

The exceptions when an array is not converted to a pointer are: as the operand of the address-of (&) operator or of sizeof, or when using the array to initialize a reference to the array. We'll see how to define a reference (or pointer) to an array in Section 7.2.4 (p. 240).

There are two other pointer conversions: A pointer to any data type can be converted to a void*, and a constant integral value of 0 can be converted to any pointer type.

Conversions to `bool`

Arithmetic and pointer values can be converted to `bool`. If the pointer or arithmetic value is zero, then the `bool` is `false`; any other value converts to `true`:

```
if (cp) /* ... */      //  true if cp is not zero
while (*cp) /* ... */  //  dereference cp and convert resulting char to bool
```

Here, the `if` converts any nonzero value of `cp` to `true`. The `while` dereferences `cp`, which yields a `char`. The null character has value zero and converts to `false`. All other `char` values convert to `true`.

Arithmetic Type and `bool` Conversions

Arithmetic objects can be converted to `bool` and `bool` objects can be converted to `int`. When an arithmetic type is converted to `bool`, zero converts as `false` and any other value converts as `true`. When a `bool` is converted to an arithmetic type, `true` becomes one and `false` becomes zero:

```
bool b = true;
int ival = b;    //  ival == 1
double pi = 3.14;
bool b2 = pi;    //  b2 is true
pi = false;      //  pi == 0
```

Conversions and Enumeration Types

Objects of an enumeration type (Section 2.7, p. 62) or an enumerator can be automatically converted to an integral type. As a result, they can be used where an integral value is required—for example, in an arithmetic expression:

```
//  point2d is 2, point2w is 3, point3d is 3, point3w is 4
enum Points { point2d = 2, point2w,
              point3d = 3, point3w };
const size_t array_size = 1024;
//  ok: pt2w promoted to int
int chunk_size = array_size * pt2w;
int array_3d = array_size * point3d;
```

The type to which an `enum` object or enumerator is promoted is machine-defined and depends on the value of the largest enumerator. Regardless of that value, an `enum` or enumerator is always promoted at least to `int`. If the largest enumerator does not fit in an `int`, then the promotion is to the smallest type larger than `int` (`unsigned int`, `long` or `unsigned long`) that can hold the enumerator value.

Conversion to `const`

A nonconst object can be converted to a `const` object, which happens when we use a nonconst object to initialize a reference to `const` object. We can also convert the address of a nonconst object (or convert a nonconst pointer) to a pointer to the related `const` type:

```
int i;
const int ci = 0;
const int &j = i;    // ok: convert non-const to reference to const int
const int *p = &ci;  // ok: convert address of non-const to address of a const
```

Conversions Defined by the Library Types

Class types can define conversions that the compiler will apply automatically. Of the library types we've used so far, there is one important conversion that we have used. When we read from an `istream` as a condition

```
string s;
while (cin >> s)
```

we are implicitly using a conversion defined by the IO library. In a condition such as this one, the expression `cin >> s` is evaluated, meaning `cin` is read. Whether the read succeeds or fails, the result of the expression is `cin`.

   The condition in the `while` expects a value of type `bool`, but it is given a value of type `istream`. That `istream` value is converted to `bool`. The effect of converting an `istream` to `bool` is to test the state of the stream. If the last attempt to read from `cin` succeeded, then the state of the stream will cause the conversion to `bool` to be `true`—the `while` test will succeed. If the last attempt failed—say because we hit end-of-file—then the conversion to `bool` will yield `false` and the `while` condition will fail.

EXERCISES SECTION 5.12.3

Exercise 5.31: Given the variable definitions on page 180, explain what conversions take place when evaluating the following expressions:

```
(a)  if (fval)
(b)  dval = fval + ival;
(c)  dval + ival + cval;
```

Remember that you may need to consider associativity of the operators in order to determine the answer in the case of expressions involving more than one operator.

5.12.4 Explicit Conversions

An explicit conversion is spoken of as a **cast** and is supported by the following set of named cast operators: **static_cast**, **dynamic_cast**, **const_cast**, and **reinterpret_cast**.

   Although necessary at times, casts are inherently dangerous constructs.

5.12.5   When Casts Might Be Useful

One reason to perform an explicit cast is to override the usual standard conversions. The following compound assignment

```
double dval;
int ival;
ival *= dval;    //  ival = ival * dval
```

converts `ival` to `double` in order to multiply it by `dval`. That double result is then truncated to `int` in order to assign it to `ival`. We can eliminate the unnecessary conversion of `ival` to `double` by explicitly casting `dval` to `int`:

```
ival *= static_cast<int>(dval);   //  converts dval to int
```

Another reason for an explicit cast is to select a specific conversion when more than one conversion is possible. We will look at this case more closely in Chapter 14.

5.12.6   Named Casts

The general form for the named cast notation is the following:

```
cast-name<type>(expression);
```

`cast-name` may be one of `static_cast`, `const_cast`, `dynamic_cast`, or `reinterpret_cast`. *type* is the target type of the conversion, and *expression* is the value to be cast. The type of cast determines the specific kind of conversion that is performed on the *expression*.

dynamic_cast

A `dynamic_cast` supports the run-time identification of objects addressed either by a pointer or reference. We cover `dynamic_cast` in Section 18.2 (p. 772).

const_cast

A `const_cast`, as its name implies, casts away the `const`ness of its expression. For example, we might have a function named `string_copy` that we are certain reads, but does not write, its single parameter of type `char*`. If we have access to the code, the best alternative would be to correct it to take a `const char*`. If that is not possible, we could call `string_copy` on a const value using a `const_cast`:

```
const  char *pc_str;
char *pc = string_copy(const_cast<char*>(pc_str));
```

Only a `const_cast` can be used to cast away `const`ness. Using any of the other three forms of cast in this case would result in a compile-time error. Similarly, it is a compile-time error to use the `const_cast` notation to perform any type conversion other than adding or removing `const`.

static_cast

Any type conversion that the compiler performs implicitly can be explicitly requested by using a static_cast:

```
double d = 97.0;
//   cast specified to indicate that the conversion is intentional
char   ch = static_cast<char>(d);
```

Such casts are useful when assigning a larger arithmetic type to a smaller type. The cast informs both the reader of the program and the compiler that we are aware of and are not concerned about the potential loss of precision. Compilers often generate a warning for assignments of a larger arithmetic type to a smaller type. When we provide the explicit cast, the warning message is turned off.

A static_cast is also useful to perform a conversion that the compiler will not generate automatically. For example, we can use a static_cast to retrieve a pointer value that was stored in a void* pointer (Section 4.2.2, p. 119):

```
void* p = &d;    //  ok: address of any data object can be stored in a void*
//  ok: converts void* back to the original pointer type
double *dp = static_cast<double*>(p);
```

When we store a pointer in a void* and then use a static_cast to cast the pointer back to its original type, we are guaranteed that the pointer value is preserved. That is, the result of the cast will be equal to the original address value.

reinterpret_cast

A reinterpret_cast generally performs a low-level reinterpretation of the bit pattern of its operands.

Beware

A reinterpret_cast is inherently machine-dependent. Safely using reinterpret_cast requires completely understanding the types involved as well as the details of how the compiler implements the cast.

As an example, in the following cast

```
int *ip;
char *pc = reinterpret_cast<char*>(ip);
```

the programmer must never forget that the actual object addressed by pc is an int, not a character array. Any use of pc that assumes it's an ordinary character pointer is likely to fail *at run time* in interesting ways. For example, using it to initialize a string object such as

```
string str(pc);
```

is likely to result in bizarre run-time behavior.

The use of pc to initialize str is a good example of why explicit casts are dangerous. The problem is that types are changed, yet there are no warnings or errors from the compiler. When we initialized pc with the address of an int, there is no error or warning from the compiler because we explicitly said the conversion was okay. Any subsequent use of pc will assume that the value it holds is a char*. The compiler has no way of knowing that it actually holds a pointer to an int. Thus, the initialization of str with pc is absolutely correct—albeit in this case meaningless or worse! Tracking down the cause of this sort of problem can prove extremely difficult, especially if the cast of ip to pc occurs in a file separate from the one in which pc is used to initialize a string.

ADVICE: AVOID CASTS

By using a cast, the programmer turns off or dampens normal type-checking (Section 2.3, p. 44). We strongly recommend that programmers avoid casts and believe that most well-formed C++ programs can be written without relying on casts.

This advice is particularly important regarding use of reinterpret_casts. Such casts are always hazardous. Similarly, use of const_cast almost always indicates a design flaw. Properly designed systems should not need to cast away const. The other casts, static_cast and dynamic_cast, have their uses but should be needed infrequently. Every time you write a cast, you should think hard about whether you can achieve the same result in a different way. If the cast is unavoidable, errors can be mitigated by limiting the scope in which the cast value is used and by documenting all assumptions about the types involved.

5.12.7 Old-Style Casts

Prior to the introduction of named cast operators, an explicit cast was performed by enclosing a type in parentheses:

```
char *pc = (char*) ip;
```

The effect of this cast is the same as using the reinterpret_cast notation. However, the visibility of this cast is considerably less, making it even more difficult to track down the rogue cast.

Standard C++ introduced the named cast operators to make casts more visible and to give the programmer a more finely tuned tool to use when casts are necessary. For example, nonpointer static_casts and const_casts tend to be safer than reinterpret_casts. As a result, the programmer (as well as readers and tools operating on the program) can clearly identify the potential risk level of each explicit cast in code.

Although the old-style cast notation is supported by Standard C++, we recommend it be used only when writing code to be compiled either under the C language or pre-Standard C++.

The old-style cast notation takes one of the following two forms:

```
type (expr); // Function-style cast notation

(type) expr; // C-language-style cast notation
```

Depending on the types involved, an old-style cast has the same behavior as a const_cast, a static_cast, or a reinterpret_cast. When used where a static_cast or a const_cast would be legal, an old-style cast does the same conversion as the respective named cast. If neither is legal, then an old-style cast performs a reinterpret_cast. For example, we might rewrite the casts from the previous section less clearly using old-style notation:

```
int ival; double dval;
ival += int (dval);   //  static_cast: converts double to int

const char* pc_str;
string_copy((char*)pc_str);   //  const_cast: casts away const

int *ip;
char *pc = (char*)ip;   //  reinterpret_cast: treats int* as char*
```

The old-style cast notation remains supported for backward compatibility with programs written under pre-Standard C++ and to maintain compatibility with the C language.

EXERCISES SECTION 5.12.7

Exercise 5.32: Given the following set of definitions,

```
char cval;      int ival;      unsigned int ui;
float fval;                     double dval;
```

identify the implicit type conversions, if any, taking place:

```
(a) cval = 'a' + 3;        (b) fval = ui - ival * 1.0;
(c) dval = ui * fval;      (d) cval = ival + fval + dval;
```

Exercise 5.33: Given the following set of definitions,

```
int ival;                           double dval;
const string *ps;      char *pc;      void *pv;
```

rewrite each of the following using a named cast notation:

```
(a) pv = (void*)ps;    (b) ival = int(*pc);
(c) pv = &dval;        (d) pc = (char*) pv;
```

CHAPTER SUMMARY

C++ provides a rich set of operators and defines their meaning when applied to values of the built-in types. Additionally, the language supports operator overloading, which allows us to define the meaning of the operators for class types. We'll see in Chapter 14 how to define operators for our own types.

To understand compound expressions—expressions involving more than one operator—it is necessary to understand precedence, associativity, and order of operand evaluation. Each operator has a precedence level and associativity. Precedence determines how operators are grouped in a compound expression. Associativity determines how operators at the same precedence level are grouped.

Most operators do not specify the order in which operands are evaluated: The compiler is free to evaluate either the left- or right-hand operand first. Often, the order of operand evaluation has no impact on the result of the expression. However, if both operands refer to the same object and one of the operands *changes* that object, then the program has a serious bug—and a bug that may be hard to find.

Finally, it is possible to write an expression that is given one type but where a value of another type is required. In such cases, the compiler will automatically apply a conversion (either built-in or defined for a class type) to transform the given type into the type that is required. Conversions can also be requested explicitly by using a cast.

DEFINED TERMS

arithmetic conversion A conversion from one arithmetic type to another. In the context of the binary arithmetic operators, arithmetic conversions usually attempt to preserve precision by converting a smaller type to a larger type (e.g., small integral types, such as `char` and `short`, are converted to `int`).

associativity Determines how operators of the same precedence are grouped. Operators can be either right associative (operators are grouped from right to left) or left associative (operators are grouped from left to right).

binary operators Operators that take two operands.

cast An explicit conversion.

compound expression An expression involving more than one operator.

const_cast A cast that converts a `const` object to the corresponding nonconst type.

conversion Process whereby a value of one type is transformed into a value of another type. The language defines conversions among the built-in types. Conversions to and from class types are also possible.

dangling pointer A pointer that refers to memory that once had an object but no longer does. Dangling pointers are the source of program errors that are quite difficult to detect.

delete expression A `delete` expression frees memory that was allocated by `new`. There are two forms of `delete`:

```
delete p;      // delete object
delete [] p;   // delete array
```

In the first case, p must be a pointer to a dynamically allocated object; in the second, p must point to the first element in a dynamically allocated array. In C++ programs, `delete` replaces the use of the C library `free` function.

dynamic_cast Used in combination with inheritance and run-time type identification. See Section 18.2 (p. 772).

expression The lowest level of computation in a C++ program. Expressions generally apply an operator to one or more operands. Each expression yields a result. Expressions can be used as operands, so we can write compound expressions requiring the evaluation of multiple operators.

implicit conversion A conversion that is automatically generated by the compiler. Given an expression that needs a particular type but has an operand of a differing type, the compiler will automatically convert the operand to the desired type if an appropriate conversion exists.

integral promotions Subset of the standard conversions that take a smaller integral type to its most closely related larger type. Integral types (e.g. short, char, etc.) are promoted to int or unsigned int.

new expression A new expression allocates memory at run time from the free store. This chapter looked at the form that allocates a single object:

```
new type;
new type(inits);
```

allocates an object of the indicated *type* and optionally initializes that object using the initializers in *inits*. Returns a pointer to the object. In C++ programs, new replaces use of the C library malloc function.

operands Values on which an expression operates.

operator Symbol that determines what action an expression performs. The language defines a set of operators and what those operators mean when applied to values of built-in type. The language also defines the precedence and associativity of each operator and specifies how many operands each operator takes. Operators may be overloaded and applied to values of class type.

operator overloading The ability to redefine an operator to apply to class types. We'll see in Chapter 14 how to define overloaded versions of operators.

order of evaluation Order, if any, in which the operands to an operator are evaluated. In most cases in C++ the compiler is free to evaluate operands in any order.

precedence Defines the order in which different operators in a compound expression are grouped. Operators with higher precedence are grouped more tightly than operators with lower precedence.

reinterpret_cast Interprets the contents of the operand as a different type. Inherently machine-dependent and dangerous.

result The value or object obtained by evaluating an expression.

static_cast An explicit request for a type conversion that the compiler would do implicitly. Often used to override an implicit conversion that the compiler would otherwise perform.

unary operators Operators that take a single operand.

~ operator The bitwise NOT operator. Inverts the bits of its operand.

, operator The comma operator. Expressions separated by a comma are evaluated left to right. Result of a comma expression is the value of the right-most expression.

?: operator The conditional operator. If-then-else expression of the form:

```
cond ? expr1 : expr2;
```

If the condition *cond* is true then *expr1* is evaluated. Otherwise, *expr2* is evaluated.

& operator Bitwise AND operator. Generates a new integral value in which each bit position is 1 if both operands have a 1 in that position; otherwise the bit is 0.

^ operator The bitwise exclusive or operator. Generates a new integral value in which each bit position is 1 if either but not both operands contain a 1 in that bit position; otherwise, the bit is 0.

| operator The bitwise OR operator. Generates a new integral value in which each bit position is 1 if either operand has a 1 in that position; otherwise the bit is 0.

++ operator The increment operator. The increment operator has two forms, prefix and postfix. Prefix increment yields an lvalue. It adds one to the operand and returns the changed value of the operand. Postfix increment yields an rvalue. It adds one to the operand and returns the original, unchanged value of the operand.

-- operator The decrement operator. has two forms, prefix and postfix. Prefix decrement yields an lvalue. It subtracts one from the operand and returns the changed value of the operand. Postfix decrement yields an rvalue. It subtracts one from the operand and returns the original, unchanged value of the operand.

<< operator The left-shift operator. Shifts bits in the left-hand operand to the left. Shifts as many bits as indicated by the right-hand operand. The right-hand operand must be zero or positive and strictly less than the number of bits in the left-hand operand.

>> operator The right-shift operator. Like the left-shift operator except that bits are shifted to the right. The right-hand operand must be zero or positive and strictly less than the number of bits in the left-hand operand.

C H A P T E R   **6**

S T A T E M E N T S

CONTENTS

Statements are analogous to sentences in a natural language. In C++ there are simple statements that execute a single task and compound statements that consist of a block of statements that execute as a unit. Like most languages, C++ provides statements for conditional execution and loops that repeatedly execute the same body of code. This chapter looks in detail at the statements supported by C++.

By default, statements are executed sequentially. Except for the simplest programs, sequential execution is inadequate. Therefore, C++ also defines a set of *flow-of-control* statements that allow statements to be executed conditionally or repeatedly. The `if` and `switch` statements support conditional execution. The `for`, `while`, and `do while` statements support repetitive execution. These latter statements are often referred to as *loops* or *iteration* statements.

6.1   Simple Statements

Most statements in C++ end with a semicolon. An expression, such as `ival + 5`, becomes an **expression statement** by following it with a semicolon. Expression statements cause the expression to be evaluated. In the case of

```
ival + 5;    // expression statement
```

evaluating this expression is useless: The result is calculated but not assigned or otherwise used. More commonly, expression statements contain expressions that when evaluated affect the program's state. Examples of such expressions are those that use assignment, increment, input, or output operators.

Null Statements

The simplest form of statement is the empty, or **null statement**. It takes the following form (a single semicolon):

```
;   // null statement
```

A null statement is useful where the language requires a statement but the program's logic does not. Such usage is most common when a loop's work can be done within the condition. For example, we might want to read an input stream, ignoring everything we read until we encounter a particular value:

```
// read until we hit end-of-file or find an input equal to sought
while (cin >> s && s != sought)
    ; // null statement
```

The condition reads a value from the standard input and implicitly tests `cin` to see whether the read was successful. Assuming the read succeeded, the second part of the condition tests whether the value we read is equal to the value in `sought`. If we found the value we want, then the `while` loop is exited; otherwise, the condition is tested again, which involves reading another value from `cin`.

 Best Practices A null statement should be commented, so that anyone reading the code can see that the statement was omitted intentionally.

Because a null statement is a statement, it is legal anywhere a statement is expected. For this reason, semicolons that might appear illegal are often nothing more than null statements:

```
// ok: second semicolon is superfluous null statement
ival = v1 + v2;;
```

This fragment is composed of two statements: the expression statement and the null statement.

> Extraneous null statements are not always harmless.

An extra semicolon following the condition in a `while` or `if` can drastically alter the programmer's intent:

```
//  disaster: extra semicolon: loop body is this null statement
while (iter != svec.end()) ; //  null statement--while body is empty!
    ++iter;        //  increment is not part of the loop
```

This program will loop indefinitely. Contrary to the indentation, the increment is not part of the loop. The loop body is a null statement caused by the extra semicolon following the condition.

6.2   Declaration Statements

Defining or declaring an object or a class is a statement. Definition statements are usually referred to as **declaration statements** although definition statement might be more accurate. We covered definitions and declarations of variables in Section 2.3 (p. 43). Class definitions were introduced in Section 2.8 (p. 63) and will be covered in more detail in Chapter 12.

6.3   Compound Statements (Blocks)

A **compound statement**, usually referred to as a **block**, is a (possibly empty) sequence of statements surrounded by a pair of curly braces. A block is a scope. Names introduced within a block are accessible only from within that block or from blocks nested inside the block. As usual, a name is visible only from its point of definition until the end of the enclosing block.

Compound statements can be used where the rules of the language require a single statement, but the logic of our program needs to execute more than one. For example, the body of a `while` or `for` loop must be a single statement. Yet, we often need to execute more than one statement in the body of a loop. We can do so by enclosing the statements in a pair of braces, thus turning the sequence of statements into a block.

As an example, recall the `while` loop from our solution to the bookstore problem on page 26:

```
//  if so, read the transaction records
while (std::cin >> trans)
    if (total.same_isbn(trans))
        //  match: update the running total
        total = total + trans;
```

```
else {
    //  no match: print & assign to total
    std::cout << total << std::endl;
    total = trans;
}
```

In the `else` branch, the logic of our program requires that we print `total` and then reset it from `trans`. An `else` may be followed by only a single statement. By enclosing both statements in curly braces, we transform them into a single (compound) statement. This statement satisfies the rules of the language and the needs of our program.

 Unlike most other statements, a block is *not* terminated by a semicolon.

Just as there is a null statement, we also can define an empty block. We do so by using a pair of curlies with no statements:

```
while (cin >> s && s != sought)
    { } //  empty block
```

EXERCISES SECTION 6.3

Exercise 6.1: What is a null statement? Give an example of when you might use a null statement.

Exercise 6.2: What is a block? Give an example of when you might use a block.

Exercise 6.3: Use the comma operator (Section 5.9, p. 168) to rewrite the `else` branch in the `while` loop from the bookstore problem so that it no longer requires a block. Explain whether this rewrite improves or diminishes the readability of this code.

Exercise 6.4: In the `while` loop that solved the bookstore problem, what effect, if any, would removing the curly brace following the `while` and its corresponding close curly have on the program?

6.4   Statement Scope

Some statements permit variable definitions within their control structure:

```
while (int i = get_num())
    cout << i << endl;
i = 0;   //  error: i is not accessible outside the loop
```

 Variables defined in a condition must be initialized. The value tested by the condition is the value of the initialized object.

Variables defined as part of the control structure of a statement are visible only until the end of the statement in which they are defined. The scope of such variables is limited to the statement body. Often the statement body itself is a block, which in turn may contain other blocks. A name introduced in a control structure is local to the statement and the scopes nested inside the statement:

```
//  index is visible only within the for statement
for (vector<int>::size_type index = 0;
                 index != vec.size(); ++index)
{ //  new scope, nested within the scope of this for statement
    int square = 0;
    if (index % 2)              // ok: index is in scope
        square = index * index;
    vec[index] = square;
}
if (index != vec.size()) // error: index is not visible here
```

If the program needs to access the value of a variable used in the control statement, then that variable must be defined outside the control structure:

```
vector<int>::size_type index = 0;
for ( /* empty */ ; index != vec.size(); ++index)
    //  as before
if (index != vec.size()) // ok: now index is in scope
    //  as before
```

> Earlier versions of C++ treated the scope of variables defined inside a for differently: Variables defined in the for header were treated as if they were defined just before the for. Older C++ programs may have code that relies on being able to access these control variables outside the scope of the for.

One advantage of limiting the scope of variables defined within a control statement to that statement is that the names of such variables can be reused without worrying about whether their current value is correct at each use. If the name is not in scope, then it is impossible to use that name with an incorrect, leftover value.

6.5 The if Statement

An **if statement** conditionally executes another statement based on whether a specified expression is true. There are two forms of the if: one with an else branch and one without. The syntactic form of the plain if is the following:

```
if (condition)
    statement
```

The *condition* must be enclosed in parentheses. It can be an expression, such as

```
if (a + b > c) {/* ... */}
```

or an initialized declaration, such as

```
//  ival only accessible within the if statement
if (int ival = compute_value()) {/* ... */}
```

As usual, *statement* could be a compound statement—that is, a block of statements enclosed in curly braces.

When a condition defines a variable, the variable must be initialized. The value of the initialized variable is converted to bool (Section 5.12.3, p. 181) and the resulting bool determines the value of the condition. The variable can be of any type that can be converted to bool, which means it can be an arithmetic or pointer type. As we'll see in Chapter 14, whether a class type can be used in a condition depends on the class. Of the types we've used so far, the IO types can be used in a condition, but the vector and string types may not be used as a condition.

To illustrate the use of the if statement, we'll find the smallest value in a vector<int>, keeping a count of how many times that minimum value occurs. To solve this problem, we'll need two if statements: one to determine whether we have a new minimum and the other to increment a count of the number of occurrences of the current minimum value:

```
if (minVal > ivec[i])  { /* process new minVal */ }
if (minVal == ivec[i]) { /* increment occurrence count */ }
```

Statement Block as Target of an if

We'll start by considering each if in isolation. One of these if statements will determine whether there is a new minimum and, if so, reset the counter and update minVal:

```
if (minVal > ivec[i]) {   // execute both statements if condition is true
    minVal = ivec[i];
    occurs = 1;
}
```

The other conditionally updates the counter. This if needs only one statement, so it need not be enclosed in curlies:

```
if (minVal == ivec[i])
    ++occurs;
```

It is a somewhat common error to forget the curly braces when multiple statements must be executed as a single statement.

In the following program, contrary to the indentation and intention of the programmer, the assignment to occurs is not part of the if statement:

```
//  error: missing curly brackets to make a block!
if (minVal > ivec[i])
    minVal = ivec[i];
    occurs = 1; // executed unconditionally: not part of the if
```

Written this way, the assignment to `occurs` will be executed unconditionally. Uncovering this kind of error can be very difficult because the text of the program looks correct.

> **Best Practices** Many editors and development environments have tools to automatically indent source code to match its structure. It is a good idea to use such tools if they are available.

6.5.1 The `if` Statement `else` Branch

Our next task is to put these `if` statements together into an execution sequence. The order of the `if` statements is significant. If we use the following order

```
if (minVal > ivec[i]) {
    minVal = ivec[i];
    occurs = 1;
}
// potential error if minVal has just been set to ivec[i]
if (minVal == ivec[i])
    ++occurs;
```

our count will always be off by 1. This code double-counts the first occurrence of the minimum.

Not only is the execution of both `if` statements on the same value potentially dangerous, it is also unnecessary. The same element cannot be both less than `minVal` and equal to it. If one condition is true, the other condition can be safely ignored. The `if` statement allows for this kind of *either-or* condition by providing an `else` clause.

The syntactic form of the **if else statement** is

```
if (condition)
    statement1
else
    statement2
```

If *condition* is true, then *statement1* is executed; otherwise, *statement2* is executed:

```
if (minVal == ivec[i])
    ++occurs;
else if (minVal > ivec[i]) {
        minVal = ivec[i];
        occurs = 1;
}
```

It is worth noting that *statement2* can be any statement or a block of statements enclosed in curly braces. In this example, *statement2* is itself an `if` statement.

Dangling `else`

There is one important complexity in using `if` statements that we have not yet covered. Notice that neither `if` directly handles the case where the current element is greater than `minVal`. Logically, ignoring these elements is fine—there is nothing to do if the element is greater than the minimum we've found so far. However, it is often the case that an `if` needs to do something on all three cases: Unique steps may be required if one value is greater than, less than, or equal to some other value. We've rewritten our loop to explicitly handle all three cases:

```
// note: indented to make clear how the else branches align with the corresponding if
if (minVal < ivec[i])
     { }                            //  empty block
else if (minVal == ivec[i])
        ++occurs;
else {                            //  minVal > ivec[i]
    minVal = ivec[i];
    occurs = 1;
}
```

This three-way test handles each case correctly. However, a simple rewrite that collapses the first two tests into a single, nested `if` runs into problems:

```
//  oops: incorrect rewrite: This code won't work!
if (minVal <= ivec[i])
    if (minVal == ivec[i])
          ++occurs;
else {        //  this else goes with the inner if, not the outer one!
    minVal = ivec[i];
    occurs = 1;
}
```

This version illustrates a source of potential ambiguity common to `if` statements in all languages. The problem, usually referred to as the **dangling-else** problem, occurs when a statement contains more `if` clauses than `else` clauses. The question then arises: To which `if` does each `else` clause belong?

The indentation in our code indicates the expectation that the `else` should match up with the outer `if` clause. In C++, however, the dangling-else ambiguity is resolved *by matching the* `else` *with the last occurring unmatched* `if`. In this case, the actual evaluation of the `if else` statement is as follows:

```
//  oops: still wrong, but now the indentation matches execution path
if (minVal <= ivec[i])
    //  indented to match handling of dangling-else
    if (minVal == ivec[i])
          ++occurs;
    else {
        minVal = ivec[i];
        occurs = 1;
    }
```

We can force an `else` to match an outer `if` by enclosing the inner `if` in a compound statement:

```
if (minVal <= ivec[i]) {
    if (minVal == ivec[i])
          ++occurs;
} else {
    minVal = ivec[i];
    occurs = 1;
}
```

Some coding styles recommend *always* using braces after any if.
Doing so avoids any possible confusion and error in later modifi-
cations of the code. At a minimum, it is nearly always a good idea
to use braces after an if (or while) when the statement in the
body is anything other than a simple expression statement, such
as an assignment or output expression.

EXERCISES SECTION 6.5.1

Exercise 6.5: Correct each of the following:
```
(a) if (ival1 != ival2)
        ival1 = ival2
    else ival1 = ival2 = 0;

(b) if (ival < minval)
        minval = ival;    // remember new minimum
        occurs = 1;       // reset occurrence counter

(c) if (int ival = get_value())
        cout << "ival = " << ival << endl;
    if (!ival)
        cout << "ival = 0\n";

(d) if (ival = 0)
        ival = get_value();
```

Exercise 6.6: What is a "dangling else"? How are else clauses resolved in C++?

6.6 The switch Statement

Deeply nested if else statements can often be correct syntactically and yet not
correctly reflect the programmer's logic. For example, mistaken else if match-
ings are more likely to pass unnoticed. Adding a new condition and associated
logic or making other changes to the statements is also hard to get right. A **switch
statement** provides a more convenient way to write deeply nested if/else logic.

Suppose that we have been asked to count how often each of the five vowels
appears in some segment of text. Our program logic is as follows:

- Read each character until there are no more characters to read

- Compare each character to the set of vowels

- If the character matches one of the vowels, add 1 to that vowel's count

- Display the results

The program was used to analyze this chapter. Here is the output:

```
Number of vowel a:    3499
Number of vowel e:    7132
Number of vowel i:    3577
Number of vowel o:    3530
Number of vowel u:    1185
```

6.6.1   Using a `switch`

We can solve our problem most directly using a `switch` statement:

```cpp
char ch;
//  initialize counters for each vowel
int aCnt = 0, eCnt = 0, iCnt = 0,
    oCnt = 0, uCnt = 0;
while (cin >> ch) {
    //  if ch is a vowel, increment the appropriate counter
    switch (ch) {
        case 'a':
            ++aCnt;
            break;
        case 'e':
            ++eCnt;
            break;
        case 'i':
            ++iCnt;
            break;
        case 'o':
            ++oCnt;
            break;
        case 'u':
            ++uCnt;
            break;
    }
}
//  print results
cout << "Number of vowel a: \t" << aCnt << '\n'
     << "Number of vowel e: \t" << eCnt << '\n'
     << "Number of vowel i: \t" << iCnt << '\n'
     << "Number of vowel o: \t" << oCnt << '\n'
     << "Number of vowel u: \t" << uCnt << endl;
```

A switch statement executes by evaluating the parenthesized expression that follows the keyword switch. That expression must yield an integral result. The result of the expression is compared with the value associated with each case. The case keyword and its associated value together are known as the **case label**. Each case label's value must be a constant expression (Section 2.7, p. 62). There is also a special case label, the default label, which we cover on page 203.

If the expression matches the value of a case label, execution begins with the first statement following that label. Execution continues normally from that statement through the end of the switch or until a break statement. If no match is found, (and if there is no default label), execution falls through to the first statement following the switch. In this program, the switch is the only statement in the body of a while. Here, falling through the switch returns control to the while condition.

We'll look at break statements in Section 6.10 (p. 212). Briefly, a break statement interrupts the current control flow. In this case, the break transfers control out of the switch. Execution continues at the first statement following the switch. In this example, as we already know, transferring control to the statement following the switch returns control to the while.

6.6.2 Control Flow within a switch

It is essential to understand that execution flows across case labels.

> It is a common misunderstanding to expect that only the statements associated with the matched case label are executed. However, execution continues *across* case boundaries until the end of the switch statement or a break is encountered.

Sometimes this behavior is indeed correct. We want to execute the code for a particular label as well as the code for following labels. More often, we want to execute only the code particular to a given label. To avoid executing code for subsequent cases, the programmer must explicitly tell the compiler to stop execution by specifying a break statement. Under most conditions, the last statement before the next case label is break. For example, here is an incorrect implementation of our vowel-counting switch statement:

```
// warning: deliberately incorrect!
switch (ch) {
    case 'a':
        ++aCnt;    // oops: should have a break statement
    case 'e':
        ++eCnt;    // oops: should have a break statement
    case 'i':
        ++iCnt;    // oops: should have a break statement
    case 'o':
        ++oCnt;    // oops: should have a break statement
    case 'u':
        ++uCnt;    // oops: should have a break statement
}
```

To understand what happens, we'll trace through this version assuming that value of ch is `'i'`. Execution begins following case `'i'`—thus incrementing iCnt. Execution does not stop there but continues across the case labels incrementing oCnt and uCnt as well. If ch had been `'e'`, then eCnt, iCnt, oCnt, and uCnt would all be incremented.

Forgetting to provide a break is a common source of bugs in switch statements.

Although it is not strictly necessary to specify a break statement after the last label of a switch, the safest course is to provide a break after every label, even the last. If an additional case label is added later, then the break is already in place.

`break` Statements Aren't Always Appropriate

There is one common situation where the programmer might wish to omit a break statement from a case label, allowing the program to *fall through* multiple case labels. That happens when two or more values are to be handled by the same sequence of actions. Only a single value can be associated with a case label. To indicate a range, therefore, we typically stack case labels following one another. For example, if we wished only to count vowels seen rather than count the individual vowels, we might write the following:

```
int vowelCnt = 0;
// ...
switch (ch)
{
    // any occurrence of a,e,i,o,u increments vowelCnt
    case 'a':
    case 'e':
    case 'i':
    case 'o':
    case 'u':
        ++vowelCnt;
        break;
}
```

Case labels need not appear on a new line. We could emphasize that the cases represent a range of values by listing them all on a single line:

```
switch (ch)
{
    // alternative legal syntax
    case 'a': case 'e': case 'i': case 'o': case 'u':
        ++vowelCnt;
        break;
}
```

Less frequently, we deliberately omit a break because we want to execute code for one case and then continue into the next case, executing that code as well.

> **Best Practices** Deliberately omitting a break at the end of a case happens rarely enough that a comment explaining the logic should be provided.

6.6.3 The default Label

The **default label** provides the equivalent of an else clause. If no case label matches the value of the switch expression and there is a default label, then the statements following the default are executed. For example, we might add a counter to track how many nonvowels we read. We'll increment this counter, which we'll name otherCnt, in the default case:

```
//  if ch is a vowel, increment the appropriate counter
switch (ch) {
    case 'a':
        ++aCnt;
        break;
    //  remaining vowel cases as before
    default:
        ++otherCnt;
        break;
}
}
```

In this version, if ch is not a vowel, execution will fall through to the default label, and we'll increment otherCnt.

> **Best Practices** It can be useful always to define a default label even if there is no processing to be done in the default case. Defining the label indicates to subsequent readers that the case was considered but that there is no work to be done.

A label may not stand alone; it must precede a statement. If a switch ends with the default case in which there is no work to be done, then the default label must be followed by a null statement.

6.6.4 switch Expression and Case Labels

The expression evaluated by a switch can be arbitrarily complex. In particular, the expression can define and intialize a variable:

```
switch(int ival = get_response())
```

In this case, ival is initialized, and the value of ival is compared with each case label. The variable ival exists throughout the entire switch statement but not outside it.

Case labels must be constant integral expressions (Section 2.7, p. 62). For example, the following labels result in compile-time errors:

```
//  illegal case label values
case 3.14:  //  noninteger
case ival:  //  nonconstant
```

It is also an error for any two case labels to have the same value.

6.6.5   Variable Definitions inside a `switch`

Variables can be defined following only the last `case` or `default` label:

```
case true:
      //  error: declaration precedes a case label
      string file_name = get_file_name();
      break;
case false:
      //  ...
```

The reason for this rule is to prevent code that might jump over the definition and initialization of a variable.

Recall that a variable can be used from its point of definition until the end of the block in which it is defined. Now, consider what would happen if we could define a variable between two case labels. That variable would continue to exist until the end of the enclosing block. It could be used by code in case labels following the one in which it was defined. If the `switch` begins executing in one of these subsequent case labels, then the variable might be used even though it had not been defined.

If we need to define a variable for a particular case, we can do so by defining the variable inside a block, thereby ensuring that the variable can be used only where it is guaranteed to have been defined and initialized:

```
case true:
      {
          //  ok: declaration statement within a statement block
          string file_name = get_file_name();
          //  ...
      }
   break;
   case false:
       //  ...
```

6.7   The `while` Statement

A **`while` statement** repeatedly executes a target statement as long as a condition is true. Its syntactic form is

```
while (condition)
        statement
```

Exercise 6.7: There is one problem with our vowel-counting program as we've implemented it: It doesn't count capital letters as vowels. Write a program that counts both lower- and uppercase letters as the appropriate vowel—that is, your program should count both 'a' and 'A' as part of aCnt, and so forth.

Exercise 6.8: Modify our vowel-count program so that it also counts the number of blank spaces, tabs, and newlines read.

Exercise 6.9: Modify our vowel-count program so that it counts the number of occurrences of the following two-character sequences: ff, fl, and fi.

Exercise 6.10: Each of the programs in the highlighted text on page 206 contains a common programming error. Identify and correct each error.

The *statement* (which is often a block) is executed as long as the *condition* evaluates as true. The *condition* may not be empty. If the first evaluation of *condition* yields false, *statement* is not executed.

The condition can be an expression or an initialized variable definition:

```
bool quit = false;
while (!quit) {                         // expression as condition
    quit = do_something();
}
while (int loc = search(name)) { // initialized variable as condition
        // do something
}
```

Any variable defined in the condition is visible only within the block associated with the while. On each trip through the loop, the initialized value is converted to bool (Section 5.12.3, p. 182). If the value evaluates as true, the while body is executed. Ordinarily, the condition itself or the loop body must do something to change the value of the expression. Otherwise, the loop might never terminate.

 Variables defined in the condition are created and destroyed on each trip through the loop.

Using a while Loop

We have already seen a number of while loops, but for completeness, here is an example that copies the contents of one array into another:

```
// arr1 is an array of ints
int *source = arr1;
size_t sz = sizeof(arr1)/sizeof(*arr1); // number of elements
int *dest = new int[sz];                    // uninitialized elements
while (source != arr1 + sz)
    *dest++ = *source++;   // copy element and increment pointers
```

CODE FOR EXERCISES IN SECTION 6.6.5

```
(a) switch (ival) {
        case 'a': aCnt++;
        case 'e': eCnt++;
        default: iouCnt++;
    }

(b) switch (ival) {
        case 1:
            int ix = get_value();
            ivec[ ix ] = ival;
            break;
        default:
            ix = ivec.size()-1;
            ivec[ ix ] = ival;
    }

(c) switch (ival) {
        case 1, 3, 5, 7, 9:
            oddcnt++;
            break;
        case 2, 4, 6, 8, 10:
            evencnt++;
            break;
    }

(d) int ival=512 jval=1024, kval=4096;
    int bufsize;
    // ...
    switch(swt) {
        case ival:
            bufsize = ival * sizeof(int);
            break;
        case jval:
            bufsize = jval * sizeof(int);
            break;
        case kval:
            bufsize = kval * sizeof(int);
            break;
    }
```

We start by initializing `source` and `dest` to point to the first element of their respective arrays. The condition in the `while` tests whether we've reached the end of the array from which we are copying. If not, we execute the body of the loop. The body contains only a single statement, which copies the element and increments both pointers so that they point to the next element in their corresponding arrays.

As we saw in the "Advice" box on page 164, C++ programmers tend to write terse expressions. The statement in the body of the `while`

```
*dest++ = *source++;
```

is a classic example. This expression is equivalent to

```
{
    *dest = *source;   // copy element
    ++dest;   // increment the pointers
    ++source;
}
```

 The assignment in the `while` loop represents a very common usage. Because such code is widespread, it is important to study this expression until its meaning is immediately clear.

6.8   The `for` Loop Statement

The syntactic form of a `for` statement is

```
for (init-statement condition; expression)
        statement
```

The *init-statement* must be a declaration statement, an expression statement, or a null statement. Each of these statements is terminated by a semicolon, so the syntactic form can also be thought of as

```
for (initializer; condition; expression)
        statement
```

although technically speaking, the semicolon after the *initializer* is part of the statement that begins the `for` header.

In general, the *init-statement* is used to initialize or assign a starting value that is modified over the course of the loop. The *condition* serves as the loop control. As long as *condition* evaluates as true, *statement* is executed. If the first evaluation of *condition* evaluates to `false`, *statement* is not executed. The *expression* usually is used to modify the variable(s) initialized in *init-statement* and tested in *condition*. It is evaluated after each iteration of the loop. If *condition* evaluates to false on the first iteration, *expression* is never executed. As usual, *statement* can be either a single or a compound statement.

EXERCISES SECTION 6.7

Exercise 6.11: Explain each of the following loops. Correct any problems you detect.

```
(a) string bufString, word;
    while (cin >> bufString >> word) { /* ... */ }

(b) while (vector<int>::iterator iter != ivec.end())
    { /* ... */ }

(c) while (ptr = 0)
        ptr = find_a_value();

(d) while (bool status = find(word))
    { word = get_next_word(); }
    if (!status)
        cout << "Did not find any words\n";
```

Exercise 6.12: Write a small program to read a sequence of strings from standard input looking for duplicated words. The program should find places in the input where one word is followed immediately by itself. Keep track of the largest number of times a single repetition occurs and which word is repeated. Print the maximum number of duplicates, or else print a message saying that no word was repeated. For example, if the input is

```
how, now now now brown cow cow
```

the output should indicate that the word "now" occurred three times.

Exercise 6.13: Explain in detail how the statement in the while loop is executed:

```
*dest++ = *source++;
```

Using a for Loop

Given the following for loop, which prints the contents of a vector,

```
for (vector<string>::size_type ind = 0;
             ind != svec.size(); ++ind) {
    cout << svec[ind];    // print current element
    // if not the last element, print a space to separate from the next one
    if (ind + 1 != svec.size())
        cout << " ";
}
```

the order of evaluation is as follows:

1. The *init-statement* is executed once at the start of the loop. In this example, ind is defined and initialized to zero.

2. Next, *condition* is evaluated. If ind is not equal to svec.size(), then the for body is executed. Otherwise, the loop terminates. If the condition is false on the first trip, then the for body is not executed.

3. If the condition is true, the `for` body executes. In this case, the `for` body prints the current element and then tests whether this element is the last one. If not, it prints a space to separate it from the next element.

4. Finally, *expression* is evaluated. In this example, `ind` is incremented by 1.

These four steps represent the first iteration of the `for` loop. Step 2 is now repeated, followed by steps 3 and 4, until the condition evaluates to `false`—that is, when `ind` is equal to `svec.size()`.

 It is worth remembering that the visibility of any object defined within the `for` header is limited to the body of the `for` loop. Thus, in this example, `ind` is inaccessible after the `for` completes.

6.8.1 Omitting Parts of the `for` Header

A `for` header can omit any (or all) of *init-statement*, *condition*, or *expression*.

The *init-statement* is omitted if an initialization is unnecessary or occurs elsewhere. For example, if we rewrote the program to print the contents of a `vector` using iterators instead of subscripts, we might, for readability reasons, move the initialization outside the loop:

```
vector<string>::iterator iter = svec.begin();
for( /* null */ ; iter != svec.end(); ++iter) {
    cout << *iter;     // print current element
    // if not the last element, print a space to separate from the next one
    if (iter+1 != svec.end())
        cout << " ";
}
```

Note that the semicolon is necessary to indicate the absence of the *init-statement*—more precisely, the semicolon represents a null *init-statement*.

If the *condition* is omitted, then it is equivalent to having written `true` as the condition:

```
for (int i = 0; /* no condition */ ; ++i)
```

It is as if the program were written as

```
for (int i = 0; true ; ++i)
```

It is essential that the body of the loop contain a `break` or `return` statement. Otherwise the loop will execute until it exhausts the system resources. Similarly, if the *expression* is omitted, then the loop must exit through a `break` or `return` or the loop body must arrange to change the value tested in the condition:

```
for (int i = 0; i != 10; /* no expression */ ) {
    // body must change i or the loop won't terminate
}
```

If the body doesn't change the value of `i`, then `i` remains 0 and the test will always succeed.

6.8.2   Multiple Definitions in the `for` Header

Multiple objects may be defined in the `init-statement`; however, only one statement may appear, so all the objects must be of the same general type:

```
const int size = 42;
int val = 0, ia[size];
// declare 3 variables local to the for loop:
// ival is an int, pi a pointer to int, and ri a reference to int
for (int ival = 0, *pi = ia, &ri = val;
        ival != size;
        ++ival, ++pi, ++ri)
                // ...
```

EXERCISES SECTION 6.8.2

Exercise 6.14: Explain each of the following loops. Correct any problems you detect.

```
(a) for (int *ptr = &ia, ix = 0;
         ix != size && ptr != ia+size;
         ++ix, ++ptr)   { /* ... */ }
(b) for (; ;) {
         if (some_condition) return;
         // ...
    }
(c) for (int ix = 0; ix != sz; ++ix)   { /* ... */ }
    if (ix != sz)
         // ...
(d) int ix;
    for (ix != sz; ++ix) { /* ... */ }
(e) for (int ix = 0; ix != sz; ++ix, ++ sz)   { /* ... */ }
```

Exercise 6.15: The `while` loop is particularly good at executing while some condition holds; for example, while the end-of-file is not reached, read a next value. The `for` loop is generally thought of as a step loop: An index steps through a range of values in a collection. Write an idiomatic use of each loop and then rewrite each using the other loop construct. If you were able to program with only one loop, which construct would you choose? Why?

Exercise 6.16: Given two `vectors` of `int`s, write a program to determine whether one `vectors` is a prefix of the other. For `vectors` of unequal length, compare the number of elements of the smaller `vector`. For example, given the `vectors` (0,1,1,2) and (0,1,1,2,3,5,8), your program should return `true`.

6.9   The `do while` Statement

We might want to write a program that interactively performs some calculation for its user. As a simple example, we might want to do sums for the user: Our program prompts the user for a pair of numbers and produces their sum. Having generated one sum, we'd like the program to give the user the option to repeat the process and generate another.

The body of this program is pretty easy. We'll need to write a prompt, then read a pair of values and print the sum of the values we read. After we print the sum, we'll ask the user whether to continue.

The hard part is deciding on a control structure. The problem is that we want to execute the loop until the user asks to exit. In particular, we want to do a sum even on the first iteration. The do while loop does exactly what we need. It guarantees that its body is always executed at least once. The syntactic form is as follows:

```
do
        statement
while (condition);
```

 Note Unlike a while statement, a do-while statement always ends with a semicolon.

The *statement* in a do is executed before *condition* is evaluated. The *condition* cannot be empty. If *condition* evaluates as false, then the loop terminates; otherwise, the loop is repeated. Using a do while, we can write our program:

```
//  repeatedly ask user for pair of numbers to sum
string rsp;   //  used in the condition; can't be defined inside the do
do {
    cout << "please enter two values: ";
    int val1, val2;
    cin  >> val1 >> val2;
    cout << "The sum of " << val1 << " and " << val2
         << " = " << val1 + val2 << "\n\n"
         << "More? [yes] [no] ";
    cin  >> rsp;
} while (!rsp.empty() && rsp[0] != 'n');
```

The body of this loop is similar to others we've written and so should be easy to follow. What might be a bit surprising is that we defined rsp before the do rather than defining it inside the loop. Had we defined rsp inside the do, then rsp would go out of scope at the close curly brace before the while. Any variable referenced inside the condition must exist before the do statement itself.

Because the condition is not evaluated until after the statement or block is executed, the do while loop does not allow variable definitions:

```
//  error: declaration statement within do condition is not supported
do {
    //  ...
    mumble(foo);
} while (int foo = get_foo()); //  error: declaration in do condition
```

If we could define variables in the condition, then any use of the variable would happen *before* the variable was defined!

Exercise 6.17: Explain each of the following loops. Correct any problems you detect.

```
(a) do
        int v1, v2;
        cout << "Please enter two numbers to sum:" ;
        cin >> v1 >> v2;
        if (cin)
            cout << "Sum is: "
                << v1 + v2 << endl;
    while (cin);

(b) do {
        // ...
    } while (int ival = get_response());

(c) do {
        int ival = get_response();
        if (ival == some_value())
            break;
    } while (ival);
     if (!ival)
        // ...
```

Exercise 6.18: Write a small program that requests two strings from the user and reports which string is lexicographically less than the other (that is, comes before the other alphabetically). Continue to solicit the user until the user requests to quit. Use the string type, the string less-than operator, and a do while loop.

6.10   The break Statement

A **break statement** terminates the nearest enclosing while, do while, for, or switch statement. Execution resumes at the statement immediately following the terminated statement. For example, the following loop searches a vector for the first occurrence of a particular value. Once it's found, the loop is exited:

```
vector<int>::iterator iter = vec.begin();
while (iter != vec.end()) {
    if (value == *iter)
        break;  // ok: found it!
    else
        ++iter;  // not found: keep looking
} // end of while
if (iter != vec.end()) // break to here ...
    // continue processing
```

In this example, the break terminates the while loop. Execution resumes at the if statement immediately following the while.

A break can appear only within a loop or switch statement or in a statement nested inside a loop or switch. A break may appear within an if only when the if is inside a switch or a loop. A break occurring outside a loop or switch is a compile-time error. When a break occurs inside a nested switch or loop statement, the enclosing loop or switch statement is unaffected by the termination of the inner switch or loop:

```
string inBuf;
while (cin >> inBuf && !inBuf.empty()) {
    switch(inBuf[0]) {
    case '-':
        // process up to the first blank
        for (string::size_type ix = 1;
                    ix != inBuf.size(); ++ix) {
            if (inBuf[ix] == ' ')
                break; // #1, leaves the for loop
            // ...
        }
        // remaining '-' processing: break #1 transfers control here
        break; // #2, leaves the switch statement
    case '+':
        // ...
    } // end switch
    // end of switch: break #2 transfers control here
} // end while
```

The break labeled #1 terminates the for loop within the hyphen case label. It does not terminate the enclosing switch statement and in fact does not even terminate the processing for the current case. Processing continues with the first statement following the for, which might be additional code to handle the hyphen case or the break that completes that section.

The break labeled #2 terminates the switch statement after handling the hyphen case but does not terminate the enclosing while loop. Processing continues after that break by executing the condition in the while, which reads the next string from the standard input.

EXERCISES SECTION 6.10

Exercise 6.19: The first program in this section could be written more succinctly. In fact, its action could be contained entirely in the condition in the while. Rewrite the loop so that it has an empty body and does the work of finding the element in the condition.

Exercise 6.20: Write a program to read a sequence of strings from standard input until either the same word occurs twice in succession or all the words have been read. Use a while loop to read the text one word at a time. Use the break statement to terminate the loop if a word occurs twice in succession. Print the word if it occurs twice in succession, or else print a message saying that no word was repeated.

6.11   The continue Statement

A **continue statement** causes the current iteration of the nearest enclosing loop to terminate. Execution resumes with the evaluation of the condition in the case of a while or do while statement. In a for loop, execution continues by evaluating the *expression* inside the for header.

For example, the following loop reads the standard input one word at a time. Only words that begin with an underscore will be processed. For any other value, we terminate the current iteration and get the next input:

```
string inBuf;
while (cin >> inBuf && !inBuf.empty()) {
        if (inBuf[0] != '_')
                continue; // get another input
        // still here? process string ...
}
```

A continue can appear only inside a for, while, or do while loop, including inside blocks nested inside such loops.

EXERCISES SECTION 6.11

Exercise 6.21:   Revise the program from the last exercise in Section 6.10 (p. 213) so that it looks only for duplicated words that start with an uppercase letter.

6.12   The goto Statement

A **goto statement** provides an unconditional jump from the goto to a labeled statement in the same function.

 Use of gotos has been discouraged since the late 1960s. gotos make it difficult to trace the control flow of a program, making the program hard to understand and hard to modify. Any program that uses a goto can be rewritten so that it doesn't need the goto.

The syntactic form of a goto statement is

```
goto label;
```

where *label* is an identifier that identifies a labeled statement. A **labeled statement** is any statement that is preceded by an identifier followed by a colon:

```
end: return;   // labeled statement, may be target of a goto
```

The identifier that forms the label may be used only as the target of a goto. For this reason, label identifiers may be the same as variable names or other identifiers in the program without interfering with other uses of those identifiers. The goto and the labeled statement to which it transfers control must be in the same function.

A goto may not jump forward over a variable definition:

```
// ...
goto end;
int ix = 10;  // error: goto bypasses declaration statement
end:
    // error: code here could use ix but the goto bypassed its declaration
    ix = 42;
```

If definitions are needed between a goto and its corresponding label, the definitions must be enclosed in a block:

```
// ...
goto end;   // ok: jumps to a point where ix is not defined
{
     int ix = 10;
     // ... code using ix
}
end: // ix no longer visible here
```

A jump backward over an already executed definition is okay. Why? Jumping over an unexecuted definition would mean that a variable could be used even though it was never defined. Jumping back to a point before a variable is defined destroys the variable and constructs it again:

```
// backward jump over declaration statement ok
  begin:
     int sz = get_size();
     if (sz <= 0) {
          goto begin;
     }
```

Note that sz is destroyed when the goto executes and is defined and initialized anew when control jumps back to begin:.

EXERCISES SECTION 6.12

Exercise 6.22: The last example in this section that jumped back to begin could be better written using a loop. Rewrite the code to eliminate the goto.

6.13 try Blocks and Exception Handling

Handling errors and other anomalous behavior in programs can be one of the most difficult parts of designing any system. Long-lived, interactive systems such as communication switches and routers can devote as much as 90 percent of their code to error detection and error handling. With the proliferation of Web-based applications that run indefinitely, attention to error handling is becoming more important to more and more programmers.

Exceptions are run-time anomalies, such as running out of memory or encountering unexpected input. Exceptions exist outside the normal functioning of the program and require immediate handling by the program.

In well-designed systems, exceptions represent a subset of the program's error handling. Exceptions are most useful when the code that detects a problem cannot handle it. In such cases, the part of the program that detects the problem needs a way to transfer control to the part of the program that can handle the problem. The error-detecting part also needs to be able to indicate what kind of problem occurred and may want to provide additional information.

Exceptions support this kind of communication between the error-detecting and error-handling parts of a program. In C++ exception handling involves:

- **throw expressions**, which the error-detecting part uses to indicate that it encountered an error that it cannot handle. We say that a throw **raises** an exceptional condition.

- **try blocks**, which the error-handling part uses to deal with an exception. A try block starts with keyword try and ends with one or more **catch clauses**. Exceptions thrown from code executed inside a try block are usually handled by one of the catch clauses. Because they "handle" the exception, catch clauses are known as **handlers**.

- A set of **exception classes** defined by the library, which are used to pass the information about an error between a throw and an associated catch.

In the remainder of this section we'll introduce these three components of exception handling. We'll have more to say about exceptions in Section 17.1 (p. 688).

6.13.1   A **throw** Expression

An exception is thrown using a throw expression, which consists of the keyword throw followed by an expression. A throw expression is usually followed by a semicolon, making it into an expression statement. The type of the expression determines what kind of exception is thrown.

As a simple example, recall the program on page 24 that added two objects of type Sales_item. That program checked whether the records it read referred to the same book. If not, it printed a message and exited.

```
Sales_item item1, item2;
std::cin >> item1 >> item2;
// first check that item1 and item2 represent the same book
if (item1.same_isbn(item2)) {
    std::cout << item1 + item2 << std::endl;
    return 0;   // indicate success
} else {
    std::cerr << "Data must refer to same ISBN"
              << std::endl;
    return -1;   // indicate failure
}
```

In a less simple program that used `Sales_items`, the part that adds the objects might be separated from the part that manages the interaction with a user. In this case, we might rewrite the test to `throw` an exception instead:

```
//  first check that data is for the same item
if (!item1.same_isbn(item2))
    throw runtime_error("Data must refer to same ISBN");
//  ok, if we're still here the ISBNs are the same
std::cout << item1 + item2 << std::endl;
```

In this code we check whether the ISBNs differ. If so, we discontinue execution and transfer control to a handler that will know how to handle this error.

A `throw` takes an expression. In this case, that expression is an object of type `runtime_error`. The `runtime_error` type is one of the standard library exception types and is defined in the `stdexcept` header. We'll have more to say about these types shortly. We create a `runtime_error` by giving it a `string`, which provides additional information about the kind of problem that occurred.

6.13.2   The `try` Block

The general form of a `try` block is

```
try {
    program-statements
} catch (exception-specifier) {
    handler-statements
} catch (exception-specifier) {
    handler-statements
} // ...
```

A `try` block begins with the keyword `try` followed by a block enclosed in braces. Following the `try` block is a list of one or more catch clauses. A catch clause consists of three parts: the keyword `catch`, the declaration of a single type or single object within parentheses (referred to as an **exception specifier**), and a block, which as usual must be enclosed in curly braces. If the catch clause is selected to handle an exception, the associated block is executed. Once the catch clause finishes, execution continues with the statement immediately following the last catch clause.

The *program-statements* inside the `try` constitute the normal logic of the program. They can contain any C++ statement, including declarations. Like any block, a `try` block introduces a local scope, and variables declared within a `try` block cannot be referred to outside the `try`, including within the catch clauses.

Writing a Handler

In the preceeding example we used a `throw` to avoid adding two `Sales_items` that represented different books. We imagined that the part of the program that added to `Sales_items` was separate from the part that communicated with the user. The part that interacts with the user might contain code something like the following to handle the exception that was thrown:

```
while (cin >> item1 >> item2) {
    try {
        // execute code that will add the two Sales_items
        // if the addition fails, the code throws a runtime_error exception
    } catch (runtime_error err) {
        // remind the user that ISBN must match and prompt for another pair
        cout << err.what()
             << "\nTry Again?  Enter y or n" << endl;
        char c;
        cin >> c;
        if (cin && c == 'n')
            break;          // break out of the while loop
    }
}
```

Following the `try` keyword is a block. That block would invoke the part of the program that processes `Sales_item` objects. That part might `throw` an exception of type `runtime_error`.

This `try` block has a single `catch` clause, which handles exceptions of type `runtime_error`. The statements in the block following the `catch` define the actions that will be executed if code inside the `try` block throws a `runtime_error`. Our `catch` handles the error by printing a message and asking the user to indicate whether to continue. If the user enters an 'n', then we break out of the `while`. Otherwise the loop continues by reading two new `Sales_items`.

The prompt to the user prints the return from `err.what()`. We know that `err` has type `runtime_error`, so we can infer that `what` is a member function (Section 1.5.2, p. 24) of the `runtime_error` class. Each of the library exception classes defines a member function named `what`. This function takes no arguments and returns a C-style character string. In the case of `runtime_error`, the C-style string that `what` returns is a copy of the `string` that was used to initialize the `runtime_error`. If the code described in the previous section threw an exception, then the output printed by this `catch` would be

```
Data must refer to same ISBN
Try Again?  Enter y or n
```

Functions Are Exited during the Search for a Handler

In complex systems the execution path of a program may pass through multiple `try` blocks before encountering code that actually throws an exception. For example, a `try` block might call a function that contains a `try`, that calls another function with its own `try`, and so on.

The search for a handler reverses the call chain. When an exception is thrown, the function that threw the exception is searched first. If no matching `catch` is found, the function terminates, and the function that called the one that threw is searched for a matching `catch`. If no handler is found, then that function also exits and the function that called it is searched; and so on back up the execution path until a catch of an appropriate type is found.

If no catch clause capable of handling the exception exists, program execution is transferred to a library function named **terminate**, which is defined in the exception header. The behavior of that function is system dependent, but it usually aborts the program.

Exceptions that occur in programs that define no try blocks are handled in the same manner: After all, if there are no try blocks, there can be no handlers for any exception that might be thrown. If an exception occurs, then terminate is called and the program (ordinarily) is aborted.

EXERCISES SECTION 6.13.2

Exercise 6.23: The bitset operation to_ulong throws an overflow_error exception if the bitset is larger than the size of an unsigned long. Write a program that generates this exception.

Exercise 6.24: Revise your program to catch this exception and print a message.

6.13.3 Standard Exceptions

The C++ library defines a set of classes that it uses to report problems encountered in the functions in the standard library. These standard exception classes are also intended to be used in the programs we write. Library exception classes are defined in four headers:

1. The exception header defines the most general kind of exception class named exception. It communicates only that an exception occurs but provides no additional information.

2. The stdexcept header defines several general purpose exception classes. These types are listed in Table 6.1 on the following page.

3. The new header defines the bad_alloc exception type, which is the exception thrown by new (Section 5.11, p. 174) if it cannot allocate memory.

4. The type_info header defines the bad_cast exception type, which we will discuss in Section 18.2 (p. 772).

Standard Library Exception Classes

The library exception classes have only a few operations. We can create, copy, and assign objects of any of the exception types. The exception, bad_alloc, and bad_cast types define only a default constructor (Section 2.3.4, p. 50); it is not possible to provide an initializer for objects of these types. The other exception types define only a single constructor that takes a string initializer. When we

Table 6.1: Standard Exception Classes Defined in `<stdexcept>`	
`exception`	The most general kind of problem.
`runtime_error`	Problem that can be detected only at run time.
`range_error`	Run-time error: result generated outside the range of values that are meaningful.
`overflow_error`	Run-time error: computation that overflowed.
`underflow_error`	Run-time error: computation that underflowed.
`logic_error`	Problem that could be detected before run time.
`domain_error`	Logic error: argument for which no result exists.
`invalid_argument`	Logic error: inappropriate argument.
`length_error`	Logic error: attempt to create an object larger than the maximum size for that type.
`out_of_range`	Logic error: used a value outside the valid range.

define any of these other exception types, we must supply a `string` argument. That `string` initializer is used to provide additional information about the error that occurred.

The exception types define only a single operation named `what`. That function takes no arguments and returns a `const char*`. The pointer it returns points to a C-style character string (Section 4.3, p. 130). The purpose of this C-style character string is to provide some sort of textual description of the exception thrown.

The contents of the C-style character array to which `what` returns a pointer depends on the type of the exception object. For the types that take a `string` initializer, the `what` function returns that `string` as a C-style character array. For the other types, the value returned varies by compiler.

6.14   Using the Preprocessor for Debugging

In Section 2.9.2 (p. 71) we learned how to use preprocessor variables to prevent header files being included more than once. C++ programmers sometimes use a technique similar to header guards to conditionally execute debugging code. The idea is that the program will contain debugging code that is executed only while the program is being developed. When the application is completed and ready to ship, the debugging code is turned off. We can write conditional debugging code using the NDEBUG preprocessor variable:

```
int main()
{
#ifndef NDEBUG
cerr << "starting main" << endl;
#endif
//  ...
```

If NDEBUG is not defined, then the program writes the message to cerr. If NDEBUG is defined, then the program executes without ever passing through the code between the #ifndef and the #endif.

By default, NDEBUG is not defined, meaning that by default, the code inside the #ifndef and #endif is processed. When the program is being developed, we leave NDEBUG undefined so that the debugging statements are executed. When the program is built for delivery to customers, these debugging statements can be (effectively) removed by defining the NDEBUG preprocessor variable. Most compilers provide a command line option that defines NDEBUG:

```
$ CC -DNDEBUG main.C
```

has the same effect as writing #define NDEBUG at the beginning of main.C.

The preprocessor defines four other constants that can be useful in debugging:

  _ _FILE_ _ name of the file.

  _ _LINE_ _ current line number.

  _ _TIME_ _ time the file was compiled.

  _ _DATE_ _ date the file was compiled.

We might use these constants to report additional information in error messages:

```
if (word.size() < threshold)
    cerr << "Error: " << __FILE__
         << " : line " << __LINE__ << endl
         << "           Compiled on " << __DATE__
         << " at " << __TIME__ << endl
         << "           Word read was " << word
         << ": Length too short" << endl;
```

If we give this program a string that is shorter than the threshold, then the following error message will be generated:

```
Error: wdebug.cc : line 21
        Compiled on Jan 12 2005 at 19:44:40
        Word read was "foo": Length too short
```

Another common debugging technique uses the NDEBUG preprocessor variable and the assert **preprocessor macro**. The assert macro is defined in the cassert header, which we must include in any file that uses assert.

A preprocessor macro acts something like a function call. The assert macro takes a single expression, which it uses as a condition:

```
assert(expr)
```

As long as NDEBUG is not defined, the assert macro evaluates the condtion and if the result is false, then assert writes a message and terminates the program. If the expression has a nonzero (e.g., true) value, then assert does nothing.

Unlike exceptions, which deal with errors that a program expects might happen in production, programmers use assert to test conditions that "cannot happen."

For example, a program that does some manipulation of input text might know that all words it is given are always longer than a threshold. That program might contain a statement such as:

```
assert(word.size() > threshold);
```

During testing the `assert` has the effect of verifying that the data are always of the expected size. Once development and test are complete, the program is built and `NDEBUG` is defined. In production code, `assert` does nothing, so there is no run-time cost. Of course, there is also no run-time check. `assert` should be used only to verify things that truly should not be possible. It can be useful as an aid in getting a program debugged but should not be used to substitute for run-time logic checks or error checking that the program should be doing.

EXERCISES SECTION 6.14

Exercise 6.25: Revise the program you wrote for the exercise in Section 6.11 (p. 214) to conditionally print information about its execution. For example, you might print each word as it is read to let you determine whether the loop correctly finds the first duplicated word that begins with an uppercase letter. Compile and run the program with debugging turned on and again with it turned off.

Exercise 6.26: What happens in the following loop:

```
string s;
while (cin >> s) {
    assert(cin);
    // process s
}
```

Explain whether this usage seems like a good application of the `assert` macro.

Exercise 6.27: Explain this loop:

```
string s;
while (cin >> s && s != sought) { }    // empty body
assert(cin);
// process s
```

CHAPTER SUMMARY

C++ provides a fairly limited number of statements. Most of these affect the flow of control within a program:

while, for, and do while statements, which implement iterative loops

if and switch, which provide conditional execution

continue, which stops the current iteration of a loop

break, which exits a loop or switch statement

goto, which transfers control to a labeled statement

try, catch, which define a try block enclosing a sequence of statements that might throw an exception. The catch clause(s) are intended to handle the exception(s) that the enclosed code might throw.

throw expressions, which exit a block of code, transferring control to an associated catch clause

There is also a return statement, which will be covered in Chapter 7.

In addition, there are expression statements and declaration statements. An expression statement causes the subject expression to be evaluated. Declarations and definitions of variables were described in Chapter 2.

DEFINED TERMS

assert Preprocessor macro that takes a single expression, which it uses as a condition. If the preprocessor variable NDEBUG is not defined, then assert evaluates the condition. If the condition is false, assert writes a message and terminates the program.

block A sequence of statements enclosed in curly braces. A block is a statement, so it can appear anywhere a statement is expected.

break statement Terminates the nearest enclosing loop or switch statement. Execution transfers to the first statement following the terminated loop or switch.

case label Integral constant value that follows the keyword case in a switch statement. No two case labels in the same switch statement may have the same value. If the value in the switch condition is equal to that in one of the case labels,

control transfers to the first statement following the matched label. Execution continues from that point until a break is encountered or it flows off the end of the switch statement.

catch clause The catch keyword, an exception specifier in parentheses, and a block of statements. The code inside a catch clause does whatever is necessary to handle an exception of the type defined in its exception specifier.

compound statement Synonym for block.

continue statement Terminates the current iteration of the nearest enclosing loop. Execution transfers to the loop condition in a while or do or to the expression in the for header.

dangling else Colloquial term used to refer to the problem of how to process nested if statements in which there are more ifs than elses. In C++, an else is always paired with the closest preceding unmatched if. Note that curly braces can be used to effectively hide an inner if so that the programmer can control with which if a given else should be matched.

declaration statement A statement that defines or declares a variable. Declarations were covered in Chapter 2.

default label The switch case label that matches any otherwise unmatched value computed in the switch condition.

exception classes Set of classes defined by the standard library to be used to represent errors. Table 6.1 (p. 220) lists the general purpose exceptions.

exception handler Code that deals with an exception raised in another part of the program. Synonym for catch clause.

exception specifier The declaration of an object or a type that indicates the kind of exceptions a catch clause can handle.

expression statement An expression followed by a semicolon. An expression statement causes the expression to be evaluated.

flow of control Execution path through a program.

goto statement Statement that causes an unconditional transfer of control to a specified labeled statement elsewhere in the program. gotos obfuscate the flow of control within a program and should be avoided.

if else statement Conditional execution of code following the if or the else, depending on the truth value of the condition.

if statement Conditional execution based on the value of the specified condition. If the condition is true, then the if body is executed. If not, control flows to the statement following the if.

labeled statement A statement preceded by a label. A label is an identifier followed by a colon.

null statement An empty statement. Indicated by a single semicolon.

preprocessor macro Function like facility defined by the preprocessor. assert is a macro. Modern C++ programs make very little use of the preprocessor macros.

raise Often used as a synonym for throw. C++ programmers speak of "throwing" or "raising" an exception interchangably.

switch statement A conditional execution statement that starts by evaluating the expression that follows the switch keyword. Control passes to the labeled statement with a case label that matches the value of the expression. If there is no matching label, execution either branches to the default label, if there is one, or falls out of the switch if there is no default label.

terminate Library function that is called if an exception is not caught. Usually aborts the program.

throw expression Expression that interrupts the current execution path. Each throw throws an object and transfers control to the nearest enclosing catch clause that can handle the type of exception that is thrown.

try block A block enclosed by the keyword try and one or more catch clauses. If the code inside the try block raises an exception and one of the catch clauses matches the type of the exception, then the exception is handled by that catch. Otherwise, the exception is handled by an enclosing try block or the program terminates.

while loop Control statement that executes its target statement as long as a specified condition is true. The statement is executed zero or more times, depending on the truth value of the condition.

C H A P T E R   **7**

F U N C T I O N S

CONTENTS

This chapter describes how to define and declare *functions*. We'll cover how arguments are passed to and values are returned from a function. We'll then look at three special kinds of functions: inline functions, class member functions, and overloaded functions. The chapter closes with a more advanced topic: function pointers.

A function can be thought of as a programmer-defined operation. Like the built-in operators, each function performs some computation and (usually) yields a result. Unlike the operators, functions have names and may take an unlimited number of operands. Like operators, functions can be overloaded, meaning that the same name may refer to multiple different functions.

7.1 Defining a Function

A function is uniquely represented by a name and a set of operand types. Its operands, referred to as *parameters*, are specified in a comma-separated list enclosed in parentheses. The actions that the function performs are specified in a block, referred to as the *function body*. Every function has an associated *return type*.

As an example, we could write the following function to find the greatest common divisor of two `int`s:

```
//  return the greatest common divisor
int gcd(int v1, int v2)
{
    while (v2) {
        int temp = v2;
        v2 = v1 % v2;
        v1 = temp;
    }
    return v1;
}
```

Here we define a function named `gcd` that returns an `int` and has two `int` parameters. To call `gcd`, we must supply two `int` values and we get an `int` in return.

Calling a Function

To invoke a function we use the **call operator**, which is a pair of parentheses. As with any operator, the call operator takes operands and yields a result. The operands to the call operator are the name of the function and a (possibly empty) comma-separated list of *arguments*. The result type of a call is the return type of the called function, and the result itself is the value returned by the function:

```
//  get values from standard input
cout << "Enter two values: \n";
int i, j;
cin >> i >> j;
//  call gcd on arguments i and j
//  and print their greatest common divisor
cout << "gcd: " << gcd(i, j) << endl;
```

If we gave this program 15 and 123 as input, the output would be 3.

Calling a function does two things: It initializes the function parameters from the corresponding arguments and transfers control to the function being invoked. Execution of the *calling* function is suspended and execution of the *called* function begins. Execution of a function begins with the (implicit) definition and initialization of its parameters. That is, when we invoke `gcd`, the first thing that happens is that variables of type `int` named `v1` and `v2` are created. These variables are initialized with the values passed in the call to `gcd`. In this case, `v1` is initialized by the value of `i` and `v2` by the value of `j`.

Function Body Is a Scope

The body of a function is a statement block, which defines the function's operation. As usual, the block is enclosed by a pair of curly braces and hence forms a new scope. As with any block, the body of a function can define variables. Names defined inside a function body are accessible only within the function itself. Such variables are referred to as **local variables**. They are "local" to that function; their names are visible only in the scope of the function. They exist only while the function is executing. Section 7.5 (p. 254) covers local variables in more detail.

Execution completes when a `return` statement is encountered. When the called function finishes, it yields as its result the value specified in the `return` statement. After the return is executed, the suspended, calling function resumes execution at the point of the call. It uses the return value as the result of evaluating the call operator and continues processing whatever remains of the statement in which the call was performed.

Parameters and Arguments

Like local variables, the parameters of a function provide named, local storage for use by the function. The difference is that parameters are defined inside the function's parameter list and are initialized by arguments passed to the function when the function is called.

An argument is an expression. It might be a variable, a literal constant or an expression involving one or more operators. We must pass exactly the same number of arguments as the function has parameters. The type of each argument must match the corresponding parameter in the same way that the type of an initializer must match the type of the object it initializes: The argument must have the same type or have a type that can be implicitly converted (Section 5.12, p. 178) to the parameter type. We'll cover how arguments match a parameter in detail in Section 7.8.2 (p. 269).

7.1.1 Function Return Type

The return type of a function can be a built-in type, such as `int` or `double`, a class type, or a compound type, such as `int&` or `string*`. A return type also can be `void`, which means that the function does not return a value. The following are example definitions of possible function return types:

```
bool is_present(int *, int);      // returns bool
int count(const string &, char);  // returns int
Date &calendar(const char*);      // returns reference to Date
void process();                    // process does not return a value
```

A function may not return another function or a built-in array type. Instead, the function may return a pointer to the function or to a pointer to an element in the array:

```
//  ok: pointer to first element of the array
int *foo_bar() { /* ... */ }
```

This function returns a pointer to `int` and that pointer could point to an element in an array.

We'll learn about function pointers in Section 7.9 (p. 276).

Functions Must Specify a Return Type

It is illegal to define or declare a function without an explicit return type:

```
//  error: missing return type
test(double v1, double v2) { /* ... */ }
```

Eariler versions of C++ would accept this program and implicitly define the return type of `test` as an `int`. Under Standard C++, this program is an error.

 In pre-Standard C++, a function without an explicit return type was assumed to return an `int`. C++ programs compiled under earlier, non-standard compilers may still contain functions that implicitly return `int`.

7.1.2   Function Parameter List

The parameter list of a function can be empty but cannot be omitted. A function with no parameters can be written either with an empty parameter list or a parameter list containing the single keyword `void`. For example, the following declarations of `process` are equivalent:

```
void process() { /* ... */ }      // implicit void parameter list

void process(void){ /* ... */ } // equivalent declaration
```

A parameter list consists of a comma-separated list of parameter types and (optional) parameter names. Even when the types of two parameters are the same, the type must be repeated:

```
int manip(int v1, v2) { /* ... */ }      // error
int manip(int v1, int v2) { /* ... */ } // ok
```

No two parameters can have the same name. Similarly, a variable local to a function may not use the same name as the name of any of the function's parameters.

Names are optional, but in a function definition, normally all parameters are named. A parameter must be named to be used.

Parameter Type-Checking

 C++ is a statically typed language (Section 2.3, p. 44). The arguments of every call are checked during compilation.

When we call a function, the type of each argument must be either the same type as the corresponding parameter or a type that can be converted (Section 5.12, p. 178) to that type. The function's parameter list provides the compiler with the type information needed to check the arguments. For example, the function gcd, which we defined on page 226, takes two parameters of type int:

```
gcd("hello", "world");   // error: wrong argument types
gcd(24312);              // error: too few arguments
gcd(42, 10, 0);          // error: too many arguments
```

Each of these calls is a compile-time error. In the first call, the arguments are of type const char*. There is no conversion from const char* to int, so the call is illegal. In the second and third calls, gcd is passed the wrong number of arguments. The function must be called with two arguments; it is an error to call it with any other number.

But what happens if the call supplies two arguments of type double? Is this call legal?

```
gcd(3.14, 6.29);          // ok: arguments are converted to int
```

In C++, the answer is yes; the call is legal. In Section 5.12.1 (p. 179) we saw that a value of type double can be converted to a value of type int. This call involves such a conversion—we want to use double values to initialize int objects. Therefore, flagging the call as an error would be too severe. Rather, the arguments are implicitly converted to int (through truncation). Because this conversion might lose precision, most compilers will issue a warning. In this case, the call becomes

```
gcd(3, 6);
```

and returns a value of 3.

A call that passes too many arguments, omits an argument, or passes an argument of the wrong type almost certainly would result in serious run-time errors. Catching these so-called interface errors at compile time greatly reduces the compile-debug-test cycle for large programs.

7.2 Argument Passing

Each parameter is created anew on each call to the function. The value used to initialize a parameter is the corresponding argument passed in the call.

 Parameters are initialized the same way that variables are. If the parameter has a nonreference type, then the argument is copied. If the parameter is a reference (Section 2.5, p. 58), then the parameter is just another name for the argument.

Exercise 7.1: What is the difference between a parameter and an argument?

Exercise 7.2: Indicate which of the following functions are in error and why. Suggest how you might correct the problems.

```
(a) int f() {
        string s;
        // ...
        return s;
    }
(b) f2(int i) { /* ... */ }
(c) int calc(int v1, int v1) /* ... */ }
(d) double square(double x) return x * x;
```

Exercise 7.3: Write a program to take two `int` parameters and generate the result of raising the first parameter to the power of the second. Write a program to call your function passing it two `int`s. Verify the result.

Exercise 7.4: Write a program to return the absolute value of its parameter.

7.2.1 Nonreference Parameters

Parameters that are plain, nonreference types are initialized by copying the corresponding argument. When a parameter is initialized with a copy, the function has no access to the actual arguments of the call. It cannot change the arguments. Let's look again at the definition of `gcd`:

```
//  return the greatest common divisor
int gcd(int v1, int v2)
{
    while (v2) {
        int temp = v2;
        v2 = v1 % v2;
        v1 = temp;
    }
    return v1;
}
```

Inside the body of the `while`, we change the values of both `v1` and `v2`. However, these changes are made to the local parameters and are not reflected in the arguments used to call `gcd`. Thus, when we call

```
gcd(i, j)
```

the values `i` and `j` are unaffected by the assignments performed inside `gcd`.

 Nonreference parameters represent local *copies* of the corresponding argument. Changes made to the parameter are made to the local copy. Once the function terminates, these local values are gone.

Pointer Parameters

A parameter can be a pointer (Section 4.2, p. 114), in which case the argument pointer is copied. As with any nonreference type parameter, changes made to the parameter are made to the local copy. If the function assigns a new pointer value to the parameter, the calling pointer value is unchanged.

Recalling the discussion in Section 4.2.3 (p. 121), the fact that the pointer is copied affects only assignments to the pointer. If the function takes a pointer to a nonconst type, then the function can assign through the pointer and change the value of the object to which the pointer points:

```
void reset(int *ip)
{
    *ip = 0;   // changes the value of the object to which ip points
    ip = 0;    // changes only the local value of ip; the argument is unchanged
}
```

After a call to `reset`, the argument is unchanged but the object to which the argument points will be 0:

```
int i = 42;
int *p = &i;
cout << "i: " << *p << '\n';   // prints i: 42
reset(p);                      // changes *p but not p
cout << "i: " << *p << endl;   // ok: prints i: 0
```

If we want to prevent changes to the value to which the pointer points, then the parameter should be defined as a pointer to `const`:

```
void use_ptr(const int *p)
{
    // use_ptr may read but not write to *p
}
```

Whether a pointer parameter points to a `const` or nonconst type affects the arguments that we can use to call the function. We can call `use_ptr` on either an `int*` or a `const int*`; we can pass only on an `int*` to `reset`. This distinction follows from the initialization rules for pointers (Section 4.2.5, p. 126). We may initialize a pointer to `const` to point to a nonconst object but may not use a pointer to nonconst to point to a `const` object.

const Parameters

We can call a function that takes a nonreference, nonconst parameter passing either a `const` or nonconst argument. For example, we could pass two `const` ints to our `gcd` function:

```
const int i = 3, j = 6;
int k = rgcd(3, 6);   // ok: k initialized to 3
```

This behavior follows from the normal initialization rules for `const` objects (Section 2.4, p. 56). Because the initialization copies the value of the initializer, we can initialize a nonconst object from a `const` object, or vice versa.

If we make the parameter a `const` nonreference type:

```
void fcn(const int i) { /* fcn can read but not write to i */ }
```

then the function cannot change its local copy of the argument. The argument is still passed as a copy so we can pass `fcn` either a `const` or nonconst object.

What may be surprising, is that although the parameter is a `const` inside the function, the compiler otherwise treats the definition of `fcn` as if we had defined the parameter as a plain `int`:

```
void fcn(const int i) { /* fcn can read but not write to i */ }
void fcn(int i) { /* ... */ }   // error: redefines fcn(int)
```

This usage exists to support compatibility with the C language, which makes no distinction between functions taking `const` or nonconst parameters.

Limitations of Copying Arguments

Copying an argument is not suitable for every situation. Cases where copying doesn't work include:

- When we want the function to be able to change the value of an argument.

- When we want to pass a large object as an argument. The time and space costs to copy the object are often too high for real-world applications.

- When there is no way to copy the object.

In these cases we can instead define the parameters as references or pointers.

EXERCISES SECTION 7.2.1

Exercise 7.5: Write a function that takes an `int` and a pointer to an `int` and returns the larger of the `int` value of the value to which the pointer points. What type should you use for the pointer?

Exercise 7.6: Write a function to swap the values pointed to by two pointers to `int`. Test the function by calling it and printing the swapped values.

7.2.2 Reference Parameters

As an example of a situation where copying the argument doesn't work, consider a function to swap the values of its two arguments:

```
// incorrect version of swap: The arguments are not changed!
void swap(int v1, int v2)
{
    int tmp = v2;
    v2 = v1;      // assigns new value to local copy of the argument
    v1 = tmp;
}                 // local objects v1 and v2 no longer exist
```

In this case, we want to change the arguments themselves. As defined, though, swap cannot affect those arguments. When it executes, swap exchanges the *local copies* of its arguments. The arguments passed to swap are unchanged:

```
int main()
{
    int i = 10;
    int j = 20;
    cout << "Before swap():\ti: "
         << i << "\tj: " << j << endl;
    swap(i, j);
    cout << "After  swap():\ti: "
         << i << "\tj: " << j << endl;
    return 0;
}
```

Compiling and executing this program results in the following output:

```
Before swap(): i: 10 j: 20
After  swap(): i: 10 j: 20
```

For swap to work as intended and swap the values of its arguments, we need to make the parameters references:

```
//  ok: swap acts on references to its arguments
void swap(int &v1, int &v2)
{
    int tmp = v2;
    v2 = v1;
    v1 = tmp;
}
```

Like all references, reference parameters refer directly to the objects to which they are bound rather than to copies of those objects. When we define a reference, we must initialize it with the object to which the reference will be bound. Reference parameters work exactly the same way. Each time the function is called, the reference parameter is created and bound to its corresponding argument. Now, when we call swap

```
swap(i, j);
```

the parameter v1 is just another name for the object i and v2 is another name for j. Any change to v1 is actually a change to the argument i. Similarly, changes to v2 are actually made to j. If we recompile main using this revised version of swap, we can see that the output is now correct:

```
Before swap(): i: 10 j: 20
After  swap(): i: 20 j: 10
```

Programmers who come to C++ from a C background are used to passing pointers to obtain access to the argument. In C++ it is safer and more natural to use reference parameters.

Using Reference Parameters to Return Additional Information

We've seen one example, swap, in which reference parameters were used to allow the function to change the value of its arguments. Another use of reference parameters is to return an additional result to the calling function.

Functions can return only a single value, but sometimes a function has more than one thing to return. For example, let's define a function named find_val that searches for a particular value in the elements of a vector of integers. It returns an iterator that refers to the element, if the element was found, or to the end value if the element isn't found. We'd also like the function to return an occurrence count if the value occurs more than once. In this case the iterator returned should be to the first element that has the value for which we're looking.

How can we define a function that returns both an iterator and an occurrence count? We could define a new type that contains an iterator and a count. An easier solution is to pass an additional reference argument that find_val can use to return a count of the number of occurrences:

```
//  returns an iterator that refers to the first occurrence of value
//  the reference parameter occurs contains a second return value
vector<int>::const_iterator find_val(
    vector<int>::const_iterator beg,     //  first element
    vector<int>::const_iterator end,     //  one past last element
    int value,                           //  the value we want
    vector<int>::size_type &occurs)      //  number of times it occurs
{
    //  res_iter will hold first occurrence, if any
    vector<int>::const_iterator res_iter = end;
    occurs = 0;   //  set occurrence count parameter
    for ( ; beg != end; ++beg)
        if (*beg == value) {
            //  remember first occurrence of value
            if (res_iter == end)
                res_iter = beg;
            ++occurs;   //  increment occurrence count
        }
    return res_iter;   //  count returned implicitly in occurs
}
```

When we call find_val, we have to pass four arguments: a pair of iterators that denote the range of elements (Section 9.2.1, p. 314) in the vector in which to look, the value to look for, and a size_type (Section 3.2.3, p. 84) object to hold the occurrence count. Assuming ivec is a vector<int>, it is an iterator of the right type, and ctr is a size_type, we could call find_val as follows:

```
it = find_val(ivec.begin(), ivec.end(), 42, ctr);
```

After the call, the value of ctr will be the number of times 42 occurs, and it will refer to the first occurrence if there is one. Otherwise, it will be equal to ivec.end() and ctr will be zero.

Using (`const`) References to Avoid Copies

The other circumstance in which reference parameters are useful is when passing a large object to a function. Although copying an argument is okay for objects of built-in data types and for objects of class types that are small in size, it is (often) too inefficient for objects of most class types or large arrays. Moreover, as we'll learn in Chapter 13, some class types cannot be copied. By using a reference parameter, the function can access the object directly without copying it.

As an example, we'll write a function that compares the length of two `string`s. Such a function needs to access the `size` of each `string` but has no need to write to the `string`s. Because `string`s can be long, we'd like to avoid copying them. Using `const` references we can avoid the copy:

```
//  compare the length of two strings
bool isShorter(const string &s1, const string &s2)
{
    return s1.size() < s2.size();
}
```

Each parameter is a reference to `const string`. Because the parameters are references the arguments are not copied. Because the parameters are `const` references, `isShorter` may not use the references to change the arguments.

> When the only reason to make a parameter a reference is to avoid copying the argument, the parameter should be `const` reference.

References to `const` Are More Flexible

It should be obvious that a function that takes a plain, nonconst reference may not be called on behalf of a `const` object. After all, the function might change the object it is passed and thus violate the `const`ness of the argument.

What may be less obvious is that we also cannot call such a function with an rvalue (Section 2.3.1, p. 45) or with an object of a type that requires a conversion:

```
//  function takes a non-const reference parameter
int incr(int &val)
{
    return ++val;
}
int main()
{
    short v1 = 0;
    const int v2 = 42;
    int v3 = incr(v1);    //  error: v1 is not an int
    v3 = incr(v2);        //  error: v2 is const
    v3 = incr(0);         //  error: literals are not lvalues
    v3 = incr(v1 + v2);   //  error: addition doesn't yield an lvalue
    int v4 = incr(v3);    //  ok: v3 is a nonconst object type int
}
```

The problem is that a nonconst reference (Section 2.5, p. 59) may be bound only to nonconst object of exactly the same type.

Parameters that do not change the value of the corresponding argument should be const references. Defining such parameters as nonconst references needlessly restricts the usefulness of a function. As an example, we might write a program to find a given character in a string:

```
//  returns index of first occurrence of c in s or s.size() if c isn't in s
//  Note: s doesn't change, so it should be a reference to const
string::size_type find_char(string &s, char c)
{
    string::size_type i = 0;
    while (i != s.size() && s[i] != c)
        ++i;                        //  not found, look at next character
    return i;
}
```

This function takes its string argument as a plain (nonconst) reference, even though it doesn't modify that parameter. One problem with this definition is that we cannot call it on a character string literal:

```
if (find_char("Hello World", 'o')) // ...
```

This call fails at compile time, even though we can convert the literal to a string.

Such problems can be surprisingly pervasive. Even if our program has no const objects and we only call find_char on behalf of string objects (as opposed to on a string literal or an expression that yields a string), we can encounter compile-time problems. For example, we might have another function is_sentence that wants to use find_char to determine whether a string represents a sentence:

```
bool is_sentence(const string &s)
{
    //  if there's a period and it's the last character in s
    //  then s is a sentence
    return (find_char(s, '.') == s.size() - 1);
}
```

As written, the call to find_char from inside is_sentence is a compile-time error. The parameter to is_sentence is a reference to const string and cannot be passed to find_char, which expects a reference to a nonconst string.

Best Practices
Reference parameters that are not changed should be references to const. Plain, nonconst reference parameters are less flexible. Such parameters may not be initialized by const objects, or by arguments that are literals or expressions that yield rvalues.

Passing a Reference to a Pointer

Suppose we want to write a function that swaps two pointers, similar to the program we wrote earlier that swaps two integers. We know that we use * to define a pointer and `&` to define a reference. The question here is how to combine these operators to obtain a reference to a pointer. Here is an example:

```
// swap values of two pointers to int
void ptrswap(int *&v1, int *&v2)
{
    int *tmp = v2;
    v2 = v1;
    v1 = tmp;
}
```

The parameter

```
int *&v1
```

should be read from right to left: `v1` is a reference to a pointer to an object of type `int`. That is, `v1` is just another name for whatever pointer is passed to `ptrswap`.

We could rewrite the `main` function from page 233 to use `ptrswap` and swap pointers to the values 10 and 20:

```
int main()
{
    int i = 10;
    int j = 20;
    int *pi = &i;   // pi points to i
    int *pj = &j;   // pj points to j
    cout << "Before ptrswap():\t*pi: "
         << *pi << "\t*pj: " << *pj << endl;
    ptrswap(pi, pj); // now pi points to j; pj points to i
    cout << "After ptrswap():\t*pi: "
         << *pi << "\t*pj: " << *pj << endl;
    return 0;
}
```

When compiled and executed, the program generates the following output:

```
Before ptrswap():    *pi: 10    *pj: 20
After ptrswap():     *pi: 20    *pj: 10
```

What happens is that the *pointer* values are swapped. When we call `ptrswap`, `pi` points to `i` and `pj` points to `j`. Inside `ptrswap` the pointers are swapped so that after `ptrswap`, `pi` points to the object `pj` had addressed. In other words, `pi` now points to `j`. Similarly, `pj` points to `i`.

7.2.3   `vector` and Other Container Parameters

Best Practices

Ordinarily, functions should not have `vector` or other library container parameters. Calling a function that has a plain, nonreference `vector` parameter will copy every element of the `vector`.

In order to avoid copying the `vector`, we might think that we'd make the parameter a reference. However, for reasons that will be clearer after reading Chapter 11,

EXERCISES SECTION 7.2.2

Exercise 7.7: Explain the difference in the following two parameter declarations:

```
void f(T);
void f(T&);
```

Exercise 7.8: Give an example of when a parameter should be a reference type. Give an example of when a parameter should not be a reference.

Exercise 7.9: Change the declaration of occurs in the parameter list of find_val (defined on page 234) to be a nonreference argument type and rerun the program. How does the behavior of the program change?

Exercise 7.10: The following program, although legal, is less useful than it might be. Identify and correct the limitation on this program:

```
bool test(string& s) { return s.empty(); }
```

Exercise 7.11: When should reference parameters be const? What problems might arise if we make a parameter a plain reference when it could be a const reference?

in practice, C++ programmers tend to pass containers by passing iterators to the elements we want to process:

```
//  pass iterators to the first and one past the last element to print
void print(vector<int>::const_iterator beg,
           vector<int>::const_iterator end)
{
    while (beg != end) {
        cout << *beg++;
        if (beg != end) cout << " ";   //  no space after last element
    }
    cout << endl;
}
```

This function prints the elements starting with one referred to by beg up to but not including the one referred to by end. We print a space after each element but the last.

7.2.4 Array Parameters

Arrays have two special properties that affect how we define and use functions that operate on arrays: We cannot copy an array (Section 4.1.1, p. 112) and when we use the name of an array it is automatically converted to a pointer to the first element (Section 4.2.4, p. 122). Because we cannot copy an array, we cannot write a function that takes an array type parameter. Because arrays are automatically converted to pointers, functions that deal with arrays usually do so indirectly by manipulating pointers to elements in the array.

Defining an Array Parameter

Let's assume that we want to write a function that will print the contents of an array of ints. We could specify the array parameter in one of three ways:

```
//  three equivalent definitions of printValues
void printValues(int*) { /* ... */ }
void printValues(int[]) { /* ... */ }
void printValues(int[10]) { /* ... */ }
```

Even though we cannot pass an array directly, we can write a function parameter that looks like an array. Despite appearances, a parameter that uses array syntax is treated as if we had written a pointer to the array element type. These three definitions are equivalent; each is interpreted as taking a parameter of type int*.

It is usually a good idea to define array parameters as pointers, rather than using the array syntax. Doing so makes it clear that what is being operated on is a pointer to an array element, not the array itself. Because an array dimension is ignored, including a dimension in a parameter definition is particularly misleading.

Parameter Dimensions Can Be Misleading

The compiler ignores any dimension we might specify for an array parameter. Relying, incorrectly, on the dimension, we might write printValues as

```
//  parameter treated as const int *, size of array is ignored
void printValues(const int ia[10])
{
    //  this code assumes array has 10 elements;
    //  disaster if argument has fewer than 10 elements!
    for (size_t i = 0; i != 10; ++i)
    {
        cout << ia[i] << endl;
    }
}
```

Although this code *assumes* that the array it is passed has at least 10 elements, nothing in the language enforces that assumption. The following calls are all legal:

```
int main()
{
    int i = 0, j[2] = {0, 1};
    printValues(&i);  //  ok: &i is int*; probable run-time error
    printValues(j);   //  ok: j is converted to pointer to 0th
                      //      element; argument has type int*;
                      //      probable run-time error
    return 0;
}
```

Even though the compiler issues no complaints, both calls are in error, and probably will fail at run time. In each case, memory beyond the array will be accessed because `printValues` assumes that the array it is passed has at least 10 elements. Depending on the values that happen to be in that memory, the program will either produce spurious output or crash.

When the compiler checks an argument to an array parameter, it checks only that the argument is a pointer and that the types of the pointer and the array elements match. The size of the array is not checked.

Array Arguments

As with any other type, we can define an array parameter as a reference or non-reference type. Most commonly, arrays are passed as plain, nonreference types, which are quietly converted to pointers. As usual, a nonreference type parameter is initialized as a copy of its corresponding argument. When we pass an array, the argument is a pointer to the first element in the array. That pointer value is copied; the array elements themselves are not copied. The function operates on a copy of the pointer, so it cannot change the value of the argument pointer. The function can, however, use that pointer to change the element values to which the pointer points. Any changes through the pointer parameter are made to the array elements themselves.

Functions that do not change the elements of their array parameter should make the parameter a pointer to const:

```
// f won't change the elements in the array
void f(const int*) { /* ... */ }
```

Passing an Array by Reference

As with any type, we can define an array parameter as a reference to the array. If the parameter is a reference to the array, then the compiler does not convert an array argument into a pointer. Instead, a reference to the array itself is passed. In this case, the array size is part of the parameter and argument types. The compiler will check that the size of the array argument matches the size of the parameter:

```
// ok: parameter is a reference to an array; size of array is fixed
void printValues(int (&arr)[10]) { /* ... */ }
int main()
{
    int i = 0, j[2] = {0, 1};
    int k[10] = {0,1,2,3,4,5,6,7,8,9};
    printValues(&i);    // error: argument is not an array of 10 ints
    printValues(j);     // error: argument is not an array of 10 ints
    printValues(k);     // ok: argument is an array of 10 ints
    return 0;
}
```

This version of `printValues` may be called only for arrays of exactly 10 ints, limiting which arrays can be passed. However, because the parameter is a reference, it is safe to rely on the size in the body of the function:

```
//  ok: parameter is a reference to an array; size of array is fixed
void printValues(int (&arr)[10])
{
    for (size_t i = 0; i != 10; ++i) {
        cout << arr[i] << endl;
    }
}
```

> The parentheses around &arr are necessary because of the higher
> precedence of the subscript operator:
>
> ```
> f(int &arr[10])     // error: arr is an array of references
> f(int (&arr)[10])   // ok: arr is a reference to an array of 10 ints
> ```

We'll see in Section 16.1.5 (p. 632) how we might write this function in a way that would allow us to pass a reference parameter to an array of any size.

Passing a Multidimensioned Array

Recall that there are no multidimensioned arrays in C++ (Section 4.4, p. 141). Instead, what appears to be a multidimensioned array is an array of arrays.

As with any array, a multidimensioned array is passed as a pointer to its zeroth element. An element in a multidimenioned array is an array. The size of the second (and any subsequent dimensions) is part of the element type and must be specified:

```
//  first parameter is an array whose elements are arrays of 10 ints
void printValues(int (matrix*)[10], int rowSize);
```

declares matrix as a pointer to an array of ten ints.

> Again, the parentheses around *matrix are necessary:
>
> ```
> int *matrix[10];      // array of 10 pointers
> int (*matrix)[10];    // pointer to an array of 10 ints
> ```

We could also declare a multidimensioned array using array syntax. As with a single-dimensioned array, the compiler ignores the first dimension and so it is best not to include it:

```
//  first parameter is an array whose elements are arrays of 10 ints
void printValues(int matrix[][10], int rowSize);
```

declares matrix to be what looks like a two-dimensional array. In fact, the parameter is a pointer to an element in an array of arrays. Each element in the array is itself an array of ten ints.

7.2.5 Managing Arrays Passed to Functions

As we've just seen, type checking for a nonreference array parameter confirms only that the argument is a pointer of the same type as the elements in the array.

Type checking does not verify that the argument actually points to an array of a specified size.

It is up to any program dealing with an array to ensure that the program stays within the bounds of the array.

There are three common programming techniques to ensure that a function stays within the bounds of its array argument(s). The first places a marker in the array itself that can be used to detect the end of the array. C-style character strings are an example of this approach. C-style strings are arrays of characters that encode their termination point with a null character. Programs that deal with C-style strings use this marker to stop processing elements in the array.

Using the Standard Library Conventions

A second approach is to pass pointers to the first and one past the last element in the array. This style of programming is inspired by techniques used in the standard library. We'll learn more about this style of programming in Part II.

Using this approach, we could rewrite `printValues` and call the new version as follows:

```
void printValues(const int *beg, const int *end)
{
    while (beg != end) {
        cout << *beg++ << endl;
    }
}
int main()
{
    int j[2] = {0, 1};
    // ok: j is converted to pointer to 0th element in j
    //     j + 2 refers one past the end of j
    printValues(j, j + 2);
    return 0;
}
```

The loop inside `printValues` looks like other programs we've written that used `vector` iterators. We march the `beg` pointer one element at a time through the array. We stop the loop when `beg` is equal to the end marker, which was passed as the second parameter to the function.

When we call this version, we pass two pointers: one to the first element we want to print and one just past the last element. The program is safe, as long as we correctly calculate the pointers so that they denote a range of elements.

Explicitly Passing a Size Parameter

A third approach, which is common in C programs and pre-Standard C++ programs, is to define a second parameter that indicates the size of the array.

Using this approach, we could rewrite `printValues` one more time. The new version and a call to it looks like:

```
//  const int ia[] is equivalent to const int* ia
//  size is passed explicitly and used to control access to elements of ia
void printValues(const int ia[], size_t size)
{
    for (size_t i = 0; i != size; ++i) {
        cout << ia[i] << endl;
    }
}
int main()
{
    int j[] = { 0, 1 };  //  int array of size 2
    printValues(j, sizeof(j)/sizeof(*j));
    return 0;
}
```

This version uses the `size` parameter to determine how many elements there are to print. When we call `printValues`, we must pass an additional parameter. The program executes safely as long as the size passed is no greater than the actual size of the array.

EXERCISES SECTION 7.2.5

Exercise 7.12: When would you use a parameter that is a pointer? When would you use a parameter that is a reference? Explain the advantages and disadvantages of each.

Exercise 7.13: Write a program to calculate the sum of the elements in an array. Write the function three times, each one using a different approach to managing the array bounds.

Exercise 7.14: Write a program to sum the elements in a `vector<double>`.

7.2.6 `main`: Handling Command-Line Options

It turns out that `main` is a good example of how C programs pass arrays to functions. Up to now, we have defined `main` with an empty parameter list:

```
int main() { ... }
```

However, we often need to pass arguments to `main`. Traditionally, such arguments are options that determine the operation of the program. For example, assuming our `main` program was in an executable file named `prog`, we might pass options to the program as follows:

```
prog -d -o ofile data0
```

The way this usage is handled is that `main` actually defines two parameters:

```
int main(int argc, char *argv[]) { ... }
```

The second parameter, `argv`, is an array of C-style character strings. The first parameter, `argc`, passes the number of strings in that array. Because the second parameter is an array, we might alternatively define `main` as

```
int main(int argc, char **argv) { ... }
```

indicating that `argv` points to a `char*`.

When arguments are passed to `main`, the first string in `argv`, if any, is always the name of the program. Subsequent elements pass additional optional strings to `main`. Given the previous command line, `argc` would be set to 5, and `argv` would hold the following C-style character strings:

```
argv[0] = "prog";
argv[1] = "-d";
argv[2] = "-o";
argv[3] = "ofile";
argv[4] = "data0";
```

EXERCISES SECTION 7.2.6

Exercise 7.15: Write a `main` function that takes two values as arguments and print their sum.

Exercise 7.16: Write a program that could accept the options presented in this section. Print the values of the arguments passed to `main`.

7.2.7 Functions with Varying Parameters

Ellipsis parameters are in C++ in order to compile C programs that use `varargs`. See your C compiler documentation for how to use `varargs`. Only simple data types from the C++ program should be passed to functions with ellipses parameters. In particular, objects of most class types are not copied properly when passed to ellipses parameters.

Ellipses parameters are used when it is impossible to list the type and number of all the arguments that might be passed to a function. Ellipses suspend type checking. Their presence tells the compiler that when the function is called, zero or more arguments may follow and that the types of the arguments are unknown. Ellipses may take either of two forms:

```
void foo(parm_list, ...);
void foo(...);
```

The first form provides declarations for a certain number of parameters. In this case, type checking is performed when the function is called for the arguments that correspond to the parameters that are explicitly declared, whereas type checking is suspended for the arguments that correspond to the ellipsis. In this first form, the comma following the parameter declarations is optional.

Most functions with an ellipsis use some information from a parameter that is explicitly declared to obtain the type and number of optional arguments provided in a function call. The first form of function declaration with ellipsis is therefore most commonly used.

7.3   The return Statement

A return statement terminates the function that is currently executing and returns control to the function that called the now-terminated function. There are two forms of return statements:

```
return;
return expression;
```

7.3.1   Functions with No Return Value

A return with no value may be used only in a function that has a return type of void. Functions that return void are not required to contain a return statement. In a void function, an implicit return takes place after the function's final statement.

Typically, a void function uses a return to cause premature termination of the function. This use of return parallels the use of the break (Section 6.10, p. 212) statement inside a loop. For example, we could rewrite our swap program to avoid doing any work if the values are identical:

```
//   ok: swap acts on references to its arguments
void swap(int &v1, int &v2)
{
    //   if values already the same, no need to swap, just return
    if (v1 == v2)
        return;
    //   ok, have work to do
    int tmp = v2;
    v2 = v1;
    v1 = tmp;
    //   no explicit return necessary
}
```

This function first checks if the values are equal and if so exits the function. If the values are unequal, the function swaps them. An implicit return occurs after the last assignment statement.

A function with a void return type ordinarily may not use the second form of the `return` statement. However, a `void` function may return the result of calling another function that returns `void`:

```
void do_swap(int &v1, int &v2)
{
    int tmp = v2;
    v2 = v1;
    v1 = tmp;
    // ok: void function doesn't need an explicit return
}
void swap(int &v1, int &v2)
{
    if (v1 == v2)
        return false; // error: void function cannot return a value
    return do_swap(v1, v2);   // ok: returns call to a void function
}
```

Attempting to return any other expression is a compile-time error.

7.3.2   Functions that Return a Value

The second form of the `return` statement provides the function's result. Every return in a function with a return type other than `void` must return a value. The value returned must have the same type as the function return type, or must have a type that can be implicitly converted to that type.

Although C++ cannot guarantee the correctness of a result, it can guarantee that every `return` from a function returns a result of the appropriate type. The following program, for example, won't compile:

```
// Determine whether two strings are equal.
// If they differ in size, determine whether the smaller
// one holds the same characters as the larger one
bool str_subrange(const string &str1, const string &str2)
{
    // same sizes: return normal equality test
    if (str1.size() == str2.size())
        return str1 == str2;   // ok, == returns bool
    // find size of smaller string
    string::size_type size = (str1.size() < str2.size())
                             ? str1.size() : str2.size();
    string::size_type i = 0;
    // look at each element up to size of smaller string
    while (i != size) {
        if (str1[i] != str2[i])
            return;   // error: no return value
    }
    // error: control might flow off the end of the function without a return
    // the compiler is unlikely to detect this error
}
```

The `return` from within the `while` loop is an error because it fails to return a value. The compiler should detect this error.

The second error occurs because the function fails to provide a `return` after the `while` loop. If we call this function with one `string` that is a subset of the other, execution would fall out of the `while`. There should be a return to handle this case. The compiler may or may not detect this error. If a program is generated, what happens at run time is undefined.

Failing to provide a `return` after a loop that does contain a `return` is particularly insidious because many compilers will not detect it. The behavior at run time is undefined.

Return from `main`

There is one exception to the rule that a function with a return type other than `void` must return a value: The `main` function is allowed to terminate without a return. If control reaches the end of `main` and there is no return, then the compiler implicitly inserts a return of 0.

Another way in which the return from `main` is special is how its returned value is treated. As we saw in Section 1.1 (p. 2), the value returned from `main` is treated as a status indicator. A zero return indicates success; most other values indicate failure. A nonzero value has a machine-dependent meaning. To make return values machine-independent, the `cstdlib` header defines two preprocessor variables (Section 2.9.2, p. 69) that we can use to indicate success or failure:

```
#include <cstdlib>
int main()
{
    if (some_failure)
        return EXIT_FAILURE;
    else
        return EXIT_SUCCESS;
}
```

Our code no longer needs to use the precise machine-dependent values. Instead, those values are defined in `cstdlib`, and our code need not change.

Returning a Nonreference Type

The value returned by a function is used to initialize a **temporary object** created at the point at which the call was made. A temporary object is an unnamed object created by the compiler when it needs a place to store a result from evaluating an expression. C++ programmers usually use the term "temporary" as an abreviation of "temporary object."

The temporary is initialized by the value returned by a function in much the same way that parameters are initialized by their arguments. If the return type is not a reference, then the return value is copied into the temporary at the call site. The value returned when a function returns a nonreference type can be a local object or the result of evaluating an expression.

As an example, we might want to write a function that, given a counter, a word, and an ending, gives us back the plural version of the word if the counter is greater than one:

```
//  return plural version of word if ctr isn't 1
string make_plural(size_t ctr, const string &word,
                                const string &ending)
{
    return (ctr == 1) ? word : word + ending;
}
```

We might use such a function to print a message with either a plural or singular ending.

This function either returns a copy of its parameter named `word` or it returns an unnamed temporary `string` that results from adding `word` and `ending`. In either case, the `return` copies that `string` to the call site.

Returning a Reference

When a function returns a reference type, the return value is not copied. Instead, the object itself is returned. As an example, consider a function that returns a reference to the shorter of its two `string` parameters:

```
//  find longer of two strings
const string &shorterString(const string &s1, const string &s2)
{
    return s1.size() < s2.size() ? s1 : s2;
}
```

The parameters and return type are references to `const string`. The `strings` are not copied either when calling the function or when returning the result.

Never Return a Reference to a Local Object

There's one crucially important thing to understand about returning a reference: Never return a reference to a local variable.

When a function completes, the storage in which the local objects were allocated is freed. A reference to a local object refers to undefined memory after the function terminates. Consider the following function:

```
//  Disaster: Function returns a reference to a local object
const string &manip(const string& s)
{
    string ret = s;
    //  transform ret in some way
    return ret;    //  Wrong: Returning reference to a local object!
}
```

This function will fail at run time because it returns a reference to a local object. When the function ends, the storage in which `ret` resides is freed. The return value refers to memory that is no longer available to the program.

 One good way to ensure that the return is safe is to ask: To what *pre-existing* object is the reference referring?

Reference Returns Are Lvalues

A function that returns a reference returns an lvalue. That function, therefore, can be used wherever an lvalue is required:

```
char &get_val(string &str, string::size_type ix)
{
    return str[ix];
}
int main()
{
    string s("a value");
    cout << s << endl;    // prints a value
    get_val(s, 0) = 'A';  // changes s[0] to A

    cout << s << endl;    // prints A value
    return 0;
}
```

It may be surprising to assign to the return of a function, but the return is a reference. As such, it is just a synonym for the element returned.

If we do not want the reference return to be modifiable, the return value should be declared as `const`:

```
const char &get_val(...
```

Never Return a Pointer to a Local Object

The return type for a function can be most any type. In particular, it is possible for a function to return a pointer. For the same reasons that it is an error to return a reference to a local object, it is also an error to return a pointer to a local object. Once the function completes, the local objects are freed. The pointer would be a dangling pointer (Section 5.11, p. 176) that refers to a nonexistent object.

7.3.3 Recursion

A function that calls itself, either directly or indirectly, is a *recursive function*. An example of a simple recursive function is one that computes the factorial of a number. The factorial of a number n is the product of the numbers from 1 to n. The factorial of 5, for example, is 120.

```
1 * 2 * 3 * 4 * 5 = 120
```

Exercise 7.17: When is it valid to return a reference? A const reference?

Exercise 7.18: What potential run-time problem does the following function have?

```cpp
string &processText() {
    string text;
    while (cin >> text) { /* ... */ }
    // ....
    return text;
}
```

Exercise 7.19: Indicate whether the following program is legal. If so, explain what it does; if not, make it legal and then explain it:

```cpp
int &get(int *arry, int index) { return arry[index]; }
int main() {
    int ia[10];
    for (int i = 0; i != 10; ++i)
        get(ia, i) = 0;
}
```

A natural way to solve this problem is recursively:

```cpp
//  calculate val!, which is 1 * 2 * 3 ... * val
int factorial(int val)
{
    if (val > 1)
        return factorial(val-1) * val;
    return 1;
}
```

A recursive function must always define a stopping condition; otherwise, the function will recurse "forever," meaning that the function will continue to call itself until the program stack is exhausted. This is sometimes called an "infinite recursion error." In the case of factorial, the stopping condition occurs when val is 1.

As another example, we can define a recursive function to find the greatest common divisor:

```cpp
//  recursive version greatest common divisor program
int rgcd(int v1, int v2)
{
    if (v2 != 0)                      //  we're done once v2 gets to zero
        return rgcd(v2, v1%v2);       //  recurse, reducing v2 on each call
    return v1;
}
```

In this case the stopping condition is a remainder of 0. If we call rgcd with the arguments (15, 123), then the result is three. Table 7.1 on the next page traces the execution.

Table 7.1: Trace of rgcd(15,123)		
v1	v2	`Return`
15	123	`rgcd(123, 15)`
123	15	`rgcd(15, 3)`
15	3	`rgcd(3, 0)`
3	0	`3`

The last call,

`rgcd(3,0)`

satisfies the stopping condition. It returns the greatest common denominator, 3. This value successively becomes the return value of each prior call. The value is said to percolate upward until the execution returns to the function that called `rgcd` in the first place.

The `main` function may *not* call itself.

EXERCISES SECTION 7.3.3

Exercise 7.20: Rewrite `factorial` as an iterative function.

Exercise 7.21: What would happen if the stopping condition in `factorial` were:

```
if (val != 0)
```

7.4 Function Declarations

Just as variables must be declared before they are used, a function must be declared before it is called. As with a variable definition (Section 2.3.5, p. 52), we can declare a function separately from its definition; a function may be defined only once but may be declared multiple times.

A function declaration consists of a return type, the function name, and parameter list. The parameter list must contain the types of the parameters but need not name them. These three elements are referred to as the **function prototype**. A function prototype describes the interface of the function.

Function prototypes provide the interface between the programmer who defines the function and programmers who use it. When we use a function, we program to the function's prototype.

Parameter names in a function declaration are ignored. If a name is given in a declaration, it should serve as a documentation aid:

```
void print(int *array, int size);
```

Function Declarations Go in Header Files

Recall that variables are declared in header files (Section 2.9, p. 67) and defined in source files. For the same reasons, functions should be declared in header files and defined in source files.

It may be tempting—and would be legal—to put a function declaration directly in each source file that uses the function. The problem with this approach is that it is tedious and error-prone. By putting function declarations into header files, we can ensure that all the declarations for a given function agree. If the interface to the function changes, only one declaration must be changed.

 Best Practices   The source file that *defines* the function should include the header that *declares* the function.

Including the header that contains a function's declaration in the same file that defines the function lets the compiler check that the definition and declaration are the same. In particular, if the definition and declaration agree as to parameter list but differ as to return type, the compiler will issue a warning or error message indicating the discrepancy.

EXERCISES SECTION 7.4

Exercise 7.22: Write the prototypes for each of the following functions:

(a) A function named `compare` with two parameters that are references to a class named `matrix` and with a return value of type `bool`.

(b) A function named `change_val` that returns a `vector<int>` iterator and takes two parameters: one is an `int` and the other is an iterator for a `vector<int>`.

Hint: When you write these prototypes, use the name of the function as an indicator as to what the function does. How does this hint affect the types you use?

Exercise 7.23: Given the following declarations, determine which calls are legal and which are illegal. For those that are illegal, explain why.

```
double calc(double);
int count(const string &, char);
int sum(vector<int>::iterator, vector<int>::iterator, int);
vector<int> vec(10);

(a) calc(23.4, 55.1);
(b) count("abcda", 'a');
(c) calc(66);
(d) sum(vec.begin(), vec.end(), 3.8);
```

7.4.1 Default Arguments

A default argument is a value that, although not universally applicable, is the argument value that is expected to be used most of the time. When we call the function, we may omit any argument that has a default. The compiler will supply the default value for any argument we omit.

A default argument is specified by providing an explicit initializer for the parameter in the parameter list. We may define defaults for one or more parameters. However, if a parameter has a default argument, all the parameters that follow it must also have default arguments.

For example, a function to create and initialize a `string` intended to simulate a window can provide default arguments for the height, width, and background character of the screen:

```
string screenInit(string::size_type height = 24,
                  string::size_type width = 80,
                  char background = ' ');
```

A function that provides a default argument for a parameter can be invoked with or without an argument for this parameter. If an argument is provided, it overrides the default argument value; otherwise, the default argument is used. Each of the following calls of `screenInit` is correct:

```
string screen;
screen = screenInit();      // equivalent to screenInit(24,80,' ')
screen = screenInit(66);    // equivalent to screenInit(66,80,' ')
screen = screenInit(66, 256);   // screenInit(66,256,' ')
screen = screenInit(66, 256, '#');
```

Arguments to the call are resolved by position, and default arguments are used to substitute for the *trailing* arguments of a call. If we want to specify an argument for `background`, we must also supply arguments for `height` and `width`:

```
screen = screenInit(, , '?'); // error, can omit only trailing arguments
screen = screenInit('?');       //  calls screenInit('?',80,' ')
```

Note that the second call, which passes a single character value, is legal. Although legal, it is unlikely to be what the programmer intended. The call is legal because `'?'` is a `char`, and a `char` can be promoted to the type of the leftmost parameter. That parameter is `string::size_type`, which is an unsigned integral type. In this call, the `char` argument is implicitly promoted to `string::size_type`, and passed as the argument to `height`.

Because `char` is an integral type (Section 2.1.1, p. 34), it is legal to pass a `char` to an `int` parameter and vice versa. This fact can lead to various kinds of confusion, one of which arises in functions that take both `char` and `int` parameters—it can be easy for callers to pass the arguments in the wrong order. Using default arguments can compound this problem.

Part of the work of designing a function with default arguments is ordering the parameters so that those least likely to use a default value appear first and those most likely to use a default appear last.

Default Argument Initializers

A default argument can be any expression of an appropriate type:

```
string::size_type screenHeight();
string::size_type screenWidth(string::size_type);
char screenDefault(char = ' ');
string screenInit(
    string::size_type height = screenHeight(),
    string::size_type width = screenWidth(screenHeight()),
    char background = screenDefault());
```

When the default argument is an expression, and the default is used as the argument, then the expression is evaluated at the time the function is called. For example, `screenDefault` is called to obtain a value for `background` every time `screenInit` is called without a third argument.

Constraints on Specifying Default Arguments

We can specify default argument(s) in either the function definition or declaration. However, a parameter can have its default argument specified only once in a file. The following is an error:

```
// ff.h
int ff(int = 0);
```

```
// ff.cc
#include "ff.h"
int ff(int i = 0) { /* ... */ } // error
```

 Default arguments ordinarily should be specified with the declaration for the function and placed in an appropriate header.

If a default argument is provided in the parameter list of a function definition, the default argument is available only for function calls in the source file that contains the function definition.

7.5   Local Objects

In C++, names have scope, and objects have **lifetimes**. To understand how functions operate, it is important to understand both of these concepts. The scope of a name is the part of the program's text in which that name is known. The lifetime of an object is the time during the program's execution that the object exists.

The names of parameters and variables defined within a function are in the scope of the function: The names are visible only within the function body. As usual, a variable's name can be used from the point at which it is declared or defined until the end of the enclosing scope.

Exercise 7.24: Which, if any, of the following declarations are errors? Why?

```
(a) int ff(int a, int b = 0, int c = 0);
(b) char *init(int ht = 24, int wd, char bckgrnd);
```

Exercise 7.25: Given the following function declarations and calls, which, if any, of the calls are illegal? Why? Which, if any, are legal but unlikely to match the programmer's intent? Why?

```
// declarations
char *init(int ht, int wd = 80, char bckgrnd = ' ');

(a) init();
(b) init(24,10);
(c) init(14, '*');
```

Exercise 7.26: Write a version of make_plural with a default argument of 's'. Use that version to print singular and plural versions of the words "success" and "failure".

7.5.1 Automatic Objects

By default, the lifetime of a local variable is limited to the duration of a single execution of the function. Objects that exist only while a function is executing are known as **automatic objects**. Automatic objects are created and destroyed on each call to a function.

The automatic object corresponding to a local variable is created when the function control path passes through the variable's definition. If the definition contains an initializer, then the object is given an initial value each time the object is created. Uninitialized local variables of built-in type have undefined values. When the function terminates, the automatic objects are destroyed.

Parameters are automatic objects. The storage in which the parameters reside is created when the function is called and is freed when the function terminates.

Automatic objects, including parameters, are destroyed at the end of the block in which they were defined. Parameters are defined in the function's block and so are destroyed when the function terminates. When a function exits, its local storage is deallocated. After the function exits, the values of its automatic objects and parameters are no longer accessible.

7.5.2 Static Local Objects

It is can be useful to have a variable that is in the scope of a function but whose lifetime persists across calls to the function. Such objects are defined as static.

A **static local object** is guaranteed to be initialized no later than the first time that program execution passes through the object's definition. Once it is created, it is not destroyed until the program terminates; local statics are not destroyed when the function ends. Local `statics` continue to exist and hold their value across calls to the function. As a trivial example, consider a function that counts how often it is called:

```
size_t count_calls()
{
    static size_t ctr = 0;   // value will persist across calls
    return ++ctr;
}
int main()
{
    for (size_t i = 0; i != 10; ++i)
        cout << count_calls() << endl;
    return 0;
}
```

This program will print the numbers from 1 through 10 inclusive.

Before `count_calls` is called for the first time, `ctr` is created and given an initial value of 0. Each call increments `ctr` and returns its current value. Whenever `count_calls` is executed, the variable `ctr` already exists and has whatever value was in the variable the last time the function exited. Thus, on the second invocation, the value is 1, on the third it is 2, and so on.

EXERCISES SECTION 7.5.2

Exercise 7.27: Explain the differences between a parameter, a local variable and a static local variable. Give an example of a program in which each might be useful.

Exercise 7.28: Write a function that returns 0 when it is first called and then generates numbers in sequence each time it is called again.

7.6   Inline Functions

Recall the function we wrote on page 248 that returned a reference to the shorter of its two `string` parameters:

```
// find longer of two strings
const string &shorterString(const string &s1, const string &s2)
{
    return s1.size() < s2.size() ? s1 : s2;
}
```

The benefits of defining a function for such a small operation include:

- It is easier to read and understand a call to `shorterString` than it would be to read and interpret an expression that used the equivalent conditional expression in place of the function call.

- If a change needs to be made, it is easier to change the function than to find and change every occurrence of the equivalent expression.

- Using a function ensures uniform behavior. Each test is guaranteed to be implemented in the same manner.

- The function can be reused rather than rewritten for other applications.

There is, however, one potential drawback to making shorterString a function: Calling a function is slower than evaluating the equivalent expression. On most machines, a function call does a lot of work: registers are saved before the call and restored after the return; the arguments are copied; and the program branches to a new location.

inline Functions Avoid Function Call Overhead

A function specified as inline (usually) is expanded "in line" at each point in the program in which it is invoked. Assuming we made shorterString an inline function, then this call

```
cout << shorterString(s1, s2) << endl;
```

would be expanded during compilation into something like

```
cout << (s1.size() < s2.size() ? s1 : s2)
    << endl;
```

The run-time overhead of making shorterString a function is thus removed.

We can define shorterString as an inline function by specifying the keyword inline before the function's return type:

```
// inline version: find longer of two strings
inline const string &
shorterString(const string &s1, const string &s2)
{
        return s1.size() < s2.size() ? s1 : s2;
}
```

The inline specification is only a *request* to the compiler. The compiler may choose to ignore this request.

In general, the inline mechanism is meant to optimize small, straight-line functions that are called frequently. Many compilers will not inline a recursive function. A 1,200-line function is also not likely to be explanded inline.

Put inline Functions in Header Files

Unlike other function definitions, inlines should be defined in header files.

To expand the code of an inline function at the point of call, the compiler must have access to the function definition. The function prototype is insufficient.

An `inline` function may be defined more than once in a program as long as the definition appears only once in a given source file and the definition is exactly the same in each source file. By putting inline functions in headers, we ensure that the same definition is used whenever the function is called and that the compiler has the function definition available at the point of call.

Whenever an `inline` function is added to or changed in a header file, every source file that uses that header must be recompiled.

EXERCISES SECTION 7.6

Exercise 7.29: Which one of the following declarations and definitions would you put in a header? In a program text file? Explain why.

```
(a) inline bool eq(const BigInt&, const BigInt&) {...}
(b) void putValues(int *arr, int size);
```

Exercise 7.30: Rewrite the `isShorter` function from page 235 as an `inline` function.

7.7 Class Member Functions

In Section 2.8 (p. 63) we began the definition of the `Sales_item` class used in solving the bookstore problem from Chapter 1. Now that we know how to define ordinary functions, we can continue to fill in our class by defining the member functions of this class.

We define member functions similarly to how we define ordinary functions. As with any function, a member function consists of four parts:

- A return type for the function

- The function name

- A (possibly empty) comma-separated list of parameters

- The function body, which is contained between a pair of curly braces

As we know, the first three of these parts constitute the function prototype. The function prototype defines all the type information related to the function: what its return type is, the function name, and what types of arguments may be passed to it. The function prototype *must* be defined within the class body. The body of the function, however, *may* be defined within the class itself or outside the class body.

With this knowledge, let's look at our expanded class definition, to which we've added two new members: the member functions `avg_price` and `same_isbn`. The `avg_price` function has an empty parameter list and returns a value of type `double`. The `same_isbn` function returns a `bool` and takes a single parameter of type reference to `const Sales_item`.

```
class Sales_item {
public:
    // operations on Sales_item objects
    double avg_price() const;
    bool same_isbn(const Sales_item &rhs) const
        { return isbn == rhs.isbn; }
// private members as before
private:
    std::string isbn;
    unsigned units_sold;
    double revenue;
};
```

We'll explain the meaning of the `const` that follows the parameter lists shortly, but first we need to explain how member functions are defined.

7.7.1   Defining the Body of a Member Function

We must declare all the members of a class within the curly braces that delimit the class definition. There is no way to subsequently add any members to the class. Members that are functions must be defined as well as declared. We can define a member function either inside or outside of the class definition. In `Sales_item`, we have one example of each: `same_isbn` is defined inside the `Sales_item` class, whereas `avg_price` is declared inside the class but defined elsewhere.

A member function that is defined inside the class is implicitly treated as an inline function (Section 7.6, p. 256).

Let's look in more detail at the definition of `same_isbn`:

```
bool same_isbn(const Sales_item &rhs) const
    { return isbn == rhs.isbn; }
```

As with any function, the body of this function is a block. In this case, the block contains a single statement that returns the result of comparing the value of the `isbn` data members of two `Sales_item` objects.

The first thing to note is that the `isbn` member is `private`. Even though these members are `private`, there is no error.

 A member function may access the `private` members of its class.

More interesting is understanding from which `Sales_item` objects does the function get the values that it compares. The function refers both to `isbn` and `rhs.isbn`. Fairly clearly, `rhs.isbn` uses the `isbn` member from the argument passed to the function. The unqualified use of `isbn` is more interesting. As we shall see, the unqualified `isbn` refers to the `isbn` member of the object on behalf of which the function is called.

Member Functions Have an Extra, Implicit Parameter

When we call a member function, we do so on behalf of an object. For example, when we called `same_isbn` in the bookstore program on page 26, we executed the `same_isbn` member on the object named `total`:

```
if (total.same_isbn(trans))
```

In this call, we pass the object `trans`. As part of executing the call, the object `trans` is used to initialize the parameter `rhs`. Thus, in this call, `rhs.isbn` is a reference to `trans.isbn`.

The same argument-binding process is used to bind the unqualified use of `isbn` to the object named `total`. Each member function has an extra, implicit parameter that binds the function to the object on which the function was called. When we call `same_isbn` on the object named `total`, that object is also passed to the function. When `same_isbn` refers to `isbn`, it is implicitly referring to the `isbn` member of the object on which the function was called. The effect of this call is to compare `total.isbn` with `trans.isbn`.

Introducing `this`

Each member function (except for `static` member functions, which we cover in Section 12.6 (p. 467)) has an extra, implicit parameter named **this**. When a member function is called, the `this` parameter is initialized with the address of the object on which the function was invoked. To understand a member function call, we might think that when we write

```
total.same_isbn(trans);
```

it is as if the compiler rewrites the call as

```
// pseudo-code illustration of how a call to a member function is translated
Sales_item::same_isbn(&total, trans);
```

In this call, the data member `isbn` inside `same_isbn` is bound to the one belonging to `total`.

Introducing `const` Member Functions

We now can understand the role of the `const` that follows the parameter lists in the declarations of the `Sales_item` member functions: That const modifies the type of the implicit `this` parameter. When we call `total.same_isbn(trans)`, the implicit `this` parameter will be a `const Sales_Item*` that points to `total`. It is as if the body of `same_isbn` were written as

```
// pseudo-code illustration of how the implicit this pointer is used
// This code is illegal: We may not explicitly define the this pointer ourselves
// Note that this is a pointer to const because same_isbn is a const member
bool Sales_item::same_isbn(const Sales_item *const this,
                           const Sales_item &rhs) const
{ return (this->isbn == rhs.isbn); }
```

A function that uses `const` in this way is called a **const member function**. Because `this` is a pointer to `const`, a `const` member function cannot change the object on whose behalf the function is called. Thus, `avg_price` and `same_isbn` may read but not write to the data members of the objects on which they are called.

A `const` object or a pointer or reference to a `const` object may be used to call only `const` member functions. It is an error to try to call a nonconst member function on a `const` object or through a pointer or reference to a `const` object.

Using the `this` Pointer

Inside a member function, we need not explicitly use the `this` pointer to access the members of the object on which the function was called. Any unqualified reference to a member of our class is assumed to be a reference through `this`:

```
bool same_isbn(const Sales_item &rhs) const
    { return isbn == rhs.isbn; }
```

The uses of `isbn` in this function are as if we had written `this->units_sold` or `this->revenue`.

The `this` parameter is defined implicitly, so it is unnecessary and in fact illegal to include the `this` pointer in the function's parameter list. However, in the body of the function we can refer to the `this` pointer explicitly. It is legal, although unnecessary, to define `same_isbn` as follows:

```
bool same_isbn(const Sales_item &rhs) const
    { return this->isbn == rhs.isbn; }
```

7.7.2 Defining a Member Function Outside the Class

Member functions defined outside the class definition must indicate that they are members of the class:

```
double Sales_item::avg_price() const
{
    if (units_sold)
        return revenue/units_sold;
    else
        return 0;
}
```

This definition is like the other functions we've seen: It has a return type of `double` and an empty parameter list enclosed in parentheses after the function name. What is new is the `const` following the parameter list and the form of the function name. The function name

```
Sales_item::avg_price
```

uses the scope operator (Section 1.2.2, p. 8) to say that we are defining the function named `avg_price` that is defined in the scope of the `Sales_item` class.

The `const` that follows the parameter list reflects the way we declared the member funcion inside the `Sales_item` header. In any definition, the return type and parameter list must match the declaration, if any, of the function. In the case of a member function, the declaration is as it appears in the class definition. If the function is declared to be a `const` member function, then the `const` after the parameter list must be included in the definition as well.

We can now fully understand the first line of this code: It says we are defining the `avg_price` function from the `Sales_item` class and that the function is a `const` member. The function takes no (explicit) parameters and returns a `double`.

The body of the function is easier to understand: It tests whether `units_sold` is nonzero and, if so, `returns` the result of dividing `revenue` by `units_sold`. If `units_sold` is zero, we can't safely do the division—dividing by zero has undefined behavior. In this program, we return 0, indicating that if there were no sales the average price would be zero. Depending on the sophistication of our error-handling strategy, we might instead throw an exception (Section 6.13, p. 215).

7.7.3 Writing the `Sales_item` Constructor

There's one more member that we need to write: a constructor. As we learned in Section 2.8 (p. 65), class data members are not initialized when the class is defined. Instead, data members are initialized through a constructor.

Constructors Are Special Member Functions

A **constructor** is a special member function that is distinguished from other member functions by having the same name as its class. Unlike other member functions, constructors have no return type. Like other member functions they take a (possibly empty) parameter list and have a function body. A class can have multiple constructors. Each constructor must differ from the others in the number or types of its parameters.

The constructor's parameters specify the initializers that may be used when creating objects of the class type. Ordinarily these initializers are used to initialize the data members of the newly created object. Constructors usually should ensure that every data member is initialized.

The `Sales_item` class needs to explicitly define only one constructor, the **default constructor**, which is the one that takes no arguments. The default constructor says what happens when we define an object but do not supply an (explicit) initializer:

```
vector<int> vi;    // default constructor: empty vector
string s;          // default constructor: empty string
Sales_item item;   // default constructor: ???
```

We know the behavior of the `string` and `vector` default constructors: Each of these constructors initializes the object to a sensible default state. The default `string` constructor generates an empty string, the one that is equal to `""`. The default `vector` constructor generates a `vector` with no elements.

Similarly, we'd like the default constructor for `Sales_items` to generate an empty `Sales_item`. Here "empty" means an object in which the isbn is the empty string and the `units_sold` and `revenue` members are initialized to zero.

Defining a Constructor

Like any other member function, a constructor is declared inside the class and may be defined there or outside the class. Our constructor is simple, so we will define it inside the class body:

```
class Sales_item {
public:
    // operations on Sales_item objects
    double avg_price() const;
    bool same_isbn(const Sales_item &rhs) const
        { return isbn == rhs.isbn; }
    // default constructor needed to initialize members of built-in type
    Sales_item(): units_sold(0), revenue(0.0) { }
// private members as before
private:
    std::string isbn;
    unsigned units_sold;
    double revenue;
};
```

Before we explain the constructor definition, note that we put the constructor in the `public` section of the class. Ordinarily, and certainly in this case, we want the constructor(s) to be part of the interface to the class. After all, we want code that uses the `Sales_item` type to be able to define and initialize `Sales_item` objects. Had we made the constructor `private`, it would not be possible to define `Sales_item` objects, which would make the class pretty useless.

As to the definition itself

```
// default constructor needed to initialize members of built-in type
Sales_item(): units_sold(0), revenue(0.0) { }
```

it says that we are defining a constructor for the `Sales_item` class that has an empty parameter list and an empty function body. The interesting part is the colon and the code between it and the curly braces that define the (empty) function body.

Constructor Initialization List

The colon and the following text up to the open curly is the **constructor initializer list**. A constructor initializer list specifies initial values for one or more data members of the class. It follows the constructor parameter list and begins with a colon. The constructor initializer is a list of member names, each of which is followed by that member's initial value in parentheses. Multiple member initializations are separated by commas.

This initializer list says that both the `units_sold` and `revenue` members should be initialized to 0. Whenever a `Sales_item` object is created, these members will start out as 0. We need not specify an initial value for the `isbn` member. Unless we say otherwise in the constructor initializer list, members that are of class type are automatically initialized by that class' default constructor. Hence, `isbn` is initialized by the `string` default constructor, meaning that `isbn` initially is the empty string. Had we needed to, we could have specified a default value for `isbn` in the initializer list as well.

Having explained the initializer list, we can now understand the constructor: Its parameter list and the function body are both empty. The parameter list is empty because we are defining the constructor that is run by default, when no initializer is present. The body is empty because there is no work to do other than initializing `units_sold` and `revenue`. The initializer list explicitly initializes `units_sold` and `revenue` to zero and implicitly initializes `isbn` to the empty `string`. Whenever we create a `Sales_item` object, the data members will start out with these values.

Synthesized Default Constructor

> If we do not explicitly define any constructors, then the compiler will generate the default constructor for us.

The compiler-created default constructor is known as a **synthesized default constructor**. It initializes each member using the same rules as are applied for variable initializations (Section 2.3.4, p. 50). Members that are of class type, such as `isbn`, are initialized by using the default constructor of the member's own class. The initial value of members of built-in type depend on how the object is defined. If the object is defined at global scope (outside any function) or is a local static object, then these members will be initialized to 0. If the object is defined at local scope, these members are uninitialized. As usual, using an uninitialized member for any purpose other than giving it a value is undefined.

> The synthesized default constructor often suffices for classes that contain only members of class type. Classes with members of built-in or compound type should usually define their own default constructors to initialize those members.

Because the synthesized constructor does not automatically initialize members of built-in type, we had to define the `Sales_item` default constructor explicitly.

7.7.4   Organizing Class Code Files

As we saw in Section 2.9 (p. 67), class declarations ordinarily are placed in headers. Usually, member functions defined outside the class are put in ordinary source files. C++ programmers tend to use a simple naming convention for headers and the associated class definition code. The class definition is put in a file named *type*.h or *type*.H, where *type* is the name of the class defined in the file. Member function definitions usually are stored in a source file whose name is the name of the class. Following this convention we put the `Sales_item` class definition in a file named `Sales_item.h`. Any program that wants to use the class must include that header. We should put the definition of our `Sales_item` functions in a file named `Sales_item.cc`. That file, like any other file that uses the `Sales_item` type, would include the `Sales_item.h` header.

EXERCISES SECTION 7.7.4

Exercise 7.31: Write your own version of the `Sales_item` class, adding two new `public` members to read and write `Sales_item` objects. These functions should operate similarly to the input and output operators used in Chapter 1. Transactions should look like the ones defined in that chapter as well. Use this class to read and write a set of transactions.

Exercise 7.32: Write a header file to contain your version of the `Sales_item` class. Use ordinary C++ conventions to name the header and any associated file needed to hold non-`inline` functions defined outside the class.

Exercise 7.33: Add a member that adds two `Sales_items`. Use the revised class to reimplement your solution to the average price problem presented in Chapter 1.

7.8 Overloaded Functions

Two functions that appear in the same scope are **overloaded** if they have the same name but have different parameter lists.

If you have written an arithmetic expression in a programming language, you have used an overloaded function. The expression

```
1 + 3
```

invokes the addition operation for integer operands, whereas the expression

```
1.0 + 3.0
```

invokes a *different* operation that adds floating-point operands. It is the compiler's responsibility, not the programmer's, to distinguish between the different operations and to apply the appropriate operation depending on the operands' types.

Similarly, we may define a set of functions that perform the same general action but that apply to different parameter types. These functions may be called without worrying about which function is invoked, much as we can add `int`s or `double`s without worrying whether integer arithmetic or floating-point arithmetic is performed.

Function overloading can make programs easier to write and to understand by eliminating the need to invent—and remember—names that exist only to help the compiler figure out which function to call. For example, a database application might well have several `lookup` functions that could do the lookup based on

name, phone number, account number, and so on. Function overloading allows
us to define a collection of functions, each named `lookup`, that differ in terms of
what values they use to do the search. We can call `lookup` passing a value of any
of several types:

```
Record lookup(const Account&);   // find by Account
Record lookup(const Phone&);     // find by Phone
Record lookup(const Name&);      // find by Name
Record r1, r2;
r1 = lookup(acct);    // call version that takes an Account
r2 = lookup(phone);   // call version that takes a Phone
```

Here, all three functions share the same name, yet they are three distinct functions.
The compiler uses the argument type(s) passed in the call to figure out which function to call.

To understand function overloading, we must understand how to define a set
of overloaded functions and how the compiler decides which function to use for a
given call. We'll review these topics in the remainder of this section.

 There may be only one instance of `main` in any program. The `main`
function may *not* be overloaded.

Distinguishing Overloading from Redeclaring a Function

If the return type and parameter list of two functions declarations match exactly,
then the second declaration is treated as a redeclaration of the first. If the parameter
lists of two functions match exactly but the return types differ, then the second
declaration is an error:

```
Record lookup(const Account&);
bool lookup(const Account&);   // error: only return type is different
```

Functions cannot be overloaded based only on differences in the return type.
Two parameter lists can be identical, even if they don't look the same:

```
// each pair declares the same function
Record lookup(const Account &acct);
Record lookup(const Account&);   // parameter names are ignored

typedef Phone Telno;
Record lookup(const Phone&);
Record lookup(const Telno&);   // Telno and Phone are the same type

Record lookup(const Phone&, const Name&);
// default argument doesn't change the number of parameters
Record lookup(const Phone&, const Name& = "");

// const is irrelevant for nonreference parameters
Record lookup(Phone);
Record lookup(const Phone);   // redeclaration
```

In the first pair, the first declaration names its parameter. Parameter names are
only a documentation aid. They do not change the parameter list.

In the second pair, it looks like the types are different, but `Telno` is not a new type; it is a synonym for `Phone`. A typedef name provides an alternative name for an existing data type; it does not create a new data type. Therefore, two parameters that differ only in that one uses a typedef and the other uses the type to which the typedef corresponds are not different.

In the third pair, the parameter lists differ only in their default arguments. A default argument doesn't change the number of parameters. The function takes two arguments, whether they are supplied by the user or by the compiler.

The last pair differs only as to whether the parameter is `const`. This difference has no effect on the objects that can be passed to the function; the second declaration is treated as a redeclaration of the first. The reason follows from how arguments are passed. When the parameter is copied, whether the parameter is `const` is irrelevant—the function executes on a copy. Nothing the function does can change the argument. As a result, we can pass a `const` object to either a `const` or nonconst parameter. The two parameters are indistinguishable.

It is worth noting that the equivalence between a parameter and a `const` parameter applies only to nonreference parameters. A function that takes a `const` reference is different from on that takes a nonconst reference. Similarly, a function that takes a pointer to a `const` type differs from a function that takes a pointer to the nonconst object of the same type.

ADVICE: WHEN NOT TO OVERLOAD A FUNCTION NAME

Although overloading can be useful in avoiding the necessity to invent (and remember) names for common operations, it is easy to take this advantage too far. There are some cases where providing different function names adds information that makes the program easier to understand. Consider a set of member functions for a `Screen` class that move `Screen`'s cursor.

```
Screen& moveHome();
Screen& moveAbs(int, int);
Screen& moveRel(int, int, char *direction);
```

It might at first seem better to overload this set of functions under the name `move`:

```
Screen& move();
Screen& move(int, int);
Screen& move(int, int, *direction);
```

However, by overloading these functions we've lost information that was inherent in the function names and by doing so may have rendered the program more obscure.

Although cursor movement is a general operation shared by all these functions, the specific nature of that movement is unique to each of these functions. `moveHome`, for example, represents a special instance of cursor movement. Which of the two calls is easier to understand for a reader of the program? Which of the two calls is easier to remember for a programmer using the `Screen` class?

```
// which is easier to understand?
myScreen.home(); // we think this one!
myScreen.move();
```

7.8.1   Overloading and Scope

We saw in the program on page 54 that scopes in C++ nest. A name declared local
to a function hides the same name declared in the global scope (Section 2.3.6, p. 54).
The same is true for function names as for variable names:

```
/*  Program for illustration purposes only:
 *  It is bad style for a function to define a local variable
 *  with the same name as a global name it wants to use
 */
string init();   // the name init has global scope
void fcn()
{
    int init = 0;        // init is local and hides global init
    string s = init(); // error: global init is hidden
}
```

Normal scoping rules apply to names of overloaded functions. If we declare a
function locally, that function hides rather than overloads the same function declared in an outer scope. As a consequence, declarations for every version of an
overloaded function must appear in the same scope.

In general, it is a bad idea to declare a function locally. Function declarations should go in header files.
   To explain how scope interacts with overloading we will violate this
practice and use a local function declaration.

As an example, consider the following program:

```
void print(const string &);
void print(double);     // overloads the print function
void fooBar(int ival)
{
    void print(int);   // new scope: hides previous instances of print
    print("Value: "); // error: print(const string &) is hidden
    print(ival); // ok: print(int) is visible
    print(3.14); // ok: calls print(int); print(double) is hidden
}
```

The declaration of print(int) in the function fooBar hides the other declarations of print. It is as if there is only one print function available: the one that
takes a single int parameter. Any use of the name print at this scope—or a scope
nested in this scope—will resolve to this instance.

When we call print, the compiler first looks for a declaration of that name. It
finds the local declaration for print that takes an int. Once the name is found,
the compiler does no further checks to see if the name exists in an outer scope.
Instead, the compiler assumes that this declaration is the one for the name we are
using. What remains is to see if the use of the name is valid

The first call passes a string literal but the function parameter is an int. A
string literal cannot be implicitly converted to an int, so the call is an error. The

`print(const string&)` function, which would have matched this call, is hidden and is not considered when resolving this call.

When we call `print` passing a `double`, the process is repeated. The compiler finds the local definition of `print(int)`. The `double` argument can be converted to an `int`, so the call is legal.

 In C++ name lookup happens before type checking.

Had we declared `print(int)` in the same scope as the other `print` functions, then it would be another overloaded version of `print`. In that case, these calls would be resolved differently:

```
void print(const string &);
void print(double);  //  overloads print function
void print(int);     //  another overloaded instance

void fooBar2(int ival)
{
    print("Value: "); //  ok: calls print(const string &)
    print(ival);      //  ok: print(int)
    print(3.14);      //  ok: calls print(double)
}
```

Now when the compiler looks for the name `print` it finds three functions with that name. On each call it selects the version of `print` that matches the argument that is passed.

7.8.2   Function Matching and Argument Conversions

Function **overload resolution** (also known as **function matching**) is the process by which a function call is associated with a specific function from a set of overloaded functions. The compiler matches a call to a function automatically by comparing the actual arguments used in the call with the parameters offered by each function in the overload set. There are three possible outcomes:

1. The compiler finds one function that is a **best match** for the actual arguments and generates code to call that function.

2. There is no function with parameters that match the arguments in the call, in which case the compiler indicates a compile-time error.

3. There is more than one function that matches and none of the matches is clearly best. This case is also an error; the call is **ambiguous**.

Most of the time it is straightforward to determine whether a particular call is legal and if so, which function will be invoked by the compiler. Often the functions in the overload set differ in terms of the number of arguments, or the types of the arguments are unrelated. Function matching gets tricky when multiple functions have parameters that are related by conversions (Section 5.12, p. 178). In these cases, programmers need to have a good grasp of the process of function matching.

7.8.3   The Three Steps in Overload Resolution

Consider the following set of functions and function call:

```
void f();
void f(int);
void f(int, int);
void f(double, double = 3.14);
f(5.6);   // calls void f(double, double)
```

Candidate Functions

The first step of function overload resolution identifies the set of overloaded functions considered for the call. The functions in this set are the **candidate functions**. A candidate function is a function with the same name as the function that is called and for which a declaration is visible at the point of the call. In this example, there are four candidate functions named `f`.

Determining the Viable Functions

The second step selects the functions from the set of candidate functions that can be called with the arguments specified in the call. The selected functions are the **viable functions**. To be viable, a function must meet two tests. First, the function must have the same number of parameters as there are arguments in the call. Second, the type of each argument must match—or be convertible to—the type of its corresponding parameter.

When a function has default arguments (Section 7.4.1, p. 253), a call may appear to have fewer arguments than it actually does. Default arguments are arguments and are treated the same way as any other argument during function matching.

For the call f(5.6), we can eliminate two of our candidate functions because of a mismatch on number of arguments. The function that has no parameters and the one that has two int parameters are not viable for this call. Our call has only one argument, and these functions have zero and two parameters, respectively.

On the other hand, the function that takes two doubles might be viable. A call to a function declaration that has a default argument (Section 7.4.1, p. 253) may omit that argument. The compiler will automatically supply the default argument value for the omitted argument. Hence, a given call might have more arguments than appear explicitly.

Having used the number of arguments to winnow the potentially viable functions, we must now look at whether the argument types match those of the parameters. As with any call, an argument might match its parameter either because the types match exactly or because there is a conversion from the argument type to the type of the parameter. In the example, both of our remaining functions are viable.

- f(int) is a viable function because a conversion exists that can convert the argument of type double to the parameter of type int.

- f(double, double) is a viable function because a default argument is provided for the function's second parameter and its first parameter is of type double, which exactly matches the type of the parameter.

If there are no viable functions, then the call is in error.

Finding the Best Match, If Any

The third step of function overload resolution determines which viable function has the best match for the actual arguments in the call. This process looks at each argument in the call and selects the viable function (or functions) for which the corresponding parameter best matches the argument. The details of "best" here will be explained in the next section, but the idea is that the closer the types of the argument and parameter are to each other, the better the match. So, for example, an exact type match is better than a match that requires a conversion from the argument type to the parameter type.

In our case, we have only one explicit argument to consider. That argument has type double. To call f(int), the argument would have to be converted from double to int. The other viable function, f(double, double), is an exact match for this argument. Because an exact match is better than a match that requires a conversion, the compiler will resolve the call f(5.6) as a call to the function that has two double parameters.

Overload Resolution with Multiple Parameters

Function matching is more complicated if there are two or more explicit arguments. Given the same functions named f, let's analyze the following call:

```
f(42, 2.56);
```

The set of viable functions is selected in the same way. The compiler selects those functions that have the required number of parameters and for which the argument types match the parameter types. In this case, the set of viable functions are f(int, int) and f(double, double). The compiler then determines argument by argument which function is (or functions are) the best match. There is a match if there is one and only one function for which

1. The match for each argument is no worse than the match required by any other viable function.

2. There is at least one argument for which the match is better than the match provided by any other viable function.

If after looking at each argument there is no single function that is preferable, then the call is in error. The compiler will complain that the call is ambiguous.

In this call, when we look only at the first argument, we find that the function f(int, int) is an exact match. To match the second function, the int argument 42 must be converted to a double. A match through a built-in conversion is "less good" than one that is exact. So, considering only this parameter, the function that takes two ints is a better match than the function that takes two doubles.

However, when we look at the second argument, then the function that takes two doubles is an exact match to the argument 2.56. Calling the version of f that takes two ints would require that 2.56 be converted from double to int. When we consider only the second parameter, then the function f(double, double) is the better match.

This call is therefore ambiguous: Each viable function is a better match on one of the arguments to the call. The compiler will generate an error. We could force a match by explicitly casting one of our arguments:

```
f(static_cast<double>(42), 2.56);  // calls f(double, double)
f(42, static_cast<int>(2.56));     // calls f(int, int)
```

Best Practices In practice, arguments should not need casts when calling overloaded functions: The need for a cast means that the parameter sets are designed poorly.

7.8.4 Argument-Type Conversions

In order to determine the best match, the compiler ranks the conversions that could be used to convert each argument to the type of its corresponding parameter. Conversions are ranked in descending order as follows:

Exercise 7.36: What is a candidate function? What is a viable function?

Exercise 7.37: Given the declarations for f, determine whether the following calls are legal. For each call list the viable functions, if any. If the call is illegal, indicate whether there is no match or why the call is ambiguous. If the call is legal, indicate which function is the best match.

```
(a)  f(2.56, 42);
(b)  f(42);
(c)  f(42, 0);
(d)  f(2.56, 3.14);
```

---

1. An exact match. The argument and parameter types are the same.

2. Match through a promotion (Section 5.12.2, p. 180).

3. Match through a standard conversion (Section 5.12.3, p. 181).

4. Match through a class-type conversion. (Section 14.9 (p. 535) covers these conversions.)

> Promotions and conversions among the built-in types can yield surprising results in the context of function matching. Fortunately, well-designed systems rarely include functions with parameters as closely related as those in the following examples.

These examples bear study to cement understanding both of function matching in particular and of the relationships among the built-in types in general.

Matches Requiring Promotion or Conversion

Promotions or conversions are applied when the type of the argument can be promoted or converted to the appropriate parameter type using one of the standard conversions.

One important point to realize is that the small integral types promote to int. Given two functions, one of which takes an int and the other a short, the int version will be a better match for a value of any integral type other than short, even though short might appear on the surface to be a better match:

```
void ff(int);
void ff(short);
ff('a');    // char promotes to int, so matches f(int)
```

A character literal is type char, and chars are promoted to int. That promoted type matches the type of the parameter of function ff(int). A char could also be converted to short, but a conversion is a "less good" match than a promotion. And so this call will be resolved as a call to ff(int).

A conversion that is done through a promotion is preferred to another standard conversion. So, for example, a char is a better match for a function taking an int than it is for a function taking a double. All other standard conversions are treated as equivalent. The conversion from char to unsigned char, for example, does not take precedence over the conversion from char to double. As a concrete example, consider:

```
extern void manip(long);
extern void manip(float);
manip(3.14);  // error: ambiguous call
```

The literal constant 3.14 is a double. That type could be converted to either long or float. Because there are two possible standard conversions, the call is ambiguous. No one standard conversion is given precedence over another.

Parameter Matching and Enumerations

Recall that an object of enum type may be initialized only by another object of that enum type or one of its enumerators (Section 2.7, p. 63). An integral object that happens to have the same value as an enumerator cannot be used to call a function expecting an enum argument:

```
enum Tokens {INLINE = 128, VIRTUAL = 129};
void ff(Tokens);
void ff(int);
int main() {
    Tokens curTok = INLINE;
    ff(128);     // exactly matches ff(int)
    ff(INLINE);  // exactly matches ff(Tokens)
    ff(curTok);  // exactly matches ff(Tokens)
    return 0;
}
```

The call that passes the literal 128 matches the version of ff that takes an int.

Although we cannot pass an integral value to a enum parameter, we can pass an enum to a parameter of integral type. When we do so, the enum value promotes to int or to a larger integral type. The actual promotion type depends on the values of the enumerators. If the function is overloaded, the type to which the enum promotes determines which function is called:

```
void newf(unsigned char);
void newf(int);
unsigned char uc = 129;
newf(VIRTUAL);  // calls newf(int)
newf(uc);       // calls newf(unsigned char)
```

The enum Tokens has only two enumerators, the largest of which has a value of 129. That value can be represented by the type unsigned char, and many compilers would store the enum as an unsigned char. However, the type of VIRTUAL is not unsigned char. Enumerators and values of an enum type, are not promoted to unsigned char, even if the values of the enumerators would fit.

When using overloaded functions with enum parameters, remember: Two enumeration types may behave quite differently during function overload resolution, depending on the value of their enumeration constants. The enumerators determine the type to which they promote. And that type is machine-dependent.

Overloading and `const` Parameters

Whether a parameter is `const` only matters when the parameter is a reference or pointer.

We can overload a function based on whether a reference parameter refers to a `const` or nonconst type. Overloading on `const` for a reference parameter is valid because the compiler can use whether the argument is `const` to determine which function to call:

```
Record lookup(Account&);
Record lookup(const Account&); // new function

const Account a(0);
Account b;

lookup(a);    // calls lookup(const Account&)
lookup(b);    // calls lookup(Account&)
```

If the parameter is a plain reference, then we may not pass a `const` object for that parameter. If we pass a `const` object, then the only function that is viable is the version that takes a `const` reference.

When we pass a nonconst object, either function is viable. We can use a nonconst object to initializer either a `const` or nonconst reference. However, initializing a `const` reference to a nonconst object requires a conversion, whereas initializing a nonconst parameter is an exact match.

Pointer parameters work in a similar way. We may pass the address of a `const` object only to a function that takes a pointer to `const`. We may pass a pointer to a nonconst object to a function taking a pointer to a `const` or nonconst type. If two functions differ only as to whether a pointer parameter points to `const` or nonconst, then the parameter that points to the nonconst type is a better match for a pointer to a nonconst object. Again, the compiler can distinguish: If the argument is `const`, it calls the function that takes a `const*`; otherwise, if the argument is a nonconst, the function taking a plain pointer is called.

It is worth noting that we cannot overload based on whether the pointer itself is `const`:

```
f(int *);
f(int *const);   // redeclaration
```

Here the `const` applies to the pointer, not the type to which the pointer points. In both cases the pointer is copied; it makes no difference whether the pointer itself is `const`. As we noted on page 267, when a parameter is passed as a copy, we cannot overload based on whether that parameter is `const`.

EXERCISES SECTION 7.8.4

Exercise 7.38: Given the following declarations,

```
void manip(int, int);
double dobj;
```

what is the rank (Section 7.8.4, p. 272) of each conversion in the following calls?

```
(a) manip('a', 'z');        (b) manip(55.4, dobj);
```

Exercise 7.39: Explain the effect of the second declaration in each one of the following sets of declarations. Indicate which, if any, are illegal.

```
(a) int calc(int, int);
    int calc(const int&, const int&);

(b) int calc(char*, char*);
    int calc(const char*, const char*);

(c) int calc(char*, char*);
    int calc(char* const, char* const);
```

Exercise 7.40: Is the following function call legal? If not, why is the call in error?

```
enum Stat { Fail, Pass };
void test(Stat);
test(0);
```

7.9 Pointers to Functions

A function pointer is just that—a pointer that denotes a function rather than an object. Like any other pointer, a function pointer points to a particular type. A function's type is determined by its return type and its parameter list. A function's name is not part of its type:

```
//  pf points to function returning bool that takes two const string references
bool (*pf)(const string &, const string &);
```

This statement declares `pf` to be a pointer to a function that takes two `const string&` parameters and has a return type of `bool`.

The parentheses around `*pf` are necessary:

```
//  declares a function named pf that returns a bool *
bool *pf(const string &, const string &);
```

Using Typedefs to Simplify Function Pointer Definitions

Function pointer types can quickly become unwieldy. We can make function pointers easier to use by defining a synonym for the pointer type using a typedef (Section 2.6, p. 61):

```
typedef bool (*cmpFcn)(const string &, const string &);
```

This definition says that cmpFcn is the name of a type that is a pointer to function. That pointer has the type "pointer to a function that returns a bool and takes two references to const string." When we need to use this function pointer type, we can do so by using cmpFcn, rather than having to write the full type definition each time.

Initializing and Assigning Pointers to Functions

When we use a function name without calling it, the name is automatically treated as a pointer to a function. Given

```
//  compares lengths of two strings
bool lengthCompare(const string &, const string &);
```

any use of lengthCompare, except as the left-hand operand of a function call, is treated as a pointer whose type is

```
bool (*)(const string &, const string &);
```

We can use a function name to initialize or assign to a function pointer:

```
cmpFcn pf1 = 0;            //  ok: unbound pointer to function
cmpFcn pf2 = lengthCompare; //  ok: pointer type matches function's type
pf1 = lengthCompare;       //  ok: pointer type matches function's type
pf2 = pf1;                 //  ok: pointer types match
```

Using the function name is equivalent to applying the address-of operator to the function name:

```
cmpFcn pf1 = lengthCompare;
cmpFcn pf2 = &lengthCompare;
```

> A function pointer may be initialized or assigned only by a function or function pointer that has the same type or by a zero-valued constant expression.

Initializing a function pointer to zero indicates that the pointer does not point to any function.

There is no conversion between one pointer to function type and another:

```
string::size_type sumLength(const string&, const string&);
bool cstringCompare(char*, char*);
//  pointer to function returning bool taking two const string&
cmpFcn pf;
pf = sumLength;        //  error: return type differs
pf = cstringCompare;   //  error: parameter types differ
pf = lengthCompare;    //  ok: function and pointer types match exactly
```

Calling a Function through a Pointer

A pointer to a function can be used to call the function to which it refers. We can use the pointer directly—there is no need to use the dereference operator to call the function

```
cmpFcn pf = lengthCompare;
lengthCompare("hi", "bye");  // direct call
pf("hi", "bye");             // equivalent call: pf1 implicitly dereferenced
(*pf)("hi", "bye");          // equivalent call: pf1 explicitly dereferenced
```

If the pointer to function is uninitialized or has a value of zero, it may not be used in a call. Only pointers that have been initialized or assigned to refer to a function can be safely used to call a function.

Function Pointer Parameters

A function parameter can be a pointer to function. We can write such a parameter in one of two ways:

```
/*  useBigger function's third parameter is a pointer to function
 *  that function returns a bool and takes two const string references
 *  two ways to specify that parameter:
 */
// third parameter is a function type and is automatically treated as a pointer to function
void useBigger(const string &, const string &,
               bool(const string &, const string &));
// equivalent declaration: explicitly define the parameter as a pointer to function
void useBigger(const string &, const string &,
               bool (*)(const string &, const string &));
```

Returning a Pointer to Function

A function can return a pointer to function, although correctly writing the return type can be a challenge:

```
// ff is a function taking an int and returning a function pointer
// the function pointed to returns an int and takes an int* and an int
int (*ff(int))(int*, int);
```

The best way to read function pointer declarations is from the inside out, starting with the name being declared.

We can figure out what this declaration means by observing that

```
ff(int)
```

says that ff is a function taking one parameter of type int. This function returns

```
int (*)(int*, int);
```

a pointer to a function that returns an `int` and takes two parameters of type `int*` and an `int`.

Typedefs can make such declarations considerably easier to read:

```
//  PF is a pointer to a function returning an int, taking an int* and an int
typedef int (*PF) (int*, int);
PF ff(int);   //  ff returns a pointer to function
```

 We can define a parameter as a function type. A function return type must be a pointer to function; it cannot be a function.

An argument to a parameter that has a function type is automatically converted to the corresponding pointer to function type. The same conversion does not happen when returning a function:

```
//  func is a function type, not a pointer to function!
typedef int func(int*, int);

void f1(func);   //  ok: f1 has a parameter of function type
func f2(int);   //  error: f2 has a return type of function type
func *f3(int);   //  ok: f3 returns a pointer to function type
```

Pointers to Overloaded Functions

It is possible to use a function pointer to refer to an overloaded function:

```
extern void ff(vector<double>);
extern void ff(unsigned int);

//  which function does pf1 refer to?
void (*pf1)(unsigned int) = &ff;   //  ff(unsigned)
```

The type of the pointer and one of the overloaded functions must match exactly. If no function matches exactly, the initialization or assignment results in a compile-time error:

```
//  error: no match: invalid parameter list
void (*pf2)(int) = &ff;

//  error: no match: invalid return type
double (*pf3)(vector<double>);
pf3 = &ff;
```

CHAPTER SUMMARY

Functions are named units of computation and are essential to structuring even modest programs. They are defined by specifying a return type, a name, a (possibly empty) list of parameters, and a function body. The function body is a block that is executed when the function is called. When a function is called, the arguments passed to the function must be compatible with the types of the corresponding parameters.

Passing an argument to a function follows the same rules as initializing a variable. Each parameter that has nonreference type is initialized as a copy of the corresponding argument. Any changes made to a (nonreference) parameter are made to the local copy, not to the argument itself.

Copying large, complex values can be expensive. To avoid the overhead of passing a copy, parameters can be specified as references. Changes made to reference parameters are reflected in the argument itself. A reference parameter that does not need to change its argument should be `const` reference.

In C++, functions may be overloaded. The same name may be used to define different functions as long as the number or types of the parameters in the functions differ. The compiler automatically figures out which function to call based the arguments in a call. The process of selecting the right function from a set of overloaded functions is referred to as function matching.

C++ provides two special kinds of functions: `inline` and member functions. Specifying `inline` on a function is a hint to the compiler to expand the function into code directly at the call point. Inline functions avoid the overhead associated with calling a function. Member functions are just that: class members that are functions. This chapter introduced simple member functions. Chapter 12 will cover member functions in more detail.

DEFINED TERMS

ambiguous call Compile-time error that results when there is not a single best match for a call to an overloaded function.

arguments Values supplied when calling a function. These values are used to initialize the corresponding parameters in the same way that variables of the same type are initialized.

automatic objects Objects that are local to a function. Automatic objects are created and initialized anew on each call and are destroyed at the end of the block in which they are defined. They no longer exist once the function terminates.

best match The single function from a set of overloaded functions that has the best

match for the arguments of a given call.

call operator The operator that causes a function to be executed. The operator is a pair of parentheses and takes two operands: The name of the function to call and a (possibly empty) comma-separated list of arguments to pass to the function.

candidate functions The set of functions that are considered when resolving a function call. The candidate functions are all the functions with the name used in the call for which a declaration is in scope at the time of the call.

const member function Function that is member of a class and that may be called for `const` objects of that type. `const` member functions may not change the data members of the object on which they operate.

constructor Member function that has the same name as its class. A constructor says how to initialize objects of its class. Constructors have no return type. Constructors may be overloaded.

constructor initializer list List used in a constructor to specify initial values for data members. The initializer list appears in the definition of a constructor between the parameter list and the constructor body. The list consists of a colon followed by a comma-separated list of member names, each of which is followed by that member's initial value in parentheses.

default constructor The constructor that is used when no explicit initializer is supplied. The compiler will synthesize a default constructor if the class defines no other constructors.

function A callable unit of computation.

function body Block that defines the actions of a function.

function matching Compiler process by which a call to an overloaded function is resolved. Arguments used in the call are compared to the parameter list of each overloaded function.

function prototype Synonym for function declaration. The name, return type, and parameter types of a function. To call a function, its prototype must have been declared before the point of call.

inline function Function that is expanded at the point of call, if possible. Inline functions avoid the normal function-calling overhead by replacing the call by the function's code.

local static objects Local object that is created and initialized once before the function is first called and whose value persists across invocations of the function.

local variables Variables defined inside a function. Local variables are accessible only within the function body.

object lifetime Every object has an associated lifetime. Objects that are defined inside a block exist from when their definition is encountered until the end of the block in which they are defined. Local static objects and global objects defined outside any function are created during program startup and are destroyed when the main function ends. Dynamically created objects that are created through a new expression exist until the memory in which they were created is freed through a corresponding delete.

overload resolution A synonym for function matching.

overloaded function A function that has the same name as at least one other function. Overloaded functions must differ in the number or type of their parameters.

parameters Variables local to a function whose initial values are supplied when the function is called.

recursive function Function that calls itself directly or indirectly.

return type The type of the value returned from a function.

synthesized default constructor If there are no constructors defined by a class, then the compiler will create (synthesize) a default constructor. This constructor default initializes each data member of the class.

temporary object Unnamed object automatically created by the compiler in the course of evaluating an expression. The phrase *temporary object* is usually abreviated as *temporary*. A temporary persists until the end of the largest expression that encloses the expression for which it was created.

this pointer Implicit parameter of a member function. this points to the object on which the function is invoked. It is a pointer to the class type. In a const member function the pointer is a pointer to const.

viable functions The subset of overloaded functions that could match a given call. Viable functions have the same number of parameters as arguments to the call and each argument type can potentially be converted to the corresponding parameter type.

CHAPTER 8

THE IO LIBRARY

In C++, input/output is provided through the library. The library defines a family of types that support IO to and from devices such as files and console windows. Additional types allow strings to act like files, which gives us a way to convert data to and from character forms without also doing IO. Each of these IO types defines how to read and write values of the built-in data types. In addition, class designers generally use the library IO facilities to read and write objects of the classes that they define. Class types are usually read and written using the same operators and conventions that the IO library defines for the built-in types.

This chapter introduces the fundamentals of the IO library. Later chapters will cover additional capabilities: Chapter 14 will look at how we can write our own input and output operators; Appendix A will cover ways to control formatting and random access to files.

Our programs have already used many IO library facilities:

- `istream` (input stream) type, which supports input operations

- `ostream` (output stream) type, which provides output operations

- `cin` (pronounced see-in) an `istream` object that reads the standard input.

- `cout` (pronounced see-out) an `ostream` object that writes to the standard output

- `cerr` (pronounced see-err) an `ostream` object that writes to the standard error. `cerr` is usually used for program error messages.

- operator `>>`, which is used to read input from an `istream` object

- operator `<<`, which is used to write output to an `ostream` object

- `getline` function, which takes a reference to an `istream` and a reference to a `string` and reads a word from the `istream` into the `string`

This chapter looks briefly at some additional IO operations, and discusses support for reading and writing files and `strings`. Appendix A covers how to control formatting of IO operations, support for random access to files, and support for unformatted IO. This primer does not describe the entire `iostream` library—in particular, we do not cover the system-specific implementation details, nor do we discuss the mechanisms by which the library manages input and output buffers or how we might write our own buffer classes. These topics are beyond the scope of this book. Instead, we'll focus on those portions of the IO library that are most useful in ordinary programs.

8.1   An Object-Oriented Library

The IO types and objects we've used so far read and write streams of data and are used to interact with a user's console window. Of course, real programs cannot be limited to doing IO solely to or from a console window. Programs often need to read or write named files. Moreover, it can be quite convenient to use the IO operations to format data in memory, thereby avoiding the complexity and run-time expense of reading or writing to a disk or other device. Applications also may have to read and write languages that require wide-character support.

Conceptually, neither the kind of device nor the character size affect the IO operations we want to perform. For example, we'd like to use `>>` to read data regardless of whether we're reading a console window, a disk file, or an in-memory string. Similarly, we'd like to use that operator regardless of whether the characters we read fit in a `char` or require the `wchar_t` (Section 2.1.1, p. 34) type.

At first glance, the complexities involved in supporting or using these different kinds of devices and different sized character streams might seem a daunting problem. To manage the complexity, the library uses **inheritance** to define a set of **object-oriented** classes. We'll have more to say about inheritance and object-oriented programming in Part IV, but generally speaking, types related by inheritance share a common interface. When one class inherits from another, we (usually) can use the same operations on both classes. More specifically, when two types are related by inheritance, we say that one class "inherits" the behavior—the interface—of its parent. In C++ we speak of the parent as the **base class** and the inheriting class as a **derived class**.

The IO types are defined in three separate headers: iostream defines the types used to read and write to a console window, fstream defines the types used to read and write named files, and sstream defines the types used to read and write in-memory strings. Each of the types in fstream and sstream is derived from a corresponding type defined in the iostream header. Table 8.1 lists the IO classes and Figure 8.1 on the next page illustrates the inheritance relationships among these types. Inheritance is usually illustrated similarly to how a family tree is displayed. The topmost circle represents a base (or parent) class. Lines connect a base class to its derived (or children) class(es). So, for example, this figure indicates that istream is the base class of ifstream and istringstream. It is also the base class for iostream, which in turn is the base class for sstream and fstream classes.

Table 8.1: IO Library Types and Headers	
Header	**Type**
iostream	istream reads from a stream
	ostream writes to a stream
	iostream reads and writes a stream; derived from istream and ostream,
fstream	ifstream, reads from a file; derived from istream
	ofstream writes to a file; derived from ostream
	fstream, reads and writes a file; derived from iostream
sstream	istringstream reads from a string; derived from istream
	ostringstream writes to a string; derived from ostream
	stringstream reads and writes a string; derived from iostream

Because the types ifstream and istringstream inherit from istream, we already know a great deal about how to use these types. Each program we've written that read an istream could be used to read a file (using the ifstream type) or a string (using the istringstream type). Similarly, programs that did output could use an ofstream or ostringstream instead of ostream. In addition to the istream and ostream types, the iostream header also defines the iostream type. Although our programs have not used this type, we actually know a good bit about how to use an iostream. The iostream type is derived from both istream and ostream. Being derived from both types means that an iostream object shares the interface of both its parent types. That is, we can use an iostream type to do both input and output to the same stream. The library also defines two types that inherit from iostream. These types can be used to read or write to a file or a string.

Using inheritance for the IO types has another important implication: As we'll see in Chapter 15, when we have a function that takes a reference to a base-class type, we can pass an object of a derived type to that function. This fact means that a function written to operate on istream& can be called with an ifstream or istringstream object. Similarly, a function that takes an ostream& can be called with an ofstream or ostringstream object. Because the IO types are related by inheritance, we can write one function and apply it to all three kinds of streams: console, disk files, or string streams.

Figure 8.1: Simplified iostream Inheritance Hierarchy

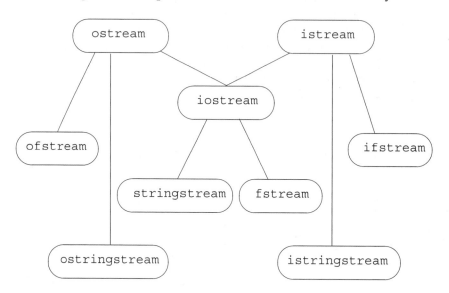

International Character Support

The stream classes described thus far read and write streams composed of type char. The library defines a corresponding set of types supporting the wchar_t type. Each class is distinguished from its char counterpart by a "w" prefix. Thus, the types wostream, wistream, and wiostream read and write wchar_t data to or from a console window. The file input and output classes are wifstream, wofstream, and wfstream. The wchar_t versions of string stream input and output are wistringstream, wostringstream, and wstringstream. The library also defines objects to read and write wide characters from the standard input and standard output. These objects are distinguished from the char counterparts by a "w" prefix: The wchar_t standard input object is named wcin; standard output is wcout; and standard error is wcerr.

Each of the IO headers defines both the char and wchar_t classes and standard input/output objects. The stream-based wchar_t classes and objects are defined in iostream, the wide character file stream types in fstream, and the wide character stringstreams in sstream.

No Copy or Assign for IO Objects

For reasons that will be more apparent when we study classes and inheritance in Parts III and IV, the library types do not allow allow copy or assignment:

```
ofstream out1, out2;
out1 = out2;   //  error: cannot assign stream objects
//  print function: parameter is copied
ofstream print(ofstream);
out2 = print(out2);   //  error: cannot copy stream objects
```

This requirement has two particularly important implications. As we'll see in Chapter 9, only element types that support copy can be stored in `vectors` or other container types. Because we cannot copy stream objects, we cannot have a `vector` (or other container) that holds stream objects.

The second implication is that we cannot have a parameter or return type that is one of the stream types. If we need to pass or return an IO object, it must be passed or returned as a pointer or reference:

```
ofstream &print(ofstream&);      //  ok: takes a reference, no copy
while (print(out2)) { /* ... */ } // ok: pass reference to out2
```

Typically, we pass a stream as a nonconst reference because we pass an IO object intending to read from it or write to it. Reading or writing an IO object changes its state, so the reference must be nonconst.

EXERCISES SECTION 8.1

Exercise 8.1: Assuming `os` is an `ofstream`, what does the following program do?

```
os << "Goodbye!" << endl;
```

What if `os` is an `ostringstream`? What if `os` is an `ifstream`?

Exercise 8.2: The following declaration is in error. Identify and correct the problem(s):

```
ostream print(ostream os);
```

8.2 Condition States

Before we explore the types defined in `fstream` and `sstream`, we need to understand a bit more about how the IO library manages its buffers and the state of a stream. Keep in mind that the material we cover in this section and the next applies equally to plain streams, file streams, or `string` streams.

Inherent in doing IO is the fact that errors can occur. Some errors are recoverable; others occur deep within the system and are beyond the scope of a program to correct. The IO library manages a set of **condition state** members that indicate whether a given IO object is in a usable state or has encountered a particular kind of error. The library also defines a set of functions and flags, listed in Table 8.2, that give us access to and let us manipulate the state of each stream.

As an example of an IO error, consider the following code:

```
int ival;
cin >> ival;
```

If we enter `Borges` on the standard input, then `cin` will be put in an error state following the unsuccessful attempt to read a string of characters as an `int`. Similarly, `cin` will be in an error state if we enter an end-of-file. Had we entered 1024, then the read would be successful and `cin` would be in a good, non-error state.

To be used for input or output, a stream must be in a non-error state. The easiest way to test whether a stream is okay is to test its truth value:

```
if (cin)
       // ok to use cin, it is in a valid state
```

```
while (cin >> word)
       // ok: read operation successful ...
```

The `if` directly tests the state of the stream. The `while` does so indirectly by testing the stream returned from the expression in the condition. If that input operation succeeds, then the condition tests `true`.

Table 8.2: IO Library Condition State	
strm::iostate	Name of the machine-dependent integral type, defined by each iostream class that is used to define the condition states.
strm::badbit	*strm*::iostate value used to indicate that a stream is corrupted.
strm::failbit	*strm*::iostate value used to indicate that an IO operation failed.
strm::eofbit	*strm*::iostate value used to indicate the a stream hit end-of-file.
s.eof()	true if eofbit in the stream s is set.
s.fail()	true if failbit in the stream s is set.
s.bad()	true if badbit in the stream s is set.
s.good()	true if the stream s is in a valid state.
s.clear()	Reset all condition values in the stream s to valid state.
s.clear(flag)	Set specified condition state(s) in s to valid. Type of flag is *strm*::iostate.
s.setstate(flag)	Add specified condition to s. Type of flag is *strm*::iostate.
s.rdstate()	Returns current condition of s as an *strm*::iostate value.

Condition States

Many programs need only know whether a stream is valid. Other programs need more fine-grained access to and control of the state of the stream. Rather than knowing that the stream is in an error state, we might want to know what kind of error was encountered. For example, we might want to distinguish between reaching end-of-file and encountering an error on the IO device.

Each stream object contains a condition state member that is managed through the `setstate` and `clear` operations. This state member has type `iostate`, which is a machine-dependent integral type defined by each `iostream` class. It is used as a collection of bits, much the way we used the `int_quiz1` variable to represent test scores in the example in Section 5.3.1 (p. 156).

Each IO class also defines three `const` values of type `iostate` that represent particular bit patterns. These `const` values are used to indicate particular kinds of IO conditions. They can be used with the bitwise operators (Section 5.3, p. 154) to test or set multiple flags in one operation.

The `badbit` indicates a system level failure, such as an unrecoverable read or write error. It is usually not possible to continue using a stream after such an error. The `failbit` is set after a recoverable error, such as reading a character when numeric data was expected. It is often possible to correct the problem that caused the `failbit` to be set. The `eofbit` is set when an end-of-file is encountered. Hitting end-of-file also sets the `failbit`.

The state of the stream is revealed by the `bad`, `fail`, `eof`, and `good` operations. If any of `bad`, `fail`, or `eof` are `true`, then testing the stream itself will indicate that the stream is in an error state. Similarly, the `good` operation returns `true` if none of the other conditions is `true`.

The `clear` and `setstate` operations change the state of the condition member. The `clear` operations put the condition back in its valid state. They are called after we have remedied whatever problem occurred and we want to reset the stream to its valid state. The `setstate` operation turns on the specified condition to indicate that a problem occurred. `setstate` leaves the existing state variables unchanged except that it adds the additional indicated state(s).

Interrogating and Controlling the State of a Stream

We might manage an input operation as follows:

```
int ival;
//  read cin and test only for EOF; loop is executed even if there are other IO failures
while (cin >> ival, !cin.eof()) {
    if (cin.bad())              //  input stream is corrupted; bail out
        throw runtime_error("IO stream corrupted");
    if (cin.fail()) {                           //  bad input
        cerr<< "bad data, try again";           //  warn the user
        cin.clear(istream::failbit);            //  reset the stream
        continue;                               //  get next input
    }
    //  ok to process ival
}
```

This loop reads `cin` until end-of-file or an unrecoverable read error occurs. The condition uses a comma operator (Section 5.9, p. 168). Recall that the comma operator executes by evaluating each operand and returns its rightmost operand as its result. The condition, therefore, reads `cin` and ignores its result. The result of the condition is the result of `!cin.eof()`. If `cin` hit end-of-file, the condition is false and we fall out of the loop. If `cin` did not hit end-of-file, we enter the loop, regardless of any other error the read might have encountered.

Inside the loop, we first check whether the stream is corrupted. If so, we exit by throwing an exception (Section 6.13, p. 215). If the input was invalid, we print a warning, and clear the `failbit` state. In this case, we execute a `continue` (Section 6.11, p. 214) to return to the start of the `while` to read another value into `ival`. If there were no errors, the rest of the loop can safely use `ival`.

Accessing the Condition State

The `rdstate` member function returns an `iostate` value that corresponds to the entire current condition state of the stream:

```
//  remember current state of cin
istream::iostate old_state = cin.rdstate();
cin.clear();
process_input();  //  use cin
cin.clear(old_state); //  now reset cin to old state
```

Dealing with Multiple States

Often we need to set or clear multiple state bits. We could do so by making multiple calls to the `setstate` or `clear` functions. Alternatively, we could use the bitwise OR (Section 5.3, p. 154) operator to generate a value to pass two or more state bits in a single call. The bitwise OR generates an integral value using the bit patterns of its operands. For each bit in the result, the bit is 1 if the corresponding bit is 1 in either of its operands. For example:

```
//  sets both the badbit and the failbit
is.setstate(ifstream::badbit | ifstream::failbit);
```

tells the object `is` to turn on both the `failbit` and the `badbit`. The argument

```
is.badbit | is.failbit
```

creates a value in which the bits corresponding to the `badbit` and to the `failbit` are both turned on—that is they are both set to 1. All other bits in the value are zero. The call to `setstate` uses this value to turn on the bits corresponding to `badbit` and `failbit` in the stream's condition state member.

8.3 Managing the Output Buffer

Each IO object manages a buffer, which is used to hold the data that the program reads and writes. When we write

```
os << "please enter a value: ";
```

the literal string is stored in the buffer associated with the stream `os`. There are several conditions that cause the buffer to be flushed—that is, written—to the actual output device or file:

Exercise 8.3: Write a function that takes and returns an `istream&`. The function should read the stream until it hits end-of-file. The function should print what it reads to the standard output. Reset the stream so that it is valid and return the stream.

Exercise 8.4: Test your function by calling it passing `cin` as an argument.

Exercise 8.5: What causes the following `while` to terminate?

```
while (cin >> i) /* . . .   */
```

1. The program completes normally. All output buffers are emptied as part of the `return` from `main`.

2. At some indeterminate time, the buffer can become full, in which case it will be flushed before writing the next value.

3. We can flush the buffer explicitly using a manipulator (Section 1.2.2, p. 7) such as `endl`.

4. We can use the `unitbuf` manipulator to set the stream's internal state to empty the buffer after each output operation.

5. We can `tie` the output stream to an input stream, in which case the output buffer is flushed whenever the associated input stream is read.

Flushing the Output Buffer

Our programs have already used the `endl` manipulator, which writes a newline and flushes the buffer. There are two other similar manipulators. The first, `flush`, is used quite frequently. It flushes the stream but adds no characters to the output. The second, `ends`, is used much less often. It inserts a null character into the buffer and then flushes it:

```
cout << "hi!" << flush;  // flushes the buffer; adds no data
cout << "hi!" << ends;   // inserts a null, then flushes the buffer
cout << "hi!" << endl;   // inserts a newline, then flushes the buffer
```

The `unitbuf` Manipulator

If we want to flush every output, it is better to use the `unitbuf` manipulator. This manipulator flushes the stream after every write:

```
cout << unitbuf << "first" << " second" << nounitbuf;
```

is equivalent to writing

```
cout << "first" << flush << " second" << flush;
```

The `nounitbuf` manipulator restores the stream to use normal, system-managed buffer flushing.

CAUTION: BUFFERS ARE NOT FLUSHED IF THE PROGRAM CRASHES

Output buffers are *not* flushed if the program terminates abnormally. When attempting to debug a program that has crashed, we often use the last output to help isolate the region of program in which the bug might occur. If the crash is after a particular print statement, then we know that the crash happened after that point in the program.

When debugging a program, it is essential to make sure that any output you *think* should have been written was actually flushed. Because the system does not automatically flush the buffers when the program crashes, it is likely that there is output that the program wrote but that has not shown up on the standard output. It is still sitting in an output buffer waiting to be printed.

If you use the last output to help locate the bug, you need to be certain that all the output really did get printed. Making sure that all output operations include an explicit flush or call to endl is the best way to ensure that you are seeing all the output that the program actually processed.

Countless hours of programmer time have been wasted tracking through code that appeared not to have executed when in fact the buffer simply had not been flushed. For this reason, we tend to use endl rather than \n when writing output. Using endl means we do not have to wonder whether output is pending when a program crashes.

Tying Input and Output Streams Together

When an input stream is tied to an output stream, any attempt to read the input stream will first flush the buffer associated output stream. The library ties cout to cin, so the statement

```
cin >> ival;
```

causes the buffer associated with cout to be flushed.

 Interactive systems usually should be sure that their input and output streams are tied. Doing so means that we are guaranteed that any output, which might include prompts to the user, has been written before attempting to read.

The tie function can be called on either istream or an ostream. It takes a pointer to an ostream and ties the argument stream to the object on which tie was called. When a stream ties itself to an ostream, then any IO operation on the stream that called tie flushes the buffer associated with the argument it passed to tie.

```
cin.tie(&cout);    // illustration only: the library ties cin and cout for us
ostream *old_tie = cin.tie();
cin.tie(0); // break tie to cout, cout no longer flushed when cin is read
cin.tie(&cerr);    // ties cin and cerr, not necessarily a good idea!
// ...
cin.tie(0);        // break tie between cin and cerr
cin.tie(old_tie); // restablish normal tie between cin and cout
```

An ostream object can be tied to only one istream object at a time. To break an existing tie, we pass in an argument of 0.

8.4   File Input and Output

The `fstream` header defines three types to support file IO:

1. `ifstream`, derived from `istream`, reads from a file.

2. `ofstream`, derived from `ostream`, writes to a file.

3. `fstream`, derived from `iostream`, reads and writes the same file.

The fact that these types are derived from the corresponding `iostream` types means that we already know most of what we need to know about how to use the `fstream` types. In particular, we can use the IO operators (`<<` and `>>`) to do formatted IO on a file, and the material covered in the previous sections on condition states apply identically to `fstream` objects.

In addition to the behavior that `fstream` types inherit, they also define two new operations of their own—`open` and `close`—along with a constructor that takes the name of a file to open. These operations can be called on objects of `fstream`, `ifstream`, or `ofstream` but not on the other IO types.

8.4.1   Using File Stream Objects

So far our programs have used the library-defined objects, `cin`, `cout`, and `cerr`. When we want to read or write a file, we must define our own objects, and bind them to the desired files. Assuming that `ifile` and `ofile` are `strings` with the names of the files we want to read and write, we might write code such as

```
//  construct an ifstream and bind it to the file named ifile
ifstream infile(ifile.c_str());
//  ofstream output file object to write file named ofile
ofstream outfile(ofile.c_str());
```

to define and open a pair of `fstream` objects. `infile` is a stream that we can read and `outfile` is a stream that we can write. Supplying a file name as an initializer to an `ifstream` or `ofstream` object has the effect of opening the specified file.

```
ifstream infile;      //  unbound input file stream
ofstream outfile;     //  unbound output file stream
```

These definitions define `infile` as a stream object that will read from a file and `outfile` as an object that we can use to write to a file. Neither object is as yet bound to a file. Before we use an `fstream` object, we must also bind it to a file to read or write:

```
infile.open("in");     //  open file named "in" in the current directory
outfile.open("out");   //  open file named "out" in the current directory
```

We bind an existing `fstream` object to the specified file by calling the `open` member. The `open` function does whatever system-specific operations are required to locate the given file and open it for reading or writing as appropriate.

Checking Whether an Open Succeeded

After opening a file, it is usually a good idea to verify that the open succeeded:

```
//  check that the open succeeded
if (!infile) {
    cerr << "error: unable to open input file: "
        << ifile << endl;
    return -1;
}
```

This condition is similar to those we've used to test whether cin had hit end-of-file or encountered some other error. When we test a stream, the effect is to test whether the object is "okay" for input or output. If the open fails, then the state of the fstream object is that it is not ready for doing IO. When we test the object

```
if (outfile) //  ok to use outfile?
```

a true return means that it is okay to use the file. Because we want to know if the file is *not* okay, we invert the return from checking the stream:

```
if (!outfile) //  not ok to use outfile?
```

Rebinding a File Stream to a New File

Once an fstream has been opened, it remains associated with the specified file. To associate the fstream with a different file, we must first close the existing file and then open a different file:

```
ifstream infile("in");    //  opens file named "in" for reading
infile.close();           //  closes "in"
infile.open("next");      //  opens file named "next" for reading
```

It is essential that we close a file stream before attempting to open a new file. The open function checks whether the stream is already open. If it is open, then it sets its internal state to indicate that a failure has happened. Subsequent attempts to use the file stream will fail.

Clearing the State of a File Stream

Consider a program that has a vector containing names of files it should open and read, doing some processing on the words stored in each file. Assuming the vector is named files, such a progam might have a loop like the following:

```
    //  for each file in the vector
    while (it != files.end()) {
        ifstream input(it->c_str());   //  open the file;
        //  if the file is ok, read and "process" the input
        if (!input)
            break;                      //  error: bail out!
        while(input >> s)               //  do the work on this file
            process(s);
        ++it;                           //  increment iterator to get next file
    }
```

Each trip through the loop constructs the ifstream named input open to read the indicated file. The initializer in the constructor uses the arrow operator (Section 5.6, p. 164) which dereferences it and fetches the c_str member from the underlying string that it currently denotes. The file is opened by the constructor, and assuming the open succeeded, we read that file until we hit end-of-file or some other error condition. At that point, input is in an error state. Any further attempt to read from input will fail. Because input is local to the while loop, it is created on each iteration. That means that it starts out each iteration in a clean state—input.good() is true.

If we wanted to avoid creating a new stream object on each trip through the while, we might move the definition of input out of the while. This simple change means that we must manage the stream state more carefully. When we encounter end-of-file, or any other error, the internal state of the stream is set so that further reads or writes are not allowed. Closing a stream does not change the internal state of the stream object. If the last read or write operation failed, the state of the object remains in a failure mode until we execute clear to reset the condition of the stream. After the clear, it is as if we had created the object afresh.

If we wish to reuse an existing stream object, our while loop must remember to close and clear the stream on each trip through the loop:

```
    ifstream input;
    vector<string>::const_iterator it = files.begin();
    //  for each file in the vector
    while (it != files.end()) {
        input.open(it->c_str());   //  open the file
        //  if the file is ok, read and "process" the input
        if (!input)
            break;                  //  error: bail out!
        while(input >> s)  //  do the work on this file
            process(s);
        input.close();              //  close file when we're done with it
        input.clear();              //  reset state to ok
        ++it;                       //  increment iterator to get next file
    }
```

Had we neglected the call to clear, this loop would read only the first file. To see why, consider what happens in this loop: First we open the indicated file. Assuming open succeeded, we read the file until we hit end-of-file or some other error condition. At that point, input is in an error state. If we close but do not clear the stream, then any subsequent input operation on `input` will fail. Once we have `closed` the file, we can `open` the next one. However, the read of `input` in the inner `while` will fail—after all, the last read from this stream hit end-of-file. The fact that the end-of-file was on a different file is irrelevant!

If we reuse a file stream to read or write more than one file, we must `clear` the stream before using it to read from another file.

EXERCISES SECTION 8.4.1

Exercise 8.6: Because `ifstream` inherits from `istream`, we can pass an `ifstream` object to a function that takes a reference to an `istream`. Use the function you wrote for the first exercise in Section 8.2 (p. 291) to read a named file.

Exercise 8.7: The two programs we wrote in this section used a `break` to exit the `while` loop if the open failed for any file in the `vector`. Rewrite these two loops to print a warning message if a file can't be opened and continue processing by getting the next file name from the `vector`.

Exercise 8.8: The programs in the previous exercise can be written without using a `continue` statement. Write the program with and without using a `continue`.

Exercise 8.9: Write a function to open a file for input and read its contents into a `vector` of `strings`, storing each line as a separate element in the `vector`.

Exercise 8.10: Rewrite the previous program to store each word in a separate element.

8.4.2 File Modes

Whenever we open a file—either through a call to `open` or as part of initializing a stream from a file name—a **file mode** is specified. Each `fstream` class defines a set of values that represent different modes in which the stream could be opened. Like the condition state flags, the file modes are integral constants that we use with the bitwise operators (Section 5.3, p. 154) to set one or more modes when we open a given file. The file stream constructors and `open` have a default argument (Section 7.4.1, p. 253) to set the file mode. The value of the default varies based on the type of the stream. Alternatively, we can supply the mode in which to open the file. Table 8.3 on the next page lists the file modes and their meanings.

The modes `out`, `trunc`, and `app` may be specifed only for files associated with an `ofstream` or an `fstream`; `in` may be specified only for files associated with either `ifstream` or `fstream`. Any file may be opened in `ate` or `binary` mode. The `ate` mode has an effect only at the open: Opening a file in `ate` mode puts the file at the end-of-file immediately after the open. A stream opened in `binary` mode processes the file as a sequence of bytes; it does no interpretation of the characters in the stream.

Table 8.3: File Modes	
in	open for input
out	open output
app	seek to the end before every write
ate	seek to the end immediately after the open
trunc	truncate an existing stream when opening it
binary	do IO operations in binary mode

By default, files associated with an ifstream are opened in in mode, which is the mode that permits the file to be read. Files opened by an ofstream are opened in out mode, which permits the file to be written. A file opened in out mode is truncated: All data stored in the file is discarded.

In effect, specifying out mode for an ofstream is equivalent to specifying both out and trunc.

The only way to preserve the existing data in a file opened by an ofstream is to specify app mode explicitly:

```
//   output mode by default; truncates file named "file1"
ofstream outfile("file1");

//   equivalent effect: "file1" is explicitly truncated
ofstream outfile2("file1", ofstream::out | ofstream::trunc);

//   append mode; adds new data at end of existing file named "file2"
ofstream appfile("file2", ofstream::app);
```

The definition of outfile2 uses the bitwise OR operator (Section 5.3, p. 154) to open inOut in both out and trunc mode.

Using the Same File for Input and Output

An fstream object can both read and write its associated file. How an fstream uses its file depends on the mode specified when we open the file.

By default, an fstream is opened with both in and out set. A file opened with both in and out mode set is not truncated. If we open the file associated with an fstream with out mode, but not in mode specified, then the file is truncated. The file is also truncated if trunc is specified, regardless of whether in is specified. The following definition opens the file copyOut in both input and output mode:

```
//   open for input and output
fstream inOut("copyOut", fstream::in | fstream::out);
```

Appendix A.3.8 (p. 837) discusses how to use a file that is opened for both input and output.

Mode Is an Attribute of a File, Not a Stream

The mode is set each time a file is opened:

```
ofstream outfile;
//   output mode set to out, "scratchpad" truncated
outfile.open("scratchpad", ofstream::out);
outfile.close();      // close outfile so we can rebind it

//   appends to file named "precious"
outfile.open("precious", ofstream::app);
outfile.close();

//   output mode set by default, "out" truncated
outfile.open("out");
```

The first call to open specifies ofstream::out. The file named "scratchpad" in the current directory is opened in output mode; the file will be truncated. When we open the file named "precious," we ask for append mode. Any data in the file remains, and all writes are done at the end of the file. When we opened "out," we did not specify an output mode explicitly. It is opened in out mode, meaning that any data currently in "out" is discarded.

 Any time open is called, the file mode is set, either explicitly or implicitly. If a mode is not specified, the default value is used.

Valid Combinations for Open Mode

Not all open modes can be specified at once. Some are nonsensical, such as opening a file setting both in and trunc. That would yield a stream we intend to read but that we have truncated so that there is no data to read. Table 8.4 lists the valid mode combinations and their meanings.

Table 8.4: File Mode Combinations	
out	open for output; deletes existing data in the file
out | app	open for output; all writes at end of file
out | trunc	same as out
in	open for input
in | out	open for both input and output; positioned to read the beginning of the file
in | out | trunc	open for both input and output, deletes existing data in the file

Any open mode combination may also include ate. The effect of adding ate to any of these modes changes only the initial position of the file. Adding ate to any of these mode combinations positions the file to the end before the first input or output operation is performed.

8.4.3 A Program to Open and Check Input Files

Several programs in this book open a given file for input. Because we need to do this work in several programs, we'll write a function, named `open_file`, to perform it. Our function takes references to an `ifstream` and a `string`. The `string` holds the name of a file to associate with the given `ifstream`:

```
//  opens in binding it to the given file
ifstream& open_file(ifstream &in, const string &file)
{
    in.close();   //  close in case it was already open
    in.clear();   //  clear any existing errors
    //   if the open fails, the stream will be in an invalid state
    in.open(file.c_str());  //  open the file we were given
    return in;  //  condition state is good if open succeeded
}
```

Because we do not know what state the stream is in, we start by calling `close` and `clear` to put the stream into a valid state. We next attempt to `open` the given file. If the open fails, the stream's condition state will indicate that the stream is unusable. We finish by returning the stream, which is either bound to the given file and ready to use or is in an error condition.

EXERCISES SECTION 8.4.3

Exercise 8.11: In the `open_file` function, explain why we call `clear` before the call to `open`. What would happen if we neglected to make this call? What would happen if we called `clear` after the `open`?

Exercise 8.12: In the `open_file` function, explain what the effect would be if the program failed to execute the `close`.

Exercise 8.13: Write a program similar to `open_file` that opens a file for output.

Exercise 8.14: Use `open_file` and the program you wrote for the first exercise in Section 8.2 (p. 291) to open a given file and read its contents.

8.5 String Streams

The `iostream` library supports in-memory input/output, in which a stream is attached to a `string` within the program's memory. That `string` can be written to and read from using the `iostream` input and output operators. The library defines three kinds of string streams:

- `istringstream`, derived from `istream`, reads from a `string`.

- `ostringstream`, derived from `ostream`, writes to a `string`.

- `stringstream`, derived from `iostream`, reads and writes a `string`.

To use any of these classes, we must include the `sstream` header.

Like the `fstream` types, these types are derived from the `iostream` types, meaning that all the operations on `iostream`s also apply to the types in `sstream`. In addition to the operations that the `sstream` types inherit, these types have a constructor that takes a `string`. The constructor copies the `string` argument into the `stringstream` object. The operations that read and write the `stringstream` read or write the `string` in the object. These classes also define a member named `str` to fetch or set the `string` value that the `stringstream` manipulates.

Note that although `fstream` and `sstream` share a common base class, they have no other interrelationship. In particular, we cannot use `open` and `close` on a `stringstream`, nor can we use `str` on an `fstream`.

Table 8.5: `stringstream`-Specific Operations	
`stringstream strm;`	Creates an unbound `stringstream`.
`stringstream strm(s);`	Creates a `stringstream` that holds a copy of the `string` s.
`strm.str()`	Returns a copy of the `string` that `strm` holds.
`strm.str(s)`	Copies the `string` s into `strm`. Returns `void`.

Using a `stringstream`

We've seen programs that need to deal with their input a word at a time or a line at a time. The first sort of programs use the `string` input operator and the second use the `getline` function. However, some programs need to do both: They have some processing to do on a per-line basis and other work that needs to be done on each word within each line. Using `stringstream`s lets us do so:

```
string line, word;      // will hold a line and word from input, respectively
while (getline(cin, line)) {      // read a line from the input into line
    // do per-line processing
    istringstream stream(line);  // bind to stream to the line we read
    while (stream >> word) {      // read a word from line
        // do per-word processing
    }
}
```

Here we use `getline` to get an entire line from the input. To get the words in each line, we bind an `istringstream` to the line that we read. We can then use the normal `string` input operator to read the words from each line.

`stringstreams` Provide Conversions and/or Formatting

One common use of `stringstream`s is when we want to obtain automatic formatting across multiple data types. For example, we might have a collection of numeric values but want their `string` representation or vice versa. The `sstream` input and output operations automatically convert an arithmetic type into its corresponding `string` representation or back again:

```
int val1 = 512, val2 = 1024;
ostringstream format_message;
//  ok: converts values to a string representation
format_message << "val1: " << val1 << "\n"
               << "val2: " << val2 << "\n";
```

Here we create an empty `ostringstream` object named `format_message` and insert the indicated text into that object. What's important is that the `int` values are automatically converted to their printable `string` equivalents. The contents of `format_message` are the characters

val1: 512\nval2: 1024

We could retrieve the numeric value by using an `istringstream` to read from the `string`. Reading an `istringstream` automatically converts from the character representation of a numeric value to its corresponding arithmetic value:

```
//  str member obtains the string associated with a stringstream
istringstream input_istring(format_message.str());

string dump;   //  place to dump the labels from the formatted message
//  extracts the stored ascii values, converting back to arithmetic types
input_istring >> dump >> val1 >> dump >> val2;

cout << val1 << " " << val2 << endl; //  prints 512 1024
```

Here we use the `str` member to obtain a copy of the `string` associated with the `ostringstream` we previously created. We bind `input_istring` to that `string`. When we read `input_istring`, the values are converted back to their original numeric representations.

> To read `input_string`, we must parse the `string` into its component parts. We want the numeric values; to get them we must read (and ignore) the labels that are interspersed with the data we want.

Because the input operator reads typed values, it is essential that the types of the objects into which we read be compatible with the types of the values read from the `stringstream`. In this case, `input_istring` had four components: The `string` value `val1:` followed by `512` followed by the `string` `val2:` followed by `1024`. As usual, when we read `strings` using the input operator, whitespace is ignored. Thus, when we read the `string` associated with `format_message`, we can ignore the newlines that are part of that value.

EXERCISES SECTION 8.5

Exercise 8.15: Use the function you wrote for the first exercise in Section 8.2 (p. 291) to print the contents of an `istringstream` object.

Exercise 8.16: Write a program to store each line from a file in a `vector<string>`. Now use an `istringstream` to read each line from the `vector` a word at a time.

CHAPTER SUMMARY

C++ uses library classes to handle input and output:

- The `iostream` classes handle stream-oriented input and output

- The `fstream` classes handle IO to named files

- The `stringstream` classes do IO to in-memory `strings`

All of these classes are related by inheritance. The input classes inherit from `istream` and the output classes from `ostream`. Thus, operations that can be performed on an `istream` object can also be performed on either an `ifstream` or an `istringstream`. Similarly for the output classes, which inherit from `ostream`.

Each IO object maintains a set of condition states that indicate whether IO can be done through this object. If an error is encountered—such as hitting end-of-file on an input stream—then the object's state will be such that no further input can be done until the error is rectified. The library provides a set of functions to set and test these states.

DEFINED TERMS

base class A class that is the parent of another class. The base class defines the interface that a derived class inherits.

condition state Flags and associated functions usable by any of the stream classes that indicate whether a given stream is usable. States and functions to get and set these states are listed in Table 8.2 (p. 288).

derived class A derived class is one that shares an interface with its parent class.

file mode Flags defined by the `fstream` classes that are specified when opening a file and control how a file can be used. Listed in Table 8.3 (p. 297).

fstream Stream object that reads or writes a named file. In addition to the normal `iostream` operations, the `fstream` class also defines `open` and `close` members. The `open` member function takes a C-style character string that names the file to open and an optional open mode argument. By default `ifstreams` are opened with `in` mode, `ofstreams` with `out` mode, and `fstreams` with `in` and `out` mode set. The `close` member closes the file to which the

stream is attached. It must be called before another file can be `opened`.

inheritance Types that are related by inheritance share a common interface. A derived class inherits properties from its base class. Chapter 15 covers inheritance.

object-oriented library A set of classes related by inheritance. Generally speaking, the base class of an object-oriented library defines an interface that is shared by the classes derived from that base class. In the IO library, the `istream` and `ostream` classes serve as base classes for the types defined in the `fstream` and `sstream` headers. We can use an object of a derived class as if it were an object of the base class. For example, we can use the operations defined for `istream` on an `ifstream` object.

stringstream Stream object that reads or writes a `string`. In addition to the normal `iostream` operations, it also defines an overloaded member named `str`. Calling `str` with no arguments returns the `string` to which the `stringstream` is attached. Calling it with a `string` attaches the `stringstream` to a copy of that `string`.

PART II

CONTAINERS AND ALGORITHMS

CONTENTS

We've said that C++ is about efficient programming with abstractions. The Standard Library is a good example: The library defines a number of container classes and a family of generic algorithms that let us write programs that are succinct, abstract, and efficient. The library worries about bookkeeping details—in particular, taking care of memory management—so that our programs can worry about the actual problems we need to solve.

In Chapter 3 we introduced the vector container type. We'll learn more in Chapter 9 about vector and the other sequential container types provided by the library. We'll also cover more operations provided by the string type. We can think of a string as a special kind of container that contains only characters. The string type supports many, but not all, of the container operations.

The library also defines several associative containers. Elements in an associative container are ordered by key rather than sequentially. The associative containers share many operations with the sequential containers and also define operations that are specific to the associative containers. The associative containers are covered in Chapter 10.

Chapter 11 introduces the generic algorithms. The algorithms typically operate on a range of elements from a container or other sequence. The algorithms library offers efficient implementations of various classical algorithms, such as searching, sorting, and other common tasks. For example, there is a copy algorithm, which copies elements from one sequence to another; find, which looks for a given element; and so on. The algorithms are generic in two ways: They they can be applied to different kinds of containers, and those containers may contain elements of most types.

The library is designed so that the container types provide a common interface: If two containers offer a similar operation, then that operation will be defined identically for both containers. For example, all the containers have an operation to return the number of elements in the container. All the containers name that operation size, and they all define a type named size_type that is the type of the value returned by size. Similarly, the algorithms have a consistent interface. For example, most algorithms operate on a range of elements specified by a pair of iterators.

Because the container operations and algorithms are defined consistently, learning the library becomes easier: Once you understand how an operation works, you can apply that same operation to other containers. More importantly, this commonality of interface leads to more flexible programs. It is often possible to take a program written to use one container type and change it to use a different container without having to rewrite code. As we'll see, the containers offer different performance tradeoffs, and the ability to change container types can be valuable when fine-tuning the performance of a system.

CHAPTER 9

SEQUENTIAL CONTAINERS

CONTENTS

This chapter completes our discussion of the standard-library sequential container types. It expands on the material from Chapter 3, which introduced the most commonly used sequential container, the `vector` type. Elements in a sequential container are stored and accessed by position. The library also defines several associative containers, which hold elements whose order depends on a key. Associative containers are covered in the next chapter.

The container classes share a common interface. This fact makes the library easier to learn; what we learn about one type applies to another. Each container type offers a different set of time and functionality tradeoffs. Often a program using one type can be fine-tuned by substituting another container without changing our code beyond the need to change type declarations.

A container holds a collection of objects of a specified type. We've used one kind of container already: the library `vector` type. It is a **sequential container**. It holds a collection of elements of a single type, making it a container. Those elements are stored and accessed by position, making it a sequential container. The order of elements in a sequential container is independent of the value of the elements. Instead, the order is determined by the order in which elements are added to the container.

The library defines three kinds of sequential containers: `vector`, `list`, and `deque` (short for "double-ended queue" and pronounced "deck"). These types differ in how elements are accessed and the relative run-time cost of adding or removing elements. The library also provides three container **adaptors**. Effectively, an adaptor *adapts* an underlying container type by defining a new interface in terms of the operations provided by the original type. The sequential container adaptors are `stack`, `queue`, and `priority_queue`.

Containers define only a small number of operations. Many additional operations are provided by the algorithms library, which we'll cover in Chapter 11. For those operations that are defined by the containers, the library imposes a common interface. The containers vary as to which operations they provide, but if two containers provide the same operation, then the interface (name and number of arguments) will be the same for both container types. The set of operations on the container types form a kind of hierarchy:

- Some operations are supported by all container types.

- Other operations are common to only the sequential or only the associative containers.

- Still others are common to only a subset of either the sequential or associative containers.

In the remainder of this chapter, we look at the sequential container types and their operations in detail.

Table 9.1: Sequential Container Types	
Sequential Containers	
`vector`	Supports fast random access
`list`	Supports fast insertion/deletion
`deque`	Double-ended queue
Sequential Container Adaptors	
`stack`	Last in/First out stack
`queue`	First in/First out queue
`priority_queue`	Priority-managed queue

9.1 Defining a Sequential Container

We already know a fair bit about how to use the sequential containers based on what we covered in Section 3.3 (p. 90). To define a container object, we must include its associated header file, which is one of

```
#include <vector>
#include <list>
#include <deque>
```

Each of the containers is a class template (Section 3.3, p. 90). To define a particular kind of container, we name the container followed by angle brackets that enclose the type of the elements the container will hold:

```
vector<string>    svec;    // empty vector that can hold strings
list<int>         ilist;   // empty list that can hold ints
deque<Sales_item> items;   // empty deque that holds Sales_items
```

Each container defines a default constructor that creates an empty container of the speicfied type. Recall that a default constructor takes no arguments.

 For reasons that shall become clear shortly, the most commonly used container constructor is the default constructor. In most programs, using the default constructor gives the best run-time performance and makes using the container easier.

9.1.1 Initializing Container Elements

In addition to defining a default constructor, each container type also supports constructors that allow us to specify initial element values.

Table 9.2: Container Constructors	
`C<T> c;`	Create an empty container named c. C is a container name, such as `vector`, and T is the element type, such as `int` or `string`. Valid for all containers.
`C c(c2);`	Create c as a copy of container c2; c and c2 must be the same container type and hold values of the same type. Valid for all containers.
`C c(b, e);`	Create c with a copy of the elements from the range denoted by iterators b and e. Valid for all containers.
`C c(n, t);`	Create c with n elements, each with value t, which must be a value of the element type of C or a type convertible to that type. **Sequential containers only.**
`C c(n);`	Create c with n value-initialized (Section 3.3.1, p. 92) elements. **Sequential containers only.**

Intializing a Container as a Copy of Another Container

When we initialize a sequential container using any constructor other than the default constructor, we must indicate how many elements the container will have. We must also supply initial values for those elements. One way to specify both the size and element values is to initialize a new container as a copy of an existing container of the same type:

```
vector<int> ivec;
vector<int> ivec2(ivec);    // ok: ivec is vector<int>
list<int>   ilist(ivec);    // error: ivec is not list<int>
vector<double> dvec(ivec);  // error: ivec holds int not double
```

> When we copy one container into another, the types must match exactly: The container type and element type must be the same.

Initializing as a Copy of a Range of Elements

Although we cannot copy the elements from one kind of container to another directly, we can do so indirectly by passing a pair of iterators (Section 3.4, p. 95). When we use iterators, there is no requirement that the container types be identical. The element types in the containers can differ as long as they are compatible. It must be possible to convert the element we copy into the type held by the container we are constructing.

The iterators denote a range of elements that we want to copy. These elements are used to initialize the elements of the new container. The iterators mark the first and one past the last element to be copied. We can use this form of initialization to copy a container that we could not copy directly. More importantly, we can use it to copy only a subsequence of the other container:

```
//  initialize slist with copy of each element of svec
list<string> slist(svec.begin(), svec.end());
//  find midpoint in the vector
vector<string>::iterator mid = svec.begin() + svec.size()/2;
//  initialize front with first half of svec: The elements up to but not including *mid
deque<string>  front(svec.begin(), mid);
//  initialize back with second half of svec: The elements *mid through end of svec
deque<string>  back(mid, svec.end());
```

Recall that pointers are iterators, so it should not be surprising that we can initialize a container from a pair of pointers into a built-in array:

```
char *words[] = {"stately", "plump", "buck", "mulligan"};
//  calculate how many elements in words
size_t words_size = sizeof(words)/sizeof(char *);
//  use entire array to initialize words2
list<string> words2(words, words + words_size);
```

Here we use `sizeof` (Section 5.8, p. 167) to calculate the size of the array. We add that size to a pointer to the first element to get a pointer to a location one past the end of the array. The initializers for `words2` are a pointer to the first element in `words` and a second pointer one past the last element in that array. The second pointer serves as a stopping condition; the location it addresses is not included in the elements to be copied.

Allocating and Initializing a Specified Number of Elements

When creating a sequential container, we may specify an explicit size and an (optional) initializer to use for the elements. The size can be either a constant or non-constant expression. The element initializer must be a valid value that can be used to initialize an object of the element type:

```
const list<int>::size_type list_size = 64;
list<string> slist(list_size, "eh?"); // 64 strings, each is eh?
```

This code initializes `slist` to have 64 elements, each with the value eh?.

As an alternative to specifying the number of elements and an element initializer, we can also specify only the size:

```
list<int> ilist(list_size);     // 64 elements, each initialized to 0
// svec has as many elements as the return value from get_word_count
extern unsigned get_word_count(const string &file_name);
vector<string> svec(get_word_count("Chimera"));
```

When we do not supply an element initializer, the library generates a value-initialized (Section 3.3.1, p. 92) one for us. To use this form of initialization, the element type must either be a built-in or compound type or be a class type that has a default constructor. If the element type does not have a default constructor, then an explicit element initializer must be specified.

 The constructors that take a size are valid *only* for sequential containers; they are not supported for the associative containers,

9.1.2 Constraints on Types that a Container Can Hold

While most types can be used as the element type of a container, there are two constraints that element types must meet:

- The element type must support assignment.

- We must be able to copy objects of the element type.

There are additional constraints on the types used as the key in an associative container, which we'll cover in Chapter 10.

Most types meet these minimal element type requirements. All of the built-in or compound types, with the exception of references, can be used as the element

---

EXERCISES SECTION 9.1.1

Exercise 9.1: Explain the following initializations. Indicate if any are in error, and if so, why.

```
int ia[7] = { 0, 1, 1, 2, 3, 5, 8 };
string sa[6] = {
    "Fort Sumter", "Manassas", "Perryville",
    "Vicksburg", "Meridian", "Chancellorsville" };
(a) vector<string> svec(sa, sa+6);
(b) list<int> ilist( ia+4, ia+6);
(c) vector<int> ivec(ia, ia+8);
(d) list<string> slist(sa+6, sa);
```

Exercise 9.2: Show an example of each of the four ways to create and initialize a vector. Explain what values each vector contains.

Exercise 9.3: Explain the differences between the constructor that takes a container to copy and the constructor that takes two iterators.

---

type. References do not support assignment in its ordinary meaning, so we cannot have containers of references.

With the exception of the IO library types (and the `auto_ptr` type, which we cover in Section 17.1.9 (p. 702)), all the library types are valid container element types. In particular, containers themselves satisfy these requirements. We can define containers with elements that are themselves containers. Our `Sales_item` type also satisfies these requirements.

The IO library types do not support copy or assignment. Therefore, we cannot have a container that holds objects of the IO types.

Container Operations May Impose Additional Requirements

The requirement to support copy and assignment is the minimal requirement on element types. In addition, some container operations impose additional requirements on the element type. If the element type doesn't support the additional requirement, then we cannot perform that operation: We can define a container of that type but may not use that particular operation.

One example of an operation that imposes a type constraint is the constructors that take a single initializer that specifies the size of the container. If our container holds objects of a class type, then we can use this constructor only if the element type has a default constructor. Most types do have a default constructor, although there are some classes that do not. As an example, assume that `Foo` is a class that does *not* define a default constructor but that does have a constructor that takes an `int` argument. Now, consider the following declarations:

```
vector<Foo> empty;       // ok: no need for element default constructor
vector<Foo> bad(10);     // error: no default constructor for Foo
vector<Foo> ok(10, 1);   // ok: each element initialized to 1
```

We can define an empty container to hold `Foo` objects, but we can define one of a given size only if we also specify an initializer for each element.

As we describe the container operations, we'll note the constraints, if any, that each container operation places on the element type.

Containers of Containers

Because the containers meet the constraints on element types, we can define a container whose element type is itself a container type. For example, we might define `lines` as a `vector` whose elements are a `vector` of `string`s:

```
// note spacing: use "> >" not ">>" when specifying a container element type
vector< vector<string> > lines;      // vector of vectors
```

Note the spacing used when specifying a container element type as a container:

```
vector< vector<string> > lines;  // ok: space required between close >
vector< vector<string>> lines;   // error: >> treated as shift operator
```

We must separate the two closing > symbols with a space to indicate that these two characters represent two symbols. Without the space, >> is treated as a single symbol, the right shift operator, and results in a compile-time error.

EXERCISES SECTION 9.1.2

Exercise 9.4: Define a `list` that holds elements that are `deque`s that hold `int`s.

Exercise 9.5: Why can we not have containers that hold `iostream` objects?

Exercise 9.6: Given a class type named `Foo` that does not define a default constructor but does define a constructor that takes `int` values, define a `list` of `Foo` that holds 10 elements.

9.2 Iterators and Iterator Ranges

The constructors that take a pair of iterators are an example of a common form used extensively throughout the library. Before we look further at the container operations, we should understand a bit more about iterators and iterator ranges.

In Section 3.4 (p. 95), we first encountered `vector` iterators. Each of the container types has several companion iterator types. Like the containers, the iterators have a common interface: If an iterator provides an operation, then the operation is supported in the same way for each iterator that supplies that operation. For example, all the container iterators let us read an element from a container, and they all do so by providing the dereference operator. Similarly, they all provide increment and decrement operators to allow us to go from one element to the next.

Table 9.3 lists the iterator operations supported by the iterators for all of the library containers.

Table 9.3: Common Iterator Operations	
`*iter`	Return a reference to the element referred to by the iterator `iter`.
`iter->mem`	Dereference `iter` and fetch the member named `mem` from the underlying element. Equivalent to `(*iter).mem`.
`++iter` `iter++`	Increment `iter` to refer to the next element in the container.
`--iter` `iter--`	Decrement `iter` to refer to the previous element in the container.
`iter1 == iter2` `iter1 != iter2`	Compare two iterators for equality (inequality). Two iterators are equal if they refer to the same element of the same container or if they are the off-the-end iterator (Section 3.4, p. 97) for the same container.

Iterators on `vector` and `deque` Support Additional Operations

There are two important sets of operations that only `vector` and `deque` support: iterator arithmetic (Section 3.4.1, p. 100) and the use of the relational operators (in addition to `==` and `!=`) to compare two iterators. These operations are summarized in Table 9.4 on the facing page.

The reason that only `vector` and `deque` support the relational operators is that only `vector` and `deque` offer fast, random access to their elements. These containers are guaranteed to let us efficiently jump directly to an element given its position in the container. Because these containers support random access by position, it is possible for their iterators to efficiently implement the arithmetic and relational operations.

For example, we could calculate the midpoint of a `vector` as follows:

```
vector<int>::iterator iter = vec.begin() + vec.size()/2;
```

On the other hand, this code

```
// copy elements from vec into ilist
list<int> ilist(vec.begin(), vec.end());
ilist.begin() + ilist.size()/2;   // error: no addition on list iterators
```

is an error. The `list` iterator does not support the arithmetic operations—addition or subtraction—nor does it support the relational (`<=`, `<`, `>=`, `>`) operators. It does support pre- and postfix increment and decrement and the equality (inequality) operators.

In Chapter 11 we'll see that the operations an iterator supports are fundamental to using the library algorithms.

Table 9.4: Operations Supported by `vector` and `deque` Iterators

`iter + n` `iter - n`	Adding (subtracting) an integral value n to (from) an iterator yields an iterator that many elements forward (backward) within the container. The resulting iterator must refer to an element in the container or one past the end of the container.
`iter1 += iter2` `iter1 -= iter2`	Compound-assignment versions of iterator addition and subtraction. Assigns the value of adding or subtracting `iter1` and `iter2` into `iter1`.
`iter1 - iter2`	Subtracting two iterators yields the number that when added to the right-hand iterator yields the left-hand iterator. The iterators must refer to elements in the same container or one past the end of the container. **Supported only for** `vector` **and** `deque`.
`>, >=, <, <=`	Relational operators on iterators. One iterator is less than another if it refers to an element whose position in the container is ahead of the one referred to by the other iterator. The iterators must refer to elements in the same container or one past the end of the container. **Supported only for** `vector` **and** `deque`.

EXERCISES SECTION 9.2

Exercise 9.7: What is wrong with the following program? How might you correct it?

```
list<int> lst1;
list<int>::iterator iter1 = lst1.begin(),
                    iter2 = lst1.end();
while (iter1 < iter2) /*  . . .   */
```

Exercise 9.8: Assuming vec_iter is bound to an element in a `vector` that holds strings, what does this statement do?

```
if (vec_iter->empty()) /*  . . .   */
```

Exercise 9.9: Write a loop to write the elements of a `list` in reverse order.

Exercise 9.10: Which, if any, of the following iterator uses are in error?

```
const vector< int > ivec(10);
vector< string >    svec(10);
list< int >         ilist(10);

(a) vector<int>::iterator     it = ivec.begin();
(b) list<int>::iterator       it = ilist.begin()+2;
(c) vector<string>::iterator it = &svec[0];
(d) for (vector<string>::iterator
            it = svec.begin(); it != 0; ++it)
            // ...
```

9.2.1 Iterator Ranges

 The concept of an iterator range is fundamental to the standard library.

An **iterator range** is denoted by a pair of iterators that refer to two elements, or to *one past the last element*, in the same container. These two iterators, often referred to as first and last, or beg and end, mark a range of elements from the container.

Although the names last and end are common, they are a bit misleading. The second iterator never refers to the last element of the range. Instead, it refers to a point one past the last element. The elements in the range include the element referred to by first and every element from first through the element just before last. If the iterators are equal, then the range is empty.

This element range is called a **left-inclusive interval**. The standard notation for such a range is

```
//  to be read as: includes first and each element up to but not including last
[ first, last )
```

indicating that the range begins with first and ends with, but does not include, last. The iterator in last may be equal to the first or may refer to an element that appears after the one referred to by first. The last iterator must not refer to an element ahead of the one referred to by first.

REQUIREMENTS ON ITERATORS FORMING AN ITERATOR RANGE

Two iterators, first and last, form an iterator range, if

- They refer to elements of, or one-past-the-end of, the same container.

- If the iterators are not equal, then it must be possible to reach last by repeatedly incrementing first. In other words, last must not precede first in the container.

 The compiler cannot itself enforce these requirements. It does not know to which container an iterator is bound, nor does it know how many elements are in a container. Failing to meet these requirements results in undefined run-time behavior.

Programming Implications of Using Left-Inclusive Ranges

The library uses left-inclusive ranges because such ranges have two convenient properties. Assuming first and last denote a valid iterator range, then

1. When first equals last, the range is empty.

2. When first is not equal to last, there is at least one element in the range, and first refers to the first element in that range. Moreover, we can advance first by incrementing it some number of times until first == last.

These properties mean that we can safely write loops such as the following to process a range of elements by testing the iterators:

```
while (first != last) {
    // safe to use *first because we know there is at least one element
    ++first;
}
```

Assuming `first` and `last` form a valid iterator range, then we know that either `first == last`, in which case the loop is exited, or the range is non-empty and `first` refers to an element. Because the condition in the `while` handles the case where the range is empty, there is no need for a special case to handle an empty range. When the range is non-empty, the loop will execute at least once. Because the loop body increments `first`, we know the loop will eventually terminate. Moreover, if we are in the loop, then we know that `*first` is safe: It must refer to an element in the non-empty range between `first` and `last`.

EXERCISES SECTION 9.2.1

Exercise 9.11: What are the constraints on the iterators that form iterator ranges?

Exercise 9.12: Write a function that takes a pair of iterators and an `int` value. Look for that value in the range and return a `bool` indicating whether it was found.

Exercise 9.13: Rewrite the program that finds a value to return an iterator that refers to the element. Be sure your function works correctly if the element does not exist.

Exercise 9.14: Using iterators, write a program to read a sequence of `strings` from the standard input into a `vector`. Print the elements in the `vector`.

Exercise 9.15: Rewrite the program from the previous exercise to use a `list`. List the changes you needed to change the container type.

9.2.2   Some Container Operations Invalidate Iterators

In the sections that follow, we'll see that some container operations change the internal state of a container or cause the elements in the container to be moved. Such operations **invalidate** all iterators that refer to the elements that are moved and may invalidate other iterators as well. Using an invalidated iterator is undefined, and likely to lead to the same kinds of problems as using a dangling pointer.

For example, each container defines one or more `erase` functions. These functions remove elements from the container. Any iterator that refers to an element that is removed has an invalid value. After all, the iterator was positioned on an element that no longer exists within the container.

When writing programs that use iterators, we must be aware of which operations can invalidate the iterators. It is a serious run-time error to use an iterator that has been invalidated.

There is no way to examine an iterator to determine whether it has been invalidated. There is no test we can perform to detect that it has gone bad. Any use of an invalidated iterator is likely to yield a run-time error, but there is no guarantee that the program will crash or otherwise make it easy to detect the problem.

When using iterators, it is usually possible to write the program so that the range of code over which an iterator must stay valid is relatively short. It is important to examine each statement in this range to determine whether elements are added or removed and adjust iterator values accordingly.

9.3   Sequence Container Operations

Each sequential container defines a set of useful typedefs and supports operations that let us

- Add elements to the container

- Delete elements from the container

- Determine the size of the container

- Fetch the first and last elements from the container, if any

9.3.1   Container Typedefs

We've used three of the container-defined types: `size_type`, `iterator`, and `const_iterator`. Each container defines these types, along with several others shown in Table 9.5.

Table 9.5: Container-Defined Typedefs	
`size_type`	Unsigned integral type large enough to hold size of largest possible container of this container type
`iterator`	Type of the iterator for this container type
`const_iterator`	Type of the iterator that can read but not write the elements
`reverse_iterator`	Iterator that addresses elements in reverse order
`const_reverse_iterator`	Reverse iterator that can read but not write the elements
`difference_type`	Signed integral type large enough to hold the difference, which might be negative, between two iterators
`value_type`	Element type
`reference`	Element's lvalue type; synonym for `value_type&`
`const_reference`	Element's const lvalue type; same as `const value_type&`

We'll have more to say about reverse iterators in Section 11.3.3 (p. 412), but briefly, a reverse iterator is an iterator that goes backward through a container and inverts the iterator operations: For example, saying ++ on a reverse iterator yields the previous element in the container.

The last three types in Table 9.5 on the facing page let us use the type of the elements stored in a container without directly knowing what that type is. If we need the element type, we refer to the container's value_type. If we need a reference to that type, we use reference or const_reference. The utility of these element-related typedefs will be more apparent when we define our own generic programs in Chapter 16.

Expressions that use a container-defined type can look intimidating:

```
// iter is the iterator type defined by list<string>
list<string>::iterator iter;
// cnt is the difference_type type defined by vector<int>
vector<int>::difference_type cnt;
```

The declaration of iter uses the scope operator to say that we want the name on the right-hand side of the :: from the scope of the left-hand side. The effect is to declare that iter has whatever type is defined for the iterator member from the list class that holds elements of type string.

EXERCISES SECTION 9.3.1

Exercise 9.16: What type should be used as the index into a vector of ints?

Exercise 9.17: What type should be used to read the elments in a list of strings?

9.3.2 begin and end Members

The begin and end operations yield iterators that refer to the first and one past the last element in the container. These iterators are most often used to form an iterator range that encompasses all the elements in the container.

Table 9.6: Container begin and end Operations	
c.begin()	Yields an iterator referring to the first element in c
c.end()	Yields an iterator referring to the one past the last element in c
c.rbegin()	Yields a reverse iterator referring to the last element in c
c.rend()	Yields a reverse iterator referring one past (i.e., before) the first element in c

There are two different versions of each of these operations: One is a const member (Section 7.7.1, p. 260) and the other is nonconst. The return type of these operations varies on whether the container is const. In each case, if the container is nonconst, then the result's type is `iterator` or `reverse_iterator`. If the object is const, then the type is prefixed by `const_`, that is, `const_iterator` or `const_reverse_iterator`. We cover reverse iterators in Section 11.3.3 (p. 412).

9.3.3 Adding Elements to a Sequential Container

In Section 3.3.2 (p. 94) we saw one way to add elements: `push_back`. Every sequential container supports `push_back`, which appends an element to the back of the container. The following loop reads one `string` at a time into `text_word`:

```
//   read from standard input putting each word onto the end of container
string text_word;
while (cin >> text_word)
    container.push_back(text_word);
```

The call to `push_back` creates a new element at the end of `container`, increasing the `size` of `container` by one. The value of that element is a copy of `text_word`. The type of `container` can be any of `list`, `vector`, or `deque`.

In addition to `push_back`, the `list` and `deque` containers support an analogous operation named `push_front`. This operation inserts a new element at the front of the container. For example,

```
list<int> ilist;
//   add elements at the end of ilist
for (size_t ix = 0; ix != 4; ++ix)
    ilist.push_back(ix);
```

uses `push_back` to add the sequence 0,1,2,3 to the end of `ilist`.

Alternatively, we could use `push_front`

```
//   add elements to the start of ilist
for (size_t ix = 0; ix != 4; ++ix)
    ilist.push_front(ix);
```

to add the elements 0, 1, 2, 3 to the beginning of `ilist`. Because each element is inserted at the new beginning of the `list`, they wind up in reverse order. After executing both loops, `ilist` holds the sequence 3,2,1,0,0,1,2,3.

KEY CONCEPT: CONTAINER ELEMENTS ARE COPIES

When we add an element to a container, we do so by copying the element value into the container. Similarly, when we initialize a container by providing a range of elements, the new container contains copies of the original range of elements. There is no relationship between the element in the container and the value from which it was copied. Subsequent changes to the element in the container have no effect on the value that was copied, and vice versa.

Table 9.7: Operations that Add Elements to a Sequential Container	
`c.push_back(t)`	Adds element with value `t` to the end of `c`. Returns `void`.
`c.push_front(t)`	Adds element with value `t` to front of `c`. Returns `void`. **Valid only for `list` or `deque`.**
`c.insert(p,t)`	Inserts element with value `t` before the element referred to by iterator `p`. Returns an iterator referring to the element that was added.
`c.insert(p,n,t)`	Inserts `n` elements with value `t` before the element referred to by iterator `p`. Returns `void`.
`c.insert(p,b,e)`	Inserts elements in the range denoted by iterators `b` and `e` before the element referred to by iterator `p`. Returns `void`.

Adding Elements at a Specified Point in the Container

The `push_back` and `push_front` operations provide convenient ways to insert a single element at the end or beginning of a sequential container. More generally, `insert` allows us to insert elements at any particular point in the container. There are three versions of `insert`. The first takes an iterator and an element value. The iterator refers to the position at which to insert the value. We could use this version of `insert` to insert an element at the beginning of a container:

```
vector<string> svec;
list<string> slist;
string spouse("Beth");
// equivalent to calling slist.push_front(spouse);
slist.insert(slist.begin(), spouse);
// no push_front on vector but we can insert before begin()
// warning: inserting anywhere but at the end of a vector is an expensive operation
svec.insert(svec.begin(), spouse);
```

The value is inserted *before* the position referred to by the iterator. The iterator can refer to any position in the container, including one past the end of the container. Because the iterator might refer to a nonexistent element off the end of the container, `insert` inserts before the position rather than after it. This code

```
slist.insert(iter, spouse); // insert spouse just before iter
```

inserts a copy of `spouse` just before the element referred to by `iter`.

This version of `insert` returns an iterator referring to the newly inserted element. We could use the return value to repeatedly insert elements at a specified position in the container:

```
list<string> lst;
list<string>::iterator iter = lst.begin();
while (cin >> word)
    iter = lst.insert(iter, word); // same as calling push_front
```

It is important to understand thoroughly how this loop operates—in particular to understand why we say that the loop is equivalent to calling push_front.

Before the loop, we initialize iter to lst.begin(). Because the list is empty, lst.begin() and lst.end() are equal, so iter refers one past the end of the (empty) list. The first call to insert puts the element we just read in front of the element referred to by iter. The value returned by insert is an iterator referring to this new element, which is now the first, and only, element in lst. We assign that iterator to iter and repeat the while, reading another word. As long as there are words to insert, each trip through the while inserts a new element ahead of iter and reassigns to iter the value of the newly inserted element. That element is always the first element, so each iteration inserts an element ahead of the first element in the list.

Inserting a Range of Elements

A second form of insert adds a specified number of identical elements at an indicated position:

```
svec.insert(svec.end(), 10, "Anna");
```

This code inserts ten elements at the end of svec and initializes each of those elements to the string "Anna".

The final form of insert adds a range of elements denoted by an iterator pair into the container. For example, given the following array of strings

```
string sarray[4] = {"quasi", "simba", "frollo", "scar"};
```

we can insert all or a subset of the array elements into our list of strings:

```
// insert all the elements in sarray at end of slist
slist.insert(slist.end(), sarray, sarray+4);
list<string>::iterator slist_iter = slist.begin();
// insert last two elements of sarray before slist_iter
slist.insert(slist_iter, sarray+2, sarray+4);
```

Inserting Elements Can Invalidate Iterators

As we'll see in Section 9.4 (p. 330), adding elements to a vector can cause the entire container to be relocated. If the container is relocated, then all iterators into the container are invalidated. Even if the vector does not have to be relocated, any iterator to an element after the one inserted is invalidated.

Iterators may be invalidated after doing any insert or push operation on a vector or deque. When writing loops that insert elements into a vector or a deque, the program must ensure that the iterator is refreshed on each trip through the loop.

Avoid Storing the Iterator Returned from `end`

When we add elements to a `vector` or `deque`, some or all of the iterators may be invalidated. It is safest to assume that all iterators are invalid. This advice is particularly true for the iterator returned by `end`. That iterator is *always* invalidated by any insertion anywhere in the container.

As an example, consider a loop that reads each element, processes it and adds a new element following the original. We want the loop to process each original element. We'll use the form of `insert` that takes a single value and returns an iterator to the element that was just inserted. After each insertion, we'll increment the iterator that is returned so that the loop is positioned to operate on the next original element. If we attempt to "optimize" the loop, by storing an iterator to the `end()`, we'll have a disaster:

```
vector<int>::iterator first = v.begin(),
                       last = v.end(); // cache end iterator
// diaster: behavior of this loop is undefined
while (first != last) {
    // do some processing
    // insert new value and reassign first, which otherwise would be invalid
    first = v.insert(first, 42);
    ++first;   // advance first just past the element we added
}
```

The behavior of this code is undefined. On many implementations, we'll get an infinite loop. The problem is that we stored the value returned by the `end` operation in a local variable named `last`. In the body of the loop, we add an element. Adding an element invalidates the iterator stored in `last`. That iterator neither refers to an element in `v` nor any longer refers to one past the last element in `v`.

 Don't cache the iterator returned from `end`. Inserting or deleting elements in a `deque` or `vector` will invalidate the cached iterator.

Rather than storing the `end` iterator, we must recompute it after each insertion:

```
// safer: recalculate end on each trip whenever the loop adds/erases elements
while (first != v.end()) {
    // do some processing
    first = v.insert(first, 42);   // insert new value
    ++first;   // advance first just past the element we added
}
```

9.3.4   Relational Operators

Each container supports the relational operators (Section 5.2, p. 152) that can be used to compare two containers. The containers must be the same kind of container and must hold elements of the same type. We can compare a `vector<int>` only with another `vector<int>`. We cannot compare a `vector<int>` with a `list<int>` or a `vector<double>`.

EXERCISES SECTION 9.3.3

Exercise 9.18: Write a program to copy elements from a `list` of `int`s into two deques. The `list` elements that are even should go into one `deque` and those that are odd into the second.

Exercise 9.19: Assuming `iv` is a `vector` of `int`s, what is wrong with the following program? How might you correct the problem(s)?

```
vector<int>::iterator mid = iv.begin() + iv.size()/2;
while (vector<int>::iterator iter != mid)
    if (iter == some_val)
        iv.insert(iter, 2 * some_val);
```

Comparing two containers is based on a pairwise comparison of the elements of the containers. The comparison uses the same relational operator as defined by the element type: Comparing two containers using `!=` uses the `!=` operator for the element type. If the element type doesn't support the operator, then the containers cannot be compared using that operator.

These operators work similarly to the `string` relationals (Section 3.2.3, p. 85):

- If both containers are the same size and all the elements are equal, then the two containers are equal; otherwise, they are unequal.

- If the containers have different sizes but every element of the shorter one is equal to the corresponding element of the longer one, then the shorter one is considered to be less than the other.

- If neither container is an initial subsequence of the other, then the comparison depends on comparing the first unequal elements.

The easiest way to understand these operators is by studying examples:

```
/*
            ivec1: 1 3 5 7 9 12
            ivec2: 0 2 4 6 8 10 12
            ivec3: 1 3 9
            ivec4: 1 3 5 7
            ivec5: 1 3 5 7 9 12
 */
// ivec1 and ivec2 differ at element [0]: ivec1 greater than ivec2
ivec1 < ivec2 // false
ivec2 < ivec1 // true

// ivec1 and ivec3 differ at element [2]: ivec1 less than ivec3
ivec1 < ivec3 // true

// all elements equal, but ivec4 has fewer elements, so ivec1 is greater than ivec4
ivec1 < ivec4 // false

ivec1 == ivec5 // true; each element equal and same number of elements
ivec1 == ivec4 // false; ivec4 has fewer elements than ivec1
ivec1 != ivec4 // true; ivec4 has fewer elements than ivec1
```

Relational Operators Use Their Element's Relational Operator

 Note We can compare two containers only if the same relational operator defined for the element types.

Each container relational operator executes by comparing pairs of elements from the two containers:

```
ivec1 < ivec2
```

Assuming ivec1 and ivec2 are vector<int>, then this comparison uses the built-in int less-than operator. If the vectors held strings, then the string less-than operator would be used.

If the vectors held objects of the Sales_item type that we used in Section 1.5 (p. 20), then the comparison would be illegal. We did not define the relational operators for Sales_item. If we have two containers of Sales_items, we could not compare them:

```
vector<Sales_item> storeA;
vector<Sales_item> storeB;

if (storeA < storeB) // error: Sales_item has no less-than operator
```

EXERCISES SECTION 9.3.4

Exercise 9.20: Write a program to compare whether a vector<int> contains the same elements as a list<int>.

Exercise 9.21: Assuming c1 and c2 are containers, what constraints does the following usage place on the element types in c1 and c2?

```
if (c1 < c2)
```

What, if any, constraints are there on c1 and c2?

9.3.5 Container Size Operations

Each container type supports four size-related operations. We used size and empty in Section 3.2.3 (p. 83): size returns the number of elements in the container; empty returns a bool that is true if size is zero and false otherwise.

The resize operation changes the number of elements in the container. If the current size is greater than the new size, then elements are deleted from the back of the container. If the current size is less than the new size, then elements are added to the back of the container:

```
list<int> ilist(10, 42);    // 10 ints: each has value 42
ilist.resize(15);           // adds 5 elements of value 0 to back of ilist
ilist.resize(25, -1);       // adds 10 elements of value -1 to back of ilist
ilist.resize(5);            // erases 20 elements from the back of ilist
```

The resize operation takes an optional element-value argument. If this argument is present, then any newly added elements receive this value. If this argument is absent, then any new elements are value initialized (Section 3.3.1, p. 92).

resize can invalidate iterators. A resize operation on a vector or deque potentially invalidates all iterators.

For any container type, if resize shrinks the container, then any iterator to an element that is deleted is invalidated.

Table 9.8: Sequential Container Size Operations

c.size()	Returns the number of elements in c. Return type is c::size_type.
c.max_size()	Returns maximum number of elements c can contain. Return type is c::size_type.
c.empty()	Returns a bool that indicates whether size is 0 or not.
c.resize(n)	Resize c so that it has n elements. If N < c.size(), the excess elements are discarded. If new elements must be added, they are value initialized.
c.resize(n,t)	Resize c to have n elements. Any elements added have value t.

EXERCISES SECTION 9.3.5

Exercise 9.22: Given that vec holds 25 elements, what does vec.resize(100) do? What if we next wrote vec.resize(10)?

Exercise 9.23: What, if any, restrictions does using resize with a single size argument place on the element types?

9.3.6 Accessing Elements

If a container is not empty, then the front and back members return references bound to the first or last elements in the container:

```
// check that there are elements before dereferencing an iterator
// or calling front or back
if (!ilist.empty()) {
    // val and val2 refer to the same element
    list<int>::reference val = *ilist.begin();
    list<int>::reference val2 = ilist.front();

    // last and last2 refer to the same element
    list<int>::reference last = *--ilist.end();
    list<int>::reference last2 = ilist.back();
}
```

This program uses two different approaches to fetch a reference to the first and last elements in `ilist`. The direct approach is to call `front` or `back`. Indirectly, we can obtain a reference to the same element by dereferencing the iterator returned by `begin` or the element one before the iterator returned by `end`. Two things are noteworthy in this program: The end iterator refers "one past the end" of the container so to fetch the last element we must first decrement that iterator. The other important point is that before calling `front` or `back` or dereferencing the iterators from `begin` or `end` we check that `ilist` isn't empty. If the list were empty all of the operations in the `if` would be undefined.

When we introduced subscripting in Section 3.3.2 (p. 94), we noted that the programmer must ensure that an element exists at the indicated subscript location. The subscript operator itself does not check. The same caution applies to using the `front` or `back` operations. If the container is empty, these operations yield an undefined result. If the container has only one element, then `front` and `back` each return a reference to that element.

Using a subscript that is out-of-range or calling `front` or `back` on an empty container are serious programming errors.

Table 9.9: Operations to Access Elements in a Sequential Container	
`c.back()`	Returns a reference to the last element in c. Undefined if c is empty.
`c.front()`	Returns a reference to the first element in c. Undefined if c is empty.
`c[n]`	Returns a reference to the element indexed by n. Undefined if n < 0 or n >= `c.size()`. **Valid only for vector and deque.**
`c.at(n)`	Returns a reference to the element indexed by n. If index is out of range, throws `out_of_range` exception. **Valid only for vector and deque.**

An alternative to subscripting is to use the `at` member. This function acts like the subscript operation but if the index is invalid, `at` throws an `out_of_range` exception (Section 6.13, p. 215):

```
vector<string> svec;  // empty vector
cout << svec[0];      // run-time error: There are no elements in svec!
cout << svec.at(0);   // throws out_of_range exception
```

EXERCISES SECTION 9.3.6

Exercise 9.24: Write a program that fetches the first element in a `vector`. Do so using `at`, the subscript operator, `front`, and `begin`. Test the program on an empty `vector`.

9.3.7 Erasing Elements

Recall that there is both a general `insert` operation that inserts anywhere in the container and specific `push_front` and `push_back` operations to add elements only at the front or back. Similarly, there is a general `erase` and specific `pop_front` and `pop_back` operations to remove elements.

Removing the First or Last Element

The `pop_front` and `pop_back` functions remove the first and last elements in the container. There is no `pop_front` operation for `vector`s. These operations remove the indicated element and return `void`.

One common use of `pop_front` is to use it together with `front` to process a container as a stack:

```
while (!ilist.empty()) {
    process(ilist.front()); //  do something with the current top of ilist
    ilist.pop_front();       //  done; remove first element
}
```

This loop is pretty simple: We use `front` to get a value to operate on and then call `pop_front` to remove that element from the `list`.

> The `pop_front` and `pop_back` return `void`; they do *not* return the value of the element popped. To examine that value, it is necessary to call `front` or `back` prior to popping the element.

Table 9.10: Operations to Remove Elements from a Sequential Container	
`c.erase(p)`	Removes element referred to by the iterator p. Returns an iterator referring to the element after the one deleted, or an off-the-end iterator if p referred to the last element. Undefined if p is an off-the-end iterator.
`c.erase(b,e)`	Removes the range of elements denoted by the iterators b and e. Returns an iterator referring after the last one in the range that was deleted, or an off-the-end iterator if e is itself an off-the-end iterator.
`c.clear()`	Removes all the elements in c. Returns `void`.
`c.pop_back()`	Removes the last element in c. Returns `void`. Undefined if c is empty.
`c.pop_front()`	Removes the first element in c. Returns `void`. Undefined if c is empty. **Valid only for list or deque.**

Removing an Element From within the Container

The more general way to remove an element, or range of elements, is through `erase`. There are two versions of `erase`: We can delete a single element referred to by an iterator or a range of elements marked by a pair of iterators. Both forms of `erase` return an iterator referring to the location after the element or range that was removed. That is, if element `j` is the element immediately after `i` and we `erase` element `i` from the container, then the iterator returned will refer to `j`.

As usual, the `erase` operations don't check their argument(s). It is up to the programmer to ensure that the iterator or iterator range is valid.

The `erase` operation is often used after finding an element that should be removed from the container. The easiest way to find a given element is to use the library `find` algorithm. We'll see more about `find` in Section 11.1 (p. 392). To use `find` or any other generic algorithm, we must include the `algorithm` header. The `find` function takes a pair of iterators that denote a range in which to look, and a value to look for within that range. `find` returns an iterator referring to the first element with that value or the off-the-end iterator:

```
string searchValue("Quasimodo");
list<string>::iterator iter =
    find(slist.begin(), slist.end(), searchValue);
if (iter != slist.end())
    slist.erase(iter);
```

Note that we check that the iterator is not the `end` iterator before erasing the element. When we ask `erase` to erase a single element, the element must exist—the behavior of `erase` is undefined if we ask it to `erase` an off-the-end iterator.

Removing All the Elements in a Container

To delete all the elements in a container, we could either call `clear` or pass the iterators from `begin` and `end` to `erase`:

```
slist.clear();  // delete all the elements within the container
slist.erase(slist.begin(), slist.end());  // equivalent
```

The iterator-pair version of `erase` lets us delete a subrange of elements:

```
// delete range of elements between two values
list<string>::iterator elem1, elem2;
// elem1 refers to val1
elem1 = find(slist.begin(), slist.end(), val1);
// elem2 refers to the first occurrence of val2 after val1
elem2 = find(elem1, slist.end(), val2);
// erase range from val1 up to but not including val2
slist.erase(elem1, elem2);
```

This code starts by calling `find` twice to obtain iterators to two elements. The iterator `elem1` refers to the first occurrence of `val1` or to the off-the-end iterator if `val1` is not present in the `list`. The iterator `elem2` refers to the first occurrence of `val2` that appears after `val1` if that element exists, otherwise, `elem2` is an off-the-end iterator. The call to `erase` removes the elements starting from the referred to by `elem1` up to but not including `elem2`.

The erase, pop_front, and pop_back functions invalidate any iterators that refer to the removed elements. For vectors, iterators to elements after the erasure point are also invalidated. For deque, if the erase does not include either the first or last element, all iterators into the deque are invalidated.

EXERCISES SECTION 9.3.7

Exercise 9.25: What happens in the program that erased a range of elements if val1 is equal to val2. What happens if either val1 or val2 or both are not present.

Exercise 9.26: Using the following definition of ia, copy ia into a vector and into a list. Use the single iterator form of erase to remove the elements with odd values from your list and the even values from your vector.

```
int ia[] = { 0, 1, 1, 2, 3, 5, 8, 13, 21, 55, 89 };
```

Exercise 9.27: Write a program to process a list of strings. Look for a particular value and, if found, remove it. Repeat the program using a deque.

9.3.8   Assignment and swap

The assignment-related operators act on the entire container. Except for swap, they can be expressed in terms of erase and insert operations. The assignment operator *erases* the entire range of elements in the left-hand container and then *inserts* the elements of the right-hand container object into the left-hand container:

```
c1 = c2;   // replace contents of c1 with a copy of elements in c2
// equivalent operation using erase and insert
c1.erase(c1.begin(), c1.end()); // delete all elements in c1
c1.insert(c1.begin(), c2.begin(), c2.end()); // insert c2
```

After the assignment, the left- and right-hand containers are equal: Even if the containers had been of unequal size, after the assignment both containers have the size of the right-hand operand.

Assignment and the assign operations invalidate all iterators into the left-hand container. swap does *not* invalidate iterators. After swap, iterators continue to refer to the same elements, although those elements are now in a different container.

Using assign

The assign operation deletes all the elements in the container and then inserts new elements as specified by the arguments. Like the constructor that copies elements from a container, the assignment operator (=) can be used to assign one

Table 9.11: Sequential Container Assignment Operations	
`c1 = c2`	Deletes elements in `c1` and copies elements from `c2` into `c1`. `c1` and `c2` must be the same type.
`c1.swap(c2)`	Swaps contents: After the call `c1` has elements that were in `c2`, and `c2` has elements that were in `c1`. `c1` and `c2` must be the same type. Execution time usually *much* faster than copying elements from `c2` to `c1`.
`c.assign(b,e)`	Replaces the elements in `c` by those in the range denoted by iterators `b` and `e`. The iterators `b` and `e` must not refer to elements in `c`.
`c.assign(n,t)`	Replaces the elements in `c` by `n` elements with value `t`.

container to another only if the container and element type are the same. If we want to assign elements of a different but compatible element type and/or from a different container type, then we must use the `assign` operation. For example, we could use `assign` to assign a range of `char*` values from a `vector` into a `list` of `string`.

Because the original elements are deleted, the iterators passed to `assign` must not refer to elements in the container on which `assign` is called.

The arguments to `assign` determine how many elements are inserted and what values the new elements will have. This statement:

```
// equivalent to slist1 = slist2
slist1.assign(slist2.begin(), slist2.end());
```

uses the version of `assign` that takes a pair of iterators. After deleting the elements in `slist1`, the function copies the elements in the range denoted by the iterators into `slist2`. Thus, this code is equivalent to assigning `slist2` to `slist1`.

The `assign` operator that takes an iterator pair lets us assign elements of one container type to another.

A second version of assign takes an integral value and an element value. It replaces the elements in the container by the specified number of elements, each of which has the specified element value

```
// equivalent to: slist1.clear();
// followed by slist1.insert(slist1.begin(), 10, "Hiya!");
slist1.assign(10, "Hiya!"); // 10 elements; each one is Hiya!
```

After executing this statement, `slist1` has 10 elements, each of which has the value `Hiya!`.

Using `swap` to Avoid the Cost of Deleting Elements

The `swap` operation swaps the values of its two operands. The types of the containers must match: The operands must be the same kind of container, and they must hold values of the same type. After the call to `swap`, the elements that had been in the right-hand operand are in the left, and vice versa:

```
vector<string> svec1(10);   // vector with 10 elements
vector<string> svec2(24);   // vector with 24 elements
svec1.swap(svec2);
```

After the `swap`, `svec1` contains 24 `string` elements and `svec2` contains 10.

 The important thing about `swap` is that it does not delete or insert any elements and is guaranteed to run in constant time. No elements are moved, and so iterators are not invalidated.

The fact that elements are not moved means that iterators are not invalidated. They refer to the same elements as they did before the swap. However, after the `swap`, those elements are in a different container. For example, had `iter` referred to the `string` at position `svec1[3]` before the `swap` it will refer to the element at position `svec2[3]` after the `swap`.

EXERCISES SECTION 9.3.8

Exercise 9.28: Write a program to assign the elements from a `list` of `char*` pointers to C-style character strings to a `vector` of `strings`.

9.4 How a `vector` Grows

When we `insert` or push an element onto a container object, the size of that object increases by one. Similarly, if we `resize` a container to be larger than its current `size`, then additional elements must be added to the container. The library takes care of allocating the memory to hold these new elements.

Ordinarily, we should not care about how a library type works: All we should care about is how to use it. However, in the case of `vectors`, a bit of the implementation leaks into its interface. To support fast random access, `vector` elements are stored contiguously—each element is adjacent to the previous element.

Given that elements are contiguous, let's think about what happens when we add an element to a `vector`: If there is no room in the `vector` for the new element, it cannot just add an element somewhere else in memory because the elements must be contiguous for indexing to work. Instead, the `vector` must allocate new memory to hold the existing elements plus the new one, copy the elements from the old location into the new space, add the new element, and deallocate the old memory. If `vector` did this memory allocation and deallocation each time we added an element, then performance would be unacceptably slow.

There is no comparable allocation issue for containers that do not hold their elements contiguously. For example, to add an element to a `list`, the library only needs to create the new element and chain it into the existing list. There is no need to reallocate or copy any of the existing elements.

One might conclude, therefore, that in general it is a good idea to use a list rather than a vector. However, the contrary is usually the case: For most applications the best container to use is a vector. The reason is that library implementors use allocation strategies that minimize the costs of storing elements contiguously. That cost is usually offset by the advantages in accessing elements that contiguous storage allows.

The way vectors achieve fast allocation is by allocating capacity beyond what is immediately needed. The vector holds this storage in reserve and uses it to allocate new elements as they are added. Thus, there is no need to reallocate the container for each new element. The exact amount of additional capacity allocated varies across different implementations of the library. This allocation strategy is dramatically more efficient than reallocating the container each time an element is added. In fact, its performance is good enough that in practice a vector usually grows more efficiently than a list or a deque.

9.4.1 capacity and reserve Members

The details of how vector handles its memory allocation are part of its implementation. However, a portion of this implementation is supported by the interface to vector. The vector class includes two members, capacity and reserve, that let us interact with the memory-allocation part of vector's implementation. The capacity operation tells us how many elements the container could hold before it must allocate more space. The reserve operation lets us tell the vector how many elements it should be prepared to hold.

 It is important to understand the difference between capacity and size. The size is the number of elements in the vector; capacity is how many it could hold before new space must be allocated.

To illustrate the interaction between size and capacity, consider the following program:

```
vector<int> ivec;
// size should be zero; capacity is implementation defined
cout << "ivec: size: " << ivec.size()
     << " capacity: "  << ivec.capacity() << endl;

// give ivec 24 elements
for (vector<int>::size_type ix = 0; ix != 24; ++ix)
    ivec.push_back(ix);

// size should be 24; capacity will be >= 24 and is implementation defined
cout << "ivec: size: " << ivec.size()
     << " capacity: "  << ivec.capacity() << endl;
```

When run on our system, this program produces the following output:

```
ivec: size: 0 capacity: 0
ivec: size: 24 capacity: 32
```

We know that the `size` of an empty `vector` is zero, and evidently our library also sets `capacity` of an empty `vector` to zero. When we add elements to the vector, we know that the `size` is the same as the number of elements we've added. The `capacity` must be at least as large as `size` but can be larger. Under this implementation, adding 24 elements one at a time results in a `capacity` of 32. Visually we can think of the current state of `ivec` as

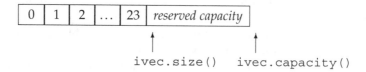

We could now `reserve` some additional space:

```
ivec.reserve(50); // sets capacity to at least 50; might be more
// size should be 24; capacity will be >= 50 and is implementation defined
cout << "ivec: size: " << ivec.size()
     << " capacity: " << ivec.capacity() << endl;
```

As the output indicates, doing so changes the `capacity` but not the `size`:

ivec: size: 24 capacity: 50

We might next use up that reserved capacity as follows:

```
// add elements to use up the excess capacity
while (ivec.size() != ivec.capacity())
    ivec.push_back(0);
// size should be 50; capacity should be unchanged
cout << "ivec: size: " << ivec.size()
     << " capacity: " << ivec.capacity() << endl;
```

Because we used only reserved capacity, there is no need for the `vector` to do any allocation. In fact, as long as there is excess capacity, the `vector` must not reallocate its elements.

The output indicates that at this point we've used up the reserved capacity, and `size` and `capacity` are equal:

ivec: size: 50 capacity: 50

If we now add another element, the `vector` will have to reallocate itself:

```
ivec.push_back(42); // add one more element
// size should be 51; capacity will be >= 51 and is implementation defined
cout << "ivec: size: " << ivec.size()
     << " capacity: " << ivec.capacity() << endl;
```

The output from this portion of the program

ivec: size: 51 capacity: 100

indicates that this `vector` implementation appears to follow a strategy of doubling the current capacity each time it has to allocate new storage.

Each implementation of `vector` is free to choose its own allocation strategy. However, it must provide the `reserve` and `capacity` functions, and it must not allocate new memory until it is forced to do so. How much memory it allocates is up to the implementation. Different libraries will implement different strategies.

Moreover, every implementation is required to follow a strategy that ensures that it is efficient to use `push_back` to populate a `vector`. Technically speaking, the execution time of creating an n-element `vector` by calling `push_back` n times on an initially empty `vector` is never more than a constant multiple of n.

EXERCISES SECTION 9.4.1

Exercise 9.29: Explain the difference between a `vector`'s capacity and its size. Why is it necessary to support the notion of capacity in a container that stores elements contiguously but not, for example, in a `list`?

Exercise 9.30: Write a program to explore the allocation stragegy followed by the library you use for `vector` objects.

Exercise 9.31: Can a container have a capacity less than its size? Is a capacity equal to its size desirable? Initially? After an element is inserted? Why or why not?

Exercise 9.32: Explain what the following program does:

```
vector<string> svec;
svec.reserve(1024);
string text_word;
while (cin >> text_word)
        svec.push_back(text_word);
svec.resize(svec.size()+svec.size()/2);
```

If the program reads 256 words, what is its likely capacity after it is resized? What if it reads 512? 1,000? 1,048?

9.5 Deciding Which Container to Use

As we saw in the previous section, allocating memory to hold elements in contiguous storage has impacts on the memory allocation strategies and overhead of a container. By using clever implementation techniques, library authors minimize this allocation overhead. Whether elements are stored contiguously has other significant impacts on:

- The costs to add or delete elements from the middle of the container

- The costs to perform nonsequential access to elements of the container

The degree to which a program does these operations should be used to determine which type of container to use. The `vector` and `deque` types provide fast non-sequential access to elements at the cost of making it expensive to add or remove elements anywhere other than the ends of the container. The `list` type supports fast insertion and deletion anywhere but at the cost of making nonsequential access to elements expensive.

How Insertion Affects Choice of Container

A `list` represents noncontiguous memory and allows for both forward and backward traversal one element at a time. It is efficient to `insert` or `erase` an element at any point. Inserting or removing an element in a `list` does not move any other elements. Random access, on the other hand, is not supported. Accessing an element requires traversing the intervening elements.

Inserting (or removing) anywhere except at the back of a `vector` requires that each element to the right of the inserted (or deleted) element be moved. For example, if we have a `vector` with 50 elements and we wish to `erase` element number 23, then each of the elements after 23 have to be moved forward by one position. Otherwise, there'd be a hole in the `vector`, and the `vector` elements would no longer be contiguous.

A `deque` is a more complicated data structure. We are guaranteed that adding or removing elements from either end of the `deque` is a fast operation. Adding or removing from the middle will be more expensive. A `deque` offers some properties of both `list` and `vector`:

- Like `vector`, it is inefficient to `insert` or `erase` elements in the middle of the `deque`.

- Unlike `vector`, a `deque` offers efficient `insert` and `erase` at the front as well as at the back.

- Unlike `list` and like `vector`, a `deque` supports fast random access to any element.

- Inserting elements at the front or back of a `deque` does not invalidate any iterators. Erasing the front or back element invalidates only iterators referring to the element(s) erased. Inserting or erasing anywhere else in the `deque` invalidates all iterators referring to elements of the `deque`.

How Access to the Elements Affects Choice of Container

Both `vector` and `deque` support efficient random access to their elements. That is, we can efficiently access element 5, then 15, then 7, and so on. Random access in a `vector` can be efficient because each access is to a fixed offset from the beginning of the `vector`. It is much slower to jump around in a `list`. the only way to move between the elements of a `list` is to sequentially follow the pointers. Moving from the 5th to the 15th element requires visiting every element between them.

In general, unless there is a good reason to prefer another container, `vector` is usually the right one to use.

Hints on Selecting Which Container to Use

There are a few rules of thumb that apply to selecting which container to use:

1. If the program requires random access to elements, use a `vector` or a `deque`.

2. If the program needs to insert or delete elements in the middle of the container, use a `list`.

3. If the program needs to insert or delete elements at the front and the back, but not in the middle, of the container, use a `deque`.

4. If we need to insert elements in the middle of the container only while reading input and then need random access to the elements, consider reading them into a `list` and then reordering the `list` as appropriate for subsequent access and copying the reordered `list` into a `vector`.

What if the program needs to randomly access and insert and delete elements in the middle of the container?

This decision will depend on the relative cost of doing random access to `list` elements versus the cost of copying elements when inserting or deleting elements in a `vector` or `deque`. In general, the predominant operation of the application (whether it does more access or more insertion or deletion) should determine the choice of container type.

Deciding which container to use may require profiling the performance of each container type doing the kinds of operations the application requires.

When you are not certain which container the application should use, try to write your code so that it uses only operations common to both `vectors` and `lists`: Use iterators, not subscripts, and avoid random access to elements. By writing your programs this way, it will be easier to change the container from a `vector` to a `list` if necessary.

9.6 `strings` Revisited

We introduced the `string` type in Section 3.2 (p. 80). Table 9.12 (p. 337) recaps the `string` operations covered in that section.

In addition to the operations we've already used, `strings` also supports most of the sequential container operations. In some ways, we can think of a `string` as a container of characters. With some exceptions, `strings` support the same operations that `vectors` support: The exceptions are that `string` does not support the operations to use the container like a stack: We cannot use the `front`, `back`, and `pop_back` operations on `strings`.

EXERCISES SECTION 9.5

Exercise 9.33: Which is the most appropriate—a vector, a deque, or a list—for the following program tasks? Explain the rationale for your choice. If there is no reason to prefer one or another container explain why not?

(a) Read an unknown number of words from a file for the purpose of generating English language sentences.

(b) Read a fixed number of words, inserting them in the container alphabetically as they are entered. We'll see in the next chapter that associative containers are better suited to this problem.

(c) Read an unknown number of words. Always insert new words at the back. Remove the next value from the front.

(d) Read an unknown number of integers from a file. Sort the numbers and then print them to standard output.

The container operations that string supports are:

- The typedefs, including the iterator types, listed in Table 9.5 (p. 316).

- The constructors listed in Table 9.2 (p. 307) except for the constructor that takes a single size parameter.

- The operations to add elements listed in Table 9.7 (p. 319) that vector supports. Note: Neither vector nor string supports push_front.

- The size operations in Table 9.8 (p. 324).

- The subscript and at operations listed in Table 9.9 (p. 325); string does not provide back or front operations listed in that table.

- The begin and end operations of Table 9.6 (p. 317).

- The erase and clear operations of Table 9.10 (p. 326); string does not support either pop_back or pop_front.

- The assignment operations in Table 9.11 (p. 329).

- Like the elements in a vector, the characters of a string are stored contiguously. Therefore, string supports the capacity and reserve operations described in Section 9.4 (p. 330).

When we say that string supports the container operations, we mean that we could take a program that manipulates a vector and rewrite that same program to operate on strings. For example, we could use iterators to print the characters of a string a line at a time to the standard output:

```
string s("Hiya!");
string::iterator iter = s.begin();
while (iter != s.end())
    cout << *iter++ << endl; // postfix increment: print old value
```

Table 9.12: string Operations Introduced in Section 3.2	
string s;	Defines a new, empty string named s.
string s(cp);	Defines a new string initialized from the null-terminated C-style string pointed to by cp.
string s(s2);	Defines a new string initialized as a copy of s2.
is >> s;	Reads a whitespace-separated string from the input stream is into s.
os << s;	Writes s to the output stream os.
getline(is, s)	Reads characters up to the first newline from input stream is into s.
s1 + s2	Concatenates s1 and s2, yielding a new string.
s1 += s2	Appends s2 to s1.
Relational Operators	The equality (== and !=) and relational (<, <=, >, and >=) can be used to compare strings. string comparison is equivalent to (case-sensitive) dictionary ordering.

Not surprisingly, this code looks almost identical to the code from page 163 that printed the elements of a vector<int>.

In addition to the operations that string shares with the containers, string supports other operations that are specific to strings. We will review these string-specific operations in the remainder of this section. These operations include additional versions of container-related operations as well as other, completely new functions. The additional functions that string provides are covered starting on page 341.

The additional versions of the container operations that string provides are defined to support attributes that are unique to strings and not shared by the containers. For example, several operations permit us to specify arguments that are pointers to character arrays. These operations support the close interaction between library strings and character arrays, whether null-terminated or not. Other versions let us use indices rather than iterators. These versions operate positionally: We specify a starting position, and in some cases a count, to specify the element or range of elements which we want to manipulate.

EXERCISES SECTION 9.6

Exercise 9.34: Use iterators to change the characters in a string to uppercase.

Exercise 9.35: Use iterators to find and to erase each capital letter from a string.

Exercise 9.36: Write a program that initializes a string from a vector<char>.

Exercise 9.37: Given that you want to read a character at a time into a string, and you know that the data you need to read is at least 100 characters long, how might you improve the performance of your program?

The `string` library defines a great number of functions, which use repeated patterns. Given the number of functions supported, this section can be mind-numbing on first reading.

Readers might want to skim the remainder of Section 9.6. Once you know what kinds of operations are available, you can return for the details when writing programs that need to use a given operation.

9.6.1 Other Ways to Construct `strings`

The `string` class supports all but one of the constructors in Table 9.2 (p. 307). The constructor that takes a single size parameter is not supported for `string`. We can create a `string`: as the empty `string`, by providing no argument; as a copy of another `string`; from a pair of iterators; or from a count and a character:

```
string s1;              //  s1 is the empty string
string s2(5, 'a');      //  s2 == "aaaaa"
string s3(s2);          //  s3 is a copy of s2
string s4(s3.begin(),
          s3.begin() + s3.size() / 2);  //  s4 == "aa"
```

In addition to these constructors, the `string` type supports three other ways to create a `string`. We have already used the constructor that takes a pointer to the first character in a null-terminated, character array. There is another constructor that takes a pointer to an element in a character array and a count of how many characters to copy. Because the constructor takes a count, the array does not have to be null-terminated:

```
char *cp = "Hiya";              //  null-terminated array
char c_array[] = "World!!!!";   //  null-terminated
char no_null[] = {'H', 'i'};    //  not null-terminated

string s1(cp);          //  s1 == "Hiya"
string s2(c_array, 5);  //  s2 == "World"
string s3(c_array + 5, 4);  //  s3 == "!!!!"
string s4(no_null);     //  runtime error: no_null not null-terminated
string s5(no_null, 2);  //  ok: s5 == "Hi"
```

We define `s1` using the constructor that takes a pointer to the first character of a null-terminated array. All the characters in that array, up to but not including the terminating null, are copied into the newly created `string`.

The initializer for `s2` uses the second constructor, taking a pointer and a count. In this case, we start at the character denoted by the pointer and copy as many characters as indicated in the second argument. `s2`, therefore, is a copy of the first five characters from the array `c_array`. Remember that when we pass an array as an argument, it is automatically converted to a pointer to its first element. Of course, we are not restricted to passing a pointer to the beginning of the array. We initialize `s3` to hold four exclamation points by passing a pointer to the first exclamation point in `c_array`.

The initializers for s4 and s5 are not C-style strings. The definition of s4 is an error. This form of initialization may be called only with a null-terminated array. Passing an array that does not contain a null is a serious error (Section 4.3, p. 130), although it is an error that the compiler cannot detect. What happens at run time is undefined.

The initialization of s5 is fine: That initializer includes a count that says how many characters to copy. As long as the count is within the size of the array, it doesn't matter whether the array is null-terminated.

Table 9.13: Additional Ways to Construct strings

string s(cp, n)	Create s as a copy of n characters from array pointed to by cp.
string s(s2, pos2)	Create s as a copy of characters in the string s2 starting at index pos2. Undefined if pos2 > s2.size().
string s(s2, pos2, len2)	
	Create s as a copy of len2 characters from s2 starting at index pos2. Undefined if pos2 > s2.size(). Regardless of the value of len2, copies at most s2.size() - pos2 characters.

Note: n, len2 *and* pos2 *are all* unsigned *values.*

Using a Substring as the Initializer

The other pair of constructors allow us to create a string as a copy of a substring of the characters in another string:

```
string s6(s1, 2);    // s6 == "ya"
string s7(s1, 0, 2); // s7 == "Hi"
string s8(s1, 0, 8); // s8 == "Hiya"
```

The first two arguments are the string from which we want to copy and a starting position. In the two-argument version, the newly created string is initialized with the characters from that position to the end of the string argument. We can also provide a third argument that specifies how many characters to copy. In this case, we copy as many characters as indicated (up to the size of the string), starting at the specified position. For example, when we create s7, we copy two characters from s1, starting at position zero. When we create s8, we copy only four characters, not the requested nine. Regardless of how many characters we ask to copy, the library copies up to the size of the string, but not more.

9.6.2 Other Ways to Change a string

Many of the container operations that string supports operate in terms of iterators. For example, erase takes an iterator or iterator range to specify which element(s) to remove from the container. Similarly, the first argument to each version of insert takes an iterator to indicate the position before which to insert the values represented by the other arguments. Although `string` supports these iterator-based operations, it also supplies operations that work in terms of an index. The index is used to indicate the starting element to `erase` or the position before which to `insert` the appropriate values. Table 9.14 lists the operations that are common to both `string` and the containers; Table 9.15 on the facing page lists the `string`-only operations.

Table 9.14: `string` Operations in Common with the Containers	
`s.insert(p, t)`	Insert copy of value t before element referred to by iterator p. Returns an iterator referring to the inserted element.
`s.insert(p, n, t)`	Insert n copies of t before p. Returns `void`.
`s.insert(p, b, e)`	Insert elements in range denoted by iterators b and e before p. Returns `void`.
`s.assign(b, e)`	Replace s by elements in range denoted by b and e. For `string`, returns s, for the containers, returns `void`.
`s.assign(n, t)`	Replace s by n copies of value t. For `string`, returns s, for the containers, returns `void`.
`s.erase(p)`	Erase element referred to by iteartor p. Returns an iterator to the element after the one deleted.
`s.erase(b, e)`	Remove elements in range denoted by b and e. Returns an iterator to the first element after the range deleted.

Position-Based Arguments

The `string`-specific versions of these operations take arguments similar to those of the additional constructors covered in the previous section. These operations let us deal with `strings` positionally and/or let us use arguments that are pointers to character arrays rather than `strings`.

For example, all containers let us specify a pair of iterators that denote a range of elements to `erase`. For `strings`, we can also specify the range by passing a starting position and count of the number of elements to `erase`. Assuming s is at least five characters long, we could erase the last five characters as follows:

```
s.erase(s.size() - 5, 5);   // erase last five characters from s
```

Similarly, we can `insert` a given number of values in a container before the element referred to by an iterator. In the case of `strings`, we can specify the insertion point as an index rather than using an iterator:

```
s.insert(s.size(), 5, '!'); // insert five exclamation points at end of s
```

Specifying the New Contents

The characters to `insert` or `assign` into the `string` can be taken from a character array or another `string`. For example, we can use a null-terminated character array as the value to `insert` or `assign` into a `string`:

```
char *cp = "Stately plump Buck";
string s;
s.assign(cp, 7);              //  s == "Stately"
s.insert(s.size(), cp + 7); //  s == "Stately plump Buck"
```

Similarly, we can `insert` a copy of one `string` into another as follows:

```
s = "some string";
s2 = "some other string";
//  3 equivalent ways to insert all the characters from s2 at beginning of s
//  insert iterator range before s.begin()
s.insert(s.begin(), s2.begin(), s2.end());
//  insert copy of s2 before position 0 in s
s.insert(0, s2);
//  insert s2.size() characters from s2 starting at s2[0] before s[0]
s.insert(0, s2, 0, s2.size());
```

Table 9.15: `string`-Specific Versions	
`s.insert(pos, n, c)`	Insert n copies of character c before element at index pos.
`s.insert(pos, s2)`	Insert copy of `string` s2 before pos.
`s.insert(pos, s2, pos2, len)`	Insert len characters from s2 starting at pos2 before pos.
`s.insert(pos, cp, len)`	Insert len characters from array pointed to by cp before pos.
`s.insert(pos, cp)`	Insert copy of null-terminated string pointed to by cp before pos.
`s.assign(s2)`	Replace s by a copy of s2.
`s.assign(s2, pos2, len)`	Replace s by a copy of len characters from s2 starting at index pos2 in s2.
`s.assign(cp, len)`	Replace s by len characters from array pointed to by cp.
`s.assign(cp)`	Replace s by null-terminated array pointed to by cp.
`s.erase(pos, len)`	Erase len characters starting at pos.

*Unless noted otherwise, all operations return a reference to **s**.*

9.6.3 `string`-Only Operations

The `string` type provides several other operations that the containers do not:

- The `substr` function that returns a substring of the current `string`

- The `append` and `replace` functions that modify the `string`

- A family of `find` functions that search the `string`

The `substr` Operation

The `substr` operation lets us retrieve a substring from a given `string`. We can pass `substr` a starting position and a count. It creates a new `string` that has that many characters, (up to the end of the `string`) from the target `string`, starting at the given position:

```
string s("hello world");
//  return substring of 5 characters starting at position 6
string s2 = s.substr(6, 5);   //  s2 = world
```

Alternatively, we could obtain the same result by writing:

```
//  return substring from position 6 to the end of s
string s3 = s.substr(6);      //  s3 = world
```

Table 9.16: Substring Operation	
`s.substr(pos, n)`	Return a `string` containing n characters from s starting at pos.
`s.substr(pos)`	Return a `string` containing characters from pos to the end of s.
`s.substr()`	Return a copy of s.

The `append` and `replace` Functions

There are six overloaded versions of `append` and ten versions of `replace`. The `append` and `replace` functions are overloaded using the same set of arguments, which are listed in Table 9.18 on the next page. These arguments specify the characters to add to the `string`. In the case of `append`, the characters are added at the end of the `string`. In the `replace` function, these characters are inserted in place a specified range of existing characters in the `string`.

The `append` operation is a shorthand way of inserting at the end:

```
string s("C++ Primer");          // initialize s to "C++ Primer"
s.append(" 3rd Ed.");            // s == "C++ Primer 3rd Ed."
// equivalent to s.append(" 3rd Ed.")
s.insert(s.size(), " 3rd Ed.");
```

The `replace` operations remove an indicated range of characters and insert a new set of characters in their place. The `replace` operations have the same effect as calling `erase` and `insert`.

The ten different versions of `replace` differ from each other in how we specify the characters to remove and in how we specify the characters to insert in their place. The first two arguments specify the range of elements to remove. We can specify the range either with an iterator pair or an index and a count. The remaining arguments specify what new characters to insert.

We can think of `replace` as a shorthand way of erasing some characters and inserting others in their place:

Table 9.17: Operations to Modify `strings` (*args* defined in Table 9.18)	
`s.append(`*args*`)`	Append *args* to s. Returns reference to s.
`s.replace(pos, len, `*args*`)`	Remove `len` characters from s starting at `pos` and replace them by characters formed by *args*. Returns reference to s. **This version does not take *args* equal to `b2, e2`.**
`s.replace(b, e, `*args*`)`	Remove characters in the range denoted by iterators `b` and `e` and replace them by *args*. Returns reference to s. **This version does not take *args* equal to `s2, pos2, len2`.**

```
//  starting at position 11, erase 3 characters and then insert "4th"
s.replace(11, 3, "4th");          // s == "C++ Primer 4th Ed."
//  equivalent way to replace "3rd" by "4th"
s.erase(11, 3);                   // s == "C++ Primer Ed."
s.insert(11, "4th");              // s == "C++ Primer 4th Ed."
```

 There is no requirement that the size of the text removed and inserted be the same.

In the previous call to `replace`, the text we inserted happens to be the same size as the text we removed. We could insert a larger or smaller `string`:

```
s.replace(11, 3, "Fourth"); // s == "C++ Primer Fourth Ed."
```

In this call we remove three characters but insert six in their place.

Table 9.18: Arguments to `append` and `replace`	
`s2`	The `string` s2.
`s2, pos2, len2`	up to `len2` characters from s2 starting at `pos2`.
`cp`	Null-terminated array pointed to by pointer `cp`.
`cp, len2`	up to `len2` characters from character array pointed to by `cp`.
`n, c`	n copies of character c.
`b2, e2`	Characters in the range formed by iterators `b2` and `e2`.

9.6.4   `string` Search Operations

The `string` class provides six search functions, each named as a variant of `find`. The operations all return a `string::size_type` value that is the index of where the match occurred, or a special value named `string::npos` if there is no match. The `string` class defines `npos` as a value that is guaranteed to be greater than any valid index.

There are four versions of each of the search operations, each of which takes a different set of arguments. The arguments to the search operations are listed in Table 9.20. Basically, these operations differ as to whether they are looking for a single character, another string, a C-style, null-terminated string, or a given number of characters from a character array.

Table 9.19: string Search Operations (Arguments in Table 9.20)	
s.find(*args*)	Find first occurrence of *args* in s.
s.rfind(*args*)	Find last occurrence of *args* in s.
s.find_first_of(*args*)	Find first occurrence of any character from *args* in s.
s.find_last_of(*args*)	Find last occurrence of any character from *args* in s.
s.find_first_not_of(*args*)	Find first character in s that is not in *args*.
s.find_last_not_of(*args*)	Find last character in s that is not in *args*.

Finding an Exact Match

The simplest of the search operations is the find function. It looks for its argument and returns the index of the first match that is found, or npos if there is no match:

```
string name("AnnaBelle");
string::size_type pos1 = name.find("Anna"); // pos1 == 0
```

Returns 0, the index at which the substring "Anna" is found in "AnnaBelle".

 By default, the find operations (and other string operations that deal with characters) use the built-in operators to compare characters in the string. As a result, these operations (and other string operations) are case sensitive.

When we look for a value in the string, case matters:

```
string lowercase("annabelle");
pos1 = lowercase.find("Anna");     // pos1 == npos
```

This code will set pos2 to npos—the string Anna does not match anna.

Table 9.20: Arguments to string find Operations	
c, pos	Look for the character c starting at position pos in s. pos defaults to 0.
s2, pos	Look for the string s2 starting at position pos in s. pos defaults to 0.
cp, pos	Look for the C-style null-terminated string pointed to by the pointer cp. Start looking starting at position pos in s. pos defaults to 0.
cp, pos, n	Look for the first n characters in the array pointed to by the pointer cp. Start looking starting at position pos in s. No default for pos or n.

Best Practices   The find operations return a string::size_type. Use an object of that type to hold the return from find.

Find Any Character

A slightly more complicated problem would be if we wanted to match any character in our search string. For example, the following locates the first digit within name:

```
string numerics("0123456789");
string name("r2d2");
string::size_type pos = name.find_first_of(numerics);
cout << "found number at index: " << pos
     << " element is " << name[pos] << endl;
```

In this example, pos is set to a value of 1 (the elements of a string, remember, are indexed beginning at 0).

Specifying Where to Start the Search

We can pass an optional starting position to the find operations. This optional argument indicates the index position from which to start the search. By default, that position is set to zero. One common programming pattern uses this optional argument to loop through a string finding all occurrences. We could rewrite our search of "r2d2" to find all the numbers in name:

```
string::size_type pos = 0;
// each trip reset pos to the next instance in name
while ((pos = name.find_first_of(numerics, pos))
              != string::npos) {
    cout << "found number at index: " << pos
         << " element is " << name[pos] << endl;
    ++pos; // move to the next character
}
```

In this case, we initialize pos to zero so that on the first trip through the while name is searched, beginning at position 0. The condition in the while resets pos to the index of the first number encountered, starting from the current value of pos. As long as the return from find_first_of is a valid index, we print our result and increment pos.

Had we neglected to increment pos at the end of this loop, then it would never terminate. To see why, consider what would happen if we didn't. On the second trip through the loop. we start looking at the character indexed by pos. That character would be a number, so find_first_of would (repeatedly) returns pos!

Note   It is essential that we increment pos. Doing so ensures that we start looking for the next number at a point *after* the number we just found.

Looking for a Nonmatch

Instead of looking for a match, we might call `find_first_not_of` to find the first position that is *not* in the search argument. For example, to find the first non-numeric character of a `string`, we can write

```
string numbers("0123456789");
string dept("03714p3");
// returns 5, which is the index to the character 'p'
string::size_type pos = dept.find_first_not_of(numbers);
```

Searching Backward

Each of the `find` operations that we've seen so far executes left to right. The library provides an analogous set of operations that look through the `string` from right to left. The `rfind` member searches for the last—that is, rightmost—occurrence of the indicated substring:

```
string river("Mississippi");
string::size_type first_pos = river.find("is");   // returns 1
string::size_type last_pos = river.rfind("is");    // returns 4
```

`find` returns an index of 1, indicating the start of the first `"is"`, while `rfind` returns an index of 4, indicating the start of the last occurrence of `"is"`.

The `find_last` Functions

The `find_last` functions operate like the corresponding `find_first` functions, except that they return the *last* match rather than the first:

- `find_last_of` searches for the last character that matches any element of the search `string`.

- `find_last_not_of` searches for the last character that does not match any element of the search `string`.

Each of these operations takes an optional second argument indicating the position within the `string` to begin searching.

9.6.5 Comparing `strings`

As we saw in Section 3.2.3 (p. 85), the `string` type defines all the relational operators so that we can compare two `strings` for equality (`==`), inequality (`!=`), and the less- or greater-than operations (`<`, `<=`, `>`, `>=`). Comparison between `strings` is lexicographical—that is, `string` comparison is the same as a case-sensitive, dictionary ordering:

```
string cobol_program_crash("abend");
string cplus_program_crash("abort");
```

EXERCISES SECTION 9.6.4

Exercise 9.38: Write a program that, given the string

```
"ab2c3d7R4E6"
```

finds each numeric character and then each alphabetic character. Write two versions of the program. The first should use `find_first_of`, and the second `find_first_not_of`.

Exercise 9.39: Write a program that, given the strings

```
string line1 = "We were her pride of 10 she named us:";
string line2 = "Benjamin, Phoenix, the Prodigal"
string line3 = "and perspicacious pacific Suzanne";

string sentence = line1 + ' ' + line2 + ' ' + line3;
```

counts the number of words in `sentence` and identifies the largest and smallest words. If several words have the largest or smallest length, report all of them.

Here `cobol_program_crash` is less than the `cplus_program_crash`. The relational operators compare two `strings` character by character until reaching a position where the two `strings` differ. The overall comparison of the `strings` depends on the comparison between these unequal characters. In this case, the first unequal characters are `'e'` and `'o'`. The letter `'e'` occurs before (is less than) `'o'` in the English alphabet and so `"abend"` is less than `"abort"`. If the `strings` are of different length, and one `string` is a substring of the other, then the shorter `string` is less than the longer.

The `compare` Functions

In addition to the relational operators, `string` provides a set of `compare` operations that perform lexicographical comparions. The results of these operations are similar to the C library `strcmp` function (Section 4.3, p. 132). Given

```
s1.compare(args);
```

`compare` returns one of three possible values:

1. A positive value if `s1` is greater than the `string` represented by *args*

2. A negative value if `s1` is less than the `string` represented by *args*

3. 0 if `s1` is equal to the `string` represented by *args*

For example

```
// returns a negative value
cobol_program_crash.compare(cplus_program_crash);
// returns a positive value
cplus_program_crash.compare(cobol_program_crash);
```

Table 9.21: `string compare` Operations

`s.compare(s2)`   Compare s to s2.

`s.compare(pos1, n1, s2)`

        Compares n1 characters starting at pos1 from s to s2.

`s.compare(pos1, n1, s2, pos2, n2)`

        Compares n1 characters starting at pos1 from s to the n2 characters starting at pos2 in s2.

`s.compare(cp)`   Compares s to the null-terminated string pointed to by cp.

`s.compare(pos1, n1, cp)`

        Compares n1 characters starting at pos1 from s to cp.

`s.compare(pos1, n1, cp, n2)`

        Compares n1 characters starting at pos1 from s to n2 characters starting from the pointer cp.

The overloaded set of six `compare` operations allows us to compare a substring of either one or both `string`s for comparison. They also let us compare a `string` to a character array or portion thereof:

```
char second_ed[] = "C++ Primer, 2nd Edition";
string third_ed("C++ Primer, 3rd Edition");
string fourth_ed("C++ Primer, 4th Edition");
// compares C++ library string to C-style string
fourth_ed.compare(second_ed);   // ok, second_ed is null-terminated
// compare substrings of fourth_ed and third_ed
fourth_ed.compare(fourth_ed.find("4th"), 3,
                  third_ed, third_ed.find("3rd"), 3);
```

The second call to `compare` is the most interesting. This call uses the version of `compare` that takes five arguments. We use `find` to locate the position of the beginning of the substring `"4th"`. We compare three characters starting at that position to a substring from `third_ed`. That substring begins at the position returned from `find` when looking for `"3rd"` and again we compare three characters. Essentially, this call compares `"4th"` to `"3rd"`.

9.7 Container Adaptors

In addition to the sequential containers, the library provides three sequential container adaptors: `queue`, `priority_queue`, and `stack`. An **adaptor** is a general concept in the library. There are container, iterator, and function adaptors. Essentially, an adaptor is a mechanism for making one thing act like another. A container adaptor takes an existing container type and makes it act like a different abstract type. For example, the `stack` adaptor takes any of the sequential containers and makes it operate as if it were a `stack`. Table 9.22 (p. 350) lists the operations and types that are common to all the container adaptors.

EXERCISES SECTION 9.6.5

Exercise 9.40: Write a program that accepts the following two `string`s:

```
string q1("When lilacs last in the dooryard bloom'd");
string q2("The child is father of the man");
```

Using the `assign` and append operations, create the `string`

```
string sentence("The child is in the dooryard");
```

Exercise 9.41: Write a program that, given the `string`s

```
string generic1("Dear Ms Daisy:");
string generic2("MrsMsMissPeople");
```

implements the function

```
string greet(string form, string lastname, string title,
             string::size_type pos, int length);
```

using the `replace` operations, where `lastname` replaces `Daisy` and `pos` indexes into `generic2` of `length` characters replacing `Ms`. For example, the following

```
string lastName("AnnaP");
string salute = greet(generic1, lastName, generic2, 5, 4);
```

returns the `string`

```
Dear Miss AnnaP:
```

To use an adaptor, we must include its associated header:

```
#include <stack>    //  stack adaptor
#include <queue>    //  both queue and priority_queue adaptors
```

Initializing an Adapator

Each adaptor defines two constructors: the default constructor that creates an empty object and a constructor that takes a container and makes a copy of that container as its underlying value. For example, assuming that `deq` is a `deque<int>`, we could use `deq` to initialize a new `stack` as follows:

```
stack<int> stk(deq);    //  copies elements from deq into stk
```

Overriding the Underlying Container Type

By default both `stack` and `queue` are implemented in terms of `deque`, and a `priority_queue` is implemented on a `vector`. We can override the default container type by naming a sequential container as a second type argument when creating the adaptor:

```
//  empty stack implemented on top of vector
stack< string, vector<string> > str_stk;
//  str_stk2 is implemented on top of vector and holds a copy of svec
stack<string, vector<string> > str_stk2(svec);
```

There are constraints on which containers can be used for a given adaptor. We can use any of the sequential containers as the underlying container for a `stack`. Thus, a `stack` can be built on a `vector`, `list`, or deque. The `queue` adaptor requires `push_front` in its underlying container, and so could be built on a `list` but not on a `vector`. A `priority_queue` requires random access and so can be built on a `vector` or a deque but not on a `list`.

Relational Operations on Adaptors

Two adaptors of the same type can be compared for equality, inequality, less-than, greater-than, less-than-equal, and greater-than-equal relationships, provided that the underlying element type supports the equality and less-than operators. For these operations, the elements are compared in turn. The first pair of unequal elements determines the less-than or greater-than relationship.

Table 9.22: Common Adaptor Operations and Types	
`size_type`	Type large enough to hold size of largest object of this type.
`value_type`	Element type.
`container_type`	Type of the underlying container on which the adaptor is implemented.
`A a;`	Create a new empty adaptor named a.
`A a(c);`	Create a new adaptor named a with a copy of the container c.
Relational Operators	Each adaptor supports all the relational operators: ==, !=, <, <=, >, >=.

9.7.1   Stack Adaptor

The operations provided by a `stack` are listed in Table 9.23 on the facing page. The following program exercises this set of five `stack` operations:

```
//  number of elements we'll put in our stack
const stack<int>::size_type stk_size = 10;
stack<int> intStack;  // empty stack
//  fill up the stack
int ix = 0;
while (intStack.size() != stk_size)
    //  use postfix increment; want to push old value onto intStack
    intStack.push(ix++);    //  intStack holds 0...9 inclusive
int error_cnt = 0;
//  look at each value and pop it off the stack
while (intStack.empty() == false) {
    int value = intStack.top();
    //  read the top element of the stack
    if (value != --ix) {
        cerr << "oops! expected " << ix
             << " received " << value << endl;
```

```
                ++error_cnt;
        }
        intStack.pop();  // pop the top element, and repeat
    }
    cout << "Our program ran with "
         << error_cnt << " errors!" << endl;
```

The declaration

```
    stack<int> intStack;  // empty stack
```

defines `intStack` to be an empty `stack` that holds integer elements. The `for` loop adds `stk_size` elements initializing each to the next integer in sequence starting from zero. The `while` loop iterates through the entire `stack`, examining the `top` value and popping it from the `stack` until the `stack` is empty.

Each container adaptor defines its own operations in terms of operations provided by the underlying container type. By default, this `stack` is implemented using a `deque` and uses `deque` operations to implement the operations of a `stack`. For example, when we execute

```
    // use postfix increment; want to push old value onto intStack
    intStack.push(ix++);   // intStack holds 0...9 inclusive
```

this operation executes by calling the `push_back` operation of the `deque` object on which `intStack` is based. Although `stack` is implemented by using a `deque`, we have no direct access to the `deque` operations. We cannot call `push_back` on a `stack`; instead, we must use the `stack` operation named `push`.

Table 9.23: Operations Supported by the Stack Container Adaptor	
`s.empty()`	Returns `true` if the `stack` is empty; false otherwise.
`s.size()`	Returns a count of the number of elements on the `stack`.
`s.pop()`	Removes, but does not return, the top element from the `stack`.
`s.top()`	Returns, but does not remove, the top element on the `stack`.
`s.push(item)`	Places a new top element on the `stack`.

9.7.2 Queue and Priority Queue

The library `queue` uses a first-in, first-out (FIFO) storage and retrieval policy. Objects entering the queue are placed in the back. The next object retrieved is taken from the front of the queue. There are two kinds of queues: the FIFO queue, which we will speak of simply as a `queue`, and a priority queue.

A `priority_queue` lets us establish a priority among the elements held in the queue. Rather than place a newly entered item at the back of the queue, the item is placed ahead of all those items with a lower priority. By default, the library uses the < operator on the element type to determine relative priorities.

A real-world example of a priority queue is the line to check luggage at an airport. Those whose flight is going to leave within the next 30 minutes are generally moved to the front of the line so that they can finish the check-in process before their plane takes off. A programming example of a priority queue is the scheduler of an operating system determining which, of a number of waiting processes, should execute next.

To use either `queue` or `priority_queue`, we must include the `queue` header. Table 9.24 lists the operations supported by `queue` and `priority_queue`.

Table 9.24: Operations Supported by Queues and Priority Queues	
`q.empty()`	Returns `true` if the `queue` is empty; false otherwise.
`q.size()`	Returns a count of the number of elements on the `queue`.
`q.pop()`	Removes, but does not return, the front element from the `queue`.
`q.front()`	Returns, but does not remove, the front element on the `queue`. **This operation can be applied only to a queue.**
`q.back()`	Returns, but does not remove, the back element on the `queue`. **This operation can be applied only to a queue.**
`q.top()`	Returns, but does not remove, the highest-priority element. **This operation can be applied only to a `priority_queue`.**
`q.push(item)`	Places a new element at the end of the `queue` or at its appropriate position based on priority in a `priority_queue`.

EXERCISES SECTION 9.7.2

Exercise 9.42: Write a program to read a series of words into a `stack`.

Exercise 9.43: Use a `stack` to process parenthesized expressions. When you see an open parenthesis, note that it was seen. When you see a close parenthesis after an open parenthesis, pop elements down to and including the open parenthesis off the `stack`. push a value onto the `stack` to indicate that a parenthesized expression was replaced.

CHAPTER SUMMARY

The C++ library defines a number of sequential container types. A container is a template type that holds objects of a given type. In a sequential container, elements are ordered and accessed by position. The sequential containers share a common, standardized interface: If two sequential containers offer a particular operation, then the operation has the same interface and meaning for both containers. All the containers provide (efficient) dynamic memory management. We may add elements to the container without worrying about where to store the elements. The container itself manages its storage.

The most commonly used container, `vector`, supports fast, random access to elements. Elements can be added and removed efficiently from the end of a `vector`. Inserting or deleting elements elsewhere can be expensive. The `deque` class is like a `vector`, but also supports fast insertion and deletion at the front of the `deque`. The `list` class supports only sequential access to elements, but it can be quite fast to insert or remove elements anywhere within the list.

The containers define surprisingly few operations. Containers define constructors, operations to add or remove elements, operations to determine the size of the container, and operations to return iterators to particular elements. Other useful operations, such as sorting or searching, are defined not by the container types but by the standard algorithms, which we shall cover in Chapter 11.

Container operations that add or remove elements can invalidate existing iterators. When mixing actions on iterators and container operations, it is essential to keep in mind whether a given container operation could invalidate the iterators. Many operations that invalidate an iterator, such as `insert` or `erase`, return a new iterator that allows the programmer to maintain a position within the container. Loops that use container operations that change the size of a container should be particularly careful in their use of iterators.

DEFINED TERMS

adaptor A library type, function, or iterator that given a type, function, or iterator, makes it act like another. There are three sequential container adaptors: `stack`, `queue`, and `priority_queue`. Each of these adaptors defines a new interface on top of an underlying sequential container.

begin Container operation that returns an iterator referring to the first element in the container, if there is one, or the off-the-end iterator ff the container is empty.

container A type that holds a collection of objects of a given type. Each library container type is a template type. To define a container, we must specify the type of the

elements stored in the container. The library containers are variable-sized.

deque Sequential container. Elements in a `deque` are accessed by their positional index. Like a `vector` in all respects except that it supports fast insertion at the front of the container as well as at the end and does not relocate elements as a result of insertions or deletions at either end.

end Container operation that returns an iterator referring to the element one past the end of the container.

invalidated iterator An iterator that refers to an element that no longer exists. Using an invalidated iterator is undefined and can cause serious run-time problems.

iterator A type whose operations support navigating among the elements of a container and examining values in the container. Each of the library containers has four companion iterator types listed in Table 9.5 (p. 316). The library iterators all support the dereference (*) and arrow (->) operators to examine the value to which the iterator refers. They also support prefix and postfix increment (++) and decrement (--) and the equality (==) and inequality (!=) operators.

iterator range A range of elements denoted by a pair of iterators. The first iterator refers to the first element in the sequence, and the second iterator refers one past the last element. If the range is empty, then the iterators are equal (and vice versa—if the iterators are equal, they denote an empty range). If the range is non-empty, then it must be possible to reach the second iterator by repeatedly incrementing the first iterator. By incrementing the iterator, each element in the sequence can be processed.

left-inclusive interval A range of values that includes its first element but not its last. Typically denoted as [i, j) meaning the sequence starting at and including i up to but excluding j.

list Sequential container. Elements in a list may be accessed only sequentially—starting from a given element, we can get to another element by incrementing or decrementing across each element between them.

Supports fast insertion (or deletion) anywhere in the list. Adding elements does not affect other elements in the list; iterators remain valid when new elements are added. When an element is removed, only the iterators to that element are invalidated.

priority_queue Adaptor for the sequential containers that yields a queue in which elements are inserted, not at the end but according to a specified priority level. By default, priority is determined by using the less-than operator for the element type.

queue Adaptor for the sequential containers that yields a type that lets us add elements to the back and remove elements from the front.

sequential container A type that holds an ordered collection of objects of a single type. Elements in a sequential container are accessed by position.

stack Adaptor for the sequential containers that yields a type that lets us add and remove elements from one end only.

vector Sequential container. Elements in a vector are accessed by their positional index. We add elements to a vector by calling push_back or insert. Adding elements to a vector might cause it be reallocated, invalidating all iterators into the vector. Adding (or removing) an element in the middle of a vector invalidates all iterators to elements after the insertion (or deletion) point.

C H A P T E R **10**

ASSOCIATIVE CONTAINERS

CONTENTS

This chapter completes our review of the standard library container types by looking at the associative containers. Associative containers differ in a fundamental respect from the sequential containers: Elements in an associative container are stored and retrieved by a key, in contrast to elements in a sequential container, which are stored and accessed sequentially by their position within the container.

Although the associative containers share much of the behavior of the sequential containers, they differ from the sequential containers in ways that support the use of keys. This chapter covers the associative containers and closes with an extended example that uses both associative and sequential containers.

Associative containers support efficient lookup and retrieval by a key. The two primary associative-container types are map and set. The elements in a map are key–value pairs: The key serves as an index into the map, and the value represents the data that are stored and retrieved. A set contains only a key and supports efficient queries to whether a given key is present.

In general, a set is most useful when we want to store a collection of distinct values efficiently, and a map is most useful when we wish to store (and possibly modify) a value associated with each key. We might use a set to hold words that we want to ignore when doing some kind of text processing. A dictionary would be a good use for a map: The word would be the key, and its definition would be the value.

An object of the map or set type may contain only a single element with a given key. There is no way to add a second element with the same key. If we need to have multiple instances with a single key, then we can use multimap or multiset, which do allow multiple elements with a given key.

The associative containers support many of the same operations as do the sequential containers. They also provide specialized operations that manage or use the key. In the sections that follow, we look at the associative container types and their operations in detail. We'll conclude the chapter by using the containers to implement a small text-query program.

Table 10.1: Associative Container Types	
map	Associative array; elements stored and retrieved by key
set	Variable-sized collection with fast retrieval by key
multimap	map in which a key can appear multiple times
multiset	set in which a key can appear multiple times

10.1   Preliminaries: the pair Type

Before we look at the associative containers, we need to know about a simple companion library type named **pair**, which is defined in the utility header.

Creating and Initializing pairs

A pair holds two data values. Like the containers, pair is a template type. Unlike the containers we've seen so far, we must supply two type names when we create a pair: A pair holds two data members, each of which has the corresponding named type. There is no requirement that the two types be the same.

```
pair<string, string> anon;        // holds two strings
pair<string, int> word_count;     // holds a string and an int
pair<string, vector<int> > line;  // holds string and vector<int>
```

When we create `pair` objects with no initializer, the default constructor value-initializes the members. Thus, anon is a `pair` of two empty `string`s, and line holds an empty `string` and an empty `vector`. The `int` value in word_count gets the value 0 and the `string` member is initialized to the empty `string`.

We can also provide initializers for each member:

```
pair<string, string> author("James", "Joyce");
```

creates a `pair` named author, in which each member has type `string`. The object named author is initialized to hold two `string`s with the values "James" and "Joyce".

The `pair` type can be unwieldy to type, so when we wish to define a number of objects of the same `pair` type, it is convenient to use a typedef (Section 2.6, p. 61):

```
typedef pair<string, string> Author;
Author proust("Marcel", "Proust");
Author joyce("James", "Joyce");
```

Table 10.2: Operations on `pairs`	
`pair<T1, T2> p1;`	Create an empty `pair` with two elements of types T1 and T2. The elements are value-initialized (Section 3.3.1, p. 92).
`pair<T1, T2> p1(v1, v2);`	Create a `pair` with types T1 and T2 initializing the `first` member from v1 and the `second` from v2.
`make_pair(v1, v2)`	Creates a new `pair` from the values v1 and v2. The type of the `pair` is inferred from the types of v1 and v2.
`p1 < p2`	Less than between two pair objects. Less than is defined as dictionary ordering: Returns `true` if p1.`first` < p2.`first` or if !(p2.`first` < p1.`first`) && p1.`second` < p2.`second`.
`p1 == p2`	Two `pairs` are equal if their `first` and `second` members are respectively equal. Uses the underlying element `==` operator.
`p.first`	Returns the (`public`) data member of p named `first`.
`p.second`	Returns the (`public`) data member of p named `second`.

Operations on `pairs`

Unlike other library types, the `pair` class gives us direct access to its data members: Its members are `public`. These members are named `first` and `second`, respectively. We can access them using the normal dot operator (Section 1.5.2, p. 25) member access notation:

```
string firstBook;
// access and test the data members of the pair
if (author.first == "James" && author.second == "Joyce")
    firstBook = "Stephen Hero";
```

The library defines only a limited number of operations on `pairs`, which are listed in Table 10.2 on the preceding page.

Generating a New `pair`

In addition to the constructors, the library defines the `make_pair` function, which generates a new `pair` from its two arguments. We might use this function to make a new `pair` to assign to an existing `pair`:

```
pair<string, string> next_auth;
string first, last;
while (cin >> first >> last) {
    // generate a pair from first and last
    next_auth = make_pair(first, last);
    // process next_auth...
}
```

This loop processes a sequence of authors. The call to `make_pair` generates a new `pair` from the names read in the `while` condition. It is equivalent to the somewhat more complicated

```
// use pair constructor to make first and last into a pair
next_auth = pair<string, string>(first, last);
```

Because the data members of `pair` are `public`, we could read the input even more directly as

```
pair<string, string> next_auth;
// read directly into the members of next_auth
while (cin >> next_auth.first >> next_auth.second) {
    // process next_auth...
}
```

EXERCISES SECTION 10.1

Exercise 10.1: Write a program to read a sequence of `strings` and `ints`, storing each into a `pair`. Store the `pairs` in a `vector`.

Exercise 10.2: There are at least three ways to create the `pairs` in the program for the previous exercise. Write three versions of the program creating the `pairs` in each way. Indicate which form you think is easier to write and understand and why.

10.2   Associative Containers

Associative containers share many, but not all, of the operations on sequential containers. Associative containers do not have the `front`, `push_front`, `pop_front`, `back`, `push_back`, or `pop_back` operations.

The operations common to sequential and associative containers are:

- The first three constructors described in Table 9.2 (p. 307):

  ```
  C<T> c;          // creates an empty container
  // c2 must be same type as c1
  C<T> c1(c2);  // copies elements from c2 into c1
  // b and e are iterators denoting a sequence
  C<T> c(b, e); // copies elements from the sequence into c
  ```

  Associative containers cannot be defined from a size, because there would be no way to know what values to give the keys.

- The relational operations described in Section 9.3.4 (p. 321).

- The `begin`, `end`, `rbegin`, and `rend` operations of Table 9.6 (p. 317).

- The typedefs listed in Table 9.5 (p. 316). Note that for `map`, the `value_type` is not the same as the element type. Instead, `value_type` is a `pair` representing the types of the keys and associated values. Section 10.3.2 (p. 361) explains the typedefs for `maps` in more detail.

- The `swap` and assignment operator described in Table 9.11 (p. 329). Associative containers do not provide the `assign` functions.

- The `clear` and `erase` operations from Table 9.10 (p. 326), except that the `erase` operation on an associative container returns `void`.

- The size operations in Table 9.8 (p. 324) except for `resize`, which we cannot use on an associative container.

Elements Are Ordered by Key

The associative container types define additional operations beyond the ones just listed. They also redefine the meaning or return type of operations that are in common with the sequential containers. The differences in these common operations reflect the use of keys in the associative containers.

> There is one important consequence of the fact that elements are ordered by key: When we iterate across an associative container, we are guaranteed that the elements are accessed in key order, irrespective of the order in which the elements were placed in the container.

EXERCISES SECTION 10.2

Exercise 10.3: Describe the differences between an associative container and a sequential container.

Exercise 10.4: Give illustrations on when a `list`, `vector`, `deque`, `map`, and `set` might be most useful.

10.3   The map Type

A map is a collection of key–value pairs. The map type is often referred to as an **associative array**: It is like the built-in array type, in that the key can be used as an index to fetch a value. It is associative in that values are associated with a particular key rather than being fetched by position in the array.

10.3.1   Defining a map

To use a map, we must include the map header. When we define a map object, we must indicate both the key and value type:

```
// count number of times each word occurs in the input
map<string, int> word_count;   // empty map from string to int
```

defines a map object word_count that is indexed by a string and that holds an associated int value.

Table 10.3: Constructors for map	
map<k, v> m;	Create an empty map named m with key and value types k and v.
map<k, v> m(m2);	Create m as a copy of m2; m and m2 must have the same key and value types.
map<k, v> m(b, e);	Create m as a copy of the elements from the range denoted by iterators b and e. Elements must have a type that can be converted to pair<const k, v>.

Constraints on the Key Type

Whenever we use an associative container, its keys have not only a type, but also an associated comparison function. By default, the library uses the < operator for the key type to compare the keys. Section 15.8.3 (p. 605) will show how we can override the default and provide our own function.

Whichever comparison function we use must define a **strict weak ordering** over the key type. We can think of a strict weak ordering as "less than," although we might choose to define a more complicated comparison function. However we define it, such a comparison function must always yield false when we compare a key with itself. Moreover, if we compare two keys, they cannot both be "less than" each other, and if k1 is "less than" k2, which in turn is "less than" k3, then k1 must be "less than" k3. If we have two keys, neither of which is "less than" the other, the container will treat them as equal. When used as a key to a map, either value could be used to access the corresponding element.

In practice, what's important is that the key type must define the < operator and that that operator should "do the right thing."

As an example, in our bookstore problem, we might add a type named ISBN that would encapsulate the rules for ISBNs. In our implementation, ISBNs are strings, which we can compare to determine which ISBN is less than another. Therefore, the ISBN type could support a < operation. Given that we had such a type, we could define a map that would allow us to efficiently search for a particular book held by a bookstore.

```
map<ISBN, Sales_item> bookstore;
```

defines a map object named bookstore that is indexed by an ISBN. Each element in the map holds an associated instance of our Sales_item class.

The key type needs to support only the < operator. There is no requirement that it support the other relational or equality operators.

EXERCISES SECTION 10.3.1

Exercise 10.5: Define a map that associates words with a list of line numbers on which the word might occur.

Exercise 10.6: Could we define a map from vector<int>::iterator to int? What about from list<int>::iterator to int? What about from pair<int, string> to int? In each case, if not, explain why not.

10.3.2 Types Defined by map

The elements of a map are key–value pairs That is, each element has two parts: its key and the value associated with that key. The value_type for a map reflects this fact. This type is more complicated than those we've seen for other containers: value_type is a pair that holds the key and value of a given element. Moreover, the key is const. For example, the value_type of the word_count array is pair<const string, int>.

Table 10.4: Types Defined by the map Class	
map<K, V>::key_type	The type of the keys used to index the map.
map<K, V>::mapped_type	The type of the values associated with the keys in the map.
map<K, V>::value_type	A pair whose first element has type const map<K, V>::key_type and second has type map<K, V>::mapped_type.

When learning the map interface, it is essential to remember that the value_type is a pair and that we can change the value but not the key member of that pair.

Dereferencing a `map` Iterator Yields a `pair`

When we dereference an iterator, we get a reference to a value of the container's
`value_type`. In the case of `map`, the `value_type` is a `pair`:

```
// get an iterator to an element in word_count
map<string, int>::iterator map_it = word_count.begin();
// *map_it is a reference to a pair<const string, int> object
cout << map_it->first;              // prints the key for this element
cout << " " << map_it->second;     // prints the value of the element
map_it->first = "new key";         // error: key is const
++map_it->second;         // ok: we can change value through an iterator
```

Dereferencing the iterator yields a `pair` object in which `first` member holds the
`const` key and `second` member holds the value.

Additional `map` Typedefs

The `map` class defines two additional types, `key_type` and `mapped_type`, that let
us access the type of either the key or the value. For `word_count`, the `key_type`
is `string` and `mapped_type` is `int`. As with the sequential containers (Section 9.3.1, p. 317), we use the scope operator to fetch a type member—for example,
`map<string, int>::key_type`.

EXERCISES SECTION 10.3.2

Exercise 10.7: What are the `mapped_type`, `key_type`, and `value_type` of a map
from `int` to `vector<int>`?

Exercise 10.8: Write an expression using a map iterator to assign a value to an element.

10.3.3   Adding Elements to a `map`

Once the `map` is defined, the next step is to populate it with the key–value element
pairs. We can do so either by using the `insert` member or by fetching an element
using the subscript operator and then assigning a value to the element returned.
In both cases, the fact that there can be only a single element for a given key affects
the behavior of these operations.

10.3.4   Subscripting a `map`

When we write

```
map <string, int> word_count; // empty map
// insert default initialzed element with key Anna; then assign 1 to its value
word_count ["Anna"] = 1;
```

the following steps take place:

1. `word_count` is searched for the element whose key is Anna. The element is not found.

2. A new key–value pair is inserted into `word_count`. The key is a `const string` holding Anna. The value is value initialized, meaning in this case that the value is 0.

3. The new key–value pair is inserted into `word_count`.

4. The newly inserted element is fetched and is given the value 1.

> Subscripting a map behaves quite differently from subscripting an array or `vector`: Using an index that is not already present *adds* an element with that index to the map.

As with other subscript operators, the map subscript takes an index (that is, a key) and fetches the value associated with that key. When we look for a key that is already in the map, then the behavior is the same for a map subscript or a `vector` subscript: The value associated with the key is returned. For maps only, if the key is not already present, *a new element is created and inserted* into the map for that key. The associated value is value-initialized: An element of class type is initialized using the default constructor for the element type; a built-in type is initialized to 0.

Using the Value Returned from a Subscript Operation

As usual, the subscript operator returns an lvalue. The lvalue it returns is the value associated with the key. We can read or write the element:

```
cout << word_count["Anna"];    // fetch element indexed by Anna; prints 1
++word_count["Anna"];          // fetch the element and add one to it
cout << word_count["Anna"];    // fetch the element and print it; prints 2
```

> Unlike `vector` or `string`, the type returned by map subscript operator differs from the type obtained by dereferencing a map iterator.

As we've seen, a map iterator returns a `value_type`, which is a `pair` that contains a `const key_type` and `mapped_type`; the subscript operator returns a value of type `mapped_type`.

Programming Implications of the Subscript Behavior

The fact that subscript adds an element if it is not already in the map allows us to write surprisingly succinct programs:

```
// count number of times each word occurs in the input
map<string, int> word_count;  // empty map from string to int
string word;
while (cin >> word)
    ++word_count[word];
```

This program creates a map that keeps track of how many times each word occurs. The while loop reads the standard input one word at a time. Each time it reads a new word, it uses that word to index word_count. If word is already in the map, then its value is incremented.

The interesting part is what happens when a word is encountered for the first time: A new element indexed by word, with an initial value of zero, is created and inserted into word_count. The value of that element is immediately incremented so that each time we insert a new word into the map it starts off with an occurrence count of one.

EXERCISES SECTION 10.3.4

Exercise 10.9: Write a program to count and print the number of times each word occurs in the input.

Exercise 10.10: What does the following program do?

```
map<int, int> m;
m[0] = 1;
```

Contrast the behavior of the previous program with this one:

```
vector<int> v;
v[0] = 1;
```

Exercise 10.11: What type can be used to subscript a map? What type does the subscript operator return? Give a concrete example—that is, define a map and then write the types that could be used to subscript the map and the type that would be returned from the subscript operator.

10.3.5 Using map::insert

The insert members operate similarly to the operations on sequential containers (Section 9.3.3, p. 318), with one important caveat: We must account for the effect of the key. The key impacts the argument types: The versions that insert a single element take a value that is a key–value pair. Similarly, for the version that takes an iterator pair, the iterators must refer to elements that are key–value pairs. The other difference is the return type from the version of insert that takes a single value, which we will cover in the remainder of this section.

Using **insert** Instead of Subscripting

When we use a subscript to add an element to a map, the value part of the element is value-initialized. Often we immediately assign to that value, which means that we've initialized and assigned the same object. Alternatively, we could insert the element directly by using the syntactically more intimidating insert member:

```
// if Anna not already in word_count, inserts new element with value 1
word_count.insert(map<string, int>::value_type("Anna", 1));
```

Table 10.5: `insert` Operations on maps	
`m.insert(e)`	e is a value of the `value_type` for m. If the key (`e.first`) is not in m, inserts a new element with value `e.second`. If the key is in m, then m is unchanged. Returns a `pair` containing a map iterator referring to the element with key `e.first` and a `bool` indicating whether the element was inserted or not.
`m.insert(beg, end)`	beg and end are iterators that denote a range of values that are key–value `pair`s with the same type as m's `value_type`. For each element in the range, if the given key is not already in m, it inserts the key and its associated value into m. Returns `void`.
`m.insert(iter, e)`	e is a value of the `value_type` for m. If the key (`e.first`) is not in m, inserts the new element using the iterator `iter` as a hint for where to begin the search for where the new element should be stored. Returns an iterator that refers to the element in m with given key.

The argument to this version of `insert`

```
map<string, int>::value_type(anna, 1)
```

is a newly created `pair` that is directly inserted into the map. Remember that `value_type` is a synonym for the type `pair<const K, V>`, where K is the key type and V is the type of the associated value. The argument to `insert` constructs a new object of the appropriate `pair` type to insert into the map. By using `insert`, we can avoid the extraneous initialization of the value that happens when we insert a new map element as a side-effect of using a subscript.

The argument to `insert` is fairly unwieldy. There are two ways to simplify it. We might use `make_pair`:

```
word_count.insert(make_pair("Anna", 1));
```

Or use a typedef:

```
typedef map<string,int>::value_type valType;
word_count.insert(valType("Anna", 1));
```

Either approach improves readability by making the call less complicated.

Testing the Return from `insert`

There can be only one element with a given key in a map. If we attempt to `insert` an element with a key that is already in the map, then `insert` does nothing. The versions of `insert` that take an iterator or iterator pair do not indicate whether or how many elements were inserted.

However, the version of `insert` that takes a single key–value `pair` does return a value. That value is a `pair` that contains an iterator that refers to the element in the map with the corresponding key, and a `bool` that indicates whether the element was inserted. If the key is already in the map, then the value is un-changed, and the `bool` portion of the return is `false`. If the key isn't present, then the element is inserted and the `bool` is `true`. In either case, the iterator refers to the element with the given key. We could rewrite our word count program to use `insert`:

```
// count number of times each word occurs in the input
map<string, int> word_count;   // empty map from string to int
string word;

while (cin >> word) {
    // inserts element with key equal to word and value 1;
    // if word already in word_count, insert does nothing
    pair<map<string, int>::iterator, bool> ret =
            word_count.insert(make_pair(word, 1));
    if (!ret.second)            // word already in word_count
        ++ret.first->second;  // increment counter
}
```

For each `word`, we attempt to `insert` it with a value 1. The `if` test examines the `bool` in the return from the `insert`. If it is `false`, then the insertion didn't happen and an element indexed by `word` was already in `word_count`. In this case we increment the value associated with that element.

Unwinding the Syntax

The definition of `ret` and the increment may be hard to decipher:

```
pair<map<string, int>::iterator, bool> ret =
        word_count.insert(make_pair(word, 1));
```

It should be easy to see that we're defining a `pair` and that the second type of the `pair` is `bool`. The first type of that `pair` is a bit harder to understand. It is the `iterator` type defined by the `map<string, int>` type.

We can understand the increment by first parenthesizing it to reflect the precedence (Section 5.10.1, p. 168) of the operators:

```
++((ret.first)->second);  // equivalent expression
```

Explaining this expression step by step, we have

- `ret` holds return value from `insert`, which is a `pair`. The `first` member of that `pair` is a map iterator referring to the key that was inserted.

- `ret.first` fetches the map iterator from the `pair` returned by `insert`.

- `ret.first->second` dereferences that iterator obtaining a `value_type` object. That object is also a `pair`, in which the `second` member is the value part of the element we added.

- `++ret.first->second` increments that value.

Putting it back together, the increment statement fetches the iterator for the element indexed by `word` and increments the value part of that element.

Exercise 10.12: Rewrite the word-count program that you wrote in the exercises for Section 10.3.4 (p. 364) to use `insert` instead of subscripting. Explain which program you think is easier to write and read. Explain your reasoning.

Exercise 10.13: Given a `map<string, vector<int> >`, write the types used as an argument and as the return value for the version of `insert` that inserts one element.

10.3.6   Finding and Retrieving a map Element

The subscript operator provides the simplest method of retrieving a value:

```
map<string,int> word_count;
int occurs = word_count["foobar"];
```

As we've seen, using a subscript has an important side effect: If that key is not already in the `map`, then subscript inserts an element with that key.

Whether this behavior is correct depends on our expectations. In this example, if "foobar" weren't already present, it would be added to the `map` with an associated value of 0. In this case, `occurs` gets a value of 0.

Our word-counting programs relied on the fact that subscripting a nonexistent element inserts that element and initializes the value to 0. There are times, though, when we want to know if an element is present but do not want the element inserted if it is not present. In such cases, we cannot use the subscript operator to determine whether the element is present.

There are two operations, `count` and `find`, that we can use to determine if a key is present without causing it to be inserted.

Table 10.6: Interrogating a map Without Changing It	
`m.count(k)`	Returns the number of occurrences of k within m.
`m.find(k)`	Returns an iterator to the element indexed by k, if there is one, or returns an off-the-end iterator (Section 3.4, p. 97) if the key is not present.

Using count to Determine Whether a Key is in the map

The `count` member for a `map` always returns either 0 or 1. A map may have only one instance of any given key, so `count` effectively indicates whether the key is present. The return from `count` is more useful for `multimaps`, which we cover in Section 10.5 (p. 375). If the return value is nonzero, we can use the subscript operator to fetch the value associated with the key without worrying that doing so will insert the element into the map:

```
int occurs = 0;
if (word_count.count("foobar"))
    occurs = word_count["foobar"];
```

Of course, executing count followed by the subscript effectively looks for the element twice. If we want to use the element if it is present, we should use find.

Retrieving an Element Without Adding It

The find operation returns an iterator to the element or the end iterator if the element is not present:

```
int occurs = 0;
map<string,int>::iterator it = word_count.find("foobar");
if (it != word_count.end())
    occurs = it->second;
```

We should use find when we want to obtain a reference to the element with the specified key if it exists, and do not want to create the element if it does not exist.

EXERCISES SECTION 10.3.6

Exercise 10.14:   What is the difference between the map operations count and find?

Exercise 10.15:   What kinds of problems would you use count to solve? When might you use find instead?

Exercise 10.16:   Define and initialize a variable to hold the result of a call to find on a map from string to vector of int.

10.3.7   Erasing Elements from a map

There are three variants of the erase operation to remove elements from a map. As with the sequential containers, we can erase a single element or a range of elements by passing erase an iterator or an iterator pair. These versions of erase are similar to the corresponding operations on sequential containers with one exception: The map operations return void, whereas those on the sequential containers return an iterator to the element following the one that was removed.

The map type supplies an additional erase operation that takes a value of the key_type and removes the element with the given key if the element exists. We could use this version to remove a specific word from word_count before printing the results:

```
// erase of a key returns number of elements removed
if (word_count.erase(removal_word))
    cout << "ok: " << removal_word << " removed\n";
else cout << "oops: " << removal_word << " not found!\n";
```

The erase function returns a count of how many elements were removed. In the case of a map, that number is either zero or one. If the return value is zero, then the element we wanted to erase was not in the map.

Table 10.7: Removing Elements from a map	
m.erase(k)	Removes the element with key k from m. Returns size_type indicating the number of elements removed.
m.erase(p)	Removes element referred to by the iterator p from m. p must refer to an actual element in m; it must not be equal to m.end(). Returns void.
m.erase(b, e)	Removes the elements in the range denoted by the iterator pair b, e. b and e must be a valid range of elements in m: b and e must refer to elements in m or one past the last element in m. b and e must either be equal—in which case the range is empty—or the element to which b refers must occur before the element referred to by e. Returns void.

10.3.8 Iterating across a map

Like any other container, map provides begin and end operations that yield iterators that we can use to traverse the map. For example, we could print the map named word_count that we built on page 363 as follows:

```
//  get iterator positioned on the first element
map<string, int>::const_iterator
                        map_it = word_count.begin();
//  for each element in the map
while (map_it != word_count.end()) {
    //  print the element key, value pairs
    cout << map_it->first << " occurs "
        << map_it->second << " times" << endl;
    ++map_it;   //  increment iterator to denote the next element
}
```

The while condition and increment for the iterator in this loop look a lot like the programs we wrote that printed the contents of a vector or a string. We initialize an iterator, map_it, to refer to the first element in word_count. As long as the iterator is not equal to the end value, we print the current element and then increment the iterator. The body of the loop is more complicated than those earlier programs because we must print both the key and value for each element.

The output of our word-count program prints the words in alphabetical order. When we use an iterator to traverse a map, the iterators yield elements in ascending key order.

10.3.9 A Word Transformation Map

We'll close this section with a program to illustrate creating, searching, and iterating across a map. Our problem is to write a program that, given one string, transforms it into another. The input to our program is two files. The first file contains several word pairs. The first word in the pair is one that might be in the input string. The second is the word to use in the output. Essentially, this file provides a set of word transformations—when we find the first word, we should replace it by the second. The second file contains the text to transform. If the contents of the word transformation file is

```
'em      them
cuz      because
gratz    grateful
i        I
nah      no
pos      supposed
sez      said
tanx     thanks
wuz      was
```

and the text we are given to transform is

```
nah i sez tanx cuz i wuz pos to
not cuz i wuz gratz
```

then the program should generate the following output:

```
no I said thanks because I was supposed to
not because I was grateful
```

The Word Transformation Program

Our solution, which appears on the next page, stores the word transformation file in a map, using the word to be replaced as the key and the word to use as the replacement as its corresponding value. We then read the input, looking up each word to see if it has a transformation. If so, we do the transformation and then print the transformed word. If not, we print the original word.

Our main program takes two arguments (Section 7.2.6, p. 243): the name of the word transformation file and the name of the file to transform. We start by checking the number of arguments. The first argument, argv[0], is always the name of the command. The file names will be in argv[1] and argv[2].

Once we know that argv[1] is valid, we call open_file (Section 8.4.3, p. 299) to open the word transformation file. Assuming the open succeeded, we read the transformation pairs. We call insert using the first word as the key and the second as the value. When the while concludes, trans_map contains the data we need to transform the input. If there's a problem with the arguments, we throw (Section 6.13, p. 215) an exception and exit the program.

Next, we call open_file to open the file we want to transform. The second while uses getline to read that file a line at a time. We read by line so that our output will have line breaks at the same position as our input file. To get the words from each line we use a nested while loop that uses an istringstream. This part of the program is similar to the sketch we wrote on page 300.

The inner while checks each word to see if it is in the transformation map. If it is, then we replace the word by its corresponding value from the map. Finally, we print the word, transformed or not. We use the bool firstword to determine whether to print a space. If it is the first word in the line, we don't print a space.

```
/*
 *  A program to transform words.
 *  Takes two arguments: The first is name of the word transformation file
 *                       The second is name of the input to transform
 */
int main(int argc, char **argv)
{
    //  map to hold the word transformation pairs:
    //  key is the word to look for in the input; value is word to use in the output
    map<string, string> trans_map;
    string key, value;

    if (argc != 3)
        throw runtime_error("wrong number of arguments");
    //  open transformation file and check that open succeeded
    ifstream map_file;
    if (!open_file(map_file, argv[1]))
        throw runtime_error("no transformation file");
    //  read the transformation map and build the map
    while (map_file >> key >> value)
        trans_map.insert(make_pair(key, value));

    //  ok, now we're ready to do the transformations
    //  open the input file and check that the open succeeded
    ifstream input;
    if (!open_file(input, argv[2]))
        throw runtime_error("no input file");

    string line;        //  hold each line from the input
    //  read the text to transform it a line at a time
    while (getline(input, line)) {
        istringstream stream(line);   //  read the line a word at a time
        string word;
        bool firstword = true;   //  controls whether a space is printed
        while (stream >> word) {
            //  ok: the actual mapwork, this part is the heart of the program
            map<string, string>::const_iterator map_it =
                                        trans_map.find(word);

            //  if this word is in the transformation map
            if (map_it != trans_map.end())
                //  replace it by the transformation value in the map
                word = map_it->second;
            if (firstword)
                firstword = false;
            else
                cout << " ";   //  print space between words
            cout << word;
        }
        cout << endl;           //  done with this line of input
    }
    return 0;
}
```

Exercise 10.17: Our transformation program uses find to look for each word:

```
map<string, string>::const_iterator map_it =
            trans_map.find(word);
```

Why do you suppose the program uses find? What would happen if it used the subscript operator instead?

Exercise 10.18: Define a map for which the key is the family surname and the value is a vector of the children's names. Populate the map with at least six entries. Test it by supporting user queries based on a surname, which should list the names of children in that family.

Exercise 10.19: Extend the map from the previous exercise by having the vector store a pair that holds a child's name and birthday. Revise the program accordingly. Test your modified test program to verify its correctness.

Exercise 10.20: List at least three possible applications in which the map type might be of use. Write the definition of each map and indicate how the elements are likely to be inserted and retrieved.

10.4 The set Type

A map is a collection of a key–value pairs, such as an address and phone number keyed to an individual's name. In contrast, a set is simply a collection of keys. For example, a business might define a set named bad_checks, to hold the names of individuals who have issued bad checks to the company. A set is most useful when we simply want to know whether a value is present. Before accepting a check, for example, that business would query bad_checks to see whether the customer's name was present.

With two exceptions, set supports the same operations as map:

- All the common container operations listed in Section 10.2 (p. 358).

- The constructors described in Table 10.3 (p. 360).

- The insert operations described in Table 10.5 (p. 365).

- The count and find operations described in Table 10.6 (p. 367).

- The erase operations described in Table 10.7 (p. 369).

The exceptions are that set does not provide a subscript operator and does not define mapped_type. In a set, the value_type is not a pair; instead it and key_type are the same type. They are each the type of the elements stored in the set. These differences reflect the fact that set holds only keys; there is no value associated with the key. As with map, the keys of a set must be unique and may not be changed.

EXERCISES SECTION 10.4

Exercise 10.21: Explain the difference between a map and a set. When might you use one or the other?

Exercise 10.22: Explain the difference between a set and a list. When might you use one or the other?

10.4.1   Defining and Using sets

To use a set, we must include the set header. The operations on sets are essentially identical to those on maps.

As with map, there can be only one element with a given key in a set. When we initialize a set from a range of elements or insert a range of elements, only one element with a given key is actually added:

```
// define a vector with 20 elements, holding two copies of each number from 0 to 9
vector<int> ivec;
for (vector<int>::size_type i = 0; i != 10; ++i) {
    ivec.push_back(i);
    ivec.push_back(i);   // duplicate copies of each number
}
// iset holds unique elements from ivec
set<int> iset(ivec.begin(), ivec.end());

cout << ivec.size() << endl;    // prints 20
cout << iset.size() << endl;    // prints 10
```

We first create a vector of ints named ivec that has 20 elements: two copies of each of the integers from 0 through 9 inclusive. We then use all the elements from ivec to initialize a set of ints. That set has only ten elements: one for each distinct element in ivec.

Adding Elements to a set

We can add elements to a set by using the insert operation:

```
set<string> set1;          // empty set
set1.insert("the");        // set1 now has one element
set1.insert("and");        // set1 now has two elements
```

Alternatively, we can insert a range of elements by providing a pair of iterators to insert. This version of insert works similarly to the constructor that takes an iterator pair—only one element with a given key is inserted:

```
set<int> iset2;    // empty set
iset2.insert(ivec.begin(), ivec.end());    // iset2 has 10 elements
```

Like the map operations, the version of insert that takes a key returns a pair containing an iterator to the element with this key and a bool indicating whether the element was added. The one that takes an iterator pair returns void.

Fetching an Element from a `set`

There is no subscript operator on `set`s. To fetch an element from a `set` by its key, we use the `find` operation. If we just want to know whether the element is present, we could also use `count`, which returns the number of elements in the `set` with a given key. Of course, for `set` that value can be only one (if the element is present) or zero (if it is not):

```
iset.find(1)     // returns iterator that refers to the element with key == 1
iset.find(11)    // returns iterator == iset.end()

iset.count(1)    // returns 1
iset.count(11)   // returns 0
```

Just as we cannot change the key part of a `map` element, the keys in a `set` are also `const`. If we have an iterator to an element of the `set`, all we can do is read it; we cannot write through it:

```
// set_it refers to the element with key == 1
set<int>::iterator set_it = iset.find(1);
*set_it = 11;                // error: keys in a set are read-only
cout << *set_it << endl;     // ok: can read the key
```

10.4.2 Building a Word-Exclusion Set

On page 369 we removed a given word from our `word_count` map. We might want to extend this approach to remove all the words in a specified file. That is, our word-count program should count only words that are not in a set of excluded words. Using `set` and `map`, this program is fairly straightforward:

```
void restricted_wc(ifstream &remove_file,
                   map<string, int> &word_count)
{
    set<string> excluded;    // set to hold words we'll ignore
    string remove_word;
    while (remove_file >> remove_word)
        excluded.insert(remove_word);
    // read input and keep a count for words that aren't in the exclusion set
    string word;
    while (cin >> word)
        // increment counter only if the word is not in excluded
        if (!excluded.count(word))
            ++word_count[word];
}
```

This program is similar to the word-count program on page 363. The difference is that we do not bother to count the common words.

The function starts by reading the file it was passed. That file contains the list of excluded words, which we store in the `set` named `excluded`. When the first `while` completes, that `set` contains an entry for each word in the input file.

The next part of the program looks a lot like our original word-count program. The important difference is that before counting each word, we check whether the word is in the exclusion set. We do this check in the `if` inside the second `while`:

```
//  increment counter only if the word is not in excluded
if (!excluded.count(word))
```

The call to `count` returns one if `word` is in `excluded` and zero otherwise. We negate the return from `count` so that the test succeeds if `word` is not in `excluded`. If `word` is not in `excluded`, we update its value in the `map`.

As in the previous version of our word count program, we rely on the fact that subscripting a `map` inserts an element if the key is not already in the `map`. Hence, the effect of

```
++word_count[word];
```

is to insert `word` into `word_count` if it wasn't already there. If the element is inserted, its value is initially set to 0. Regardless of whether the element had to be created, the value is then incremented.

EXERCISES SECTION 10.4.2

Exercise 10.23: Write a program that stores the excluded words in a `vector` instead of in a `set`. What are the advantages to using a `set`?

Exercise 10.24: Write a program that generates the non-plural version of a word by stripping the `'s'` off the end of the word. Build an exclusion set to recognize words in which the trailing `'s'` should not be removed. Two examples of words to place in this set are `success`, `class`. Use this exclusion set to write a program that strips plural suffixes from its input but leaves words in the exclusion set unchanged.

Exercise 10.25: Define a `vector` of books you'd like to read within the next six months and a set of titles that you've read. Write a program that chooses a next book for you to read from the `vector`, provided that you have not yet read it. When it returns the selected title to you, it should enter the title in the set of books read. If in fact you end up putting the book aside, provide support for removing the title from the set of books read. At the end of our virtual six months, print the set of books read and those books that were not read.

10.5 The `multimap` and `multiset` Types

Both `map` and `set` can contain only a single instance of each key. The types `multiset` and a `multimap` allow multiple instances of a key. In a phone directory, for example, someone might wish to provide a separate listing for each phone number associated with an individual. A listing of available texts by an author might provide a separate listing for each title. The `multimap` and `multiset` types are defined in the same headers as the corresponding single-element versions: the `map` and `set` headers, respectively.

The operations supported by `multimap` and `multiset` are the same as those on `map` and `set`, respectively, with one exception: `multimap` does not support subscripting. We cannot subscript a `multimap` because there may be more than one value associated with a given key. The operations that are common to both `map` and `multimap` or `set` and `multiset` change in various ways to reflect the fact that there can be multiple keys. When using either a `multimap` or `multiset`, we must be prepared to handle multiple values, not just a single value.

10.5.1   Adding and Removing Elements

The `insert` operations described in Table 10.5 (p. 365) and the `erase` operations described in Table 10.7 (p. 369) are used to add and remove elements of a `multimap` or `multiset`.

Because keys need not be unique, `insert` always adds an element. As an example, we might define a `multimap` to map authors to titles of the books they have written. The map might hold multiple entries for each author:

```cpp
// adds first element with key Barth
authors.insert(make_pair(
  string("Barth, John"),
  string("Sot-Weed Factor")));
// ok: adds second element with key Barth
authors.insert(make_pair(
  string("Barth, John"),
  string("Lost in the Funhouse")));
```

The version of `erase` that takes a key removes *all* elements with that key. It returns a count of how many elements were removed. The versions that take an iterator or an iterator pair remove only the indicated element(s). These versions return `void`:

```cpp
multimap<string, string> authors;
string search_item("Kazuo Ishiguro");
// erase all elements with this key; returns number of elements removed
multimap<string, string>::size_type cnt =
                    authors.erase(search_item);
```

10.5.2   Finding Elements in a `multimap` or `multiset`

We noted that `map`s and `set`s store their elements in order. The `multimap` and `multiset` types do so as well. As a result, when a `multimap` or `multiset` has multiple instances of a given key, those instances will be adjacent elements within the container.

We are guaranteed that iterating across a `multimap` or `multiset` returns all the elements with a given key in sequence.

Finding an element in a `map` or a `set` is a simple matter—the element is or is not in the container. For `multimap` and `multiset` the process is more complicated: the element may be present many times. For example, given our map from author to titles, we might want to find and print all the books by a particular author.

It turns out that there are three strategies we might use to find and print all the books by a given author. Each of these strategies relies on the fact that we know that all the entries for a given author will be adjacent within the `multimap`.

We'll start by presenting a strategy that uses only functions we've already seen. This version turns out to require the most code, so we will continue by exploring more compact alternatives.

Using `find` and `count`

We could solve our problem using `find` and `count`. The `count` function tells us how many times a given key occurs, and the `find` operation returns an iterator that refers to the first instance of the key we're looking for:

```
//   author we'll look for
string search_item("Alain de Botton");
//   how many entries are there for this author
typedef multimap<string, string>::size_type sz_type;
sz_type entries = authors.count(search_item);
//   get iterator to the first entry for this author
multimap<string,string>::iterator iter =
                       authors.find(search_item);
//   loop through the number of entries there are for this author
for (sz_type cnt = 0; cnt != entries; ++cnt, ++iter)
        cout << iter->second << endl; //  print each title
```

We start by determining how many entries there are for the author by calling `count` and getting an iterator to the first element with this key by calling `find`. The number of iterations of the `for` loop depends on the number returned from `count`. In particular, if the `count` was zero, then the loop is never executed.

A Different, Iterator-Oriented Solution

Another, more elegant strategy uses two associative container operations that we haven't seen yet: `lower_bound` and `upper_bound`. These operations, listed in Table 10.8 (p. 379), apply to all associative containers. They can be used with (plain) `map`s or `set`s but are most often used with `multimap`s or `multiset`s. Each of these operations takes a key and returns an iterator.

Calling `lower_bound` and `upper_bound` on the same key yields an iterator range (Section 9.2.1, p. 314) that denotes all the elements with that key. If the key is in the container, the iterators will differ: the one returned from `lower_bound` will refer to the first instance of the key, whereas `upper_bound` will return an iterator referring just after the last instance. If the element is not in the `multimap`, then `lower_bound` and `upper_bound` will return equal iterators; both will refer to the point at which the key could be inserted without disrupting the order.

Of course, the iterator returned from these operations might be the off-the-end iterator for the container itself. If the element we look for has the largest key in the `multimap`, then `upper_bound` on that key returns the off-the-end iterator. If the key is not present and is larger than any key in the `multimap`, then the return from `lower_bound` will also be the off-the-end iterator.

 The iterator returned from `lower_bound` may or may not refer to an element with the given key. If the key is not in the container, then `lower_bound` refers to the first point at which this key could be inserted while preserving the element order within the container.

Using these operations, we could rewrite our program as follows:

```
//   definitions of authors and search_item as above
//   beg and end denote range of elements for this author
typedef multimap<string, string>::iterator authors_it;
authors_it beg = authors.lower_bound(search_item),
           end = authors.upper_bound(search_item);
//   loop through the number of entries there are for this author
while (beg != end) {
    cout << beg->second << endl; //   print each title
    ++beg;
}
```

This program does the same work as the previous one that used `count` and `find` but accomplishes its task more directly. The call to `lower_bound` positions `beg` so that it refers to the first element matching `search_item` if there is one. If there is no such element, then `beg` refers to first element with a key larger than `search_item`. The call to `upper_bound` sets end to refer to the element with the key just beyond the last element with the given key.

 These operations say nothing about whether the key is present. The important point is that the return values act like an iterator range.

If there is no element for this key, then `lower_bound` and `upper_bound` will be equal: They will both refer to the same element or they will both point one past the end of the `multimap`. They both will refer to the point at which this key could be inserted while maintaining the container order.

If there are elements with this key, then `beg` will refer to the first such element. We can increment `beg` to traverse the elements with this key. The iterator in end will signal when we've seen all the elements. When `beg` equals end, we have seen every element with this key.

Given that these iterators form a range, we can use the same kind of `while` loop that we've used to traverse other ranges. The loop is executed zero or more times and prints the entries, if any, for the given author. If there are no elements, then `beg` and end are equal and the loop is never executed. Otherwise, we know that the increment to `beg` will eventually reach end and that in the process we will print each record associated with this author.

Table 10.8: Associative Container Operations Returning Iterators	
`m.lower_bound(k)`	Returns an iterator to the first element with key not less than k.
`m.upper_bound(k)`	Returns an iterator to the first element with key greater than k.
`m.equal_range(k)`	Returns a `pair` of iterators. The `first` member is equivalent to `m.lower_bound(k)` and `second` is equivalent to `m.upper_bound(k)`.

The `equal_range` Function

It turns out that there is an even more direct way to solve this problem: Instead of calling `upper_bound` and `lower_bound`, we can call `equal_range`. This function returns a `pair` of iterators. If the value is present, then the first iterator refers to the first instance of the key and the second iterator refers one past the last instance of the key. If no matching element is found, then both the first and second iterator refer to the position where this key could be inserted.

We could use `equal_range` to modify our program once again:

```
//  definitions of authors and search_item as above
//  pos holds iterators that denote range of elements for this key
pair<authors_it, authors_it>
                  pos = authors.equal_range(search_item);
//  loop through the number of entries there are for this author
while (pos.first != pos.second) {
    cout << pos.first->second << endl;  //  print each title
    ++pos.first;
}
```

This program is essentially identical to the previous one that used `upper_bound` and `lower_bound`. Instead of using local variables, `beg` and `end`, to hold the iterator range, we use the `pair` returned by `equal_range`. The `first` member of that `pair` holds the same iterator as the one `lower_bound` would have returned. The iterator that `upper_bound` would have returned is in the `second` member.

Thus, in this program `pos.first` is equivalent to `beg`, and `pos.second` is equivalent to `end`.

10.6 Using Containers: Text-Query Program

To conclude this chapter, we'll implement a simple text-query program.

Our program will read a file specified by the user and then allow the user to search the file for words that might occur in it. The result of a query will be the number of times the word occurs and a list of lines on which it appears. If a word occurs more than once on the same line, our program should be smart enough to display that line only once. Lines should be displayed in ascending order—that is, line 7 should be displayed before line 9, and so on.

Exercise 10.26: Write a program that populates a `multimap` of authors and their works. Use `find` to find an element in the `multimap` and `erase` that element. Be sure your program works correctly if the element you look for is not in the `map`.

Exercise 10.27: Repeat the program from the previous exercise, but this time use `equal_range` to get iterators so that you can `erase` a range of elements.

Exercise 10.28: Using the `multimap` from the previous exercise, write a program to generate the list of authors whose name begins with the each letter in the alphabet. Your output should look something like:

```
Author Names Beginning with 'A':
Author, book, book, ...
...
Author Names Beginning with 'B':
...
```

Exercise 10.29: Explain the meaning of the operand `pos.first->second` used in the output expression of the final program in this section.

For example, we might read the file that contains the input for this chapter and look for the word "element." The first few lines of the output would be:

```
element occurs 125 times
    (line 62) element with a given key.
    (line 64) second element with the same key.
    (line 153) element |==| operator.
    (line 250) the element type.
    (line 398) corresponding element.
```

followed by the remaining 120 or so lines in which the word "element" occurs.

10.6.1 Design of the Query Program

A good way to start the design of a program is to list the program's operations. Knowing what operations we need to provide can then help us see what data structures we'll need and how we might implement those actions. Starting from requirements, the tasks our program needs to support include:

1. It must allow the user to indicate the name of a file to process. The program will store the contents of the file so that we can display the original line in which each word appears.

2. The program must break each line into words and remember all the lines in which each word appears. When it prints the line numbers, they should be presented in ascending order and contain no duplicates.

3. The result of querying for a particular word should be the line numbers on which that word appeared.

4. To print the text in which the word appeared, it must be possible to fetch the line from the input file corresponding to a given line number.

Data Structure

We'll implement our program as a simple class that we'll name `TextQuery`. Our requirements can be met quite neatly by using various containers:

1. We'll use a `vector<string>` to store a copy of the entire input file. Each line in the input file will be an element in this `vector`. That way, when we want to print a line, we can fetch it by using the line number as an index.

2. We'll store each word's line numbers in a `set`. Using a `set` will guarantee that there is only one entry per line and that the line numbers will be automatically stored in ascending order.

3. We'll use a `map` to associate each word with the `set` of line numbers on which the word appears.

Our class will have two data members: a `vector` to hold the input file and a `map` to associate each input word with the `set` of line numbers on which it appears.

Operations

The requirements also lead fairly directly to an interface for our class. However, we have one important design decision to make first: The function that does the query will need to return a `set` of line numbers. What type should it use to do so?

We can see that doing the query will be simple: We'll index into the `map` to obtain the associated `set`. The only question is how to return the `set` that we find. The safest design is to return a copy of that `set`. However, doing so means that each element in the `set` must be copied. Copying the `set` could be expensive if we process a very large file. Other possible return values are a `pair` of iterators into the `set`, or a `const` reference to the `set`. For simplicity, we'll return a copy, noting that this decision is one that we might have to revisit if the copy is too expensive in practice.

The first, third, and fourth tasks are actions programmers using our class will perform. The second task is internal to the class. Mapping these tasks to member functions, we'll have three `public` functions in the class interface:

- `read_file` takes an `ifstream&`, which it reads a line at a time, storing the lines in the `vector`. Once it has read all the input, `read_file` will create the `map` that associates each word to the line numbers on which it appears.

- `run_query` takes a `string` and returns the `set` of line numbers on which that `string` appears.

- `text_line` takes a line number and returns the corresponding text for that line from the input file.

Neither `run_query` nor `text_line` changes the object on which it runs, so we'll define these operations as `const` member functions (Section 7.7.1, p. 260).

To do the work of `read_file`, we'll also define two `private` functions to read the input file and build the `map`:

- `store_file` will read the file and store the data in our `vector`.

- `build_map` will break each line into words and build the `map`, remembering the line number on which each word appeared.

10.6.2 `TextQuery` Class

Having worked through our design, we can now write our `TextQuery` class:

```
class TextQuery {
public:
    //   typedef to make declarations easier
    typedef std::vector<std::string>::size_type line_no;
    /*   interface:
     *     read_file builds internal data structures for the given file
     *     run_query finds the given word and returns set of lines on which it appears
     *     text_line returns a requested line from the input file
     */
    void read_file(std::ifstream &is)
                { store_file(is); build_map(); }
    std::set<line_no> run_query(const std::string&) const;
    std::string text_line(line_no) const;
private:
    //   utility functions used by read_file
    void store_file(std::ifstream&); //  store input file
    void build_map(); //  associated each word with a set of line numbers
    //   remember the whole input file
    std::vector<std::string> lines_of_text;
    //   map word to set of the lines on which it occurs
    std::map< std::string, std::set<line_no> > word_map;
};
```

The class directly reflects our design decisions. The only part we hadn't described is the typedef that defines an alias for `size_type` of `vector`.

For the reasons described on page 80, this class definition uses fully qualified `std::` names for all references to library entities.

The `read_file` function is defined inside the class. It calls `store_file` to read and store the input file and `build_map` to build the `map` from words to line numbers. We'll define the other functions in Section 10.6.4 (p. 385). First, we'll write a program that uses this class to solve our text-query problem.

EXERCISES SECTION 10.6.2

Exercise 10.30: The member functions of `TextQuery` use only capabilities that we have already covered. Without looking ahead, write your own versions of the member functions. Hint: The only tricky part is what to return from `run_query` if the line number set is empty. The solution is to construct and return a new (temporary) `set`.

10.6.3 Using the `TextQuery` Class

The following `main` program uses a `TextQuery` object to perform a simple query session with the user. Most of the work in this program involves managing the interaction with the user: prompting for the next search word and calling the `print_results` function—which we shall write next—to print the results.

```
//   program takes single argument specifying the file to query
int main(int argc, char **argv)
{
    //   open the file from which user will query words
    ifstream infile;
    if (argc < 2 || !open_file(infile, argv[1])) {
        cerr << "No input file!" << endl;
        return EXIT_FAILURE;
    }
    TextQuery tq;
    tq.read_file(infile);   //   builds query map
    //   iterate with the user: prompt for a word to find and print results
    //   loop indefinitely; the loop exit is inside the while
    while (true) {
        cout << "enter word to look for, or q to quit: ";
        string s;
        cin >> s;
        //   stop if hit eof on input or a 'q' is entered
        if (!cin || s == "q") break;
        //   get the set of line numbers on which this word appears
        set<TextQuery::line_no> locs = tq.run_query(s);
        //   print count and all occurrences, if any
        print_results(locs, s, tq);
    }
    return 0;
}
```

Preliminaries

This program checks that `argv[1]` is valid and then uses the `open_file` function (Section 8.4.3, p. 299) to open the file we're given as an argument to `main`. We test the stream to determine whether the input file is okay. If not, we generate an appropriate message and exit, returning `EXIT_FAILURE` (Section 7.3.2, p. 247) to indicate that an error occurred.

Once we have opened the file, it is a simple matter to build up the `map` that will support queries. We define a local variable named `tq` to hold the file and associated data structures:

```
TextQuery tq;
tq.read_file(infile);   // builds query map
```

We call the `read_file` operation on `tq`, passing it the file opened by `open_file`.

After `read_file` completes, `tq` holds our two data structures: the `vector` that corresponds to the input file and the `map` from word to set of line numbers. That `map` contains an entry for each unique word in the input file. The `map` associates with each word the `set` of line numbers on which that word appeared.

Doing the Search

We want the program to let the user look for more than one word in each session, so we wrap the prompt in a `while` loop:

```
//   iterate with the user: prompt for a word to find and print results
//   loop indefinitely; the loop exit is inside the while          .
while (true) {
    cout << "enter word to look for, or q to quit: ";
    string s;
    cin >> s;
    //   stop if hit eof on input or a 'q' is entered
    if (!cin || s == "q") break;
    //   get the set of line numbers on which this word appears
    set<TextQuery::line_no> locs = tq.run_query(s);
    //   print count and all occurrences, if any
    print_results(locs, s, tq);
}
```

The test in the `while` is the boolean literal `true`, which means that the test always succeeds. We exit the loop through the `break` after the test on `cin` and the value read into `sought`. The loop exits when `cin` hits an error or end-of-file or when the user enters a `'q'` to quit.

Once we have a word to look for, we ask `tq` for the `set` of line numbers on which that word appears. We pass that `set` along with the word we are looking for and the `TextQuery` object to the `print_results` function. That function will write the output of our program.

Printing the Results

What remains is to define the `print_results` function:

```
void print_results(const set<TextQuery::line_no>& locs,
                   const string& sought, const TextQuery &file)
{
    //   if the word was found, then print count and all occurrences
    typedef set<TextQuery::line_no> line_nums;
```

```
            line_nums::size_type size = locs.size();
            cout << "\n" << sought << " occurs "
                 << size << " "
                 << make_plural(size, "time", "s") << endl;
            // print each line in which the word appeared
            line_nums::const_iterator it = locs.begin();
            for ( ; it != locs.end(); ++it) {
                cout << "\t(line "
                     // don't confound user with text lines starting at 0
                     << (*it) + 1 << ") "
                     << file.text_line(*it) << endl;
            }
    }
}
```

The function starts by defining a typedef to simplify the use of the line number set. Our output first reports how many matches were found, which we know from the size of the set. We call make_plural (Section 7.3.2, p. 248) to print time or times, depending on whether that size is equal to one.

The messiest part of the program is the for loop that processes locs to print the line numbers on which the word was found. The only subtlety here is remembering to change the line numbers into more human-friendly counting. When we stored the text, we stored the first line as line number zero, which is consistent with how C++ containers and arrays are numbered. Most users think of the first line as line number 1, so we systematically add one to our stored line numbers to convert to this more common notation.

EXERCISES SECTION 10.6.3

Exercise 10.31: What is the output of main if we look for a word that is not found?

10.6.4 Writing the Member Functions

What remains is to write the definitions of the member functions that were not defined inside the class.

Storing the Input File

Our first task is to read the file that our user wishes to query. Using string and vector operations, this task is handled easily:

```
    // read input file: store each line as element in lines_of_text
    void TextQuery::store_file(ifstream &is)
    {
        string textline;
        while (getline(is, textline))
            lines_of_text.push_back(textline);
    }
```

Because we want to store the file a line at a time, we use `getline` to read our input. We push each line we read onto the `lines_of_text vector`.

Building the Word `map`

Each element in the `vector` holds a line of text. To build the `map` from words to line numbers, we need to break each line into its individual words. We again use an `istringstream` in ways outlined in the program on page 300:

```
//  finds whitespace-separated words in the input vector
//    and puts the word in word_map along with the line number
void TextQuery::build_map()
{
    //  process each line from the input vector
    for (line_no line_num = 0;
                 line_num != lines_of_text.size();
                 ++line_num)
    {
        //  we'll use line to read the text a word at a time
        istringstream line(lines_of_text[line_num]);
        string word;
        while (line >> word)
            //  add this line number to the set;
            //  subscript will add word to the map if it's not already there
            word_map[word].insert(line_num);
    }
}
```

The `for` loop marches through `lines_of_text` a line at a time. We start by binding an `istringstream` object named `line` to the current line and use the `istringstream` input operator to read each word on the line. Remember that that operator, like the other `istream` operators, ignores whitespace. Thus, the `while` reads each whitespace-separated word from `line` into `word`.

The last part of this function is similar to our word-count programs. We use `word` to subscript the `map`. If `word` was not already present, then the subscript operator adds `word` to the `word_map`, giving it an inital value that is the empty set. Regardless of whether `word` was added, the return value from the subscript is a `set`. We then call `insert` to add the current line number. If the word occurs more than once in the same line, then the call to `insert` does nothing.

Supporting Queries

The `run_query` function handles the actual queries:

```
set<TextQuery::line_no>
TextQuery::run_query(const string &query_word) const
{
    //  Note: must use find and not subscript the map directly
    //  to avoid adding words to word_map!
    map<string, set<line_no> >::const_iterator
                      loc = word_map.find(query_word);
```

```
            if (loc == word_map.end())
                return set<line_no>();   //  not found, return empty set
            else
                //  fetch and return set of line numbers for this word
                return loc->second;
    }
```

The `run_query` function takes a reference to a `const string` and uses that value to index the `word_map`. Assuming the `string` is found, it returns the `set` of line numbers associated with the `string`. Otherwise, it returns an empty `set`.

Using the Return from `run_query`

Once we've run the `run_query` function, we get back a set of line numbers on which the word we sought appears. In addition to printing how many times each word appears, we also want to print the line on which the word appeared. The `text_line` function lets us do so:

```
string TextQuery::text_line(line_no line) const
{
    if (line < lines_of_text.size())
        return lines_of_text[line];
    throw std::out_of_range("line number out of range");
}
```

This function takes a line number and returns the input text line corresponding to that line number. Because the code using our `TextQuery` class cannot do so—`lines_of_text` is `private`—we first check that the line we are asked for is in range. If it is, we return the corresponding line. If it is not, we `throw` an `out_of_range` exception.

EXERCISES SECTION 10.6.4

Exercise 10.32: Reimplement the text-query program to use a `vector` instead of a `set` to hold the line numbers. Note that because lines appear in ascending order, we can append a new line number to the `vector` only if the last element of the `vector` isn't that line number. What are the performance and design characteristics of the two solutions? Which do you feel is the preferred design solution? Why?

Exercise 10.33: Why doesn't the `TextQuery::text_line` function check whether its argument is negative?

CHAPTER SUMMARY

The elements in an associative container are ordered and accessed by key. The associative containers support efficient lookup and retrieval of elements by key. The use of a key distinguishes them from the sequential containers, in which elements are accessed positionally.

The map and multimap types store elements that are key–value pairs. These types use the library pair class, defined in the utility header, to represent these pairs. Dereferencing a map or multimap iterator yields a value that is a pair. The first member of the pair is a const key, and the second member is a value associated with that key. The set and multiset types store keys. The map and set types allow only one element with a given key. The multimap and multiset types allow multiple elements with the same key.

The associative containers share many operations with the sequential containers. However, the associative containers define some new operations and redefine the meaning or return types of some operations that are in common with the sequential containers. The differences in the operations reflect the use of keys in associative containers.

Elements in an associative container can be accessed by iterators. The library guarantees that iterators access elements in order by key. The begin operation yields the element with the lowest key. Incrementing that iterator yields elements in nondescending order.

DEFINED TERMS

associative array Array whose elements are indexed by key rather than positionally. We say that the array maps a key to its associated value.

associative container A type that holds a collection of objects that supports efficient lookup by key.

key_type Type defined by the associative containers that is the type for the keys used to store and retrieve values. For a map, key_type is the type used to index the map. For set, key_type and value_type are the same.

map Associative container type that defines an associative array. Like vector, map is a class template. A map, however, is defined with two types: the type of the key and the type of the associated value. In a map a given key may appear only once. Each key is associated with a particular value. Dereferencing a map iterator yields a pair that holds a const key and its associated value.

mapped_type Type defined by map and multimap that is the type for the values stored in the map.

multimap Associative container similar to map except that in a multimap, a given key may appear more than once.

multiset Associative container type that holds keys. In a multiset, a given key may appear more than once.

pair Type that holds two public data members named first and second. The pair type is a template type that takes two type parameters that are used as the types of these members.

set Associative container that holds keys. In a set, a given key may appear only once.

strict weak ordering Relationship among the keys used in an associative container. In a strict weak ordering, it is possible to compare any two values and determine which of the two is less than the other. If neither value is less than the other, then the two values are considered equal. See Section 10.3.1 (p. 360).

value_type The type of the element stored in a container. For `set` and `multiset`, `value_type` and `key_type` are the same. For `map` and `multimap`, this type is a `pair` whose `first` member has type `const` `key_type` and whose `second` member has type `mapped_type`.

* operator The dereference operator when applied to a `map`, `set`, `multimap`, or `multiset` iterator yields a `value_type`. Note, that for `map` and `multimap` the `value_type` is a `pair`.

[ ] operator Subscript operator. When applied to a `map`, `[]` takes an index that must be a `key_type` (or type that can be converted to `key_type`) value. Yields a `mapped_type` value.

CHAPTER **11**

GENERIC ALGORITHMS

CONTENTS

The library containers define a surprisingly small set of operations. Rather than adding lots of functionality to the containers, the library instead provides a set of algorithms, most of which are independent of any particular container type. These algorithms are "generic:" They operate on different types of containers and on elements of various types.

The generic algorithms, and a more detailed look at iterators, form the subject matter of this chapter.

The standard containers define few operations. For the most part they allow us to add and remove elements; to access the first or last element; to obtain and in some cases reset the size of the container; and to obtain iterators to the first and one past the last element.

We can imagine many other useful operations one might want to do on the elements of a container. We might want to sort a sequential container, or find a particular element, or find the largest or smallest element, and so on. Rather than define each of these operations as members of each container type, the standard library defines a set of **generic algorithms**: "algorithms" because they implement common operations; and "generic" because they operate across multiple container types—not only library types such as `vector` or `list`, but also the built-in array type, and, as we shall see, over other kinds of sequences as well. The algorithms also can be used on container types we might define ourselves, as long as our types conform to the standard library conventions.

Most of the algorithms operate by traversing a range of elements bounded by two iterators. Typically, as the algorithm traverses the elements in the range, it operates on each element. The algorithms obtain access to the elements through the iterators that denote the range of elements to traverse.

11.1   Overview

Suppose we have a `vector` of `int`s, named `vec`, and we want to know if it holds a particular value. The easiest way to answer this question is to use the library `find` operation:

```
//  value we'll look for
int search_value = 42;
//  call find to see if that value is present
vector<int>::const_iterator result =
        find(vec.begin(), vec.end(), search_value);
//  report the result
cout << "The value " << search_value
    << (result == vec.end()
            ? " is not present" : " is present")
    << endl;
```

The call to `find` takes two iterators and a value. It tests each element in the range (Section 9.2.1, p. 314) denoted by its iterator arguments. As soon as it sees an element that is equal to the given value, `find` returns an iterator referring to that element. If there is no match, then `find` returns its second iterator to indicate failure. We can test whether the return is equal to the second argument to determine whether the element was found. We do this test in the output statement, which uses the conditional operator (Section 5.7, p. 165) to report whether the value was found.

Because `find` operates in terms of iterators, we can use the same `find` function to look for values in any container. For example, we can use `find` to look for a value in a `list` of `int` named `lst`:

```
//  call find to look through elements in a list
list<int>::const_iterator result =
        find(lst.begin(), lst.end(), search_value);
cout << "The value " << search_value
     << (result == lst.end()
            ? " is not present" : " is present")
     << endl;
```

Except for the type of `result` and the iterators passed to `find`, this code is identical to the program that used `find` to look at elements of a `vector`.

Similarly, because pointers act like iterators on built-in arrays, we can use `find` to look in an array:

```
int ia[6] = {27, 210, 12, 47, 109, 83};
int search_value = 83;
int *result = find(ia, ia + 6, search_value);
cout << "The value " << search_value
     << (result == ia + 6
            ? " is not present" : " is present")
     << endl;
```

Here we pass a pointer to the first element in `ia` and another pointer that is six elements past the start of `ia` (that is, one past the last element of `ia`). If the pointer returned is equal to `ia + 6` then the search is unsuccessful; otherwise, the pointer points to the value that was found.

If we wish to pass a subrange, we pass iterators (or pointers) to the first and one past the last element of that subrange. For example, in this invocation of `find`, only the elements `ia[1]` and `ia[2]` are searched:

```
//  only search elements ia[1] and ia[2]
int *result = find(ia + 1, ia + 3, search_value);
```

How the Algorithms Work

Each generic algorithm is implemented independently of the individual container types. The algorithms are also largely, but not completely, independent of the types of the elements that the container holds. To see how the algorithms work, let's look a bit more closely at `find`. Its job is to find a particular element in an unsorted collection of elements. Conceptually the steps that `find` must take include:

1. Examine each element in turn.

2. If the element is equal to the value we want, then return an iterator that refers to that element.

3. Otherwise, examine the next element, repeating step 2 until either the value is found or all the elements have been examined.

4. If we have reached the end of the collection and we have not found the value, return a value that indicates that the value was not found.

The Standard Algorithms Are Inherently Type-Independent

The algorithm, as we've stated it, is independent of the type of the container: Nothing in our description depends on the container type. Implicitly, the algorithm does have one dependency on the element type: We must be able to compare elements. More specifically, the requirements of the algorithm are:

1. We need a way to traverse the collection: We need to be able to advance from one element to the next.

2. We need to be able to know when we have reached the end of the collection.

3. We need to be able to compare each element to the value we want.

4. We need a type that can refer to an element's position within the container or that can indicate that the element was not found.

Iterators Bind Algorithms to Containers

The generic algorithms handle the first requirement, container traversal, by using iterators. All iterators support the increment operator to navigate from one element to the next, and the dereference operator to access the element value. With one exception that we'll cover in Section 11.3.5 (p. 416), the iterators also support the equality and inequality operators to determine whether two iterators are equal.

For the most part, the algorithms each take (at least) two iterators that denote the range of elements on which the algorithm is to operate. The first iterator refers to the first element, and the second iterator marks one past the last element. The element addressed by the second iterator, sometimes referred to as the **off-the-end iterator**, is not itself examined; it serves as a sentinel to terminate the traversal.

The off-the-end iterator also handles requirement 4 by providing a convenient return value that indicates that the search element wasn't found. If the value isn't found, then the off-the-end iterator is returned; otherwise, the iterator that refers to the matching element is returned.

Requirement 3, value comparison, is handled in one of two ways. By default, the find operation requires that the element type define operator ==. The algorithm uses that operator to compare elements. If our type does not support the == operator, or if we wish to compare elements using a different test, we can use a second version of find. That version takes an extra argument that is the name of a function to use to compare the elements.

The algorithms achieve type independence by never using container operations; rather, all access to and traversal of the elements is done through the iterators. The actual container type (or even whether the elements are stored in a container) is unknown.

The library provides more than 100 algorithms. Like the containers, the algorithms have a consistent architecture. Understanding the design of the algorithms makes learning and using them easier than memorizing all 100+ algorithms. In this chapter we'll both illustrate the use of the algorithms and describe the unifying principles used by the library algorithms. Appendix A lists all the algorithms classified by how they operate.

KEY CONCEPT: ALGORITHMS *Never* EXECUTE CONTAINER OPERATIONS

The generic algorithms do not themselves execute container operations. They operate solely in terms of iterators and iterator operations. The fact that the algorithms operate in terms of iterators and not container operations has a perhaps surprising but essential implication: When used on "ordinary" iterators, algorithms never change the size of the underlying container. As we'll see, algorithms may change the values of the elements stored in the container, and they may move elements around within the container. They do not, however, ever add or remove elements directly.

As we'll see in Section 11.3.1 (p. 406), there is a special class of iterator, the inserters, that do more than traverse the sequence to which they are bound. When we assign to these iterators, they execute insert operations on the underlying container. When an algorithm operates on one of these iterators, the iterator may have the effect of adding elements to the container. The algorithm itself, however, never does so.

11.2 A First Look at the Algorithms

Before covering the structure of the algorithms library, let's look at a couple of examples. We've already seen the use of `find`; in this section we'll use a few additional algorithms. To use a generic algorithm, we must include the `algorithm` header:

```
#include <algorithm>
```

The library also defines a set of generalized numeric algorithms, using the same conventions as the generic algorithms. To use these algorithms we include the `numeric` header:

```
#include <numeric>
```

With only a handful of exceptions, all the algorithms operate over a range of elements. We'll refer to this range as the "input range." The algorithms that take an input range always use their first two parameters to denote that range. These parameters are iterators used to denote the first and one past the last element that we want to process.

Although most algorithms are similar in that they operate over an input range, they differ in how they use the elements in that range. The most basic way to understand the algorithms is to know whether they read elements, write elements, or rearrange the order of the elements. We'll look at samples of each kind of algorithm in the remainder of this section.

11.2.1 Read-Only Algorithms

A number of the algorithms read, but never write to, the elements in their input range. `find` is one such algorithm. Another simple, read-only algorithm is `accumulate`, which is defined in the `numeric` header. Assuming `vec` is a vector of `int` values, the following code

```
// sum the elements in vec starting the summation with the value 42
int sum = accumulate(vec.begin(), vec.end(), 42);
```

sets `sum` equal to the sum of the elements in `vec` plus 42. `accumulate` takes three parameters. The first two specify a range of elements to sum. The third is an initial value for the sum. The `accumulate` function sets an internal variable to the initial value. It then adds the value of each element in the range to that initial value. The algorithm returns the result of the summation. The return type of `accumulate` is the type of its third argument.

The third argument, which specifies the starting value, is necessary because `accumulate` knows nothing about the element types that it is accumulating. Therefore, it has no way to invent an appropriate starting value or associated type.

There are two implications of the fact that `accumulate` doesn't know about the types over which it sums. First, we must pass an initial starting value because otherwise `accumulate` cannot know what starting value to use. Second, the type of the elements in the container must match or be convertible to the type of the third argument. Inside `accumulate`, the third argument is used as the starting point for the summation; the elements in the container are successively added into this sum. It must be possible to add the element type to the type of the sum.

As an example, we could use `accumulate` to concatenate the elements of a vector of `strings`:

```
// concatenate elements from v and store in sum
string sum = accumulate(v.begin(), v.end(), string(""));
```

The effect of this call is to concatenate each element in `vec` onto a `string` that starts out as the empty string. Note that we explicitly create a `string` as the third parameter. Passing a character-string literal would be a compile-time error. If we passed a string literal, the summation type would be `const char*` but the `string` addition operator (Section 3.2.3, p. 86) for operands of type `string` and `const char*` yields a `string` not a `const char*`.

Using `find_first_of`

In addition to `find`, the library defines several other, more complicated searching algorithms. Several of these are similar to the `find` operations of the `string` class (Section 9.6.4, p. 343). One such is `find_first_of`. This algorithm takes two pairs of iterators that denote two ranges of elements. It looks in the first range for a match to any element from the second range and returns an iterator denoting the first element that matches. If no match is found, it returns the end iterator of the first range. Assuming that `roster1` and `roster2` are two `list`s of names, we could use `find_first_of` to count how many names are in both lists:

```
//    program for illustration purposes only:
//    there are much faster ways to solve this problem
size_t cnt = 0;
list<string>::iterator it = roster1.begin();
//    look in roster1 for any name also in roster2
while ((it = find_first_of(it, roster1.end(),
               roster2.begin(), roster2.end()))
                    != roster1.end()) {
     ++cnt;
     //    we got a match, increment it to look in the rest of roster1
     ++it;
}
cout << "Found " << cnt
     << " names on both rosters"  << endl;
```

The call to `find_first_of` looks for any element in `roster2` that matches an element from the first range—that is, it looks for an element in the range from `it` to `roster1.end()`. The function returns the first element in that range that is also in the second range. On the first trip through the `while`, we look in the entire range of `roster1`. On second and subsequent trips, we look in that part of `roster1` that has not already been matched.

In the condition, we check the return from `find_first_of` to see whether we found a matching name. If we got a match, we increment our counter. We also increment `it` so that it refers to the next element in `roster1`. We know we're done when `find_first_of` returns `roster1.end()`, which it does if there is no match.

KEY CONCEPT: ITERATOR ARGUMENT TYPES

In general, the generic algorithms operate on iterator pairs that denote a range of elements in a container (or other sequence). The types of the arguments that denote the range must match exactly, and the iterators themselves must denote a range: They must refer to elements in the same container (or to the element just past the end of that container), and if they are unequal, then it must be possible to reach the second iterator by repeatedly incrementing the first iterator.

Some algorithms, such as `find_first_of`, take two pairs of iterators. The iterator types in each pair must match exactly, but there is no requirement that the type of the two pairs match each other. In particular, the elements can be stored in different kinds of sequences. What is required is that we be able to compare elements from the two sequences.

In our program, the types of `roster1` and `roster2` need not match exactly: `roster1` could be a `list` while `roster2` was a `vector`, `deque`, or other sequence that we'll learn about later in this chapter. What is required is that we be able to compare the elements from these two sequences using the `==` operator. If `roster1` is a `list<string>`, then `roster2` could be a `vector<char*>` because the `string` library defines `==` on a `string` and a `char*`.

Exercise 11.3: Use `accumulate` to sum the elements in a `vector<int>`.

Exercise 11.4: Assuming v is a `vector<double>` what, if anything, is wrong with calling `accumulate<v.begin(), v.end(), 0)`?

Exercise 11.5: What would happen if the program that called `find_first_of` did not increment `it`?

11.2.2 Algorithms that Write Container Elements

Some algorithms write element values. When using algorithms that write elements, we must take care to ensure that the sequence into which the algorithm writes is at least as large as the number of elements being written.

Some algorithms write directly into the input sequence. Others take an additional iterator that denotes a destination. Such algorithms use the destination iterator as a place in which to write output. Still a third kind writes a specified number of elements to some sequence.

Writing to the Elements of the Input Sequence

The algorithms that write to their input sequence are inherently safe—they write only as many elements as are in the specified input range.

A simple example of an algorithm that writes to its input sequence is `fill`:

```
fill(vec.begin(), vec.end(), 0);   //  reset each element to 0
//   set subsequence of the range to 10
fill(vec.begin(), vec.begin() + vec.size()/2, 10);
```

`fill` takes a pair of iterators that denote a range in which to write copies of its third parameter. It executes by setting each element in the range to the given value. Assuming that the input range is valid, then the writes are safe. The algorithm writes only to elements known to exist in the input range itself.

Algorithms Do Not Check Write Operations

The `fill_n` function takes an iterator, a count, and a value. It writes the specified number of elements with the given value starting at the element referred to by the iterator. The `fill_n` function assumes that it is safe to write the specified number of elements. It is a fairly common beginner mistake to call `fill_n` (or similar algorithms that write to elements) on a container that has no elements:

```
vector<int> vec;   //  empty vector
//   disaster: attempts to write to 10 (nonexistent) elements in vec
fill_n(vec.begin(), 10, 0);
```

This call to `fill_n` is a disaster. We specified that ten elements should be written, but there are no such elements—vec is empty. The result is undefined and will probably result in a serious run-time failure.

> Algorithms that write a specified number of elements or that write to a destination iterator do not check whether the destination is large enough to hold the number of elements being written.

Introducing `back_inserter`

One way to ensure that an algorithm has enough elements to hold the output is to use an **insert iterator**. An insert iterator is an iterator that *adds* elements to the underlying container. Ordinarily, when we assign to a container element through an iterator, we assign to the element to which the iterator refers. When we assign through an insert iterator, a new element equal to the right-hand value is added to the container.

We'll have more to say about insert iterators in Section 11.3.1 (p. 406). However, in order to illustrate how to safely use algorithms that write to a container, we will use **`back_inserter`**. Programs that use `back_inserter` must include the `iterator` header.

The `back_inserter` function is an iterator adaptor. Like the container adaptors (Section 9.7, p. 348), an iterator adaptor takes an object and generates a new object that adapts the behavior of its argument. In this case, the argument to `back_inserter` is a reference to a container. `back_inserter` generates an insert iterator bound to that container. When we attempt to assign to an element through that iterator, the assignment calls `push_back` to add an element with the given value to the container. We can use `back_inserter` to generate an iterator to use as the destination in `fill_n`:

```cpp
vector<int> vec;  // empty vector
// ok: back_inserter creates an insert iterator that adds elements to vec
fill_n(back_inserter(vec), 10, 0);  // appends 10 elements to vec
```

Now, each time `fill_n` writes a value, it will do so through the insert iterator generated by `back_inserter`. The effect will be to call `push_back` on `vec`, adding ten elements to the end of `vec`, each of which has the value 0.

Algorithms that Write to a Destination Iterator

A third kind of algorithm writes an unknown number of elements to a destination iterator. As with `fill_n`, the destination iterator refers to the first element of a sequence that will hold the output. The simplest such algorithm is `copy`. This algorithm takes three iterators: The first two denote an input range and the third refers to an element in the destination sequence. It is essential that the destination passed to `copy` be at least as large as the input range. Assuming `ilst` is a `list` holding `int`s, we might `copy` it into a `vector`:

```cpp
vector<int> ivec;  // empty vector
// copy elements from ilst into ivec
copy(ilst.begin(), ilst.end(), back_inserter(ivec));
```

`copy` reads elements from the input range, copying them to the destination.

Of course, this example is a bit inefficient: Ordinarily if we want to create a new container as a copy of an existing container, it is better to use an input range directly as the initializer for a newly constructed container:

```
//  better way to copy elements from ilst
vector<int> ivec(ilst.begin(), ilst.end());
```

Algorithm _copy Versions

Several algorithms provide so-called "copying" versions. These algorithms do some processing on the elements of their input sequence but do not change the original elements. Instead, a new sequence is written that contains the result of processing the elements of the original.

The `replace` algorithm is a good example. This algorithm reads and writes to an input sequence, replacing a given value by a new value. The algorithm takes four parameters: a pair of iterators denoting the input range and a pair of values. It substitutes the second value for each element that is equal the first:

```
//  replace any element with value of 0 by 42
replace(ilst.begin(), ilst.end(), 0, 42);
```

This call replaces all instances of 0 by the 42. If we wanted to leave the original sequence unchanged, we would call `replace_copy`. That algorithm takes a third iterator argument denoting a destination in which to write the adjusted sequence:

```
//  create empty vector to hold the replacement
vector<int> ivec;
//  use back_inserter to grow destination as needed
replace_copy(ilst.begin(), ilst.end(),
             back_inserter(ivec), 0, 42);
```

After this call, `ilst` is unchanged, and `ivec` contains a copy of `ilst` with the exception that every element in `ilst` with the value 0 has the value 42 in `ivec`.

11.2.3 Algorithms that Reorder Container Elements

Suppose we want to analyze the words used in a set of children's stories. For example, we might want know how many words contain six or more characters. We want to count each word only once, regardless of how many times it appears or whether it appears in multiple stories. We'd like to be able to print the words in size order, and we want the words to be in alphabetic order within a given size.

We'll assume that we have read our input and stored the text of each book in a `vector` of `strings` named `words`. How might we solve the part of the problem that involves counting word occurrences? To solve this problem, we'd need to:

1. Eliminate duplicate copies of each word

2. Order the words based on size

3. Count the words whose size is 6 or greater

Exercise 11.6: Using `fill_n`, write a program to set a sequence of `int` values to 0.

Exercise 11.7: Determine if there are any errors in the following programs and, if so, correct the error(s):

```
(a)  vector<int> vec; list<int> lst; int i;
     while (cin >> i)
         lst.push_back(i);
     copy(lst.begin(), lst.end(), vec.begin());

(b)  vector<int> vec;
     vec.reserve(10);
     fill_n(vec.begin(), 10, 0);
```

Exercise 11.8: We said that algorithms do not change the size of the containers over which they operate. Why doesn't the use of `back_inserter` invalidate this claim?

We can use generic algorithms in each of these steps.

For purposes of illustration, we'll use the following simple story as our input:

```
the quick red fox jumps over the slow red turtle
```

Given this input, our program should produce the following output:

```
1 word 6 characters or longer
```

Eliminating Duplicates

Assuming our input is in a `vector` named `words`, our first subproblem is to eliminate duplicates from the `words`:

```
//  sort words alphabetically so we can find the duplicates
sort(words.begin(), words.end());
/*  eliminate duplicate words:
 *  unique reorders words so that each word appears once in the
 *      front portion of words and returns an iterator one past the unique range;
 *  erase uses a vector operation to remove the nonunique elements
 */
vector<string>::iterator end_unique =
            unique(words.begin(), words.end());
words.erase(end_unique, words.end());
```

Our input `vector` contains a copy of every word used in each story. We start by sorting this `vector`. The `sort` algorithm takes two iterators that denote the range of elements to sort. It uses the `<` operator to compare the elements. In this call we ask that the entire `vector` be sorted.

After the call to `sort`, our `vector` elements are ordered:

```
fox jumps over quick red red slow the the turtle
```

Note that the words `red` and `the` are duplicated.

Using `unique`

Once `words` is sorted, our problem is to keep only one copy of each word that is used in our stories. The `unique` algorithm is well suited to this problem. It takes two iterators that denote a range of elements. It rearranges the elements in the input range so that adjacent duplicated entries are eliminated and returns an iterator that denotes the end of the range of the unique values.

After the call to `unique`, the `vector` holds

words

fox	jumps	over	quick	red	slow	the	turtle	the	turtle

last_word
(One past last unique element)

Note that the size of `words` is unchanged. It still has ten elements; only the order of these elements has changed. The call to `unique` "removes" adjacent duplicates. We put remove in quotes because `unique` doesn't remove any elements. Instead, it overwrites adjacent duplicates so that the unique elements are copied into the front of the sequence. The iterator returned by `unique` denotes one past the end of the range of unique elements.

Using Container Operations to Remove Elements

If we want to eliminate the duplicate items, we must use a container operation, which we do in the call to `erase`. This call erases the elements starting with the one to which `end_unique` refers through the end of `words`. After this call, `words` contains the eight unique words from the input.

 Algorithms never directly change the size of a container. If we want to add or remove elements, we must use a container operation.

It is worth noting that this call to `erase` would be safe even if there were no duplicated words in our `vector`. If there were no duplicates, then `unique` would return `words.end()`. Both arguments in the call to `erase` would have the same value, `words.end()`. The fact that the iterators are equal would mean that the range to `erase` would be empty. Erasing an empty range has no effect, so our program is correct even if the input has no duplicates.

Defining Needed Utility Functions

Our next subproblem is to count how many words are of length six or greater. To solve this problem, we'll use two additional generic algorithms: `stable_sort` and `count_if`. To use each of these algorithms we'll need a companion utility function, known as a **predicates**. A predicate is a function that performs some test and returns a type that can be used in a condition to indicate success or failure.

The first predicate we need will be used to sort the elements based on size. To do this sort, we need to define a predicate function that compares two `strings` and returns a `bool` indicating whether the first is shorter in length than the second:

```
// comparison function to be used to sort by word length
bool isShorter(const string &s1, const string &s2)
{
    return s1.size() < s2.size();
}
```

The other function we need will determine whether a given `string` is of length six or greater:

```
// determine whether a length of a given word is 6 or more
bool GT6(const string &s)
{
    return s.size() >= 6;
}
```

Although this function solves our problem, it is unnecessarily limited—the function hardwires the size into the function itself. If we wanted to find out how many words were of another length, we'd have to write another function. We could easily write a more general comparison function that took two parameters, the `string` and the size. However, the function we pass to `count_if` takes a single argument, so we cannot use the more general approach in this program. We'll see a better way to write this part of our solution in Section 14.8.1 (p. 531).

Sorting Algorithms

The library defines four different sort algorithms, of which we've used the simplest, `sort`, to sort `words` into alphabetical order. In addition to `sort`, the library also defines a `stable_sort` algorithm. A `stable_sort` maintains the original order among equal elements. Ordinarily, we don't care about the relative order of equal elements in a sorted sequence. After all, they're equal. However, in this case, we have defined "equal" to mean "the same length." Elements that have the same length can still be distinct when viewed alphabetically. By calling `stable_sort`, we maintain alphabetic order among those elements that have the same length.

Both `sort` and `stable_sort` are overloaded functions. One version uses the `<` operator for the element type to do the comparison. We used this version of `sort` to sort `words` before looking for duplicate elements. The second version takes a third parameter: the name of a predicate to use when comparing elements. That function must take two arguments of the same type as the element type and return a value that can be tested in a condition. We will use this second version, passing our `isShorter` function to compare elements:

```
// sort words by size, but maintain alphabetic order for words of the same size
stable_sort(words.begin(), words.end(), isShorter);
```

After this call, `words` is sorted by element size, but the words of each length are also still in alphabetical order:

words

| fox | red | the | over | slow | jumps | quick | turtle |

Counting Words of Length Six or More

Now that we've reordered our `vector` by word size, our remaining problem is to count how many words are of length six or greater. The `count_if` algorithm handles this problem:

```
vector<string>::size_type wc =
            count_if(words.begin(), words.end(), GT6);
```

`count_if` executes by reading the range denoted by its first two parameters. It passes each value that it reads to the predicate function represented by its third argument. That function must take a single argument of the element type and must return a value that can be tested as a condition. The algorithm returns a count of the number of elements for which the function succeeded. In this case, `count_if` passes each word to `GT6`, which returns the `bool` value `true` if the word's length is six or more.

Putting It All Together

Having looked at the program in detail, here is the program as a whole:

```
//   comparison function to be used to sort by word length
bool isShorter(const string &s1, const string &s2)
{
    return s1.size() < s2.size();
}
//   determine whether a length of a given word is 6 or more
bool GT6(const string &s)
{
    return s.size() >= 6;
}
int main()
{
    vector<string> words;
    //   copy contents of each book into a single vector
    string next_word;
    while (cin >> next_word) {
        //   insert next book's contents at end of words
        words.push_back(next_word);
    }
    //   sort words alphabetically so we can find the duplicates
    sort(words.begin(), words.end());
    /*   eliminate duplicate words:
     *   unique reorders words so that each word appears once in the
     *      front portion of words and returns an iterator one past the unique range;
     *   erase uses a vector operation to remove the nonunique elements
     */
    vector<string>::iterator end_unique =
            unique(words.begin(), words.end());
    words.erase(end_unique, words.end());
```

```
    //  sort words by size, but maintain alphabetic order for words of the same size
    stable_sort(words.begin(), words.end(), isShorter);
    vector<string>::size_type wc =
               count_if(words.begin(), words.end(), GT6);
    cout << wc << " " << make_plural(wc, "word", "s")
        << " 6 characters or longer" << endl;
    return 0;
}
```

We leave as an exercise the problem of printing the words in size order.

EXERCISES SECTION 11.2.3

Exercise 11.9: Implement the program to count words of size 4 or greater, including printing the list of unique words in the input. Test your program by running it on the program's source file.

Exercise 11.10: The library defines a `find_if` function. Like `find`, the `find_if` function takes a pair of iterators that indicates a range over which to operate. Like `count_if`, it also takes a third parameter that names a predicate that can be used to test each element in the range. `find_if` returns an iterator that refers to the first element for which the function returns a nonzero value. It returns its second iterator argument if there is no such element. Use the `find_if` function to rewrite the portion of our program that counted how many words are greater than length six.

Exercise 11.11: Why do you think the algorithms don't change the size of containers?

Exercise 11.12: Why was it be necessary to use `erase` rather than define a generic algorithm that could remove elements from the container?

11.3   Revisiting Iterators

In Section 11.2.2 (p. 398) we saw that the library defines iterators that are independent of a particular container. In fact, there are three additional kinds of iterators:

- **insert iterators**: These iterators are bound to a container and can be used to insert elements to the container.

- **`iostream` iterators**: These iterators can be bound to input or output streams and used to iterate through the associated IO stream.

- **reverse iterators**: These iterators move backward, rather than forward. Each container type defines its own `reverse_iterator` types, which are retuned by the `rbegin` and `rend` functions.

These iterator types are defined in the `iterator` header.

This section will look at each of these kinds of iterators and show how they can be used with the generic algorithms. We'll also take a look at how and when to use the container `const_iterators`.

11.3.1 Insert Iterators

In Section 11.2.2 (p. 398) we saw that we can use `back_inserter` to create an iterator that adds elements to a container. The `back_inserter` function is an example of an **inserter**. An inserter is an iterator adaptor (Section 9.7, p. 348) that takes a container and yields an iterator that inserts elements into the specified container. When we assign through an insert iterator, the iterator inserts a new element. There are three kinds of inserters, which differ as to where elements are inserted:

- `back_inserter`, which creates an iterator that uses `push_back`.

- `front_inserter`, which uses `push_front`.

- `inserter`, which uses `insert`. In addition to a container, `inserter` takes a second argument: an iterator indicating the position ahead of which insertion should begin.

`front_inserter` Requires `push_front`

`front_inserter` operates similarly to `back_inserter`: It creates an iterator that treats assignment as a call to `push_front` on its underlying container.

> We can use `front_inserter` *only* if the container has a `push_front` operation. Using `front_inserter` on a `vector`, or other container that does not have `push_front`, is an error.

`inserter` Yields an Iterator that Inserts at a Given Place

The `inserter` adaptor provides a more general form. This adaptor takes both a container and an iterator denoting a position at which to do the insertion:

```
//  position an iterator into ilst
list<int>::iterator it =
                 find(ilst.begin(), ilst.end(), 42);
//  insert replaced copies of ivec at that point in ilst
replace_copy(ivec.begin(), ivec.end(),
             inserter(ilst, it), 100, 0);
```

We start by using `find` to locate an element in `ilst`. The call to `replace_copy` uses an `inserter` that will insert elements into `ilst` just before of the element denoted by the iterator returned from `find`. The effect of the call to `replace_copy` is to copy the elements from `ivec`, replacing each value of `100` by `0`. The elements are inserted just ahead of the element denoted by `it`.

When we create an `inserter`, we say where to insert new elements. Elements are always inserted in *front* of the position denoted by the iterator argument to `inserter`.

We might think that we could simulate the effect of `front_inserter` by using `inserter` and the `begin` iterator for the container. However, an `inserter` behaves quite differently from `front_inserter`. When we use `front_inserter`, the elements are always inserted ahead of the then first element in the container. When we use `inserter`, elements are inserted ahead of a specific position. Even if that position initially is the first element, as soon as we insert an element in front of that element, it is no longer the one at the beginning of the container:

```
list<int> ilst, ilst2, ilst3;      // empty lists
// after this loop ilst contains: 1 2 3 4
for (list<int>::size_type i = 0; i != 4; ++i)
    ilst.push_front(i);
// after copy ilst2 contains: 4 3 2 1
copy(ilst.begin(), ilst.end(), front_inserter(ilst2));
// after copy, ilst3 contains: 1 2 3 4
copy(ilst.begin(), ilst.end(),
            inserter(ilst3, ilst3.begin()));
```

When we copy into `ilst2`, elements are always inserted ahead of any other element in the `list`. When we copy into `ilst3`, elements are inserted at a fixed point. That point started out as the head of the `list`, but as soon as even one element is added, it is no longer the first element.

Recalling the discussion in Section 9.3.3 (p. 318), it is important to understand that using `front_inserter` results in the elements appearing in the destination in reverse order.

EXERCISES SECTION 11.3.1

Exercise 11.13: Explain the differences among the three insert iterators.

Exercise 11.14: Write a program that uses `replace_copy` to copy a sequence from one container to another, replacing elements with a given value in the first sequence by the specified new value. Write the program to use an `inserter`, a `back_inserter` and a `front_inserter`. Discuss how the output sequence varies in each case.

Exercise 11.15: The algorithms library defines a function named `unique_copy` that operates like `unique`, except that it takes a third iterator denoting a sequence into which to copy the unique elements. Write a program that uses `unique_copy` to copy the unique elements from a `list` into an initially empty `vector`.

11.3.2 `iostream` Iterators

Even though the `iostream` types are not containers, there are iterators that can be used with `iostream` objects: An **istream_iterator** reads an input stream, and an **ostream_iterator** writes an output stream. These iterators treat their corresponding stream as a sequence of elements of a specified type. Using a stream iterator, we can use the generic algorithms to read (or write) data to (or from) stream objects.

The stream iterators define only the most basic of the iterator operations: increment, dereference, and assignment. In addition, we can compare two `istream` iterators for equality (or inequality). There is no comparison for `ostream` iterators.

Defining Stream Iterators

The stream iterators are class templates: An `istream_iterator` can be defined for any type for which the input operator (the `>>` operator) is defined. Similarly, an `ostream_iterator` can be defined for any type that has an output operator (the `<<` operator).

Table 11.1: `iostream` Iterator Constructors	
`istream_iterator<T> in(strm);`	Create `istream_iterator` that reads objects of type `T` from input stream `strm`.
`istream_iterator<T> in;`	Off-the-end iterator for `istream_iterator`.
`ostream_iterator<T> in(strm);`	Create `ostream_iterator` that writes objects of type `T` to the output stream `strm`.
`ostream_iterator<T> in(strm, delim);`	Create `ostream_iterator` that writes objects of type `T` to the output stream `strm` using `delim` as a separator between elements. `delim` is a null-terminated character array.

When we create a stream iterator, we must specify the type of objects that the iterator will read or write:

```
istream_iterator<int> cin_it(cin);    // reads ints from cin
istream_iterator<int> end_of_stream;  // end iterator value
// writes Sales_items from the ofstream named outfile
// each element is followed by a space
ofstream outfile;
ostream_iterator<Sales_item> output(outfile, " ");
```

We must bind an `ostream_iterator` to a specific stream. When we create an `istream_iterator`, we can bind it to a stream. Alternatively, we can supply no argument, which creates an iterator that we can use as the off-the-end value. There is no off-the-end iterator for `ostream_iterator`.

When we create an `ostream_iterator`, we may (optionally) provide a second argument that specifies a delimiter to use when writing elements to the output stream. The delimiter must be a C-style character string. Because it is a C-style string, it must be null-terminated; otherwise, the behavior is undefined.

Operations on `istream_iterators`

Constructing an `istream_iterator` bound to a stream positions the iterator so that the first dereference reads the first value from the stream.

Table 11.2: `istream_iterator` Operations

`it1 == it2` `it1 != it2`	Equality (inequality) between two `istream_iterators`. The iterators must read the same type. Two iterators are equal if they are both the end value. Two non-end-of-stream iterators are equal if they are constructed using the same input stream.
`*it`	Returns the value read from the stream.
`it->mem`	Synonym for `(*it).mem`. Returns member, `mem`, of the object read from the stream.
`++it` `it++`	Advances the iterator by reading the next value from the input stream using the » operator for the element type. As usual, the prefix version advances the stream and returns a reference to the incremented iterator. The postfix version advances the stream but returns the old value.

As an example, we could use an `istream_iterator` to read the standard input into a `vector`:

```
istream_iterator<int> in_iter(cin);   // read ints from cin
istream_iterator<int> eof;            // istream "end" iterator

// read until end of file, storing what was read in vec
while (in_iter != eof)
        // increment advances the stream to the next value
        // dereference reads next value from the istream
        vec.push_back(*in_iter++);
```

This loop reads `ints` from `cin`, and stores what was read in `vec`. On each trip the loop checks whether `in_iter` is the same as `eof`. That iterator was defined as the empty `istream_iterator`, which is used as the end iterator. An iterator bound to a stream is equal to the end iterator once its associated stream hits end-of-file or encounters another error.

The hardest part of this program is the argument to `push_back`, which uses the dereference and postfix increment operators. Precedence rules (Section 5.5, p. 163) say that the result of the increment is the operand to the dereference. Incrementing an `istream_iterator` advances the stream. However, the expression uses the postfix increment, which yields the *old* value of the iterator. The effect of the increment is to read the next value from the stream but return an iterator that refers to the previous value read. We dereference that iterator to obtain that value.

What is more interesting is that we could rewrite this program as:

```
istream_iterator<int> in_iter(cin);   // read ints from cin
istream_iterator<int> eof;            // istream "end" iterator
vector<int> vec(in_iter, eof);        // construct vec from an iterator range
```

Here we construct `vec` from a pair of iterators that denote a range of elements. Those iterators are `istream_iterators`, which means that the range is obtained by reading the associated stream. The effect of this constructor is to read `cin` until it hits end-of-file or encounters an input that is not an `int`. The elements that are read are used to construct `vec`.

Using `ostream_iterators` and `ostream_iterators`

We can use an `ostream_iterator` to write a sequence of values to a stream in much the same way that we might use an iterator to assign a sequence of values to the elements of a container:

```
//  write one string per line to the standard output
ostream_iterator<string> out_iter(cout, "\n");
//  read strings from standard input and the end iterator
istream_iterator<string> in_iter(cin), eof;
//  read until eof and write what was read to the standard output
while (in_iter != eof)
    //  write value of in_iter to standard output
    //  and then increment the iterator to get the next value from cin
    *out_iter++ = *in_iter++;
```

This program reads `cin`, writing each word it reads on separate line on `cout`.

We start by defining an `ostream_iterator` to write `strings` to `cout`, following each `string` by a newline. We define two `istream_iterators` that we'll use to read `strings` from `cin`. The `while` loop works similarly to our previous example. This time, instead of storing the values we read into a `vector`, we print them to `cout` by assigning the values we read to `out_iter`.

The assignment works similarly to the one in the program on page 205 that copied one array into another. We dereference both iterators, assigning the right-hand value into the left, incrementing each iterator. The effect is to write what was read to `cout` and then increment each iterator, reading the next value from `cin`.

Using `istream_iterators` with Class Types

We can create an `istream_iterator` for any type for which an input operator (`>>`) exists. For example, we might use an `istream_iterator` to read a sequence of `Sales_item` objects to sum:

```
istream_iterator<Sales_item> item_iter(cin), eof;
Sales_item sum;       //  initially empty Sales_item
sum = *item_iter++; //  read first transaction into sum and get next record
while (item_iter != eof) {
    if (item_iter->same_isbn(sum))
        sum = sum + *item_iter;
    else {
        cout << sum << endl;
        sum = *item_iter;
    }
    ++item_iter;  //  read next transaction
}
cout << sum << endl;   //  remember to print last set of records
```

This program binds `item_iter` to `cin` and says that the iterator will read objects of type `Sales_item`. The program next reads the first record into `sum`:

```
sum = *item_iter++; //  read first transaction into sum and get next record
```

This statement uses the dereference operator to fetch the first record from the standard input and assigns that value to sum. It increments the iterator, causing the stream to read the next record from the standard input.

The while loop executes until we hit end-of-file on cin. Inside the while, we compare the isbn of the record we just read with sum's isbn. The first statement in the while uses the arrow operator to dereference the istream iterator and obtain the most recently read object. We then run the same_isbn member on that object and the object in sum.

If the isbns are the same, we increment the totals in sum. Otherwise, we print the current value of sum and reset it as a copy of the most recently read transaction. The last step in the loop is to increment the iterator, which in this case causes the next transaction to be read from the standard input. The loop continues until an error or end-of-file is encountered. Before exiting we remember to print the values associated with the last ISBN in the input.

Limitations on Stream Iterators

The stream iterators have several important limitations:

- It is not possible to read from an ostream_iterator, and it is not possible to write to an istream_iterator.

- Once we assign a value to an ostream_iterator, the write is committed. There is no way to subsequently change a value once it is assigned. Moreover, each distinct value of an ostream_iterator is expected to be used for output exactly once.

- There is no -> operator for ostream_iterator.

Using Stream Iterators with the Algorithms

As we know, the algorithms operate in terms of iterator operations. And as we've seen, stream iterators define at least some of the iterator operations. Because the stream iterators support iterator operations, we can use them with at least some of the generic algorithms. As an example, we could read numbers from the standard input and write the unique numbers we read on the standard output:

```
istream_iterator<int> cin_it(cin);    // reads ints from cin
istream_iterator<int> end_of_stream;  // end iterator value
// initialize vec from the standard input:
vector<int> vec(cin_it, end_of_stream);

sort(vec.begin(), vec.end());

// writes ints to cout using " " as the delimiter
ostream_iterator<int> output(cout, " ");

// write only the unique elements in vec to the standard output
unique_copy(vec.begin(), vec.end(), output);
```

If the input to this program is

```
23 109 45 89 6 34 12 90 34 23 56 23 8 89 23
```

then the output would be

```
6 8 12 23 34 45 56 89 90 109
```

The program creates vec from the iterator pair, input and end_of_stream. The effect of this initializer is to read cin until end-of-file or an error occurs. The values read are stored in vec.

Once the input is read and vec initialized, we call sort to sort the input. Duplicated items from the input will be adjacent after the call to sort.

The program uses unique_copy, which is a copying version of unique. It copies the unique values in its input range to the destination iterator. This call uses our output iterator as the destination. The effect is to copy the unique values from vec to cout, following each value by a space.

EXERCISES SECTION 11.3.2

Exercise 11.16: Rewrite the program on 410 to use the copy algorithm to write the contents of a file to the standard output.

Exercise 11.17: Use a pair of istream_iterators to initialize a vector of ints.

Exercise 11.18: Write a program to read a sequence of integer numbers from the standard input using an istream_iterator. Write the odd numbers into one file, using an ostream_iterator. Each value should be followed by a space. Write the even numbers into a second file, also using an ostream_iterator. Each of these values should be placed on a separate line.

11.3.3 Reverse Iterators

A reverse iterator is an iterator that traverses a container backward. That is, it traverses from the last element toward the first. A reverse iterator inverts the meaning of increment (and decrement): ++ on a reverse iterator accesses the previous element; -- accesses the next element.

Recall that each container defines begin and end members. These members return respectively an iterator to the first element of the container and an iterator one past the last element of the container. The containers also define rbegin and rend, which return reverse iterators to the last element in the container and one "past" (that is, one before) the beginning of the container. As with ordinary iterators, there are both const and nonconst reverse iterators. Figure 11.1 on the facing page illustrates the relationship between these four iterators on a hypothetical vector named vec.

Given a vector that contains the numbers from 0 to 9 in ascending order

```
vector<int> vec;
for (vector<int>::size_type i = 0; i != 10; ++i)
    vec.push_back(i);   // elements are 0,1,2,...9
```

the following for loop prints the elements in reverse order:

Figure 11.1: Comparing `begin`/`end` and `rbegin`/`rend` Iterators

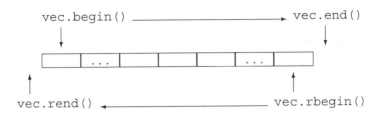

```
//  reverse iterator of vector from back to front
vector<int>::reverse_iterator r_iter;
for (r_iter = vec.rbegin();  // binds r_iter to last element
        r_iter != vec.rend();  // rend refers 1 before 1st element
        ++r_iter)              // decrements iterator one element
      cout << *r_iter << endl;// prints 9,8,7,...0
```

Although it may seem confusing to have the meaning of the increment and decrement operators reversed, doing so lets us use the algorithms transparently to process a container forward or backward. For example, we could sort our `vector` in descending order by passing `sort` a pair of reverse iterators:

```
//  sorts vec in "normal" order
sort(vec.begin(), vec.end());
//  sorts in reverse: puts smallest element at the end of vec
sort(vec.rbegin(), vec.rend());
```

Reverse Iterators Require Decrement Operators

Not surprisingly, we can define a reverse iterator only from an iterator that supports `--` as well as `++`. After all, the purpose of a reverse iterator is to move the iterator backward through the sequence. The iterators on the standard containers all support decrement as well as increment. However, the stream iterators do not, because it is not possible to move backward through a stream. Therefore, it is not possible to create a reverse iterator from a stream iterator.

Relationship between Reverse Iterators and Other Iterators

Suppose we have a `string` named `line` that contains a comma-separated list of words, and we want to print the first word in `line`. Using `find`, this task is easy:

```
//  find first element in a comma-separated list
string::iterator comma = find(line.begin(), line.end(), ',');
cout << string(line.begin(), comma) << endl;
```

If there is a comma in `line`, then `comma` refers to that comma; otherwise it is `line.end()`. When we print the `string` from `line.begin()` to `comma` we print characters up to the comma, or the entire `string` if there is no comma.

If we wanted the last word in the list, we could use reverse iterators instead:

```
// find last element in a comma-separated list
string::reverse_iterator rcomma =
                        find(line.rbegin(), line.rend(), ',');
```

Because we pass `rbegin()` and `rend()`, this call starts with the last character in `line` and searches backward. When `find` completes, if there is a comma, then `rcomma` refers to the last comma in the line—that is it refers to the first comma found in the backward search. If there is no comma, then `rcomma` is `line.rend()`.

The interesting part comes when we try to print the word we found. The direct attempt

```
// wrong: will generate the word in reverse order
cout << string(line.rbegin(), rcomma) << endl;
```

generates bogus output. For example, had our input been

FIRST,MIDDLE,LAST

then this statement would print `TSAL`!

Figure 11.2 illustrates the problem: We are using reverse iterators, and such iterators process the `string` backward. To get the right output, we need to transform the reverse iterators `line.rbegin()` and `rcomma` into normal iterators that go forward. There is no need to transform `line.rbegin()` as we already know that the result of that transformation would be `line.end()`. We can transform `rcomma` by calling `base`, which is a member of each reverse iterator type:

```
// ok: get a forward iterator and read to end of line
cout << string(rcomma.base(), line.end()) << endl;
```

Given the same preceeding input, this statement prints `LAST` as expected.

Figure 11.2: Relationship between Reverse and Ordinary Iterators

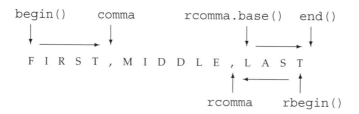

The objects shown in Figure 11.2 visually illustrate the relationship between ordinary and reverse iterators. For example, `rcomma` and `rcomma.base()` refer to different elements, as do `line.rbegin()` and `line.end()`. These differences are needed to ensure that the range of elements whether processed forward or backward is the same. Technically speaking, the relationship between normal and reverse iterators is designed to accommodate the properties of a left-inclusive range (Section 9.2.1, p. 314), so that [line.rbegin(), rcomma) and [rcomma.base(), line.end()) refer to the same elements in line.

> The fact that reverse iterators are intended to represent ranges and that these ranges are asymmetric has an important consequence. When we initialize or assign a reverse iterator from a plain iterator, the resulting iterator does not refer to the same element as the original.

EXERCISES SECTION 11.3.3

Exercise 11.19: Write a program that uses reverse_iterators to print the contents of a vector in reverse order.

Exercise 11.20: Now print the elements in reverse order using ordinary iterators.

Exercise 11.21: Use find to find the last element in a list of ints with value 0.

Exercise 11.22: Given a vector that has 10 elements, copy the elements from position 3 through 7 in reverse order to a list.

11.3.4 const Iterators

Careful readers will have noted that in the program on page 392 that used find, we defined result as a const_iterator. We did so because we did not intend to use the iterator to change a container element.

On the other hand, we used a plain, nonconst iterator to hold the return from find_first_of on page 397, even though we did not intend to change any container elements in that program either. The difference in treatment is subtle and deserves an explanation.

The reason is that in the second case, we use the iterator as an argument to find_first_of:

```
find_first_of(it, roster1.end(),
              roster2.begin(), roster2.end())
```

The input range for this call is specified by it and the iterator returned from a call to roster1.end(). Algorithms require the iterators that denote a range to have *exactly* the same type. The iterator returned by roster1.end() depends on the type of roster1. If that container is a const object, then the iterator is const_iterator; otherwise, it is the plain iterator type. In this program, roster1 was not const, and so end returns an iterator.

If we defined it as a const_iterator, the call to find_first_of would not compile. The types of the iterators used to denote the range would not have been identical. it would have been a const_iterator, and the iterator returned by roster1.end() would be iterator.

11.3.5 The Five Iterator Categories

Iterators define a common set of operations, but some iterators are more powerful than other iterators. For example, `ostream_iterators` support only increment, dereference, and assignment. Iterators on `vectors` support these operations and the decrement, relational, and arithmetic operators as well. As a result, we can classify iterators based on the set of operations they provide.

Similarly, we can categorize algorithms by the kinds of operations they require from their iterators. Some, such as `find`, require only the ability to read through the iterator and to increment it. Others, such as `sort`, require the ability to read, write, and randomly access elements. The iterator operations required by the algorithms are grouped into five categories. These five categories correspond to five categories of iterators, which are summarized in Table 11.3.

Table 11.3: Iterator Categories	
Input iterator	Read, but not write; increment only
Output iterator	Write, but not read; increment only
Forward iterator	Read and write; increment only
Bidirectional iterator	Read and write; increment and decrement
Random access iterator	Read and write; full iterator arithmetic

1. **Input iterators** can read the elements of a container but are not guaranteed to be able to write into a container. An input iterator must provide the following minimum support:

   - Equality and inequality operators (`==`, `!=`) to compare two iterators.
   - Prefix and postfix increment (`++`) to advance the iterator.
   - Dereference operator (`*`) to read an element; dereference may appear only on the right-hand side of an assignment.
   - The arrow operator (`->`) as a synonym for (`*it`)`.member`—that is, dereference the iterator and fetch a member from the underlying object.

   Input iterators may be used only sequentially; there is no way to examine an element once the input iterator has been incremented. Generic algorithms requiring only this level of support include `find` and `accumulate`. The library `istream_iterator` type is an input iterator.

2. **Output iterators** can be thought of as having complementary functionality to input iterators; An output iterator can be used to write an element but it is not guaranteed to support reading. Output iterators require:

   - Prefix and postfix increment (`++`) to advance the iterator.
   - Dereference (`*`), which may appear only as the left-hand side of an assignment. Assigning to a dereferenced output iterator writes to the underlying element.

Output iterators may require that each iterator value must be written exactly once. When using an output iterator, we should use * once and only once on a given iterator value. Output iterators are generally used as a third argument to an algorithm and mark the position where writing should begin. For example, the `copy` algorithm takes an output iterator as its third parameter and copies elements from its input range to the destination indicated by the output iterator. The `ostream_iterator` type is an output iterator.

3. **Forward iterators** read from and write to a given container. They move in only one direction through the sequence. Forward iterators support all the operations of both input iterators and output iterators. In addition, they can read or write the same element multiple times. We can copy a forward iterator to remember a place in the sequence so as to return to that place later. Generic algorithms that require a forward iterator include `replace`.

4. **Bidirectional iterators** read from and write to a container in both directions. In addition to supporting all the operations of a forward iterator, a bidirectional iterator also supports the prefix and postfix decrement (`--`) operators. Generic algorithms requiring a bidirectional iterator include `reverse`. All the library containers supply iterators that at a minimum meet the requirements for a bidirectional iterator.

5. **Random-access iterators** provide access to any position within the container in constant time. These iterators support all the functionality of bidirectional iterators. In addition, random-access iterators support:

   - The relational operators `<`, `<=`, `>`, and `>=` to compare the relative positions of two iterators.

   - Addition and subtraction operators `+`, `+=`, `-`, and `-=` between an iterator and an integral value. The result is the iterator advanced (or retreated) the integral number of elements within the container.

   - The subtraction operator `-` when applied to two iterators, which yields the distance between two iterators.

   - The subscript operator `iter[n]` as a synonym for `*(iter + n)`.

Generic algorithms requiring a random-access iterator include the `sort` algorithms. The `vector`, `deque`, and `string` iterators are random-access iterators, as are pointers when used to access elements of a built-in array.

With the exception of output iterators, the iterator categories form a sort of hierarchy: Any iterator of a higher category can be used where an iterator of lesser power is required. We can call an algorithm requiring an input iterator with an input iterator or a forward, bidirectional, or random-access iterator. Only a random-access iterator may be passed to an algorithm requiring a random-access iterator.

The `map`, `set`, and `list` types provide bidirectional iterators. Iterators on `string`, `vector`, and `deque` are random-access iterators, as are pointers bound to arrays. An `istream_iterator` is an input iterator, and an `ostream_iterator` is an output iterator.

KEY CONCEPT: ASSOCIATIVE CONTAINERS AND THE ALGORITHMS

Although the map and set types provide bidirectional iterators, we can use only a subset of the algorithms on associative containers. The problem is that the key in an associative container is const. Hence, any algorithm that writes to elements in the sequence cannot be used on an associative container. We may use iterators bound to associative containers only to supply arguments that will be read.

 When dealing with the algorithms, it is best to think of the iterators on associative containers as if they were input iterators that also support decrement, not as full bidirectional iterators.

The C++ standard specifies the minimum iterator category for each iterator parameter of the generic and numeric algorithms. For example, find—which implements a one-pass, read-only traversal over a container—minimally requires an input iterator. The replace function requires a pair of iterators that are at least forward iterators. The first two iterators to replace_copy must be at least forward. The third, which represents a destination, must be at least an output iterator.

For each parameter, the iterator must be at least as powerful as the stipulated minimum. Passing an iterator of a lesser power results in an error; passing an stronger iterator type is okay.

 Errors in passing an invalid category of iterator to an algorithm are not guaranteed to be caught at compile-time.

EXERCISES SECTION 11.3.5

Exercise 11.23: List the five iterator categories and the operations that each supports.

Exercise 11.24: What kind of iterator does a list have? What about a vector?

Exercise 11.25: What kinds of iterators do you think copy requires? What about reverse or unique?

Exercise 11.26: Explain why each of the following is incorrect. Identify which errors should be caught during compilation.

```
(a) string sa[10];
    const vector<string> file_names(sa, sa+6);
    vector<string>::iterator it = file_names.begin()+2;

(b) const vector<int> ivec;
    fill(ivec.begin(), ivec.end(), ival);

(c) sort(ivec.begin(), ivec.rend());

(d) sort(ivec1.begin(), ivec2.end());
```

11.4 Structure of Generic Algorithms

Just as there is a consistent design pattern behind the containers, there is a common design underlying the algorithms. Understanding the design behind the library makes it easier to learn and easier to use the algorithms. Because there are more than 100 algorithms, it is much better to understand their structure than to memorize the whole list of algorithms.

The most fundamental property of any algorithm is the kind(s) of iterators it expects. Each algorithm specifies for each of its iterator parameters what kind of iterator can be supplied. If a parameter must be a random-access iterator, then we can provide an iterator for a `vector` or a `deque`, or we can supply a pointer into an array. Iterators on the other containers cannot be used with such algorithms.

A second way is to classify the algorithms is as we did in the beginning of this chapter. We can categorize them by what actions they take on the elements:

- Some are read-only and leave element values and ordering unchanged.

- Others assign new values to specific elements.

- Others move values from one element to another.

As we'll see in the remainder of this section, there are two additional patterns to the algorithms: One pattern is defined by the parameters the algorithms take; the other is defined by two function naming and overloading conventions.

11.4.1 Algorithm Parameter Patterns

Superimposed on any other classification of the algorithms is a set of parameter conventions. Understanding these parameter conventions can aid in learning new algorithms—by knowing what the parameters mean, you can concentrate on understanding the operation the algorithm performs. Most of algorithms take one of the following four forms:

```
alg(beg, end, other parms);
alg(beg, end, dest, other parms);
alg(beg, end, beg2, other parms);
alg(beg, end, beg2, end2, other parms);
```

where *alg* is the name of the algorithm, and `beg` and `end` denote the range of elements on which the algorithm operates. We typically refer to this range as the "input range" of the algorithm. Although nearly all algorithms take an input range, the presence of the other parameters depends on the work being performed. The common ones listed here—`dest`, `beg2` and `end2`—are all iterators. When used, these iterators fill similar roles. In addition to these iterator parameters, some algorithms take additional, noniterator parameters that are algorithm-specific.

Algorithms with a Single Destination Iterator

A `dest` parameter is an iterator that denotes a destination used to hold the output. Algorithms *assume* that it is safe to write as many elements as needed.

When calling these algorithms, it is essential to ensure that the output container is sufficiently large to hold the output, which is why they are frequently called with insert iterators or `ostream_iterators`. If we call these algorithms with a container iterator, the algorithm assumes there are as many elements as needed in that container.

If `dest` is an iterator on a container, then the algorithm writes its output to existing elements within the container. More commonly, `dest` is bound to an insert iterator (Section 11.3.1, p. 406) or an `ostream_iterator`. An insert iterator adds elements to the container, ensuring that there is enough space. An `ostream_iterator` writes to an output stream, again presenting no problem regardless of how many elements are written.

Algorithms with a Second Input Sequence

Algorithms that take either `beg2` alone or `beg2` and `end2` use these iterators to denote a second input range. These algorithms typically use the elements from the second range in combination with the input range to perform a computation. When an algorithm takes both `beg2` and `end2`, these iterators are used to denote the entire second range. That is, the algorithm takes two completely specified ranges: the input range denoted by `beg` and `end`, and a second input range denoted by `beg2` and `end2`.

Algorithms that take `beg2` but not `end2` treat `beg2` as the first element in the second input range. The end of this range is not specified. Instead, these algorithms *assume* that the range starting at `beg2` is at least as large as the one denoted by `beg`, `end`.

As with algorithms that write to `dest`, algorithms that take `beg2` alone *assume* that the sequence beginning at `beg2` is as large as the range denoted by `beg` and `end`.

11.4.2   Algorithm Naming Conventions

The library uses a set of consistent naming and overload conventions that can simplify learning the library. There are two important patterns. The first involves algorithms that test the elements in the input range, and the second applies to those that reorder elements within the input range.

Distinguishing Versions that Take a Value or a Predicate

Many algorithms operate by testing elements in their input range. These algorithms typically use one of the standard relational operators, either `==` or `<`. Most of the algorithms provide a second version that allows the programmer to override the use of the operator and instead to supply a comparison or test function.

Algorithms that reorder the container elements use the `<` operator. These algorithms define a second, overloaded version that takes an additional parameter representing a different operation to use to order the elements:

```
sort(beg, end);         // use < operator to sort the elements
sort(beg, end, comp);   // use function named comp to sort the elements
```

Algorithms that test for a specific value use the == operator by default. These algorithms provide a second named—not overloaded—version with a parameter that is a predicate (Section 11.2.3, p. 402). Algorithms that take a predicate have the suffix _if appended:

```
find(beg, end, val);        // find first instance of val in the input range
find_if(beg, end, pred);    // find first instance for which pred is true
```

These algorithms both find the first instance of a specific element in the input range. The find algorithm looks for a specific value; the find_if algorithm looks for a value for which pred returns a nonzero value.

The reason these algorithms provide a named version rather than an over-loaded one is that both versions take the same number of parameters. In the case of the ordering algorithms, it is easy to disambiguate a call based solely on the number of parameters. In the case of algorithms that look for a specific element, the number of parameters is the same whether testing for a value or testing a predicate. Overloading ambiguities (Section 7.8.2, p. 269) would therefore be possible, albeit rare, and so the library provides two named versions for these algorithms rather than relying on overloading.

Distinguishing Versions that Copy from Those that Do Not

Independently of whether an algorithm tests its elements, the algorithm may re-arrange elements within the input range. By default, such algorithms write the rearranged elements back into their input range. These algorithms also provide a second, named version that writes to a specified output destination. These algorithms append _copy to their names:

```
reverse(beg, end);
reverse_copy(beg, end, dest);
```

The reverse function does what its name implies: It reverses the order of the elements in the input sequence. The first version reverses the elements in the input sequence itself. The second version, reverse_copy, makes a copy of the elements, placing them in reverse order in the sequence that begins at dest.

11.5 Container-Specific Algorithms

The iterators on list are bidirectional, not random access. Because the list container does not support random access, we cannot use the algorithms that require random-access iterators. These algorithms include the sort-related algorithms. There are other algorithms, defined generically, such as merge, remove, reverse, and unique, that can be used on lists but at a cost in performance. These algorithms can be implemented more efficiently if they can take advantage of how lists are implemented.

EXERCISES SECTION 11.4.2

Exercise 11.27: The library defines the following algorithms:

```
replace(beg, end, old_val, new_val);
replace_if(beg, end, pred, new_val);
replace_copy(beg, end, dest, old_val, new_val);
replace_copy_if(beg, end, dest, pred, new_val);
```

Based only on the names and parameters to these functions, describe the operation that these algorithms perform.

Exercise 11.28: Assume `lst` is a container that holds 100 elements. Explain the following program fragment and fix any bugs you think are present.

```
vector<int> vec1;
reverse_copy(lst.begin(), lst.end(), vec1.begin());
```

It is possible to write much faster algorithms if the internal structure of the `list` can be exploited. Rather than relying solely on generic operations, the library defines a more elaborate set of operations for `list` than are supported for the other sequential containers. These `list`-specific operations are described in Table 11.4 on the next page. Generic algorithms not listed in the table that take bidirectional or weaker iterators execute equally efficiently on `list`s as on other containers.

 Best Practices The `list` member versions should be used in preference to the generic algorithms when applied to a `list` object.

Most of the `list`-specific algorithms are similar—but not identical—to their counterparts that we have already seen in their generic forms:

```
l.remove(val);        // removes all instances of val from l
l.remove_if(pred);    // removes all instances for which pred is true from l
l.reverse();          // reverses the order of elements in l
l.sort();             // use element type < operator to compare elements
l.sort(comp);         // use comp to compare elements
l.unique();           // uses element == to remove adjacent duplicates
l.unique(comp);       // uses comp to remove duplicate adjacent copies
```

There are two crucially important differences between the `list`-specific operations and their generic counterparts. One difference is that the `list` versions of `remove` and `unique` change the underlying container; the indicated elements are actually removed. For example, second and subsequent duplicate elements are removed from the list by `list::unique`.

 Note Unlike the corresponding generic algorithms, the `list`-specific operations do add and remove elements.

The other difference is that the `list` operations, `merge` and `splice`, are destructive on their arguments. When we use the generic version of `merge`, the

Table 11.4: `list`-Specific Operations

`lst.merge(lst2)`
`lst.merge(lst2, comp)`

> Merges elements from `lst2` onto `lst`. Both lists must be sorted. Elements are removed from `lst2`. After the merge, `lst2` is empty. Returns `void`. The first version uses the `<` operator; the second version uses the specified comparison.

`lst.remove(val)`
`lst.remove_if(unaryPred)`

> Removes, by calling `lst.erase`, each element that equals a specified value or for which the specified predicate returns a nonzero value. Returns `void`.

`lst.reverse()`   Reverses the order of the elements in `lst`.

`lst.sort`   Sorts the elements of the `lst`.
`lst.splice(iter, lst2)`
`lst.splice(iter, lst2, iter2)`
`lst.splice(iter, beg, end)`

> Moves element(s) from `lst2` into `lst` just before the element (in `lst`) referred to by the iterator `iter`. Removes element(s) that are moved from `lst2`. The first version moves all elements from `lst2` into `lst`; after the splice, `lst2` is empty. `lst` and `lst2` may not be the same `list`. The second version moves only the element referred to by `iter2`, which must refer to an element in `lst2`. In this case, `lst2` and `lst` could be the same `list`. That is, `splice` can be used to move an element within a single `list`. The third version moves the elements in the range denoted by the iterators `beg` and `end`. As usual, `beg` and `end` must refer to a valid range. The iterators can refer to a range in any `list`, including `lst`. If the iterators refer to `lst`, the operation is undefined if `iter` refers to an element in the range.

`lst.unique()`
`lst.unique(binaryPred)`

> Deletes, by calling `erase`, consecutive copies of the same value. The first version uses `==` to determine if elements are equal; the second uses the specified predicate.

merged sequence is written to a destination iterator, and the two input sequences are left unchanged. In the case of the `merge` function that is a member of `list`, the argument `list` is destroyed—elements are moved from the argument and removed as they are merged into the `list` object on which `merge` was called.

EXERCISES SECTION 11.5

Exercise 11.29: Reimplement the program that eliminated duplicate words that we wrote in Section 11.2.3 (p. 400) to use a `list` instead of a `vector`.

CHAPTER SUMMARY

One of the more important contributions from the standardization process for C++ was the creation and expansion of the standard library. The containers and algorithms libraries are a cornerstone of the standard library. The library defines more than 100 algorithms. Fortunately, the algorithms have a consistent architecture, which makes learning and using them easier.

The algorithms are type independent: They generally operate on a sequence of elements that can be stored in a library container type, a built-in array, or even a generated sequence, such as by reading or writing to a stream. Algorithms achieve their type independence by operating in terms of iterators. Most algorithms take a pair of iterators denoting a range of elements as the first two arguments. Additional iterator arguments might include an output iterator denoting a destination, or another iterator or iterator pair denoting a second input sequence.

Iterators can be categorized by the operations that they support. There are five iterator categories: input, output, forward, bidirectional, and random access. An iterator belongs to a particular category if it supports the operations required for that iterator category.

Just as iterators are categorized by their operations, iterator parameters to the algorithms are categorized by the iterator operations they require. Algorithms that only read their sequences often require only input iterator operations. Those that write to a destination iterator often require only the actions of an output iterator, and so on.

Algorithms that look for a value often have a second version that looks for an element for which a predicate returns a nonzero value. For such algorithms, the name of the second version has the suffix _if. Similarly, many algorithms provide so-called copying versions. These write the (transformed) elements to an output sequence rather than writing back into the input range. Such versions have names that end with _copy.

A third pattern is whether algorithms read, write, or reorder elements. Algorithms *never* directly change the size of the sequences on which they operate. (If an argument is an insert iterator, then that iterator might add elements, but the algorithm does not do so directly.) They may copy elements from one position to another but cannot directly add or remove elements.

DEFINED TERMS

back_inserter Iterator adaptor that takes a reference to a container and generates an insert iterator that uses push_back to add elements to the specified container.

bidirectional iterator Same operations as forward iterators plus the ability to use -- to move backward through the sequence.

forward iterator Iterator that can read and write elements, but does not support --.

front_inserter Iterator adaptor that given a container, generates an insert iterator that uses push_front to add elements to the beginning of that container.

generic algorithms Type-independent algorithms.

input iterator Iterator that can read but not write elements.

insert iterator Iterator that uses a container operation to insert elements rather than overwrite them. When a value is assigned to an insert iterator, the effect is to insert the element with that value into the sequence.

inserter Iterator adaptor that takes an iterator and a reference to a container and generates an insert iterator that uses `insert` to add elements just ahead of the element referred to by the given iterator.

istream_iterator Stream iterator that reads an input stream.

iterator categories Conceptual organization of iterators based on the operations that an iterator supports. Iterator categories form a hierarchy, in which the more powerful categories offer the same operations as the lesser categories. The algorithms use iterator categories to specify what operations the iterator arguments must support. As long as the iterator provides at least that level of operation, it can be used. For example, some algorithms require only input iterators. Such algorithms can be called on any iterator other than one that meets only the output iterator requirements. Algorithms that require random-access iterators can be used only on iterators that support random-access operations.

off-the-end iterator An iterator that marks the end of a range of elements in a sequence. The off-the-end iterator is used as a sentinel and refers to an element one past the last element in the range. The off-the-end iterator may refer to a nonexistent element, so it must never be dereferenced.

ostream_iterator Iterator that writes to an output stream.

output iterator Iterator that can write but not read elements.

predicate Function that returns a type that can be converted to `bool`. Often used by the generic algorithms to test elements. Predicates used by the library are either unary (taking one argument) or binary (taking two).

random-access iterator Same operations as bidirectional iterators plus the ability to use the relational operators to compare iterator values and the ability to do arithmetic on iterators, thus supporting random access to elements.

reverse iterator Iterator that moves backward through a sequence. These iterators invert the meaning of ++ and --.

stream iterator Iterator that can be bound to a stream.

PART **III**

CLASSES AND DATA ABSTRACTION

CONTENTS

Classes are central to most C++ programs: Classes let us define our own types that are customized for the problems we need to solve, resulting in applications that are easier to write and understand. Well-designed class types can be as easy to use as the built-in types.

A class defines data and function members: The data members store the state associated with objects of the class type, and the functions perform operations that give meaning to the data. Classes let us separate implementation and interface. The interface specifies the operations that the class supports. Only the implementor of the class need know or care about the details of the implementation. This separation reduces the bookkeeping aspects that make programming tedious and error-prone.

Class types often are referred to as *abstract data types*. An abstract data type treats the data (state) and operations on that state as a single unit. We can think abstractly about what the class does, rather than always having to be aware of how the class operates. Abstract data types are fundamental to both object-oriented and generic programming.

Chapter 12 begins our detailed coverage of how classes are defined. This chapter covers topics fundamental to any use of classes: class scope, data hiding, and constructors. It also introduces some new class features: friends, uses of the implicit `this` pointer, and the role of `static` and `mutable` members.

Classes in C++ control what happens when objects are initialized, copied, assigned, and destroyed. In this respect, C++ differs from many other languages, many of which do not give class designers the ability to control these operations. Chapter 13 covers these topics.

Chapter 14 looks at operator overloading, which allows operands of class types to be used with the built-in operators. Operator overloading is one of the ways whereby C++ lets us create new types that are as intuitive to use as are the built-in types. This chapter also presents another special kind of class member function—conversion functions—which define implicit conversions from objects of class type. The compiler applies these conversions in the same contexts— and for the same reasons—as it does with conversions among the built-in types.

CHAPTER **12**

CLASSES

In C++ we use classes to define our own **abstract data types**. By defining types that mirror concepts in the problems we are trying to solve, we can make our programs easier to write, debug, and modify.

This chapter continues the coverage of classes begun in Chapters 2 and 5. We'll cover in more detail the importance of data abstraction, which lets us hide the internal representation of an object while still allowing `public` operations to be performed on the object.

We'll also explain more about class scope, constructors, and the `this` pointer. We also introduce three new class-related features: `friends`, and `mutable` and `static` members.

Classes are the most important feature in C++. Early versions of the language were named "C with Classes," emphasizing the central role of the class facility. As the language evolved, support for building classes increased. A primary goal of the language design has been to provide features that allow programmers to define their own types that are as easy and intuitive to use as the built-in types. This chapter presents many of the basic features of classes.

12.1   Class Definitions and Declarations

Starting from Chapter 1, our programs have used classes. The library types we've used—`vector`, `istream`, `string`—are all class types. We've also defined some simple classes of our own, such as the `Sales_item` and `TextQuery` classes. To recap, let's look again at the `Sales_item` class:

```
class Sales_item {
public:
    // operations on Sales_item objects
    double avg_price() const;
    bool same_isbn(const Sales_item &rhs) const
        { return isbn == rhs.isbn; }
    // default constructor needed to initialize members of built-in type
    Sales_item(): units_sold(0), revenue(0.0) { }
private:
    std::string isbn;
    unsigned units_sold;
    double revenue;
};

double Sales_item::avg_price() const
{
    if (units_sold)
        return revenue/units_sold;
    else
        return 0;
}
```

12.1.1   Class Definitions: A Recap

In writing this class in Section 2.8 (p. 63) and Section 7.7 (p. 258), we already learned a fair bit about classes.

 Most fundamentally, a class defines a new type and a new scope.

Class Members

Each class defines zero or more members. Members can be either data, functions, or type definitions.

A class may contain multiple public, private, and protected sections. We've already used the public and private access labels: Members defined in the public section are accessible to all code that uses the type; those defined in the private section are accessible to other class members. We'll have more to say about protected when we discuss inheritance in Chapter 15.

All members must be declared inside the class; there is no way to add members once the class definition is complete.

Constructors

When we create an object of a class type, the compiler automatically uses a constructor (Section 2.3.3, p. 49) to initialize the object. A constructor is a special member function that has the same name as the class. Its purpose is to ensure that each data member is set to sensible initial values.

A constructor generally should use a constructor initializer list (Section 7.7.3, p. 263), to initialize the data members of the object:

```
//  default constructor needed to initialize members of built-in type
Sales_item(): units_sold(0), revenue(0.0) {  }
```

The constructor initializer list is a list of member names and parenthesized initial values. It follows the constructor's parameter list and begins with a colon.

Member Functions

Member functions must be declared, and optionally may be defined, inside the class; functions defined inside the class are inline (Section 7.6, p. 256) by default.

Member functions defined outside the class must indicate that they are in the scope of the class. The definition of Sales_item::avg_price uses the scope operator (Section 1.2.2, p. 8) to indicate that the definition is for the avg_price function of the Sales_item class.

Member functions take an extra implicit argument that binds the function to the object on behalf of which the function is called—when we write

```
trans.avg_price()
```

we are calling the avg_price function on the object named trans. If trans is a Sales_item object, then references to a member of the Sales_item class inside the avg_price function are to the members in trans.

Member functions may be declared const by putting the const keyword following the parameter list:

```
double avg_price() const;
```

A const member may not change the data members of the object on which it operates. The const must appear in both the declaration and definition. It is a compile-time error for the const to be indicated on one but not the other.

Exercise 12.1: Write a class named `Person` that represents the name and address of a person. Use a `string` to hold each of these elements.

Exercise 12.2: Provide a constructor for `Person` that takes two `strings`.

Exercise 12.3: Provide operations to return the name and address. Should these functions be `const`? Explain your choice.

Exercise 12.4: Indicate which members of `Person` you would declare as `public` and which you would declare as `private`. Explain your choice.

12.1.2 Data Abstraction and Encapsulation

The fundamental ideas behind classes are **data abstraction** and **encapsulation**.

Data abstraction is a programming (and design) technique that relies on the separation of interface and implementation. The class designer must worry about how a class is implemented, but programmers that use the class need not know about these details. Instead, programmers who use a type need to know only the type's interface; they can think *abstractly* about what the type does rather than concretely about how the type works.

Encapsulation is a term that describes the technique of combining lower-level elements to form a new, higher-level entity. A function is one form of encapsulation: The detailed actions performed by the function are *encapsulated* in the larger entity that is the function itself. Encapsulated elements hide the details of their implementation—we may call a function but have no access to the statements that it executes. In the same way, a class is an encapsulated entity: It represents an aggregation of several members, and most (well-designed) class types hide the members that implement the type.

If we think about the library `vector` type, it is an example of both data abstraction and encapsulation. It is abstract in that to use it, we think about its interface—about the operations that it can perform. It is encapsulated because we have no access to the details of how the type is represented nor to any of its implementation artifacts. An array, on the other hand, is similar in concept to a `vector` but is neither abstract nor encapsulated. We manipulate an array directly by accessing the memory in which the array is stored.

Access Labels Enforce Abstraction and Encapsulation

In C++ we use access labels (Section 2.8, p. 65) to define the abstract interface to the class and to enforce encapsulation. A class may contain zero or more access labels:

- Members defined after a `public` label are accessible to all parts of the program. The data-abstraction view of a type is defined by its `public` members.

- Members defined after a `private` label are not accessible to code that uses the class. The `private` sections encapsulate (e.g., hide) the implementation from code that uses the type.

There are no restrictions on how often an access label may appear. Each access label specifies the access level of the succeeding member definitions. The specified access level remains in effect until the next access label is encountered or the closing right brace of the class body is seen.

A class may define members before any access label is seen. The access level of members defined after the open curly of the class and before the first access label depend on how the class is defined. If the class is defined with the `struct` keyword, then members defined before the first access label are `public`; if the class is defined using the `class` keyword, then the members are `private`.

ADVICE: CONCRETE AND ABSTRACT TYPES

Not all types need to be abstract. The library `pair` class is a good example of a useful, well-designed class that is concrete rather than abstract. A concrete class is a class that exposes, rather than hides, its implementation.

Some classes, such as `pair`, really have no abstract interface. The `pair` type exists to bundle two data members into a single object. There is no need or advantage to hiding the data members. Hiding the members in a class like `pair` would only complicate the use of the type.

Even so, such types often have member functions. In particular, it is a good idea for any class that has data members of built-in or compound type to define constructor(s) to initialize those members. The user of the class could initialize or assign to the data members but it is less error-prone for the class to do so.

Different Kinds of Programming Roles

Programmers tend to think about the people who will run their applications as "users." Applications are designed for and evolve in response to feedback from those who ultimately "use" the applications. Classes are thought of in a similar way: A class designer designs and implements a class for "users" of that class. In this case, the "user" is a programmer, not the ultimate user of the application.

Authors of successful applications do a good job of understanding and implementing the needs of the application's users. Similarly, well-designed, useful classes are designed with a close attention to the needs of the users of the class.

In another way, the division between class designer and class user reflects the division between users of an application and the designers and implementors of the application. Users care only if the application meets their needs in a cost-effective way. Similarly, users of a class care only about its interface. Good class designers define a class interface that is intuitive and easy to use. Users care about the implementation only in so far as the implementation affects their use of the class. If the implementation is too slow or puts burdens on users of the class, then the users must care. In well-designed classes, only the class designer worries about the implementation.

In simple applications, the user of a class and the designer of the class might be one and the same person. Even in such cases, it is useful to keep the roles distinct. When designing the interface to a class, the class designer should think about how easy it will be to use the class. When using the class, the designer shouldn't think about how the class works.

C++ programmers tend to speak of "users" interchangably as users of the application or users of a class.

When referring to a "user," the context makes it clear which kind of user is meant. If we speak of "user code" or the "user" of the `Sales_item` class, we mean a programmer who is using a class in writing an application. If we speak of the "user" of the bookstore application, we mean the manager of the store who is running the application.

KEY CONCEPT: BENEFITS OF DATA ABSTRACTION AND ENCAPSULATION

Data abstraction and encapsulation provide two important advantages:

- Class internals are protected from inadvertent user-level errors, which might corrupt the state of the object.

- The class implementation may evolve over time in response to changing requirements or bug reports without requiring change in user-level code.

By defining data members only in the `private` section of the class, the class author is free to make changes in the data. If the implementation changes, only the class code needs to be examined to see what affect the change may have. If data are `public`, then any function that directly accesses the data members of the old representation might be broken. It would be necessary to locate and rewrite all those portions of code that relied on the old representation before the program could be used again.

Similarly, if the internal state of the class is `private`, then changes to the member data can happen in only a limited number of places. The data is protected from mistakes that users might introduce. If there is a bug that corrupts the object's state, the places to look for the bug are localized: When data are `private`, only a member function could be responsible for the error. The search for the mistake is limited, greatly easing the problems of maintenance and program correctness.

If the data are `private` and if the interface to the member functions does not change, then user functions that manipulate class objects require no change.

Because changing a class definition in a header file effectively changes the text of every source file that includes that header, code that uses a class must be recompiled when the class changes.

12.1.3   More on Class Definitions

The classes we've defined so far have been simple; yet they have allowed us to explore quite a bit of the language support for classes. There remain a few more details about the basics of writing a class that we shall cover in the remainder of this section.

Exercise 12.5: What are the access labels supported by C++ classes? What kinds of members should be defined after each access label? What, if any, are the constraints on where and how often an access label may appear inside a class definition?

Exercise 12.6: How do classes defined with the `class` keyword differ from those defined as `struct`?

Exercise 12.7: What is encapsulation? Why it is useful?

Multiple Data Members of the Same Type

As we've seen, class data members are declared similarly to how ordinary variables are declared. One way in which member declarations and ordinary declarations are the same is that if a class has multiple data members with the same type, these members can be named in a single member declaration.

For example, we might define a type named `Screen` to represent a window on a computer. Each `Screen` would have a `string` member that holds the contents of the window, and three `string::size_type` members: one that specifies the character on which the cursor currently rests, and two others that specify the height and width of the window. We might define the members of this class as:

```
class Screen {
public:
    //  interface member functions
private:
    std::string contents;
    std::string::size_type cursor;
    std::string::size_type height, width;
};
```

Using Typedefs to Streamline Classes

In addition to defining data and function members, a class can also define its own local names for types. Our `Screen` will be a better abstraction if we provide a typedef for `std::string::size_type`:

```
class Screen {
public:
    //  interface member functions
    typedef std::string::size_type index;
private:
    std::string contents;
    index cursor;
    index height, width;
};
```

Type names defined by a class obey the standard access controls of any other member. We put the definition of `index` in the `public` part of the class because we want users to use that name. Users of class `Screen` need not know that we use a `string` as the underlying implementation. By defining `index`, we hide this detail of how `Screen` is implemented. By making the type `public`, we let our users use this name.

Member Functions May Be Overloaded

Another way our classes have been simple is that they have defined only a few member functions. In particular, none of our classes have needed to define overloaded versions of any of their member functions. However, as with nonmember functions, a member function may be overloaded (Section 7.8, p. 265).

With the exception of overloaded operators (Section 14.9.5, p. 547)—which have special rules—a member function overloads only other member functions of its own class. A class member function is unrelated to, and cannot overload, ordinary nonmember functions or functions declared in other classes. The same rules apply to overloaded member functions as apply to plain functions: Two overloaded members cannot have the same number and types of parameters. The function-matching (Section 7.8.2, p. 269) process used for calls of nonmember overloaded functions also applies to calls of overloaded member functions.

Defining Overloaded Member Functions

To illustrate overloading, we might give our `Screen` class two overloaded members to return a given character from the window. One version will return the character currently denoted by the cursor and the other returns the character at a given row and column:

```
class Screen {
public:
    typedef std::string::size_type index;
    //  return character at the cursor or at a given position
    char get() const { return contents[cursor]; }
    char get(index ht, index wd) const;
    //  remaining members
private:
    std::string contents;
    index cursor;
    index height, width;
};
```

As with any overloaded function, we select which version to run by supplying the appropriate number and/or types of arguments to a given call:

```
Screen myscreen;
char ch = myscreen.get();// calls Screen::get()
ch = myscreen.get(0,0);  // calls Screen::get(index, index)
```

Explicitly Specifying `inline` Member Functions

Member functions that are defined inside the class, such as the `get` member that takes no arguments, are automatically treated as `inline`. That is, when they are called, the compiler will attempt to expand the function inline (Section 7.6, p. 256). We can also explicitly declare a member function as `inline`:

```
class Screen {
public:
    typedef std::string::size_type index;
    //  implicitly inline when defined inside the class declaration
    char get() const { return contents[cursor]; }
    //  explicitly declared as inline; will be defined outside the class declaration
    inline char get(index ht, index wd) const;
    //  inline not specified in class declaration, but can be defined inline later
    index get_cursor() const;
    //  ...
};
//  inline declared in the class declaration; no need to repeat on the definition
char Screen::get(index r, index c) const
{
    index row = r * width;       //  compute the row location
    return contents[row + c];    //  offset by c to fetch specified character
}
//  not declared as inline in the class declaration, but ok to make inline in definition
inline Screen::index Screen::get_cursor() const
{
    return cursor;
}
```

We can specify that a member is `inline` as part of its declaration inside the class body. Alternatively, we can specify `inline` on the function definition that appears outside the class body. It is legal to specify `inline` both on the declaration and definition. One advantage of defining `inline` functions outside the class is that it can make the class easier to read.

> As with other `inline`s, the definition of an `inline` member function must be visible in every source file that calls the function. The definition for an `inline` member function that is not defined within the class body ordinarily should be placed in the same header file in which the class definition appears.

12.1.4 Class Declarations versus Definitions

A class is completely defined once the closing curly brace appears. Once the class is defined, all the class members are known. The size required to store an object of the class is known as well. A class may be defined only once in a given source file. When a class is defined in multiple files, the definition in each file must be identical.

By putting class definitions in header files, we can ensure that a class is defined the same way in each file that uses it. By using header guards (Section 2.9.2, p. 69), we ensure that even if the header is included more than once in the same file, the class definition will be seen only once.

It is possible to declare a class without defining it:

```cpp
class Screen; // declaration of the Screen class
```

This declaration, sometimes referred to as a **forward declaration**, introduces the name `Screen` into the program and indicates that `Screen` refers to a class type. After a declaration and before a definition is seen, the type `Screen` is an **incompete type**—it's known that `Screen` is a type but not known what members that type contains.

 An incomplete type can be used only in limited ways. Objects of the type may not be defined. An incomplete type may be used to define only pointers or references to the type or to declare (but not define) functions that use the type as a paremeter or return type.

A class must be fully defined before objects of that type are created. The class must be defined—and not just declared—so that the compiler can know how much storage to reserve for an object of that class type. Similarly, the class must be defined before a reference or pointer is used to access a member of the type.

Using Class Declarations for Class Members

A data member can be specified to be of a class type only if the definition for the class has already been seen. If the type is incomplete, a data member can be only a pointer or a reference to that class type.

Because a class is not defined until its class body is complete, a class cannot have data members of its own type. However, a class is considered declared as soon as its class name has been seen. Therefore, a class can have data members that are pointers or references to its own type:

```
class LinkScreen {
    Screen window;
    LinkScreen *next;
    LinkScreen *prev;
};
```

 A common use of class forward declarations is to write classes that are mutually dependent on one another. We'll see an example of such usage in Section 13.4 (p. 486).

EXERCISES SECTION 12.1.4

Exercise 12.11: Define a pair of classes X and Y, in which X has a pointer to Y, and Y has an object of type X.

Exercise 12.12: Explain the difference between a class declaration and definition. When would you use a class declaration? A class definition?

12.1.5 Class Objects

When we define a class, we are defining a type. Once a class is defined, we can define objects of that type. Storage is allocated when we define objects, but (ordinarily) not when we define types:

```
class Sales_item {
public:
    //  operations on Sales_item objects
private:
    std::string isbn;
    unsigned units_sold;
    double revenue;
};
```

defines a new type, but does not allocate any storage. When we define an object

```
Sales_item item;
```

the compiler allocates an area of storage sufficient to contain a Sales_item object. The name item refers to that area of storage. Each object has its own copy of the class data members. Modifying the data members of item does not change the data members of any other Sales_item object.

Defining Objects of Class Type

After a class type has been defined, the type can be used in two ways:

- Using the class name directly as a type name

- Specifying the keyword `class` or `struct`, followed by the class name:

```
Sales_item item1;        //  default initialized object of type Sales_item
class Sales_item item1;  //  equivalent definition of item1
```

Both methods of referring to a class type are equivalent. The second method is inherited from C and is also valid in C++. The first, more concise form was introduced by C++ to make class types easier to use.

Why a Class Definition Ends in a Semicolon

We noted on page 64 that a class definition ends with a semicolon. A semicolon is required because we can follow a class definition by a list of object definitions. As always, a definition must end in a semicolon:

```
class Sales_item { /* ... */ };
class Sales_item { /* ... */ } accum, trans;
```

Best Practices

Ordinarily, it is a bad idea to define an object as part of a class definition. Doing so obscures what's happening. It is confusing to readers to combine definitions of two different entities—the class and a variable—in a single statement.

12.2 The Implicit `this` Pointer

As we saw in Section 7.7.1 (p. 260), member functions have an extra implicit parameter that is a pointer to an object of the class type. This implicit parameter is named `this`, and is bound to the object on which the member function is called. Member functions may not define the `this` parameter; the compiler does so implicitly. The body of a member function may explicitly use the `this` pointer, but is not required to do so. The compiler treats an unqualified reference to a class member as if it had been made through the `this` pointer.

When to Use the `this` Pointer

Although it is usually unnecessary to refer explicitly to `this` inside a member function, there is one case in which we must do so: when we need to refer to the object as a whole rather than to a member of the object. The most common case where we must use `this` is in functions that return a reference to the object on which they were invoked.

The `Screen` class is a good example of the kind of class that might have operations that should return references. So far our class has only a pair of `get` operations. We might logically add:

- A pair of set operations to set either a specified character or the character denoted by the cursor to a given value

- A move operation that, given two index values, moves the cursor to that new position

Ideally, we'd like users to be able to concatenate a sequence of these actions into a single expression:

```
//  move cursor to given position, and set that character
myScreen.move(4,0).set('#');
```

We'd like this statement to be equivalent to

```
myScreen.move(4,0);
myScreen.set('#');
```

Returning *this

To allow us to call move and set in a single expression, each of our new operations must return a reference to the object on which it executes:

```
class Screen {
public:
        //  interface member functions
        Screen& move(index r, index c);
        Screen& set(char);
        Screen& set(index, index, char);
        //  other members as before
};
```

Notice that the return type of these functions is Screen&, which indicates that the member function returns a reference to an object of its own class type. Each of these functions returns the object on which it was invoked. We'll use the this pointer to get access to the object. Here is the implementation for two of our new members:

```
Screen& Screen::set(char c)
{
    contents[cursor] = c;
    return *this;
}
Screen& Screen::move(index r, index c)
{
    index row = r * width; // row location
    cursor = row + c;
    return *this;
}
```

The only interesting part in this function is the return statement. In each case, the function returns *this. In these functions, this is a pointer to a nonconst Screen. As with any pointer, we can access the object to which this points by dereferencing the this pointer.

Returning *this from a const Member Function

In an ordinary nonconst member function, the type of this is a const pointer (Section 4.2.5, p. 126) to the class type. We may change the value to which this points but cannot change the address that this holds. In a const member function, the type of this is a const pointer to a const class-type object. We may change neither the object to which this points nor the address that this holds.

> We cannot return a plain reference to the class object from a const member function. A const member function may return *this only as a const reference.

As an example, we might add a display operation to our Screen class. This function should print contents on a given ostream. Logically, this operation should be a const member. Printing the contents doesn't change the object. If we make display a const member of Screen, then the this pointer inside display will be a const Screen* const.

However, as we can with the move and set operations, we'd like to be able to use the display in a series of actions:

```
// move cursor to given position, set that character and display the screen
myScreen.move(4,0).set('#').display(cout);
```

This usage implies that display should return a Screen reference and take a reference to an ostream. If display is a const member, then its return type must be const Screen&.

Unfortunately, there is a problem with this design. If we define display as a const member, then we could call display on a nonconst object but would not be able to embed a call to display in a larger expression. The following code would be illegal:

```
Screen myScreen;
// this code fails if display is a const member function
// display return a const reference; we cannot call set on a const
myScreen.display().set('*');
```

The problem is that this expression runs set on the object returned from display. That object is const because display returns its object as a const. We cannot call set on a const object.

Overloading Based on const

To solve this problem we must define two display operations: one that is const and one that isn't. We can overload a member function based on whether it is const for the same reasons that we can overload a function based on whether a pointer parameter points to const (Section 7.8.4, p. 275). A const object will use only the const member. A nonconst object could use either member, but the nonconst version is a better match.

While we're at it, we'll define a private member named do_display to do the actual work of printing the Screen. Each of the display operations will call this function and then return the object on which it is executing:

```
class Screen {
public:
    //  interface member functions
    //  display overloaded on whether the object is const or not
    Screen& display(std::ostream &os)
                    { do_display(os); return *this; }
    const Screen& display(std::ostream &os) const
                    { do_display(os); return *this; }
private:
        //  single function to do the work of displaying a Screen,
        //  will be called by the display operations
        void do_display(std::ostream &os) const
                        { os << contents; }
    //  as before
};
```

Now, when we embed `display` in a larger expression, the nonconst version will be called. When we `display` a `const` object, then the `const` version is called:

```
Screen myScreen(5,3);
const Screen blank(5, 3);
myScreen.set('#').display(cout);   //  calls nonconst version
blank.display(cout);               //  calls const version
```

Mutable Data Members

It sometimes (but not very often) happens that a class has a data member that we want to be able to modify, even inside a `const` member function. We can indicate such members by declaring them as `mutable`.

A **mutable data member** is a member that is never `const`, even when it is a member of a `const` object. Accordingly, a `const` member function may change a `mutable` member. To declare a data member as mutable, the keyword `mutable` must precede the declaration of the member:

```
class Screen {
public:
//  interface member functions
private:
    mutable size_t access_ctr; //  may change in a const members
    //  other data members as before
};
```

We've given `Screen` a new data member named `access_ctr` that is `mutable`. We'll use `access_ctr` to track how often `Screen` member functions are called:

```
void Screen::do_display(std::ostream& os) const
{
    ++access_ctr;      //  keep count of calls to any member function
    os << contents;
}
```

Even though `do_display` is `const`, it can increment `access_ctr`. That member is a `mutable` member, so any member function, including `const` functions, can change the value of `access_ctr`.

ADVICE: USE PRIVATE UTILITY FUNCTIONS FOR COMMON CODE

Some readers might be surprised that we bothered to define a separate `do_display` operation. After all, the calls to `do_display` aren't much simpler than the action done inside `do_display`. Why bother? We do so for several reasons:

1. A general desire to avoid writing the same code in more than one place.

2. The `display` operation can be expected to become more complicated as our class evolves. As the actions involved become more complex, it makes more obvious sense to write those actions in one place, not two.

3. It is likely that we might want to add debugging information to `do_display` during development that would be eliminated in the final product version of the code. It will be easier to do so if only one definition of `do_display` needs to be changed to add or remove the debugging code.

4. There needn't be any overhead involved in this extra function call. We made `do_display` inline, so the run-time performance between calling `do_display` or putting the code directly into the `display` operations should be identical.

In practice, well-designed C++ programs tend to have lots of small functions such as `do_display` that are called to do the "real" work of some other set of functions.

EXERCISES SECTION 12.2

Exercise 12.13: Extend your version of the `Screen` class to include the `move`, `set`, and `display` operations. Test your class by executing the expression:

```
// move cursor to given position, set that character and display the screen
myScreen.move(4,0).set('#').display(cout);
```

Exercise 12.14: It is legal but redundant to refer to members through the `this` pointer. Discuss the pros and cons of explicitly using the `this` pointer to access members.

12.3   Class Scope

Every class defines its own new scope and a unique type. The declarations of the class members within the class body introduce the member names into the scope of their class. Two different classes have two different class scopes.

 Even if two classes have exactly the same member list, they are different types. The members of each class are distinct from the members of any other class (or any other scope).

For example:

```
class First {
public:
    int memi;
    double memd;
};

class Second {
public:
    int memi;
    double memd;
};

First obj1;
Second obj2 = obj1;  // error: obj1 and obj2 have different types
```

Using a Class Member

Outside the class scope, members may be accessed only through an object or a pointer using member access operators dot or arrow, respectively. The left-hand operand to these operators is a class object or a pointer to a class object, respectively. The member name that follows the operator must be declared in the scope of the associated class:

```
Class obj;        // Class is some class type
Class *ptr = &obj;
// member is a data member of that class
ptr->member;      // fetches member from the object to which ptr points
obj.member;       // fetches member from the object named obj
// memfcn is a function member of that class
ptr->memfcn();  // runs memfcn on the object to which ptr points
obj.memfcn();     // runs memfcn on the object named obj
```

Some members are accessed using the member access operators; others are accessed directly from the class using the scope operator, (::). Ordinary data or function members must be accessed through an object. Members that define types, such as Screen::index, are accessed using the scope operator.

Scope and Member Definitions

Member definitions behave as if they are in the scope of the class, even if the member is defined outside the class body. Recall that member definitions that appear outside the class body must indicate the class in which the member appears:

```
double Sales_item::avg_price() const
{
    if (units_sold)
        return revenue/units_sold;
    else
        return 0;
}
```

Here we use the fully qualified name `Sales_item::avg_price` to indicate that
the definition is for the `avg_price` member in the scope of the `Sales_item` class.
Once the fully qualified name of the member is seen, the definition is known to be
in class scope. Because the definition is in class scope, we can refer to `revenue` and
`units_sold` without having to write `this->revenue` or `this->units_sold`.

Parameter Lists and Function Bodies Are in Class Scope

In a member function defined outside the class, the parameter list and member-
function body both appear after the member name. These are defined inside the
class scope and so may refer to other class members without qualification—for
example, the definition of the two-parameter version of `get` in class `Screen`:

```
char Screen::get(index r, index c) const
{
    index row = r * width;        // compute the row location
    return contents[row + c];     // offset by c to fetch specified character
}
```

This function uses the type name `index` defined inside `Screen` to name the types
of its parameters. Because the parameter list is inside the scope of class `Screen`,
there is no need to specify that we want `Screen::index`. It is implicit that the
one we want is the one defined in the current class scope. Similarly, the uses of
`index`, `width`, and `contents` all refer to names declared inside class `Screen`.

Function Return Types Aren't Always in Class Scope

In contrast to the parameter types, the return type appears before the member
name. If the function is defined outside the class body, then the name used for the
return type is outside the class scope. If the return type uses a type defined by the
class, it must use the fully qualified name. For example, consider the `get_cursor`
function:

```
class Screen {
public:
    typedef std::string::size_type index;
    index get_cursor() const;
};
inline Screen::index Screen::get_cursor() const
{
    return cursor;
}
```

The return type of this function is `index`, which is a type name defined inside the
`Screen` class. If we define `get_cursor` outside the class body, the code is not
in the class scope until the function name has been processed. When the return
type is seen, its name is used outside of the class scope. We must use the fully
qualified type name, `Screen::index` to specify that we want the name `index`
that is defined inside class `Screen`.

12.3.1 Name Lookup in Class Scope

In the programs we've written so far, **name lookup** (the process of finding which declaration is matched to a given use of a name) has been relatively straightforward:

1. First, look for a declaration of the name in the block in which the name was used. Only names declared before the use are considered.

2. If the name isn't found, the enclosing scope(s) are searched.

If no declaration is found, then the program is in error. In C++ programs, all names must be declared before they are used.

   Class scopes may seem to behave a bit differently, but in reality they obey this same rule. Confusion can arise due to the way names are resolved inside a function defined within the class body itself.

Class definitions are actually processed in two phases:

1. First, the member declarations are compiled.

2. Only after all the class members have been seen are the definitions themselves compiled.

   Of course, the names used in class scope do not always have to be class member names. Name lookup in class scope finds names declared in other scopes as well. During name lookup, if a name used in class scope does not resolve to a class member name, the scopes surrounding the class or member definition are searched to find a declaration for the name.

Name Lookup for Class Member Declarations

Names used in the declarations of a class member are resolved as follows:

- The declarations of the class members that appear before the use of the name are considered.

- If the lookup in step 1 is not successful, the declarations that appear in the scope in which the class is defined, and that appear before the class definition itself, are considered.

For example:

```
typedef double Money;
class Account {
public:
    Money balance() { return bal; }
private:
    Money bal;
    // ...
};
```

When processing the declaration of the `balance` function, the compiler first looks for a declaration of `Money` in the scope of the class `Account`. The compiler considers only declarations that appear before the use of `Money`. Because no member declaration is found, the compiler then looks for a declaration of `Money` in global scope. Only the declarations located before the definition of the class `Account` are considered. The declaration for the global typedef `Money` is found and is used for the return type of the function `balance` and the data member `bal`.

 Names of types defined in a class must be seen before they are used as the type of a data member or as the return type or parameter type(s) of a member function.

The compiler handles member declarations in the order in which they appear in the class. As usual, a name must be defined before it can be used. Moreover, once a name has been used as the name of a type, that name may not be redefined:

```
typedef double Money;
class Account {
public:
    Money balance() { return bal; }   // uses global definition of Money
private:
    // error: cannot change meaning of Money
    typedef long double Money;
    Money bal;
    // ...
};
```

Name Lookup in Class Member Definitions

A name used in the body of a member function is resolved as follows:

1. Declarations in the member-function local scopes are considered first.

2. If the a declaration for the name is not found in the member function, the declarations for all the class members are considered.

3. If a declaration for the name is not found in the class, the declarations that appear in scope before the member function definition are considered.

Class Members Follow Normal Block-Scope Name Lookup

Programs that illustrate how name lookup works often have to rely on bad practices. The next several programs contain bad style deliberately.

The following function uses the same name for a parameter and a member, which normally should be avoided. We do so here to show how names are resolved:

```
//  Note: This code is for illustration purposes only and reflects bad practice
//  It is a bad idea to use the same name for a parameter and a member
int height;
class Screen {
public:
    void dummy_fcn(index height) {
        cursor = width * height; //  which height? The parameter
    }
private:
    index cursor;
    index height, width;
};
```

When looking for a declaration for the name `height` used in the definition of `dummy_fcn`, the compiler first looks in the local scope of that function. A function parameter is declared in the local scope of its function. The name `height` used in the body of `dummy_fcn` refers to this parameter declaration.

In this case, the `height` parameter hides the member named `height`.

Even though the class member is hidden, it is still possible to use it by qualifying the member's name with the name of its class or by using the `this` pointer explicitly.

If we wanted to override the normal lookup rules, we could do so:

```
//  bad practice: Names local to member functions shouldn't hide member names
void dummy_fcn(index height) {
    cursor = width * this->height;  //  member height
    //  alternative way to indicate the member
    cursor = width * Screen::height; //  member height
}
```

After Function Scope, Look in Class Scope

If we wanted to use the member named `height`, a much better way to do so would be to give the parameter a different name:

```
//  good practice: Don't use member name for a parameter or other local variable
void dummy_fcn(index ht) {
    cursor = width * height;  //  member height
}
```

Now when the compiler looks for the name `height`, it will not find that name in the function. The compiler next looks in the `Screen` class. Because `height` is used inside a member function, the compiler looks at all the member declarations. Even though the declaration of `height` appears after its use inside `dummy_fcn`, the compiler resolves this use to the data member named `height`.

After Class Scope, Look in the Surrounding Scope

If the compiler doesn't find the name in function or class scope, it looks for the name in the surrounding scope. In our example, declarations in global scope that appear before the definition of the `Screen` include a global object named `height`. However, that object is hidden.

 Even though the global object is hidden, it is still possible to use it by qualifying the name with the global scope resolution operator.

```
//   bad practice: Don't hide names that are needed from surrounding scopes
void dummy_fcn(index height) {
    cursor = width * ::height;//   which height? The global one
}
```

Names Are Resolved Where They Appear within the File

When a member is defined outside the class definition, the third step of name lookup not only considers the declarations in global scope that appear before the definition of class Screen, but also considers the global scope declarations that appear before the member function definition—for example:

```
class Screen {
public:
    // ...
    void setHeight(index);
private:
    index height;
};

Screen::index verify(Screen::index);

void Screen::setHeight(index var) {
    //  var: refers to the parameter
    //  height: refers to the class member
    //  verify: refers to the global function
    height = verify(var);
}
```

Notice that the declaration of the global function `verify` is not visible before the definition of the class `Screen`. However, the third step of name lookup considers the surrounding scope declarations that appear before the member definition, and the declaration for the global function `verify` is found.

Exercise 12.17: What would happen if we put the typedef in the `Screen` class as the last line in the class?

Exercise 12.18: Explain the following code. Indicate which definition of `Type` or `initVal` is used for each use of those names. If there are any errors, say how you would fix the program.

```
typedef string Type;
Type initVal();

class Exercise {
public:
    // ...
    typedef double Type;
    Type setVal(Type);
    Type initVal();
private:
    int val;
};

Type Exercise::setVal(Type parm) {
    val = parm + initVal();
}
```

The definition of the member function `setVal` is in error. Apply the necessary changes so that the class `Exercise` uses the global typedef `Type` and the global function `initVal`.

12.4 Constructors

Constructors (Section 2.3.3, p. 49) are special member functions that are executed whenever we create new objects of a class type. The job of a constructor is to ensure that the data members of each object start out with sensible initial values. Section 7.7.3 (p. 262) showed how we define a constructor:

```
class Sales_item {
public:
    // operations on Sales_item objects
    // default constructor needed to initialize members of built-in type
    Sales_item(): units_sold(0), revenue(0.0) { }
private:
    std::string isbn;
    unsigned units_sold;
    double revenue;
};
```

This constructor uses the constructor initializer list to initialize the `units_sold` and `revenue` members. The `isbn` member is implicitly initialized by the `string` default constructor as an empty string.

Constructors have the same name as the name of the class and may not specify a return type. Like any other function, they may define zero or more parameters.

Constructors May Be Overloaded

There is no constraint on the number of constructors we may declare for a class, provided that the parameter list of each constructor is unique. How can we know which or how many constructors to define? Ordinarily, constructors differ in ways that allow the user to specify differing ways to initialize the data members.

For example, we might logically extend our `Sales_item` class by providing two additional constructors: one that would let users provide an initial value for the isbn and another that would let them initialize the object by reading an istream object:

```
class Sales_item;
//  other members as before
public:
    //  added constructors to initialize from a string or an istream
    Sales_item(const std::string&);
    Sales_item(std::istream&);
    Sales_item();
};
```

Arguments Determine Which Constructor to Use

Our class now defines three constructors. We could use any of these constructors when defining new objects:

```
//  uses the default constructor:
//  isbn is the empty string; units_sold and revenue are 0
Sales_item empty;
//  specifies an explicit isbn; units_sold and revenue are 0
Sales_item Primer_3rd_Ed("0-201-82470-1");
//  reads values from the standard input into isbn, units_sold, and revenue
Sales_item Primer_4th_ed(cin);
```

The argument type(s) used to initialize an object determines which constructor is used. In the definition of empty, there is no initializer, so the default constructor is run. The constructor that takes a single string argument is used to initialize Primer_3rd_ed; the one that takes a reference to an istream initializes Primer_4th_ed.

Constructors Are Executed Automatically

The compiler runs a constructor whenever an object of the type is created:

```
//  constructor that takes a string used to create and initialize variable
Sales_item Primer_2nd_ed("0-201-54848-8");
//  default constructor used to initialize unnamed object on the heap
Sales_item *p = new Sales_item();
```

In the first case, the constructor that takes a `string` is run to initialize the variable named `Primer_2nd_ed`. In the second case, a new `Sales_item` object is allocated dynamically. Assuming that the allocation succeeds, then the object is initialized by running the default constructor.

Constructors for `const` Objects

A constructor may not be declared as `const` (Section 7.7.1, p. 260):

```
class Sales_item {
public:
    Sales_item() const;     // error
};
```

There is no need for a `const` constructor. When we create a `const` object of a class type, an ordinary constructor is run to initialize the `const` object. The job of the constructor is to initialize an object. A constructor is used to initialize an object regardless of whether the object is `const`.

EXERCISES SECTION 12.4

Exercise 12.19: Provide one or more constructors that allows the user of this class to specify initial values for none or all of the data elements of this class:

```
class NoName {
public:
    //  constructor(s) go here ...
private:
    std::string  *pstring;
    int          ival;
    double       dval;
};
```

Explain how you decided how many constructors were needed and what parameters they should take.

Exercise 12.20: Choose one of the following abstractions (or an abstraction of your own choosing). Determine what data is needed in the class. Provide an appropriate set of constructors. Explain your decisions.

    (a) `Book`   (b) `Date`   (c) `Employee`
    (d) `Vehicle`   (e) `Object`   (f) `Tree`

12.4.1 The Constructor Initializer

Like any other function, a constructor has a name, a parameter list, and a function body. Unlike other functions, a constructor may also contain a constructor initializer list:

```
//  recommended way to write constructors using a constructor initializer
Sales_item::Sales_item(const string &book):
    isbn(book), units_sold(0), revenue(0.0) { }
```

The constructor initializer starts with a colon, which is followed by a comma-separated list of data members each of which is followed by an initializer inside parentheses. This constructor initializes the isbn member to the value of its book parameter and initializes units_sold and revenue to 0. As with any member function, constructors can be defined inside or outside of the class. The constructor initializer is specified only on the constructor definition, not its declaration.

The constructor initializer is a feature that many reasonably experienced C++ programmers have not mastered.

One reason constructor initializers are hard to understand is that it is usually legal to omit the initializer list and *assign* values to the data members inside the constructor body. For example, we could write the Sales_item constructor that takes a string as

```
//  legal but sloppier way to write the constructor:
//  no constructor initializer
Sales_item::Sales_item(const string &book)
{
    isbn = book;
    units_sold = 0;
    revenue = 0.0;
}
```

This constructor assigns, but does not explicitly initialize, the members of class Sales_item. Regardless of the lack of an explicit initializer, the isbn member is initialized before the constructor is executed. This constructor implicitly uses the default string constructor to initialize isbn. When the body of the constructor is executed, the isbn member already has a value. That value is overwritten by the assignment inside the constructor body.

Conceptually, we can think of a constructor as executing in two phases: (1) the initialization phase and (2) a general computation phase. The computation phase consists of all the statements within the body of the constructor.

Data members of class type are *always* initialized in the initialization phase, regardless of whether the member is initialized explicitly in the constructor initializer list. Initialization happens *before* the computation phase begins.

Each member that is not explicitly mentioned in the constructor initializer is initialized using the same rules as those used to initialize variables (Section 2.3.4, p. 50). Data members of class type are initialized by running the type's default constructor. The initial value of members of built-in or compound type depend on the scope of the object: At local scope those members are uninitialized, at global scope they are initialized to 0.

The two versions of the `Sales_item` constructor that we wrote in this section have the same effect: Whether we initialized the members in the constructor initializer list or assigned to them inside the constructor body, the end result is the same. After the constructor completes, the three data members hold the same values. The difference is that the version that uses the constructor initializer *initializes* its data members. The version that does not define a constructor initializer *assigns* values to the data members in the body of the constructor. How significant this distinction is depends on the type of the data member.

Constructor Initializers Are Sometimes Required

If an initializer is not provided for a class member, then the compiler implicitly uses the default constructor for the member's type. If that class does not have a default constructor, then the attempt by the compiler to use it will fail. In such cases, an initializer must be provided in order to initialize the data member.

> Some members *must* be initialized in the constructor initializer. For such members, assigning to them in the constructor body doesn't work. Members of a class type that do not have a default constructor and members that are `const` or reference types *must* be initialized in the constructor initializer *regardless of type*.

Because members of built-in type are not implicitly initialized, it may seem that it doesn't matter whether these members are initialized or assigned. With two exceptions, using an initializer is equivalent to assigning to a nonclass data member both in result and in performance.

For example, the following constructor is in error:

```
class ConstRef {
public:
    ConstRef(int ii);
private:
    int i;
    const int ci;
    int &ri;
};
//   no explicit constructor initializer: error ri is uninitialized
ConstRef::ConstRef(int ii)
{                    //  assignments:
    i = ii;     //  ok
    ci = ii;    //  error: cannot assign to a const
    ri = i;     //  assigns to ri which was not bound to an object
}
```

Remember that we can initialize but not assign to `const` objects or objects of reference type. By the time the body of the constructor begins executing, initialization is complete. Our only chance to initialize `const` or reference data members is in the constructor initializer. The correct way to write the constructor is

```
//   ok: explicitly initialize reference and const members
ConstRef::ConstRef(int ii): i(ii), ci(i), ri(ii) {  }
```

Order of Member Initialization

Not surprisingly, each member may be named only once in the constructor initializer. After all, what might it mean to give a member two initial values? What may be more surprising is that the constructor initializer list specifies only the values used to initialize the members, not the order in which those initializations are performed. The order in which members are initialized is the order in which the members are defined. The first member is initialized first, then the next, and so on.

The order of initialization often doesn't matter. However, if one member is initialized in terms of another, then the order in which members are initialized is crucially important.

Consider the following class:

```
class X {
    int i;
    int j;
public:
    // run-time error: i is initialized before j
    X(int val): j(val), i(j) { }
};
```

In this case, the constructor initializer is written to make it *appear* as if j is initialized with `val` and then j is used to initialize i. However, i is initialized first. The effect of this initializer is to initialize i with the as yet uninitialized value of j!

Some compilers are kind enough to generate a warning if the data members are listed in the constructor initializer in a different order from the order in which the members are declared.

It is a good idea to write constructor initializers in the same order as the members are declared. Moreover, when possible, avoid using members to initialize other members.

It is often the case that we can avoid any problems due to order of execution for initializers by (re)using the constructor's parameters rather than using the object's data members. For example, it would be better to write the constructor for X as

```
X(int val): i(val), j(val) { }
```

In this version, the order in which i and j are initialized doesn't matter.

Initializers May Be Any Expression

An initializer may be an arbitrarily complex expression. As an example, we could give our Sales_item class a new constructor that takes a string representing the isbn, an unsigned representing the number of books sold, and a double representing the price at which each of these books was sold:

```
Sales_item(const std::string &book, int cnt, double price):
    isbn(book), units_sold(cnt), revenue(cnt * price) { }
```

This initializer for revenue uses the parameters representing price and number sold to calculate the object's revenue member.

Initializers for Data Members of Class Type

When we initialize a member of class type, we are specifying arguments to be passed to one of the constructors of that member's type. We can use any of that type's constructors. For example, our Sales_item class could initialize isbn using any of the string constructors (Section 9.6.1, p. 338). Instead of using the empty string, we might decide that the default value for isbn should be a value that represents an impossibly high value for an ISBN. We could initialize isbn to a string of ten 9s:

```
// alternative definition for Sales_item default constructor
Sales_item(): isbn(10, '9'), units_sold(0), revenue(0.0) {}
```

This initializer uses the string constructor that takes a count and a character and generates a string holding that character repeated that number of times.

EXERCISES SECTION 12.4.1

Exercise 12.21: Write the default constructor using a constructor initializer for class that contains the following members: a const string, an int, a double*, and an ifstream&. Initialize the string to hold the name of the class.

Exercise 12.22: The following initializer is in error. Identify and fix the problem.

```
struct X {
    X (int i, int j): base(i), rem(base % j) { }
    int rem, base;
};
```

Exercise 12.23: Assume we have a class named NoDefault that has a constructor that takes an int but no default constructor. Define a class C that has a member of type NoDefault. Define the default constructor for C.

12.4.2   Default Arguments and Constructors

Let's look again at our definitions for the default constructor and the constructor
that takes a `string`:

```
Sales_item(const std::string &book):
            isbn(book), units_sold(0), revenue(0.0) { }
Sales_item(): units_sold(0), revenue(0.0) { }
```

These constructors are almost the same: The only difference is that the constructor
that takes a `string` parameter uses the parameter to initialize `isbn`. The default
constructor (implicitly) uses the `string` default constructor to initialize `isbn`.

   We can combine these constructors by supplying a default argument for the
`string` initializer:

```
class Sales_item {
public:
    // default argument for book is the empty string
    Sales_item(const std::string &book = ""):
            isbn(book), units_sold(0), revenue(0.0) { }
    Sales_item(std::istream &is);
    // as before
};
```

Here we define only two constructors, one of which provides a default argument
for its parameter. The constructor that takes a default argument for its single
`string` parameter will be run for either of these definitions:

```
Sales_item empty;
Sales_item Primer_3rd_Ed("0-201-82470-1");
```

In the case of `empty`, the default argument is used, whereas `Primer_3rd_ed`
supplies an explicit argument.

   Each version of our class provides the same interface: They both initialize a
`Sales_item` to the same values given a `string` or given no initializer.

Best
Practices

> We prefer to use a default argument because it reduces code dupli-
> cation.

12.4.3   The Default Constructor

The default constructor is used whenever we define an object but do not supply
an initializer. A constructor that supplies default arguments for all its parameters
also defines the default constructor.

The Synthesized Default Constructor

If a class defines even one constructor, then the compiler will not generate the default constructor. The basis for this rule is that if a class requires control to initialize
an object in one case, then the class is likely to require control in all cases.

EXERCISES SECTION 12.4.2

Exercise 12.24: Using the version of `Sales_item` from page 458 that defined two constructors, one of which has a default argument for its single `string` parameter, determine which constructor is used to initialize each of the following variables and list the values of the data members in each object:

```
Sales_item first_item(cin);

int main() {
    Sales_item next;
    Sales_item last("9-999-99999-9");
}
```

Exercise 12.25: Logically, we might want to supply `cin` as a default argument to the constructor that takes an `istream&`. Write the constructor declaration that uses `cin` as a default argument.

Exercise 12.26: Would it be legal for both the constructor that takes a `string` and the one that takes an `istream&` to have default arguments? If not, why not?

The compiler generates a default constructor automatically only if a class defines *no* constructors.

The **synthesized default constructor** initializes members using the same rules as those that apply for how variables are initialized. Members that are of class type are initialized by running each member's own default constructor. Members of built-in or compound type, such as pointers and arrays, are initialized only for objects that are defined at global scope. When objects are defined at local scope, then members of built-in or compound type are *uninitialized*.

If a class contains data members of built-in or compound type, then the class should not rely on the synthesized default constructor. It should define its own constructor to initialize these members.

Moreover, every constructor should provide initializers for members of built-in or compound type. A constructor that does not initialize a member of built-in or compound type leaves that member in an undefined state. Using an undefined member in any way other than as the target of an assignment is an error. If every constructor sets every member to an explicit, known state, then member functions can distinguish between an empty object and one that has actual values.

Classes Should Usually Define a Default Constructor

In certain cases, the default constructor is applied implicitly by the compiler. If the class has no default constructor, then the class may not be used in these contexts. To illustrate the cases where a default constructor is required, assume we have a class named `NoDefault` that does not define its own default constructor but does have a constructor that takes a `string` argument. Because the class defines a constructor, the compiler will not synthesize the default constructor. The fact that `NoDefault` has no default constructor means:

1. Every constructor for every class that has a `NoDefault` member must explicitly initialize the `NoDefault` member by passing an initial `string` value to the `NoDefault` constructor.

2. The compiler will not synthesize the default constructor for classes that have members of type `NoDefault`. If such classes want to provide a default, they must define one explicitly, and that constructor must explicitly initialize their `NoDefault` member.

3. The `NoDefault` type may not be used as the element type for a dynamically allocated array.

4. Statically allocated arrays of type `NoDefault` must provide an explicit initializer for each element.

5. If we have a container such as `vector` that holds `NoDefault` objects, we cannot use the constructor that takes a size without also supplying an element initializer.

Best Practices

In practice, it is almost always right to provide a default constructor if other constructors are being defined. Ordinarily the initial values given to the members in the default constructor should indicate that the object is "empty."

Using the Default Constructor

Beware

A common mistake among programmers new to C++ is to declare an object initialized with the default constructor as follows:

```
//  oops! declares a function, not an object
Sales_item myobj();
```

The declaration of `myobj` compiles without complaint. However, when we try to use `myobj`

```
Sales_item myobj();     //  ok: but defines a function, not an object
if (myobj.same_isbn(Primer_3rd_ed))   //  error: myobj is a function
```

the compiler complains that we cannot apply member access notation to a function! The problem is that our definition of `myobj` is interpreted by the compiler as a declaration of a function taking no parameters and returning an object of type `Sales_item`—hardly what we intended! The correct way to define an object using the default constructor is to leave off the trailing, empty parentheses:

```
//  ok: defines a class object ...
Sales_item myobj;
```

On the other hand, this code is fine:

```
// ok: create an unnamed, empty Sales_item and use to initialize myobj
Sales_item myobj = Sales_item();
```

Here we create and value-initialize a `Sales_item` object and to use it to initialize `myobj`. The compiler value-initializes a `Sales_item` by running its default constructor.

EXERCISES SECTION 12.4.3

Exercise 12.27: Which, if any, of the following statements are untrue? Why?

(a) A class must provide at least one constructor.
(b) A default constructor is a constructor with no parameters for its parameter list.
(c) If there are no meaningful default values for a class, the class should not provide a default constructor.
(d) If a class does not define a default constructor, the compiler generates one automatically, initializing each data member to the default value of its associated type.

12.4.4 Implicit Class-Type Conversions

As we saw in Section 5.12 (p. 178), the language defines several automatic conversions among the built-in types. We can also define how to implicitly convert an object from another type to our class type or to convert from our class type to another type. We'll see in Section 14.9 (p. 535) how to define conversions *from* a class type to another type. To define an implicit conversion *to* a class type, we need to define an appropriate constructor.

> A constructor that can be called with a single argument defines an implicit conversion from the parameter type to the class type.

Let's look again at the version of `Sales_item` that defined two constructors:

```
class Sales_item {
public:
    // default argument for book is the empty string
    Sales_item(const std::string &book = ""):
                isbn(book), units_sold(0), revenue(0.0) { }
    Sales_item(std::istream &is);
    // as before
};
```

Each of these constructors defines an implicit conversion. Accordingly, we can use a `string` or an `istream` where an object of type `Sales_item` is expected:

```
string null_book = "9-999-99999-9";
// ok: builds a Sales_item with 0 units_sold and revenue from
//     and isbn equal to null_book
item.same_isbn(null_book);
```

This program uses an object of type `string` as the argument to the `Sales_item` `same_isbn` function. That function expects a `Sales_item` object as its argument. The compiler uses the `Sales_item` constructor that takes a `string` to generate a new `Sales_item` object from `null_book`. That newly generated (temporary) `Sales_item` is passed to `same_isbn`.

Whether this behavior is desired depends on how we think our users will use the conversion. In this case, it might be a good idea. The `string` in `book` probably represents a nonexistent ISBN, and the call to `same_isbn` can detect whether the `Sales_item` in `item` represents a null `Sales_item`. On the other hand, our user might have mistakenly called `same_isbn` on `null_book`.

More problematic is the conversion from `istream` to `Sales_item`:

```
// ok: uses the Sales_item istream constructor to build an object
//     to pass to same_isbn
item.same_isbn(cin);
```

This code implicitly converts `cin` to a `Sales_item`. This conversion executes the `Sales_item` constructor that takes an `istream`. That constructor creates a (temporary) `Sales_item` object by reading the standard input. That object is then passed to `same_isbn`.

This `Sales_item` object is a temporary (Section 7.3.2, p. 247). We have no access to it once `same_isbn` finishes. Effectively, we have constructed an object that is discarded after the test is complete. This behavior is almost surely a mistake.

Supressing Implicit Conversions Defined by Constructors

We can prevent the use of a constructor in a context that requires an implicit conversion by declaring the constructor `explicit`:

```
class Sales_item {
public:
    // default argument for book is the empty string
    explicit Sales_item(const std::string &book = ""):
            isbn(book), units_sold(0), revenue(0.0) { }
    explicit Sales_item(std::istream &is);
    // as before
};
```

The `explicit` keyword is used only on the constructor declaration inside the class. It is not repeated on a definition made outside the class body:

```
// error: explicit allowed only on constructor declaration in class header
explicit Sales_item::Sales_item(istream& is)
{
    is >> *this; // uses Sales_item input operator to read the members
}
```

Now, neither constructor can be used to implicitly create a `Sales_item` object. Neither of our previous uses will compile:

```
item.same_isbn(null_book);    // error: string constructor is explicit
item.same_isbn(cin);          // error: istream constructor is explicit
```

> When a constructor is declared `explicit`, the compiler will *not* use it
> as a conversion operator.

Explicitly Using Constructors for Conversions

An `explicit` constructor can be used to generate a conversion as long as we do
so explicitly:

```
string null_book = "9-999-99999-9";
// ok: builds a Sales_item with 0 units_sold and revenue from
//     and isbn equal to null_book
item.same_isbn(Sales_item(null_book));
```

In this code, we create a `Sales_item` from `null_book`. Even though the constructor is `explicit`, this usage is allowed. Making a constructor `explicit`
turns off only the use of the constructor implicitly. Any constructor can be used to
explicitly create a temporary object.

> Ordinarily, single-parameter constructors should be `explicit` un-
> less there is an obvious reason to want to define an implicit conver-
> sion. Making constructors `explicit` may avoid mistakes, and a
> user can explicitly construct an object when a conversion is useful.

EXERCISES SECTION 12.4.4

Exercise 12.28: Explain whether the `Sales_item` constructor that takes a `string`
should be explicit. What would be the benefits of making the constructor explicit?
What would be the drawbacks?

Exercise 12.29: Explain what operations happen during the following definitions:

```
string null_isbn = "9-999-99999-9";
Sales_item null1(null_isbn);
Sales_item null("9-999-99999-9");
```

Exercise 12.30: Compile the following code:

```
f(const vector<int>&);
int main() {
    vector<int> v2;
    f(v2);   // should be ok
    f(42);   // should be an error
    return 0;
}
```

What can we infer about the `vector` constructors based on the error on the second call
to `f`? If the call succeeded, then what would you conclude?

12.4.5 Explicit Initialization of Class Members

Although most objects are initialized by running an appropriate constructor, it is possible to initialize the data members of simple nonabstract classes directly. Members of classes that define no constructors and all of whose data members are `public` may be initialized in the same way that we initialize array elements:

```
struct Data {
    int ival;
    char *ptr;
};
// val1.ival = 0; val1.ptr = 0
Data val1 = { 0, 0 };
// val2.ival = 1024;
// val2.ptr = "Anna Livia Plurabelle"
Data val2 = { 1024, "Anna Livia Plurabelle" };
```

The initializers are used in the declaration order of the data members. The following, for example, is an error because `ival` is declared before `ptr`:

```
// error: can't use "Anna Livia Plurabelle" to initialize the int ival
Data val2 = { "Anna Livia Plurabelle" , 1024 };
```

This form of initialization is inherited from C and is supported for compatibility with C programs. There are three significant drawbacks to explicitly initializing the members of an object of class type:

1. It requires that all the data members of the class be `public`.

2. It puts the burden on the programmer to initialize every member of every object. Such initialization is tedious and error-prone because it is easy to forget an initializer or to supply an inappropriate initializer.

3. If a member is added or removed, all initializations have to be found and updated correctly.

 Best Practices It is almost always better to define and use constructors. When we provide a default constructor for the types we define, we allow the compiler to automatically run that constructor, ensuring that every class object is properly initialized prior to the first use of that object.

EXERCISES SECTION 12.4.5

Exercise 12.31: The data members of `pair` are `public`, yet this code doesn't compile. Why?

```
pair<int, int> p2 = {0, 42};  // doesn't compile, why?
```

12.5   Friends

In some cases, it is convenient to let specific nonmember functions access the private members of a class while still preventing general access. For example, overloaded operators, such as the input or output operators, often need access to the private data members of a class. For reasons we'll see in Chapter 14 these operators might not be members of the class. Yet, even if they are not members of the class, they are "part of the interface" to the class.

The **friend** mechanism allows a class to grant access to its nonpublic members to specified functions or classes. A friend declaration begins with the keyword friend. It may appear only within a class definition. Friend declarations may appear anywhere in the class: Friends are not members of the class granting friendship, and so they are not affected by the access control of the section in which they are declared.

 Ordinarily it is a good idea to group friend declarations together either at the beginning or end of the class definition.

Friendship: An Example

Imagine that in addition to the `Screen` class we had a window manager that manages a group of `Screens` on a given display. That class logically might need access to the internal data of the `Screen` objects it manages. Assuming that `Window_Mgr` is the name of the window-management class, `Screen` could let `Window_Mgr` access its members as follows:

```
class Screen {
    //  Window_Mgr members can access private parts of class Screen
    friend class Window_Mgr;
    //  ...rest of the Screen class
};
```

The members of `Window_Mgr` can refer directly to the `private` members of `Screen`. For example, `Window_Mgr` might have a function to relocate a `Screen`:

```
Window_Mgr&
Window_Mgr::relocate(Screen::index r, Screen::index c,
                     Screen& s)
{
    //  ok to refer to height and width
    s.height += r;
    s.width += c;
    return *this;
}
```

In absence of the friend declaration, this code would be in error: It would not be allowed to use the `height` and `width` members of its parameter named `s`. Because `Screen` grants friendship to `Window_Mgr`, all the members of `Screen` are accessible to the functions in `Window_Mgr`.

A friend may be an ordinary, nonmember function, a member function of another previously defined class, or an entire class. In making a class a friend, all the member functions of the friend class are given access to the nonpublic members of the class granting friendship.

Making Another Class' Member Function a Friend

Instead of making the entire `Window_Mgr` class a friend, `Screen` could have specified that only the `relocate` member was allowed access:

```
class Screen {
    // Window_Mgr must be defined before class Screen
    friend Window_Mgr&
        Window_Mgr::relocate(Window_Mgr::index,
                             Window_Mgr::index,
                             Screen&);
    // ...rest of the Screen class
};
```

When we declare a member function to be a friend, the name of the function must be qualified by the name of the class of which it is a member.

Friend Declarations and Scope

Interdependencies among friend declarations and the definitions of the friends can require some care in order to structure the classes correctly. In the previous example, class `Window_Mgr` must have been defined. Otherwise, class `Screen` could not name a `Window_Mgr` function as a friend. However, the `relocate` function itself can't be defined until class `Screen` has been defined—after all, it was made a friend in order to access the members of class `Screen`.

More generally, to make a member function a friend, the class containing that member must have been defined. On the other hand, a class or nonmember function need not have been declared to be made a friend.

 A friend declaration introduces the named class or nonmember function into the surrounding scope. Moreover, a friend function may be *defined* inside the class. The scope of the function is exported to the scope enclosing the class definition.

Class names and functions (definitions or declarations) introduced in a friend can be used as if they had been previously declared:

```
class X {
    friend class Y;
    friend void f() { /* ok to define friend function in the class body */ }
};
class Z {
    Y *ymem;    // ok: declaration for class Y introduced by friend in X
    void g() { return ::f(); } // ok: declaration of f introduced by X
};
```

Overloaded Functions and Friendship

A class must declare as a friend each function in a set of overloaded functions that it wishes to make a friend:

```
// overloaded storeOn functions
extern std::ostream& storeOn(std::ostream &, Screen &);
extern BitMap& storeOn(BitMap &, Screen &);
class Screen {
    // ostream version of storeOn may access private parts of Screen objects
    friend std::ostream& storeOn(std::ostream &, Screen &);
    // ...
};
```

Class `Screen` makes the version of `storeOn` that takes an `ostream&` its friend. The version that takes a `BitMap&` has no special access to `Screen`.

EXERCISES SECTION 12.5

Exercise 12.32: What is a friend function? A friend class?

Exercise 12.33: When are friends useful? Discuss the pros and cons of using friends.

Exercise 12.34: Define a nonmember function that adds two `Sales_item` objects.

Exercise 12.35: Define a nonmember function that reads an `istream` and stores what it reads into a `Sales_item`.

12.6 `static` Class Members

It is sometimes necessary for all the objects of a particular class type to access a global object. Perhaps a count is needed of how many objects of a particular class type have been created at any one point in the program, or the global object may be a pointer to an error-handling routine for the class, or it may be a pointer to the free-store memory for objects of this class type.

However, making the object global violates encapsulation: The object exists to support the implementation of a particular class abstraction. If the object is global, general user code can modify the value. Rather than defining a generally accessible global object, a class can define a **class `static` member**.

Ordinary, non`static` data members exist in each object of the class type. Unlike ordinary data members, a `static` data member exists independently of any object of its class; each `static` data member is an object associated with the class, not with the objects of that class.

Just as a class may define shared `static` data members, it may also define `static` member functions. A `static` member function has no `this` parameter. It may directly access the `static` members of its class but may not directly use the non`static` members.

Advantages of Using Class `static` Members

There are three advantages to using `static` members rather than globals:

1. The name of a `static` member is in the scope of the class, thereby avoiding name collisions with members of other classes or global objects.

2. Encapsulation can be enforced. A `static` member can be a private member; a global object cannot.

3. It is easy to see by reading the program that a `static` member is associated with a particular class. This visibility clarifies the programmer's intentions.

Defining `static` Members

A member is made `static` by prefixing the member declaration with the keyword `static`. The `static` members obey the normal public/private access rules.

As an example, consider a simple class intended to represent a bank account. Each account has a balance and an owner. Each account earns interest monthly, but the interest rate applied to each account is always the same. We could write this class as

```
class Account {
public:
    // interface functions here
    void applyint() { amount += amount * interestRate; }
    static double rate() { return interestRate; }
    static void rate(double);   // sets a new rate
private:
    std::string owner;
    double amount;
    static double interestRate;
    static double initRate();
};
```

Each object of this class has two data members: `owner` and `amount`. Objects do not have data members that correspond to `static` data members. Instead, there is a single `interestRate` object that is shared by all objects of type `Account`.

Using a Class `static` Member

A `static` member can be invoked directly from the class using the scope operator or indirectly through an object, reference, or pointer to an object of its class type.

```
Account ac1;
Account *ac2 = &ac1;

// equivalent ways to call the static member rate function
double rate;
rate = ac1.rate();        // through an Account object or reference
rate = ac2->rate();       // through a pointer to an Account object
rate = Account::rate();   // directly from the class using the scope operator
```

As with other members, a class member function can refer to a class `static` member without the use of the scope operator:

```
class Account {
public:
    //  interface functions here
    void applyint() { amount += amount * interestRate; }
};
```

Exercise 12.36: What is a `static` class member? What are the advantages of `static` members? How do they differ from ordinary members?

Exercise 12.37: Write your own version of the `Account` class.

12.6.1 `static` Member Functions

Our `Account` class has two `static` member functions named `rate`, one of which was defined inside the class. When we define a `static` member outside the class, we do not respecify the `static` keyword. The keyword appears only with the declaration inside the class body:

```
void Account::rate(double newRate)
{
    interestRate = newRate;
}
```

`static` Functions Have No `this` Pointer

A `static` member is part of its class but not part of any object. Hence, a `static` member function does not have a `this` pointer. Referring to `this` either explicitly or implicitly by using a nonstatic member is a compile-time error.

Because a `static` member is not part of any object, `static` member functions may not be declared as `const`. After all, declaring a member function as `const` is a promise not to modify the object of which the function is a member. Finally, `static` member functions may also not be declared as virtual. We'll learn about virtual functions in Section 15.2.4 (p. 566).

12.6.2 `static` Data Members

`static` data members can be declared to be of any type. They can be `const`s, references, arrays, class types, and so forth.

`static` data members must be defined (exactly once) outside the class body. Unlike ordinary data members, `static` members are not initialized through the class constructor(s) and instead should be initialized when they are defined.

Exercise 12.38: Define a class named Foo that has a single data member of type int. Give the class a constructor that takes an int value and initializes the data member from that value. Give it a function that returns the value of its data member.

Exercise 12.39: Given the class Foo defined in the previous exercise, define another class Bar with two static data elements: one of type int and another of type Foo.

Exercise 12.40: Using the classes from the previous two exercises, add a pair of static member functions to class Bar. The first static, named FooVal, should return the value of class Bar's static member of type Foo. The second member, named callsFooVal, should keep a count of how many times xval is called.

 The best way to ensure that the object is defined exactly once is to put the definition of static data members in the same file that contains the definitions of the class noninline member functions.

static data members are defined in the same way that other class members and other variables are defined. The member is defined by naming its type followed by the fully qualified name of the member.

We might define interestRate as follows:

```
// define and initialize static class member
double Account::interestRate = initRate();
```

This statement defines the static object named interestRate that is a member of class Account and has type double. Like other member definitions, the definition of a static member is in class scope once the member name is seen. As a result, we can use the static member function named initRate directly without qualification as the initializer for rate. Note that even though initRate is private, we can use this function to initialize interestRate. The definition of interestRate, like any other member definition, is in the scope of the class and hence has access to the private members of the class.

 As with any class member, when we refer to a class static member outside the class body, we must specify the class in which the member is defined. The static keyword, however, is used *only* on the declaration inside the class body. Definitions are not labeled static.

Integral const static Members Are Special

Ordinarily, class static members, like ordinary data members, cannot be initialized in the class body. Instead, static data members are normally initialized when they are defined.

One exception to this rule is that a const static data member of integral type can be initialized within the class body as long as the initializer is a constant expression:

```
class Account {
public:
    static double rate() { return interestRate; }
    static void rate(double);   // sets a new rate
private:
    static const int period = 30;   // interest posted every 30 days
    double daily_tbl[period]; // ok: period is constant expression
};
```

A `const static` data member of integral type initialized with a constant value is a constant expression. As such, it can be used where a constant expression is required, such as to specify the dimension for the array member `daily_tbl`.

 Note When a `const static` data member is initialized in the class body, the data member must still be defined outside the class definition.

When an initializer is provided inside the class, the definition of the member must not specify an initial value:

```
// definition of static member with no initializer;
// the initial value is specified inside the class definition
const int Account::period;
```

`static` Members Are Not Part of Class Objects

Ordinary members are part of each object of the given class. `static` members exist independently of any object and are not part of objects of the class type. Because `static` data members are not part of any object, they can be used in ways that would be illegal for non`static` data members.

As an example, the type of a `static` data member can be the class type of which it is a member. A non`static` data member is restricted to being declared as a pointer or a reference to an object of its class:

```
class Bar {
public:
    // ...
private:
    static Bar mem1; // ok
    Bar *mem2;       // ok
    Bar mem3;        // error
};
```

Similarly, a `static` data member can be used as a default argument:

```
class Screen {
public:
    // bkground refers to the static member
    // declared later in the class definition
    Screen& clear(char = bkground);
private:
    static const char bkground = '#';
};
```

A nonstatic data member may not be used as a default argument because its value cannot be used independently of the object of which it is a part. Using a nonstatic data member as a default argument provides no object from which to obtain the member's value and so is an error.

Exercise 12.41: Given the classes Foo and Bar that you wrote for the exercises to Section 12.6.1 (p. 470), initialize the static members of Foo. Initialize the int member to 20 and the Foo member to 0.

Exercise 12.42: Which, if any, of the following static data member declarations and definitions are errors? Explain why.

```
// example.h
class Example {
public:
    static double rate = 6.5;

    static const int vecSize = 20;
    static vector<double> vec(vecSize);
};

// example.C
#include "example.h"
double Example::rate;
vector<double> Example::vec;
```

CHAPTER SUMMARY

Classes are the most fundamental feature in C++. Classes let us define new types that are tailored to our own applications, making our programs shorter and easier to modify.

Data abstraction—the ability to define both data and function members—and encapsulation—the ability to protect class members from general access—are fundamental to classes. Member functions define the interface to the class. We encapsulate the class by making the data and functions used by the implementation of a class `private`.

Classes may define constructors, which are special member functions that control how objects of the class are initialized. Constructors may be overloaded. Every constructor should initialize every data member. Constructors should use a constructor initializer list to initialize the data members. Initializer lists are lists of name–value pairs where the name is a member and the value is an initial value for that member.

Classes may grant access to their nonpublic members to other classes or functions. A class grants access by making the class or function a friend.

Classes may also define `mutable` or `static` members. A `mutable` member is a data member that is never `const`; its value may be changed inside a `const` member function. A `static` member can be either function or data; `static` members exist independently of the objects of the class type.

DEFINED TERMS

abstract data type A data structure that uses encapsulation to hide its implementation, allowing programmers using the type to think *abstractly* about what the type does rather than *concretely* about how the type is represented. Classes in C++ can be used to define abstract data types.

access label A `public` or `private` label that defines whether the following members are accessible to users of the class or only to the friends and members of the class. Each label sets the access protection for the members declared up to the next label. Labels may appear multiple times within the class.

class C++ mechanism for defining our own abstract data types. Classes may have data, function or type members. A class defines a new type and a new scope.

class declaration A class may be declared before it is defined. A class declaration is the keyword `class` (or `struct`) followed by the class name followed by a semicolon. A class that is declared but not defined is an incomplete type.

class keyword In a class defined following the `class` keyword, the initial implicit access label is `private`.

class scope Each class defines a scope. Class scopes are more complicated than other scopes—member functions defined within the class body may use names that appear after the definition.

concrete class A class that exposes its implementation.

const member function A member function that may not change an object's ordinary (i.e., neither `static` nor `mutable`) data members. The `this` pointer in a `const` member is a pointer to `const`. A member function may be overloaded based on whether the function is `const`.

constructor initializer list Specifies initial values of the data members of a class. The members are initialized to the values specified in the initializer list before the body of the constructor executes. Class members that are not initialized in the initializer list are implicitly initialized by using their default constructor.

conversion constructor A nonexplicit constructor that can be called with a single argument. A conversion constructor is used implicitly to convert from the argument's type to the class type.

data abstraction Programming technique that focuses on the interface to a type. Data abstraction allows programmers to ignore the details of how a type is represented and to think instead about the operations that the type can perform. Data abstraction is fundamental to both object-oriented and generic programming.

default constructor The constructor that is used when no initializer is specified.

encapsulation Separation of implementation from interface; encapsulation hides the implementation details of a type. In C++, encapsulation is enforced by preventing general user access to the private parts of a class.

explicit constructor Constructor that can be called with a single argument but that may not be used to perform an implicit conversion. A constructor is made explicit by prepending the keyword explicit to its declaration.

forward declaration Declaration of an as yet undefined name. Most often used to refer to the declaration of a class that appears prior to the definition of that class. See incomplete type.

friend Mechanism by which a class grants access to its nonpublic members. Both classes and functions may be named as friends. friends have the same access rights as members.

incomplete type A type that has been declared but not yet defined. It is not possible use an incomplete type to define a variable or class member. It is legal to define references or pointers to incomplete types.

member function Class member that is a function. Ordinary member functions are bound to an object of the class type through the implicit this pointer. Static member functions are not bound to an object and have no this pointer. Member functions may be overloaded, provided that the versions of the function are distinguished by number or type of their parameters.

mutable data member Data member that is never const, even when it is a member of a const object. A mutable member can be changed inside a const function.

name lookup The process by which the use of a name is matched to its corresponding declaration.

private members Members defined after a private access label; accessible only to the friends and other class members. Data members and utility functions used by the class that are not part of the type's interface are usually declared private.

public members Members defined after a public access label; public members are accessible to any user of the class. Ordinarily, only the functions that define the interface to the class should be defined in the public sections.

static member Data or function member that is not a part of any object but is shared by all objects of a given class.

struct keyword In a class defined following the struct keyword, the initial implicit access label is public.

synthesized default constructor The default constructor created (synthesized) by the compiler for classes that do not define any constructors. This constructor initializes members of class type by running that class's default constructor; members of built-in type are uninitialized.

CHAPTER 13

COPY CONTROL

Each type, whether a built-in or class type, defines the meaning of a (possibly empty) set of operations on objects of that type. We can add two int values, run size on a vector, and so on. These operations define what can be done with objects of the given type.

Each type also defines what happens when objects of the type are created. Initialization of objects of class type is defined by constructors. Types also control what happens when objects of the type are copied, assigned, or destroyed. Classes control these actions through special member functions: the copy constructor, the assignment operator, and the destructor. This chapter covers these operations.

When we define a new type, we specify—explicitly or implicitly—what happens when objects of that type are copied, assigned, and destroyed. We do so by defining special members: the copy constructor, the assignment operator, and the destructor. If we do not explicitly define the copy constructor or the assignment operator, the compiler will (usually) define them for us.

The **copy constructor** is a special constructor that has a single parameter that is a (usually `const`) reference to the class type. The copy constructor is used explicitly when we define a new object and initialize it from an object of the same type. It is used implicitly when we pass or return objects of that type to or from functions.

The **destructor** is complementary to the constructors: It is applied automatically when an object goes out of scope or when a dynamically allocated object is deleted. The destructor is used to free resources acquired when the object was constructed or during the lifetime of the object. Regardless of whether a class defines its own destructor, the compiler automatically executes the destructors for the `nonstatic` data members of the class.

We'll learn more about operator overloading in the next chapter, but in this chapter we cover the **assignment operator**. Like constructors, the assignment operator may be overloaded by specifying different types for the right-hand operand. The version whose right-hand operand is of the class type is special: If we do not write one, the compiler will synthesize one for us.

Collectively, the copy constructor, assignment operator, and destructor are referred to as **copy control**. The compiler automatically implements these operations, but the class may define its own versions.

Copy control is an essential part of defining any C++ class. Programmers new to C++ are often confused by having to define what happens when objects are copied, assigned, or destroyed. This confusion is compounded because if we do not explicitly define these operations, the compiler defines them for us—although they might not behave as we intend.

Often the compiler-synthesized copy-control functions are fine—they do exactly the work that needs to be done. But for some classes, relying on the default definitions leads to disaster. Frequently, the most difficult part of implementing the copy-control operations is recognizing when we need to override the default versions. One especially common case that requires the class to define its own the copy-control members is if the class has a pointer member.

13.1   The Copy Constructor

The constructor that takes a single parameter that is a (usually `const`) reference to an object of the class type itself is called the copy constructor. Like the default constructor, the copy constructor can be implicitly invoked by the compiler. The copy constructor is used to

- Explicitly or implicitly initialize one object from another of the same type

- Copy an object to pass it as an argument to a function

- Copy an object to return it from a function

- Initialize the elements in a sequential container

- Initialize elements in an array from a list of element initializers

Forms of Object Definition

Recall that C++ supports two forms of initialization (Section 2.3.3, p. 48): direct and copy. Copy-initialization uses the = symbol, and direct-initialization places the initializer in parentheses.

The copy and direct forms of initialization, when applied to objects of class type, are subtly different. Direct-initialization directly invokes the constructor matched by the arguments. Copy-initialization always involves the copy constructor. Copy-initialization first uses the indicated constructor to create a temporary object (Section 7.3.2, p. 247). It then uses the copy constructor to copy that temporary into the one we are creating:

```
string null_book = "9-999-99999-9";   // copy-initialization
string dots(10, '.');                  // direct-initialization

string empty_copy = string();          // copy-initialization
string empty_direct;                   // direct-initialization
```

For objects of class type, copy-initialization can be used only when specifying a single argument or when we explicitly build a temporary object to copy.

When `dots` is created, the `string` constructor that takes a count and a character is called and directly initializes the members in `dots`. To create `null_book`, the compiler first creates a temporary by invoking the `string` constructor that takes a C-style character string parameter. The compiler then uses the `string` copy constructor to initialize `null_book` as a copy of that temporary.

The initialization of `empty_copy` and `empty_direct` both call the `string` default constructor. In the first case, the default constructor creates a temporary object, which is then used by the copy constructor to initialize `empty_copy`. In the second case, the default constructor is run directly on `empty_direct`.

The copy form of initialization is primarily supported for compatibility with C usage. When it can do so, the compiler is permitted (but not obligated) to skip the copy constructor and create the object directly.

Usually the difference between direct- or copy-initialization is at most a matter of low-level optimization. However, for types that do not support copying, or when using a constructor that is nonexplicit (Section 12.4.4, p. 462) the distinction can be essential:

```
ifstream file1("filename");   // ok: direct initialization
ifstream file2 = "filename";  // error: copy constructor is private
// This initialization is okay only if
// the Sales_item(const string&) constructor is not explicit
Sales_item item = string("9-999-99999-9");
```

The initialization of `file1` is fine. The `ifstream` class defines a constructor that can be called with a C-style string. That constructor is used to initialize `file1`.

The seemingly equivalent initialization of `file2` uses copy-initialization. That definition is not okay. We cannot copy objects of the IO types (Section 8.1, p. 287), so we cannot use copy-initialization on objects of these types.

Whether the initialization of `item` is okay depends on which version of our `Sales_item` class we are using. Some versions define the constructor that takes a `string` as `explicit`. If the constructor is explicit, then the initialization fails. If the constructor is not explicit, then the initialization is fine.

Parameters and Return Values

As we know, when a parameter is a nonreference type (Section 7.2.1, p. 230), the argument is copied. Similarly, a nonreference return value (Section 7.3.2, p. 247) is returned by copying the value in the `return` statement.

When the parameter or return type is a class type, the copy is done by the copy constructor. For example, consider our `make_plural` function from page 248:

```
//  copy constructor used to copy the return value;
//  parameters are references, so they aren't copied
string make_plural(size_t, const string&, const string&);
```

This function implicitly uses the `string` copy constructor to return the plural version of a given word. The parameters are `const` references; they are not copied.

Initializing Container Elements

The copy constructor is used to initialize the elements in a sequential container. For example, we can initialize a container using a single parameter that represents a size (Section 3.3.1, p. 92). This form of construction uses both the default constructor and the copy constructor for the element container:

```
//  default string constructor and five string copy constructors invoked
vector<string> svec(5);
```

The compiler initializes `svec` by first using the default `string` constructor to create a temporary value. The copy constructor is then used to copy the temporary into each element of `svec`.

As a general rule (Section 9.1.1, p. 307), unless you intend to use the default initial value of the container elements, it is more efficient to allocate an empty container and add elements as the values for those elements become known.

Constructors and Array Elements

If we provide no element initializers for an array of class type, then the default constructor is used to initialize each element. However, if we provide explicit element initializers using the normal brace-enclosed array initialization list (Section 4.1.1, p. 111), then each element is initialized using copy-initialization. An element of the appropriate type is created from the specified value, and then the copy constructor is used to copy that value to the corresponding element:

```
Sales_item primer_eds[] = { string("0-201-16487-6"),
                            string("0-201-54848-8"),
                            string("0-201-82470-1"),
                            Sales_item()
                          };
```

A value that can be used to invoke a single-argument constructor for the element type can be specified directly, as in the initializers for the first three elements. If we wish to specify no arguments or multiple arguments, we need to use the full constructor syntax, as we do in the initializer for the last element.

EXERCISES SECTION 13.1

Exercise 13.1: What is a copy constructor? When is it used?

Exercise 13.2: The second initialization below fails to compile. What can we infer about the definition of vector?

```
vector<int> v1(42);   // ok: 42 elements, each 0
vector<int> v2 = 42;  // error: what does this error tell us about vector?
```

Exercise 13.3: Assuming Point is a class type with a public copy constructor, identify each use of the copy constructor in this program fragment:

```
Point global;

Point foo_bar(Point arg)
{
    Point local = arg;
    Point *heap = new Point(global);
    *heap = local;
    Point pa[ 4 ] = { local, *heap };
    return *heap;
}
```

13.1.1   The Synthesized Copy Constructor

If we do not otherwise define the copy constructor, the compiler synthesizes one for us. Unlike the synthesized default constructor (Section 12.4.3, p. 458), a copy constructor is synthesized even if we define other constructors. The behavior of the **synthesized copy constructor** is to **memberwise initialize** the new object as a copy of the original object.

By memberwise, we mean that taking each nonstatic member in turn, the compiler copies the member from the existing object into the one being created. With one exception, the type of each member determines what it means to copy it. The synthesized copy constructor directly copies the value of members of built-in type. Members of class type are copied by using the copy constructor for that class. The one exception concerns array members. Even though we ordinarily cannot copy an array, if a class has a member that is an array, then the synthesized copy constructor will copy the array. It does so by copying each element.

The simplest conceptual model of memberwise initialization is to think of the synthesized copy constructor as one in which each data member is initialized in the constructor initializer list. For example, given our `Sales_item` class, which has three data members

```
class Sales_item {
// other members and constructors as before
private:
    std::string isbn;
    int units_sold;
    double revenue;
};
```

the synthesized `Sales_item` copy constructor would look something like:

```
Sales_item::Sales_item(const Sales_item &orig):
    isbn(orig.isbn),              // uses string copy constructor
    units_sold(orig.units_sold), // copies orig.units_sold
    revenue(orig.revenue)        // copy orig.revenue
    {    }                        // empty body
```

13.1.2 Defining Our Own Copy Constructor

The copy constructor is the constructor that takes a single parameter that is a (usually `const`) reference to the class type:

```
class Foo {
public:
    Foo();              // default constructor
    Foo(const Foo&);    // copy constructor
    // ...
};
```

Usually the parameter is a `const` reference, although we can also define the copy constructor to take a nonconst reference. Because the constructor is used (implicitly) to pass and return objects to and from functions, it usually should not be made `explicit` (Section 12.4.4, p. 462). The copy constructor should copy the members from its argument into the object that is being constructed.

For many classes, the synthesized copy constructor does exactly the work that is needed. Classes that contain only members that are of class type or members that are of built-in (but not pointer type) often can be copied without explicitly defining the copy constructor.

However, some classes *must* take control of what happens when objects are copied. Such classes often have a data member that is a pointer or that represents another resource that is allocated in the constructor. Other classes have bookkeeping that must be done whenever a new object is created. In both these cases, the copy constructor must be defined.

Often the hardest part about defining a copy constructor is recognizing that a copy constructor is needed. Defining the constructor is usually pretty easy once the need for the constructor is recognized. The copy constructor itself is defined like any other constructor: It has the same name as the name of the class, it has no return value, it may (should) use a constructor initializer to initialize the members of the newly created object, and it may do any other necessary work inside a function body.

We'll look at examples of classes that require class-defined copy constructors in later sections. Section 13.4 (p. 486) looks at a pair of classes that require an explicit copy constructor to handle bookkeeping associated with a simple message-handling application; classes with members that are pointers are covered in Section 13.5 (p. 492).

EXERCISES SECTION 13.1.2

Exercise 13.4: Given the following sketch of a class, write a copy constructor that copies all the elements. Copy the object to which `pstring` points, not the pointer.

```
struct NoName {
    NoName(): pstring(new std::string), i(0), d(0) { }
private:
    std::string  *pstring;
    int      i;
    double d;
};
```

Exercise 13.5: Which class definition is likely to need a copy constructor?

(a) A `Point3w` class containing four float members
(b) A `Matrix` class in which the actual matrix is allocated dynamically within the constructor and is deleted within its destructor
(c) A `Payroll` class in which each object is provided with a unique ID
(d) A `Word` class containing a `string` and a `vector` of line and column location pairs

Exercise 13.6: The parameter of the copy constructor does not strictly need to be `const`, but it does need to be a reference. Explain the rationale for this restriction. For example, explain why the following definition could not work.

```
Sales_item::Sales_item(const Sales_item rhs);
```

13.1.3 Preventing Copies

Some classes need to prevent copies from being made at all. For example, the `iostream` classes do not permit copying (Section 8.1, p. 287). It might seem that if we want to forbid copies, we could omit the copy constructor. However, if we don't define a copy constructor, the compiler will synthesize one.

To prevent copies, a class must explicitly declare its copy constructor as `private`.

If the copy constructor is private, then user code will not be allowed to copy objects of the class type. The compiler will reject any attempt to make a copy.

However, the friends and members of the class could still make copies. If we want to prevent copies even within the friends and members, we can do so by declaring a (`private`) copy constructor but not defining it.

It is legal to declare but not define a member function. However, any attempt to *use* an undefined member results in a link-time failure. By declaring (but not defining) a `private` copy constructor, we can forestall any attempt to copy an object of the class type: Attempts to make copies in user code will be flagged as an error at compile time, and attempts to make copies in member functions or friends will result in an error at link time.

Most Classes Should Define Copy and Default Constructors

Classes that do not define the default constructor and/or the copy constructor impose serious limits on users of the class. Objects of classes that do not allow copies may be passed to (or returned from) a function only as a reference. They also may not be used as elements in a container.

It is usually best to define—either implicitly or explicitly—the default and copy constructors. The default constructor is synthesized only if there are no other constructors. If the copy constructor is defined, then the default constructor must be defined as well.

13.2   The Assignment Operator

Just as classes control how objects are initialized, they also define what happens when objects of their type are assigned:

```
Sales_item trans, accum;
trans = accum;
```

As with the copy constructor, the compiler synthesizes an assignment operator if the class does not define its own.

Introducing Overloaded Assignment

Before we look at the synthesized assignment operator, we need to know a bit about **overloaded operators**, which we cover in detail in Chapter 14.

Overloaded operators are functions that have the name `operator` followed by the symbol for the operator being defined. Hence, we define assignment by defining a function named `operator=`. Like any other function, an operator function has a return type and a parameter list. The parameter list must have the same number of parameters (including the implicit `this` parameter if the operator is a member) as the operator has operands. Assignment is binary, so the operator function has two parameters: The first parameter corresponds to the left-hand operand, and the second to the right-hand operand.

Most operators may be defined as member or nonmember functions. When an operator is a member function, its first operand is implicitly bound to the `this` pointer. Some operators, assignment among them, must be members of the class for which the operator is defined. Because assignment must be a member of its class, `this` is bound to a pointer to the left-hand operand. The assignment operator, therefore, takes a single parameter that is an object of the same class type. Usually, the right-hand operand is passed as a `const` reference.

The return type from the assignment operator should be the same as the return from assignment for the built-in types (Section 5.4.1, p. 160). Assignment to a built-in type returns a reference to its left-hand operand. Therefore, the assignment operator also returns a reference to the same type as its class.

For example, the assignment operator for `Sales_item` might be declared as

```
class Sales_item {
public:
    // other members as before
    // equivalent to the synthesized assignment operator
    Sales_item& operator=(const Sales_item &);
};
```

The Synthesized Assignment Operator

The **synthesized assignment operator** operates similarly to the synthesized copy constructor. It performs **memberwise assignment**: Each member of the right-hand object is assigned to the corresponding member of the left-hand object. Except for arrays, each member is assigned in the usual way for its type. For arrays, each array element is assigned.

As an example, the synthesized `Sales_item` assignment operator would look something like:

```
// equivalent to the synthesized assignment operator
Sales_item&
Sales_item::operator=(const Sales_item &rhs)
{
    isbn = rhs.isbn;                // calls string::operator=
    units_sold = rhs.units_sold;    // uses built-in int assignment
    revenue = rhs.revenue;          // uses built-in double assignment
    return *this;
}
```

The synthesized assignment operator assigns each member in turn, using the built-in or class-defined assignment operator as appropriate to the type of the member. The operator returns *this, which is a reference to the left-hand object.

Copy and Assign Usually Go Together

Classes that can use the synthesized copy constructor usually can use the synthesized assignment operator as well. Our `Sales_item` class has no need to define either the copy constructor or the assignment operator: The synthesized versions of these operators work fine.

However, a class may define its own assignment operator. In general, if a class needs a copy constructor, it will also need an assignment operator.

 In fact, these operations should be thought of as a unit. If we require one, we almost surely require the other.

We'll see examples of classes that need to define their own assignment operators in Section 13.4 (p. 486) and Section 13.5 (p. 492).

EXERCISES SECTION 13.2

Exercise 13.7: When does a class need to define an assignment operator?

Exercise 13.8: For each type listed in the first exercise in Section 13.1.2 (p. 481) indicate whether the class would need an assignment operator.

Exercise 13.9: The first exercise in Section 13.1.2 (p. 481) included a skeletal definition for class `NoName`. Determine whether that class needs an assignment operator. If so, implement it.

Exercise 13.10: Define an `Employee` class that contains the employee's name and a unique employee identifier. Give the class a default constructor and a constructor that takes a `string` representing the employee's name. If the class needs a copy constructor or assignment operator, implement those functions as well.

13.3   The Destructor

One purpose of a constructor is to provide for the automatic acquisition of a resource. For example, a constructor might allocate a buffer or open a file. Having allocated the resource in the constructor, we need a corresponding operation that automatically deallocates or otherwise releases the resource. The destructor is a special member function that can be used to do whatever resource deallocation is needed. It serves as the complement to the constructors of the class.

When a Destructor Is Called

The destructor is called automatically whenever an object of its class is destroyed:

```
//   p points to default constructed object
Sales_item *p = new Sales_item;
{                                 // new scope
    Sales_item item(*p);   // copy constructor copies *p into item
    delete p;              // destructor called on object pointed to by p
}                             // exit local scope; destructor called on item
```

Variables such as item are destroyed automatically when they go out of scope. Hence, the destructor on item is run when the close curly is encountered.

An object that is dynamically allocated is destroyed only when a pointer pointing to the object is deleted. If we do not delete a pointer to a dynamically allocated object, then the destructor is never run on that object. The object will persist forever, leading to a memory leak. Moreover, any resources used inside the object will also not be released.

> The destructor is *not* run when a reference or a pointer to an object goes out of scope. The destructor is run only when a pointer to a dynamically allocated object is deleted or when an actual object (not a reference to the object) goes out of scope.

Destructors are also run on the elements of class type in a container—whether a library container or built-in array—when the container is destroyed:

```
{
    Sales_item *p = new Sales_item[10]; // dynamically allocated
    vector<Sales_item> vec(p, p + 10);  // local object
    // ...
    delete [] p; // array is freed; destructor run on each element
}   // vec goes out of scope; destructor run on each element
```

The elements in the container are always destroyed in reverse order: The element indexed by size() - 1 is destroyed first, followed by the one indexed by size() - 2 and so on until element [0], which is destroyed last.

When to Write an Explicit Destructor

Many classes do not require an explicit destructor. In particular, a class that has a constructor does not necessarily need to define its own destructor. Destructors are needed only if there is work for them to do. Ordinarily they are used to relinquish resources acquired in the constructor or during the lifetime of the object.

> A useful rule of thumb is that if a class needs a destructor, it will also need the assignment operator and a copy constructor. This rule is often referred to as the **Rule of Three**, indicating that if you need a destructor, then you need all three copy-control members.

A destructor is not limited only to relinquishing resources. A destructor, in general, can perform any operation that the class designer wishes to have executed subsequent to the last use of an object of that class.

The Synthesized Destructor

Unlike the copy constructor or assignment operator, the compiler always synthesizes a destructor for us. The synthesized destructor destroys each nonstatic member in the reverse order from that in which the object was created. In consequence, it destroys the members in reverse order from which they are declared in the class. For each member that is of class type, the synthesized destructor invokes that member's destructor to destroy the object.

Destroying a member of built-in or compound type has no effect. In particular, the synthesized destructor does *not* delete the object pointed to by a pointer member.

How to Write a Destructor

Our `Sales_item` class is an example of a class that allocates no resources and so does not need its own destructor. Classes that do allocate resources usually need to define a destructor to free those resources. The destructor is a member function with the name of the class prefixed by a tilde (~). It has no return value and takes no parameters. Because it cannot specify any parameters, it cannot be overloaded. Although we can define multiple class constructors, we can provide only a single destructor to be applied to all objects of our class.

An important difference between the destructor and the copy constructor or assignment operator is that even if we write our own destructor, the synthesized destructor is still run. For example, we might write the following empty destructor for class `Sales_item`:

```
class Sales_item {
public:
    //  empty; no work to do other than destroying the members,
    //  which happens automatically
    ~Sales_item() { }
    //  other members as before
};
```

When objects of type `Sales_item` are destroyed, this destructor, which does nothing, would be run. After it completes, the synthesized destructor would also be run to destroy the members of the class. The synthesized destructor destroys the `string` member by calling the `string` destructor, which frees the memory used to hold the isbn. The `units_sold` and `revenue` members are of built-in type, so the synthesized destructor does nothing to destroy them.

13.4   A Message-Handling Example

As an example of a class that needs to control copies in order to do some bookkeeping, we'll sketch out two classes that might be used in a mail-handling application. These classes, `Message` and `Folder`, represent, respectively, email (or other) messages and directories in which a message might appear. A given `Message` might appear in more than one `Folder`. We'll have `save` and `remove` operations on `Message` that save or remove that message in the specified `Folder`.

Rather than putting a copy of each `Message` into each `Folder`, we'll have each `Message` hold a `set` of pointers to the `Folders` in which this `Message` appears. Each `Folder` will also store pointers to the `Messages` it contains. Figure 13.1 (p. 488) illustrates the data structure we'll implement.

When we create a new `Message`, we will specify the contents of the message but no `Folder`. Calling `save` will put a `Message` in a `Folder`.

EXERCISES SECTION 13.3

Exercise 13.11: What is a destructor? What does the synthesized destructor do? When is a destructor synthesized? When must a class define its own destructor?

Exercise 13.12: Determine whether the `NoName` class skteched in the exercises on page 481, is likely to need a destructor. If so, implement it.

Exercise 13.13: Determine whether the `Employee` class, defined in the exercises on page 484, needs a destructor. If so, implement it.

Exercise 13.14: A good way to understand copy-control members and constructors is to define a simple class with these members in which each member prints its name:

```
struct Exmpl {
    Exmpl() { std::cout << "Exmpl()" << std::endl; }
    Exmpl(const Exmpl&)
      { std::cout << "Exmpl(const Exmpl&)" << std::endl; }
    // ...
};
```

Write a class like `Exmpl`, giving it the copy-control members and other constructors. Now write a program using objects of type `Exmpl` in various ways: pass them as non-reference and reference parameters; dynamically allocate them; put them in containers, and so forth. Studying which constructors and copy-control members are executed and when can be helpful in cementing your understanding of these concepts.

Exercise 13.15: How many destructor calls occur in the following code fragment?

```
void fcn(const Sales_item *trans, Sales_item accum)
{
    Sales_item item1(*trans), item2(accum);
    if (!item1.same_isbn(item2)) return;
    if (item1.avg_price() <= 99) return;
    else if (item2.avg_price() <= 99) return;
    // ...
}
```

When we copy a `Message`, we'll copy both the contents of the original message and the set of `Folder` pointers. We must also add a pointer to this `Message` to each of the `Folders` that points to the original `Message`.

Assigning one `Message` to another behaves similarly to copying a `Message`: After the assignment, the contents and set of `Folders` will be the same. We'll start by removing the existing left-hand `message` from the `Folders` it was in prior to the assignment. Once the old `Message` is gone, we'll copy the contents and set of `Folders` from the right-hand operand into the left. We'll also have to add a pointer to the left-hand `Message` to each `Folder` in this set.

When we destroy a `Message`, we must update each `Folder` that points to the `Message`. Once the `Message` goes away, those pointers will be no good, so we must remove the pointer to this `Message` from each `Folder` in the `Message`'s own `set` of `Folder` pointers.

Figure 13.1: Message and Folder Class Design

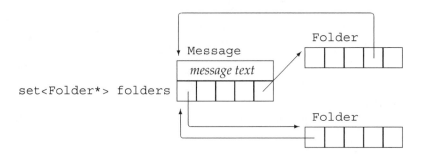

Looking at this list of operations, we can see that the destructor and the assignment operator share the work of removing messages from the list of Folders that had held a given Message. Similarly, the copy constructor and the assignment operator share the work of adding a Message to a given list of Folders. We'll define a pair of private utility functions to do these tasks.

The Message Class

Given this design, we can write a fair bit of our Message class:

```
class Message {
public:
    // folders is initialized to the empty set automatically
    Message(const std::string &str = ""):
                contents (str) { }
    // copy control: we must manage pointers to this Message
    // from the Folders pointed to by folders
    Message(const Message&);
    Message& operator=(const Message&);
    ~Message();

    // add/remove this Message from specified Folder's set of messages
    void save(Folder&);
    void remove(Folder&);
private:
    std::string contents;        // actual message text
    std::set<Folder*> folders;  // Folders that have this Message

    // Utility functions used by copy constructor, assignment, and destructor:
    // Add this Message to the Folders that point to the parameter
    void put_Msg_in_Folders(const std::set<Folder*>&);
    // remove this Message from every Folder in folders
    void remove_Msg_from_Folders();
};
```

The class defines two data members: `contents`, which is a `string` that holds the actual message, and `folders`, which is a `set` of pointers to the `Folders` in which this `Message` appears.

The constructor takes a single `string` parameter representing the contents of the message. The constructor stores a copy of the message in `contents` and (implicitly) initializes the `set` of `Folders` to the empty set. This constructor provides a default argument, which is the empty string, so it also serves as the `Message` default constructor.

The utility functions provide the actions shared among the copy-control members. The `put_Msg_in_Folders` function adds a copy of its own `Message` to the `Folders` that point to the given `Message`. After this function completes, each `Folder` that points to the parameter will also point to this `Message`. This function will be used by both the copy constructor and the assignment operator.

The `remove_Msg_from_Folders` function is used by the assignment operator and destructor. It removes the pointer to this `Message` from each of the `Folders` in the `folders` member.

Copy Control for the `Message` Class

When we copy a `Message`, we have to add the newly created `Message` to each `Folder` that holds the `Message` from which we're copying. This work is beyond what the synthesized constructor would do for us, so we must define our own copy constructor:

```
Message::Message(const Message &m):
    contents(m.contents), folders(m.folders)
{
    // add this Message to each Folder that points to m
    put_Msg_in_Folders(folders);
}
```

The copy constructor initializes the data members of the new object as copies of the members from the old. In addition to these initializations—which the synthesized copy constructor would have done for us—we must also iterate through `folders`, adding this `Message` to each `Folder` in that set. The copy constructor uses the `put_Msg_in_Folder` function to do this work.

> When we write our own copy constructor, we must explicitly copy any members that we want copied. An explicitly defined copy constructor copies nothing automatically.

As with any other constructor, if we do not initialize a class member, then that member is initialized using the member's default constructor. Default initialization in a copy constructor does *not* use the member's copy constructor.

The `put_Msg_in_Folders` Member

`put_Msg_in_Folders` iterates through the pointers in the `folders` member of the parameter `rhs`. These pointers denote each `Folder` that points to `rhs`. We need to add a pointer to this `Message` to each of those `Folders`.

The function does this work by looping through rhs.folders, calling the
Folder member named addMsg. That function will do whatever it takes to add a
pointer to this Message to that Folder:

```
//  add this Message to Folders that point to rhs
void Message::put_Msg_in_Folders(const set<Folder*> &rhs)
{
    for(std::set<Folder*>::const_iterator beg = rhs.begin();
                                     beg != rhs.end(); ++beg)
        (*beg)->addMsg(this);   //  *beg points to a Folder
}
```

The only tricky part in this function is the call to addMsg:

```
(*beg)->addMsg(this);   //  *beg points to a Folder
```

That call starts with (*beg), which dereferences the iterator. Dereferencing the
iterator yields a pointer to a Folder. The expression then applies the arrow operator to the Folder pointer in order to run the addMsg operation. We pass this,
which points to the Message we want to add to the Folder.

Message Assignment Operator

Assignment is more complicated than the copy constructor. Like the copy constructor, assignment must assign the contents and update folders to match
that of the right-hand operand. It must also add this Message to each of the
Folders that points to the rhs. We can use our put_Msg_in_Folders function to do this part of the assignment.

Before copying from the rhs, we must first remove this Message from each of
the Folders that currently point to it. We'll need to iterate through folders, removing the pointer to this Message from each Folder in folders. The function
named remove_Msg_from_Folders will do this work.

Given remove_Msg_from_Folders and put_Msg_in_Folders, which do
the real work, the assignment operator itself is fairly simple:

```
Message& Message::operator=(const Message &rhs)
{
    if (&rhs != this) {
        remove_Msg_from_Folders(); // update existing Folders
        contents = rhs.contents;   // copy contents from rhs
        folders = rhs.folders;     // copy Folder pointers from rhs
        // add this Message to each Folder in rhs
        put_Msg_in_Folders(rhs.folders);
    }
    return *this;
}
```

The assignment operator starts by checking that the left- and right-hand operands
are not the same. We do this check for reasons that will become apparent as we
walk through the rest of the function. Assuming that the operands are different
objects, we call remove_Msg_from_Folders to remove this Message from each

of the `Folders` in the `folders` member. Once that work is done, we have to assign the `contents` and `folders` members from the right-hand operand to this object. Finally, we call `put_Msg_in_Folders` to add a pointer to this `Message` in each of the `Folders` that also point to `rhs`.

Now that we've seen work that `remove_Msg_from_Folders` does, we can see why we start the assignment operator by checking that the objects are different. Assignment involves obliterating the left-hand operand. Once the members of the left-hand operand are destroyed, those in the right-hand operand are assigned to the corresponding left-hand members. If the objects were the same, then destroying the left-hand members would also destroy the right-hand members!

It is crucially important for assignment operators to work correctly, even when an object is assigned to iself. A common way to ensure this behavior is by checking explicitly for self-assignment.

The `remove_Msg_from_Folders` Member

The implementation of the `remove_Msg_from_Folders` function is similar to that of `put_Msg_in_Folders`, except that this time we'll call `remMsg` to remove this `Message` from each `Folder` pointed to by `folders`:

```
//  remove this Message from corresponding Folders
void Message::remove_Msg_from_Folders()
{
    //  remove this message from corresponding folders
    for(std::set<Folder*>::const_iterator beg =
            folders.begin(); beg != folders.end(); ++beg)
        (*beg)->remMsg(this);   //  *beg points to a Folder
}
```

The `Message` Destructor

The remaining copy-control function that we must implement is the destructor:

```
Message::~Message()
{
    remove_Msg_from_Folders();
}
```

Given the `remove_Msg_from_Folders` function, writing the destructor is trivial. We call that function to clean up `folders`. The system automatically invokes the `string` destructor to free `contents` and the `set` destructor to clean up the memory used to hold the `folders` member. Thus, the only work for the `Message` destructor is to call `remove_Msg_from_Folders`.

The assignment operator often does the same work as is needed in the copy constructor and destructor. In such cases, the common work should be put in `private` utility functions.

Exercise 13.16: Write the `Message` class as described in this section.

Exercise 13.17: Add functions to the `Message` class that are analogous to the `Folder` operations `addMsg` and `remMsg`. These functions, which could be named `addFldr` and `remFldr`, should take a pointer to a `Folder` and insert that pointer into `folders`. These functions can be `private` because they will be used only in the implementation of the `Folder` class.

Exercise 13.18: Write the corresponding `Folder` class. That class should hold a `set<Message*>` that contains elements that point to `Messages`.

Exercise 13.19: Add a `save` and `remove` operation to the `Message` and `Folder` classes. These operations should take a `Folder` and add (or remove) that `Folder` to (from) the set of `Folders` that point to this `Message`. The operation must also update the `Folder` to know that it points to this `Message`, which can be done by calling `addMsg` or `remMsg`.

13.5 Managing Pointer Members

This book generally advocates the use of the standard library. One reason we do so is that using the standard library greatly reduces the need for pointers in modern C++ programs. However, many applications still require the use of pointers, particularly in the implementation of classes. Classes that contain pointers require careful attention to copy control. The reason they must do so is that copying a pointer copies only the address in the pointer. Copying a pointer does not copy the object to which the pointer points.

When designing a class with a pointer member, the first decision a class author must make is what behavior that pointer should provide. When we copy one pointer to another, the two pointers point to the same object. When two pointers point to the same object, it is possible to use either pointer to change the underlying object. Similarly, it is possible for one pointer to `delete` the object even though the user of the other pointer still thinks the underlying object exists.

By default, a pointer member has the same behavior as a pointer object. However, through different copy-control strategies we can implement different behavior for pointer members. Most C++ classes take one of three approaches to managing pointer members:

1. The pointer member can be given normal pointerlike behavior. Such classes will have all the pitfalls of pointers but will require no special copy control.

2. The class can implement so-called "smart pointer" behavior. The object to which the pointer points is shared, but the class prevents dangling pointers.

3. The class can be given valuelike behavior. The object to which the pointer points will be unique to and managed separately by each class object.

In this section we look at three classes that implement each of these different approaches to managing their pointer members.

A Simple Class with a Pointer Member

To illustrate the issues involved, we'll implement a simple class that contains an int and a pointer:

```
//  class that has a pointer member that behaves like a plain pointer
class HasPtr {
public:
    //  copy of the values we're given
    HasPtr(int *p, int i): ptr(p), val(i) { }
    //  const members to return the value of the indicated data member
    int *get_ptr() const { return ptr; }
    int get_int() const { return val; }
    //  nonconst members to change the indicated data member
    void set_ptr(int *p) { ptr = p; }
    void set_int(int i) { val = i; }
    //  return or change the value pointed to, so ok for const objects
    int get_ptr_val() const { return *ptr; }
    void set_ptr_val(int val) const { *ptr = val; }
private:
    int *ptr;
    int val;
};
```

The HasPtr constructor takes two parameters, which it copies into HasPtr's data members. The class provides simple accessor functions: The const functions get_int and get_ptr return the value of the int and pointer members, respectively; the set_int and set_ptr members let us change these members, giving a new value to the int or making the pointer point to a different object. We also define the get_ptr_val and set_ptr_val members. These members get and set the underlying value to which the pointer points.

Default Copy/Assignment and Pointer Members

Because the class does not define a copy constructor, copying one HasPtr object to another copies both members:

```
int obj = 0;
HasPtr ptr1(&obj, 42);   //  int* member points to obj, val is 42
HasPtr ptr2(ptr1);       //  int* member points to obj, val is 42
```

After the copy, the pointers in ptr1 and ptr1 both address the same object and the int values in each object are the same. However, the behavior of these two members appears quite different, because the value of a pointer is distinct from the value of the object to which it points. After the copy, the int values are distinct and independent, whereas the pointers are intertwined.

Classes that have pointer members and use default synthesized copy control have all the pitfalls of ordinary pointers. In particular, the class itself has no way to avoid dangling pointers.

Pointers Share the Same Object

When we copy an arithmetic value, the copy is independent from the original. We can change one copy without changing the other:

```
ptr1.set_int(0);      // changes val member only in ptr1
ptr2.get_int();       // returns 42
ptr1.get_int();       // returns 0
```

When we copy a pointer, the address values are distinct, but the pointers point to the same underlying object. If we call set_ptr_val on either object, the underlying object is changed for both:

```
ptr1.set_ptr_val(42); // sets object to which both ptr1 and ptr2 point
ptr2.get_ptr_val();    // returns 42
```

When two pointers point to the same object, either one can change the value of the shared object.

Dangling Pointers Are Possible

Because our class copies the pointers directly, it presents our users with a potential problem: HasPtr stores the pointer it was given. It is up to the user to guarantee that the object to which that pointer points stays around as long as the HasPtr object does:

```
int *ip = new int(42);  // dynamically allocated int initialized to 42
HasPtr ptr(ip, 10);     // HasPtr points to same object as ip does
delete ip;              // object pointed to by ip is freed
ptr.set_ptr_val(0);     // disaster: The object to which HasPtr points was freed!
```

The problem here is that ip and the pointer inside ptr both point to the same object. When that object is deleted, the pointer inside HasPtr no longer points to a valid object. However, there is no way to know that the object is gone.

EXERCISES SECTION 13.5

Exercise 13.20: Given the original version of the HasPtr class that relies on the default definitions for copy-control, describe what happens in the following code:

```
int i = 42;
HasPtr p1(&i, 42);
HasPtr p2 = p1;
cout << p2.get_ptr_val() << endl;
p1.set_ptr_val(0);
cout << p2.get_ptr_val() << endl;
```

Exercise 13.21: What would happen if we gave our HasPtr class a destructor that deleted its pointer member?

13.5.1 Defining Smart Pointer Classes

In the previous section we defined a simple class that held a pointer and an int. The pointer member behaved in all ways like any other pointer. Any changes made to the object to which the pointer pointed were made to a single, shared object. If the user deleted that object, then our class had a dangling pointer. Its pointer member pointed at an object that no longer existed.

An alternative to having a pointer member behave exactly like a pointer is to define what is sometimes referred to as a **smart pointer** class. A smart pointer behaves like an ordinary pointer except that it adds functionality. In this case, we'll give our smart pointer the responsibility for deleting the shared object. Users will dynamically allocate an object and pass the address of that object to our new HasPtr class. The user may still access the object through a plain pointer but must not delete the pointer. The HasPtr class will ensure that the object is deleted when the last HasPtr that points to it is destroyed.

In other ways, our HasPtr will behave like a plain pointer. In particular, when we copy a HasPtr object, the copy and the original will point to the same underlying object. If we change that object through one copy, the value will be changed when accessed through the other.

Our new HasPtr class will need a destructor to delete the pointer. However, the destructor cannot delete the pointer unconditionally. If two HasPtr objects point to the same underlying object, we don't want to delete the object until both objects are destroyed. To write the destructor, we need to know whether this HasPtr is the last one pointing to a given object.

Introducing Use Counts

A common technique used in defining smart pointers is to use a **use count**. The pointerlike class associates a counter with the object to which the class points. The use count keeps track of how many objects of the class share the same pointer. When the use count goes to zero, then the object is deleted. A use count is sometimes also referred to as a **reference count**.

Each time a new object of the class is created, the pointer is initialized and the use count is set to 1. When an object is created as a copy of another, the copy constructor copies the pointer and increments the associated use count. When an object is assigned to, the assignment operator decrements the use count of the object to which the left-hand operand points (and deletes that object if the use count goes to zero) and increments the use count of the object pointed to by the right-hand operand. Finally, when the destructor is called, it decrements the use count and deletes the underlying object if the count goes to zero.

The only wrinkle is deciding where to put the use count. The counter cannot go directly into our HasPtr object. To see why, consider what happens in the following case:

```
int obj;
HasPtr p1(&obj, 42);
HasPtr p2(p1);   // p1 and p2 both point to same int object
HasPtr p3(p1);   // p1, p2, and p3 all point to same int object
```

If the use count is stored in a `HasPtr` object, how can we update it correctly when p3 is created? We could increment the count in p1 and copy that count into p3, but how would we update the counter in p2?

The Use-Count Class

There are two classic strategies for implementing a use count, one of which we will use here; the other approach is described in Section 15.8.1 (p. 599). In the approach we use here, we'll define a separate concrete class to encapsulate the use count and the associated pointer:

```
//  private class for use by HasPtr only
class U_Ptr {
    friend class HasPtr;
    int *ip;
    size_t use;
    U_Ptr(int *p): ip(p), use(1) { }
    ~U_Ptr() { delete ip; }
};
```

All the members of this class are `private`. We don't intend ordinary users to use the `U_Ptr` class, so we do not give it any `public` members. The `HasPtr` class is made a friend so that its members will have access to the members of `U_Ptr`.

The class is pretty simple, although the concept of how it works can be slippery. The `U_Ptr` class holds the pointer and the use count. Each `HasPtr` will point to a `U_Ptr`. The use count will keep track of how many `HasPtr` objects point to each `U_Ptr` object. The only functions `U_Ptr` defines are its constructor and destructor. The constructor copies the pointer, which the destructor deletes. The constructor also sets the use count to 1, indicating that a `HasPtr` object points to this `U_Ptr`.

Assuming we just created a `HasPtr` object from a pointer that pointed to an `int` value of 42, we might picture the objects as follows:

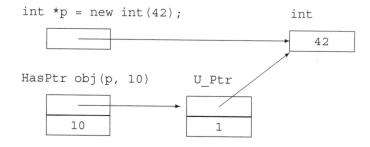

If we copy this object, then the objects will be as shown on the next page.

Using the Use-Counted Class

Our new `HasPtr` class holds a pointer to a `U_Ptr`, which in turn points to the actual underlying `int` object. Each member must be changed to reflect the fact that the class points to a `U_Ptr` rather than an `int*`.

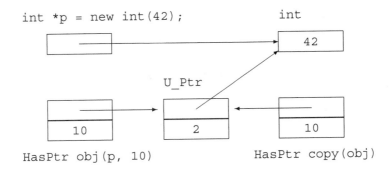

We'll look first at the constructors and copy-control members:

```
/*  smart pointer class: takes ownership of the dynamically allocated
 *             object to which it is bound
 *  User code must dynamically allocate an object to initialize a HasPtr
 *  and must not delete that object; the HasPtr class will delete it
 */
class HasPtr {
public:
    // HasPtr owns the pointer; p must have been dynamically allocated
    HasPtr(int *p, int i): ptr(new U_Ptr(p)), val(i) { }
    // copy members and increment the use count
    HasPtr(const HasPtr &orig):
        ptr(orig.ptr), val(orig.val) { ++ptr->use; }
    HasPtr& operator=(const HasPtr&);
    // if use count goes to zero, delete the U_Ptr object
    ~HasPtr() { if (--ptr->use == 0) delete ptr; }
private:
    U_Ptr *ptr;          //  points to use-counted U_Ptr class
    int val;
};
```

The `HasPtr` constructor that takes a pointer and an `int` uses its pointer parameter to create a new `U_Ptr` object. After the `HasPtr` constructor completes, the `HasPtr` object points to a newly allocated `U_Ptr` object. That `U_Ptr` object stores the pointer we were given. The use count in that new `U_Ptr` is 1, indicating that only one `HasPtr` object points to it.

The copy constructor copies the members from its parameter and increments the use count. After the constructor completes, the newly created object points to the same `U_Ptr` object as the original and the use count of that `U_Ptr` object is incremented by one.

The destructor checks the use count in the underlying `U_Ptr` object. If the use count goes to 0, then this is the last `HasPtr` object that points to this `U_Ptr`. In this case, the `HasPtr` destructor deletes its `U_Ptr` pointer. Deleting that pointer has the effect of calling the `U_Ptr` destructor, which in turn deletes the underlying `int` object.

Assignment and Use Counts

The assignment operator is a bit more complicated than the copy constructor:

```
HasPtr& HasPtr::operator=(const HasPtr &rhs)
{
    ++rhs.ptr->use;      //  increment use count on rhs first
    if (--ptr->use == 0)
        delete ptr;      //  if use count goes to 0 on this object, delete it
    ptr = rhs.ptr;       //  copy the U_Ptr object
    val = rhs.val;       //  copy the int member
    return *this;
}
```

Here we start by incrementing the use count in the right-hand operand. Then we decrement and check the use count on this object. As with the destructor, if this is the last object pointing to the U_Ptr, we delete the object, which in turn destroys the underlying int. Having decremented (and possibly destroyed) the existing value in the left-hand operand, we then copy the pointer from rhs into this object. As usual, assignment returns a reference to this object.

 This assignment operator guards against self-assignment by incrementing the use count of rhs before decrementing the use count of the left-hand operand.

If the left and right operands are the same, the effect of this assignment operator will be to increment and then immediately decrement the use count in the underlying U_Ptr object.

Changing Other Members

The other members that access the int* now need to change to get to the int indirectly through the U_Ptr pointer:

```
class HasPtr {
public:
        //  copy control and constructors as before
        //  accessors must change to fetch value from U_Ptr object
        int *get_ptr() const { return ptr->ip; }
        int get_int() const { return val; }
        //  change the appropriate data member
        void set_ptr(int *p) { ptr->ip = p; }
        void set_int(int i) { val = i; }
        //  return or change the value pointed to, so ok for const objects
        //  Note: *ptr->ip is equivalent to * (ptr->ip)
        int get_ptr_val() const { return *ptr->ip; }
        void set_ptr_val(int i) { *ptr->ip = i; }
private:
        U_Ptr *ptr;          //  points to use-counted U_Ptr class
        int val;
};
```

The functions that get and set the `int` member are unchanged. Those that operate on the pointer have to dereference the `U_Ptr` to get to the underlying `int*`.

When we copy `HasPtr` objects, the `int` member behaves the same as in our first class. Its value is copied; the members are independent. The pointer members in the copy and the original still point to the same underlying object. A change made to that object will affect the value as seen by either `HasPtr` object. However, users of `HasPtr` do not need to worry about dangling pointers. As long as they let the `HasPtr` class take care of freeing the object, the class will ensure that the object stays around as long as there are `HasPtr` objects that point to it.

ADVICE: MANAGING POINTER MEMBERS

Objects with pointer members often need to define the copy-control members. If we rely on the synthesized versions, then the class puts a burden on its users. Users must ensure that the object to which the member points stays around for at least as long as the object that points to it does.

To manage a class with pointer members, we must define all three copy-control members: the copy constructor, assignment operator, and the destructor. These members can define either pointerlike or valuelike behavior for the pointer member.

Valuelike classes give each object its own copy of the underlying values pointed to by pointer members. The copy constructor allocates a new element and copies the value from the object it is copying. The assignment operator destroys the existing object it holds and copies the value from its right-hand operand into its left-hand operand. The destructor destroys the object.

As an alternative to defining either valuelike behavior or pointerlike behavior some classes are so-called "smart pointers." These classes share the same underlying value between objects, thus providing pointerlike behavior. But they use copy-control techniques to avoid some of the pitfalls of regular pointers. To implement smart pointer behavior, a class needs to ensure that the underlying object stays around until the last copy goes away. Use counting (Section 13.5.1, p. 495), is a common technique for managing smart pointer classes. Each copy of the same underlying value is given a use count. The copy constructor copies the pointer from the old object into the new one and increments the use count. The assignment operator decrements the use count of the left-hand operand and increments the count of the right-hand operand. If the use count of the left-hand operand goes to zero, the assignment operator must delete the object to which it points. Finally, the assignment operator copies the pointer from the right-hand operand into its left-hand operand. The destructor decrements the use count and deletes the underlying object if the count goes to zero.

 These approaches to managing pointers occur so frequently that programmers who use classes with pointer members must be thoroughly familiar with these programming techniques.

13.5.2 Defining Valuelike Classes

A completely different approach to the problem of managing pointer members is to give them **value semantics**. Simply put, classes with value semantics define

EXERCISES SECTION 13.5.1

Exercise 13.22: What is a use count?

Exercise 13.23: What is a smart pointer? How does a smart pointer class differ from one that implements plain pointer behavior?

Exercise 13.24: Implement your own version of the use-counted `HasPtr` class.

objects that behave like the arithmetic types: When we copy a valuelike object, we get a new, distinct copy. Changes made to the copy are not reflected in the original, and vice versa. The `string` class is an example of a valuelike class.

To make our pointer member behave like a value, we must copy the object to which the pointer points whenever we copy the `HasPtr` object:

```
/*
 *  Valuelike behavior even though HasPtr has a pointer member:
 *  Each time we copy a HasPtr object, we make a new copy of the
 *  underlying int object to which ptr points.
 */
class HasPtr {
public:
    //  no point to passing a pointer if we're going to copy it anyway
    //  store pointer to a copy of the object we're given
    HasPtr(const int &p, int i): ptr(new int(p)), val(i) {}

    //  copy members and increment the use count
    HasPtr(const HasPtr &orig):
       ptr(new int (*orig.ptr)), val(orig.val) { }

    HasPtr& operator=(const HasPtr&);
    ~HasPtr() { delete ptr; }
    //  accessors must change to fetch value from Ptr object
    int get_ptr_val() const { return *ptr; }
    int get_int() const { return val; }

    //  change the appropriate data member
    void set_ptr(int *p) { ptr = p; }
    void set_int(int i)  { val = i; }

    //  return or change the value pointed to, so ok for const objects
    int *get_ptr() const { return ptr; }
    void set_ptr_val(int p) const { *ptr = p; }
private:
    int *ptr;         //  points to an int
    int val;
};
```

The copy constructor no longer copies the pointer. It now allocates a new `int` object and initializes that object to hold the same value as the object of which it is a copy. Each object always holds its own, distinct copy of its `int` value. Because each object holds its own copy, the destructor unconditionally deletes the pointer.

The assignment operator doesn't need to allocate a new object. It just has to remember to assign a new value to the object to which its `int` pointer points rather than assigning to the pointer itself:

```
HasPtr& HasPtr::operator=(const HasPtr &rhs)
{
    // Note: Every HasPtr is guaranteed to point at an actual int;
    //     We know that ptr cannot be a zero pointer
    *ptr = *rhs.ptr;        // copy the value pointed to
    val = rhs.val;          // copy the int
    return *this;
}
```

In other words, we change the value pointed to but not the pointer.

As always, the assignment operator must be correct even if we're assigning an object to itself. In this case, the operations are inherently safe even if the left- and right-hand objects are the same. Thus, there is no need to explicitly check for self-assignment.

EXERCISES SECTION 13.5.2

Exercise 13.25: What is a valuelike class?

Exercise 13.26: Implement your own version of a valuelike `HasPtr` class.

Exercise 13.27: The valuelike `HasPtr` class defines each of the copy-control members. Describe what would happen if the class defined

(a) The copy constructor and destructor but no assignment operator.
(b) The copy constructor and assignment operator but no destructor.
(c) The destructor but neither the copy constructor nor assignment operator.

Exercise 13.28: Given the following classes, implement a default constructor and the necessary copy-control members.

```
(a) class TreeNode {           (b) class BinStrTree {
    public:                        public:
        // ...                         // ...
    private:                       private:
        std::string value;             TreeNode *root;
        int        count;          };
        TreeNode   *left;
        TreeNode   *right;
    };
```

CHAPTER SUMMARY

In addition to defining the operations on objects of its type, a class also defines what it means to copy, assign, or destroy objects of the type. Special member functions—the copy constructor, the assignment operator, and the destructor—define these operations. Collectively these operations are referred to as the "copy control" functions.

If a class does not define one or more of these operations, the compiler will define them automatically. The synthesized operations perform memberwise initialization, assignment, or destruction: Taking each member in turn, the synthesized operation does whatever is appropriate to the member's type to copy, assign, or destroy that member. If the member is a class type, the synthesized operation calls the corresponding operation for that class (e.g., the copy constructor calls the member's copy constructor, the destructor calls its destructor, etc.). If the member is a built-in type or a pointer, the member is copied or assigned directly; the destructor does nothing to destroy members of built-in or pointer type. If the member is an array, the elements in the array are copied, assigned, or destroyed in a manner appropriate to the element type.

Unlike the copy constructor and assignment operator, the synthesized destructor is created and run, regardless of whether the class defines its own destructor. The synthesized destructor is run after the class-defined destructor, if there is one, completes.

The hardest part of defining the copy-control functions is often simply recognizing that they are necessary.

Classes that allocate memory or other resources almost always require that the class define the copy-control members to manage the allocated resource. If a class needs a destructor, then it almost surely needs to define the copy constructor and assignment operator as well.

DEFINED TERMS

assignment operator The assignment operator can be overloaded to define what it means to assign one object of a class type to another of the same type. The assignment operator must be a member of its class and should return a reference to its object. The compiler synthesizes the assignment operator if the class does not explicitly define one.

copy constructor Constructor that initializes a new object as a copy of another object of the same type. The copy constructor is applied implicitly to pass objects to or from a function by value. If we do not define the

copy constructor, the compiler synthesizes one for us.

copy control Special members that control what happens when object of class type are copied, assigned, and destroyed. The compiler synthesizes appropriate definitions for these operations if the class does not otherwise define them.

destructor Special member function that cleans up an object when the object goes out of scope or is deleted. The compiler automatically destroys each member. Members of class type are destroyed by invoking their destructor; no explicit work is done to destroy members of built-in or compound type. In particular, the object pointed to by a pointer member is not deleted by the automatic work done by the destructor.

memberwise assignment Term used to describe how the synthesized assignment operator works. The assignment operator assigns, member by member, from the old object to the new. Members of built-in or compound type are assigned directly. Those that are of class type are assigned by using the member's assignment operator.

memberwise initialization Term used to described how the synthesized copy constructor works. The constructor copies, member by member, from the old object to the new. Members of built-in or compound type are copied directly. Those that are of class type are copied by using the member's copy constructor.

overloaded operator Function that redefines one of the C++ operators to operate on object(s) of class type. This chapter showed how to define the assignment operator; Chapter 14 covers overloaded operators in more detail.

reference count Synonym for use count.

Rule of Three Shorthand for the rule of thumb that if a class needs a nontrivial destructor then it almost surely also needs to define its own copy constructor and an assignment operator.

smart pointer A class that behaves like a pointer but provides other functionality as well. One common form of smart pointer takes a pointer to a dynamically allocated object and assumes responsibility for deleting that object. The user allocates the object, but the smart pointer class deletes it. Smart pointer classes require that the class implement the copy-control members to manage a pointer to the shared object. That object

is deleted only when the last smart pointer pointing to it is destroyed. Use counting is the most popular way to implement smart pointer classes.

synthesized assignment operator A version of the assignment operator created (synthesized) by the compiler for classes that do not explicitly define one. The synthesized assignment operator memberwise assigns the right-hand operand to the left.

synthesized copy constructor The copy constructor created (synthesized) by the compiler for classes that do not explicitly define the copy constructor. The synthesized copy constructor memberwise initializes the new object from the existing one.

use count Programming technique used in copy-control members. A use count is stored along with a shared object. A separate class is created that points to the shared object and manages the use count. The constructors, other than the copy constructor, set the state of the shared object and set the use count to one. Each time a new copy is made—either in the copy constructor or the assignment operator—the use count is incremented. When an object is destroyed—either in the destructor or as the left-hand side of the assignment operator—the use count is decremented. The assignment operator and the destructor check whether the decremented use count has gone to zero and, if so, they destroy the object.

value semantics Description of the copy-control behavior of classes that mimic the way arithmetic types are copied. Copies of valuelike objects are independent: Changes made to a copy have no effect on the original object. A valuelike class that has a pointer member must define its own copy-control members. The copy-control operations copy the object to which the pointer points. Valuelike classes that contain only other valuelike classes or built-in types often can rely on the synthesized copy-control members.

C H A P T E R **14**

OVERLOADED OPERATIONS AND CONVERSIONS

CONTENTS

In Chapter 5 we saw that C++ defines a large number of operators and automatic conversions among the built-in types. These facilities allow programmers to write a rich set of mixed-type expressions.

C++ lets us redefine the meaning of the operators when applied to objects of class type. It also lets us define conversion operations for class types. Class-type conversions are used like the built-in conversions to implicitly convert an object of one type to another type when needed.

505

Operator overloading allows the programmer to define versions of the operators for operands of class type. Chapter 13 covered the importance of the assignment operator and showed how to define the assignment operator. We first used overloaded operators in Chapter 1, when our programs used the shift operators (>> and <<) for input and output and the addition operator (+) to add two `Sales_items`. We'll finally see in this chapter how to define these overloaded operators.

Through operator overloading, we can redefine most of the operators from Chapter 5 to work on objects of class type. Judicious use of operator overloading can make class types as intuitive to use as the built-in types. For example, the standard library defines several overloaded operators for the container classes. These classes define the subscript operator to access data elements and * and -> to dereference container iterators. The fact that these library types have the same operators makes using them similar to using built-in arrays and pointers. Allowing programs to use expressions rather than named functions can make the programs much easier to write and read. As an example, compare

```
cout << "The sum of " << v1 << " and " << v2
     << " is " << v1 + v2 << endl;
```

to the more verbose code that would be necessary if IO used named functions:

```
// hypothetical expression if IO used named functions
cout.print("The sum of ").print(v1).
     print(" and ").print(v2).print(" is ").
     print(v1 + v2).print("\n").flush();
```

14.1   Defining an Overloaded Operator

Overloaded operators are functions with special names: the keyword `operator` followed by the symbol for the operator being defined. Like any other function, an overloaded operator has a return type and a parameter list.

```
Sales_item operator+(const Sales_item&, const Sales_item&);
```

declares the addition operator that can be used to "add" two `Sales_item` objects and yields a copy of a `Sales_item` object.

With the exception of the function-call operator, an overloaded operator has the same number of parameters (including the implicit `this` pointer for member functions) as the operator has operands. The function-call operator takes any number of operands.

Overloaded Operator Names

Table 14.1 on the next page lists the operators that may be overloaded. Those that may not be overloaded are listed in Table 14.2.

New operators may not be created by concatenating other legal symbols. For example, it would be illegal to attempt to define an `operator**` to provide exponentiation. Overloading `new` and `delete` is described in Chapter 18 (p. 753).

Table 14.1: Overloadable Operators					
+	-	*	/	%	^
&	|	~	!	,	=
<	>	<=	>=	++	--
<<	>>	==	!=	&&	||
+=	-=	/=	%=	^=	&=
|=	*=	<<=	>>=	[]	()
->	->*	new	new []	delete	delete []

Table 14.2: Operators That Cannot Be Overloaded			
::	.*	.	?:

Overloaded Operators Must Have an Operand of Class Type

The meaning of an operator for the built-in types may not be changed. For example, the built-in integer addition operation cannot be redefined:

```
//  error: cannot redefine built-in operator for ints
int operator+(int, int);
```

Nor may additional operators be defined for the built-in data types. For example, an `operator+` taking two operands of array types cannot be defined.

> An overloaded operator must have at least one operand of class or enumeration (Section 2.7, p. 62) type. This rule enforces the requirement that an overloaded operator may not redefine the meaning of the operators when applied to objects of built-in type.

Precedence and Associativity Are Fixed

The precedence (Section 5.10.1, p. 168), associativity, or number of operands of an operator cannot be changed. Regardless of the type of the operands and regardless of the definition of what the operations do, this expression

```
x == y + z;
```

always binds the arguments `y` and `z` to `operator+` and uses that result as the right-hand operand to `operator==`.

Four symbols (`+`, `-`, `*`, and `&`) serve as both unary and binary operators. Either or both of these operators can be overloaded. Which operator is being defined is controlled by the number of operands. Default arguments for overloaded operators are illegal, except for `operator()`, the function-call operator.

Short-Ciruit Evaluation Is Not Preserved

Overloaded operators make no guarantees about the order in which operands are evaluated. In particular, the operand-evaluation guarantees of the built-in logical AND, logical OR (Section 5.2, p. 152), and comma (Section 5.9, p. 168) operators are not preserved. Both operands to an overloaded version of && or || are always evaluated. The order in which those operands are evaluated is not stipulated. The order in which the operands to the comma are evaluated is also not defined. For this reason, it is usually a bad idea to overload &&, ||, or the comma operator.

Class Member versus Nonmember

Most overloaded operators may be defined as ordinary nonmember functions or as class member functions.

> Overloaded functions that are members of a class may appear to have one less parameter than the number of operands. Operators that are member functions have an implicit this parameter that is bound to the first operand.

An overloaded unary operator has no (explicit) parameter if it is a member function and one parameter if it is a nonmember function. Similarly, an overloaded binary operator would have one parameter when defined as a member and two parameters when defined as a nonmember function.

The Sales_item class offers a good example of member and nonmember binary operators. We know that the class has an addition operator. Because it has an addition operator, we ought to define a compound-assignment (+=) operator as well. This operator will add the value of one Sales_item object into another.

Ordinarily we define the arithmetic and relational operators as nonmember functions and we define assignment operators as members:

```
// member binary operator: left-hand operand bound to implicit this pointer
Sales_item& Sales_item::operator+=(const Sales_item&);
// nonmember binary operator: must declare a parameter for each operand
Sales_item operator+(const Sales_item&, const Sales_item&);
```

Both addition and compound assignment are binary operators, yet these functions define a different number of parameters. The reason for the discrepancy is the this pointer.

When an operator is a member function, this points to the left-hand operand. Thus, the nonmember operator+ defines two parameters, both references to const Sales_item objects. Even though compound assignment is a binary operator, the member compound-assignment operator takes only one (explicit) parameter. When the operator is used, a pointer to the left-hand operand is automatically bound to this and the right-hand operand is bound to the function's sole parameter.

It is also worth noting that compound assignment returns a reference and the addition operator returns a Sales_item object. This difference matches the return types of these operators when applied to arithmetic types: Addition yields an rvalue and compound assignment returns a reference to the left-hand operand.

Operator Overloading and Friendship

When operators are defined as nonmember functions, they often must be made friends (Section 12.5, p. 465) of the class(es) on which they operate. We'll see later in this chapter two reasons why operators might be defined as nonmembers. In such cases, the operator often needs access to the private parts of the class.

Our `Sales_item` class is again a good example of why some operators need to be friends. It defines one member operator and has three nonmember operators. Those nonmember operators, which need access to the private data members, are declared as friends:

```
class Sales_item {
    friend std::istream& operator>>
                    (std::istream&, Sales_item&);
    friend std::ostream& operator<<
                    (std::ostream&, const Sales_item&);
public:
    Sales_item& operator+=(const Sales_item&);
};
Sales_item operator+(const Sales_item&, const Sales_item&);
```

That the input and output operators need access to the `private` data should not be surprising. After all, they read and write those members. On the other hand, there is no need to make the addition operator a friend. It can be implemented using the `public` member `operator+=`.

Using Overloaded Operators

We can use an overloaded operator in the same way that we'd use the operator on operands of built-in type. Assuming `item1` and `item2` are `Sales_item` objects, we might print their sum in the same way that we'd print the sum of two `int`s:

```
cout << item1 + item2 << endl;
```

This expression implicitly calls the `operator+` that we defined for `Sales_items`.

We also can call an overloaded operator function in the same way that we call an ordinary function: We name the function and pass an appropriate number of arguments of the appropriate type:

```
//  equivalent direct call to nonmember operator function
cout << operator+(item1, item2) << endl;
```

This call has the same effect as the expression that added `item1` and `item2`.

We call a member operator function the same way we call any other member function: We name an object on which to run the function and then use the dot or arrow operator to fetch the function we wish to call passing the required number and type of arguments. In the case of a binary member operator function, we must pass a single operand:

```
item1 += item2;             //  expression based "call"
item1.operator+=(item2);    //  equivalent call to member operator function
```

Each of these statements adds the value of `item2` into `item1`. In the first case, we implicitly call the overloaded operator function using expression syntax. In the second, we call the member operator function on the object `item1`.

EXERCISES SECTION 14.1

Exercise 14.1: In what ways does an overloaded operator differ from a built-in operator? In what ways are overloaded operators the same as the built-in operators?

Exercise 14.2: Write declarations for the overloaded input, output, addition and compound-assignment operators for `Sales_item`.

Exercise 14.3: Explain the following program, assuming that the `Sales_item` constructor that takes a `string` is not `explicit`. Explain what happens if that constructor is `explicit`.

```
string null_book = "9-999-99999-9";
Sales_item item(cin);
item += null_book;
```

Exercise 14.4: Both the `string` and `vector` types define an overloaded `==` that can be used to compare objects of those types. Identify which version of `==` is applied in each of the following expressions:

```
string s; vector<string> svec1, svec2;
"cobble" == "stone"
svec1[0] == svec2[0];
svec1 == svec2
```

14.1.1 Overloaded Operator Design

When designing a class there are some useful rules of thumb to keep in mind when deciding which, if any, overloaded operators to provide.

Don't Overload Operators with Built-in Meanings

The assignment, address of, and comma operators have default meanings for operands of class types. If there is no overloaded version specified, the compiler defines its own version of these operators:

- The synthesized assignment operator (Section 13.2, p. 482) does memberwise assignment: It uses each member's own assignment operator to assign each member in turn.

- By default the address of (`&`) and comma (`,`) operators execute on class type objects the same way they do on objects of built-in type. The address of operator returns the address in memory of the object to which it is applied. The comma operator evaluates each expression from left to right and returns the value of its rightmost operand.

- The built-in logical AND (`&&`) and OR (`||`) operators apply short-circuit evaluation (Section 5.2, p. 152). If the operator is redefined, the short-circuit nature of the operators is lost.

The meaning of these operators can be changed by redefining them for operands of a given class type.

Best Practices

> It is usually *not* a good idea to overload the comma, address-of, logical AND, or logical OR operators. These operators have built-in meanings that are useful and become inaccessible if we define our own versions.

We sometimes must define our own version of assignment. When we do so, it should behave analogously to the synthesized operators: After an assignment, the values in the left-hand and right-hand operands should be the same and the operator should return a reference to its left-hand operand. Overloaded assignment should customize the built-in meaning of assignment, not circumvent it.

Most Operators Have No Meaning for Class Objects

Operators other than assignment, address-of, and comma have no meaning when applied to an operand of class type unless an overloaded definition is provided. When designing a class, we decide which, if any, operators to support.

The best way to design operators for a class is first to design the class' public interface. Once the interface is defined, it is possible to think about which operations should be defined as overloaded operators. Those operations with a logical mapping to an operator are good candidates. For example,

- An operation to test for equality should use `operator==`.

- Input and output are normally done by overloading the shift operators.

- An operation to test whether the object is empty could be represented by the logical NOT operator, `operator!`.

Compound Assignment Operators

If a class has an arithmetic (Section 5.1, p. 149) or bitwise (Section 5.3, p. 154) operator, then it is usually a good idea to provide the corresponding compound-assignment operator as well. For example, our `Sales_item` class defined the + operator. Logically, it also should define +=. Needless to say, the += operator should be defined to behave the same way the built-in operators do: Compound assignment should behave as + followed by =.

Equality and Relational Operators

Classes that will be used as the key type of an associative container should define the < operator. The associative containers by default use the < operator of the key type. Even if the type will be stored only in a sequential container, the class ordinarily should define the equality (==) and less-than (<) operators. The reason

---

CAUTION: USE OPERATOR OVERLOADING JUDICIOUSLY

Each operator has an associated meaning from its use on the built-in types. Binary +, for example, is strongly identified with addition. Mapping binary + to an analogous operation for a class type can provide a convenient notational shorthand. For example, the library `string` type, following a convention common to many programming languages, uses + to represent concatenation—"adding" one string to the other.

Operator overloading is most useful when there is a logical mapping of a built-in operator to an operation on our type. Using overloaded operators rather than inventing named operations can make our programs more natural and intuitive. Overuse or outright abuse of operator overloading can make our classes incomprehensible.

Obvious abuses of operator overloading rarely happen in practice. As an example, no responsible programmer would define `operator+` to perform subtraction. More common, but still inadvisable, are uses that contort an operator's "normal" meaning to force a fit to a given type. Operators should be used only for operations that are likely to be unambiguous to users. An operator with ambiguous meaning, in this sense, is one that supports equally well a number of different interpretations.

 Best Practices — When the meaning of an overloaded operator is not obvious, it is better to give the operation a name. It is also usually better to use a named function rather than an operator for operations that are rarely done. If the operation is unusual, the brevity of using an operator is unnecessary.

---

is that many algorithms assume that these operators exist. As an example, the `sort` algorithm uses `<` and `find` uses `==`.

If the class defines the equality operator, it should also define `!=`. Users of the class will assume that if they can compare for equality, they can also compare for inequality. The same argument applies to the other relational operators as well. If the class defines `<`, then it probably should define all four relational operators (`>`, `>=`, `<`, and `<=`).

Choosing Member or Nonmember Implementation

When designing the overloaded operators for a class, we must choose whether to make each operator a class member or an ordinary nonmember function. In some cases, the programmer has no choice; the operator must be a member. In other cases, there are some rules of thumb that can help guide the decision. The following guidelines can be of help when deciding whether to make an operator a member or an ordinary nonmember function:

- The assignment (`=`), subscript (`[]`), call (`()`), and member access arrow (`->`) operators must be defined as members. Defining any of these operators as a nonmember function is flagged at compile time as an error.

- Like assignment, the compound-assignment operators ordinarily ought to be members of the class. Unlike assignment, they are not required to be so and the compiler will not complain if a nonmember compound-assignment operator is defined.

- Other operators that change the state of their object or that are closely tied to their given type—such as increment, decrement, and dereference—usually should be members of the class.

- Symmetric operators, such as the arithmetic, equality, relational, and bitwise operators, are best defined as ordinary nonmember functions.

EXERCISES SECTION 14.1.1

Exercise 14.5: List the operators that must be members of a class.

Exercise 14.6: Explain why and whether each of the following operators should be class members:
   (a) +   (b) +=   (c) ++   (d) ->   (e) <<   (f) &&   (g) ==   (h) ()

14.2 Input and Output Operators

Classes that support I/O ordinarily should do so by using the same interface as defined by the `iostream` library for the built-in types. Thus, many classes provide overloaded instances of the input and output operators.

14.2.1 Overloading the Output Operator <<

 To be consistent with the IO library, the operator should take an `ostream&` as its first parameter and a reference to a `const` object of the class type as its second. The operator should return a reference to its `ostream` parameter.

The general skeleton of an overloaded output operator is

```
//  general skeleton of the overloaded output operator
ostream&
operator <<(ostream& os, const ClassType &object)
{
    // any special logic to prepare object

    // actual output of members
    os <<  // ...

    // return ostream object
    return os;
}
```

The first parameter is a reference to an `ostream` object on which the output will be generated. The `ostream` is nonconst because writing to the stream changes its state. The parameter is a reference because we cannot copy an `ostream` object.

The second parameter ordinarily should be a `const` reference to the class type we want to print. The parameter is a reference to avoid copying the argument. It can be `const` because (ordinarily) printing an object should not change it. By making the parameter a `const` reference, we can use a single definition to print `const` and nonconst objects.

The return type is an `ostream` reference. Its value is usually the `ostream` object against which the output operator is applied.

The `Sales_item` Output Operator

We can now write the `Sales_item` output operator:

```
ostream&
operator<<(ostream& out, const Sales_item& s)
{
    out << s.isbn << "\t" << s.units_sold << "\t"
        << s.revenue << "\t" <<  s.avg_price();
    return out;
}
```

Printing a `Sales_item` entails printing its three data elements and the computed average sales price. Each element is separated by a tab. After printing the values, the operator returns a reference to the `ostream` it just wrote.

Output Operators Usually Do Minimal Formatting

Class designers face one significant decision about output: whether and how much formatting to perform.

 Best Practices Generally, output operators should print the contents of the object, with minimal formatting. They should not print a newline.

The output operators for the built-in types do little if any formatting and do not print newlines. Given this treatment for the built-in types, users expect class output operators to behave similarly. By limiting the output operator to printing just the contents of the object, we let the users determine what if any additional formatting to perform. In particular, an output operator should not print a newline. If the operator does print a newline, then users would be unable to print descriptive text along with the object on the same line. By having the output operator perform minimal formatting, we let users control the details of their output.

IO Operators Must Be Nonmember Functions

When we define an input or output operator that conforms to the conventions of the `iostream` library, we must make it a nonmember operator. Why?

We cannot make the operator a member of our own class. If we did, then the left-hand operand would have to be an object of our class type:

```
// if operator<< is a member of Sales_item
Sales_item item;
item << cout;
```

This usage is the opposite of the normal way we use output operators defined for other types.

If we want to support normal usage, then the left-hand operand must be of type `ostream`. That means that if the operator is to be a member of any class, it must be a member of class `ostream`. However, that class is part of the standard library. We—and anyone else who wants to define IO operators—can't go adding members to a class in the library.

Instead, if we want to use the overloaded operators to do IO for our types, we must define them as a nonmember functions. IO operators usually read or write the nonpublic data members. As a consequence, classes often make the IO operators friends.

EXERCISES SECTION 14.2.1

Exercise 14.7: Define an output operator for the following `CheckoutRecord` class:

```
class CheckoutRecord {
public:
    // ...
private:
    double book_id;
    string title;
    Date date_borrowed;
    Date date_due;
    pair<string,string> borrower;
    vector< pair<string,string>* > wait_list;
};
```

Exercise 14.8: In the exercises to Section 12.4 (p. 451) you wrote a sketch of one of the following classes:
    (a) `Book`   (b) `Date`   (c) `Employee`
    (d) `Vehicle` (e) `Object` (f) `Tree`
Write the output operator for the class you chose.

14.2.2 Overloading the Input Operator >>

Similar to the output operator, the input operator takes a first parameter that is a reference to the stream from which it is to read, and returns a reference to that same stream. Its second parameter is a `nonconst` reference to the object into which to read. The second parameter must be `nonconst` because the purpose of an input operator is to read data into this object.

A more important, and less obvious, difference between input and output operators is that input operators must deal with the possibility of errors and end-of-file.

The `Sales_item` Input Operator

The `Sales_item` input operator looks like:

```
istream&
operator>>(istream& in, Sales_item& s)
{
    double price;
    in >> s.isbn >> s.units_sold >> price;
    //  check that the inputs succeeded
    if (in)
        s.revenue = s.units_sold * price;
    else
        s = Sales_item();   //  input failed: reset object to default state
    return in;
}
```

This operator reads three values from its `istream` parameter: a `string` value, which it stores in the `isbn` member of its `Sales_item` parameter; an `unsigned`, which it stores in the `units_sold` member; and a `double`, which it stores in a local named `price`. Assuming the reads succeed, the operator uses `price` and `units_sold` to set the object's `revenue` member.

Errors During Input

Our `Sales_item` input operator reads the expected values and checks whether an error occurred. The kinds of errors that might happen include:

1. Any of the read operations could fail because an incorrect value was provided. For example, after reading `isbn`, the input operator assumes that the next two items will be numeric data. If nonnumeric data is input, that read and any subsequent use of the stream will fail.

2. Any of the reads could hit end-of-file or some other error on the input stream.

Rather than checking each read, we check once before using the data we read:

```
//  check that the inputs succeeded
if (in)
    s.revenue = s.units_sold * price;
else
    s = Sales_item();   //  input failed: reset object to default state
```

If one of the reads failed, then `price` would be uninitialized. Hence, before using `price`, we check that the input stream is still valid. If it is, we do the calculation and store it in `revenue`. If there was an error, we do not worry about which input failed. Instead, we reset the entire object as if it were an empty `Sales_item`. We do so by creating a new, unnamed `Sales_item` constructed using the default constructor and assigning that value to `s`. After this assignment, `s` will have an empty `string` for its `isbn` member, and its `revenue` and `units_sold` members will be zero.

Handling Input Errors

If an input operator detects that the input failed, it is often a good idea to make sure that the object is in a usable and consistent state. Doing so is particularly important if the object might have been partially written before the error occurred.

For example, in the `Sales_item` input operator, we might successfully read a new `isbn`, and then encounter an error on the stream. An error after reading `isbn` would mean that the `units_sold` and `revenue` members of the old object were unchanged. The effect would be to associate a different `isbn` with that data.

In this operator, we avoid giving the parameter an invalid state by resetting it to the empty `Sales_item` if an error occurs. A user who needs to know whether the input succeeded can test the stream. If the user ignores the possibility of an input error, the object is in a usable state—its members are all all defined. Similarly, the object won't generate misleading results—its data are internally consistent.

 Best Practices | When designing an input operator, it is important to decide what to do about error-recovery, if anything.

Indicating Errors

In addition to handling any errors that might occur, an input operator might need to set the condition state (Section 8.2, p. 287) of its input `istream` parameter. Our input operator is quite simple—the only errors we care about are those that could happen during the reads. If the reads succeed, then our input operator is correct and has no need to do additional checking.

Some input operators do need to do additional checking. For example, our input operator might check that the `isbn` we read is in an appropriate format. We might have read data successfully, but these data might not be suitable when interpreted as an ISBN. In such cases, the input operator might need to set the condition state to indicate failure, even though technically speaking the actual IO was successful. Usually an input operator needs to set only the `failbit`. Setting `eofbit` would imply that the file was exhausted, and setting `badbit` would indicate that the stream was corrupted. These errors are best left to the IO library itself to indicate.

14.3 Arithmetic and Relational Operators

Ordinarily, we define the arithmetic and relational operators as nonmember functions, as we do here with our `Sales_item` addition operator:

```
// assumes that both objects refer to the same isbn
Sales_item
operator+(const Sales_item& lhs, const Sales_item& rhs)
{
    Sales_item ret(lhs);    // copy lhs into a local object that we'll return
    ret += rhs;             // add in the contents of rhs
    return ret;             // return ret by value
}
```

EXERCISES SECTION 14.2.2

Exercise 14.9: Describe the behavior of the `Sales_item` input operator if given the following input:

(a) `0-201-99999-9 10 24.95`
(b) `10 24.95 0-210-99999-9`

Exercise 14.10: What is wrong with the following `Sales_item` input operator?

```
istream& operator>>(istream& in, Sales_item& s)
{
    double price;
    in >> s.isbn >> s.units_sold >> price;
    s.revenue = s.units_sold * price;
    return in;
}
```

What would happen if we gave this operator the data in the previous exercise?

Exercise 14.11: Define an input operator for the `CheckoutRecord` class defined in the exercises for Section 14.2.1 (p. 515). Be sure the operator handles input errors.

The addition operator doesn't change the state of either operand; the operands are references to `const` objects. Instead, it generates and returns a new `Sales_item` object, which is initialized as a copy of `lhs`. We use the `Sales_item` compound-assignment operator to add in the value of `rhs`.

 Note that to be consistent with the built-in operator, addition returns an rvalue, not a reference.

An arithmetic operator usually generates a new value that is the result of a computation on its two operands. That value is distinct from either operand and is calculated in a local variable. It would be a run-time error to return a reference to that variable.

 Classes that define both an arithmetic operator and the related compound assignment ordinarily ought to implement the arithmetic operator by using the compound assignment.

It is simpler and more efficient to implement the arithmetic operator (e.g., +) in terms of the compound-assignment operator (e.g., +=) rather than the other way around. As an example, consider our `Sales_item` operators. If we implemented += by calling +, then += would needlessly create and destroy a temporary to hold the result from +.

14.3.1 Equality Operators

Ordinarily, classes in C++ use the equality operator to mean that the objects are equivalent. That is, they usually compare every data member and treat two objects

EXERCISES SECTION 14.3

Exercise 14.12: Write the `Sales_item` operators so that + does the actual addition and += calls +. Discuss the disadvantages of this approach compared to the way the operators were implemented in this section.

Exercise 14.13: Which other arithmetic operators, if any, do you think `Sales_item` ought to support? Define those that you think the class should include.

as equal if and only if all corresponding members are the same. In line with this design philosophy, our `Sales_item` equality operator should compare the `isbn` as well as the sales figures:

```
inline bool
operator==(const Sales_item &lhs, const Sales_item &rhs)
{
    //  must be made a friend of Sales_item
    return lhs.units_sold == rhs.units_sold &&
           lhs.revenue == rhs.revenue &&
        lhs.same_isbn(rhs);
}
inline bool
operator!=(const Sales_item &lhs, const Sales_item &rhs)
{
    return !(lhs == rhs); //  != defined in terms of operator==
}
```

The definition of these functions is trivial. More important are the design principles that these functions embody:

- If a class defines the == operator, it defines it to mean that two objects contain the same data.

- If a class has an operation to determine whether two objects of the type are equal, it is usually right to define that function as `operator==` rather than inventing a named operation. Users will expect to be able to compare objects using ==, and doing so is easier than remembering a new name.

- If a class defines `operator==`, it should also define `operator!=`. Users will expect that if they can use one operator, then the other will also exist.

- The equality and inequality operators should almost always be defined in terms of each other. One operator should do the real work to compare objects. The other should call the one that does the real work.

Classes that define `operator==` are easier to use with the standard library. Some algorithms, such as `find`, use the == operator by default. If a class defines ==, then these algorithms can be used on that class type without any specialization.

14.3.2   Relational Operators

Classes for which the equality operator is defined also often have relational operators. In particular, because the associative containers and some of the algorithms use the less-than operator, it can be quite useful to define an `operator<`.

Although we might think our `Sales_item` class should support the relational operators, it turns out that it probably should not. The reasons are somewhat subtle and deserve understanding.

As we'll see in Chapter 15, we might want to use an associative container to hold `Sales_item` transactions. When we put objects into the container, we'd want them ordered by ISBN, and wouldn't care whether the sales data in two records were different.

However, if we were to define `operator<` as comparison on `isbn`, that definition would be incompatible with the obvious definition of `==`. If we had two transactions for the same ISBN, neither record would be less than the other. Yet, if the sales figures in those objects were different, then these objects would be `!=`. Ordinarily, if we have two objects, neither of which is less than the other, then we expect that those objects are equal.

Because the logical definition of `<` is inconsistent with the logical definition of `==`, it is better not to define `<` at all. We'll see in Chapter 15 how to use a separate named function to compare `Sales_items` when we want to store them in an associative container.

> The associative containers, as well as some of the algorithms, use the `<` operator by default. Ordinarily, the relational operators, like the equality operators, should be defined as nonmember functions.

14.4   Assignment Operators

We covered the assignment of one object of class type to another object of its type in Section 13.2 (p. 482). The class assignment operator takes a parameter that is the class type. Usually the parameter is a `const` reference to the class type. However, the parameter could be the class type or a `nonconst` reference to the class type. This operator will be synthesized by the compiler if we do not define it ourselves. The class assignment operator must be a member of the class so the compiler can know whether it needs to synthesize one.

Additional assignment operators that differ by the type of the right-hand operand can be defined for a class type. For example, the library `string` class defines three assignment operators: In addition to the class assignment operator, which takes a `const string&` as its right-hand operand, the `string` class defines versions of assignment that take a C-style character string or a `char` as the right-hand operand. These might be used as follows:

```
string car ("Volks");
car = "Studebaker";    // string = const char*
string model;
model = 'T';           // string = char
```

To support these operations, the `string` class contains members that look like

```
//  illustration of assignment operators for class string
class string {
public:
    string& operator=(const string &);  // s1 = s2;
    string& operator=(const char *);     // s1 = "str";
    string& operator=(char);             // s1 = 'c';
    // ....
};
```

Assignment operators can be overloaded. Unlike the compound-assignment operators, every assignment operator, regardless of parameter type, must be defined as a member function.

Assignment Should Return a Reference to `*this`

The `string` assignment operators return a reference to `string`, which is consistent with assignment for the built-in types. Moreover, because assignment returns a reference there is no need to create and destroy a temporary copy of the result. The return value is usually a reference to the left-hand operand. For example, here is the definition of the `Sales_item` compound-assignment operator:

```
//  assumes that both objects refer to the same isbn
Sales_item& Sales_item::operator+=(const Sales_item& rhs)
{
    units_sold += rhs.units_sold;
    revenue += rhs.revenue;
    return *this;
}
```

Ordinarily, assignment operators and compound-assignment operators ought to return a reference to the left-hand operand.

EXERCISES SECTION 14.4

Exercise 14.14: Define a version of the assignment operator that can assign an `isbn` to a `Sales_item`.

Exercise 14.15: Define the class assignment operator for the `CheckoutRecord` introduced in the exercises to Section 14.2.1 (p. 515).

Exercise 14.16: Should `CheckoutRecord` define any other assignment operators? If so, explain which types should be used as operands and why. Implement the assignment operators for those types.

14.5   Subscript Operator

Classes that represent containers from which individual elements can be retrieved usually define the subscript operator, `operator[]`. The library classes, `string` and `vector`, are examples of classes that define the subscript operator.

 The subscript operator must be defined as a class member function.

Providing Read and Write Access

One complication in defining the subscript operator is that we want it to do the right thing when used as either the left- or right-hand operand of an assignment. To appear on the left-hand side, it must yield an lvalue, which we can achieve by specifying the return type as a reference. As long as subscript returns a reference, it can be used on either side of an assignment.

It is also a good idea to be able to subscript `const` and nonconst objects. When applied to a `const` object, the return should be a `const` reference so that it is not usable as the target of an assignment.

 Ordinarily, a class that defines subscript needs to define two versions: one that is a nonconst member and returns a reference and one that is a `const` member and returns a `const` reference.

Prototypical Subscript Operator

The following class defines the subscript operator. For simplicity, we assume the data `Foo` holds are stored in a `vector<int>`:

```
class Foo {
public:
    int &operator[](const size_t);
    const int &operator[](const size_t) const;
    //  other interface members
private:
    vector<int> data;
    //  other member data and private utility functions
};
```

The subscript operators themselves would look something like:

```
int& Foo::operator[](const size_t index)
{
    return data[index];    //  no range checking on index
}
const int& Foo::operator[](const size_t index) const
{
    return data[index];    //  no range checking on index
}
```

14.6 Member Access Operators

To support pointerlike classes, such as iterators, the language allows the dereference (`*`) and arrow (`->`) operators to be overloaded.

 Operator arrow must be defined as a class member function. The dereference operator is not required to be a member, but it is usually right to make it a member as well.

Building a Safer Pointer

The dereference and arrow operators are often used in classes that implement smart pointers (Section 13.5.1, p. 495). As an example, let's assume that we want to define a class type to represent a pointer to an object of the `Screen` type that we wrote in Chapter 12. We'll name this class `ScreenPtr`.

Our `ScreenPtr` class will be similar to our second `HasPtr` class. Users of `ScreenPtr` will be expected to pass a pointer to a dynamically allocated `Screen`. The `ScreenPtr` class will own that pointer and arrange to `delete` the underlying object when the last `ScreenPtr` referring to it goes away. In addition, we will not give our `ScreenPtr` class a default constructor. This way we'll know that a `ScreenPtr` object will always refer to a `Screen`. Unlike a built-in pointer, there will be no unbound `ScreenPtr`s. Applications can use `ScreenPtr` objects without first testing whether they refer to a `Screen` object.

As does the `HasPtr` class, the `ScreenPtr` class will use-count its pointer. We'll define a companion class to hold the pointer and its associated use count:

```
// private class for use by ScreenPtr only
class ScrPtr {
    friend class ScreenPtr;
    Screen *sp;
    size_t use;
    ScrPtr(Screen *p): sp(p), use(1) { }
    ~ScrPtr() { delete sp; }
};
```

This class looks a lot like the `U_Ptr` class and has the same role. `ScrPtr` holds the pointer and associated use count. We make `ScreenPtr` a friend so that it can access the use count. The `ScreenPtr` class manages the use count:

```
/*
 *  smart pointer: Users pass to a pointer to a dynamically allocated Screen, which
 *                 is automatically destroyed when the last ScreenPtr goes away
 */
class ScreenPtr {
public:
    //  no default constructor: ScreenPtrs must be bound to an object
    ScreenPtr(Screen *p): ptr(new ScrPtr(p)) { }
    //  copy members and increment the use count
    ScreenPtr(const ScreenPtr &orig):
        ptr(orig.ptr) { ++ptr->use; }
    ScreenPtr& operator=(const ScreenPtr&);
    //  if use count goes to zero, delete the ScrPtr object
    ~ScreenPtr() { if (--ptr->use == 0) delete ptr; }
private:
    ScrPtr *ptr;             //  points to use-counted ScrPtr class
};
```

Because there is no default constructor, every object of type `ScreenPtr` must provide an initializer. The initializer must be another `ScreenPtr` or a pointer to a dynamically allocated `Screen`. The constructor allocates a new `ScrPtr` object to hold that pointer and an associated use count.

An attempt to define a `ScreenPtr` with no initializer is in error:

```
ScreenPtr p1; // error: ScreenPtr has no default constructor
ScreenPtr ps(new Screen(4,4)); // ok: ps points to a copy of myScreen
```

Supporting Pointer Operations

Among the fundamental operations a pointer supports are dereference and arrow. We can give our class these operations as follows:

```
class ScreenPtr {
public:
    //  constructor and copy control members as before
    Screen &operator*() { return *ptr->sp; }
    Screen *operator->() { return ptr->sp; }

    const Screen &operator*() const { return *ptr->sp; }
    const Screen *operator->() const { return ptr->sp; }
private:
    ScrPtr *ptr;             //  points to use-counted ScrPtr class
};
```

Overloading the Dereference Operator

The dereference operator is a unary operator. In this class, it is defined as a member so it has no explicit parameters. The operator returns a reference to the `Screen` to which this `ScreenPtr` points.

As with the subscript operator, we need both `const` and nonconst versions of the dereference operator. These differ in their return types: The `const` member returns a reference to `const` to prevent users from changing the underlying object.

Overloading the Arrow Operator

Operator arrow is unusual. It may appear to be a binary operator that takes an object and a member name, dereferencing the object in order to fetch the member. Despite appearances, the arrow operator takes no explicit parameter.

There is no second parameter because the right-hand operand of -> is not an expression. Rather, the right-hand operand is an identifier that corresponds to a member of a class. There is no obvious, useful way to pass an identifier as a parameter to a function. Instead, the compiler handles the work of fetching the member.

When we write

```
point->action();
```

precedence rules make it equivalent to writing

```
(point->action)();
```

In other words, we want to call the result of evaluating point->action. The compiler evaluates this code as follows:

1. If point is a pointer to a class object that has a member named action, then the compiler writes code to call the action member of that object.

2. Otherwise, if point is an object of a class that defines operator->, then point->action is the same as point.operator->()->action. That is, we execute operator->() on point and then repeat these three steps, using the result of executing operator-> on point.

3. Otherwise, the code is in error.

Using Overloaded Arrow

We can use a ScreenPtr object to access members of a Screen as follows:

```
ScreenPtr p(&myScreen);  // copies the underlying Screen
p->display(cout);
```

Because p is a ScreenPtr, the meaning of p->display is the same as evaluating (p.operator->())->display. Evaluating p.operator->() calls the operator-> from class ScreenPtr, which returns a pointer to a Screen object. That pointer is used to fetch and run the display member of the object to which the ScreenPtr points.

Constraints on the Return from Overloaded Arrow

 The overloaded arrow operator *must* return either a pointer to a class type or an object of a class type that defines its own operator arrow.

If the return type is a pointer, then the built-in arrow operator is applied to that pointer. The compiler dereferences the pointer and fetches the indicated member from the resulting object. If the type pointed to does not define that member, then the compiler generates an error.

If the return value is another object of class type (or reference to such an object), then the operator is applied recursively. The compiler checks whether the type of the object returned has a member arrow and if so, applies that operator. Otherwise, the compiler generates an error. This process continues until either a pointer to an object with the indicated member is returned or some other value is returned, in which case the code is in error.

EXERCISES SECTION 14.6

Exercise 14.20: In our sketch for the `ScreenPtr` class, we declared but did not define the assignment operator. Implement the `ScreenPtr` assignment operator.

Exercise 14.21: Define a class that holds a pointer to a `ScreenPtr`. Define the overloaded arrow operator for that class.

Exercise 14.22: A smart pointer probably should define the equality and inequality operators to test whether two pointers are equal or unequal. Add these operations to the `ScreenPtr` class.

14.7   Increment and Decrement Operators

The increment (++) and decrement (--) operators are most often implemented for classes, such as iterators, that provide pointerlike behavior on the elements of a sequence. As an example, we might define a class that points to an array and provides checked access to elements in that array. Ideally, our checked-pointer class could be used on arrays of any type, which we'll learn how to do in Chapter 16 when we cover class templates. For now, our class will handle arrays of `ints`:

```
/*
 *  smart pointer: Checks access to elements throws an out_of_range
 *                 exception if attempt to access a nonexistent element
 *  users allocate and free the array
 */
class CheckedPtr {
public:
        // no default constructor; CheckedPtrs must be bound to an object
        CheckedPtr(int *b, int *e): beg(b), end(e), curr(b) { }
        // dereference and increment operations
private:
        int* beg;     // pointer to beginning of the array
        int* end;     // one past the end of the array
        int* curr;    // current position within the array
};
```

Like `ScreenPtr`, this class has no default constructor. We must supply pointers to an array when we create a `CheckedPtr`. A `CheckedPtr` has three data members:

beg, which points to the first element in the array; end, which points one past the end of the array; and curr, which points to the array element to which this CheckedPtr object currently refers.

The constructor takes two pointers: one pointing to the beginning of the array and the other one past the end of the array. The constructor initializes beg and end from these pointers and initializes curr to point to the first element.

Defining the Increment/Decrement Operators

There is no language requirement that the increment or decrement operators be made members of the class. However, because these operators change the state of the object on which they operate, our preference is to make them members.

Before we can define the overloaded increment and decrement operators for CheckedPtr, we must think about one more thing. For the built-in types, there are both prefix and postfix versions of the increment and decrement operators. Not surprisingly, we can define both the prefix and postfix instances of these operators for our own classes as well. We'll look at the prefix versions first and then implement the postfix ones.

Defining Prefix Increment/Decrement Operators

The declarations for the prefix operators look as one might expect:

```
class CheckedPtr {
public:
    CheckedPtr& operator++();          //  prefix operators
    CheckedPtr& operator--();
    //  other members as before
};
```

For consistency with the built-in operators, the prefix operations should return a reference to the incremented or decremented object.

This increment operator ensures that the user can't increment past the end of the array by checking curr against end. We throw an out_of_range exception if the increment would move curr past end; otherwise, we increment curr and return a reference to the object:

```
//  prefix: return reference to incremented/decremented object
CheckedPtr& CheckedPtr::operator++()
{
    if (curr == end)
        throw out_of_range
                ("increment past the end of CheckedPtr");
    ++curr;                          //  advance current state
    return *this;
}
```

The decrement operator behaves similarly, except that it decrements `curr` and checks whether the decrement would move `curr` past `beg`:

```
CheckedPtr& CheckedPtr::operator--()
{
    if (curr == beg)
        throw out_of_range
            ("decrement past the beginning of CheckedPtr");
    --curr;                    // move current state back one element
    return *this;
}
```

Differentiating Prefix and Postfix Operators

There is one problem with defining both the prefix and postfix operators: They each take the same number and type of parameters. Normal overloading cannot distinguish between whether the operator we're defining is the prefix version or the postfix.

To solve this problem, the postfix operator functions take an extra (unused) parameter of type `int`. When we use the postfix operator, the compiler supplies 0 as the argument for this parameter. Although our postfix function could use this extra parameter, it usually should not. That parameter is not needed for the work normally performed by a postfix operator. Its sole purpose is to distinguish the definition of the postfix function from the prefix version.

Defining the Postfix Operators

We can now add the postfix operators to `CheckedPtr`:

```
class CheckedPtr {
public:
    // increment and decrement
    CheckedPtr operator++(int);      // postfix operators
    CheckedPtr operator--(int);
    // other members as before
};
```

Best Practices
For consistency with the built-in operators, the postfix operators should return the old (unincremented or undecremented) value. That value is returned as a value, not a reference.

The postfix operators might be implemented as follows:

```
// postfix: increment/decrement object but return unchanged value
CheckedPtr CheckedPtr::operator++(int)
{
    // no check needed here, the call to prefix increment will do the check
    CheckedPtr ret(*this);     // save current value
    ++*this;                   // advance one element, checking the increment
    return ret;                // return saved state
}
```

```
CheckedPtr CheckedPtr::operator--(int)
{
    // no check needed here, the call to prefix decrement will do the check
    CheckedPtr ret(*this);   // save current value
    --*this;                 // move backward one element and check
    return ret;              // return saved state
}
```

The postfix versions are a bit more involved than the prefix operators. They have to remember the current state of the object before incrementing the object. These operators define a local CheckedPtr, which is initialized as a copy of *this—that is, ret is a copy of the current state of this object.

Having kept a copy of the current state, the operator calls its own prefix operator to do the increment or decrement, respectively:

```
++*this
```

calls the CheckedPtr prefix increment operator on this object. That operator checks that the increment is safe and either increments curr or throws an exception. Assuming no exception was thrown, the postfix function completes by returning the stored copy in ret. Thus, after the return, the object itself has been advanced, but the value returned reflects the original, unincremented value.

Because these operators are implemented by calling the prefix versions, there is no need to check that the curr is in range. That check, and the throw if necessary, is done inside the corresponding prefix operator.

 The int parameter is not used, so we do not give it a name.

Calling the Postfix Operators Explicitly

As we saw on page 509, we can explicitly call an overloaded operator rather than using it as an operator in an expression. If we want to call the postfix version using a function call, then we must pass a value for the integer argument:

```
CheckedPtr parr(ia, ia + size);   // ia points to an array of ints
parr.operator++(0);               // call postfix operator++
parr.operator++();                // call prefix operator++
```

The value passed usually is ignored but is necessary to alert the compiler that the postfix version is desired.

 Ordinarily it is best to define both the prefix and postfix versions. Classes that define only the prefix version or only the postfix version will surprise users who are accustomed to being able to use either form.

EXERCISES SECTION 14.7

Exercise 14.23: The class `CheckedPtr` represents a pointer that points to an array of `int`s. Define an overloaded subscript and dereference for this class. Have the operator ensure that the `CheckedPtr` is valid: It should not be possible to dereference or index one past the end of the array.

Exercise 14.24: Should the dereference or subscript operators defined in the previous exercise also check whether an attempt is being made to dereference or index one before the beginning of the array? If not, why not? If so, why?

Exercise 14.25: To behave like a pointer to an array, our `CheckedPtr` class should implement the equality and relational operators to determine whether two `CheckedPtr`s are equal, or whether one is less-than another, and so on. Add these operations to the `CheckedPtr` class.

Exercise 14.26: Define addition and subtraction for `ScreenPtr` so that these operators implement pointer arithmetic (Section 4.2.4, p. 123).

Exercise 14.27: Discuss the pros and cons of allowing an empty array argument to the `CheckedPtr` constructor.

Exercise 14.28: We did not define a `const` version of the increment and decrement operators. Why?

Exercise 14.29: We also didn't implement arrow. Why?

Exercise 14.30: Define a version of `CheckedPtr` that holds an array of `Screen`s. Implement the overloaded increment, decrement, dereference, and arrow operators for this class.

14.8 Call Operator and Function Objects

The function-call operator can be overloaded for objects of class type. Typically, the call operator is overloaded for classes that represent an operation. For example, we could define a struct named `absInt` that encapsulates the operation of converting a value of type `int` to its absolute value:

```
struct absInt {
    int operator()(int val) {
        return val < 0 ? -val : val;
    }
};
```

This class is simple. It defines a single operation: the function-call operator. That operator takes a single parameter and returns the absolute value of its parameter.

We use the call operator by applying an argument list to an object of the class type, in a way that looks like a function call:

```
int i = -42;
absInt absObj;  // object that defines function call operator
unsigned int ui = absObj(i);   // calls absInt::operator(int)
```

Even though `absObj` is an object and not a function, we can make a "call" on that object. The effect is to run the overloaded call operator defined by the object `absObj`. That operator takes an `int` value and returns its absolute value.

 The function-call operator must be declared as a member function. A class may define multiple versions of the call operator, each of which differs as to the number or types of their parameters.

Objects of class types that define the call operator are often referred to as **function objects**—that is, they are objects that act like functions.

EXERCISES SECTION 14.8

Exercise 14.31: Define a function object to perform an if-then-else operation: The function object should take three parameters. It should test its first parameter and if that test succeeds, it should return its second parameter, otherwise, it should return its third parameter.

Exercise 14.32: How many operands may an overloaded function-call operator take?

14.8.1 Using Function Objects with Library Algorithms

Function objects are most often used as arguments to the generic algorithms. As an example, recall the problem we solved in Section 11.2.3 (p. 400). That program analyzed words in a set of stories, counting how many of them were of size six or greater. One part of that solution involved defining a function to determine whether a given `string` was longer than six characters in length:

```
//  determine whether a length of a given word is 6 or more
bool GT6(const string &s)
{
    return s.size() >= 6;
}
```

We used `GT6` as an argument to the `count_if` algorithm to count the number of words for which `GT6` returned `true`:

```
vector<string>::size_type wc =
            count_if(words.begin(), words.end(), GT6);
```

Function Objects Can Be More Flexible than Functions

There was a serious problem with our implementation: It hardwired the number six into the definition of the `GT6` function. The `count_if` algorithm runs a function that takes a single parameter and returns a `bool`. Ideally, we'd pass both the `string` and the size we wanted to test. In that way, we could use the same code to count strings of differing sizes.

We could gain the flexibility we want by defining GT6 as a class with a function-call member. We'll name this class GT_cls to distinguish it from the function:

```
// determine whether a length of a given word is longer than a stored bound
class GT_cls {
public:
    GT_cls(size_t val = 0): bound(val) { }
    bool operator()(const string &s)
                        { return s.size() >= bound; }
private:
    std::string::size_type bound;
};
```

This class has a constructor that takes an integral value and remembers that value in its member named bound. If no value is provided, the constructor sets bound to zero. The class also defines the call operator, which takes a string and returns a bool. That operator compares the length of its string argument to the value stored in its data member bound.

Using a GT_cls Function Object

We can do the same count as before but this time we'll use an object of type GT_cls rather than the GT6 function:

```
cout << count_if(words.begin(), words.end(), GT_cls(6))
     << " words 6 characters or longer" << endl;
```

This call to count_if passes a temporary object of type GT_cls rather than the function named GT6. We initialize that temporary using the value 6, which the GT_cls constructor stores in its bound member. Now, each time count_if calls its function parameter, it uses the call operator from GT_cls. That call operator tests the size of its string argument against the value in bound.

Using the function object, we can easily revise our program to test against another value. We need to change only the argument to the constructor for the object we pass to count_if. For example, we could count the number of words of length five or greater by revising our program as follows:

```
cout << count_if(words.begin(), words.end(), GT_cls(5))
     << " words 5 characters or longer" << endl;
```

More usefully, we could count the number of words with lengths greater than one through ten:

```
for (size_t i = 0; i != 11; ++i)
    cout << count_if(words.begin(), words.end(), GT(i))
         << " words " << i
         << " characters or longer" << endl;
```

To write this program using a function—instead of a function object—would require that we write ten different functions, each of which would test against a different value.

14.8.2 Library-Defined Function Objects

The standard library defines a set of arithmetic, relational, and logical function-object classes, which are listed in Table 14.3 on the following page. The library also defines a set of function adaptors that allow us to specialize or extend the function-object classes defined by the library or those that we define ourselves. The library function-object types are defined in the functional header.

Each Class Represents a Given Operator

Each of the library function-object classes represents an operator—that is, each class defines the call operator that applies the named operation. For example, plus is a template type that represents the addition operator. The call operator in the plus template applies + to a pair of operands.

Different function-object classes define call operators that perform different operations. Just as plus defines a call operator that executes the + operator; the modulus class defines a call operator that applies the binary % operator; the equal_to class applies ==; and so on.

There are two **unary function-object** classes: unary minus (negate<Type>) and logical NOT (logical_not<Type>). The remaining library function objects are **binary function-object** classes representing the binary operators. The call operators defined for the binary operators expect two parameters of the given type; the unary function-object types define a call operator that takes a single argument.

The Template Type Represents the Operand(s) Type

Each of the function-object classes is a class template to which we supply a single type. As we know from the sequential containers such as vector, a class template is a class that can be used on a variety of types. The template type for the function-object classes specifies the parameter type for the call operator.

For example, plus<string> applies the string addition operator to string objects; for `plus<int>` the operands are `int`s; `plus<Sales_item>` applies + to `Sales_items`; and so on:

```
plus<int> intAdd;        // function object that can add two int values
negate<int> intNegate;   // function object that can negate an int value
// uses intAdd::operator(int, int) to add 10 and 20
int sum = intAdd(10, 20);       // sum = 30
// uses intNegate::operator(int) to generate -10 as second parameter
// to intAdd::operator(int, int)
sum = intAdd(10, intNegate(10));  // sum = 0
```

Table 14.3: Library Arithmetic Function Objects	
Arithmetic Function Objects Types	
`plus<Type>`	*applies +*
`minus<Type>`	*applies -*
`multiplies<Type>`	*applies * *
`divides<Type>`	*applies /*
`modulus<Type>`	*applies %*
`negate<Type>`	*applies -*
Relational Function Objects Types	
`equal_to<Type>`	*applies ==*
`not_equal_to<Type>`	*applies !=*
`greater<Type>`	*applies >*
`greater_equal<Type>`	*applies >=*
`less<Type>`	*applies <*
`less_equal<Type>`	*applies <=*
Logical Function Object Types	
`logical_and<Type>`	*applies &&*
`logical_or<Type>`	*applies |*
`logical_not<Type>`	*applies !*

Using a Library Function Object with the Algorithms

Function objects are often used to override the default operator used by an algorithm. For example, by default, `sort` uses `operator<` to sort a container in ascending order. To sort the container in descending order, we could pass the function object `greater`. That class generates a call operator that invokes the greater-than operator of the underlying element type. If `svec` is a `vector<string>`

```
// passes temporary function object that applies > operator to two strings
sort(svec.begin(), svec.end(), greater<string>());
```

sorts the `vector` in descending order. As usual, we pass a pair of iterators to denote the sequence that should be sorted. The third argument is used to pass a predicate (Section 11.2.3, p. 402) function to use to compare elements. That argument is a temporary of type `greater<string>`, which is a function object that applies the `>` operator to two `string` operands.

14.8.3 Function Adaptors for Function Objects

The standard library provides a set of **function adaptors** with which to specialize and extend both unary and binary function objects. The function adaptors are divided into the following two categories.

1. Binders: A **binder** is a function adaptor that converts a binary function object into a unary function object by binding one of the operands to a given value.

2. Negators: A **negator** is a function adaptor that reverses the truth value of a predicate function object.

The library defines two binder adaptors: `bind1st` and `bind2nd`. Each binder takes a function object and a value. As you might expect, `bind1st` binds the given value to the first argument of the binary function object, and `bind2nd` binds the value to the second. For example, to count all the elements within a container that are less than or equal to `10`, we would pass `count_if` the following:

```
count_if(vec.begin(), vec.end(),
         bind2nd(less_equal<int>(), 10));
```

The third argument to `count_if` uses the `bind2nd` function adaptor. That adaptor returns a function object that applies the `<=` operator using 10 as the right-hand operand. This call to `count_if` counts the number of elements in the input range that are less than or equal to 10.

The library also provides two negators: `not1` and `not2`. Again, as you might expect, `not1` reverses the truth value of a unary predicate function object, and `not2` reverses the truth value of a binary predicate function object.

To negate our binding of the `less_equal` function object, we would write

```
count_if(vec.begin(), vec.end(),
         not1(bind2nd(less_equal<int>(), 10)));
```

Here we first bind the second operand of the `less_equal` object to `10`, effectively transforming that binary operation into a unary operation. We then negate the return from the operation using `not1`. The effect is that each element will be tested to see if it is `<=` to 10. Then, the truth value of that result will be negated. In effect, this call counts those elements that are not `<=` to 10.

14.9 Conversions and Class Types

In Section 12.4.4 (p. 461) we saw that a nonexplicit constructor that can be called with one argument defines an implicit conversion. The compiler will use that conversion when an object of the argument type is supplied and an object of the class type is needed. Such constructors define conversions to the class type.

In addition to defining conversions *to* a class type, we can also define conversions *from* the class type. That is, we can define a conversion operator that, given an object of the class type, will generate an object of another type. As with other conversions, the compiler will apply this conversion automatically. Before showing how to define such conversions, we'll look at why they might be useful.

14.9.1   Why Conversions Are Useful

Assume that we want to define a class, which we'll name SmallInt, to implement safe small integers. Our class will allow us to define objects that could hold the same range of values as an 8-bit unsigned char—that is, 0 to 255. This class would catch under- and overflow errors and so would be safer to use than a built-in unsigned char.

We'd want our class to define all the same operations as are supported by an unsigned char. In particular, we'd want to define the five arithmetic operators (+, -, *, /, and %) and the corresponding compound-assignment operators; the four relational operators (<, <=, >, and >=); and the equality operators (== and !=). Evidently, we'd need to define 16 operators.

Supporting Mixed-Type Expressions

Moreover, we'd like to be able to use these operators in mixed-mode expressions. For example, it should be possible to add two SmallInt objects and also possible to add any of the arithmetic types to a SmallInt. We could come close by defining three instances for each operator:

```
int operator+(int, const SmallInt&);
int operator+(const SmallInt&, int);
SmallInt operator+(const SmallInt&, const SmallInt&);
```

Because there is a conversion to int from any of the arithmetic types, these three functions would cover our desire to support mixed mode use of SmallInt objects. However, this design only approximates the behavior of built-in integer arithmetic. It wouldn't properly handle mixed-mode operations for the floating-point types, nor would it properly support addition of `long`, `unsigned int`, or `unsigned long`. The problem is that this design converts all arithmetic types—even those bigger than `int`—to `int` and does an `int` addition.

Conversions Reduce the Number of Needed Operators

Even ignoring the issue of floating-point or large integral operands, if we implemented this design, we'd have to define 48 operators! Fortunately, C++ provides a mechanism by which a class can define its own conversions that can be applied to objects of its class type. For `SmallInt`, we could define a conversion from `SmallInt` to type `int`. If we define the conversion, then we won't need to define any of the arithmetic, relational, or equality operators. Given a conversion to `int`, a `SmallInt` object could be used anywhere an `int` could be used.

If there were a conversion to `int`, then

```
SmallInt si(3);
si + 3.14159;      // convert si to int, then convert to double
```

would be resolved by

1. Converting `si` to an `int`.

2. Converting the resulting `int` to `double` and adding it to the double literal constant `3.14159`, yielding a `double` value.

14.9.2 Conversion Operators

A **conversion operator** is a special kind of class member function. It defines a conversion that converts a value of a class type to a value of some other type. A conversion operator is declared in the class body by specifying the keyword `operator` followed by the type that is the target type of the conversion:

```
class SmallInt {
public:
    SmallInt(int i = 0): val(i)
    { if (i < 0 || i > 255)
        throw std::out_of_range("Bad SmallInt initializer");
    }
    operator int() const { return val; }
private:
    std::size_t val;
};
```

A conversion function takes the general form

```
operator type();
```

where *type* represents the name of a built-in type, a class type, or a name defined by a typedef. Conversion functions can be defined for any type (other than `void`) that could be a function return type. In particular, conversions to an array or function type are not permitted. Conversions to pointer types—both data and function pointers—and to reference types are allowed.

 A conversion function must be a member function. The function may not specify a return type, and the parameter list must be empty.

All of the following declarations are errors:

```
operator int(SmallInt &);      // error: nonmember

class SmallInt {
public:
    int operator int();        // error: return type
    operator int(int = 0);     // error: parameter list
    // ...
};
```

Although a conversion function does not specify a return type, each conversion function must explicitly return a value of the named type. For example, `operator int` returns an `int`; if we defined an `operator Sales_item`, it would return a `Sales_item`; and so on.

 Conversion operations ordinarily should not change the object they are converting. As a result, conversion operators usually should be defined as `const` members.

Using a Class-Type Conversion

Once a conversion exists, the compiler will call it automatically (Section 5.12.1, p. 179) in the same places that a built-in conversion would be used:

- In expressions:

```
SmallInt si;
double dval;
si >= dval          // si converted to int and then convert to double
```

- In conditions:

```
if (si)             // si converted to int and then convert to bool
```

- When passing arguments to or returning values from a function:

```
int calc(int);
SmallInt si;
int i = calc(si);   // convert si to int and call calc
```

- As operands to overloaded operators:

```
// convert si to int then call opeator<< on the int value
cout << si << endl;
```

- In an explicit cast:

```
int ival;
SmallInt si = 3.541;
// instruct compiler to cast si to int
ival = static_cast<int>(si) + 3;
```

Class-Type Conversions and Standard Conversions

When using a conversion function, the converted type need not exactly match the needed type. A class-type conversion can be followed by a standard conversion (Section 5.12.3, p. 181) if needed to obtain the desired type. For example, in the comparison between a `SmallInt` and a `double`

```
SmallInt si;
double dval;
si >= dval           //  si converted to int and then convert to double
```

`si` is first converted from a `SmallInt` to an `int`, and then the `int` value is converted to `double`.

Only One Class-Type Conversion May Be Applied

 A class-type conversion may not be followed by another class-type conversion. If more than one class-type conversion is needed then the code is in error.

For example, assume we had another class, `Integral`, that could be converted to `SmallInt` but that had no conversion to `int`:

```
//  class to hold unsigned integral values
class Integral {
public:
    Integral(int i = 0): val(i) { }
    operator SmallInt() const { return val % 256; }
private:
    std::size_t val;
};
```

We could use an `Integral` where a `SmallInt` is needed, but not where an `int` is required:

```
int calc(int);
Integral intVal;
SmallInt si(intVal);   // ok: convert intVal to SmallInt and copy to si
int i = calc(si);      // ok: convert si to int and call calc
int j = calc(intVal);  // error: no conversion to int from Integral
```

When we create `si`, we use the `SmallInt` copy constructor. First `int_val` is converted to a `SmallInt` by invoking the `Integral` conversion operator to generate a temporary value of type `SmallInt`. The (synthesized) `SmallInt` copy constructor then uses that value to initialize `si`.

The first call to `calc` is also okay: The argument `si` is automatically converted to `int`, and the `int` value is passed to the function.

The second call is an error: There is no direct conversion from `Integral` to `int`. To get an `int` from an `Integral` would require two class-type conversions: first from `Integral` to `SmallInt` and then from `SmallInt` to `int`. However, the language allows only one class-type conversion, so the call is in error.

Standard Conversions Can Precede a Class-Type Conversion

When using a constructor to perform an implicit conversion (Section 12.4.4, p. 462), the parameter type of the constructor need not exactly match the type supplied. For example, the following code invokes the constructor `SmallInt(int)` defined in class `SmallInt` to convert `sobj` to the type `SmallInt`:

```
void calc(SmallInt);
short sobj;
//  sobj promoted from short to int
//  that int converted to SmallInt through the SmallInt(int) constructor
calc(sobj);
```

If needed, a standard conversion sequence can be applied to an argument before a constructor is called to perform a class-type conversion. To call the function `calc()`, a standard conversion is applied to convert `dobj` from type `double` to type `int`. The `SmallInt(int)` constructor is then invoked to convert the result of the conversion to the type `SmallInt`.

EXERCISES SECTION 14.9.2

Exercise 14.40: Write operators that could convert a `Sales_item` to `string` and to `double`. What values do you think these operators should return? Do you think these conversions are a good idea? Explain why or why not.

Exercise 14.41: Explain the difference between these two conversion operators:

```
class Integral {
public:
    const int();
    int() const;
};
```

Are either of these conversions too restricted? If so, how might you make the conversion more general?

Exercise 14.42: Define a conversion operator to `bool` for the `CheckoutRecord` class from the exercises in Section 14.2.1 (p. 515).

Exercise 14.43: Explain what the `bool` conversion operator does. Is that the only possible meaning for this conversion for the `CheckoutRecord` type? Explain whether you think this conversion is a good use of a conversion operation.

14.9.3   Argument Matching and Conversions

The rest of this chapter covers a somewhat advanced topic. It can be safely skipped on first reading.

Class-type conversions can be a boon to implementing and using classes. By defining a conversion to int for SmallInts, we made the class easier to implement and easier to use. The int conversion lets users of SmallInt use all the arithmetic and relational operators on SmallInt objects. Moreover, users can safely write expressions that intermix SmallInts and other arithmetic types. The class implementor's job is made much easier by defining a single conversion operator instead of having to define 48 (or more) overloaded operators.

Class-type conversions can also be a great source of compile-time errors. Problems arise when there are multiple ways to convert from one type to another. If there are several class-type conversions that could be used, the compiler must figure out which one to use for a given expression. In this section, we look at how class-type conversions are used to match an argument to its corresponding parameter. We look first at how parameters are matched for functions that are not overloaded and then look at overloaded functions.

Used carefully, class-type conversions can greatly simplify both class and user code. Used too freely, they can lead to mysterious compile-time errors that can be hard to understand and hard to avoid.

Argument Matching and Multiple Conversion Operators

To illustrate how conversions on values of class type interact with function matching, we'll add two additional conversions to our SmallInt class. We'll add a second constructor that takes a double and also define a second conversion operator to convert SmallInt to double:

```
//  unwise class definition:
//  multiple constructors and conversion operators to and from the built-in types
//  can lead to ambiguity problems
class SmallInt {
public:
    //  conversions to SmallInt from int and double
    SmallInt(int = 0);
    SmallInt(double);

    //  Conversions to int or double from SmallInt
    //  Usually it is unwise to define conversions to multiple arithmetic types
    operator int() const { return val; }
    operator double() const { return val; }
    //  ...
private:
    std::size_t val;
};
```

Ordinarily it is a bad idea to give a class conversions to or from two built-in types. We do so here to illustrate the pitfalls involved.

Consider the simple case where we call a function that is not overloaded:

```
void compute(int);
void fp_compute(double);
void extended_compute(long double);

SmallInt si;
compute(si);              // SmallInt::operator int() const
fp_compute(si);           // SmallInt::operator double() const
extended_compute(si);     // error: ambiguous
```

Either conversion operator could be used in the call to `compute`:

1. `operator int` generates an exact match to the parameter type.

2. `operator double` followed by the standard conversion from `double` to `int` matches the parameter type.

An exact match is a better conversion than one that requires a standard conversion. Hence, the first conversion sequence is better. The conversion function `SmallInt::operator int()` is chosen to convert the argument.

Similarly, in the second call, `fp_compute` could be called using either conversion. However, the conversion to `double` is an exact match; it requires no additional standard conversion.

The final call to `extended_compute` is ambiguous. Either conversion function could be used, but each would have to be followed by a standard conversion to get to `long double`. Hence, neither conversion is better than the other, so the call is ambiguous.

If two conversion operators could be used in a call, then the rank of the standard conversion (Section 7.8.4, p. 272), if any, *following* the conversion function is used to select the best match.

Argument Matching and Conversions by Constructors

Just as there might be two conversion operators, there can also be two constructors that might be applied to convert a value to the target type of a conversion.

Consider the `manip` function, which takes an argument of type `SmallInt`:

```
void manip(const SmallInt &);

double d; int i; long l;

manip(d);      // ok: use SmallInt(double) to convert the argument
manip(i);      // ok: use SmallInt(int) to convert the argument
manip(l);      // error: ambiguous
```

In the first call, we could use either of the `SmallInt` constructors to convert d to a value of type `SmallInt`. The int constructor requires a standard conversion on d, whereas the `double` constructor is an exact match. Because an exact match is better than a standard conversion, the constructor `SmallInt(double)` is used for the conversion.

In the second call, the reverse is true. The `SmallInt(int)` constructor provides an exact match—no additional conversion is needed. To call the `SmallInt` constructor that takes a `double` would require that i first be converted to `double`. For this call, the int constructor would be used to convert the argument.

The third call is ambiguous. Neither constructor is an exact match for `long`. Each would require that the argument be converted before using the constructor:

1. standard conversion (`long` to `double`) followed by `SmallInt(double)`

2. standard conversion (`long` to `int`) followed by `SmallInt(int)`

These conversion sequences are indistinguishable, so the call is ambiguous.

> When two constructor-defined conversions could be used, the rank of the standard conversion, if any, required on the constructor argument is used to select the best match.

Ambiguities When Two Classes Define Conversions

When two classes define conversions to each other, ambiguities are likely:

```
class Integral;
class SmallInt {
public:
    SmallInt(Integral); // convert from Integral to SmallInt
    // ...
};
class Integral {
public:
    operator SmallInt() const; // convert from SmallInt to Integral
    // ...
};
void compute(SmallInt);
Integral int_val;
compute(int_val);    // error: ambiguous
```

The argument int_val can be converted to a `SmallInt` in two different ways. The compiler could use the `SmallInt` constructor that takes an `Integral` object or it could use the `Integral` conversion operation that converts an `Integral` to a `SmallInt`. Because these two functions are equally good, the call is in error.

In this case, we cannot use a cast to resolve the ambiguity—the cast itself could use either the conversion operation or the constructor. Instead, we would need to explicitly call the conversion operator or the constructor:

```
compute(int_val.operator SmallInt()); // ok: use conversion operator
compute(SmallInt(int_val));            // ok: use SmallInt constructor
```

Moreover, conversions that we might think would be ambiguous can be legal for what seem like trivial reasons. For example, our `SmallInt` class constructor copies its `Integral` argument. If we change the constructor so that it takes a reference to `const Integral`

```
class SmallInt {
public:
SmallInt(const Integral&);
};
```

our call to `compute(int_val)` is no longer ambiguous! The reason is that using the `SmallInt` constructor requires binding a reference to `int_val`, whereas using class `Integral`'s conversion operator avoids this extra step. This small difference is enough to tip the balance in favor of using the conversion operator.

 Best Practices The best way to avoid ambiguities or surprises is to avoid writing pairs of classes where each offers an implicit conversion to the other.

CAUTION: AVOID OVERUSE OF CONVERSION FUNCTIONS

As with using overloaded operators, judicious use of conversion operators can greatly simplify the job of a class designer and make using a class easier. However, there are two potential pitfalls: Defining too many conversion operators can lead to ambiguous code, and some conversions can be confusing rather than helpful.

The best way to avoid ambiguities is to ensure that there is at most one way to convert one type to another. The best way to do that is to limit the number of conversion operators. In particular there should be only one conversion to a built-in type.

Conversion operators can be misleading when they are used where there is no obvious single mapping between the class type and the conversion type. In such cases, providing a conversion function may be confusing to the user of the class.

As an example, if we had a class that represented a `Date`, we might think it would be a good idea to provide a conversion from `Date` to `int`. However, what value should the conversion function return? The function might return the julian date, which is the sequence number of the current date starting from 0 as January 1. But should the year precede the day or follow it? That is, would January 31, 1986 be represented as 1986031 or 311986? Alternatively, the conversion operator might return an `int` representing the day count since some epoch point. The counter might count days since January 1, 1971 or some other starting point.

The problem is that whatever choice is made, the use of `Date` objects will be ambiguous because there is no single one-to-one mapping between an object of type `Date` and a value of type `int`. In such cases, it is better not to define the conversion operator. Instead, the class ought to define one or more ordinary members to extract the information in these various forms.

14.9.4 Overload Resolution and Class Arguments

As we have just seen, the compiler automatically applies a class conversion operator or constructor when needed to convert an argument to a function. Class conversion operators, therefore, are considered during function resolution. Function overload resolution (Section 7.8.2, p. 269) consists of three steps:

1. Determine the set of candidate functions: These are the functions with the same name as the function being called.

2. Select the viable functions: These are the candidate functions for which the number and type of the function's parameters match the arguments in the call. When selecting the viable functions, the compiler also determines which conversion operations, if any, are needed to match each parameter.

3. The best match function is selected. To determine the best match, the type conversions needed to convert argument(s) to the type of the corresponding parameter(s) are ranked. For arguments and parameters of class type, the set of possible conversions includes class-type conversions.

Standard Conversions Following Conversion Operator

Which function is the best match can depend on whether one or more class-type conversions are involved in matching different functions.

> If two functions in the overload set can be matched *using the same conversion function*, then the rank of the standard conversion sequence that follows or precedes the conversion is used to determine which function has the best match.
>
> Otherwise, if *different conversion operations* could be used, then the conversions are considered equally good matches, regardless of the rank of any standard conversions that might or might not be required.

On page 541 we looked at the effect of class-type conversions on calls to functions that are not overloaded. Now, we'll look at similar calls but assume that the functions are overloaded:

```
void compute(int);
void compute(double);
void compute(long double);
```

Assuming we use our original SmallInt class that only defines one conversion operator—the conversion to int—then if we pass a SmallInt to compute, the call is matched to the version of compute that takes an int.

All three compute functions are viable:

- compute(int) is viable because SmallInt has a conversion to int. That conversion is an exact match for the parameter.

- compute(double) and compute(long double) are also viable, by using the conversion to int followed by the appropriate standard conversion to either double or long double.

Because all three functions would be matched using the *same* class-type conversion, the rank of the standard conversion, if any, is used to determine the best match. Because an exact match is better than a standard conversion, the function `compute(int)` is chosen as the best viable function.

 The standard conversion sequence following a class-type conversion is used as a selection criterion only if the two conversion sequences use the same conversion operation.

Multiple Conversions and Overload Resolution

We can now see one reason why adding a conversion to `double` is a bad idea. If we use the revised `SmallInt` class that defines conversions to both `int` and `double`, then calling `compute` on a `SmallInt` value is ambiguous:

```
class SmallInt {
public:
    // Conversions to int or double from SmallInt
    // Usually it is unwise to define conversions to multiple arithmetic types
    operator int() const { return val; }
    operator double() const { return val; }
    // ...
private:
    std::size_t val;
};
void compute(int);
void compute(double);
void compute(long double);

SmallInt si;
compute(si);      // error: ambiguous
```

In this case we could use the `operator int` to convert `si` and call the version of `compute` that takes an `int`. Or we could use `operator double` to convert `si` and call `compute(double)`.

The compiler will not attempt to distinguish between two different class-type conversions. In particular, even if one of the calls required a standard conversion following the class-type conversion and the other were an exact match, the compiler would still flag the call as an error.

Explicit Constructor Call to Disambiguate

A programmer who is faced with an ambiguous conversion can use a cast to indicate explicitly which conversion operation to apply:

```
void compute(int);
void compute(double);

SmallInt si;
compute(static_cast<int>(si)); // ok: convert and call compute(int)
```

This call is now legal because it explicitly says which conversion operation to apply to the argument. The type of the argument is forced to `int` by the cast. That type exactly matches the parameter of the first version of `compute` that takes an `int`.

Standard Conversions and Constructors

Let's look at overload resolution when multiple conversion constructors exist:

```
class SmallInt {
public:
    SmallInt(int = 0);
};
class Integral {
public:
    Integral(int = 0);
};
void manip(const Integral&);
void manip(const SmallInt&);
manip(10);    //  error: ambiguous
```

The problem is that both classes, Integral and SmallInt, provide constructors that take an int. Either constructor could be used to match a version of manip. Hence, the call is ambiguous: It could mean convert the int to Integral and call the first version of manip, or it could mean convert the int to a SmallInt and call the second version.

This call would be ambiguous even if one of the classes defined a constructor that required a standard conversion for the argument. For example, if SmallInt defined a constructor that took a short instead of an int, the call manip(10) would require a standard conversion from int to short before using that constructor. The fact that one call requires a standard conversion and the other does not is immaterial when selecting among overloaded versions of a call. The compiler will not prefer the direct constructor; the call would still be ambiguous.

Explicit Constructor Call to Disambiguate

The caller can disambiguate by explicitly constructing a value of the desired type:

```
manip(SmallInt(10));    //  ok: call manip(SmallInt)
manip(Integral(10));    //  ok: call manip(Integral)
```

Needing to use a constructor or a cast to convert an argument in a call to an overloaded function is a sign of bad design.

14.9.5 Overloading, Conversions, and Operators

Overloaded operators are overloaded functions. The same process that is used to resolve a call to an overloaded function is used to determine which operator—built-in or class-type—to apply to a given expression. Given code such as

```
ClassX sc;
int iobj = sc + 3;
```

Exercise 14.44: Show the possible class-type conversion sequences for each of the following initializations. What is the outcome of each initialization?

```
class LongDouble {
    operator double();
    operator float();
};
LongDouble ldObj;
(a) int ex1 = ldObj;          (b) float ex2 = ldObj;
```

Exercise 14.45: Which calc() function, if any, is selected as the best viable function for the following call? Show the conversion sequences needed to call each function and explain why the best viable function is selected.

```
class LongDouble {
public
    LongDouble(double);
    // ...
};
void calc(int);
void calc(LongDouble);
double dval;

calc(dval); // which function?
```

there are four possibilities:

- There is an overloaded addition operator that matches ClassX and int.

- There are conversions to convert sc and/or to convert an int to types for which + is defined. If so, this expression will use the conversion(s) followed by applying the appropriate addition operator.

- The expression is ambiguous because both a conversion operator and an overloaded version of + are defined.

- The expression is invalid because there is neither a conversion nor an overloaded + to use.

Overload Resolution and Operators

 The fact that member and nonmember functions are possible changes how the set of candidate functions is selected.

Overload resolution (Section 7.8.2, p. 269) for operators follows the usual three-step process:

1. Select the candidate functions.

2. Select the viable functions including identifying potential conversions sequences for each argument.

3. Select the best match function.

Candidate Functions for Operators

As usual, the set of candidate functions consists of all functions that have the name of the function being used, and that are visible from the place of the call. In the case of an operator used in an expression, the candidate functions include the built-in versions of the operator along with all the ordinary nonmember versions of that operator. In addition, if the left-hand operand has class type, then the candidate set will contain the overloaded versions of the operator, if any, defined by that class.

 Ordinarily, the candidate set for a call includes only member functions or nonmember functions but not both. When resolving the use of an operator, it is possible for both nonmember and member versions of the operator to be candidates.

When resolving a call to a named function (as opposed to the use of an operator), the call itself determines the scope of names that will be considered. If the call is through an object of a class type (or through a reference or pointer to such an object), then only the member functions of that class are considered. Member and nonmember functions with the same name do *not* overload one another. When we use an overloaded operator, the call does not tell us anything about the scope of the operator function that is being used. Therefore, both member and nonmember versions must be considered.

CAUTION: CONVERSIONS AND OPERATORS

Correctly designing the overloaded operators, conversion constructors, and conversion functions for a class requires some care. In particular, ambiguities are easy to generate if a class defines both conversion operators and overloaded operators. A few rules of thumb can be helpful:

1. Never define mutually converting classes—that is, if class Foo has a constructor that takes an object of class Bar, do not give class Bar a conversion operator to type Foo.

2. Avoid conversions to the built-in arithmetic types. In particular, if you do define a conversion to an arithmetic type, then

   - Do not define overloaded versions of the operators that take arithmetic types. If users need to use these operators, the conversion operation will convert objects of your type, and then the built-in operators can be used.

   - Do not define a conversion to more than one arithmetic type. Let the standard conversions provide conversions to the other arithmetic types.

The easiest rule of all: Avoid defining conversion functions and limit nonexplicit constructors to those that are "obviously right."

Conversions Can Cause Ambiguity with Built-In Operators

Let's extend our SmallInt class once more. This time, in addition to a conversion operator to int and a constructor from int, we'll give our class an overloaded addition operator:

```
class SmallInt {
public:
    SmallInt(int = 0);  // convert from int to SmallInt
    // conversion to int from SmallInt
    operator int() const { return val; }
    // arithmetic operators
    friend SmallInt
    operator+(const SmallInt&, const SmallInt&);
private:
    std::size_t val;
};
```

Now we could use this class to add two SmallInts, but we will run into ambiguity problems if we attempt to perform mixed-mode arithmetic:

```
SmallInt s1, s2;
SmallInt s3 = s1 + s2;      // ok: uses overloaded operator+
int i = s3 + 0;             // error: ambiguous
```

The first addition uses the overloaded version of + that takes two SmallInt values. The second addition is ambiguous. The problem is that we could convert 0 to a SmallInt and use the SmallInt version of +, or we could convert s3 to int and use the built-in addition operator on ints.

Providing both conversion functions to an arithmetic type and overloaded operators for the same class type may lead to ambiguities between the overloaded operators and the built-in operators.

Viable Operator Functions and Conversions

We can understand the behavior of these two calls by listing the viable functions for each call. In the first call, there are two viable addition operators:

- operator+(const SmallInt&, const SmallInt&)

- The built-in operator+(int, int)

The first addition requires no conversions on either argument—s1 and s2 match exactly the types of the parameters. Using the built-in addition operator for this addition would require conversions on both arguments. Hence, the overloaded operator is a better match for both arguments and is the one that is called. For the second addition

```
int i = s3 + 0;             // error: ambiguous
```

the same two functions are viable. In this case, the overloaded version of + matches
the first argument exactly, but the built-in version is an exact match for the second
argument. The first viable function is better for the left operand, whereas the second viable function is better for the right operand. The call is flagged as ambiguous
because no best viable function can be found.

EXERCISES SECTION 14.9.5

Exercise 14.46: Which `operator+`, if any, is selected as the best viable function for
the addition operation in `main`? List the candidate functions, the viable functions, and
the type conversions on the arguments for each viable function.

```
class Complex {
    Complex(double);
    // ...
};
class LongDouble {
    friend LongDouble operator+(LongDouble&, int);
public:
    LongDouble(int);
    operator double();
    LongDouble operator+(const complex &);
    // ...
};
LongDouble operator+(const LongDouble &, double);

LongDouble ld(16.08);
double res = ld + 15.05; // which operator+ ?
```

Chapter Summary

Chapter 5 described the rich set of operators that C++ defines for the built-in types. That chapter also covered the standard conversions, which automatically convert operands from one type to another.

We can define a similarly rich set of expressions for objects of our own types (i.e., class or enumeration types) by defining overloaded versions of the built-in operators. An overloaded operator must have at least one operand of class or enumeration type. An overloaded operator has the same number of operands, associativity, and precedence as the corresponding operator when applied to the built-in types.

Most overloaded operators can be defined as class members or as ordinary non-member functions. The assignment, subscript, call, and arrow operators must be class members. When an operator is defined as a member, it is a normal member function. In particular, member operators have an implicit `this` pointer, which is bound to the first (only operand for unary operators, left-hand operand for binary operators) operand.

Objects of classes that overload `operator()`, the function call operator, are known as "function objects." Such objects are often used to define predicate functions to be used in combination with the standard algorithms.

Classes can define conversions that will be applied automatically when an object of one type is used where an object of a different type is needed. Constructors that take a single parameter and are not designated as `explicit` (Section 12.4.4, p. 462) define conversions from the class type to other types. Overloaded operator conversion functions define conversions from other types to the class type. Conversion operators must be members of the class that they convert. They have no parameters and define no return value. Conversion operators return a value of the type of the operator—for example, `operator int` returns an `int`.

Both overloaded operators and class-type conversions can make types easier and more natural to use. However, care should be taken to avoid designing operators or conversions that are not obvious to users of the type and to avoid defining multiple conversions between one type and another.

Defined Terms

binary function object A class that has a function-call operator and represents one of the binary operators, such as one of the arithmetic or relational operators.

binder An adaptor that binds an operand of a specified function object. For example, `bind2nd(minus<int>(), 2)` generates a unary function object that subtracts two from its operand.

class-type conversion Conversions to or from class types. Non-explicit constructors

that take a single parameter define a conversion from the parameter type to the class type. Conversion operators define conversions from the class type to the type specified by the operator.

conversion operators Conversion operators are member functions that define conversions from the class type to another type. Conversion operators must be a member of their class. They do not specify a return type and take no parameters. They return a value of the type of the conversion operator. That is, `operator int` returns an `int`, `operator Sales_item` returns a `Sales_item`, and so on.

function adaptor Library type that provides a new interface for a function object.

function object Object of a class that defines an overloaded call operator. Function objects can be used where functions are normally expected.

negator An adaptor that negates the value returned by the specified function object. For example, `not2(equal_to<int>())` generates a function object that is equivalent to `not_equal_to<int>`.

smart pointer A class that defines pointer-like behavior and other functionality, such as reference counting, memory management, or more thorough checking. Such classes typically define overloaded versions of dereference (`operator*`) and member access (`operator->`).

unary function object A class that has a function-call operator and represents one of the unary operators, unary minus or logical NOT.

P A R T **IV**

OBJECT-ORIENTED AND GENERIC PROGRAMMING

CONTENTS

Part IV extends the discussion of Part III by covering how C++ supports object-oriented and generic programming.

Chapter 15 covers inheritance and dynamic binding. Along with data abstraction, inheritance and dynamic binding are fundamental to object-oriented programming.

Chapter 16 covers function and class templates. Templates let us write generic classes and functions that are independent of type.

Writing our own object-oriented or generic types requires a fairly good understanding of C++. Fortunately, we can use OO and generic types without understanding the details of how to build them. In fact, the standard library uses the facilities we'll study in Chapters 15 and 16 extensively, and we've used the library types and algorithms without needing to know how they are implemented. Readers, therefore, should understand that Part IV covers advanced topics. Writing templates or object-oriented classes requires a good understanding of the basics of C++ and a good grasp of how to define more basic classes.

C H A P T E R   **15**
O B J E C T - O R I E N T E D
P R O G R A M M I N G

CONTENTS

Object-oriented programming is based on three fundamental concepts: data abstraction, inheritance, and dynamic binding. In C++ we use classes for data abstraction and class derivation to inherit one class from another: A derived class inherits the members of its base class(es). Dynamic binding lets the compiler determine at run time whether to use a function defined in the base or derived class.

Inheritance and dynamic binding streamline our programs in two ways: They make it easier to define new classes that are similar, but not identical, to other classes, and they make it easier for us to write programs that can ignore the details of how those similar types differ.

Many applications are characterized by concepts that are related but slightly different. For example, our bookstore might offer different pricing strategies for different books. Some books might be sold only at a given price. Others might be sold subject to some kind of discount strategy. We might give a discount to purchasers who buy a specified number of copies of the book. Or we might give a discount for only the first few copies purchased but charge full price for any bought beyond a given limit.

Object-oriented programming (OOP) is a good match to this kind of application. Through inheritance we can define types that model the different kinds of books. Through dynamic binding we can write applications that use these types but that can ignore the type-dependent differences.

The ideas of inheritance and dynamic binding are conceptually simple but have profound implications for how we build our applications and for the features that programming languages must support. Before covering how C++ supports OOP, we'll look at the concepts that are fundamental to this style of programming.

15.1   OOP: An Overview

The key idea behind OOP is **polymorphism**. Polymorphism is derived from a Greek word meaning "many forms." We speak of types related by inheritance as polymorphic types, because in many cases we can use the "many forms" of a derived or base type interchangeably. As we'll see, in C++, polymorphism applies only to references or pointers to types related by inheritance.

Inheritance

Inheritance lets us define classes that model relationships among types, sharing what is common and specializing only that which is inherently different. Members defined by the **base class** are inherited by its **derived classes**. The derived class can use, without change, those operations that do not depend on the specifics of the derived type. It can redefine those member functions that do depend on its type, specializing the function to take into account the peculiarities of the derived type. Finally, a derived class may define additional members beyond those it inherits from its base class.

Classes related by inheritance are often described as forming an **inheritance hierarchy**. There is one class, referred to as the root, from which all the other classes inherit, directly or indirectly. In our bookstore example, we will define a base class, which we'll name `Item_base`, to represent undiscounted books. From `Item_base` we will inherit a second class, which we'll name `Bulk_item`, to represent books sold with a quantity discount.

At a minimum, these classes will define the following operations:

- an operation named `book` that will return the ISBN

- an operation named `net_price` that returns the price for purchasing a specified number of copies of a book

Classes derived from `Item_base` will inherit the `book` function without change: The derived classes have no need to redefine what it means to fetch the ISBN. On the other hand, each derived class will need to define its own version of the `net_price` function to implement an appropriate discount pricing strategy.

In C++, a base class must indicate which of its functions it intends for its derived classes to redefine. Functions defined as **virtual** are ones that the base expects its derived classes to redefine. Functions that the base class intends its children to inherit are not defined as virtual.

Given this discussion, we can see that our classes will define three (`const`) member functions:

- A nonvirtual function, `std::string book()`, that returns the ISBN. It will be defined by `Item_base` and inherited by `Bulk_item`.

- Two versions of the virtual function, `double net_price(size_t)`, to return the total price for a given number of copies of a specific book. Both `Item_base` and `Bulk_item` will define their own versions of this function.

Dynamic Binding

Dynamic binding lets us write programs that use objects of any type in an inheritance hierarchy without caring about the objects' specific types. Programs that use these classes need not distinguish between functions defined in the base or in a derived class.

For example, our bookstore application would let a customer select several books in a single sale. When the customer was done shopping, the application would calculate the total due. One part of figuring the final bill would be to print for each book purchased a line reporting the total quantity and sales price for that portion of the purchase.

We might define a function named `print_total` to manage this part of the application. The `print_total` function, given an item and a count, should print the ISBN and the total price for purchasing the given number of copies of that particular book. The output of this function should look like:

```
ISBN: 0-201-54848-8 number sold: 3 total price: 98
ISBN: 0-201-82470-1 number sold: 5 total price: 202.5
```

Our `print_total` function might look something like the following:

```
// calculate and print price for given number of copies, applying any discounts
void print_total(ostream &os,
                 const Item_base &item, size_t n)
{
    os << "ISBN: " << item.book() // calls Item_base::book
       << "\tnumber sold: " << n << "\ttotal price: "
       // virtual call: which version of net_price to call is resolved at run time
       << item.net_price(n) << endl;
}
```

The function's work is trivial: It prints the results of calling `book` and `net_price` on its `item` parameter. There are two interesting things about this function.

First, even though its second parameter is a reference to Item_base, we can pass either an Item_base object or a Bulk_item object to this function.

Second, because the parameter is a reference and the net_price function is virtual, the call to net_price will be resolved at run time. The version of net_price that is called will depend on the type of the argument passed to print_total. When the argument to print_total is a Bulk_item, the version of net_price that is run will be the one defined in Bulk_item that applies a discount. If the argument is an Item_base object, then the call will be to the version defined by Item_base.

> In C++, dynamic binding happens when a virtual function is called through a reference (or a pointer) to a base class. The fact that a reference (or pointer) might refer to either a base- or a derived-class object is the key to dynamic binding. Calls to virtual functions made through a reference (or pointer) are resolved at run time: The function that is called is the one defined by the actual type of the object to which the reference (or pointer) refers.

15.2   Defining Base and Derived Classes

In many ways, base and derived classes are defined like other classes we have already seen. However, there are some additional features that are required when defining classes in an inheritance hierarchy. This section will present those features. Subsequent sections will see how use of these features impacts classes and the programs we write using inherited classes.

15.2.1   Defining a Base Class

Like any other class, a base class has data and function members that define its interface and implementation. In the case of our (very simplified) bookstore pricing application, our Item_base class defines the book and net_price functions and needs to store an ISBN and the standard price for the book:

```
//  Item sold at an undiscounted price
//  derived classes will define various discount strategies
class Item_base {
public:
    Item_base(const std::string &book = "",
              double sales_price = 0.0):
                    isbn(book), price(sales_price) { }
    std::string book() const { return isbn; }
    //  returns total sales price for a specified number of items
    //  derived classes will override and apply different discount algorithms
    virtual double net_price(std::size_t n) const
                { return n * price; }
    virtual ~Item_base() { }
```

```
private:
    std::string isbn;    // identifier for the item
protected:
    double price;        // normal, undiscounted price
};
```

For the most part, this class looks like others we have seen. It defines a constructor along with the functions we have already described. That constructor uses default arguments (Section 7.4.1, p. 253), which allows it to be called with zero, one, or two arguments. It initializes the data members from these arguments.

The new parts are the `protected` access label and the use of the `virtual` keyword on the destructor and the `net_price` function. We'll explain virtual destructors in Section 15.4.4 (p. 587), but for now it is worth noting that classes used as the root class of an inheritance hierarchy generally define a virtual destructor.

Base-Class Member Functions

The `Item_base` class defines two functions, one of which is preceded by the keyword `virtual`. The purpose of the `virtual` keyword is to enable dynamic binding. By default, member functions are nonvirtual. Calls to nonvirtual functions are resolved at compile time. To specify that a function is virtual, we precede its return type by the keyword `virtual`. Any nonstatic member function, other than a constructor, may be virtual. The `virtual` keyword appears only on the member-function declaration inside the class. The `virtual` keyword may not be used on a function definition that appears outside the class body.

We'll have more to say about virtual functions in Section 15.2.4 (p. 566).

 Best Practices A base class usually should define as virtual any function that a derived class will need to redefine.

Access Control and Inheritance

In a base class, the `public` and `private` labels have their ordinary meanings: User code may access the `public` members and may not access the `private` members of the class. The `private` members are accessible only to the members and friends of the base class. A derived class has the same access as any other part of the program to the `public` and `private` members of its base class: It may access the `public` members and has no access to the `private` members.

Sometimes a class used as a base class has members that it wants to allow its derived classes to access, while still prohibiting access to those same members by other users. The **protected access label** is used for such members. A `protected` member may be accessed by a derived object but may not be accessed by general users of the type.

Our `Item_base` class expects its derived classes to redefine the `net_price` function. To do so, those classes will need access to the `price` member. Derived classes are expected to access `isbn` in the same way as ordinary users: through the `book` access function. Hence, the `isbn` member is `private` and is inaccessible to classes that inherit from `Item_base`.

Exercise 15.1: What is a virtual member?

Exercise 15.2: Define the `protected` access label. How does it differ from `private`?

Exercise 15.3: Define your own version of the `Item_base` class.

Exercise 15.4: A library has different kinds of materials that it lends out—books, CDs, DVDs, and so forth. Each of the different kinds of lending material has different check-in, check-out, and overdue rules. The following class defines a base class that we might use for this application. Identify which functions are likely to be defined as virtual and which, if any, are likely to be common among all lending materials. (Note: we assume that `LibMember` is a class representing a customer of the library, and `Date` is a class representing a calendar day of a particular year.)

```
class Library {
public:
    bool check_out(const LibMember&);
    bool check_in (const LibMember&);
    bool is_late(const Date& today);
    double apply_fine();
    ostream& print(ostream& = cout);
    Date due_date() const;
    Date date_borrowed() const;
    string title() const;
    const LibMember& member() const;
};
```

15.2.2 `protected` Members

The `protected` access label can be thought of as a blend of `private` and `public`:

- Like `private` members, `protected` members are inaccessible to users of the class.

- Like `public` members, the `protected` members are accessible to classes derived from this class.

In addition, `protected` has another important property:

- A derived object may access the `protected` members of its base class *only* through a derived object. The derived class has no special access to the `protected` members of base type objects.

As an example, let's assume that `Bulk_item` defines a member function that takes a reference to a `Bulk_item` object and a reference to an `Item_base` object. This function may access the `protected` members of its own object as well as those of its `Bulk_item` parameter. However, it has no special access to the `protected` members in its `Item_base` parameter:

```
void Bulk_item::memfcn(const Bulk_item &d, const Item_base &b)
{
    // attempt to use protected member
    double ret = price;  // ok: uses this->price
    ret = d.price;  // ok: uses price from a Bulk_item object
    ret = b.price;  // error: no access to price from an Item_base
}
```

The use of d.price is okay, because the reference to price is through an object of type Bulk_item. The use of b.price is illegal because Bulk_item has no special access to objects of type Item_base.

KEY CONCEPT: CLASS DESIGN AND PROTECTED MEMBERS

In the absence of inheritance, a class has two kinds of users: members of the class itself and the users of that class. This separation between kinds of users is reflected in the division of the class into private and public access levels. Users may access only the public interface; class members and friends may access both the public and private members.

Under inheritance, there is now a third kind of user of a class: programmers who will define new classes that are derived from the class. The provider of a derived class often (but not always) needs access to the (ordinarily private) base-class implementation. To allow that access while still preventing general access to the implementation, an additional access label, protected, is provided. The data and function members in a protected section of a class remain inaccessible to the general program, yet are accessible to the derived class. Anything placed within a private section of the base class is accessible only to the class itself and its friends. The private members are not accessible to the derived classes.

When designing a class to serve as a base class, the criteria for designating a member as public do not change: It is still the case that interface functions should be public and data generally should not be public. A class designed to be inherited from must decide which parts of the implementation to declare as protected and which should be private. A member should be made private if we wish to prevent subsequently derived classes from having access to that member. A member should be made protected if it provides an operation or data that a derived class will need to use in its implementation. In other words, the interface to the derived type is the combination of both the protected and public members.

15.2.3 Derived Classes

To define a derived class, we use a **class derivation list** to specify the base class(es). A class derivation list names one or more base classes and has the form

```
class classname: access-label base-class
```

where *access-label* is one of public, protected, or private, and *base-class* is the name of a previously defined class. As we'll see, a derivation list might name more than one base class. Inheritance from a single base class is most common and is the topic of this chapter. Section 17.3 (p. 731) covers use of multiple base classes.

We'll have more to say about the access label used in a derivation list in Section 15.2.5 (p. 570). For now, what's useful to know is that the access label determines the access to the inherited members. When we want to inherit the interface of a base class, then the derivation should be `public`.

A derived class inherits the members of its base class and may define additional members of its own. Each derived object contains two parts: those members that it inherits from its base and those it defines itself. Typically, a derived class (re)defines only those aspects that differ from or extend the behavior of the base.

Defining a Derived Class

In our bookstore application, we will derive `Bulk_item` from `Item_base`, so `Bulk_item` will inherit the `book`, `isbn`, and `price` members. `Bulk_item` must redefine its `net_price` function and define the data members needed for that operation:

```
//  discount kicks in when a specified number of copies of same book are sold
//  the discount is expressed as a fraction used to reduce the normal price
class Bulk_item : public Item_base {
public:
    //  redefines base version so as to implement bulk purchase discount policy
    double net_price(std::size_t) const;
private:
    std::size_t min_qty;    //  minimum purchase for discount to apply
    double discount;        //  fractional discount to apply
};
```

Each `Bulk_item` object contains four data elements: It inherits `isbn` and `price` from `Item_base` and defines `min_qty` and `discount`. These latter two members specify the minimum quantity and the discount to apply once that number of copies are purchased. The `Bulk_item` class also needs to define a constructor, which we shall do in Section 15.4 (p. 580).

Derived Classes and `virtual` Functions

Ordinarily, derived classes redefine the virtual functions that they inherit, although they are not requried to do so. If a derived class does not redefine a virtual, then the version it uses is the one defined in its base class.

A derived type must include a declaration for each inherited member it intends to redefine. Our `Bulk_item` class says that it will redefine the `net_price` function but will use the inherited version of `book`.

With one exception, the declaration (Section 7.4, p. 251) of a virtual function in the derived class must exactly match the way the function is defined in the base. That exception applies to virtuals that return a reference (or pointer) to a type that is itself a base class. A virtual function in a derived class can return a reference (or pointer) to a class that is publicly derived from the type returned by the base-class function.

For example, the `Item_base` class might define a virtual function that returned an `Item_base*`. If it did, then the instance defined in the `Bulk_item` class could be defined to return either an `Item_base*` or a `Bulk_item*`. We'll see an example of this kind of virtual in Section 15.9 (p. 607).

 Once a function is declared as virtual in a base class it remains virtual; nothing the derived classes do can change the fact that the function is virtual. When a derived class redefines a virtual, it may use the `virtual` keyword, but it is not required to do so.

Derived Objects Contain Their Base Classes as Subobjects

A derived object consists of multiple parts: the (`nonstatic`) members defined in the derived class itself plus the subobjects made up of the (`nonstatic`) members of its base class. We can think of our `Bulk_item` class as consisting of two parts as represented in Figure 15.1.

Figure 15.1: Conceptual Structure of a `Bulk_item` Object

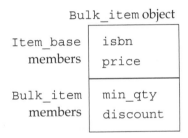

 There is no requirement that the compiler lay out the base and derived parts of an object contiguously. Hence, Figure 15.1 is a conceptual, not physical, representation of how classes work.

Functions in the Derived May Use Members from the Base

As with any member function, a derived class function can be defined inside the class or outside, as we do here for the `net_price` function:

```
//   if specified number of items are purchased, use discounted price
double Bulk_item::net_price(size_t cnt) const
{
    if (cnt >= min_qty)
        return cnt * (1 - discount) * price;
    else
        return cnt * price;
}
```

This function generates a discounted price: If the given quantity is more than `min_qty`, we apply the `discount` (which was stored as a fraction) to the `price`.

Because each derived object has a base-class part, classes may access the `public` and `protected` members of its base class as if those members were members of the derived class itself.

A Class Must Be Defined to Be Used as a Base Class

A class must be defined before it can be used as a base class. Had we declared, but not defined, `Item_base`, we could not use it as our base class:

```
class Item_base;   // declared but not defined
```

```
// error: Item_base must be defined
class Bulk_item : public Item_base { ... };
```

The reason for this restriction should already be easy to see: Each derived class contains, and may access, the members of its base class. To use those members, the derived class must konw what they are. One implication of this rule is that it is impossible to derive a class from itself.

Using a Derived Class as a Base Class

A base class can itself be a derived class:

```
class Base { /* ... */ };
class D1: public Base { /* ... */ };
class D2: public D1 { /* ... */ };
```

Each class inherits all the members of its base class. The most derived type inherits the members of its base, which in turn inherits the members of its base and so on up the inheritance chain. Effectively, the most derived object contains a subobject for each of its **immediate-base** and **indirect-base** classes.

Declarations of Derived Classes

If we need to declare (but not yet define) a derived class, the declaration contains the class name but does not include its derivation list. For example, the following forward declaration of `Bulk_item` results in a compile-time error:

```
// error: a forward declaration must not include the derivation list
class Bulk_item : public Item_base;
```

The correct forward declarations are:

```
// forward declarations of both derived and nonderived class
class Bulk_item;
class Item_base;
```

15.2.4 `virtual` and Other Member Functions

By default, function calls in C++ do not use dynamic binding. To trigger dynamic binding, two conditions must be met: First, only member functions that are specified as virtual can be dynamically bound. By default, member functions are not

EXERCISES SECTION 15.2.3

Exercise 15.5: Which of the following declarations, if any, are incorrect?

```
class Base { ... };

(a) class Derived : public Derived { ... };
(b) class Derived : Base { ... };
(c) class Derived : private Base { ... };
(d) class Derived : public Base;
(e) class Derived inherits Base { ... };
```

Exercise 15.6: Write your own version of the `Bulk_item` class.

Exercise 15.7: We might define a type to implement a limited discount strategy. This class would give a discount for books purchased up to a limit. If the number of copies purchased exceeds that limit, then the normal price should be applied to any books purchased beyond the limit. Define a class that implements this strategy.

virtual; nonvirtual functions are not dynamically bound. Second, the call must be made through a reference or a pointer to a base-class type. To understand this requirement, we need to understand what happens when we use a reference or pointer to an object that has a type from an inheritance hierarchy.

Derived to Base Conversions

Because every derived object contains a base part, we can bind a base-type reference to the base-class part of a derived object. We can also use a pointer to base to point to a derived object:

```
// function with an Item_base reference parameter
double print_total(const Item_base&, size_t);
Item_base item;           // object of base type
// ok: use pointer or reference to Item_base to refer to an Item_base object
print_total(item, 10); // passes reference to an Item_base object
Item_base *p = &item;     // p points to an Item_base object

Bulk_item bulk;           // object of derived type
// ok: can bind a pointer or reference to Item_base to a Bulk_item object
print_total(bulk, 10); // passes reference to the Item_base part of bulk
p = &bulk;                // p points to the Item_base part of bulk
```

This code uses the same base-type pointer to point to an object of the base type and to an object of the derived type. It also calls a function that expects a reference to the base type, passing an object of the base-class type and also passing an object of the derived type. Both uses are fine, because every derived object has a base part.

Because we can use a base-type pointer or reference to refer to a derived-type object, when we use a base-type reference or pointer, we don't know the type of the object to which the pointer or reference is bound: A base-type reference or pointer might refer to an object of base type or an object of derived type. Regardless of which actual type the object has, the compiler treats the object as if it is a base type object. Treating a derived object as if it were a base is safe, because every derived object has a base subobject. Also, the derived class inherits the operations of the base class, meaning that any operation that might be performed on a base object is available through the derived object as well.

> The crucial point about references and pointers to base-class types is that the **static type**—the type of the reference or pointer, which is knowable at compile time—and the **dynamic type**—the type of the object to which the pointer or reference is bound, which is knowable only at run time—may differ.

Calls to `virtual` Functions May Be Resolved at Run time

Binding a base-type reference or pointer to a derived object has no effect on the underlying object. The object itself is unchanged and remains a derived object. The fact that the actual type of the object might differ from the static type of the reference or pointer addressing that object is the key to dynamic binding in C++.

When a virtual function is called through a reference or pointer, the compiler generates code to *decide at run time* which function to call. The function that is called is the one that corresponds to the dynamic type. As an example, let's look again at the `print_total` function:

```
//   calculate and print price for given number of copies, applying any discounts
void print_total(ostream &os,
                 const Item_base &item, size_t n)
{
    os << "ISBN: " << item.book() //  calls Item_base::book
       << "\tnumber sold: " << n << "\ttotal price: "
       //  virtual call: which version of net_price to call is resolved at run time
       << item.net_price(n) << endl;
}
```

Because the `item` parameter is a reference and `net_price` is virtual, the version of `net_price` that is called in `item.net_price(n)` depends at run time on the actual type of the argument bound to the `item` parameter:

```
Item_base base;
Bulk_item derived;
//  print_total makes a virtual call to net_price
print_total(cout, base, 10);     //  calls Item_base::net_price
print_total(cout, derived, 10);  //  calls Bulk_item::net_price
```

In the first call, the `item` parameter is bound, at run time, to an object of type `Item_base`. As a result, the call to `net_price` inside `print_total` calls the version defined in `Item_base`. In the second call, `item` is bound to an object of type `Bulk_item`. In this call, the version of `net_price` called from `print_total` will be the one defined by the `Bulk_item` class.

KEY CONCEPT: POLYMORPHISM IN C++

The fact that the static and dynamic types of references and pointers can differ is the cornerstone of how C++ supports polymorphism.

When we call a function defined in the base class through a base-class reference or pointer, we do not know the precise type of the object on which the function is executed. The object on which the function executes might be of the base type or it might be an object of a derived type.

If the function called is nonvirtual, then regardless of the actual object type, the function that is executed is the one defined by the base type. If the function is virtual, then the decision as to which function to run is delayed until run time. The version of the virtual function that is run is the one defined by the type of the object to which the reference is bound or to which the pointer points.

From the perspective of the code that we write, we need not care. As long as the classes are designed and implemented correctly, the operations will do the right thing whether the actual object is of base or derived type.

On the other hand, an object is not polymorphic—its type is known and unchanging. The dynamic type of an object (as opposed to a reference or pointer) is always the same as the static type of the object. The function that is run, virtual or nonvirtual, is the one defined by the type of the object.

 Virtuals are resolved at run time *only* if the call is made through a reference or pointer. Only in these cases is it possible for an object's dynamic type to be unknown until run time.

Nonvirtual Calls Are Resolved at Compile Time

Regardless of the actual type of the argument passed to `print_total`, the call of `book` is resolved at compile time to `Item_base::book`.

 Even if `Bulk_item` defined its own version of the `book` function, this call would call the one from the base class.

Nonvirtual functions are *always* resolved at compile time based on the type of the object, reference, or pointer from which the function is called. The type of `item` is reference to `const Item_base`, so a call to a nonvirtual function on that object will call the one from `Item_base` regardless of the type of the actual object to which `item` refers at run time.

Overriding the Virtual Mechanism

In some cases, we want to override the virtual mechanism and force a call to use a particular version of a virtual function. We can do so by using the scope operator:

```
Item_base *baseP = &derived;
// calls version from the base class regardless of the dynamic type of baseP
double d = baseP->Item_base::net_price(42);
```

This code forces the call to `net_price` to be resolved to the version defined in `Item_base`. The call will be resolved at compile time.

Only code inside member functions should ever need to use the scope operator to override the virtual mechanism.

Why might we wish to override the virtual mechanism? The most common reason is when a derived-class virtual calls the version from the base. In such cases, the base-class version might do work common to all types in the hierarchy. Each derived type adds only whatever is particular to its own type.

For example, we might define a Camera hierarchy with a virtual display operation. The display function in the Camera class would display information common to all Cameras. A derived class, such as PerspectiveCamera, would need to display both that common information and the information unique to PerspectiveCamera. Rather than duplicate the Camera operations within PerspectiveCamera's implementation of display, we could explicitly invoke the Camera version to display the common information. In a case such as this one, we'd know exactly which instance to invoke, so there would be no need to go through the virtual mechanism.

When a derived virtual calls the base-class version, it *must* do so explicitly using the scope operator. If the derived function neglected to do so, then the call would be resolved at run time and would be a call to itself, resulting in an infinite recursion.

Virtual Functions and Default Arguments

Like any other function, a virtual function can have default arguments. As usual, the value, if any, of a default argument used in a given call is determined at compile time. If a call omits an argument that has a default value, then the value that is used is the one defined by the type through which the function is called, irrespective of the object's dynamic type. When a virtual is called through a reference or pointer to base, then the default argument is the value specified in the declaration of the virtual in the base class. If a virtual is called through a pointer or reference to derived, the default argument is the one declared in the version in the derived class.

Using different default arguments in the base and derived versions of the same virtual is almost guaranteed to cause trouble. Problems are likely to arise when the virtual is called through a reference or pointer to base, but the version that is executed is the one defined by the derived. In such cases, the default argument defined for the base version of the virtual will be passed to the derived version, which was defined using a different default argument.

15.2.5 Public, Private, and Protected Inheritance

Access to members defined within a derived class is controlled in exactly the same way as access is handled for any other class (Section 12.1.2, p. 432). A derived class may define zero or more access labels that specify the access level of the members following that label. Access to the members the class inherits is controlled by a

EXERCISES SECTION 15.2.4

Exercise 15.8: Given the following classes, explain each `print` function:

```
struct base {
    string name() { return basename; }
    virtual void print(ostream &os) { os << basename; }
private:
    string basename;
};

struct derived {
    void print() { print(ostream &os); os << " " << mem; }
private:
    int mem;
};
```

If there is a problem in this code, how would you fix it?

Exercise 15.9: Given the classes in the previous exercise and the following objects, determine which function is called at run time:

```
base bobj;      base *bp1 = &base;      base &br1 = bobj;
derived dobj;   base *bp2 = &doboj;     base &br2 = dobj;

(a) bobj.print();    (b) dobj.print();    (c) bp1->name();
(d) bp2->name();     (e) br1.print();     (f) br2.print();
```

combination of the access level of the member in the base class and the access label used in the derived class' derivation list.

 Each class controls access to the members it defines. A derived class may further restrict but may not loosen the access to the members that it inherits.

The base class itself specifies the minimal access control for its own members. If a member is `private` in the base class, then only the base class and its friends may access that member. The derived class has no access to the `private` members of its base class, nor can it make those members accessible to its own users. If a base class member is `public` or `protected`, then the access label used in the derivation list determines the access level of that member in the derived class:

- In **public inheritance**, the members of the base retain their access levels: The `public` members of the base are `public` members of the derived and the `protected` members of the base are `protected` in the derived.

- In **protected inheritance**, the `public` and `protected` members of the base class are `protected` members in the derived class.

- In **private inheritance**, all the members of the base class are `private` in the derived class.

As an example, consider the following hierarchy:

```
class Base {
public:
    void basemem();    // public member
protected:
    int i;             // protected member
    // ...
};
struct Public_derived : public Base {
    int use_base() { return i; }  // ok: derived classes can access i
    // ...
};
struct Private_derived : private Base {
    int use_base() { return i; }  // ok: derived classes can access i
};
```

All classes that inherit from Base have the same access to the members in Base, regardless of the access label in their derivation lists. The derivation access label controls the access that *users* of the derived class have to the members inherited from Base:

```
Base b;
Public_derived d1;
Private_derived d2;

b.basemem();   // ok: basemem is public
d1.basemem();  // ok: basemem is public in the derived class
d2.basemem();  // error: basemem is private in the derived class
```

Both Public_derived and Private_derived inherit the basemem function. That member retains its access level when the inheritance is public, so d1 can call basemem. In Private_derived, the members of Base are private; users of Private_derived may not call basemem.

The derivation access label also controls access from indirectly derived classes:

```
struct Derived_from_Private : public Private_derived {
    // error: Base::i is private in Private_derived
    int use_base() { return i; }
};
struct Derived_from_Public : public Public_derived {
    // ok: Base::i remains protected in Public_derived
    int use_base() { return i; }
};
```

Classes derived from Public_derived may access i from the Base class because that member remains a protected member in Public_derived. Classes derived from Private_derived have no such access. To them all the members that Private_base inherited from Base are private.

Interface versus Implementation Inheritance

A `publicly` derived class inherits the interface of its base class; it has the same interface as its base class. In well-designed class hierarchies, objects of a `publicly` derived class can be used wherever an object of the base class is expected.

Classes derived using either `private` or `protected` do not inherit the base-class interface. Instead, these derivations are often referred to as implementation inheritance. The derived class uses the inherited class in its implementation but does not expose the fact of the inheritance as part of its interface.

As we'll see in Section 15.3 (p. 577), whether a class uses interface or implementation inheritance has important implications for users of the derived class.

 By far the most common form of inheritance is `public`.

KEY CONCEPT: INHERITANCE VERSUS COMPOSITION

The design of inheritance hierarchies is a complex topic in its own right and well beyond the scope of this language primer. However, there is one important design guide that is so fundamental that every programmer should be familiar with it.

When we define one class as publicly inherited from another, the derived class should reflect a so-called "Is A" relationship to the base class. In our bookstore example, our base class represents the concept of a book sold at a stipulated price. Our `Bulk_item` is a kind of book, but one with a different pricing strategy.

Another common relationship among types is a so-called "Has A" relationship. Our bookstore classes have a price and they have an ISBN. Types related by a "Has A" relationship imply membership. Thus, our bookstore classes are composed from members representing the price and the ISBN.

Exempting Individual Members

When inheritance is `private` or `protected`, the access level of members of the base may be more restrictive in the derived class than it was in the base:

```
class Base {
public:
    std::size_t size() const { return n; }
protected:
    std::size_t n;
};
class Derived : private Base { . . . };
```

 The derived class can restore the access level of an inherited member. The access level cannot be made more or less restrictive than the level originally specified within the base class.

In this hierarchy, `size` is `public` in `Base` but `private` in `Derived`. To make size public in Derived we can add a using declaration for it to a public section in Derived. By changing the definition of Derived as follows, we can make the size member accessible to users and n accessible to classes subsequently derived from Derived:

```
class Derived : private Base {
public:
    // maintain access levels for members related to the size of the object
    using Base::size;
protected:
    using Base::n;
    // ...
};
```

Just as we can use a using declaration (Section 3.1, p. 78) to use names from the std namespace, we may also use a using declaration to access a name from a base class. The form is the same except that the left-hand side of the scope operator is a class name instead of a namespace name.

Default Inheritance Protection Levels

In Section 2.8 (p. 65) we learned that classes defined with the struct and class keywords have different default access levels. Similarly, the default inheritance access level differs depending on which keyword is used to define the derived class. A derived class defined using the class keyword has private inheritance. A class is defined with the struct keyword, has public inheritance:

```
class Base { /* ... */ };
struct D1 : Base { /* ... */ };   // public inheritance by default
class D2 : Base { /* ... */ };    // private inheritance by default
```

It is a common misconception to think that there are deeper differences between classes defined using the struct keyword and those defined using class. The only differences are the default protection level for members and the default protection level for a derivation. There are no other distinctions:

```
class D3 : public Base {
public:
    /* ... */
};
// equivalent definition of D3
struct D3 : Base {      // inheritance public by default
    /* ... */           // initial member access public by default
};
struct D4 : private Base {
private:
    /* ... */
};
// equivalent definition of D4
class D4 : Base {       // inheritance private by default
    /* ... */           // initial member access private by default
};
```

Although private inheritance is the default when using the `class` keyword, it is also relatively rare in practice. Because private inheritance is so rare, it is usually a good idea to explicitly specify `private`, rather than rely on the default. Being explicit makes it clear that private inheritance is intended and not an oversight.

EXERCISES SECTION 15.2.5

Exercise 15.10: In the exercises to Section 15.2.1 (p. 562) you wrote a base class to represent the lending policies of a library. Assume the library offers the following kinds of lending materials, each with its own check-out and check-in policy. Organize these items into an inheritance hierarchy:

book	audio book	record
children's puppet	sega video game	video
cdrom book	nintendo video game	rental book
sony playstation video game		

Exercise 15.11: Choose one of the following general abstractions containing a family of types (or choose one of your own). Organize the types into an inheritance hierarchy:

(a) Graphical file formats (such as gif, tiff, jpeg, bmp)
(b) Geometric primitives (such as box, circle, sphere, cone)
(c) C++ language types (such as class, function, member function)

Exercise 15.12: For the class you chose in the previous exercise, identify some of the likely virtual functions as well as `public` and `protected` members.

15.2.6 Friendship and Inheritance

As with any other class, a base or derived class can make other class(es) or function(s) friends (Section 12.5, p. 465). Friends may access the class' `private` and `protected` data.

Note Friendship is not inherited. Friends of the base have no special access to members of its derived classes. If a base class is granted friendship, only the base has special access. Classes derived from that base have no access to the class granting friendship.

Each class controls friendship to its own members:

```
class Base {
    friend class Frnd;
protected:
    int i;
};
```

```
//  Frnd has no access to members in D1
class D1 : public Base {
protected:
    int j;
};
class Frnd {
public:
    int mem(Base b) { return b.i; } // ok: Frnd is friend to Base
    int mem(D1 d) { return d.i; }    // error: friendship doesn't inherit
};
//  D2 has no access to members in Base
class D2 : public Frnd {
public:
    int mem(Base b) { return b.i; } // error: friendship doesn't inherit
};
```

If a derived class wants to grant access to its members to the friends of its base class, the derived class must do so explicitly: Friends of the base have no special access to types derived from that base class. Similarly, if a base and its derived types all need access to another class, that class must specifically grant access to the base and each derived class.

15.2.7   Inheritance and Static Members

If a base class defines a `static` member (Section 12.6, p. 467) there is only one such member defined for the entire hierarchy. Regardless of the number of classes derived from the base class, there exists a single instance of each `static` member.

`static` members obey normal access control: If the member is `private` in the base class, then derived classes have no access to it. Assuming the member is accessible, we can access the `static` member either through the base or derived class. As usual, we can use either the scope operator or the dot or arrow member access operators.

```
struct Base {
    static void statmem();    // public by default
};
struct Derived : Base {
    void f(const Derived&);
};
void Derived::f(const Derived &derived_obj)
{
    Base::statmem();     // ok: Base defines statmem
    Derived::statmem();  // ok: Derived inherits statmem
    //  ok: derived objects can be used to access static from base
    derived_obj.statmem();  // accessed through Derived object
    statmem();              // accessed through this class
```

15.3 Conversions and Inheritance

Understanding conversions between base and derived types is essential to understanding how object-oriented programming works in C++.

As we've seen, every derived object contains a base part, which means that we can execute operations on a derived object as if it were a base object. Because a derived object is also a base, there is an automatic conversion from a reference to a derived type to a reference to its base type(s). That is, we can convert a reference to a derived object to a reference to its base subobject and likewise for pointers.

Base-type objects can exist either as independent objects or as part of a derived object. Therefore, a base object might or might not be part of a derived object. As a result, there is no (automatic) conversion from reference (or pointer) to base to reference (or pointer) to derived.

The situation with respect to conversions of objects (as opposed to references or pointers) is more complicated. Although we can usually use an object of a derived type to initialize or assign an object of the base type, there is no direct conversion from an object of a derived type to an object of the base type.

15.3.1 Derived-to-Base Conversions

If we have an object of a derived type, we can use its address to assign or initialize a pointer to the base type. Similarly, we can use a reference or object of the derived type to initialize a reference to the base type. Pedantically speaking, there is no similar conversion for objects. The compiler will not automatically convert an object of derived type into an object of the base type.

It is, however, usually possible to use a derived-type object to initialize or assign an object of base type. The difference between initializing and/or assigning an object and the automatic conversion that is possible for a reference or pointer is subtle and must be well understood.

Conversion to a Reference is Not the Same as Converting an Object

As we've seen, we can pass an object of derived type to a function expecting a reference to base. We might therefore think that the object is converted. However, that is not what happens. When we pass an object to a function expecting a reference, the reference is bound directly to that object. Although it appears that we are passing an object, the argument is actually a reference to that object. The object itself is not copied and the conversion doesn't change the derived-type object in any way. It remains a derived-type object.

When we pass a derived object to a function expecting a base-type object (as opposed to a reference) the situation is quite different. In that case, the parameter's type is fixed—both at compile time and run time it will be a base-type object. If we call such a function with a derived-type object, then the base-class portion of that derived object is copied into the parameter.

It is important to understand the difference between converting a derived object to a base-type reference and using a derived object to initialize or assign to a base-type object.

Using a Derived Object to Initialize or Assign a Base Object

When we initialize or assign an object of base type, we are actually calling a function: When we initialize, we're calling a constructor; when we assign, we're calling an assignment operator.

When we use a derived-type object to initialize or assign a base object, there are two possibilities. The first (albeit unlikely) possibility is that the base class might explicitly define what it means to copy or assign an object of the derived type to an object of the base type. It would do so by defining an appropriate constructor or assignment operator:

```
class Derived;
class Base {
public:
    Base(const Derived&); // create a new Base from a Derived
    Base &operator=(const Derived&); // assign from a Derived
    // ...
};
```

In this case, the definition of these members would control what happens when a Derived object is used to initialize or assign to a Base object.

However, it is uncommon for classes to define explicitly how to initialize or assign an object of the base type from an object of derived type. Instead, base classes ususally define (either explicitly or implicitly) their own copy constructor and assignment operator (Chapter 13). These members take a parameter that is a (const) reference to the base type. Because there is a conversion from reference to derived to reference to base, these copy-control members can be used to initialize or assign a base object from a derived object:

```
Item_base item;          //  object of base type
Bulk_item bulk;          //  object of derived type
```

```
//  ok: uses Item_base::Item_base(const Item_base&) constructor
Item_base item(bulk);  //  bulk is "sliced down" to its Item_base portion
//  ok: calls Item_base::operator=(const Item_base&)
item = bulk;               //  bulk is "sliced down" to its Item_base portion
```

When we call the `Item_base` copy constructor or assignment operator on an object of type `Bulk_item`, the following steps happen:

- The `Bulk_item` object is converted to a reference to `Item_base`, which means only that an `Item_base` reference is bound to the `Bulk_item` object.

- That reference is passed as an argument to the copy constructor or assignment operator.

- Those operators use the `Item_base` part of `Bulk_item` to initialize and assign, respectively, the members of the `Item_base` on which the constructor or assignment was called.

- Once the operator completes, the object is an `Item_base`. It contains a copy of the `Item_base` part of the `Bulk_item` from which it was initialized or assigned, but the `Bulk_item` parts of the argument are ignored.

In these cases, we say that the `Bulk_item` portion of `bulk` is "sliced down" as part of the initialization or assignment to `item`. An `Item_base` object contains only the members defined in the base class. It does not contain the members defined by any of its derived types. There is no room in an `Item_base` object for the derived members.

Accessibility of Derived-to-Base Conversion

Like an inherited member function, the conversion from derived to base may or may not be accessible. Whether the conversion is accessible depends on the access label specified on the derived class' derivation.

 To determine whether the conversion to base is accessible, consider whether a `public` member of the base class would be accessible. If so, the conversion is accessible; otherwise, it is not.

If the inheritance is `public`, then both user code and member functions of subsequently derived classes may use the derived-to-base conversion. If a class is derived using `private` or `protected` inheritance, then user code may not convert an object of derived type to a base type object. If the inheritance is `private`, then classes derived from the `privately` inherited class may not convert to the base class. If the inheritance is `protected`, then the members of subsequently derived classes may convert to the base type.

Regardless of the derivation access label, a `public` member of the base class is accessible to the derived class itself. Therefore, the derived-to-base conversion is always accessible to the members and friends of the derived class itself.

15.3.2   Conversions from Base to Derived

There is no automatic conversion from the base class to a derived class. We cannot use a base object when a derived object is required:

```
Item_base base;
Bulk_item* bulkP = &base;    // error: can't convert base to derived
Bulk_item& bulkRef = base;   // error: can't convert base to derived
Bulk_item bulk = base;       // error: can't convert base to derived
```

The reason that there is no (automatic) conversion from base type to derived type is that a base object might be just that—a base. It does not contain the members of the derived type. If we were allowed to assign a base object to a derived type, then we might attempt to use that derived object to access members that do not exist.

What is sometimes a bit more surprising is that the restriction on converting from base to derived exists even when a base pointer or reference is actually bound to a derived object:

```
Bulk_item bulk;
Item_base *itemP = &bulk;    // ok: dynamic type is Bulk_item
Bulk_item *bulkP = itemP;    // error: can't convert base to derived
```

The compiler has no way to know at compile time that a specific conversion will actually be safe at run time. The compiler looks only at the static types of the pointer or reference to determine whether a conversion is legal.

In those cases when we *know* that the conversion from base to derived is safe, we can use a `static_cast` (Section 5.12.4, p. 183) to override the compiler. Alternatively, we could request a conversion that is checked at run time by using a `dynamic_cast`, which is covered in Section 18.2.1 (p. 773).

15.4   Constructors and Copy Control

The fact that each derived object consists of the (non`static`) members defined in the derived class plus one or more base-class subobjects affects how derived-type objects are constructed, copied, assigned, and destroyed. When we construct, copy, assign, or destroy an object of derived type, we also construct, copy, assign, or destroy those base-class subobjects.

Constructors and the copy-control members are not inherited; each class defines its own constructor(s) and copy-control members. As is the case for any class, synthesized versions of the default constructor and the copy-control members will be used if the class does not define its own versions.

15.4.1   Base-Class Constructors and Copy Control

Constructors and copy control for base classes that are not themselves a derived class are largely unaffected by inheritance. Our `Item_base` constructor looks like many we've seen before:

```
Item_base(const std::string &book = "",
          double sales_price = 0.0):
                  isbn(book), price(sales_price) { }
```

The only impact inheritance has on base-class constructors is that there is a new kind of user that must be considered when deciding which constructors to offer. Like any other member, constructors can be made `protected` or `private`. Some classes need special constructors that are intended only for their derived classes to use. Such constructors should be made `protected`.

15.4.2 Derived-Class Constructors

Derived constructors are affected by the fact that they inherit from another class. Each derived constructor initializes its base class in addition to initializing its own data members.

The Synthesized Derived-Class Default Constructor

A derived-class synthesized default constructor (Section 12.4.3, p. 458) differs from a nonderived constructor in only one way: In addition to initializing the data members of the derived class, it also initializes the base part of its object. The base part is initialized by the default constructor of the base class.

For our `Bulk_item` class, the synthesized default constructor would execute as follows:

1. Invoke the `Item_base` default constructor, which initializes the `isbn` member to the empty string and the `price` member to zero.

2. Initialize the members of `Bulk_item` using the normal variable initialization rules, which means that the `qty` and `discount` members would be uninitialized.

Defining a Default Constructor

Because `Bulk_item` has members of built-in type, we should define our own default constructor:

```
class Bulk_item : public Item_base {
public:
    Bulk_item(): min_qty(0), discount(0.0) { }
    // as before
};
```

This constructor uses the constructor initializer list (Section 7.7.3, p. 263) to initialize its `min_qty` and `discount` members. The constructor initializer also implicitly invokes the `Item_base` default constructor to initialize its base-class part.

The effect of running this constructor is that first the `Item_base` part is initialized using the `Item_base` default constructor. That constructor sets `isbn` to the empty string and `price` to zero. After the `Item_base` constructor finishes, the members of the `Bulk_item` part are initialized, and the (empty) body of the constructor is executed.

Passing Arguments to a Base-Class Constructor

In addition to the default constructor, our `Item_base` class lets users initialize the `isbn` and `price` members. We'd like to support the same initialization for `Bulk_item` objects. In fact, we'd like our users to be able to specify values for the entire `Bulk_item`, including the discount rate and quantity.

The constructor initializer list for a derived-class constructor may initialize only the members of the derived class; it may not directly initialize its inherited members. Instead, a derived constructor indirectly initializes the members it inherits by including its base class in its constructor initializer list:

```cpp
class Bulk_item : public Item_base {
public:
    Bulk_item(const std::string& book, double sales_price,
              std::size_t qty = 0, double disc_rate = 0.0):
                  Item_base(book, sales_price),
                  min_qty(qty), discount(disc_rate) { }
    // as before
};
```

This constructor uses the two-parameter `Item_base` constructor to initialize its base subobject. It passes its own `book` and `sales_price` arguments to that constructor. We might use this constructor as follows:

```cpp
// arguments are the isbn, price, minimum quantity, and discount
Bulk_item bulk("0-201-82470-1", 50, 5, .19);
```

`bulk` is built by first running the `Item_base` constructor, which initializes `isbn` and `price` from the arguments passed in the `Bulk_item` constructor initializer. After the `Item_base` constructor finishes, the members of `Bulk_item` are initialized. Finally, the (empty) body of the `Bulk_item` constructor is run.

> The constructor initializer list supplies initial values for a class' base class and members. It does not specify the order in which those initializations are done. The base class is initialized first and then the members of the derived class are initialized in the order in which they are declared.

Using Default Arguments in a Derived Constructor

Of course, we might write these two `Bulk_item` constructors as a single constructor that takes default arguments:

```cpp
class Bulk_item : public Item_base {
public:
    Bulk_item(const std::string& book, double sales_price,
              std::size_t qty = 0, double disc_rate = 0.0):
                  Item_base(book, sales_price),
                  min_qty(qty), discount(disc_rate) { }
    // as before
};
```

Here we provide defaults for each parameter so that the constructor might be used with zero to four arguments.

Only an Immediate Base Class May Be Initialized

A class may initialize only its own immediate base class. An immediate base class is the class named in the derivation list. If class C is derived from class B, which is derived from class A, then B is the immediate base of C. Even though every C object contains an A part, the constructors for C may not initialize the A part directly. Instead, class C initializes B, and the constructor for class B in turn initializes A. The reason for this restriction is that the author of class B has specified how to construct and initialize objects of type B. As with any user of class B, the author of class C has no right to change that specification.

As a more concrete example, our bookstore might have several discount strategies. In addition to a bulk discount, it might offer a discount for purchases up to a certain quantity and then charge the full price thereafter. Or it might offer a discount for purchases above a certain limit but not for purchases up to that limit.

Each of these discount strategies is the same in that it requires a quantity and a discount amount. We might support these differing strategies by defining a new class named Disc_item to store the quantity and the discount amount. This class would not define a net_price function but would serve as a base class for classes such as Bulk_item that define the different discount strategies.

> **KEY CONCEPT: REFACTORING**
>
> Adding Disc_item to the Item_base hierarchy is an example of refactoring. Refactoring involves redesigning a class hierarchy to move operations and/or data from one class to another. Refactoring happens most often when classes are redesigned to add new functionality or handle other changes in that application's requirements.
>
> Refactoring is common in OO applications. It is noteworthy that even though we changed the inheritance hierarchy, code that uses the Bulk_item or Item_base classes would not need to change. However, when classes are refactored, or changed in any other way, any code that uses those classes must be recompiled.

To implement this design, we first need to define the Disc_item class:

```
//   class to hold discount rate and quantity
//   derived classes will implement pricing strategies using these data
class Disc_item : public Item_base {
public:
    Disc_item(const std::string& book = "",
                double sales_price = 0.0,
                std::size_t qty = 0, double disc_rate = 0.0):
                    Item_base(book, sales_price),
                    quantity(qty), discount(disc_rate) { }
protected:
    std::size_t quantity;   //   purchase size for discount to apply
    double discount;        //   fractional discount to apply
};
```

This class inherits from `Item_base` and defines its own members, `discount` and `quantity`. Its only member function is the constructor, which initializes its `Item_base` base class and the members defined by `Disc_item`.

Next, we can reimplement `Bulk_item` to inherit from `Disc_item`, rather than inheriting directly from `Item_base`:

```cpp
// discount kicks in when a specified number of copies of same book are sold
// the discount is expressed as a fraction to use to reduce the normal price
class Bulk_item : public Disc_item {
public:
    Bulk_item(const std::string& book = "",
                double sales_price = 0.0,
                std::size_t qty = 0, double disc_rate = 0.0):
            Disc_item(book, sales_price, qty, disc_rate) { }
    // redefines base version so as to implement bulk purchase discount policy
    double net_price(std::size_t) const;
};
```

The `Bulk_item` class now has a direct base class, `Disc_item`, and an indirect base class, `Item_base`. Each `Bulk_item` object has three subobjects: an (empty) `Bulk_item` part and a `Disc_item` subobject, which in turn has an `Item_base` base subobject.

Even though `Bulk_item` has no data members of its own, it defines a constructor in order to obtain values to use to initialize its inherited members.

A derived constructor may initialize only its immediate base class. Naming `Item_base` in the `Bulk_item` constructor initializer would be an error.

> **KEY CONCEPT: RESPECTING THE BASE-CLASS INTERFACE**
>
> The reason that a constructor can initialize only its immediate base class is that each class defines its own interface. When we define `Disc_item`, we specify how to initialize a `Disc_item` by defining its constructors. Once a class has defined its interface, all interactions with objects of that class should be through that interface, even when those objects are part of a derived object.
>
> For similar reasons, derived-class constructors may not initialize and should not assign to the members of its base class. When those members are `public` or `protected`, a derived constructor could assign values to its base class members inside the constructor body. However, doing so would violate the interface of the base. Derived classes should respect the initialization intent of their base classes by using constructors rather than assigning to these members in the body of the constructor.

15.4.3 Copy Control and Inheritance

Like any other class, a derived class may use the synthesized copy-control members described in Chapter 13. The synthesized operations copy, assign, or destroy the base-class part of the object along with the members of the derived part. The

---

EXERCISES SECTION 15.4.2

Exercise 15.14: Redefine the `Bulk_item` and `Item_base` classes so that they each need to define only a single constructor.

Exercise 15.15: Identify the base- and derived-class constructors for the library class hierarchy described in the first exercise on page 575.

Exercise 15.16: Given the following base class definition,

```
struct Base {
    Base(int val): id(val) { }
protected:
    int id;
};
```

explain why each of the following constructors is illegal.

```
(a) struct C1 : public Base {
        C1(int val): id(val) { }
    };
(b) struct C2 : public C1 {
        C2(int val): Base(val), C1(val){ }
    };
(c) struct C3 : public C1 {
        C3(int val): Base(val) { }
    };
(d) struct C4 : public Base {
        C4(int val) : Base(id + val){ }
    };
(e) struct C5 : public Base {
        C5() { }
    };
```

---

base part is copied, assigned, or destroyed by using the base class' copy constructor, assignment operator, or destructor.

Whether a class needs to define the copy-control members depends entirely on the class' own direct members. A base class might define its own copy control while the derived uses the synthesized versions or vice versa.

Classes that contain only data members of class type or built-in types other than pointers usually can use the synthesized operations. No special control is required to copy, assign, or destroy such members. Classes with pointer members often need to define their own copy control to manage these members.

Our `Item_base` class and its derived classes can use the synthesized versions of the copy-control operations. When a `Bulk_item` is copied, the (synthesized) copy constructor for `Item_base` is invoked to copy the isbn and price members. The isbn member is copied by using the string copy constructor; the price member is copied directly. Once the base part is copied, then the derived part is copied. Both members of `Bulk_item` are doubles, and these members are copied directly. The assignment operator and destructor are handled similarly.

Defining a Derived Copy Constructor

 If a derived class explicitly defines its own copy constructor or assignment operator, that definition completely overrides the defaults. The copy constructor and assignment operator for inherited classes are responsible for copying or assigning their base-class components as well as the members in the class itself.

If a derived class defines its own copy constructor, that copy constructor usually should explicitly use the base-class copy constructor to initialize the base part of the object:

```
class Base { /* ... */ };
class Derived: public Base {
public:
    // Base::Base(const Base&) not invoked automatically
    Derived(const Derived& d):
        Base(d) /* other member initialization */ { /*... */ }
};
```

The initializer `Base(d)` converts (Section 15.3, p. 577) the derived object, d, to a reference to its base part and invokes the base-class copy constructor. Had the initializer for the base class been omitted,

```
// probably incorrect definition of the Derived copy constructor
Derived(const Derived& d) /* derived member initizations */
                          { /* ... */ }
```

the effect would be to run the `Base` default constructor to initialize the base part of the object. Assuming that the initialization of the `Derived` members copied the corresponding elements from d, then the newly constructed object would be oddly configured: Its `Base` part would hold default values, while its `Derived` members would be copies of another object.

Derived-Class Assignment Operator

As usual, the assignment operator is similar to the copy constructor: If the derived class defines its own assignment operator, then that operator must assign the base part explicitly:

```
// Base::operator=(const Base&) not invoked automatically
Derived &Derived::operator=(const Derived &rhs)
{
    if (this != &rhs) {
        Base::operator=(rhs); // assigns the base part
        // do whatever needed to clean up the old value in the derived part
        // assign the members from the derived
    }
    return *this;
}
```

The assignment operator must, as always, guard against self-assignment. Assuming the left- and right-hand operands differ, then we call the `Base` class assignment operator to assign the base-class portion. That operator might be defined by the class or it might be the synthesized assignment operator. It doesn't matter—we can call it directly. The base-class operator will free the old value in the base part of the left-hand operand and will assign the new values from `rhs`. Once that operator finishes, we continue doing whatever is needed to assign the members in the derived class.

Derived-Class Destructor

The destructor works differently from the copy constructor and assignment operator: The derived destructor is never responsible for destroying the members of its base objects. The compiler always implicitly invokes the destructor for the base part of a derived object. Each destructor does only what is necessary to clean up its own members:

```
class Derived: public Base {
public:
    // Base::~Base invoked automatically
    ~Derived() { /* do what it takes to clean up derived members */ }
};
```

Objects are destroyed in the opposite order from which they are constructed: The derived destructor is run first, and then the base-class destructors are invoked, walking back up the inheritance hierarchy.

15.4.4 Virtual Destructors

The fact that destructors for the base parts are invoked automatically has an important consequence for the design of base classes.

When we `delete` a pointer that points to a dynamically allocated object, the destructor is run to clean up the object before the memory for that object is freed. When dealing with objects in an inheritance hierarchy, it is possible that the static type of the pointer might differ from the dynamic type of the object that is being deleted. We might `delete` a pointer to the base type that actually points to a derived object.

If we `delete` a pointer to base, then the base-class destructor is run and the members of the base are cleaned up. If the object really is a derived type, then the behavior is undefined. To ensure that the proper destructor is run, the destructor must be virtual in the base class:

```
class Item_base {
public:
    // no work, but virtual destructor needed
    // if base pointer that points to a derived object is ever deleted
    virtual ~Item_base() { }
};
```

If the destructor is virtual, then when it is invoked through a pointer, which destructor is run will vary depending on the type of the object to which the pointer points:

```
Item_base *itemP = new Item_base; //  same static and dynamic type
delete itemP;                     //  ok: destructor for Item_base called
itemP = new Bulk_item;            //  ok: static and dynamic types differ
delete itemP;                     //  ok: destructor for Bulk_item called
```

Like other virtual functions, the virtual nature of the destructor is inherited. Therefore, if the destructor in the root class of the hierarchy is virtual, then the derived destructors will be virtual as well. A derived destructor will be virtual whether the class explicitly defines its destructor or uses the synthesized destructor.

Destructors for base classes are an important exception to the Rule of Three (Section 13.3, p. 485). That rule says that if a class needs a destructor, then the class almost surely needs the other copy-control members. A base class almost always needs a destructor so that it can make the destructor virtual. If a base class has an empty destructor in order to make it virtual, then the fact that the class has a destructor is not an indication that the assignment operator or copy constructor is also needed.

 Best Practices The root class of an inheritance hierarchy should define a virtual destructor even if the destructor has no work to do.

Constructors and Assignment Are Not Virtual

Of the copy-control members, only the destructor should be defined as virtual. Constructors cannot be defined as virtual. Constructors are run before the object is fully constructed. While the constructor is running, the object's dynamic type is not complete.

Although we can define a virtual operator= member function in the base class, doing so does not affect the assignment operators used in the derived classes. Each class has its own assignment operator. The assignment operator in a derived class has a parameter that has the same type as the class itself. That type must differ from the parameter type for the assignment operator in any other class in the hierarchy.

Making the assignment operator virtual is likely to be confusing because a virtual function must have the same parameter type in base and derived classes. The base-class assignment operator has a parameter that is a reference to its own class type. If that operator is virtual, then each class gets a virtual member that defines an operator= that takes a base object. But this operator is not the same as the assignment operator for the derived class.

 Making the class assignment operator virtual is likely to be confusing and unlikely to be useful.

Beware

EXERCISES SECTION 15.4.4

Exercise 15.17: Describe the conditions under which a class should have a virtual destructor.

Exercise 15.18: What operations must a virtual destructor perform?

Exercise 15.19: What if anything is likely to be incorrect about this class definition?

```
class AbstractObject {
public:
    virtual void doit();
    // other members not including any of the copy-control functions
};
```

Exercise 15.20: Recalling the exercise from Section 13.3 (p. 487) in which you wrote a class whose copy-control members printed a message, add print statements to the constructors of the `Item_base` and `Bulk_item` classes. Define the copy-control members to do the same job as the synthesized versions but that also print a message. Now write programs using objects and functions that use the `Item_base` types. In each case, predict what objects will be created and destroyed and compare your predictions with what your programs generate. Continue experimenting until you can correctly predict which copy-control members are executed for a given bit of code.

15.4.5 Virtuals in Constructors and Destructors

A derived object is constructed by first running a base-class constructor to initialize the base part of the object. While the base-class constructor is executing, the derived part of the object is uninitialized. In effect, the object is not yet a derived object.

When a derived object is destroyed, its derived part is destroyed first, and then its base parts are destroyed in the reverse order of how they were constructed.

In both cases, while a constructor or destructor is running, the object is incomplete. To accommodate this incompleteness, the compiler treats the object as if its type changes during construction or destruction. Inside a base-class constructor or destructor, a derived object is treated as if it were an object of the base type.

The type of an object during construction and destruction affects the binding of virtual functions.

> If a virtual is called from inside a constructor or destructor, then the version that is run is the one defined for the type of the constructor or destructor itself.

This binding applies to a virtual whether the virtual is called directly by the constructor (or destructor) or is called indirectly from a function that the constructor (or destructor) called.

To understand this behavior, consider what would happen if the derived-class version of a virtual function were called from a base-class constructor (or destructor). The derived version of the virtual probably accesses members of the derived object. After all, if the derived-class version didn't need to use members from the derived object, the derived class could probably use the definition from the base class. However, the members of the derived part of the object aren't initialized while the base constructor (or destructor) is running. In practice, if such access were allowed, the program would probably crash.

15.5   Class Scope under Inheritance

Each class maintains its own scope (Section 12.3, p. 444) within which the names of its members are defined. Under inheritance, the scope of the derived class is nested within the scope of its base classes. If a name is unresolved within the scope of the derived class, the enclosing base-class scope(s) are searched for a definition of that name.

It is this hierarchical nesting of class scopes under inheritance that allows the members of the base class to be accessed directly as if they are members of the derived class. When we write

```
Bulk_item bulk;
cout << bulk.book();
```

the use of the name book is resolved as follows:

1. bulk is an object of the Bulk_item class. The Bulk_item class is searched for book. That name is not found.

2. Because Bulk_item is derived from Item_Base, the Item_Base class is searched next. The name book is found in the Item_base class. The reference is resolved successfully.

15.5.1   Name Lookup Happens at Compile Time

The static type of an object, reference, or pointer determines the actions that the object can perform. Even when the static and dynamic types might differ, as can happen when a reference or pointer to a base type is used, the static type determines what members can be used. As an example, we might add a member to the Disc_item class that returns a pair holding the minimum (or maximum) quantity and the discounted price:

```
class Disc_item : public Item_base {
public:
    std::pair<size_t, double> discount_policy() const
        { return std::make_pair(quantity, discount); }
    // other members as before
};
```

We can access discount_policy only through an object, pointer, or reference of type Disc_item or a class derived from Disc_item:

```
Bulk_item bulk;
Bulk_item *bulkP = &bulk;    // ok: static and dynamic types are the same
Item_base *itemP = &bulk;    // ok: static and dynamic types differ

bulkP->discount_policy();     // ok: bulkP has type Bulk_item*

itemP->discount_policy();     // error: itemP has type Item_base*
```

The call through `itemP` is an error because a pointer (reference or object) to a base type can access only the base parts of an object and there is no `discount_policy` member defined in the base class.

EXERCISES SECTION 15.5.1

Exercise 15.21: Redefine your `Item_base` hierarchy to include a `Disc_item` class.

Exercise 15.22: Redefine `Bulk_item` and the class you implemented in the exercises from Section 15.2.3 (p. 567) that represents a limited discount strategy to inherit from `Disc_item`.

15.5.2   Name Collisions and Inheritance

Although a base-class member can be accessed directly as if it were a member of the derived class, the member retains its base-class membership. Normally we do not care which actual class contains the member. We usually need to care only when a base- and derived-class member share the same name.

A derived-class member with the same name as a member of the base class hides direct access to the base-class member.

```
struct Base {
    Base(): mem(0) { }
protected:
    int mem;
};
struct Derived : Base {
    Derived(int i): mem(i) { }         // initializes Derived::mem
    int get_mem() { return mem; }      // returns Derived::mem
protected:
    int mem;     // hides mem in the base
};
```

The reference to `mem` inside `get_mem` is resolved to the name inside `Derived`. Were we to write

```
Derived d(42);
cout << d.get_mem() << endl;           // prints 42
```

then the output would be `42`.

Using the Scope Operator to Access Hidden Members

We can access a hidden base-class member by using the scope operator:

```
struct Derived : Base {
    int get_base_mem() { return Base::mem; }
};
```

The scope operator directs the compiler to look for mem starting in Base.

 Best Practices When designing a derived class, it is best to avoid name collisions with members of the base class whenever possible.

EXERCISES SECTION 15.5.2

Exercise 15.23: Given the following base- and derived-class definitions

```
struct Base {
    foo(int);
protected:
    int bar;
    double foo_bar;
};

struct Derived : public Base {
    foo(string);
    bool bar(Base *pb);
    void foobar();
protected:
    string bar;
};
```

identify the errors in each of the following examples and how each might be fixed:

```
(a) Derived d; d.foo(1024);
(b) void Derived::foobar() { bar = 1024; }
(c) bool Derived::bar(Base *pb)
        { return foo_bar == pb->foo_bar; }
```

15.5.3   Scope and Member Functions

A member function with the same name in the base and derived class behaves the same way as a data member: The derived-class member hides the base-class member within the scope of the derived class. The base member is hidden, *even if the prototypes of the functions differ*:

```
struct Base {
    int memfcn();
};
```

```
struct Derived : Base {
    int memfcn(int);     // hides memfcn in the base
};
Derived d; Base b;
b.memfcn();              // calls Base::memfcn
d.memfcn(10);            // calls Derived::memfcn
d.memfcn();              // error: memfcn with no arguments is hidden
d.Base::memfcn();        // ok: calls Base::memfcn
```

The declaration of `memfcn` in `Derived` hides the declaration in `Base`. Not surprisingly, the first call through b, which is a `Base` object, calls the version in the base class. Similarly, the second call through d calls the one from `Derived`. What can be surprising is the third call:

> `d.memfcn();` // error: Derived has no memfcn that takes no arguments

To resolve this call, the compiler looks for the name `memfcn`, which it finds in the class `Derived`. Once the name is found, the compiler looks no further. This call does not match the definition of `memfcn` in `Derived`, which expects an `int` argument. The call provides no such argument and so is in error.

Recall that functions declared in a local scope do not overload functions defined at global scope (Section 7.8.1, p. 268). Similarly, functions defined in a derived class do *not* overload members defined in the base. When the function is called through a derived object, the arguments must match a version of the function defined in the derived class. The base class functions are considered only if the derived does not define the function at all.

Overloaded Functions

As with any other function, a member function (virtual or otherwise) can be overloaded. A derived class can redefine zero or more of the versions it inherits.

If the derived class redefines any of the overloaded members, then only the one(s) redefined in the derived class are accessible through the derived type.

If a derived class wants to make all the overloaded versions available through its type, then it must either redefine all of them or none of them.

Sometimes a class needs to redefine the behavior of only some of the versions in an overloaded set, and wants to inherit the meaning for others. It would be tedious in such cases to have to redefine every base-class version in order to redefine the ones that the class needs to specialize.

Instead of redefining every base-class version that it inherits, a derived class can provide a `using` declaration (Section 15.2.5, p. 574) for the overloaded member. A `using` declaration specifies only a name; it may not specify a parameter list. Thus, a `using` declaration for a base-class member function name adds all the overloaded instances of that function to the scope of the derived-class. Having brought all the names into its scope, the derived class need redefine only those functions that it truly must define for its type. It can use the inherited definitions for the others.

15.5.4 Virtual Functions and Scope

Recall that to obtain dynamic binding, we must call a virtual member through a reference or a pointer to a base class. When we do so, the compiler looks for the function in the base class. Assuming the name is found, the compiler checks that the arguments match the parameters.

We can now understand why virtual functions must have the same prototype in the base and derived classes. If the base member took different arguments than the derived-class member, there would be no way to call the derived function from a reference or pointer to the base type. Consider the following (artificial) collection of classes:

```cpp
class Base {
public:
    virtual int fcn();
};
class D1 : public Base {
public:
    //  hides fcn in the base; this fcn is not virtual
    int fcn(int);  //  parameter list differs from fcn in Base
    //  D1 inherits definition of Base::fcn()
};
class D2 : public D1 {
public:
    int fcn(int);  //  nonvirtual function hides D1::fcn(int)
    int fcn();     //  redefines virtual fcn from Base
};
```

The version of fcn in D1 does not redefine the virtual fcn from Base. Instead, it hides fcn from the base. Effectively, D1 has two functions named fcn: The class inherits a virtual named fcn from the Base and defines its own, nonvirtual member named fcn that takes an int parameter. However, the virtual from the Base cannot be called from a D1 object (or reference or pointer to D1) because that function is hidden by the definition of fcn(int).

The class D2 redefines both functions that it inherits. It redefines the virtual version of fcn originally defined in Base and the nonvirtual defined in D1.

Calling a Hidden Virtual through the Base Class

When we call a function through a base-type reference or pointer, the compiler looks for that function in the base class and ignores the derived classes:

```cpp
Base bobj;  D1 d1obj;  D2 d2obj;
Base *bp1 = &bobj, *bp2 = &d1obj, *bp3 = &d2obj;
```

```
bp1->fcn();  //  ok: virtual call, will call Base::fcn at run time
bp2->fcn();  //  ok: virtual call, will call Base::fcn at run time
bp3->fcn();  //  ok: virtual call, will call D2::fcn at run time
```

All three pointers are pointers to the base type, so all three calls are resolved by looking in `Base` to see if `fcn` is defined. It is, so the calls are legal. Next, because `fcn` is virtual, the compiler generates code to make the call at run time based on the actual type of the object to which the reference or pointer is bound. In the case of `bp2`, the underlying object is a `D1`. That class did not redefine the virtual version of `fcn` that takes no arguments. The call through `bp2` is made (at run time) to the version defined in `Base`.

> **KEY CONCEPT: NAME LOOKUP AND INHERITANCE**
>
> Understanding how function calls are resolved is crucial to understanding inheritance hierarchies in C++. The following four steps are followed:
>
> 1. Start by determining the static type of the object, reference, or pointer through which the function is called.
>
> 2. Look for the function in that class. If it is not found, look in the immediate base class and continue up the chain of classes until either the function is found or the last class is searched. If the name is not found in the class or its enclosing base classes, then the call is in error.
>
> 3. Once the name is found, do normal type-checking (Section 7.1.2, p. 229) to see if this call is legal given the definition that was found.
>
> 4. Assuming the call is legal, the compiler generates code. If the function is virtual and the call is through a reference or pointer, then the compiler generates code to determine which version to run based on the dynamic type of the object. Otherwise, the compiler generates code to call the function directly.

15.6   Pure Virtual Functions

The `Disc_item` class that we wrote on page 583 presents an interesting problem: That class inherits the `net_price` function from `Item_base` but does not redefine it. We didn't redefine `net_price` because there is no meaning to ascribe to that function for the `Disc_item` class. A `Disc_item` doesn't correspond to any discount strategy in our application. This class exists solely for other classes to inherit from it.

We don't intend for users to define `Disc_item` objects. Instead, `Disc_item` objects should exist only as part of an object of a type derived from `Disc_item`. However, as defined, there is nothing that prevents users from defining a plain `Disc_item` object. That leaves open the question of what would happen if a user did create a `Disc_item` and invoked `net_price` function on it. We now know from the scope discussion in the previous section that the effect would be to call the `net_price` function inherited from `Item_base`, which generates the undiscounted price.

Exercise 15.24: Why is it that, given

```
Bulk_item bulk;
Item_base item(bulk);
Item_base *p = &bulk;
```

the expression

```
p->net_price(10);
```

invokes the `Bulk_item` instance of `net_price`, whereas

```
item.net_price(10);
```

invokes the `Item_base` instance?

Exercise 15.25: Assume `Derived` inherits from `Base` and that `Base` defines each of the following functions as virtual. Assuming `Derived` intends to define its own version of the virtual, determine which declarations in `Derived` are in error and specify what's wrong.

```
(a) Base* Base::copy(Base*);
    Base* Derived::copy(Derived*);
(b) Base* Base::copy(Base*);
    Derived* Derived::copy(Base*);
(c) ostream& Base::print(int, ostream&=cout);
    ostream& Derived::print(int, ostream&);
(d) void Base::eval() const;
    void Derived::eval();
```

It's hard to say what behavior users might expect from calling `net_price` on a `Disc_item`. The real problem is that we'd rather they couldn't create such objects at all. We can enforce this design intent and correctly indicate that there is no meaning for the `Disc_item` version of `net_price` by making `net_price` a **pure virtual function**. A pure virtual function is specified by writing = 0 after the function parameter list:

```
class Disc_item : public Item_base {
public:
    double net_price(std::size_t) const = 0;
};
```

Defining a virtual as pure indicates that the function provides an interface for subsequent types to override but that the version in this class will never be called. As importantly, users will not be able to create objects of type `Disc_item`.

An attempt to create an object of an abstract base class is a compile-time error:

```
// Disc_item declares pure virtual functions
Disc_item discounted;   // error: can't define a Disc_item object
Bulk_item bulk;         // ok: Disc_item subobject within Bulk_item
```

Note   A class containing (or inheriting) one or more pure virtual functions is an **abstract base class**. We may not create objects of an abstract type except as parts of objects of classes derived from the abstract base.

EXERCISES SECTION 15.6

Exercise 15.26: Make your version of the `Disc_item` class an abstract class.

Exercise 15.27: Try to define an object of type `Disc_item` and see what errors you get from the compiler.

15.7 Containers and Inheritance

We'd like to use containers (or built-in arrays) to hold objects that are related by inheritance. However, the fact that objects are not polymorphic (Section 15.3.1, p. 577) affects how we can use containers with types in an inheritance hierarchy.

As an example, our bookstore application would probably have the notion of a basket that represents the books a customer is buying. We'd like to be able to store the purchases in a `multiset` (Section 10.5, p. 375). To define the `multiset`, we must specify the type of the objects that the container will hold. When we put an object in a container, the element is copied (Section 9.3.3, p. 318).

If we define the `multiset` to hold objects of the base type

```
multiset<Item_base> basket;
Item_base base;
Bulk_item bulk;
basket.insert(base);   // ok: add copy of base to basket
basket.insert(bulk);   // ok: but bulk sliced down to its base part
```

then when we add objects that are of the derived type, only the base portion of the object is stored in the container. Remember, when we copy a derived object to a base object, the derived object is sliced down (Section 15.3.1, p. 577).

The elements in the container are `Item_base` objects. Regardless of whether the element was made as a copy of a `Bulk_item` object, when we calculate the `net_price` of an element the element would be priced without a discount. Once the object is put into the `multiset`, it is no longer a derived object.

Beware   Because derived objects are "sliced down" when assigned to a base object, containers and types related by inheritance do not mix well.

We cannot fix this problem by defining the container to hold derived objects. In this case, we couldn't put objects of `Item_base` into the container—there is no standard conversion from base to derived type. We could explicitly cast a base-type object into a derived and add the resulting object to the container. However, if we did so, disaster would strike when we tried to use such an element. In this case, the element would be treated as if it were a derived object, but the members of the derived part would be uninitialized.

The only viable alternative would be to use the container to hold pointers to our objects. This strategy works—but at the cost of pushing onto our users the problem of managing the objects and pointers. The user must ensure that the objects pointed to stay around for as long as the container. If the objects are dynamically allocated, then the user must ensure that they are properly freed when the container goes away. The next section presents a better and more common solution to this problem.

EXERCISES SECTION 15.7

Exercise 15.28: Define a `vector` to hold objects of type `Item_base` and copy a number of objects of type `Bulk_item` into the `vector`. Iterate over the `vector` and generate the `net_price` for the elements in the container.

Exercise 15.29: Repeat your program, but this time store pointers to objects of type `Item_base`. Compare the resulting sum.

Exercise 15.30: Explain any discrepancy in the amount generated by the previous two programs. If there is no discrepancy, explain why there isn't one.

15.8   Handle Classes and Inheritance

One of the ironies of object-oriented programming in C++ is that we cannot use objects to support it. Instead, we must use pointers and references, not objects. For example, in the following code fragment,

```
void get_prices(Item_base object,
                const Item_base *pointer,
                const Item_base &reference)
{
    // which version of net_price is called is determined at run time
    cout << pointer->net_price(1) << endl;
    cout << reference.net_price(1) << endl;

    // always invokes Item_base::net_price
    cout << object.net_price(1) << endl;
}
```

the invocations through `pointer` and `reference` are resolved at run time based on the dynamic types of the object to which they are bound.

Unfortunately, using pointers or references puts a burden on the users of our classes. We saw one such burden in the previous section that discussed the interactions between objects of inherited types and containers.

A common technique in C++ is to define a so-called cover or **handle** class. The handle class stores and manages a pointer to the base class. The type of the object to which that pointer points will vary; it can point at either a base- or a derived-type object. Users access the operations of the inheritance hierarchy through the handle. Because the handle uses its pointer to execute those operations, the behavior of virtual members will vary at run time depending on the kind of object to which the handle is actually bound. Users of the handle thus obtain dynamic behavior but do not themselves have to worry about managing the pointer.

Handles that cover an inheritance hierarchy have two important design considerations:

- As with any class that holds a pointer (Section 13.5, p. 492), we must decide what to do about copy control. Handles that cover an inheritance hierarchy typically behave like either a smart pointer (Section 13.5.1, p. 495) or a value (Section 13.5.2, p. 499).

- The handle class determines whether the handle interface will hide the inheritance hierarchy or expose it. If the hierarchy is not hidden, users must know about and use objects in the underlying hierarchy.

There is no one right choice among these options; the decisions depend on the details of the hierarchy and how the class designer wants programmers to interact with those class(es). In the next two sections, we'll implement two different kinds of handles that address these design questions in different ways.

15.8.1 A Pointerlike Handle

As our first example, we'll define a pointerlike handle class, named `Sales_item`, to represent our `Item_base` hierarchy. Users of `Sales_item` will use it as if it were a pointer: Users will bind a `Sales_item` to an object of type `Item_base` and will then use the * and -> operations to execute `Item_base` operations:

```
// bind a handle to a Bulk_item object
Sales_item item(Bulk_item("0-201-82470-1", 35, 3, .20));

item->net_price(); // virtual call to net_price function
```

However, users won't have to manage the object to which the handle points; the `Sales_item` class will do that part of the job. When users call a function through a `Sales_item`, they'll get polymorphic behavior.

Defining the Handle

We'll give our class three constructors: a default constructor, a copy constructor, and a constructor that takes an `Item_base`. This third constructor will copy the `Item_base` and ensure that the copy stays around as long as the `Sales_item` does. When we copy or assign a `Sales_item`, we'll copy the pointer rather than copying the object. As with our other pointerlike handle classes, we'll use a use count to manage the copies.

The use-counted classes we've used so far have used a companion class to store the pointer and associated use count. In this class, we'll use a different design, as illustrated in Figure 15.2. The `Sales_item` class will have two data members, both of which are pointers: One pointer will point to the `Item_base` object and the other will point to the use count. The `Item_base` pointer might point to an `Item_base` object or an object of a type derived from `Item_base`. By pointing to the use count, multiple `Sales_item` objects can share the same counter.

Figure 15.2: Use-Count Strategy for the `Sales_item` Handle Class

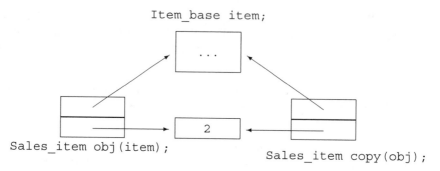

In addition to managing the use count, the `Sales_item` class will define the dereference and arrow operators:

```
//   use counted handle class for the Item_base hierarchy
class Sales_item {
public:
    //   default constructor: unbound handle
    Sales_item(): p(0), use(new std::size_t(1)) { }
    //   attaches a handle to a copy of the Item_base object
    Sales_item(const Item_base&);
    //   copy control members to manage the use count and pointers
    Sales_item(const Sales_item &i):
                        p(i.p), use(i.use) { ++*use; }
    ~Sales_item() { decr_use(); }
    Sales_item& operator=(const Sales_item&);
    //   member access operators
    const Item_base *operator->() const { if (p) return p;
        else throw std::logic_error("unbound Sales_item"); }
    const Item_base &operator*() const { if (p) return *p;
        else throw std::logic_error("unbound Sales_item"); }
private:
    Item_base *p;           //   pointer to shared item
    std::size_t *use;       //   pointer to shared use count
    //   called by both destructor and assignment operator to free pointers
    void decr_use()
        { if (--*use == 0) { delete p; delete use; } }
};
```

Use-Counted Copy Control

The copy-control members manipulate the use count and the `Item_base` pointer as appropriate. Copying a `Sales_item` involves copying the two pointers and incrementing the use count. The destructor decrements the use count and destroys the pointers if the count goes to zero. Because the assignment operator will need to do the same work, we implement the destructor's actions in a private utility function named `decr_use`.

The assignment operator is a bit more complicated than the copy constructor:

```
// use-counted assignment operator; use is a pointer to a shared use count
Sales_item&
Sales_item::operator=(const Sales_item &rhs)
{
    ++*rhs.use;
    decr_use();
    p = rhs.p;
    use = rhs.use;
    return *this;
}
```

The assignment operator acts like the copy constructor in that it increments the use count of the right-hand operand and copies the pointer. It also acts like the destructor in that we first have to decrement the use count of the left-hand operand and then delete the pointers if the use count goes to zero.

As usual with an assignment operator, we must protect against self-assignment. This operator handles self-assignment by first incrementing the use count in the right-hand operand. If the left- and right-hand operands are the same, the use count will be at least 2 when `decr_use` is called. That function decrements and checks the use count of the left-hand operand. If the use count goes to zero, then `decr_use` will free the `Item_base` and `use` objects currently in this object. What remains is to copy the pointers from the right-hand to the left-hand operand. As usual, our assignment operator returns a reference to the left-hand operand.

Aside from the copy-control members, the only other functions `Sales_item` defines are the operator functions, `operator*` and `operator->`. Users will access `Item_base` members through these operators. Because these operators return a pointer and reference, respectively, functions called through these operators will be dynamically bound.

We define only the `const` versions of these operators because the `public` members in the underlying `Item_base` hierarchy are all `const`.

Constructing the Handle

Our handle has two constructors: the default constructor, which creates an unbound `Sales_item`, and a second constructor, which takes an object to which it attaches the handle.

The first constructor is easy: We set the `Item_base` pointer to 0 to indicate that this handle is not attached to any object. The constructor allocates a new use counter and initializes it to 1.

The second constructor is more difficult. We'd like users of our handle to create their own objects, to which they could attach a handle. The constructor will allocate a new object of the appropriate type and copy the parameter into that newly allocated object. That way the `Sales_item` class will own the object and can guarantee that the object is not deleted until the last `Sales_item` attached to the object goes away.

15.8.2 Cloning an Unknown Type

To implement the constructor that takes an `Item_base`, we must first solve a problem: We do not know the actual type of the object that the constructor is given. We know that it is an `Item_base` or an object of a type derived from `Item_base`. Handle classes often need to allocate a new copy of an existing object *without knowing the precise type* of the object. Our `Sales_item` constructor is a good example.

> The common approach to solving this problem is to define a virtual operation to do the copy, which we'll name `clone`.

To support our handle class, we'll need to add `clone` to each of the types in the hierarchy, starting with the base class, which must define the function as virtual:

```
class Item_base {
public:
    virtual Item_base* clone() const
                          { return new Item_base(*this); }
};
```

Each class must now redefine the virtual. Because the function exists to generate a new copy of an object of the class, we'll define the return type to reflect the type of the class itself:

```
class Bulk_item : public Item_base {
public:
    Bulk_item* clone() const
        { return new Bulk_item(*this); }
};
```

On page 564 we said there is one exception to the requirement that the return type of the derived class must match exactly that of the base class instance. That exception supports cases such as this one. If the base instance of a virtual function returns a reference or pointer to a class type, the derived version of the virtual may return a class `publicly` derived from the class returned by the base class instance (or a pointer or a reference to a class type).

Defining the Handle Constructors

Once the `clone` function exists, we can write the `Sales_item` constructor:

```
Sales_item::Sales_item(const Item_base &item):
            p(item.clone()), use(new std::size_t(1)) { }
```

Like the default constructor, this constructor allocates and initializes its use count. It calls `clone` on its parameter to generate a (virtual) copy of that object. If the argument is an `Item_base`, then the `clone` function for `Item_base` is run; if the argument is a `Bulk_item`, then the `Bulk_item clone` is executed.

EXERCISES SECTION 15.8.2

Exercise 15.31: Define and implement the `clone` operation for the limited discount class implemented in the exercises for Section 15.2.3 (p. 567).

Exercise 15.32: In practice, our programs are unlikely to run correctly the first time we run them or the first time we run them against real data. It is often useful to incorporate a debugging strategy into the design of our classes. Implement a virtual `debug` function for our `Item_base` class hierarchy that displays the data members of the respective classes.

Exercise 15.33: Given the version of the `Item_base` hierarchy that includes the `Disc_item` abstract base class, indicate whether the `Disc_item` class should implement the `clone` function. If not, why not? If so, why?

Exercise 15.34: Modify your debug function to let users turn debugging on or off. Implement the control two ways:

(a) By defining a parameter to the `debug` function
(b) By defining a class data member that allows individual objects to turn on or turn off the display of debugging information

---

15.8.3 Using the Handle

Using `Sales_item` objects, we could more easily write our bookstore application. Our code wouldn't need to manage pointers to the `Item_base` objects, yet the code would obtain virtual behavior on calls made through a `Sales_item`.

As an example, we could use `Item_base` objects to solve the problem proposed in Section 15.7 (p. 597). We could use `Sales_items` to keep track of the purchases a customer makes, storing a `Sales_item` representing each purchase in a `multiset`. When the customer was done shopping, we would total the sale.

Comparing Two `Sales_items`

Before writing the function to total a sale, we need to define a way to compare `Sales_items`. To use `Sales_item` as the key in an associative container, we must be able to compare them (Section 10.3.1, p. 360). By default, the associative containers use the less-than operator on the key type. However, for the same reasons discussed about our original `Sales_item` type in Section 14.3.2 (p. 520), defining `operator<` for the `Sales_item` handle would be a bad idea: We want to take only the ISBN into account when we use `Sales_item` as a key, but want to consider all data members when determining equality.

Fortunately, the associative containers allow us to specify a function (or function object (Section 14.8, p. 530)) to use as the comparison function. We do so similarly to the way we passed a separate function to the `stable_sort` algorithm in Section 11.2.3 (p. 403). In that case, we needed only to pass an additional argument to `stable_sort` to provide a comparison function to use in place of the `<` operator. Overriding an associative container's comparison function is a bit more complicated because, as we shall see, we must supply the comparison function when we define the container object.

Let's start with the easy part, which is to define a function to use to compare `Sales_item` objects:

```
// compare defines item ordering for the multiset in Basket
inline bool
compare(const Sales_item &lhs, const Sales_item &rhs)
{
    return lhs->book() < rhs->book();
}
```

Our `compare` function has the same interface as the less-than operator. It returns a `bool` and takes two `const` references to `Sales_item`s. It compares the parameters by comparing their ISBNs. This function uses the `Sales_item ->` operator, which returns a pointer to an `Item_base` object. That pointer is used to fetch and run the `book` member, which returns the ISBN.

Using a Comparator with an Associative Container

If we think a bit about how the comparison function is used, we'll realize that it must be stored as part of the container. The comparison function is used by any operation that adds or finds an element in the container. In principle, each of these operations could take an optional extra argument that represented the comparison function. However, this strategy would be error-prone: If two operations used different comparison functions, then the ordering would be inconsistent. It's impossible to predict what would happen in practice.

To work effectively, an associative container needs to use the same comparison function for every operation. Yet, it is unreasonable to expect users to remember the comparison function every time, especially when there is no way to check that each call uses the same comparison function. Therefore, it makes sense for the container to remember the comparison function. By storing the comparator in the container object, we are assured that every operation that compares elements will do so consistently.

For the same reasons that the container needs to know the element type, it needs to know the comparator type in order to store the comparator. In principle, the container could infer this type by assuming that the comparator is pointer to a function that returns a `bool` and takes references to two objects of the `key_type` of the container. Unfortunately, this inferred type would be overly restrictive. For one thing, we should allow the comparator to be a function object as well as a plain function. Even if we were willing to require that the comparator be a function, the inferred type would still be too restrictive. After all, the comparison function might return an `int` or any other type that can be used in a condition. Similarly, the parameter type need not exactly match the `key_type`. Any parameter type that is convertible to the `key_type` should also be allowed.

So, to use our `Sales_item` comparison function, we must specify the comparator type when we define the `multiset`. In our case, that type is a function that returns a `bool` and takes two const `Sales_item` references.

We'll start by defining a typedef that is a synonym for this type (Section 7.9, p. 276):

```
// type of the comparison function used to order the multiset
typedef bool (*Comp)(const Sales_item&, const Sales_item&);
```

This statement defines `Comp` as a synonym for the pointer to function type that matches the comparison function we wish to use to compare `Sales_item` objects.

Next we'll need to define a `multiset` that holds objects of type `Sales_item` and that uses this `Comp` type for its comparison function. Each constructor for the associative containers allows us to supply the name of the comparison function. We can define an empty `multiset` that uses our `compare` function as follows:

```
std::multiset<Sales_item, Comp> items(compare);
```

This definition says that `items` is a `multiset` that holds `Sales_item` objects and uses an object of type `Comp` to compare them. The `multiset` is empty—we supplied no elements—but we did supply a comparison function named `compare`. When we add or look for elements in `items` our `compare` function will be used to order the `multiset`.

Containers and Handle Classes

Now that we know how to supply a comparison function, we'll define a class, named `Basket`, to keep track of a sale and calculate the purchase price:

```
class Basket {
    // type of the comparison function used to order the multiset
    typedef bool (*Comp)(const Sales_item&, const Sales_item&);
public:
    // make it easier to type the type of our set
    typedef std::multiset<Sales_item, Comp> set_type;
    // typedefs modeled after corresponding container types
    typedef set_type::size_type size_type;
    typedef set_type::const_iterator const_iter;
    Basket(): items(compare) { }   // initialze the comparator
    void add_item(const Sales_item &item)
                        { items.insert(item); }
    size_type size(const Sales_item &i) const
                        { return items.count(i); }
    double total() const;   // sum of net prices for all items in the basket
private:
    std::multiset<Sales_item, Comp> items;
};
```

This class holds the customer's purchases in a `multiset` of `Sales_item` objects. We use a `multiset` to allow the customer to buy multiple copies of the same book.

The class defines a single constructor, the `Basket` default constructor. The class needs its own default constructor to pass `compare` to the `multiset` constructor that builds the `items` member.

The operations that the `Basket` class defines are fairly simple: `add_item` takes a reference to a `Sales_item` and puts a copy of that item into the `multiset`; `item_count` returns the number of records for this ISBN in the basket for a given ISBN. In addition to the operations, `Basket` defines three typedefs to make it easier to use its `multiset` member.

Using the Handle to Execute a Virtual Function

The only complicated member of class `Basket` is the `total` function, which returns the price for all the items in the basket:

```
double Basket::total() const
{
    double sum = 0.0;        // holds the running total

    /* find each set of items with the same isbn and calculate
     * the net price for that quantity of items
     *  iter refers to first copy of each book in the set
     *  upper_bound refers to next element with a different isbn
     */
    for (const_iter iter = items.begin();
                    iter != items.end();
                    iter = items.upper_bound(*iter))
    {
        // we know there's at least one element with this key in the Basket
        // virtual call to net_price applies appropriate discounts, if any
        sum += (*iter)->net_price(items.count(*iter));
    }
    return sum;
}
```

The `total` function has two interesting parts: the call to the `net_price` function, and the structure of the `for` loop. We'll look at each in turn.

When we call `net_price`, we need to tell it how many copies of a given book are being purchased. The `net_price` function uses this argument to determine whether the purchase qualifies for a discount. This requirement implies that we'd like to process the `multiset` in chunks—processing all the records for a given title in one chunk and then the set of those for the next title and so on. Fortunately, `multiset` is well suited to this problem.

Our `for` loop starts by defining and initializing `iter` to refer to the first element in the `multiset`. We use the `multiset count` member (Section 10.3.6, p. 367) to determine how many elements in the `multiset` have the same key (e.g., same `isbn`) and use that number as the argument to the call to `net_price`.

The interesting bit is the "increment" expression in the `for`. Rather than the usual loop that reads each element, we advance `iter` to refer to the next key. We skip over all the elements that match the current key by calling `upper_bound` (Section 10.5.2, p. 377). The call to `upper_bound` returns the iterator that refers to the element just past the last one with the same key as in `iter`. That iterator we get back denotes either the end of the set or the next unique book. We test the new value of `iter`. If `iter` is equal to `items.end()`, we drop out of the `for`. Otherwise, we process the next book.

The body of the `for` calls the `net_price` function. That call can be a bit tricky to read:

```
sum += (*iter)->net_price(items.count(*iter));
```

We dereference `iter` to get the underlying `Sales_item` to which we apply the overloaded arrow operator from the `Sales_item` class. That operator returns the underlying `Item_base` object to which the handle is attached. From that object we call `net_price`, passing the `count` of items with the same `isbn`. The `net_price` function is virtual, so the version of the pricing function that is called depends on the type of the underlying `Item_base` object.

EXERCISES SECTION 15.8.3

Exercise 15.35: Write your own version of the `compare` function and `Basket` class and use them to manage a sale.

Exercise 15.36: What is the underlying type of `Basket::const_iter`?

Exercise 15.37: Why did we define the `Comp` typedef in the `private` part of `Basket`?

Exercise 15.38: Why did we define two `private` sections in `Basket`?

15.9 Text Queries Revisited

As a final example of inheritance, we'll extend our text query application from Section 10.6 (p. 379). The class we developed there let us look for occurrences of a given word in a text file. We'd like to extend the system to support more complex queries.

For illustration purposes, we'll run queries against the following simple story:

```
Alice Emma has long flowing red hair.
Her Daddy says when the wind blows
through her hair, it looks almost alive,
like a fiery bird in flight.
A beautiful fiery bird, he tells her,
magical but untamed.
"Daddy, shush, there is no such thing,"
she tells him, at the same time wanting
him to tell her more.
Shyly, she asks, "I mean, Daddy, is there?"
```

Our system should support:

1. Word queries that find a single word. All lines in which the word appears should be displayed in ascending order:

   ```
   Executed Query for: Daddy
   match occurs 3 times:
   (line 2) Her Daddy says when the wind blows
   (line 7) "Daddy, shush, there is no such thing,"
   (line 10) Shyly, she asks, "I mean, Daddy, is there?"
   ```

2. Not queries, using the ~ operator. All lines that do not match the query are displayed:

   ```
   Executed Query for: ~(Alice)
   match occurs 9 times:
   (line 2) Her Daddy says when the wind blows
   (line 3) through her hair, it looks almost alive,
   (line 4) like a fiery bird in flight.
   . . .
   ```

3. Or queries, using the | operator. All lines in which either of two queries match are displayed:

   ```
   Executing Query for: (hair | Alice)
   match occurs 2 times:
   (line 1) Alice Emma has long flowing red hair.
   (line 3) through her hair, it looks almost alive,
   ```

4. And queries, using the & operator. All lines in which both queries match are displayed.

   ```
   Executed query: (hair & Alice)
   match occurs 1 time:
   (line 1) Alice Emma has long flowing red hair.
   ```

Moreover, these elements can be combined, as in

```
fiery & bird | wind
```

Our system will not be sophisticated enough to read these expressions. Instead, we'll build them up inside a C++ program. Hence, we'll evaluate compound expressions such as this example using normal C++ precedence rules. The evaluation of this query will match a line in which `fiery` and `bird` appear or one in which `wind` appears. It will not match a line on which `fiery` or `bird` appears alone:

```
Executing Query for: ((fiery & bird) | wind)
match occurs 3 times:
(line 2) Her Daddy says when the wind blows
(line 4) like a fiery bird in flight.
(line 5) A beautiful fiery bird, he tells her,
```

Our output will print the query, using parentheses to indicate the way in which the query was interpreted. As with our original implementation, our system must be smart enough not to display the same line more than once.

15.9.1 An Object-Oriented Solution

We might think that we could use the `TextQuery` class from page 382 to represent our word queries. We might then derive our other queries from that class.

However, this design would be flawed. Conceptually, a "not" query is not a kind of word query. Instead, a not query "has a" query (word query or any other kind of query) whose value it negates.

This observation suggests that we model our different kinds of queries as independent classes that share a common base class:

```
WordQuery   // Shakespeare
NotQuery    // ~Shakespeare
OrQuery     // Shakespeare | Marlowe
AndQuery    // William & Shakespeare
```

Instead of inheriting from `TextQuery`, we will use that class to hold the file and build the associated `word_map`. We'll use the query classes to build up expressions that will ultimately run queries against the file in a `TextQuery` object.

Abstract Interface Class

We have identified four kinds of query classes. These classes are conceptually siblings. Each class shares the same abstract interface, which suggests that we'll need to define an abstract base class (Section 15.6, p. 595) to represent the operations performed by a query. We'll name our abstract class `Query_base`, indicating that its role is to serve as the root of our query hierarchy.

We'll derive `WordQuery` and `NotQuery` directly from our abstract base. The `AndQuery` and `OrQuery` classes share one property that the other classes in our system do not: They each have two operands. To model this fact, we'll add another abstract class, named `BinaryQuery`, to our hierarchy to represent queries with two operands. The `AndQuery` and `OrQuery` classes will inherit from the `BinaryQuery` class, which in turn will inherit from `Query_base`. These decisions give us the class design represented in Figure 15.3 on the next page.

Operations

Our `Query_base` classes exist mostly to represent kinds of queries; they do little actual work. We'll reuse our `TextQuery` class to store the file, build the query `map`, and search for each word. Our query types need only two operations:

1. An `eval` operation to return the `set` of matching line numbers. This operation takes a `TextQuery` object on which to execute the query.

2. A `display` operation that takes a reference to an `ostream` and prints the query that a given object performs on that stream.

We'll define each of these operations as pure `virtual` functions (Section 15.6, p. 595) in the `Query_base` class. Each of our derived classes will have to define its own version of these functions.

Figure 15.3: `Query_base` Inheritance Hierarchy

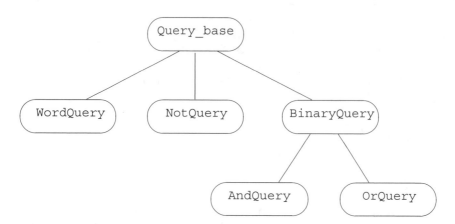

15.9.2   A Valuelike Handle

Our program will deal with evaluating queries, not with building them. However, we need to be able to create queries in order to run our program. The simplest way to do so is to write C++ expressions to create queries directly. For example, we'd like to be able to write code such as

```
Query q = Query("fiery") & Query("bird") | Query("wind");
```

to generate the compound query previously described.

   This problem description implicitly suggests that user-level code won't use our inherited classes directly. Instead, we'll define a handle class named `Query`, which will hide the hierarchy. User code will execute in terms of the handle; user code will only indirectly manipulate `Query_base` objects.

   As with our `Sales_item` handle, our `Query` handle will hold a pointer to an object of a type in an inheritance hierarchy. The `Query` class will also point to a use count, which we'll use to manage the object to which the handle points.

   In this case, our handle will completely hide the underlying inheritance hierarchy. Users will create and manipulate `Query_base` objects only indirectly through operations on `Query` objects. We'll define three overloaded operators on `Query` objects and a `Query` constructor that will dynamically allocate a new `Query_base` object. Each operator will bind the generated `Query_base` object to a `Query` handle: The `&` operator will generate a `Query` bound to a new `AndQuery`; the `|` operator will generate a `Query` bound to a new `OrQuery`; and the `~` operator will generate a `Query` bound to a new `NotQuery`. We'll give `Query` a constructor that takes a `string`. This constructor will generate a new `WordQuery`.

   The `Query` class will provide the same operations as the `Query_base` classes: `eval` to evaluate the associated query, and `display` to print the query. It will define an overloaded output operator to display the associated query.

Table 15.1: Query Program Design: A Recap	
`TextQuery`	Class that reads a specified file and builds an associated lookup map. That class provides a `query_text` operation that takes a `string` argument and returns a `set` of line numbers on which the argument appears.
`Query_base`	Abstract base class for the query classes.
`Query`	Use-counted handle class, which points to an object of a type derived from `Query_base`.
`WordQuery`	Class derived from `Query_base` that looks for a given word.
`NotQuery`	Class derived from `Query_base` that returns the set of lines in which its `Query` operand does not appear.
`BinaryQuery`	Abstract base type derived from `Query_base` that represents queries with two `Query` operands.
`OrQuery`	Class derived from `BinaryQuery` that returns the union of the line numbers in which its two operands appear.
`AndQuery`	Class derived from `BinaryQuery` that returns the intersection of the line numbers in which its two operands appear.
`q1 & q2`	Returns a `Query` bound to a new `AndQuery` object that holds `q1` and `q2`.
`q1	q2`	Returns a `Query` bound to a new `OrQuery` object that holds `q1` and `q2`.
`~q`	Returns a `Query` bound to a new `NotQuery` object that holds `q`.
`Query q(s)`	Binds the `Query` q to a new `WordQuery` that holds the `string` s.

Our Design: A Recap

It is often the case, especially when new to designing object-oriented systems, that understanding the design is the hardest part. Once we're comfortable with the design, the implementation flows naturally.

It is important to realize that much of the work in this application consists of building objects to represent the user's query. As illustrated in Figure 15.4 on the following page, an expression such as

```
Query q = Query("fiery") & Query("bird") | Query("wind");
```

generates ten objects: five `Query_base` objects and their associated handles. The five `Query_base` objects are three `WordQuery`s, an `OrQuery`, and an `AndQuery`.

Once the tree of objects is built up, evaluating (or displaying) a given query is basically a process (managed for us by the compiler) of following these links, asking each object in the tree to evaluate (or display) itself. For example, if we call `eval` on q (i.e., on the root of this tree), then `eval` will ask the `OrQuery` to which it points to `eval` itself. Evaluating this `OrQuery` calls `eval` on its two operands, which in turn calls `eval` on the `AndQuery` and `WordQuery` that looks for the word `wind`, and so on.

Figure 15.4: Objects Created by Query Expressions

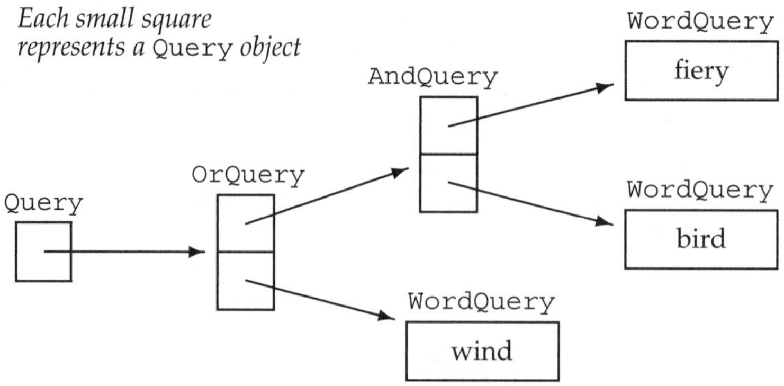

Each small square represents a Query *object*

Objects Created by the Expression
Query("fiery") & Query("bird") | Query("wind");

EXERCISES SECTION 15.9.2

Exercise 15.39: Given that s1, s2, s3 and s4 are all strings, determine what objects are created in the following uses of the Query class:

```
(a) Query(s1) | Query(s2) & ~ Query(s3);
(b) Query(s1) | (Query(s2) & ~ Query(s3));
(c) (Query(s1) & (Query(s2)) | (Query(s3) & Query(s4)));
```

15.9.3 The Query_base Class

Now that we've explained our design, we'll start our implementation by defining the Query_base class:

```
// private, abstract class acts as a base class for concrete query types
class Query_base {
    friend class Query;
protected:
    typedef TextQuery::line_no line_no;
    virtual ~Query_base() { }
private:
    // eval returns the |set| of lines that this Query matches
    virtual std::set<line_no>
        eval(const TextQuery&) const = 0;
    // display prints the query
    virtual std::ostream&
        display(std::ostream& = std::cout) const = 0;
};
```

The class defines two interface members: `eval` and `display`. Both are pure `virtual` functions (Section 15.6, p. 595), which makes this class abstract. There will be no objects of type `Query_base` in our applications.

Users and the derived classes will use the `Query_base` class only through the `Query` handle. Therefore, we made our `Query_base` interface `private`. The (virtual) destructor (Section 15.4.4, p. 587) and the typedef are `protected` so that the derived types can access these members. The destructor is used (implicitly) by the derived-class destructors and so must be accessible to them.

We grant friendship to the `Query` handle class. Members of that class will call the virtuals in `Query_base` and so must have access to them.

15.9.4 The `Query` Handle Class

Our `Query` handle will be similar to the `Sales_item` class in that it will hold a pointer to the `Query_base` and a pointer to a use count. As in the `Sales_item` class, the copy-control members of `Query` will manage the use count and the `Query_base` pointer.

Unlike the `Sales_item` class, `Query` will provide the only interface to the `Query_base` hierarchy. Users will not directly access any of the members of `Query_base` or its derived classes. This design decision leads to two differences between `Query` and `Sales_item`. The first is that the `Query` class won't define overloaded versions of dereference and arrow operators. The `Query_base` class has no `public` members. If the `Query` handle defined the dereference or arrow operators, they would be of no use! Any attempt to use those operators to access a `Query_base` member would fail. Instead, `Query` must define its own versions of the `Query_base` interface functions `eval` and `display`.

The other difference results from how we intend objects of the hierarchy to be created. Our design says that objects derived from `Query_base` will be created only through operations on the `Query` handle. This difference results in different constructors being required for the `Query` class than were used in the `Sales_item` handle.

The `Query` Class

Given the preceeding design, the `Query` class itself is quite simple:

```
// handle class to manage the Query_base inheritance hierarchy
class Query {
    // these operators need access to the Query_base* constructor
    friend Query operator~(const Query &);
    friend Query operator|(const Query&, const Query&);
    friend Query operator&(const Query&, const Query&);
public:
    Query(const std::string&);  // builds a new WordQuery

    // copy control to manage pointers and use counting
    Query(const Query &c): q(c.q), use(c.use) { ++*use; }
    ~Query() { decr_use(); }
    Query& operator=(const Query&);
```

```
              // interface functions: will call corresponding Query_base operations
              std::set<TextQuery::line_no>
                 eval(const TextQuery &t) const { return q->eval(t); }
              std::ostream &display(std::ostream &os) const
                                         { return q->display(os); }
          private:
              Query(Query_base *query): q(query),
                                        use(new std::size_t(1)) { }
              Query_base *q;
              std::size_t *use;
              void decr_use()
              { if (--*use == 0) { delete q; delete use; } }
          };
```

We start by naming as friends the operators that create `Query` objects. We'll see shortly why these operators need to be friends.

In the `public` interface for `Query`, we declare, but cannot yet define, the constructor that takes a `string`. That constructor creates a `WordQuery` object, so we cannot define the constructor until we have defined the `WordQuery` class.

The next three members handle copy control and are the same as the corresponding members of the `Sales_item` class.

The last two `public` members represent the interface for `Query_base`. In each case, the `Query` operation uses its `Query_base` pointer to call the respective `Query_base` operation. These operations are virtual. The actual version that is called is determined at run time and will depend on the type of the object to which `q` points.

The `private` implementation of `Query` includes a constructor that takes a pointer to a `Query_base` object. This constructor stores in `q` the pointer it is given and allocates a new use counter, which it initializes to one. This constructor is `private` because we don't intend general user code to define `Query_base` objects. Instead, the constructor is needed for the operators that create `Query` objects. Because the constructor is `private`, the operators had to be made friends.

The `Query` Overloaded Operators

The `|`, `&` and `~` operators create `OrQuery`, `AndQuery`, and `NotQuery` objects, respectively:

```
    inline Query operator&(const Query &lhs, const Query &rhs)
    {
        return new AndQuery(lhs, rhs);
    }
    inline Query operator|(const Query &lhs, const Query &rhs)
    {
        return new OrQuery(lhs, rhs);
    }
    inline Query operator~(const Query &oper)
    {
        return new NotQuery(oper);
    }
```

Each of these operations dynamically allocates a new object of a type derived from `Query_base`. The `return` (implicitly) uses the `Query` constructor that takes a pointer to a `Query_base` to create the `Query` object from the `Query_base` pointer that the operation allocates. For example the `return` statement in the `~` operator is equivalent to

```
// allocate a new NotQuery object
// convert the resulting pointer to NotQuery to a pointer to Query_base
Query_base *tmp = new NotQuery(expr);
return Query(tmp); // use Query constructor that takes a pointer to Query_base
```

There is no operator to create a `WordQuery`. Instead, we gave our `Query` class a constructor that takes a `string`. That constructor generates a `WordQuery` to look for the given `string`.

The `Query` Output Operator

We'd like users to be able to print `Query`s using the normal (overloaded) output operator. However, we also need the print operation to be virtual—printing a `Query` should print the `Query_base` object to which the `Query` points. There's only one problem: only member functions can be virtual, but the output operator cannot be a member of the `Query_base` classes (Section 14.2.1, p. 514).

To obtain the necessary virtual behavior, our `Query_base` classes defined a virtual `display` member, which the `Query` output operator will use:

```
inline std::ostream&
operator<<(std::ostream &os, const Query &q)
{
    return q.display(os);
}
```

When we write

```
Query andq = Query(sought1) & Query(sought2);
cout << "\nExecuted query: " << andq << endl;
```

the `Query` output operator is invoked. That operator calls

```
q.display(os)
```

with q referring to the `Query` object that points to this `AndQuery`, and os bound to `cout`. When we write

```
Query name(sought);
cout << "\nExecuted Query for: " << name << endl;
```

the `WordQuery` instance of `display` is called. More generally, a call

```
Query query = some_query;
cout << query << endl;
```

invokes the instance of `display` associated with the object that `query` addresses at that point in the execution of our program.

15.9.5 The Derived Classes

We next need to implement our concrete query classes. The one interesting part about these classes is how they are represented. The WordQuery class is most straightforward. Its job is to hold the search word.

The other classes operate on one or two Query operands. A NotQuery negates the result of another Query. Both AndQuery and OrQuery have two operands, which are actually stored in their common base class, BinaryQuery.

In each of these classes, the operand(s) could be an object of any of the concrete Query_base classes: A NotQuery could be applied to a WordQuery, an AndQuery, an OrQuery, or another NotQuery. To allow this flexibility, the operands must be stored as pointers to Query_base that might point to any one of the concrete Query_base classes.

However, rather than storing a Query_base pointer, our classes will themselves use the Query handle. Just as user code is simplified by using a handle, we can simplify our own class code by using the same handle class. We'll make the Query operand const because once a given Query_base object is built, there are no operations that can change the operand(s).

Now that we know the design for these classes, we can implement them.

The WordQuery Class

A WordQuery is a kind of Query_base that looks for a specified word in a given query map:

```
class WordQuery: public Query_base {
    friend class Query; // Query uses the WordQuery constructor
    WordQuery(const std::string &s): query_word(s) { }

    // concrete class: WordQuery defines all inherited pure virtual functions
    std::set<line_no> eval(const TextQuery &t) const
                         { return t.run_query(query_word); }
    std::ostream& display (std::ostream &os) const
                             { return os << query_word; }
    std::string query_word;    // word for which to search
};
```

Like Query_base, WordQuery has no public members; WordQuery must make Query a friend to allow Query to access the WordQuery constructor.

Each of the concrete query classes must define the inherited pure virtual functions. The WordQuery operations are simple enough to define in the class body. The eval member calls the query_text member of its TextQuery parameter passing it the string that was used to create this WordQuery. To display a WordQuery, we print the query_word.

The NotQuery Class

A NotQuery holds a const Query, which it negates:

```
class NotQuery: public Query_base {
    friend Query operator~(const Query &);
```

```
        NotQuery(Query q): query(q) { }
        // concrete class: NotQuery defines all inherited pure virtual functions
        std::set<line_no> eval(const TextQuery&) const;
        std::ostream& display(std::ostream &os) const
            { return os << "~(" << query << ")"; }
        const Query query;
    };
```

The `Query` overloaded `~` operator is made a friend to allow that operator to create a new `NotQuery` object. To `display` a `NotQuery`, we print the `~` symbol followed by the underlying `Query`. We parenthesize the output to ensure that precedence is clear to the reader.

The use of the output operator in the `display` operation is ultimately a virtual call to a `Query_base` object:

```
// uses the Query output operator, which calls Query::display
// that funtion makes a virtual call to Query_base::display
{ return os << "~(" << query << ")"
```

The `eval` member is complicated enough that we will implement it outside the class body. The `eval` function appears in Section 15.9.6 (p. 620).

The `BinaryQuery` Class

The `BinaryQuery` class is an abstract class that holds the data needed by the two query types, `AndQuery` and `OrQuery`, that operate on two operands:

```
class BinaryQuery: public Query_base {
protected:
    BinaryQuery(Query left, Query right, std::string op):
        lhs(left), rhs(right), oper(op) { }
    // abstract class: BinaryQuery doesn't define eval
    std::ostream& display(std::ostream &os) const
    { return os << "(" << lhs  << " " << oper << " "
                        << rhs << ")"; }
    const Query lhs, rhs;    // right- and left-hand operands
    const std::string oper; // name of the operator
};
```

The data in a `BinaryQuery` are the two `Query` operands and the operator symbol to use when displaying the query. These data are all declared `const`, because the contents of a query should not change once it has been constructed. The constructor takes the two operands and the operator symbol, which it stores in the appropriate data members.

To `display` a `BinaryOperator`, we print the parenthesized expression consisting of the left-hand operand, followed by the operator, followed by the right-hand operand. As when we displayed a `NotQuery`, the overloaded `<<` operator that is used to print `left` and `right` ultimately makes a virtual call to the underlying `Query_base display`.

> The BinaryQuery class does not define the eval function and so in-herits a pure virtual. As such, BinaryQuery is also an abstract class, and we cannot create objects of BinaryQuery type.

The AndQuery and OrQuery Classes

The AndQuery and OrQuery classes are nearly identical:

```
class AndQuery: public BinaryQuery {
    friend Query operator&(const Query&, const Query&);
    AndQuery(Query left, Query right):
                        BinaryQuery(left, right, "&") { }
    // concrete class: AndQuery inherits display and defines remaining pure virtual
    std::set<line_no> eval(const TextQuery&) const;
};

class OrQuery: public BinaryQuery {
    friend Query operator|(const Query&, const Query&);
    OrQuery(Query left, Query right):
                BinaryQuery(left, right, "|") { }
    // concrete class: OrQuery inherits display and defines remaining pure virtual
    std::set<line_no> eval(const TextQuery&) const;
};
```

These classes make the respective operator a friend and define a constructor to create their BinaryQuery base part with the appropriate operator. They inherit the BinaryQuery definition of display, but each defines its own version of the eval function.

EXERCISES SECTION 15.9.5

Exercise 15.40: For the expression built in Figure 15.4 (p. 612)

(a) List the constructors executed in processing this expression.
(b) List the calls to display and to the overloaded << operator that are made in exe-cuting cout << q.
(c) List the calls to eval made when evaluating q.eval.

15.9.6   The eval Functions

The heart of the query class hierarchy are the eval virtual functions. Each of these functions calls eval on its operand(s) and then applies its own logic: The AndQuery eval operation returns the union of the results of its two operands; OrQuery returns the intersection. The NotQuery is more complicated: It must return the line numbers not in its operand's set.

OrQuery::eval

An OrQuery merges the set of line numbers returned by its two operands—its result is the union of the results for its two operands:

```
// returns union of its operands' result sets
set<TextQuery::line_no>
OrQuery::eval(const TextQuery& file) const
{
    // virtual calls through the Query handle to get result sets for the operands
    set<line_no> right = rhs.eval(file),
                 ret_lines = lhs.eval(file);   // destination to hold results
    // inserts the lines from right that aren't already in ret_lines
    ret_lines.insert(right.begin(), right.end());

    return ret_lines;
}
```

The eval function starts by calling eval on each of its Query operands. Those calls call Query::eval, which in turn makes a virtual call to eval on the underlying Query_base object. Each of these calls yields a set of line numbers in which its operand appears. We then call insert on ret_lines, passing a pair of iterators denoting the set returned from evaluating the right-hand operand. Because ret_lines is a set, this call adds the elements from right that are not also in left into ret_lines. After the call to insert, ret_lines contains each line number that was in either of the left or right sets. We complete the function by returning ret_lines.

AndQuery::eval

The AndQuery version of eval uses one of the library algorithms that performs setlike operations. These algorithms are described in the Library Appendix, in Section A.2.8 (p. 821):

```
// returns intersection of its operands' result sets
set<TextQuery::line_no>
AndQuery::eval(const TextQuery& file) const
{
    // virtual calls through the Query handle to get result sets for the operands
    set<line_no> left = lhs.eval(file),
                 right = rhs.eval(file);
    set<line_no> ret_lines;   // destination to hold results
    // writes intersection of two ranges to a destination iterator
    // destination iterator in this call adds elements to ret
    set_intersection(left.begin(), left.end(),
                     right.begin(), right.end(),
                     inserter(ret_lines, ret_lines.begin()));
    return ret_lines;
}
```

This version of eval uses the set_intersection algorithm to find the lines in common to both queries: That algorithm takes five iterators: The first four denote two input ranges, and the last denotes a destination. The algorithm writes each element that is in both of the two input ranges into the destination. The destination in this call is an insert iterator (Section 11.3.1, p. 406) which inserts new elements into ret_lines.

NotQuery::eval

NotQuery finds each line of the text within which the operand is not found. To support this function, we need the TextQuery class to add a member to return the size of the file, so that we can know what line numbers exist.

```
//   returns lines not in its operand's result set
set<TextQuery::line_no>
NotQuery::eval(const TextQuery& file) const
{
      //   virtual call through the Query handle to eval
      set<TextQuery::line_no> has_val = query.eval(file);

      set<line_no> ret_lines;

      //   for each line in the input file, check whether that line is in has_val
      //   if not, add that line number to ret_lines
      for (TextQuery::line_no n = 0; n != file.size(); ++n)
          if (has_val.find(n) == has_val.end())
              ret_lines.insert(n);
      return ret_lines;
}
```

As in the other eval functions, we start by calling eval on this object's operand. That call returns the set of line numbers on which the operand appears. What we want is the set of line numbers on which the operand does not appear. We obtain that set by looking at each line number in the input file. We use the size member that must be added to TextQuery to control the for loop. That loop adds each line number to ret_lines that does not appear in has_val. Once we've processed all the line numbers, we return ret_lines.

EXERCISES SECTION 15.9.6

Exercise 15.41: Implement the Query and Query_base classes, and add the needed size operation to the TextQuery class from Chapter 10. Test your application by evaluating and printing a query such as the one in Figure 15.4 (p. 612).

Exercise 15.42: Design and implement one of the following enhancements:

(a) Introduce support for evaluating words based on their presence within the same sentence rather than the same line.

(b) Introduce a history system in which the user can refer to a previous query by number, possibly adding to it or combining it with another.

(c) Rather than displaying the count of matches and all the matching lines, allow the user to indicate a range of lines to display, both for intermediate query evaluation and the final query.

CHAPTER SUMMARY

The ideas of inheritance and dynamic binding are simple but powerful. Inheritance lets us write new classes that share behavior with their base class(es) but redefine that behavior as needed. Dynamic binding lets the compiler decide at run time which version of a function to run based on an object's dynamic type. The combination of inheritance and dynamic binding lets us write type-independent programs that have type-specific behavior.

In C++, dynamic binding applies *only* to functions declared as virtual when called through a reference or pointer. It is common for C++ programs to define handle classes to interface to an inheritance hierarchy. These classes allocate and manage pointers to objects in the inheritance hierarchy, thus obtaining dynamic behavior while shielding user code from having to deal with pointers.

Inherited objects are composed of base-class part(s) and a derived-class part. Inherited objects are constructed, copied, and assigned by constructing, copying, and assigning the base part(s) of the object before handling the derived part. Because a derived object contains a base part, it is possible to convert a reference or pointer to a derived type to a reference or pointer to its base type.

Base classes usually should define a virtual destructor even if the class otherwise has no need for a destructor. The destructor must be virtual if a pointer to a base is ever deleted when it actually addresses a derived-type object.

DEFINED TERMS

abstract base class Class that has or inherits one or more pure virtual functions. It is not possible to create objects of an abstract base-class type. Abstract base classes exist to define an interface. Derived classes will complete the type by defining type-specific implementations for the pure virtuals defined in the base.

base class Class from which another class inherits. The members of the base class become members of the derived class.

class derivation list Used by a class definition to indicate that the class is a derived class. A derivation list includes an optional access level and names the base class. If no access label is specified, the type of inheritance depends on the keyword used to define the derived class. By default, if the derived class is defined with the `struct` keyword, then the base class is inherited `publicly`. If the class is defined using the `class` keyword, then the base class is inherited `privately`.

derived class A class that inherits from another class. The members of the base class are also members of the derived class. A derived class can redefine the members of its base and can define new members. A derived-class scope is nested in the scope of its base class(es), so the derived class can access members of the base class directly. Members defined in the derived with the same name as members in the base hide those base members; in particular, member functions in the derived do not overload members from the base. A hidden member in the base can be accessed using the scope operator.

direct base class Synonym for immediate base class.

dynamic binding Delaying until run time the selection of which function to run. In C++, dynamic binding refers to the run-time choice of which `virtual` function to run based on the underlying type of the object to which a reference or pointer is bound.

dynamic type Type at run time. Pointers and references to base-class types can be bound to objects of derived type. In such cases the static type is reference (or pointer) to base, but the dynamic type is reference (or pointer) to derived.

handle class Class that provides an interface to another class. Commonly used to allocate and manage a pointer to an object of an inheritance hierarchy.

immediate base class A base class from which a derived class inherits directly. The immediate base is the class named in the derivation list. The immediate base may itself be a derived class.

indirect base class A base class that is not immediate. A class from which the immediate base class inherits, directly or indirectly, is an indirect base class to the derived class.

inheritance hierarchy Term used to describe the relationships among classes related by inheritance that share a common base class.

object-oriented programming Term used to describe programs that use data abstraction, inheritance, and dynamic binding.

polymorphism A term derived from a Greek word that means "many forms." In object-oriented programming, polymorphism refers to the ability to obtain type-specific behavior based on the dynamic type of a reference or pointer.

private inheritance A form of implementation inheritance in which the `public` and `protected` members of a `private` base class are `private` in the derived.

protected access label Members defined after a `protected` label may be accessed by class members and friends and by the members (but not friends) of a derived class. `protected` members are not accessible to ordinary users of the class.

protected inheritance In `protected` inheritance the `protected` and `public` members of the base class are `protected` in the derived class.

public inheritance The `public` interface of the base class is part of the `public` interface of the derived class.

pure virtual A virtual function declared in the class header using `= 0` at the end of the function's parameter list. A pure virtual is one that need not be (but may be) defined by the class. A class with a pure virtual is an abstract class. If a derived class does not define its own version of an inherited pure virtual, then the derived class is abstract as well.

refactoring Redesigning programs to collect related parts into a single abstraction, replacing the original code by uses of the new abstraction. In OO programs, refactoring frequently happens when redesigning the classes in an inheritance hierarchy. Refactoring often occurs in response to a change in requirements. In general, classes are refactored to move data or function members to the highest common point in the hierarchy to avoid code duplication.

sliced Term used to describe what happens when an object of derived type is used to initialize or assign an object of the base type. The derived portion of the object is "sliced down," leaving only the base portion, which is assigned to the base.

static type Compile-time type. Static type of an object is the same as its dynamic type. The dynamic type of an object to which a reference or pointer refers may differ from the static type of the reference or pointer.

virtual function A member function that defines type-specific behavior. Calls to a virtual made through a reference or pointer are resolved at run time, based on the type of the object to which the reference or pointer is bound.

C H A P T E R   16

T EMPLATES   AND   G ENERIC
P ROGRAMMING

CONTENTS

Generic programming involves writing code in a way that is independent of any particular type. When we use a generic program we supply the type(s) or value(s) on which that instance of the program will operate. The library containers, iterators, and algorithms described in Part II are examples of generic programming. There is a single definition of each container, such as `vector`, but we can define many different kinds of `vectors` that differ by the element type that the `vector` contains.

Templates are the foundation of generic programming. We can, and have, used templates without understanding how they are defined. In this chapter we'll see how we can define our own template classes and functions.

Generic programming, like object-oriented programming, relies on a form of polymorphism. The polymorphism in OOP applies at run time to classes related by inheritance. We can write code that uses such classes in ways that ignore the type differences among the base and derived classes. As long as we use references or pointers to the base type, we can use the same code on objects of the base type or a type derived from that type.

Generic programming lets us write classes and functions that are polymorphic across unrelated types at compile time. A single class or function can be used to manipulate objects of a variety of types. The standard library containers, iterators, and algorithms are good examples of generic programming. The library defines each of the containers, iterators, and algorithms in a type-independent manner. We can use library classes and functions on most any kind of type. For example, we can define a `vector` of `Sales_item` objects even though the designers of `vector` could have had no knowledge of our application-specific class.

In C++, templates are the foundation for generic programming. A template is a blueprint or formula for creating a class or a function. For example, the standard library defines a single class template that defines what it means to be a `vector`. That template is used to generate any number of type-specific `vector` classes—for example, `vector<int>` or `vector<string>`. Part II showed how to use generic types and functions; this chapter shows how we can define our own templates.

16.1   Template Definitions

Let's imagine that we want to write a function to compare two values and indicate whether the first is less than, equal to, or greater than the second. In practice, we'd want to define several such functions, each of which could compare values of a given type. Our first attempt might be to define several overloaded functions:

```
// returns 0 if the values are equal, -1 if v1 is smaller, 1 if v2 is smaller
int compare(const string &v1, const string &v2)
{
    if (v1 < v2) return -1;
    if (v2 < v1) return 1;
    return 0;
}
int compare(const double &v1, const double &v2)
{
    if (v1 < v2) return -1;
    if (v2 < v1) return 1;
    return 0;
}
```

These functions are nearly identical: The only difference between them is the type of their parameters. The function body is the same in each function.

Having to repeat the body of the function for each type that we compare is tedious and error-prone. More importantly, we need to know *in advance* all the types that we might ever want to `compare`. This strategy cannot work if we want to be able to use the function on types that we don't know about.

16.1.1   Defining a Function Template

Rather than defining a new function for each type, we can define a single **function template**. A function template is a type-independent function that is used as a formula for generating a type-specific version of the function. For example, we might write a function template named `compare`, which would tell the compiler how to generate specific versions of `compare` for the types that we want to compare.

The following is a template version of `compare`:

```
//   implement strcmp-like generic compare function
//   returns 0 if the values are equal, 1 if v1 is larger, -1 if v1 is smaller
template <typename T>
int compare(const T &v1, const T &v2)
{
    if (v1 < v2) return -1;
    if (v2 < v1) return 1;
    return 0;
}
```

A template definition starts with the keyword `template` followed by a **template parameter list**, which is a comma-separated list of one or more **template parameters** bracketed by the less-than (<) and greater-than (>) tokens.

 The template parameter list cannot be empty.

Template Parameter List

The template parameter list acts much like a function parameter list. A function parameter list defines local variable(s) of a specified type but leaves those variables uninitialized. At run time, arguments are supplied that initialize the parameters.

Analogously, template parameters represent types or values we can use in the definition of a class or function. For example, our `compare` function declares one type parameter named `T`. Inside `compare`, we can use the name `T` to refer to a type. Which *actual type* `T` represents is determined by the compiler based on how the function is used.

A template parameter can be a **type parameter**, which represents a type, or a **nontype parameter**, which represents a constant expression. A nontype parameter is declared following a type specifier. We'll see more about nontype parameters in Section 16.1.5 (p. 632). A type parameter is defined following the keyword `class` or `typename`. For example, `class T` is a type parameter named `T`. There is no difference between `class` and `typename` in this context.

Using a Function Template

When we use a function template, the compiler infers what **template argument(s)** to bind to the template parameter(s). Once the compiler determines the actual template argument(s), it **instantiates** an instance of the function template for us.

Essentially, the compiler figures out what type to use in place of each type parameter and what value to use in place of each nontype parameter. Having deduced the actual template arguments, it generates and compiles a version of the function using those arguments in place of the corresponding template parameters. The compiler takes on the tedium of (re)writing the function for each type we use.

Given the calls

```
int main()
{
    //  T is int;
    //  compiler instantiates int compare(const int&, const int&)
    cout << compare(1, 0) << endl;
    //  T is string;
    //  compiler instantiates int compare(const string&, const string&)
    string s1 = "hi", s2 = "world";
    cout << compare(s1, s2) << endl;
    return 0;
}
```

the compiler will instantiate two different versions of `compare`. The compiler will create one version that replaces `T` by `int` and a second version that uses `string` in place of `T`.

`inline` Function Templates

A function template can be declared `inline` in the same way as a nontemplate function. The specifier is placed following the template parameter list and before the return type. It is not placed in front of the `template` keyword.

```
//  ok: inline specifier follows template parameter list
template <typename T> inline T min(const T&, const T&);
//  error: incorrect placement of inline specifier
inline template <typename T> T min(const T&, const T&);
```

EXERCISES SECTION 16.1.1

Exercise 16.1: Write a template that returns the absolute value of its parameter. Call the template on values of at least three different types. Note: until we discuss how the compiler handles template instantiation in Section 16.3 (p. 643), you should put each template definition and all uses of that template in the same file.

Exercise 16.2: Write a function template that takes a reference to an `ostream` and a value, and writes the value to the stream. Call the function on at least four different types. Test your program by writing to `cout`, to a file, and to a `stringstream`.

Exercise 16.3: When we called `compare` on two `strings`, we passed two `string` objects, which we initialized from string literals. What would happen if we wrote:

```
compare("hi", "world");
```

16.1.2 Defining a Class Template

Just as we can define function templates, we can also define class templates.

To illustrate class templates, we'll implement our own version of the standard library queue (Section 9.7, p. 348) class. User programs ought to use the standard queue class, not the one we define here.

Our `Queue` must be able to hold objects of different types, so we'll define it as a **class template**. The operations our `Queue` will support are a subset of the interface of the standard `queue`:

- `push` to add an item to the back of the queue

- `pop` to remove the item at the head of the queue

- `front` to return a reference to the element at the head of the queue

- `empty` to indicate whether there are any elements in the queue

We'll look at how we might implement our `Queue` in Section 16.4 (p. 647), but we can start by defining its interface:

```
template <class Type> class Queue {
public:
     Queue();                         //  default constructor
     Type &front();                   //  return element from head of Queue
     const Type &front() const;
     void push(const Type &);         //  add element to back of Queue
     void pop();                      //  remove element from head of Queue
     bool empty() const;              //  true if no elements in the Queue
private:
     //  ...
};
```

A class template is a template, so it must begin with the keyword `template` followed by a template parameter list. Our `Queue` template takes a single template type parameter named `Type`.

With the exception of the template parameter list, the definition of a class template looks like any other class. A class template may define data, function, and type members; it may use access labels to control access to those members; it defines constructors and destructors; and so on. In the definition of the class and its members, we can use the template parameters as stand-ins for types or values that will be supplied when the class is used.

For example, our `Queue` template has one template type parameter. We can use that parameter anywhere a type name can be used. In this template definition, we use `Type` to name the return type from the overloaded `front` operations and as the parameter type for the `push` operation.

Using a Class Template

In contrast to calling a function template, when we use a class template, we must explicitly specify arguments for the template parameters:

```
Queue<int> qi;              // Queue that holds ints
Queue< vector<double> > qc; // Queue that holds vectors of doubles
Queue<string> qs;           // Queue that holds strings
```

The compiler uses the arguments to instantiate a type-specific version of the class. Essentially, the compiler rewrites our Queue class replacing Type by the specified actual type provided by the user. In this case, the compiler will instantiate three classes: a version of Queue with Type replaced by int, a second Queue class that uses vector<double> in place of Type, and a third that replaces Type by string.

EXERCISES SECTION 16.1.2

Exercise 16.4: What is a function template? What is a class template?

Exercise 16.5: Define a function template to return the larger of two values.

Exercise 16.6: Similar to our a simplified version of queue, write a class template named List that is a simplified version of the standard list class.

16.1.3 Template Parameters

As with a function parameter, the name chosen by the programmer for a template parameter has no intrinsic meaning. In our example, we named compare's template type parameter T, but we could have named it anything:

```
// equivalent template definition
template <class Glorp>
int compare(const Glorp &v1, const Glorp &v2)
{
    if (v1 < v2) return -1;
    if (v2 < v1) return 1;
    return 0;
}
```

This code defines the same compare template as before.

The only meaning we can ascribe to a template parameter is to distinguish whether the parameter is a type parameter or a nontype parameter. If it is a type parameter, then we know that the parameter represents an as yet unknown type. If it is a nontype parameter, we know it is an as yet unknown value.

When we wish to use the type or value that a template parameter represents, we use the same name as the corresponding template parameter. For example, all references to Glorp in the compare function template will be resolved to the same type when the function is instantiated.

Template Parameter Scope

The name of a template parameter can be used after it has been declared as a template parameter and until the end of the template declaration or definition.

Template parameters follow normal name-hiding rules. A template parameter with the same name as an object, function, or type declared in global scope hides the global name:

```
typedef double T;
template <class T> T calc(const T &a, const T &b)
{
    // tmp has the type of the template parameter T
    // not that of the global typedef
    T tmp = a;
    // ...
    return tmp;
}
```

The global typedef that defines T as double is hidden by the type parameter named T. Thus, tmp is not a double. Instead, the type of tmp is whatever type gets bound to the template parameter T.

Restrictions on the Use of a Template Parameter Name

A name used as a template parameter may not be reused within the template:

```
template <class T> T calc(const T &a, const T &b)
{
    typedef double T; // error: redeclares template parameter T
    T tmp = a;
    // ...
    return tmp;
}
```

This restriction also means that the name of a template parameter can be used only once within the same template parameter list:

```
// error: illegal reuse of template parameter name V
template <class V, class V> V calc(const V&, const V&);
```

Of course, just as we can reuse function parameter names, the name of a template parameter can be reused across different templates:

```
// ok: reuses parameter type name across different templates
template <class T> T calc(const T&, const T&);

template <class T> int compare(const T&, const T&);
```

Template Declarations

As with any other function or class, we can declare a template without defining it. A declaration must indicate that the function or class is a template:

```
// declares compare but does not define it
template <class T> int compare(const T&, const T&);
```

The names of the template parameters need not be the same across declarations and the definition of the same template:

```
//   all three uses of calc refer to the same function template
//   forward declarations of the template
template <class T> T calc(const T&, const T&);
template <class U> U calc(const U&, const U&);
//   actual definition of the template
template <class Type>
Type calc(const Type& a, const Type& b) { /* ... */ }
```

Each template type parameter must be preceded either by the keyword `class` or `typename`; each nontype parameter must be preceded by a type name. It is an error to omit the keyword or a type specifier:

```
//   error: must precede U by either typename or class
template <typename T, U> T calc(const T&, const U&);
```

EXERCISES SECTION 16.1.3

Exercise 16.7: Explain each of the following function template definitions and identify whether any are illegal. Correct each error that you find.

```
(a) template <class T, U, typename V> void f1(T, U, V);
(b) template <class T> T f2(int &T);
(c) inline template <class T> T foo(T, unsigned int*);
(d) template <class T> f4(T, T);
(e) typedef char Ctype;
    template <typename Ctype> Ctype f5(Ctype a);
```

Exercise 16.8: Explain which, if any, of the following declarations are errors and why.

```
(a) template <class Type> Type bar(Type, Type);
    template <class Type> Type bar(Type, Type);
(b) template <class T1, class T2> void bar(T1, T2);
    template <class C1, typename C2> void bar(C1, C2);
```

Exercise 16.9: Write a template that acts like the library `find` algorithm. Your template should take a single type parameter that will name the type for a pair of iterators that should be parameters to the function. Use your function to find a given value in a `vector<int>` and in a `list<string>`.

16.1.4   Template Type Parameters

Type parameters consist of the keyword `class` or the keyword `typename` followed by an identifier. In a template parameter list, these keywords have the same meaning: They indicate that the name that follows represents a type.

A template type parameter can be used as a type specifier anywhere in the template, in exactly the same way as a built-in or class type specifier. In particular, it can be used to name the return type or a function parameter type, and for variable declarations or casts inside the function body:

```
//  ok: same type used for the return type and both parameters
template <class T> T calc(const T& a, const T& b)
{
    //  ok: tmp will have same type as the parameters & return type
    T tmp = a;
    //  ...
    return tmp;
}
```

Distinction Between `typename` and `class`

In a function template parameter list, the keywords `typename` and `class` have the same meaning and can be used interchangeably. Both keywords can be used in the same template parameter list:

```
//  ok: no distinction between typename and class in template parameter list
template <typename T, class U> calc (const T&, const U&);
```

It may seem more intuitive to use the keyword `typename` instead of the keyword `class` to designate a template type parameter; after all, we can use built-in (nonclass types) types as the actual type parameter. Moreover, `typename` more clearly indicates that the name that follows is a type name. However, the keyword `typename` was added to C++ as part of Standard C++, so older programs are more likely to use the keyword `class` exclusively.

Designating Types inside the Template Definition

In addition to defining data or function members, a class may define type members. For example, the library container classes define various types, such as `size_type`, that allow us to use the containers in a machine-independent way. When we want to use such types inside a function template, we must tell the compiler that the name we are using refers to a type. We must be explicit because the compiler (and a reader of our program) cannot tell by inspection when a name defined by a type parameter is a type or a value. As an example, consider the following function:

```
template <class Parm, class U>
Parm fcn(Parm* array, U value)
{
    Parm::size_type * p; // If Parm::size_type is a type, then a declaration
                         //  If Parm::size_type is an object, then multiplication
}
```

We know that `size_type` must be a member of the type bound to `Parm`, but we do not know whether `size_type` is the name of a type or a data member. By default, the compiler assumes that such names name data members, not types.

If we want the compiler to treat `size_type` as a type, then we must explicitly tell the compiler to do so:

```
template <class Parm, class U>
Parm fcn(Parm* array, U value)
{
    typename Parm::size_type * p; // ok: declares p to be a pointer
}
```

We tell the compiler to treat a member as a type by prefixing uses of the member name with the keyword `typename`. By writing `typename Parm::size_type` we say that member `size_type` of the type bound to `Parm` is the name of a type. Of course, this declaration puts an obligation on the types used to instantiate `fcn`: Those types must have a member named `size_type` that is a type.

> If there is any doubt as to whether `typename` is necessary to indicate that a name is a type, it is a good idea to specify it. There is no harm in specifying `typename` before a type, so if the `typename` was unnecessary, it won't matter.

EXERCISES SECTION 16.1.4

Exercise 16.10: What, if any, are the differences between a type parameter that is declared as a `typename` and one that is declared as a `class`?

Exercise 16.11: When must `typename` be used?

Exercise 16.12: Write a function template that takes a pair of values that represent iterators of unknown type. Find the value that occurs most frequently in the sequence.

Exercise 16.13: Write a function that takes a reference to a container and prints the elements in that container. Use the container's `size_type` and `size` members to control the loop that prints the elements.

Exercise 16.14: Rewrite the function from the previous exercise to use iterators returned from `begin` and `end` to control the loop.

16.1.5   Nontype Template Parameters

A template parameter need not be a type. In this section we'll look at nontype parameters as used by function templates. We'll look at nontype parameters for class templates in Section 16.4.2 (p. 655) after we've seen more about how class templates are implemented.

Nontype parameters are replaced by values when the function is called. The type of that value is specified in the template parameter list. For example, the following function template declares `array_init` as a function template with one type and one nontype template parameter. The function itself takes a single parameter, which is a reference to an array (Section 7.2.4, p. 240):

```
//  initialize elements of an array to zero
template <class T, size_t N> void array_init(T (&parm)[N])
{
    for (size_t i = 0; i != N; ++i) {
        parm[i] = 0;
    }
}
```

A template nontype parameter is a constant value inside the template definition. A nontype parameter can be used when constant expressions are required—for example, as we do here—to specify the size of an array.

When `array_init` is called, the compiler figures out the value of the nontype parameter from the array argument:

```
int x[42];
double y[10];
array_init(x);   //  instantiates array_init(int(&)[42]
array_init(y);   //  instantiates array_init(double(&)[10]
```

The compiler will instantiate a separate version of `array_init` for each kind of array used in a call to `array_init`. For the program above, the compiler instantiates two versions of `array_init`: The first instance has its parameter bound to `int[42]`, and in the other, that parameter is bound to `double[10]`.

Type Equivalence and Nontype Parameters

Expressions that evaluate to the same value are considered equivalent template arguments for a template nontype parameter. The following calls to `array_init` both refer to the same instantiation, `array_init<int, 42>`:

```
int x[42];
const int sz = 40;
int y[sz + 2];
array_init(x);   //  instantiates array_init(int(&)[42])
array_init(y);   //  equivalent instantiation
```

EXERCISES SECTION 16.1.5

Exercise 16.15: Write a function template that can determine the size of an array.

Exercise 16.16: Rewrite the `printValues` function from page 240 as a function template that could be used to print the contents of arrays of varying sizes.

16.1.6 Writing Generic Programs

When we write a template, the code may not be overtly type-specific, but template code always makes some assumptions about the types that will be used. For example, although our `compare` function is technically valid for any type, in practice the instantiated version might be illegal.

Whether the generated program is legal depends on the operations used in the function and the operations supported by the type or types used. Our `compare` function has has three statements:

```
if (v1 < v2) return -1;    // < on two objects of type T
if (v2 < v1) return 1;     // < on two objects of type T
return 0;                  // return int; not dependent on T
```

The first two statements contain code that implicitly depends on the parameter type. The `if` tests use the < operator on the parameters. The type of those parameters isn't known until the compiler sees a call to `compare` and `T` is bound to an actual type. Which < operator is used depends entirely on the argument type.

If we call `compare` on an object that does not support the < operator, then the call will be invalid:

```
Sales_item item1, item2;
//   error: no < on Sales_item
cout << compare(item1, item2) << endl;
```

The program is in error. The `Sales_item` type does not define the < operator, so the program won't compile.

The operations performed inside a function template constrains the types that can be used to instantiate the function. It is up to the programmer to guarantee that the types used as the function arguments actually support any operations that are used, and that those operations behave correctly in the context in which the template uses them.

Writing Type-Independent Code

The art of writing good generic code is beyond the scope of this language primer. However, there is one overall guideline that is worth noting.

When writing template code, it is useful to keep the number of requirements placed on the argument types as small as possible.

Simple though it is, our `compare` function illustrates two important principles for writing generic code:

- The parameters to the template are `const` references.

- The tests in the body use only < comparisons.

By making the parameters `const` references, we allow types that do not allow copying. Most types—including the built-in types and, except for the IO types, all the library types we've used—do allow copying. However, there can be class types that do not allow copying. By making our parameters `const` references, we ensure that such types can be used with our `compare` function. Moreover, if `compare` is called with large objects, then this design will also make the function run faster.

Some readers might think it would be more natural for the comparisons to be done using both the < and > operators:

```
// expected comparison
if (v1 < v2) return -1;
if (v1 > v2) return 1;
return 0;
```

However, by writing the code as

```
// expected comparison
if (v1 < v2) return -1;
if (v2 < v1) return 1;   // equivalent to v1 > v2
return 0;
```

we reduce the requirements on types that can be used with our compare function. Those types must support <, but they need not also support >.

EXERCISES SECTION 16.1.6

Exercise 16.17: In the "Key Concept" box on page 95, we noted that as a matter of habit C++ programmers prefer using ! = to using <. Explain the rationale for this habit.

Exercise 16.18: In this section we noted that we deliberately wrote the test in compare to avoid requiring a type to have both the < and > operators. On the other hand, we tend to assume that types will have both == and ! =. Explain why this seeming discrepancy in treatment actually reflects good programming style.

CAUTION: COMPILE-TIME ERRORS AT LINK-TIME

In general, when compiling a template, there are three stages during which the compiler might flag an error: The first is when we compile the template definition itself. The compiler generally can't find many errors at this stage. Syntax errors, such as forgetting a semicolon or misspelling a variable name, can be detected.

The second error-detection time is when the compiler sees a use of the template. At this stage, there is still not much the compiler can check. For a call to a function template, many compilers check only that the number and types of the arguments are appropriate. The compiler can detect that there are too many or too few arguments. It can also detect whether two arguments that are supposed to have the same type do so. For a class template, the compiler can check that the right number of template arguments are provided but not much else.

The third time when errors are generated is during instantiation. It is only then that type-related errors can be found. Depending on how the compiler manages instantiation, which we'll cover on page 643, these errors may be reported at link time.

It is important to realize that when we compile a template definition, we do not know much about how valid the program is. Similarly, we may obtain compiler errors even after we have successfully compiled each file that uses the template. It is not uncommon to detect errors only during instantiation, which may happen at link-time.

16.2 Instantiation

A template is a blueprint; it is not itself a class or a function. The compiler uses the template to generate type-specific versions of the specified class or function. The process of generatng a type-specific instance of a template is known as instantiation. The term reflects the notion that a new "instance" of the template type or function is created.

A template is instantiated when we use it. A class template is instantiated when we refer to the an actual template class type, and a function template is instantiated when we call it or use it to initialize or assign to a pointer to function.

Instantiating a Class

When we write

```
Queue<int> qi;
```

the compiler automatially creates a class named `Queue<int>`. In effect, the compiler creates the `Queue<int>` class by rewriting the `Queue` template, replacing every occurrence of the template parameter `Type` by the type `int`. The instantiated class is as if we had written:

```
//  simulated version of Queue instantiated for type int
template <class Type> class Queue<int> {
public:
    Queue();                        //  this bound to Queue<int>*
    int &front();                   //  return type bound to int
    const int &front() const;       //  return type bound to int
    void push(const int &);         //  parameter type bound to int
    void pop();                     //  type invariant code
    bool empty() const;             //  type invariant code
private:
    // ...
};
```

To create a `Queue` class for objects of type `string`, we'd write:

```
Queue<string> qs;
```

In this case, each occurrence of `Type` would be replaced by `string`.

 Each instantiation of a class template constitutes an independent class type. The `Queue` instantiation for the type `int` has no relationship to nor any special access to the members of any other `Queue` type.

Class Template Arguments Are Required

When we want to use a class template, we must always specify the template arguments explicitly.

```
Queue qs;    // error: which template instantiation?
```

A class template does not define a type; only a specific instantiation defines a type. We define a specific instantiation by providing a template argument to match each template parameter. Template arguments are specified in a comma-separated list and bracketed by the (<) and (>) tokens:

```
Queue<int> qi;      // ok: defines Queue that holds ints
Queue<string> qs;   // ok: defines Queue that holds strings
```

The type defined by a template class always includes the template argument(s). For example, Queue is not a type; Queue<int> or Queue<string> are.

Function-Template Instantiation

When we use a function template, the compiler will usually infer the template arguments for us:

```
int main()
{
    compare(1, 0);       // ok: binds template parameter to int
    compare(3.14, 2.7);  // ok: binds template parameter to double
    return 0;
}
```

This program instantiates two versions of compare: one where T is replaced by int and the other where it is replaced by double. The compiler essentially writes for us these two instances of compare:

```
int compare(const int &v1, const int &v2)
{
    if (v1 < v2) return -1;
    if (v2 < v1) return 1;
    return 0;
}
int compare(const double &v1, const double &v2)
{
    if (v1 < v2) return -1;
    if (v2 < v1) return 1;
    return 0;
}
```

16.2.1 Template Argument Deduction

To determine which functions to instantiate, the compiler looks at each argument. If the corresponding parameter was declared with a type that is a type parameter, then the compiler infers the type of the parameter from the type of the argument. In the case of compare, both arguments have the same template type: they were each declared using the type parameter T.

In the first call, compare(1, 0), those arguments are type int; in the second, compare(3.14, 2.7), they have type double. The process of determining the types and values of the template arguments from the type of the function arguments is called **template argument deduction**.

Multiple Type Parameter Arguments Must Match Exactly

A template type parameter may be used as the type of more than one function parameter. In such cases, template type deduction must generate the same template argument type for each corresponding function argument. If the deduced types do not match, then the call is an error:

```
template <typename T>
int compare(const T& v1, const T& v2)
{
    if (v1 < v2) return -1;
    if (v2 < v1) return 1;
    return 0;
}
int main()
{
    short si;
    //  error: cannot instantiate compare(short, int)
    //  must be: compare(short, short) or
    //           compare(int, int)
    compare(si, 1024);
    return 0;
}
```

This call is in error because the arguments to compare don't have the same type. The template argument deduced from the first argument is short; the one for the second is int. These types don't match, so template argument deduction fails.

If the designer of compare wants to allow normal conversions on the arguments, then the function must be defined with two type parameters:

```
//  argument types can differ, but must be compatible
template <typename A, typename B>
int compare(const A& v1, const B& v2)
{
    if (v1 < v2) return -1;
    if (v2 < v1) return 1;
    return 0;
}
```

Now the user may supply arguments of different types:

```
short si;
compare(si, 1024); // ok: instantiates compare(short, int)
```

However, a < operator must exist that can compare values of those types.

Limited Conversions on Type Parameter Arguments

Consider the following calls to compare:

```
short s1, s2;
int i1, i2;
compare(i1, i2);    // ok: instantiate compare(int,  int)
compare(s1, s2);    // ok: instantiate compare(short, short)
```

The first call generates an instance of `compare` with `T` bound to `int`. A new instance is created for the second call, binding `T` to `short`.

Had `compare(int, int)` been an ordinary nontemplate function, then the second call would match that function. The `short` arguments would be promoted (Section 5.12.2, p. 180) to `int`. Because `compare` is a template, a new function is instantiated with the type parameter bound to `short`.

In general, arguments are not converted to match an existing instantiation; instead, a new instance is generated. There are only two kinds of conversions that the compiler will perform rather than generating a new instantiation:

- `const` conversions: A function that takes a reference or pointer to a `const` can be called with a reference or pointer to nonconst object, respectively, without generating a new instantiation. If the function takes a nonreference type, then `const` is ignored on either the parameter type or the argument. That is, the same instantiation will be used whether we pass a `const` or nonconst object to a function defined to take a nonreference type.

- array or function to pointer conversions: If the template parameter is not a reference type, then the normal pointer conversion will be applied to arguments of array or function type. An array argument will be treated as a pointer to its first element, and a function argument will be treated as a pointer to the function's type.

As examples, consider calls to the functions `fobj` and `fref`. The `fobj` function copies its parameters, whereas `fref`'s parameters are references:

```
template <typename T> T fobj(T, T);        // arguments are copied
template <typename T>
T fref(const T&, const T&);                 // reference arguments
string s1("a value");
const string s2("another value");
fobj(s1, s2);       // ok: calls f(string, string), const is ignored
fref(s1, s2);       // ok: nonconst object s1 converted to const reference
int a[10], b[42];
fobj(a, b); // ok: calls f(int*, int*)
fref(a, b); // error: array types don't match; arguments aren't converted to pointers
```

In the first case, we pass a `string` and a `const string` as arguments. Even though these types do not match exactly, both calls are legal. In the call to `fobj`, the arguments are copied, so whether the original object is `const` doesn't matter. In the call to `fref`, the parameter type is a reference to `const`. Conversion to `const` for a reference parameter is one of the acceptable conversions, so this call is also okay.

In the next case, we pass array arguments in which the arrays are different sizes. In the call to `fobj`, the fact that the arrays are different doesn't matter. Both arrays are converted to pointers. The template parameter type in `fobj` is `int*`. The call to `fref`, however, is illegal. When the parameter is a reference (Section 7.2.4, p. 240), the arrays are not converted to pointers. The types of `a` and `b` don't match, so the call is in error.

Normal Conversions Apply for Nontemplate Arguments

 The restriction on type conversions applies only to those arguments whose types are template parameters.

Normal conversions (Section 7.1.2, p. 229) are allowed for parameters defined using ordinary types. The following function template sum has two parameters:

```
template <class Type> Type sum(const Type &op1, int op2)
{
    return op1 + op2;
}
```

The first parameter, op1, has a template parameter type. Its actual type cannot be known until the function is used. The type of the second parameter, op2, is known: It's int.

Because the type of op2 is fixed, normal conversions can be applied to arguments passed to op2 when sum is called:

```
double d = 3.14;
string s1("hiya"), s2(" world");
sum(1024, d);  // ok: instantiates sum(int, int), converts d to int
sum(1.4, d);   // ok: instantiates sum(double, int), converts d to int
sum(s1, s2);   // error: s2 cannot be converted to int
```

In the first two calls, the type of the second argument dd is not the same as the type of the corresponding function parameter. However, these calls are okay: There is a conversion from double to int. Because the type of the second parameter does not depend on a template parameter, the compiler will implicitly convert dd. The first call causes the function sum(int, int) to be instantiated; sum(double, int) is instantiated by the second call.

The third call is an error. There is no conversion from string to int. Using a string argument to match an int parameter is, as usual, illegal.

Template Argument Deduction and Function Pointers

We can use a function template to initialize or assign to a function pointer (Section 7.9, p. 276). When we do so, the compiler uses the type of the pointer to instantiate a version of the template with the appropriate template argument(s).

As an example, assume we have a function pointer that points to a function returning an int that takes two parameters, each of which is a reference to a const int. We could use that pointer to point to an instantiation of compare:

```
template <typename T> int compare(const T&, const T&);
// pf1 points to the instantiation int compare(const int&, const int&)
int (*pf1)(const int&, const int&) = compare;
```

The type of pf1 is "pointer to function returning an int taking two parameters of type const int&." The type of the parameters in pf1 determines the type of the template argument for T. The template argument for T is int. The pointer pf1 refers to the instantiation with T bound to int.

When the address of a function-template instantiation is taken, the context must be such that it allows a unique type or value to be determined for each template parameter.

It is an error if the template arguments cannot be determined from the function pointer type. For example, assume we have two functions named `func`. Each function takes a pointer to function argument. The first version of `func` takes a pointer to a function that has two `const string` reference parameters and returns a `string`. The second version of `func` takes a pointer to a function taking two `const int` reference parameters and returning an `int`. We cannot use `compare` as an argument to `func`:

```
// overloaded versions of func; each take a different function pointer type
void func(int(*)(const string&, const string&));
void func(int(*)(const int&, const int&));

func(compare); // error: which instantiation of compare?
```

The problem is that by looking at the type of `func`'s parameter, it is not possible to determine a unique type for the template argument. The call to `func` could instantiate either of the following functions:

```
compare(const string&, const string&)
compare(const int&, const int&)
```

Because it is not possible to identify a unique instantiation for the argument to `func`, this call is a compile-time (or link-time) error.

EXERCISES SECTION 16.2.1

Exercise 16.19: What is instantiation?

Exercise 16.20: What happens during template argument deduction?

Exercise 16.21: Name two type conversions allowed on function arguments involved in template argument deduction.

Exercise 16.22: Given the following templates

```
template <class Type>
Type calc(const Type* array, int size);
template <class Type>
Type fcn(Type p1, Type p2;
```
which ones of the following calls, if any, are errors? Why?
```
double dobj;    float fobj;    char cobj;
int ai[5] = { 511, 16, 8, 63, 34 };

(a) calc(cobj, 'c');
(b) calc(dobj, fobj);
(c) fcn(ai, cobj);
```

16.2.2   Function-Template Explicit Arguments

In some situations, it is not possible to deduce the types of the template arguments. This problem arises most often when a function return type must be a type that differs from any used in the parameter list. In such situations, it is necessary to override the template argument deduction mechanism and explicitly specify the types or values to be used for the template parameters.

Specifying an Explicit Template Argument

Consider the following problem. We wish to define a function template called `sum` that takes arguments of two differnt types. We'd like the return type to be large enough to contain the sum of two values of any two types passed in any order. How can we do that? How should we specify `sum`'s return type?

```
// T or U as the return type?
template <class T, class U> ??? sum(T, U);
```

In this case, the answer is that neither parameter works all the time. Using either parameter is bound to fail at some point:

```
// neither T nor U works as return type
sum(3, 4L); // second type is larger; want U sum(T, U)
sum(3L, 4); // first type is larger; want T sum(T, U)
```

One approach to solving this problem would be to force callers of `sum` to cast (Section 5.12.4, p. 183) the smaller type to the type we wish to use as the result:

```
// ok: now either T or U works as return type
int i; short s;
sum(static_cast<int>(s), i); // ok: instantiates int sum(int, int)
```

Using a Type Parameter for the Return Type

An alternative way to specify the return type is to introduce a third template parameter that must be explicitly specified by our caller:

```
// T1 cannot be deduced: it doesn't appear in the function parameter list
template <class T1, class T2, class T3>
T1 sum(T2, T3);
```

This version adds a template parameter to specify the return type. There is only one catch: There is no argument whose type can be used to infer the type of `T1`. Instead, the caller must explicitly provide an argument for this parameter on each call to `sum`.

We supply an explicit template argument to a call in much the same way that we define an instance of a class template. Explicit template arguments are specified in a comma-separated list, bracketed by the less-than (`<`) and greater-than (`>`) tokens. The list of explicit template types appears after the function name and before the argument list:

```
// ok T1 explicitly specified; T2 and T3 inferred from argument types
long val3 = sum<long>(i, lng); // ok: calls long sum(int, long)
```

This call explicitly specifies the type for `T1`. The compiler deduces the types for `T2` and `T3` from the arguments passed in the call.

Explicit template argument(s) are matched to corresponding template parameter(s) from left to right; the first template argument is matched to the first template parameter, the second argument to the second parameter, and so on. An explicit template argument may be omitted only for the trailing (rightmost) parameters, assuming these can be deduced from the function parameters. If our `sum` function had been written as

```
//  poor design: Users must explicitly specify all three template parameters
template <class T1, class T2, class T3>
T3 alternative_sum(T2, T1);
```

then we would always have to specify arguments for all three parameters:

```
//  error: can't infer initial template parameters
long val3 = alternative_sum<long>(i, lng);
//  ok: All three parameters explicitly specified
long val2  = alternative_sum<long, int, long>(i, lng);
```

Explicit Arguments and Pointers to Function Templates

Another example where explicit template arguments would be useful is the ambiguous program from page 641. We could disambiguate that case by using explicit template argument:

```
template <typename T> int compare(const T&, const T&);
//  overloaded versions of func; each take a different function pointer type
void func(int(*)(const string&, const string&));
void func(int(*)(const int&, const int&));
func(compare<int>); //  ok: explicitly specify which version of compare
```

As before, we want to pass an instantiation of `compare` in the call to the overloaded function named `func`. It is not possible to select which instantiation of `compare` to pass by looking at the parameter lists for the different versions of `func`. Two different instantiations of `compare` could satisfy the call. The explicit template argument indicates which instantiation of `compare` should be used and which `func` function is called.

16.3   Template Compilation Models

When the compiler sees a template definition, it does not generate code immediately. The compiler produces type-specific instances of the template only when it sees a use of the template, such as when a function template is called or an object of a class template is defined.

Ordinarily, when we call a function, the compiler needs to see only a declaration for the function. Similarly, when we define an object of class type, the class definition must be available, but the definitions of the member functions need not be present. As a result, we put class definitions and function declarations in header files and definitions of ordinary and class-member functions in source files.

Exercise 16.23: The library max function takes a single type parameter. Could you call max passing it an int and a double? If so, how? If not, why not?

Exercise 16.24: In Section 16.2.1 (p. 638) we saw that the arguments to the version of compare that has a single template type parameter must match exactly. If we wanted to call the function with compatible types, such as int and short, we could use an explicit template argument to specify either int or short as the parameter type. Write a program that uses the version of compare that has one template parameter. Call compare using an explicit template argument that will let you pass arguments of type int and short.

Exercise 16.25: Use an explicit template argument to make it sensible to call compare passing two string literals.

Exercise 16.26: Given the following template definition for sum

```
template <class T1, class T2, class T3> T1 sum(T2, T3);
```

explain each of the following calls. Indicate which, if any, are errors. For each error, explain what is wrong.

```
double dobj1, dobj2; float fobj1, fobj2; char cobj1, cobj2;

(a)  sum(dobj1, dobj2);
(b)  sum<double, double, double>(fobj1, fobj2);
(c)  sum<int>(cobj1, cobj2);
(d)  sum<double, ,double>(fobj2, dobj2);
```

Templates are different: To generate an instantiation, the compiler must have access to the source code that defines the template. When we call a function template or a member function of a class template, the compiler needs the function definition. It needs the code we normally put in the source files.

Standard C++ defines two models for compiling template code. In each of these models, we structure our programs in largely the same way: Class definitions and function declarations go in header files, and function and member definitions go in source files. The two models differ in how the definitions from the source files are made available to the compiler. As of this writing, all compilers support the first model, known as the "inclusion" model; only some compilers support the second, "separate compilation" model.

 To compile code that uses your own class and function templates, you must consult your compiler's user's guide to see how your compiler handles instantiation.

Inclusion Compilation Model

In the **inclusion compilation model**, the compiler must see the definition for any template that is used. Typically, we make the definitions available by adding a

#include directive to the headers that declare function or class templates. That
#include brings in the source file(s) that contain the associated definitions:

```
// header file utlities.h
#ifndef UTLITIES_H    // header gaurd (Section 2.9.2, p. 69)
#define UTLITIES_H
template <class T> int compare(const T&, const T&);
// other declarations

#include "utilities.cc"    // get the definitions for compare etc.
#endif

// implemenatation file utlities.cc
template <class T> int compare(const T &v1, const T &v2)
{
    if (v1 < v2) return -1;
    if (v2 < v1) return 1;
    return 0;
}
// other definitions
```

This strategy lets us maintain the separation of header files and implementation
files but ensures that the compiler will see both files when compiling code that
uses the templates.

Some, especially older, compilers that use the inclusion model may generate
multiple instantiations. If two or more separately compiled source files use the
same template, these compilers will generate an instantiation for the template in
each file. Ordinarily, this approach implies that a given template will be instantiated more than once. At link time, or during a prelink phase, the compiler selects
one instantiation, discarding the others. In such cases, compile-time performance
can be significantly degraded if there are a lot of files that instantiate the same
template. This compile-time degradation is unlikely to be a problem on modern
computers for many applications. However, in the context of large systems, the
compile-time hit may become important.

Such compilers often support mechanisms that avoid the compile-time overhead implicit in multiple instantiations of the same template. The way compilers
optimize compile-time performance varies from one compiler to the next. If compile time for programs using templates is too burdensome, consult your compiler's
user's guide to see what support your compiler offers to avoid redundant instantiations.

Separate Compilation Model

In the **separate compilation model**, the compiler keeps track of the associated template definitions for us. However, we must tell the compiler to remember a given
template definition. We use the **export keyword** to do so.

The export keyword indicates that a given definition might be needed to generate instantiations in other files. A template may be defined as exported only once
in a program. The compiler figures out how to locate the template definition when

it needs to generate these instantiations. The `export` keyword need not appear on the template declaration.

Ordinarily, we indicate that a function template is `exported` as part of its definition. We do so by including the keyword `export` before the `template` keyword:

```
//  the template definition goes in a separately-compiled source file
export template <typename Type>
Type sum(Type t1, Type t2)   /* ...*/
```

The declaration for this function template, should, as usual, be put in a header. The declaration must not specify `export`.

Using `export` on a class template is a bit more complicated. As usual, the class declaration must go in a header file. The class body in the header should not use the `export` keyword. If we used `export` in the header, then that header could be used by only one source file in the program.

Instead, we `export` the class in the class implementation file:

```
//  class template header goes in shared header file
template <class Type> class Queue { ... };
```
```
//  Queue.cc implementation file declares Queue as exported
export template <class Type> class Queue;
#include "Queue.h"
//  Queue member definitions
```

The members of an exported class are automatically declared as exported. It is also possible to declare individual members of a class template as exported. In this case, the keyword `export` is not specified on the class template itself. It is specified only on the specific member definitions to be exported. The definition of exported member functions need not be visible when the member is used. The definitions of any nonexported member must be treated as in the inclusion model: The definition should be placed inside the header that defines the class template.

EXERCISES SECTION 16.3

Exercise 16.27: Determine which compilation model your compiler uses. Write and call a function template to find the median value in a `vector` that holds objects of unknown type. (Note: The median is a value such that half the elements are larger than the median, and half are smaller.) Structure your program in the normal way: The function definition should go in one file, a declaration for it in a header, which the code that defines and uses the function template should include.

Exercise 16.28: Where would you place the definitions for the member functions and `static` data members of your class templates if the compiler you use supports the separation compilation model? Explain why.

Exercise 16.29: Where would you put those template member definitions if your compiler uses the inclusion model? Explain why.

> ### CAUTION: NAME LOOKUP IN CLASS TEMPLATES
>
> Compiling templates is a surprisingly difficult task. Fortunately, it is a task handled by compiler writers. Unfortunately, some of that complexity is pushed onto users of templates: Templates contain two kinds of names:
>
> 1. Those that do not depend on a template parameter
>
> 2. Those that do depend on a template parameter
>
> It is up to the template designer to ensure that all names that do not depend on a template parameter are defined in the same scope as the template itself.
>
> It is up to *users* of a template to ensure that declarations for all functions, types, and operators associated with the types used to instantiate the template are visible. This responsibility means that the user must ensure that these declarations are visible when a member of a class template or a function template is instantiated.
>
> Both of these requirements are easily satisfied by well-structured programs that make appropriate use of headers. Authors of templates should provide a header that contains declarations for all the names used in the class template or in the definitions of its members. Before defining a template on a particular type or using a member of that template, the user must ensure that the header for the template type and the header that defines the type used as the element type are included.

16.4   Class Template Members

So far we have seen only how to declare the interface members of our `Queue` class template. In this section, we'll look at how we might implement the class.

> The standard library implements `queue` as an adaptor (Section 9.7, p. 348) on top of another container. To emphasize the programming points involved in using a lower-level data structure, we'll implement our `Queue` class as a linked list. In practice, using a library container in our implementation would probably be a better decision.

`Queue` Implementation Strategy

Our implementation, shown in Figure 16.1 on the next page, uses two classes:

1. Class `QueueItem` will represent a node in `Queue`'s linked list. This class has two data members: `item` and `next`:

   - `item` holds the value of the element in the `Queue`; its type varies with each instance of `Queue`.

   - `next` is a pointer to the next `QueueItem` object in the queue.

   Each element in the `Queue` is stored in a `QueueItem` object.

2. Class `Queue` will provide the interface functions described in Section 16.1.2 (p. 627). The `Queue` class will also have two data members: `head` and `tail`. These members are pointers to `QueueItem`.

As do the standard containers, our `Queue` class will copy the values it's given.

Figure 16.1: `Queue` Implementation

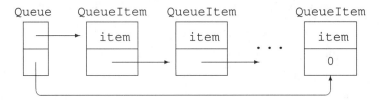

The `QueueItem` Class

We'll start our implementation by writing the `QueueItem` class:

```
template <class Type> class QueueItem {
// private class: no public section
    QueueItem(const Type &t): item(t), next(0) { }
    Type item;              // value stored in this element
    QueueItem *next;        // pointer to next element in the Queue
};
```

As it stands, this class is already complete: It holds two data elements, which its constructor initializes. Like `Queue`, `QueueItem` is a class template. The class uses its template parameter to name the type of its `item` member. The value of each element in the `Queue` will be stored in `item`.

Each time we instantiate a `Queue` class, the same version of `QueueItem` will be instantiated as well. For example, if we create `Queue<int>`, then a companion class, `QueueItem<int>`, will be instantiated.

Class `QueueItem` is a private class—it has no public interface. We intend this class to be used to implement `Queue` and have not built it for general use. Hence, it has no public members. We'll need to make class `Queue` a friend of `QueueItem` so that its members can access the members of `QueueItem`. We'll see how to do so in Section 16.4.4 (p. 658).

 Inside the scope of a class template, we may refer to the class using its unqualified name.

The `Queue` Class

We can now flesh out our `Queue` class:

```
template <class Type> class Queue {
public:
    // empty Queue
    Queue(): head(0), tail(0) { }
    // copy control to manage pointers to QueueItems in the Queue
    Queue(const Queue &Q): head(0), tail(0)
                                { copy_elems(Q); }
    Queue& operator=(const Queue&);
    ~Queue() { destroy(); }
```

```
        //  return element from head of Queue
        //  unchecked operation: front on an empty Queue is undefined
        Type& front()           { return head->item; }
        const Type &front() const { return head->item; }

        void push(const Type &);    //  add element to back of Queue
        void pop();                 //  remove element from head of Queue

        bool empty() const {        //  true if no elements in the Queue
            return head == 0;
        }
    private:
        QueueItem<Type> *head;      //  pointer to first element in Queue
        QueueItem<Type> *tail;      //  pointer to last element in Queue

        //  utility functions used by copy constructor, assignment, and destructor
        void destroy();             //  delete all the elements
        void copy_elems(const Queue&); //  copy elements from parameter
    };
```

In addition to the interface members, we have added the three copy-control members (Chapter 13) and associated utility functions used by those members. The `private` utility functions `destroy` and `copy_elems` will do the work of freeing the elements in the `Queue` and copying elements from another `Queue` into this one. The copy-control members are needed to manage the data members, `head` and `tail`, which are pointers to the first and last elements in the `Queue`. These elements are values of type `QueueItem<Type>`.

The class implements several of its member functions:

- The default constructor sets both `head` and `tail` pointers to zero, indicating that the `Queue` is currently empty.

- The copy constructor initializes `head` and `tail`, and calls `copy_elems` to copy the elements from its initializer.

- The `front` functions return the value at the head of the `Queue`. These functions do no checking: As with the analogous operations in the standard `queue`, users may not run `front` on an empty `Queue`.

- The `empty` function returns the result of comparing `head` with zero. If `head` is zero, the `Queue` is empty; otherwise, it is not.

References to a Template Type in the Scope of the Template

For the most part, this class definition should be familiar. It differs little from other classes that we have defined. What is new is the use (or lack thereof) of the template type parameter in references to the `Queue` and `QueueItem` types.

Ordinarily, when we use the name of a class template, we must specify the template parameters. There is one exception to this rule: Inside the scope of the class itself, we may use the unqualified name of the class template. For example, in the declarations of the default and copy constructor the name `Queue` is a shorthand notation that stands for `Queue<Type>`. Essentially the compiler infers that when we refer to the name of the class, we are referring to the same version. Hence, the copy constructor definition is really equivalent to writing:

```
Queue<Type>(const Queue<Type> &Q): head(0), tail(0)
              { copy_elems(Q); }
```

The compiler performs no such inference for the template parameter(s) for other templates used within the class. Hence, we must specify the type parameter when declaring pointers to the companion QueueItem class:

```
QueueItem<Type> *head;        //  pointer to first element in Queue
QueueItem<Type> *tail;        //  pointer to last element in Queue
```

These declarations say that for a given instantiation of class Queue, head and tail point to an object of type QueueItem instantiated for the same template parameter. That is, the type of head and tail inside the Queue< int > instantiation is QueueItem< int >*. It would be an error to omit the template parameter in the definition of the head and tail members:

```
QueueItem *head; //  error: which version of QueueItem?
QueueItem *tail; //  error: which version of QueueItem?
```

EXERCISES SECTION 16.4

Exercise 16.30: Identify which, if any, of the following class template declarations (or declaration pairs) are illegal.

```
(a) template <class Type> class C1;
    template <class Type, int size> class C1;
(b) template <class T, U, class V> class C2;
(c) template <class C1, typename C2> class C3 { };
(d) template <typename myT, class myT> class C4 { };
(e) template <class Type, int *ptr> class C5;
    template <class T, int *pi> class C5;
```

Exercise 16.31: The following definition of List is incorrect. How would you fix it?

```
template <class elemType> class ListItem;

template <class elemType> class List {
public:
    List<elemType>();
    List<elemType>(const List<elemType> &);
    List<elemType>& operator=(const List<elemType> &);
    ~List();
    void insert(ListItem *ptr, elemType value);
    ListItem *find(elemType value);
private:
    ListItem *front;
    ListItem *end;
};
```

16.4.1 Class-Template Member Functions

The definition of a member function of a class template has the following form:

- It must start with the keyword `template` followed by the template parameter list for the class.

- It must indicate the class of which it is a member.

- The class name must include its template parameters.

From these rules, we can see that a member function of class `Queue` defined outside the class will start as

```
template <class T> ret-type Queue<T>::member-name
```

The destroy Function

To illustrate a class template member function defined outside its class, let's look at the `destroy` function:

```
template <class Type> void Queue<Type>::destroy()
{
    while (!empty())
        pop();
}
```

This definition can be read from left to right as:

- Defining a function template with a single type parameter named `Type`

- that returns `void`,

- which is in the scope of the `Queue<Type>` class template.

The use of `Queue<Type>` preceding the scope operator (`::`) names the class to which the member function belongs.

Following the member-function name is the function definition. In the case of `destroy`, the function body looks very much like an ordinary nontemplate function definition. Its job is to walk the list of entries in this `Queue`, calling `pop` to remove each item.

The pop Function

The pop member removes the value at the front of the `Queue`:

```
template <class Type> void Queue<Type>::pop()
{
    // pop is unchecked: Popping off an empty Queue is undefined
    QueueItem<Type>* p = head;  // keep pointer to head so we can delete it
    head = head->next;          // head now points to next element
    delete p;                   // delete old head element
}
```

The pop function assumes that users do not call pop on an empty Queue. The job of pop is to remove the element at the start of the Queue. We must reset the head pointer to point to the next element in the Queue, and then delete the element that had been at the head. The only tricky part is remembering to keep a separate pointer to that element so we can delete it after resetting the head pointer.

The push Function

The push member places a new item at the back of the queue:

```
template <class Type> void Queue<Type>::push(const Type &val)
{
    // allocate a new QueueItem object
    QueueItem<Type> *pt = new QueueItem<Type>(val);
    // put item onto existing queue
    if (empty())
        head = tail = pt;       // the queue now has only one element
    else {
        tail->next = pt;        // add new element to end of the queue
        tail = pt;
    }
}
```

This function starts by allocating a new QueueItem, which is initialized from the value we were passed. There's actually a surprising bit of work going on in this statement:

1. The QueueItem constructor copies its argument into the QueueItem's item member. As do the standard containers, our Queue class stores copies of the elements it is given.

2. If item is a class type, the initialization of item uses the copy constructor of whatever type item has.

3. The QueueItem constructor also initializes the next pointer to 0 to indicate that this element points to no other QueueItem.

Because we're adding the element at the end of the Queue, setting next to 0 is eactly what we want.

Having created and initialized a new element, we must next hook it into the Queue. If the Queue is empty, then both head and tail should point to this new element. If there are already other elements in the Queue, then we make the current tail element point to this new element. The old tail is no longer the last element, which we indicate by making tail point to the newly constructed element as well.

The copy Function

Aside from the assignment operator, which we leave as an exercise, the only remaining function to write is copy_elems. This function is designed to be used by the assignment operator and copy constructor. Its job is to copy the elements from its parameter into this Queue:

```
template <class Type>
void Queue<Type>::copy_elems(const Queue &orig)
{
    // copy elements from orig into this Queue
    // loop stops when pt == 0, which happens when we reach orig.tail
    for (QueueItem<Type> *pt = orig.head; pt; pt = pt->next)
        push(pt->item);   // copy the element
}
```

We copy the elements in a `for` loop that starts by setting `pt` equal to the parameter's `head` pointer. The `for` continues until `pt` is 0, which happens after we get to the element that is the last one in `orig`. For each element in `orig`, we `push` a copy of value in that element onto this `Queue` and advance `pt` to point to the next element in `orig`.

Instantiation of Class-Template Member Functions

Member functions of class templates are themselves function templates. Like any other function template, a member function of a class template is used to generate instantiations of that member. Unlike other function templates, the compiler does not perform template-argument deduction when instantiating class template member functions. Instead, the template parameters of a class template member function are determined by the type of the object on which the call is made. For example, when we call the `push` member of an object of type `Queue<int>`, the `push` function that is instantiated is

```
void Queue<int>::push(const int &val)
```

The fact that member-function template parameters are fixed by the template arguments of the object means that calling a class template member function is more flexible than comparable calls to function templates. Normal conversions are allowed on arguments to function parameters that were defined using the template parameter:

```
Queue<int> qi;    // instantiates class Queue<int>
short s = 42;
int i = 42;
// ok: s converted to int and passed to push
qi.push(s); // instantiates Queue<int>::push(const int&)
qi.push(i); // uses Queue<int>::push(const int&)
f(s);       // instantiates f(const short&)
f(i);       // instantiates f(const int&)
```

When Classes and Members Are Instantiated

Member functions of a class template are instantiated only for functions that are used by the program. If a function is never used, then that member function is never instantiated. This behavior implies that types used to instantiate a template need to meet only the requirements of the operations that are actually used. As an example, recall the sequential container constructor (Section 9.1.1, p. 309) that takes only a size parameter. That constructor uses the default constructor for the element type. If we have a type that does not define the default constructor, we may still define a container to hold this type. However, we may not use the constructor that takes only a size.

When we define an object of a template type, that definition causes the class template to be instantiated. Defining an object also instantiates whichever constructor was used to initialize the object, along with any members called by that constructor:

```
//  instantiates Queue<int> class and Queue<int>::Queue()
Queue<string> qs;
qs.push("hello");   // instantiates Queue<int>::push
```

The first statement instantiates the Queue<string> class and its default constructor. The next statement instantiates the push member function.

The instantiation of the push member:

```
template <class Type> void Queue<Type>::push(const Type &val)
{
    //  allocate a new QueueItem object
    QueueItem<Type> *pt = new QueueItem<Type>(val);
    //  put item onto existing queue
    if (empty())
        head = tail = pt;     //  the queue now has only one element
    else {
        tail->next = pt;      //  add new element to end of the queue
        tail = pt;
    }
}
```

in turn instantiates the companion QueueItem<string> class and its constructor.

The QueueItem members in Queue are pointers. Defining a pointer to a class template doesn't instantiate the class; the class is instantiated only when we use such a pointer. Thus, QueueItem is not instantiated when we create a Queue object. Instead, the QueueItem class is instanatiated when a Queue member such as front, push, or pop is used.

EXERCISES SECTION 16.4.1

Exercise 16.32: Implement the assignment operator for class Queue.

Exercise 16.33: Explain how the next pointers in the newly created Queue get set during the copy_elems function.

Exercise 16.34: Write the member function definitions of the List class that you defined for the exercises in Section 16.1.2 (p. 628).

Exercise 16.35: Write a generic version of the CheckedPtr class described in Section 14.7 (p. 526).

16.4.2   Template Arguments for Nontype Parameters

Now that we've seen more about how class templates are implemented, we can look at nontype parameters for class templates. We'll do so by defining a new version of the Screen class first introduced in Chapter 12. In this case, we'll redefine Screen to be a template, parameterized by its height and width:

```
template <int hi, int wid>
class Screen {
public:
    // template nontype parameters used to initialize data members
    Screen(): screen(hi * wid, '#'), cursor (0),
              height(hi), width(wid) { }
    // ...
private:
    std::string               screen;
    std::string::size_type cursor;
    std::string::size_type height, width;
};
```

This template has two parameters, both of which are nontype parameters. When users define Screen objects, they must provide a constant expression to use for each of these parameters. The class uses these parameters in the default constructor to set the size of the default Screen.

As with any class template, the parameter values must be explicitly stated whenever we use the Screen type:

```
Screen<24,80> hp2621;  // screen 24 lines by 80 characters
```

The object hp2621 uses the template instantiation Screen<24,80>. The template argument for hi is 24, and the argument for wid is 80. In both cases, the template argument is a constant expression.

 Nontype template arguments must be compile-time constant expressions.

16.4.3   Friend Declarations in Class Templates

There are three kinds of friend declarations that may appear in a class template. Each kind of declaration declares friendship to one or more entities:

1. A friend declaration for an ordinary nontemplate class or function, which grants friendship to the specific named class or function.

2. A friend declaration for a class template or function template, which grants access to all instances of the friend.

3. A friend declaration that grants access only to a specific instance of a class or function template.

Exercise 16.36: Explain what instantiations, if any, are caused by each labeled statement.

```
template <class T> class Stack { };
void f1(Stack<char>);                        // (a)
class Exercise {
    Stack<double> &rsd;                      // (b)
    Stack<int>    si;                        // (c)
};
int main() {
    Stack<char> *sc;                         // (d)
    f1(*sc);                                 // (e)
    int iObj = sizeof(Stack< string >);      // (f)
}
```

Exercise 16.37: Identify which, if any, of the following template instantiations are valid. Explain why the instantiation isn't valid.

```
template <class T, int size> class Array { /* . . . */ };
template <int hi, int wid> class Screen { /* . . . */ };
(a) const int hi = 40, wi = 80; Screen<hi, wi+32> sObj;
(b) const int arr_size = 1024;  Array<string, arr_size> a1;
(c) unsigned int asize = 255;   Array<int, asize> a2;
(e) const double db = 3.1415;   Array<double, db> a3;
```

Ordinary Friends

A nontemplate class or function can be a friend to a class template:

```
template <class Type> class Bar {
    //  grants access to ordinary, nontemplate class and function
    friend class FooBar;
    friend void fcn();
    // ...
};
```

This declaration says that the members of `FooBar` and the function `fcn` may access the `private` and `protected` members of any instantiation of class `Bar`.

General Template Friendship

A friend can be a class or function template:

```
template <class Type> class Bar {
    //  grants access to Foo1 or templ_fcn1 parameterized by any type
    template <class T> friend class Foo1;
    template <class T> friend void templ_fcn1(const T&);
    // ...
};
```

These friend declarations use a different type parameter than does the class itself. That type parameter refers to the type parameter of `Foo1` and `templ_fcn1`. In both these cases, an unlimited number of classes and functions are made friends to `Bar`. The friend declaration for `Foo1` says that any instance of `Foo1` may access the private elements of any instance of `Bar`. Similarly, any instance of `templ_fcn1` may access any instance of `Bar`.

This friend declaration establishes a one-to-many mapping between each instantiation of `Bar` and its friends, `Foo1` and `templ_fcn1`. For each instantiation of `Bar`, all instantiations of `Foo1` or `templ_fcn1` are friends.

Specific Template Friendship

Rather than making all instances of a template a friend, a class can grant access to only a specific instance:

```
template <class T> class Foo2;
template <class T> void templ_fcn2(const T&);
template <class Type> class Bar {
    //  grants access to a single specific instance parameterized by char*
    friend class Foo2<char*>;
    friend void templ_fcn2<char*>(char* const &);
    // ...
};
```

Even though `Foo2` itself is a class template, friendship is extended only to the specific instance of `Foo2` that is parameterized by `char*`. Similarly, the friend declaration for `templ_fcn2` says that only the instance of that function parameterized by `char*` is a friend to class `Bar`. The specific instantiations of `Foo2` and `templ_fcn2` parameterized by `char*` can access every instantiation of `Bar`.

More common are friend declarations of the following form:

```
template <class T> class Foo3;
template <class T> void templ_fcn3(const T&);
template <class Type> class Bar {
    //  each instantiation of Bar grants access to the
    //  version of Foo3 or templ_fcn3 instantiated with the same type
    friend class Foo3<Type>;
    friend void templ_fcn3<Type>(const Type&);
    // ...
};
```

These friends define friendship between a particular instantiation of `Bar` and the instantiation of `Foo3` or `templ_fcn3` that uses the same template argument. Each instantiation of `Bar` has a single associated `Foo3` and `templ_fcn3` friend:

```
Bar<int> bi;     // Foo3<int> and templ_fcn3<int> are friends
Bar<string> bs;  // Foo3<string>, templ_fcn3<string> are friends
```

Only those versions of `Foo3` or `templ_fcn3` that have the same template argument as a given instantiation of `Bar` are friends. Thus, `Foo3<int>` may access the private parts of `Bar<int>` but not of `Bar<string>` or any other instantiation of `Bar`.

Declaration Dependencies

When we grant access to all instances of a given template, there need not be a declaration for that class or function template in scope. Essentially, the compiler treats the friend declaration as a declaration of the class or function as well.

When we want to restrict friendship to a specific instantiation, then the class or function must have been declared before it can be used in a friend declaration:

```
template <class T> class A;
template <class T> class B {
public:
    friend class A<T>;      //  ok: A is known to be a template
    friend class C;         //  ok: C must be an ordinary, nontemplate class
    template <class S> friend class D; //  ok: D is a template
    friend class E<T>;      //  error: E wasn't declared as a template
    friend class F<int>;  //  error: F wasn't declared as a template
};
```

If we have not previously told the compiler that the friend is a template, then the compiler will infer that the friend is an ordinary nontemplate class or function.

16.4.4   `Queue` and `QueueItem` Friend Declarations

Our `QueueItem` class is not intended to be used by the general program: All its members are private. In order for `Queue` to use `QueueItem`, `QueueItem` must make `Queue` a friend.

Making a Class Template a Friend

As we have just seen, when making a class template a friend, the class designer must decide how wide to make that friendship. In the case of `QueueItem`, we need to decide whether `QueueItem` should grant friendship to all `Queue` instances or only to a specific instance.

Making every `Queue` a friend of each `QueueItem` is too broad. It makes no sense to allow a `Queue` instantiated with the type `string` to access members of a `QueueItem` instantiated with type `double`. The `Queue<string>` instantiation should be a friend only to the instantiation of the `QueueItem` for `strings`. That is, we want a one-to-one mapping between a `Queue` and `QueueItem` for each type of `Queue` that is instantiated:

```
// declaration that Queue is a template needed for friend declaration in QueueItem
template <class Type> class Queue;
template <class Type> class QueueItem {
    friend class Queue<Type>;
    // ...
};
```

This declaration establishes the desired one-to-one mapping; only the `Queue` class that is instantiated with the same type as `QueueItem` is made a friend.

The `Queue` Output Operator

One operation that might be useful to add to our `Queue` interface is the ability to print the contents of a `Queue` object. We'll do so by providing an overloaded instance of the output operator. This operator will walk the list of elements in the `Queue` and print the value in each element. We'll print the elements inside a pair of brackets.

Because we want to be able to print the contents of `Queue`s of any type, we need to make the output operator a template as well:

```
template <class Type>
ostream& operator<<(ostream &os, const Queue<Type> &q)
{
    os << "< ";
    QueueItem<Type> *p;
    for (p = q.head; p; p = p->next)
            os << p->item << " ";
    os <<">";
    return os;
}
```

If a `Queue` of type `int` contains the values 3, 5, 8, and 13, the output of this `Queue` displays as follows:

```
< 3 5 8 13 >
```

If the `Queue` is empty, the `for` loop body is never executed. The effect will be to print an empty pair of brackets if the `Queue` is empty.

Making a Function Template a Friend

The output operator needs to be a friend of both the `Queue` and `QueueItem` classes. It uses the `head` member of class `Queue` and the `next` and `item` members of class `QueueItem`. Our classes grant friendship to the specific instance of the output operator instantiated with the same type:

```
// function template declaration must precede friend declaration in QueueItem
template <class T>
std::ostream& operator<<(std::ostream&, const Queue<T>&);

template <class Type> class QueueItem {
    friend class Queue<Type>;
    // needs access to item and next
    friend std::ostream&
    operator<< <Type> (std::ostream&, const Queue<Type>&);
    // ...
};
template <class Type> class Queue {
    // needs access to head
    friend std::ostream&
    operator<< <Type> (std::ostream&, const Queue<Type>&);
};
```

Each friend declaration grants access to the corresponding instantiation of the `operator<<`. That is, the output operator that prints a `Queue<int>` is a friend to class `Queue<int>` (and `QueueItem<int>`). It is not a friend to any other `Queue` type.

Type Dependencies and the Output Operator

The `Queue` output `operator<<` relies on the `operator<<` of `item` to actually print each element:

```
os << p->item << " ";
```

When we use `p->item` as an operand of the `<<` operator, we are using the `<<` defined for whatever type `item` has.

This code is an example of a type dependency between `Queue` and the element type that `Queue` holds. In effect, each type bound to `Queue` that uses the `Queue` output operator must itself have an output operator. There is no language mechanism to specify or enforce that dependency in the definition of `Queue` itself. It is legal to create a `Queue` for a class that does not define the output operator but it is a compile-time (or link-time) error to print a `Queue` holding such a type.

EXERCISES SECTION 16.4.4

Exercise 16.38: Write a `Screen` class template that uses nontype parameters to define the height and width of the `Screen`.

Exercise 16.39: Implement input and output operators for the template `Screen` class.

Exercise 16.40: Which, if any, friends are necessary in class `Screen` to make the input and output operators work? Explain why each friend declaration, if any, was needed.

Exercise 16.41: The friend declaration for `operator<<` in class `Queue` was

```
friend std::ostream&
operator<< <Type> (std::ostream&, const Queue<Type>&);
```

What would be the effect of writing the `Queue` parameter as `const Queue&` rather than `const Queue<Type>&`?

Exercise 16.42: Write an input operator that reads an `istream` and puts the values it reads into a `Queue`.

16.4.5   Member Templates

Any class (template or otherwise) may have a member that is itself a class or function template. Such members are referred to as **member templates**. Member templates may not be virtual.

One example of a member template is the `assign` (Section 9.3.8, p. 328) member of the standard containers. The version `assign` that takes two iterators uses a template parameter to represent the type of its iterator parameters. Another member template example is the container constructor that takes two iterators (Section 9.1.1, p. 307). This constructor and the `assign` member allow containers to be built from sequences of different but compatible element types and/or different container types. Having implemented our own `Queue` class, we now can understand the design of these standard container members a bit better.

Consider the `Queue` copy constructor: It takes a single parameter that is a reference to a `Queue<Type>`. If we wanted to create a `Queue` by copying elements from a `vector`, we could not do so; there is no conversion from `vector` to `Queue`. Similarly, if we wanted to copy elements from a `Queue<short>` into a `Queue<int>`, we could not do so. Again, even though we can convert a `short` to an `int`, there is no conversion from `Queue<short>` to `Queue<int>`. The same logic applies to the `Queue` assignment operator, which also takes a parameter of type `Queue<Type>&`.

The problem is that the copy constructor and assignment operator fix both the container and element type. We'd like to define a constructor and an `assign` member that allow both the container and element type to vary. When we need a parameter type to vary, we need to define a function template. In this case, we'll define the constructor and `assign` member to take a pair of iterators that denote a range in some other sequence. These functions will have a single template type parameter that represents an iterator type.

The standard queue class does not define these members: `queue` doesn't support building or assigning a queue from another container. We define these members here for illustration purposes only.

Defining a Member Template

A template member declaration looks like the declaration of any template:

```
template <class Type> class Queue {
public:
    //  construct a Queue from a pair of iterators on some sequence
    template <class It>
    Queue(It beg, It end):
            head(0), tail(0) { copy_elems(beg, end); }
    //  replace current Queue by contents delimited by a pair of iterators
    template <class Iter> void assign(Iter, Iter);
    //  rest of Queue class as before
private:
    //  version of copy to be used by assign to copy elements from iterator range
    template <class Iter> void copy_elems(Iter, Iter);
};
```

The member declaration starts with its own template parameter list. The constructor and `assign` member each have a single template type parameter. These functions use that type parameter as the type for their function parameters, which are iterators denoting a range of elements to copy.

Defining a Member Template Outside the Class

Like nontemplate members, a member template can be defined inside or outside
of its enclosing class or class template definition. We have defined the constructor
inside the class body. Its job is to copy the elements from the iterator range formed
by its iterator arguments. It does so by calling the iterator version of `copy_elems`
to do the actual copy.

When we define a member template outside the scope of a class template, we
must include both template parameter lists:

```
template <class T> template <class Iter>
void Queue<T>::assign(Iter beg, Iter end)
{
    destroy();                 // remove existing elements in this Queue
    copy_elems(beg, end);  // copy elements from the input range
}
```

When a member template is a member of a class template, then its definition must
include the class-template parameters as well as its own template parameters. The
class-template parameter list comes first, followed by the member's own template
parameter list. The definition of `assign` starts with

```
template <class T> template <class Iter>
```

The first template parameter list—`template<class T>`—is that of the class template. The second template parameter list—`template<class Iter>`—is that of
the member template.

The actions of our `assign` function are quite simple: It first calls `destroy`,
which, as we've seen, frees the existing members of this `Queue`. The `assign` member then calls a new utility function named `copy_elems` to do the work of copying
elements from the input range. That function is also a member template:

```
template <class Type> template <class It>
void Queue<Type>::copy_elems(It beg, It end)
{
    while (beg != end) {
        push(*beg);
        ++beg;
    }
}
```

The iterator version of `copy_elems` walks through an input range denoted by a
pair of iterators. It calls `push` on each element in that range, which actually adds
the element to the `Queue`.

Because `assign` erases elements in the existing container, it is essential that the iterators passed to `assign` refer to elements in a different
container. The standard container `assign` members and iterator constructors have the same restrictions.

Member Templates Obey Normal Access Control

A member template follows the same access rules as any other class members. If the member template is private, then only member functions and friends of the class can use that member template. Because the function member template `assign` is a public member, it can be used by the entire program; `copy_elems` is private, so it can be accessed only by the friends and members of `Queue`.

Member Templates and Instantiation

Like any other member, a member template is instantiated only when it is used in a program. The instantiation of member templates of class templates is a bit more complicated than the instantiation of plain member functions of class templates. Member templates have two kinds of template parameters: Those that are defined by the class and those defined by the member template itself. The class template parameters are fixed by the type of the object through which the function is called. The template parameters defined by the member act like parameters of ordinary function templates. These parameters are resolved through normal template argument deduction (Section 16.2.1, p. 637).

To understand how instantiation works, let's look at uses of these members to copy and assign elements from an array of `short`s or a `vector<int>`:

```
short a[4] = { 0, 3, 6, 9 };
// instantiates Queue<int>::Queue(short *, short *)
Queue<int> qi(a, a + 4);  // copies elements from a into qi

vector<int> vi(a, a + 4);
// instantiates Queue<int>::assign(vector<int>::iterator,
//                               vector<int>::iterator)
qi.assign(vi.begin(), vi.end());
```

Because we are constructing an object of type `Queue<int>`, we know that the compiler will instantiate the iterator-based constructor for `Queue<int>`. The type of the constructor's own template parameter is deduced by the compiler from the type of a and a + 4. That type is pointer to `short`. Thus, the definition of qi instantiates

```
void Queue<int>::Queue(short *, short *);
```

The effect of this constructor is to copy the elements of type `short` from the array named a into qi.

The call to `assign` instantiates a member of qi, which has type `Queue<int>`. Thus, this call instantiates the `Queue<int>` member named `assign`. That function is itself a function template. As with any other function template, the compiler deduces the template argument for `assign` from the arguments to the call. The type deduced is `vector<int>::iterator`, meaning that this call instantiates

```
void Queue<int>::assign(vector<int>::iterator,
                        vector<int>::iterator);
```

16.4.6 The Complete `Queue` Class

For completeness, here is the final definition of our `Queue` class:

```
//  declaration that Queue is a template needed for friend declaration in QueueItem
template <class Type> class Queue;
//  function template declaration must precede friend declaration in QueueItem
template <class T>
std::ostream& operator<<(std::ostream&, const Queue<T>&);

template <class Type> class QueueItem {
    friend class Queue<Type>;
    //  needs access to item and next
    friend std::ostream&         //  defined on page 659
    operator<< <Type> (std::ostream&, const Queue<Type>&);
//  private class: no public section
    QueueItem(const Type &t): item(t), next(0) { }
    Type item;                 //  value stored in this element
    QueueItem *next;           //  pointer to next element in the Queue
};

template <class Type> class Queue {
    //  needs access to head
    friend std::ostream&         //  defined on page 659
    operator<< <Type> (std::ostream&, const Queue<Type>&);
public:
    //  empty Queue
    Queue(): head(0), tail(0) { }
    //  construct a Queue from a pair of iterators on some sequence
    template <class It>
    Queue(It beg, It end):
          head(0), tail(0) { copy_elems(beg, end); }
    //  copy control to manage pointers to QueueItems in the Queue
    Queue(const Queue &Q): head(0), tail(0)
                                     { copy_elems(Q); }
    Queue& operator=(const Queue&); //  left as exercise for the reader
    ~Queue() { destroy(); }

    //  replace current Queue by contents delimited by a pair of iterators
    template <class Iter> void assign(Iter, Iter);

    //  return element from head of Queue
    //  unchecked operation: front on an empty Queue is undefined
    Type& front()              { return head->item; }
    const Type &front() const { return head->item; }

    void push(const Type &);// defined on page 652
    void pop();                //  defined on page 651
    bool empty() const {             //  true if no elements in the Queue
        return head == 0;
    }
private:
    QueueItem<Type> *head;       //  pointer to first element in Queue
    QueueItem<Type> *tail;       //  pointer to last element in Queue
```

```
        // utility functions used by copy constructor, assignment, and destructor
        void destroy();                    // defined on page 651
        void copy_elems(const Queue&);    // defined on page 652
        // version of copy to be used by assign to copy elements from iterator range
        // defined on page 662
        template <class Iter> void copy_elems(Iter, Iter);
};

// Inclusion Compilation Model: include member function definitions as well
#include "Queue.cc"
```

Members that are not defined in the class itself can be found in earlier sections of
this chapter; the comment following such members indicates the page on which
the definition can be found.

EXERCISES SECTION 16.4.6

Exercise 16.43: Add the `assign` member and a constructor that takes a pair of iterators to your `List` class.

Exercise 16.44: We implemented our own `Queue` class in order to illustrate how class
templates are implemented. One way in which our implementation could be simplified would be to define `Queue` on top of one of the existing library container types.
That way, we could avoid having to manage the allocation and deallocation of the
`Queue` elements. Reimplement `Queue` using `std::list` to hold the actual `Queue`
elements.

16.4.7 `static` Members of Class Templates

A class template can declare `static` members (Section 12.6, p. 467) in the same
way as any other class:

```
template <class T> class Foo {
public:
    static std::size_t count() { return ctr; }
    // other interface members
private:
    static std::size_t ctr;
    // other implementation members
};
```

defines a class template named `Foo` that among other members has a `public`
`static` member function named `count` and a `private static` data member
named `ctr`.

Each instantiation of class `Foo` has its own `static` member:

```
// Each object shares the same Foo<int>::ctr and Foo<int>::count members
Foo<int> fi, fi2, fi3;

// has static members Foo<string>::ctr and Foo<string>::count
Foo<string> fs;
```

Each instantiation represents a distinct type, so there is one `static` shared among the objects of any given instantiation. Hence, any objects of type `Foo<int>` share the same `static` member `ctr`. Objects of type `Foo<string>` share a different `ctr` member.

Using a `static` Member of a Class Template

As usual, we can access a `static` member of a class template through an object of the class type or by using the scope operator to access the member directly. Of course, when we attempt to use the `static` member through the class, we must refer to an actual instantiation:

```
Foo<int> fi, fi2;                // instantiates Foo<int> class
size_t ct = Foo<int>::count();   // instantiates Foo<int>::count
ct = fi.count();                 // ok: uses Foo<int>::count
ct = fi2.count();                // ok: uses Foo<int>::count
ct = Foo::count();               // error: which template instantiation?
```

Like any other member function, a `static` member function is instantiated only if it is used in a program.

Defining a `static` Member

As with any other `static` data member, there must be a definition for the data member that appears outside the class. In the case of a class template `static`, the member definition must inidicate that it is for a class template:

```
template <class T>
size_t Foo<T>::ctr = 0;  // define and initialize ctr
```

A `static` data member is defined like any other member of a class template that is defined outside the class. It begins with the keyword `template` followed by the class template parameter list and the class name. In this case, the name of the `static` data member is prefixed by `Foo<T>::`, which indicates that the member belongs to the class template `Foo`.

16.5   A Generic Handle Class

This example represents a fairly sophisticated use of C++. Understanding it requires understanding both inheritance and templates fairly well. It may be useful to delay studying this example until you are comfortable with these features. On the other hand, this example provides a good test of your understanding of these features.

In Chapter 15 we defined two handle classes: the `Sales_item` (Section 15.8, p. 598) class and the `Query` (Section 15.9, p. 607) class. These classes managed pointers to objects in an inheritance hierarchy. Users of the handle did not have to manage the pointers to those objects. User code was written in terms of the handle class. The handle dynamically allocated and freed objects of the related inheritance classes and forwarded all "real" work back to the classes in the underlying inheritance hierarchy.

These handles were similar to but different from each other: They were similar in that each defined use-counted copy control to manage a pointer to an object of a type in an inheritance hierarchy. They differed with respect to the interface they provided to users of the inheritance hierarchy.

The use-counting implementation was the same in both classes. This kind of problem is well suited to generic programming: We could define a class template to manage a pointer and do the use-counting. Our otherwise unrelated `Sales_item` and `Query` types could be simplified by using that template to do the common use-counting work. The handles would remain different as to whether they reveal or hide the underlying inheritance hierarchy.

In this section, we'll implement a **generic handle class** to provide the operations that manage the use count and the underlying objects. Then we'll rewrite the `Sales_item` class, showing how it could use the generic handle rather than defining its own use-counting operations.

16.5.1 Defining the Handle Class

Our `Handle` class will behave like a pointer: Copying a `Handle` will not copy the underlying object. After the copy, both `Handles` will refer to the same underlying object. To create a `Handle`, a user will be expected to pass the address of a dynamically allocated object of the type (or a type derived from that type) managed by the `Handle`. From that point on, the `Handle` will "own" the given object. In particular, the `Handle` class will assume responsibility for deleting that object once there are no longer any `Handles` attached to it.

Given this design, here is an implementation of our generic `Handle`:

```
/*  generic handle class: Provides pointerlike behavior. Although access through
 *  an unbound Handle is checked and throws a runtime_error exception.
 *  The object to which the Handle points is deleted when the last Handle goes away.
 *  Users should allocate new objects of type T and bind them to a Handle.
 *  Once an object is bound to a Handle, the user must not delete that object.
 */
template <class T> class Handle {
public:
    // unbound handle
    Handle(T *p = 0): ptr(p), use(new size_t(1)) { }
    // overloaded operators to support pointer behavior
    T& operator*();
    T* operator->();
    const T& operator*() const;
    const T* operator->() const;
    // copy control: normal pointer behavior, but last Handle deletes the object
    Handle(const Handle& h): ptr(h.ptr), use(h.use)
                                        { ++*use; }
```

```
        Handle& operator=(const Handle&);
        ~Handle() { rem_ref(); }
    private:
        T* ptr;             //  shared object
        size_t *use;        //  count of how many Handles point to *ptr
        void rem_ref()
            { if (--*use == 0) { delete ptr; delete use; } }
    };
```

This class looks like our other handles, as does the assignment operator.

```
    template <class T>
    inline Handle<T>& Handle<T>::operator=(const Handle &rhs)
    {
        ++*rhs.use;         //  protect against self-assignment
        rem_ref();          //  decrement use count and delete pointers if needed
        ptr = rhs.ptr;
        use = rhs.use;
        return *this;
    }
```

The only other members our class will define are the dereference and member access operators. These operators will be used to access the underlying object. We'll provide a measure of safety by having these operations check that the Handle is actually bound to an object. If not, an attempt to access the object will throw an exception.

The nonconst versions of these operators look like:

```
    template <class T> inline T& Handle<T>::operator*()
    {
        if (ptr) return *ptr;
        throw std::runtime_error
                    ("dereference of unbound Handle");
    }
    template <class T> inline T* Handle<T>::operator->()
    {
        if (ptr) return ptr;
        throw std::runtime_error
                    ("access through unbound Handle");
    }
```

The const versions would be similar and are left as an exercise.

16.5.2   Using the Handle

We intend this class to be used by other classes in their internal implementations. However, as an aid to understanding how the Handle class works, we'll look at a simpler example first. This example illustrates the behavior of the Handle by allocating an int and binding a Handle to that newly allocated object:

```
{    // new scope
     // user allocates but must not delete the object to which the Handle is attached
     Handle<int> hp(new int(42));
     { // new scope
          Handle<int> hp2 = hp;      // copies pointer; use count incremented
          cout << *hp << " " << *hp2 << endl;     // prints 42 42
          *hp2 = 10;                 // changes value of shared underlying int
     }    // hp2 goes out of scope; use count is decremented
     cout << *hp << endl;      // prints 10
}    // hp goes out of scope; its destructor deletes the int
```

Even though the user of `Handle` allocates the `int`, the `Handle` destructor will delete it. In this code, the `int` is deleted at the end of the outer block when the last `Handle` goes out of scope. To access the underlying object, we apply the `Handle` `*` operator. That operator returns a reference to the underlying `int` object.

Using a `Handle` to Use-Count a Pointer

As an example of using `Handle` in a class implementation, we might reimplement our `Sales_item` class (Section 15.8.1, p. 599). This version of the class defines the same interface, but we can eliminate the copy-control members by replacing the pointer to `Item_base` by a `Handle<Item_base>`:

```
class Sales_item {
public:
     // default constructor: unbound handle
     Sales_item(): h() { }
     // copy item and attach handle to the copy
     Sales_item(const Item_base &item): h(item.clone()) { }
     // no copy control members: synthesized versions work
     // member access operators: forward their work to the Handle class
     const Item_base& operator*() const { return *h; }
     const Item_base* operator->() const
                              { return h.operator->(); }
private:
     Handle<Item_base> h;     // use-counted handle
};
```

Although the interface to the class is unchanged, its implementation differs considerably from the original:

- Both classes define a default constructor and a constructor that takes a `const` reference to an `Item_base` object.

- Both define overloaded `*` and `->` operators as `const` members.

The `Handle`-based version of `Sales_item` has a single data member. That data member is a `Handle` attached to a copy of the `Item_base` object given to the constructor. Because this version of `Sales_item` has no pointer members, there is no need for copy-control members. This version of `Sales_item` can safely use the synthesized copy-control members. The work of managing the use-count and associated `Item_base` object is done inside `Handle`.

Because the interface is unchanged, there is no need to change code that uses `Sales_item`. For example, the program we wrote in Section 15.8.3 (p. 603) can be used without change:

```
double Basket::total() const
{
    double sum = 0.0;        //  holds the running total
    /*  find each set of items with the same isbn and calculate
     *  the net price for that quantity of items
     *  iter refers to first copy of each book in the set
     *  upper_bound refers to next element with a different isbn
     */
    for (const_iter iter = items.begin();
                     iter != items.end();
                     iter = items.upper_bound(*iter))
    {
        //  we know there's at least one element with this key in the Basket
        //  virtual call to net_price applies appropriate discounts, if any
        sum += (*iter)->net_price(items.count(*iter));
    }
    return sum;
}
```

It's worthwhile to look in detail at the statement that calls `net_price`:

```
sum += (*iter)->net_price(items.count(*iter));
```

This statement uses operator `->` to fetch and run the `net_price` function. What's important to understand is how this operator works:

- `(*iter)` returns h, our use-counted handle member.

- `(*iter)->` therefore uses the overloaded arrow operator of the handle class

- The compiler evaluates `h.operator->()`, which in turn yields the pointer to `Item_base` that the `Handle` holds.

- The compiler dereferences that `Item_base` pointer and calls the `net_price` member for the object to which the pointer points.

EXERCISES SECTION 16.5.2

Exercise 16.49: Implement the version of the `Sales_item` handle presented here that uses the generic `Handle` class to manage the pointer to `Item_base`.

Exercise 16.50: Rerun the function to total a sale. List all changes you had to make to get your code to work.

Exercise 16.51: Rewrite the `Query` class from Section 15.9.4 (p. 613) to use the generic `Handle` class. Note that you will need to make the `Handle` a friend of the `Query_base` class to let it access the `Query_base` destructor. List and explain all other changes you made to get the programs to work.

16.6 Template Specializations

The rest of this chapter covers a somewhat advanced topic. It can be safely skipped on first reading.

It is not always possible to write a single template that is best suited for every possible template argument with which the template might be instantiated. In some cases, the general template definition is simply wrong for a type. The general definition might not compile or might do the wrong thing. At other times, we may be able to take advantage of some specific knowledge about a type to write a more efficient function than the one that is instantiated from the template.

Our `compare` function and our `Queue` class are both good examples of the problem: Neither works correctly when used with C-style character strings. Let's look again at our `compare` function template:

```
template <typename T>
int compare(const T &v1, const T &v2)
{
    if (v1 < v2) return -1;
    if (v2 < v1) return 1;
    return 0;
}
```

If we call this template definition on two `const char*` arguments, the function compares the pointer values. It will tell us the relative positions in memory of these two pointers but says nothing about the contents of the arrays to which the pointers point.

To get be able to use `compare` with character strings, we would have to provide a specialized definition that knows how to compare C-style strings. The fact that these versions are specialized is transparent to users of these templates. Calls to a specialized function or use of a specialized class are indistinguishable from uses of a version instantiated from the general template.

16.6.1 Specializing a Function Template

A **template spacialization** is a separate definition in which the actual type(s) or value(s) of one or more template parameter(s) is (are) specified. The form of a specialization is:

- The keyword `template` followed by an empty bracket pair (`< >`),

- followed by the template name and a bracket pair specifying the template parameters(s) that this specialization defines,

- the function parameter list,

- and the function body.

The following program defines a specialization of `compare` when the template parameter type is bound to `const char*`:

```
//   special version of compare to handle C-style character strings
template <>
int compare<const char*>(const char* const &v1,
                         const char* const &v2)
{
    return strcmp(v1, v2);
}
```

The declaration for the specialization must match that of the corresponding template. In this case, the template has one type parameter and two function parameters. The function parameters are `const` references to the type parameter. Here we are fixing the type parameter to `const char*`; our function parameters, therefore, are `const` references to a `const char*`.

Now when we call `compare`, passing it two character pointers, the compiler will call our specialized version. It will call the generic version for any other argument types (including plain `char*`):

```
const char *cp1 = "world", *cp2 = "hi";
int i1, i2;
compare(cp1, cp2); //  calls the specialization
compare(i1, i2);   //  calls the generic version instantiated with int
```

Declaring a Template Specialization

As with any function, we can declare a function template specialization without defining it. A template specialization declaration looks like the definition but omits the function body:

```
//   declaration of function template explicit specialization
template<>
int compare<const char*>(const char* const&,
                         const char* const&);
```

This declaration consists of an empty template parameter list (`template<>`) followed by the return type, the function name (optionally) followed by explicit template argument(s) specified inside a pair of angle brackets, and the function parameter list. A template specialization must always include the empty template parameter specifier, `template<>`, and it must include the function parameter list. If the template arguments can be inferred from the function parameter list, there is no need to explicitly specify the template arguments:

```
// error: invalid specialization declarations
// missing template<>
int compare<const char*>(const char* const&,
                         const char* const&);
```

```
// error: function parameter list missing
template<> int compare<const char*>;
```

```
// ok: explicit template argument const char* deduced from parameter types
template<> int compare(const char* const&,
                       const char* const&);
```

Function Overloading versus Template Specializations

Omitting the empty template parameter list, `template<>`, on a specialization may have surprising effects. If the specialization syntax is missing, then the effect is to declare an overloaded nontemplate version of the function:

```
// generic template definition
template <class T>
int compare(const T& t1, const T& t2) { /* ... */ }
```

```
// OK: ordinary function declaration
int compare(const char* const&, const char* const&);
```

The definition of `compare` does not define a template specialization. Instead, it declares an ordinary function with a return type and a parameter list that could match those of a template instantiation.

We'll look at the interaction of overloading and templates in more detail in the next section. For now, what's important to know is that when we define a nontemplate function, normal conversions are applied to the arguments. When we specialize a template, conversions are not applied to the argument types. In a call to a specialized version of a template, the argument type(s) in the call must match the specialized version function parameter type(s) exactly. If they don't, then the compiler will instantiate an instantiation for the argument(s) from the template definition.

Duplicate Definitions Cannot Always Be Detected

If a program consists of more than one file, the declaration for a template specialization must be visible in every file in which the specialization is used. A function template cannot be instantiated from the generic template definition in some files and be specialized for the same set of template arguments in other files.

Best Practices

As with other function declarations, declarations for template specializations should be included in a header file. That header should then be included in every source file that uses the specialization.

Ordinary Scope Rules Apply to Specializations

Before we can declare or define a specialization, a declaration for the template that it specializes must be in scope. Similarly, a declaration for the specialization must be in scope before that version of the template is called:

```
// define the general compare template
template <class T>
int compare(const T& t1, const T& t2) { /* ... */ }

int main() {
    // uses the generic template definition
    int i = compare("hello", "world");
    // ...
}

// invalid program: explicit specialization after call
template<>
int compare<const char*>(const char* const& s1,
                         const char* const& s2)
{ /* ... */ }
```

This program is in error because a call that would match the specialization is made before the specialization is declared. When the compiler sees a call, it must know to expect a specialization for this version. Otherwise, the compiler is allowed to instantiate the function from the template definition.

Note

A program cannot have both an explicit specialization and an instantiation for the same template with the same set of template arguments.

It is an error for a specialization to appear after a call to that instance of the template has been seen.

EXERCISES SECTION 16.6.1

Exercise 16.52: Define a function template `count` to count the number of occurrences of some value in a `vector`.

Exercise 16.53: Write a program to call the `count` function defined in the previous exercise passing it first a `vector` of `doubles`, then a `vector` of `ints`, and finally a `vector` of `chars`.

Exercise 16.54: Introduce a specialized template instance of the `count` function to handle `strings`. Rerun the program you wrote to call the function template instantiations.

16.6.2   Specializing a Class Template

Our `Queue` class has a problem similar to the one in `compare` when used with C-style strings. In this case, the problem is in the `push` function. That function copies the value it's given to create a new element in the `Queue`. By default, copying a C-style character string copies only the pointer, not the characters. Copying a pointer in this case has all the problems that shared pointers have in other contexts. The most serious is that if the pointer points to dynamic memory, it's possible for the user to delete the array to which the pointer points.

Defining a Class Specialization

One way to provide the right behavior for `Queue`'s of C-style strings is to define a specialized version of the entire class for `const char*`:

```
/*  definition of specialization for const char*
 *  this class forwards its work to Queue<string>;
 *  the push function translates the const char* parameter to a string
 *  the front functions return a string rather than a const char*
 */
template<> class Queue<const char*> {
public:
    //  no copy control: Synthesized  versions work for this class
    //  similarly, no need for explicit default constructor either
    void push(const char*);
    void pop()                {real_queue.pop();}
    bool empty() const        {return real_queue.empty();}

    //  Note: return type does not match template parameter type
    std::string front()       {return real_queue.front();}
    const std::string &front() const
                              {return real_queue.front();}
private:
    Queue<std::string> real_queue; //  forward calls to real_queue
};
```

This implementation gives `Queue` a single data element: a `Queue` of `string`s. The various members delegate their work to this member—for example, `pop` is implemented by calling `pop` on `real_queue`.

This version of the class does not define the copy-control members. Its only data element has a class type that does the right thing when copied, assigned, or destroyed; we can use the synthesized copy-control members.

Our `Queue` class implements mostly, but not entirely, the same interface as the template version of `Queue`. The difference is that we return a `string` rather than a `char*` from the `front` members. We do so to avoid having to manage the character array that would be required if we wanted to return a pointer.

It is worth noting that a specialization may define completely different members than the template itself. If a specialization fails to define a member from the template, that member may not be used on objects of the specilization type. The member definitions of the class template are not used to create the definitions for the members of an explicit specialization.

> A class template specialization ought to define the same interface as the template it specializes. Doing otherwise will surprise users when they attempt to use a member that is not defined.

Class Specialization Definition

> When a member is defined outside the class specialization, it is not preceded by the tokens `template<>`.

Our class defines only one member outside the class:

```
void Queue<const char*>::push(const char* val)
{
    return real_queue.push(val);
}
```

Although it does little obvious work, this function implicitly copies the character array to which `val` points. The copy is made in the call to `real_queue.push`, which creates a new `string` from the `const char*` argument. That argument uses the `string` constructor that takes a `const char*`. The `string` constructor copies the characters from the array pointed to by `val` into an unnamed `string` that will be stored in the element we `push` onto `real_queue`.

EXERCISES SECTION 16.6.2

Exercise 16.55: The comments on the specialized version of `Queue` for `const char*` note that there is no need to define the default constructor or copy-control members. Explain why the synthesized members suffice for this version of `Queue`.

Exercise 16.56: We explained the generic behavior of `Queue` if it is not specialized for `const char*`. Using the generic `Queue` template, explain what happens in the following code:

```
Queue<const char*> q1;
q1.push("hi"); q1.push("bye"); q1.push("world");
Queue<const char*> q2(q1);   // q2 is a copy of q1

Queue<const char*> q3;         // empty Queue
q1 = q3;
```

In particular, say what the values of q1 and q2 are after the initialization of q2 and after the assignment to q3.

Exercise 16.57: Our specialized `Queue` returns `strings` from the `front` function rather than `const char*`. Why do you suppose we did so? How might you implement the `Queue` to return a `const char*`? Discuss the pros and cons of each approach.

16.6.3 Specializing Members but Not the Class

If we look a bit more deeply at our class, we can see that we can simplify our code: Rather than specializing the whole template, we can specialize just the push and pop members. We'll specialize push to copy the character array and pop to free the memory we used for that copy:

```
template <>
void Queue<const char*>::push(const char *const &val)
{
    //  allocate a new character array and copy characters from val
    char* new_item = new char[strlen(val) + 1];
    strncpy(new_item, val, strlen(val) + 1);
    //  store pointer to newly allocated and initialized element
    QueueItem<const char*> *pt =
        new QueueItem<const char*>(new_item);
    //  put item onto existing queue
    if (empty())
        head = tail = pt;     //  queue has only one element
    else {
        tail->next = pt;      //  add new element to end of queue
        tail = pt;
    }
}
template <>
void Queue<const char*>::pop()
{
    //  remember head so we can delete it
    QueueItem<const char*> *p = head;
    delete head->item;        //  delete the array allocated in push
    head = head->next;        //  head now points to next element
    delete p;                 //  delete old head element
}
```

Now, the class type Queue<const char*> will be instantiated from the generic class template definition, with the exception of the push and pop functions. When we call push or pop on a Queue<const char*>, then the specialized version will be called. When we use any other member, the generic one will be instantiated for const char* from the class template.

Specialization Declarations

Member specializations are declared just as any other function template specialization. They must start with an empty template parameter list:

```
//  push and pop specialized for const char*
template <>
void Queue<const char*>::push(const char* const &);

template <> void Queue<const char*>::pop();
```

These declarations should be placed in the Queue header file.

EXERCISES SECTION 16.6.3

Exercise 16.58: The specialization of Queue presented in the previous subsection and the specialization in this subsection of push and pop apply only to Queues of const char*. Implement these two different ways of specializing Queue that could be used with plain char*.

Exercise 16.59: If we go the route of specializing only the push function, what value is returned by front for a Queue of C-style character strings?

Exercise 16.60: Discuss the pros and cons of the two designs: defining a specialized version of the class for const char* versus specializing only the push and pop functions. In particular, compare and contrast the behavior of front and the possibility of errors in user code corrupting the elements in the Queue.

16.6.4 Class-Template Partial Specializations

If a class template has more than one template parameter, we might want to specialize some but not all of the template parameters. We can do so using a class template partial specialization:

```
template <class T1, class T2>
class some_template {
    // ...
};
// partial specialization: fixes T2 as int and allows T1 to vary
template <class T1>
class some_template<T1, int> {
    // ...
};
```

A class template **partial specialization** is itself a template. The definition of a partial specialization looks like a template definition. Such a definition begins with the keyword template followed by a template parameter list enclosed by angle brackets (< >). The parameter list of a partial specialization is a subset of the parameter list of the corresponding class template definition. The partial specialization for some_template has only one template type parameter named T1. The second template argument for T2 is known to be int. The template parameter list for the partial specialization only lists the parameters for which the template arguments are still unknown.

Using a Class-Template Partial Specialization

The partial specialization has the same name as the class template to which it corresponds—namely, some_template. The name of the class template must be followed by a template argument list. In the previous example, the template argument list is <T1, int>. Because the argument value for the first template parameter is unknown, the argument list uses the name of the template parameter

T1 as a placeholder. The other argument is the type int, for which the template is partially specialized.

As with any other class template, a partial specialization is instantiated implicitly when used in a program:

```
some_template<int, string> foo;   // uses template
some_template<string, int> bar;   // uses partial specialization
```

Notice that the type of the second variable, some_template parameterized by string and int, could be instantiated from the generic class template definition as well as from the partial specialization. Why is it that the partial specialization is chosen to instantiate the template? When a parital specialization is declared, the compiler chooses the template definition that is the most specialized for the instantiation. When no partial specialization can be used, the generic template definition is used. The instantiated type of foo does not match the partial specialization provided. Thus, the type of foo must be instantiated from the general class template, binding int to T1 and string to T2. The partial specialization is only used to instantiate some_template types with a second type of int.

The definition of a partial specialization is completely disjointed from the definition of the generic template. The partial specialization may have a completely different set of members from the generic class template. The generic definitions for the members of a class template are never used to instantiate the members of the class template partial specialization.

16.7 Overloading and Function Templates

A function template can be overloaded: We can define multiple function templates with the same name but differing numbers or types of parameters. We also can define ordinary nontemplate functions with the same name as a function template.

Of course, declaring a set of overloaded function templates does not guarantee that they can be called successfully. Overloaded function templates may lead to ambiguities.

Function Matching and Function Templates

The steps used to resolve a call to an overloaded function in which there are both ordinary functions and function templates are as follows:

1. Build the set of candidate functions for this function name, including:

   (a) Any ordinary function with the same name as the called function.

   (b) Any function-template instantiation for which template argument deduction finds template arguments that match the function arguments used in the call.

2. Determine which, if any, of the ordinary functions are viable (Section 7.8.2, p. 269). Each template instance in the candidate set is viable, because template argument deduction ensures that the function could be called.

3. Rank the viable functions by the kinds of conversions, if any, required to make the call, remembering that the conversions allowed to call an instance of a template function are limited.

   (a) If only one function is selected, call this function.

   (b) If the call is ambiguous, remove any function template instances from the set of viable functions.

4. Rerank the viable functions excluding the function template instantiations.

   • If only one function is selected, call this function.

   • Otherwise, the call is ambiguous.

An Example of Function-Template Matching

Consider the following set of overloaded ordinary and function templates:

```
// compares two objects
template <typename T> int compare(const T&, const T&);
// compares elements in two sequences
template <class U, class V> int compare(U, U, V);
// plain functions to handle C-style character strings
int compare(const char*, const char*);
```

The overload set contains three functions: The first template handles simple values, the second template compares elements from two sequences, and the third is an ordinary function to handle C-style character strings.

Resolving Calls to Overloaded Function Templates

We could call these functions on a variety of types:

```
// calls compare(const T&, const T&) with T bound to int
compare(1, 0);
// calls compare(U, U, V), with U and V bound to vector<int>::iterator
vector<int> ivec1(10), ivec2(20);
compare(ivec1.begin(), ivec1.end(), ivec2.begin());
int ia1[] = {0,1,2,3,4,5,6,7,8,9};
// calls compare(U, U, V) with U bound to int*
// and V bound to vector<int>::iterator
compare(ia1, ia1 + 10, ivec1.begin());
// calls the ordinary function taking const char* parameters
const char const_arr1[] = "world", const_arr2[] = "hi";
compare(const_arr1, const_arr2);
// calls the ordinary function taking const char* parameters
char ch_arr1[] = "world", ch_arr2[] = "hi";
compare(ch_arr1, ch_arr2);
```

We'll look at each call in turn:

`compare(1, 0)`: Both arguments have type `int`. The candidate functions are the first template instantiated with `T` bound to `int` and the ordinary function named `compare`. The ordinary function, however, isn't viable—we cannot pass an `int` to a parameter expecting a `char*`. The instantiated function using `int` is an exact match for the call, so it is selected.

`compare(ivec1.begin(), ivec1.end(), ivec2.begin())`
`compare(ia1, ia1 + 10, ivec1.begin())`: In these calls, the only viable function is the instantiation of the template that has three parameters. Neither the template with two arguments nor the ordinary nonoverloaded function can match these calls.

`compare(const_arr1, const_arr2)`: This call, as expected, calls the ordinary function. Both that function and the first template with `T` bound to `const char*` are viable. Both are also exact matches. By rule 3b, we know that the ordinary function is preferred. We eliminate the instance of the template from consideration, leaving just the ordinary function as viable.

`compare(ch_arr1, ch_arr2)`: This call also is bound to the ordinary function. The candidates are the version of the function template with `T` bound to `char*` and the ordinary function that takes `const char*` arguments. Both functions require a trivial conversion to convert the arrays, `ch_arr1` and `ch_arr2`, to pointers. Because both functions are equal matches, the plain function is preferred to the template version.

Conversions and Overloaded Function Templates

It can be difficult to design a set of overloaded functions in which some are templates and others are ordinary functions. Doing so requires deep understanding of the relationships among types and in particular of the implicit conversions that may or may not take place when templates are involved.

Let's look at two examples of why it is hard to design overloaded functions that work properly when there are both template and nontemplate versions in the overload set. First, consider a call to `compare` using pointers instead of the arrays themselves:

```
char *p1 = ch_arr1, *p2 = ch_arr2;
compare(p1, p2);
```

This call matches the template version! Ordinarily, we expect to get the same function whether we pass an array or a pointer to an element to that array. In this case, however, the function template is an exact match for the call, binding `char*` to `T`. The plain version still requires a conversion from `char*` to `const char*`, so the function template is preferred.

Another change that has surprising results is what happens if the template version of `compare` has a parameter of type `T` instead of a `const` reference to `T`:

```
template <typename T> int compare2(T, T);
```

In this case, if we have an array of plain `char`; then, whether we pass the array itself or a pointer, the template version is called. The only way to call the non-

template version is when the arguments are arrays of `const char` or pointers to
`const char*`:

```
//  calls compare (T,  T) with T bound to char*
compare(ch_arr1, ch_arr2);
//  calls compare (T,  T) with T bound to char*
compare(p1, p2);
//  calls the ordinary function taking const  char* parameters
compare(const_arr1, const_arr2);

const char *cp1 = const_arr1, *cp2 = const_arr2;
//  calls the ordinary function taking const  char* parameters
compare(cp1, cp2);
```

In these cases, the plain function and the function template are exact matches. As
always, when the match is equally good, the nonoverloaded version is preferred.

> It is hard to design overloaded function sets involving both function
> templates and nontemplate functions. Because of the likelihood of
> surprise to users of the functions, it is almost always better to define
> a function-template specialization (Section 16.6, p. 671) than to use
> a nontemplate version.

EXERCISES SECTION 16.7

Exercise 16.61: Implement the three versions of `compare`. Include a print statement
in each function that indicates which function is being called. Use these functions to
check your answers to the remaining questions.

Exercise 16.62: Given the `compare` functions and variables defined in this section,
explain which function is called, and why, for each of these calls:

```
compare(ch_arr1, const_arr1);
compare(ch_arr2, const_arr2);
compare(0, 0);
```

Exercise 16.63: For each of the following calls, list the candidate and viable functions.
Indicate whether the call is valid and if so which function is called.

```
template <class T> T calc(T, T);
double calc(double, double);
template <> char calc<char>(char, char);

int ival; double dval; float fd;
calc(0, ival);            calc(0.25, dval);
calc(0, fd);              calc (0, 'J');
}
```

CHAPTER SUMMARY

Templates are a distinctive feature of C++ and are fundamental to the library. A template is a type-independent blueprint that the compiler uses to generate a variety of type-specific instances. We write the template once, and the compiler instantiates the template for the type or types with which we use the template. We can write both function templates and class templates.

Function templates are the base on which the algorithms library is built. Class templates are the base on which the library container and iterator types are built.

Compiling templates requires assistance from the programming environment. The language defines two broad strategies for instantiating templates: the inclusion model and the separate compilation model. These models have impacts on how we build our systems in so far as they dictate whether template definitions go in header files or source files. At this time, all compilers implement the inclusion model, while only some implement the separate compilation model. Your compiler's user's guide should specify how your system manages templates.

An explicit template argument lets us fix the type or value of one or more template parameters. Explicit arguments are useful in letting us design functions in which a template type need not be inferred from a corresponding argument and lets us allow conversions on the arguments.

A template specialization is a specialized definition that defines a distinct version of the template that binds one or more parameters to specified types or values. Specializations are useful when there are types for which the default template definition does not apply.

DEFINED TERMS

class template A class definition that can be used to define a set of type-specific classes. Class templates are defined using the `template` keyword followed by a comma-separated list of one or more parameters enclosed in < and > brackets.

export keyword Keyword used to indicate that the compiler must remember the location of the associated template definition. Used by compilers that support the separate-compilation model of template instantiation. The `export` keyword ordinarily goes with a function definition; a class is normally declared as `exported` in the associated class implementation file. A template may be defined with the `export` keyword only once in a program.

function template A definition for a function that can be used for a variety of types. A function template is defined using the `template` keyword followed by a comma-separated list of template one or more parameters enclosed in < and > brackets.

generic handle class A class that holds and manages a pointer to another class. A generic handle takes a single type parameter and allocates and manages a pointer to an object of that type. The handle class defines the necessary copy control members. It also defines the dereference (*) and arrow (->) member access operators to provide access to the underlying object. A generic handle requires no knowledge of the type it manages.

inclusion compilation model Mechanism used by compilers to find template definitions that relies on template definitions being *included* in each file that uses the template. Typically, template definitions are stored in a header, and that header must be included in any file that uses the template.

instantiation Compiler process whereby the actual template argument(s) are used to generate a specific instance of the template in which the parameter(s) are replaced by the corresponding argument(s). Functions are instantiated automatically based on the arguments used in a call. Template arguments must be provided explicitly whenever a class template is used.

member template A member of a class or class template that is a function template. A member template may not be virtual.

nontype parameter A template parameter that represents a value. When a function template is instantiated, each nontype parameter is bound to a constant expression as indicated by the arguments used in the call. When a class template is instantiated, each nontype parameter is bound to a constant expression as indicated by the arguments used in the class instantiation.

partial specialization A version of a class template in which some some but not all of the template parameters are specified.

separate compilation model Mechanism used by compilers to find template definitions that allows template definitions and declarations to be stored in independent files. Template declarations are placed in a header, and the definition appears only once in the program, typically in a source file. The compiler implements whatever programming environment support is necessary to find that source file and instantiate the versions of the template used by the program.

template argument Type or value specified when using a template type, such as when defining an object or naming a type in a cast.

template argument deduction Process by which the compiler determines which function template to instantiate. The compiler examines the types of the arguments that were specified using a template parameter. It automatically instantiates a version of the function with those types or values bound to the template parameters.

template parameter A name specifed in the template parameter list that may be used inside the definition of a template. Template parameters can be type or nontype parameters. To use a class template, actual arguments must be specified for each template parameter. The compiler uses those types or values to instantiate a version of the class in which uses of the parameter(s) are replaced by the actual argument(s). When a function template is used, the compiler deduces the template arguments from the arguments in the call and instantiates a specific function using the deduced template arguments.

template parameter list List of type or nontype parameters (separated by commas) to be used in the definition or declaration of a template.

template specialization Redefinition of a class template or a member of a class template in which the template parameters are specified. A template specialization may not appear until after the class that it specializes has been defined. A template specialization must appear before any use of the template for the specialized arguments is used.

type parameter Name used in a template parameter list to represent a type. When the template is instantiated, each type parameter is bound to an actual type. In a function template, the types are inferred from the argument types or are explicitly specified in the call. Type arguments must be specified for a class template when the class is used.

P A R T V

ADVANCED TOPICS

CONTENTS

Part V covers additional features that, although useful in the right context, are not needed by every C++ programmer. These features divide into two clusters: those that are useful for large-scale problems and those that are applicable to specialized problems rather than general ones.

Chapter 17 covers exception handling, namespaces, and multiple inheritance. These features tend to be most useful in the context of large-scale problems.

Even programs simple enough to be written by a single author can benefit from exception handling, which is why we introduced the basics of exception handling in Chapter 6. However, the need to deal with unexpected run-time errors tends to be more important and harder to manage in problems that require large programming teams. In Chapter 17 we review some additional useful exception-handling facilities. We also look in more detail at how exceptions are handled and the implications of exceptions on resource allocation and destruction. We also show how we can define and use our own exception classes.

Large-scale applications often use code from multiple independent vendors. Combining independently developed libraries would be difficult (if not impossible) if vendors had to put the names they define into a single namespace. Independently developed libraries would almost inevitably use names in common with one another; a name defined in one library would conflict with the use of that name in another library. To avoid name collisions, we can define names inside a `namespace`.

Right from the beginning of this book we have used namespaces. Whenever we use a name from the standard library, we are using a name defined in the namespace named `std`. Chapter 17 shows how we can define our own namespaces.

Chapter 17 closes by looking at an important but infrequently used language feature: multiple inheritance. Multiple inheritance is most useful for fairly complicated inheritance hierarchies.

Chapter 18 covers several specialized tools and techniques. These tools and techniques are applicable to particular kinds of problems.

The first part of Chapter 18 shows how classes can define their own optimized memory management. We next look at C++ support for run-time type identification (RTTI). These facilities let us determine the actual type of an object at run-time.

Next, we look at how we can define and use pointers to class members. Pointers to class members differ from pointers to ordinary data or functions. Ordinary pointers only vary based on the type of the object or function. Pointers to members must also reflect the class to which the member belongs.

We then look at three additional aggregate types: unions, nested classes, and local classes.

The chapter closes by looking briefly at a collection of features that are inherently nonportable: the `volatile` qualifier, bit-fields, and linkage directives.

C H A P T E R 17

T O O L S F O R L A R G E P R O G R A M S

CONTENTS

C++ is used on problems that have a wide range in complexity. It is used on problems small enough to be solved by a single programmer after a few hours' work to problems requiring enormous systems consisting of tens of millions of lines of code developed and modified over many years. The facilities we covered in the earlier parts of this book are equally useful across this range of programming problems.

The language includes some features that are most useful on systems once problems get to be more complex than those that an individual can manage. These features—exception handling, namespaces, and multiple inheritance—are the topic of this chapter.

Large-scale programming places greater demands on programming languages than do the needs of systems that can be developed by small teams of programmers. Among the needs that distinguish large-scale applications are:

1. Stricter up-time requirements and the need for more robust error detection and error handling. Error handling often must span independently developed subsystems.

2. The ability to structure programs that are composed of libraries developed more or less independently.

3. The need to deal with more complicated application concepts.

Three features in C++ are aimed at these needs: exception handling, namespaces, and multiple inheritance. This chapter looks at these three facilities.

17.1   Exception Handling

Exception handling allows independently developed parts of a program to communicate about and handle problems that arise during execution of the program. One part of the program can detect a problem that that part of the program cannot resolve. The problem-detecting part can pass the problem along to another part that is prepared to handle what went wrong.

 Exceptions let us separate problem detection from problem resolution. The part of the program that detects a problem need not know how to deal with it.

In C++, exception handling relies on the problem-detecting part throwing an object to a handler. The type and contents of that object allow the two parts to communicate about what went wrong.

Section 6.13 (p. 215) introduced the basic concepts and mechanics of using exceptions in C++. In that section, we hypothesized that a more complex bookstore application might use exceptions to communicate about problems. For example, the Sales_item addition operator might throw an exception if the isbn members of its operands didn't match:

```
//  throws exception if both objects do not refer to the same isbn
Sales_item
operator+(const Sales_item& lhs, const Sales_item& rhs)
{
    if (!lhs.same_isbn(rhs))
        throw runtime_error("Data must refer to same ISBN");
    //  ok, if we're still here the ISBNs are the same so it's okay to do the addition
    Sales_item ret(lhs);    //  copy lhs into a local object that we'll return
    ret += rhs;             //  add in the contents of rhs
    return ret;             //  return a copy of ret
}
```

Those parts of the program that added `Sales_item` objects would use a `try` block in order to catch an exception if one occured:

```
// part of the application that interacts with the user
Sales_item item1, item2, sum;
while (cin >> item1 >> item2) {   // read two transactions
    try {
        sum = item1 + item2;        // calculate their sum
        // use sum
    } catch (const runtime_error &e) {
        cerr << e.what() << " Try again.\n"
            << endl;
    }
}
```

In this section we'll expand our coverage of these basics and cover some additional exception-handling facilities. Effective use of exception handling requires understanding what happens when an exception is thrown, what happens when it is caught, and the meanings of the objects used to communicate what went wrong.

17.1.1 Throwing an Exception of Class Type

An exception is **raised** by **throwing** an object. The type of that object determines which handler will be invoked. The selected handler is the one nearest in the call chain that matches the type of the object.

Exceptions are thrown and caught in ways that are similar to how arguments are passed to functions. An exception can be an object of any type that can be passed to a nonreference parameter, meaning that it must be possible to copy objects of that type.

Recall that when we pass an argument of array or function type, that argument is autmatically converted to an pointer. The same automatic conversion happens for objects that are thrown. As a consequence, there are no exceptions of array or function types. Instead, if we `throw` an array, the thrown object is converted to a pointer to the first element in the array. Similarly, if we throw a function, the function is converted to a pointer to the function (Section 7.9, p. 276).

When a `throw` is executed, the statement(s) following the `throw` are not executed. Instead, control is transferred from the `throw` to the matching `catch`. That `catch` might be local to the same function or might be in a function that directly or indirectly called the function in which the exception occurred. The fact that control passes from one location to another has two important implications:

1. Functions along the call chain are prematurely exited. Section 17.1.2 (p. 691) discusses what happens when functions are exited due to an exception.

2. In general, the storage that is local to a block that throws an exception is not around when the exception is handled.

Because local storage is freed while handling an exception, the object that is thrown is not stored locally. Instead, the throw expression is used to initialize a special object referred to as the **exception object**. The exception object is managed by the compiler and is guaranteed to reside in space that will be accessible to whatever `catch` is invoked. This object is created by a `throw`, and is initialized as a copy of the expression that is thrown. The exception object is passed to the corresponding `catch` and is destroyed after the exception is completely handled.

The exception object is created by copying the result of the thrown expression; that result must be of a type that can be copied.

Beware

Exception Objects and Inheritance

In practice, many applications throw expressions whose type comes from an inheritance hierarchy. As we'll see in Section 17.1.7 (p. 697), the standard exceptions (Section 6.13, p. 215) are defined in an inheritance hierarchy. What's important to know at this point is how the form of the `throw` expression interacts with types related by inheritance.

When an exception is thrown, the static, compile-time type of the thrown object determines the type of the exception object.

Note

Ordinarily, the fact that the object is thrown using its static type is not an issue. When we throw an exception, we usually construct the object we are going to throw at the throw point. That object represents what went wrong, so we know the precise exception type.

Exceptions and Pointers

The one case where it matters that a throw expression throws the static type is if we dereference a pointer in a throw. The result of dereferencing a pointer is an object whose type matches the type of the pointer. If the pointer points to a type from an inheritance hierarchy, it is possible that the type of the object to which the pointer points is different from the type of the pointer. Regardless of the object's actual type, the type of the exception object matches the static type of the pointer. If that pointer is a base-class type pointer that points to a derived-type object, then that object is sliced down (Section 15.3.1, p. 577); only the base-class part is thrown.

A problem more serious than slicing the object may arise if we `throw` the pointer itself. In particular, it is always an error to `throw` a pointer to a local object for the same reasons as it is an error to return a pointer to a local object (Section 7.3.2, p. 249) from a function. When we `throw` a pointer, we must be certain that the object to which the pointer points will exist when the handler is entered.

If we `throw` a pointer to a local object and the handler is in another function, then the object to which the pointer points will no longer exist when the handler is executed. Even if the handler is in the same function, we must be sure that the object to which the pointer points exists at the site of the `catch`. If the pointer points to an object in a block that is exited before the `catch`, then that local object will have been destroyed before the `catch`.

It is usually a bad idea to throw a pointer: Throwing a pointer requires that the object to which the pointer points exist wherever the corresponding handler resides.

EXERCISES SECTION 17.1.1

Exercise 17.1: What is the type of the exception object in the following throws:

```
(a) range_error r("error");   (b) exception *p = &r;
    throw r;                       throw *p;
```

Exercise 17.2: What would happen if the second throw were written as throw p?

17.1.2 Stack Unwinding

When an exception is thrown, execution of the current function is suspended and the search begins for a matching catch clause. The search starts by checking whether the throw itself is located inside a try block. If so, the catch clauses associated with that try are examined to see if one of them matches the thrown object. If a matching catch is found, the exception is handled. If no catch is found, the current function is exited—its memory is freed and local objects are destroyed—and the search continues in the calling function.

If the call to the function that threw is in a try block, then the catch clauses associated with that try are examined. If a matching catch is found, the exception is handled. If no matching catch is found, the calling function is also exited, and the search continues in the function that called this one.

This process, known as **stack unwinding**, continues up the chain of nested function calls until a catch clause for the exception is found. As soon as a catch clause that can handle the exception is found, that catch is entered, and execution continues within this handler. When the catch completes, execution continues at the point immediately after the last catch clause associated with that try block.

Destructors Are Called for Local Objects

During stack unwinding, the function containing the throw, and possibly other functions in the call chain, are exited prematurely. In general, these functions will have created local objects that ordinarily would be destroyed when the function exited. When a function is exited due to an exception, the compiler guarantees that the local objects are properly destroyed. As each function exits, its local storage is freed. Before releasing the memory, any local object that was created before the exception occurred is destroyed. If the local object is of class type, the destructor for this object is called automatically. As usual, the compiler does no work to destroy an object of built-in type.

> During stack unwinding, the memory used by local objects is freed and
> destructors for local objects of class type are run.

If a block directly allocates a resource, and the exception occurs before that
resource is freed, that resource will not be freed during stack unwinding. For example, a block might dynamically allocate memory through a call to `new`. If the
block exits due to an exception, the compiler does not `delete` the pointer. The
allocated memory will not be freed.

Resources allocated by an object of class type generally will be properly freed.
Destructors for local objects are run; resources allocated by class-type objects ordinarily are freed by their destructor. Section 17.1.8 (p. 700) describes a programming
technique that uses classes to manage resource allocation in the face of exceptions.

Destructors Should Never `throw` Exceptions

Destructors are often executed during stack unwinding. When destructors are executing, the exception has been raised but not yet handled. It is unclear what should
happen if a destructor itself throws a new exception during this process. Should
the new exception supersede the earlier exception that has not yet been handled?
Should the exception in the destructor be ignored?

The answer is that while stack unwinding is in progress for an exception, a
destructor that throws another exception of its own that it does not also handle,
causes the library **terminate** function is called. Ordinarily, `terminate` calls
abort, forcing an abnormal exit from the entire program.

Because `terminate` ends the program, it is usually a very bad idea for a destructor to do anything that might cause an exception. In practice, because destructors free resources, it is unlikely that they throw exceptions. The standard library
types all guarantee that their destructors will not raise an exception.

Exceptions and Constructors

Unlike destructors, it is often the case that something done inside a constructor
might throw an exception. If an exception occurs while constructing an object, then
the object might be only partially constructed. Some of its members might have
been initialized, and others might not have been initialized before the exception
occurs. Even if the object is only partially constructed, we are guaranteed that the
constructed members will be properly destroyed.

Similarly, an exception might occur when initializing the elements of an array
or other container type. Again, we are guaranteed that the constructed elements
will be destroyed.

Uncaught Exceptions Terminate the Program

An exception cannot remain unhandled. An exception is an important enough
event that the program cannot continue executing normally. If no matching `catch`
is found, then the program calls the library `terminate` function.

17.1.3   Catching an Exception

The **exception specifier** in a **catch clause** looks like a parameter list that contains exactly one parameter. The exception specifier is a type name followed by an optional parameter name.

The type of the specifier determines what kinds of exceptions the handler can catch. The type must be a complete type: It must either be a built-in type or a programmer-defined type that has already been defined. A forward declaration for the type is not sufficient.

An exception specifier can omit the parameter name when a catch needs to know only the type of the exception in order to handle it. If the handler needs information beyond what type of exception occurred, then its exception specifier will include a parameter name. The catch uses the name to get access to the exception object.

Finding a Matching Handler

During the search for a matching catch, the catch that is found is not necessarily the one that matches the exception best. Instead, the catch that is selected is the first catch found that can handle the exception. As a consequence, in a list of catch clauses, the most specialized catch must appear first.

The rules for when an exception matches a catch exception specifier are much more restrictive than the rules used for matching arguments with parameter types. Most conversions are not allowed—the types of the exception and the catch specifier must match exactly with only a few possible differences:

- Conversions from nonconst to const are allowed. That is, a throw of a nonconst object can match a catch specified to take a const reference.

- Conversions from derived type to base type are allowed.

- An array is converted to a pointer to the type of the array; a function is converted to the appropriate pointer to function type.

No other conversions are allowed when looking for a matching catch. In particular, neither the standard arithmetic conversions nor conversions defined for class types are permitted.

Exception Specifiers

When a catch is entered, the catch parameter is initialized from the exception object. As with a function parameter, the exception-specifier type might be a reference. The exception object itself is a copy of the object that was thrown. Whether the exception object is copied again into the catch site depends on the exception-specifier type.

If the specifier is not a reference, then the exception object is copied into the catch parameter. The catch operates on a local copy of the exception object. Any changes made to the catch parameter are made to the copy, not to the exception object itself. If the specifier is a reference, then like a reference parameter, there is no separate `catch` object; the `catch` parameter is just another name for the exception object. Changes made to the `catch` parameter are made to the exception object.

Exception Specifiers and Inheritance

Like a parameter declaration, an exception specifier for a base class can be used to `catch` an exception object of a derived type. Again, like a parameter declaration, the static type of the exception specifier determines the actions that the `catch` clause may perform. If the exception object thrown is of derived-class type but is handled by a `catch` that takes a base-class type, then the `catch` cannot use any members that are unique to the derived type.

 Best Practices Usually, a `catch` clause that handles an exception of a type related by inheritance ought to define its parameter as a reference.

If the `catch` parameter is a reference type, then the `catch` object accesses the exception object directly. The static type of the `catch` object and the dynamic type of the exception object to which it refers might differ. If the specifier is not a reference, then the `catch` object is a copy of the exception object. If the `catch` object in an object of the base type and the exception object has derived type, then the exception object is sliced down (Section 15.3.1, p. 577) to its base-class subobject.

Moreover, as we saw in Section 15.2.4 (p. 566), objects (as opposed to references) are not polymorphic. When we use a virtual function on an object rather than through a reference, the object's static and dynamic type are the same; the fact that the function is virtual makes no difference. Dynamic binding happens only for calls through a reference or pointer, not calls on an object.

Ordering of Catch Clauses Must Reflect Type Hierarchy

When exception types are organized in class hierarchies, users may choose the level of granularity with which their applications will deal with an exception. For example, an application that merely wants to do cleanup and exit might define a single try block that encloses the code in `main` with a `catch` such as the following:

```
catch(exception &e) {
    //  do cleanup
    //  print a message
    cerr << "Exiting: " << e.what() << endl;
    size_t status_indicator = 42;   //  set and return an
    return(status_indicator);       //  error indicator
}
```

Other programs with more rigorous uptime requirements might need finer control over exceptions. Such applications will clear whatever caused the exception and continue processing.

Because `catch` clauses are matched in the order in which they appear, programs that use exceptions from an inheritance hierarchy must order their `catch` clauses so that handlers for a derived type occurs before a `catch` for its base type.

Multiple `catch` clauses with types related by inheritance must be ordered from most derived type to least derived.

EXERCISES SECTION 17.1.3

Exercise 17.3: Explain why this `try` block is incorrect. Correct it.

```
try {
      // use of the C++ standard library
} catch(exception) {
      // ...
} catch(const runtime_error &re) {
      // ...
} catch(overflow_error eobj) { /* ... */ }
```

17.1.4 Rethrow

It is possible that a single `catch` cannot completely handle an exception. After some corrective actions, a `catch` may decide that the exception must be handled by a function further up the chain of function calls. A `catch` can pass the exception out to another `catch` further up the list of function calls by **rethrowing** the exception. A rethrow is a `throw` that is not followed by a type or an expression:

```
throw;
```

An empty `throw` rethrows the exception object. An empty `throw` can appear only in a `catch` or in a function called (directly or indirectly) from a `catch`. If an empty `throw` is encountered when a handler is not active, `terminate` is called.

Although the rethrow does not specify its own exception, an exception object is still passed up the chain. The exception that is thrown is the original exception object, not the `catch` parameter. When a `catch` parameter is a base type, then we cannot know the actual type thrown by a rethrow expression. That type depends on the dynamic type of the exception object, not the static type of the `catch` parameter. For example, a rethrow from a `catch` with a parameter of base type might actually `throw` an object of the derived type.

In general, a `catch` might change its parameter. If, after changing its parameter, the `catch` rethrows the exception, then those changes will be propagated only if the exception specifier is a reference:

```
catch (my_error &eObj) {        // specifier is a reference type
      eObj.status = severeErr; // modifies the exception object
      throw; // the status member of the exception object is severeErr
} catch (other_error eObj) { // specifier is a nonreference type
      eObj.status = badErr;     // modifies local copy only
      throw; // the status member of the exception rethrown is unchanged
}
```

17.1.5   The Catch-All Handler

A function may want to perform some action before it exits with a thrown exception, even though it cannot handle the exception that is thrown. Rather than provide a specific `catch` clause for every possible exception, and because we can't know all the exceptions that might be thrown, we can use a **catch-all** `catch` clause. A catch-all clause has the form `(...)`. For example:

```
//   matches any exception that might be thrown
catch (...) {
      //   place our code here
}
```

A catch-all clause matches any type of exception.

A `catch(...)` is often used in combination with a rethrow expression. The `catch` does whatever local work can be done and then rethrows the exception:

```
void manip() {
      try {
            //   actions that cause an exception to be thrown
      }
      catch (...) {
            //   work to partially handle the exception
            throw;
      }
}
```

A `catch(...)` clause can be used by itself or as one of several catch clauses.

> If a `catch(...)` is used in combination with other `catch` clauses, it must be last; otherwise, any `catch` clause that followed it could never be matched.

17.1.6   Function Try Blocks and Constructors

In general, exceptions can occur at any point in the program's execution. In particular, an exception might occur in a constructor, or while processing a constructor initializer. Constructor initializers are processed before the constructor body is entered. A `catch` clause inside the constructor body cannot handle an exception that might occur while processing a constructor initializer.

To handle an exception from a constructor initializer, we must write the constructor as a **function try block**. A function try block lets us associate a group of `catch` clauses with the function as a whole. As an example, we might wrap our `Handle` constructor from Chapter 16 in a try block to detect a failure in `new`:

```
template <class T> Handle<T>::Handle(T *p)
try : ptr(p), use(new size_t(1))
{
      //   empty function body
} catch(const std::bad_alloc &e)
      { handle_out_of_memory(e); }
```

EXERCISES SECTION 17.1.5

Exercise 17.4: Given a basic C++ program,

```
int main() {
      // use of the C++ standard library
}
```

modify `main` to catch any exception thrown by functions in the C++ standard library. The handlers should print the error message associated with the exception before calling `abort` (defined in the header `cstdlib`) to terminate `main`.

Exercise 17.5: Given the following exception types and `catch` clauses, write a `throw` expression that creates an exception object that could be caught by each `catch` clause.

```
(a)  class exceptionType { };
     catch(exceptionType *pet) { }
(b)  catch(...) { }
(c)  enum mathErr { overflow, underflow, zeroDivide };
     catch(mathErr &ref) { }
(d)  typedef int EXCPTYPE;
     catch(EXCPTYPE) { }
```

Notice that the keyword `try` precedes the member initialization list, and the compound statement of the try block encompasses the constructor function body. The `catch` clause can handle exceptions thrown either from within the member initialization list or from within the constructor body.

 The only way for a constructor to handle an exception from a constructor initializer is to write the constructor as a function try block.

17.1.7 Exception Class Hierarchies

Section 6.13 (p. 215) introduced the standard-library exception classes. What that section did not cover is that these classes are related by inheritance. The inheritance hierarchy is portrayed in Figure 17.1 on the following page.

The only operation the `exception` types define is a virtual member named `what`. That function returns a `const char*`. It typically returns the message used when constructing the exception object at the throw site. Because `what` is virtual if we catch a base-type reference, a call to the `what` function will execute the version appropriate to the dynamic type of the exception object.

Exception Classes for a Bookstore Application

The standard exception classes can be used for quite a number of applications. In addition, applications often extend the `exception` hierarchy by deriving additional types from `exception` or one of the intermediate base classes. These newly derived classes can represent exception types specific to the application domain.

Figure 17.1: Standard exception Class Hierarchy

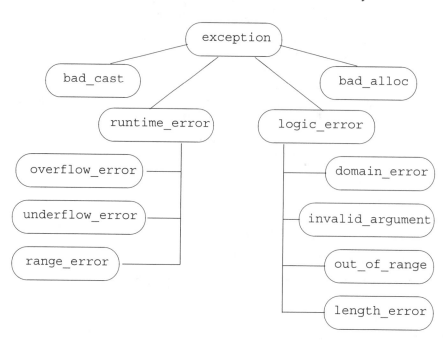

If we were building a real bookstore application, our classes would have been much more complex than the ones presented in this primer. One way in which they might be more elaborate would be in their handling of exceptions. In fact, we probably would have defined our own hierarchy of exceptions to represent application-specific problems that might arise. Our design might include classes such as

```
//  hypothetical exception classes for a bookstore application
class out_of_stock: public std::runtime_error {
public:
    explicit out_of_stock(const std::string &s):
                        std::runtime_error(s) { }
};
class isbn_mismatch: public std::logic_error {
public:
    explicit isbn_mismatch(const std::string &s):
                        std::logic_error(s) { }
    isbn_mismatch(const std::string &s,
        const std::string &lhs, const std::string &rhs):
        std::logic_error(s), left(lhs), right(rhs) { }
    const std::string left, right;
    // Section 17.1.10 (p. 706) explains the destructor and why we need one
    virtual ~isbn_mismatch() throw() { }
};
```

Here we defined our application-specific exception types by deriving them from the standard exception classes. As with any hierarchy, we can think of the exception classes as being organized into layers. As the hierarchy becomes deeper, each layer becomes a more specific exception. For example, the first and most general layer of the hierarchy is represented by class exception. All we know when we catch an object of this type is that something has gone wrong.

The second layer specializes exception into two broad categories: run-time or logic errors. Our bookstore exception classes represent an even more specialized layer. The class out_of_stock represents something that can go wrong at run time that is particular to our application. It would be used to signal that an order cannot be fulfilled. The isbn_mismatch exception is a more particular form of logic_error. In principle, a program could detect that the ISBNs don't match by calling same_isbn.

Using Programmer-Defined Exception Types

We use our own exception classes in the same way that we use one of the standard library classes. One part of the program throws an object of one of these types, and another part catches and handles the indicated problem. As an example, we might define the overloaded addition operator for our Sales_item class to throw an error of type isbn_mismatch if it detected that the ISBNs didn't match:

```
//  throws exception if both objects do not refer to the same isbn
Sales_item
operator+(const Sales_item& lhs, const Sales_item& rhs)
{
    if (!lhs.same_isbn(rhs))
        throw isbn_mismatch("isbn mismatch",
                            lhs.book(), rhs.book());
    Sales_item ret(lhs);    //  copy lhs into a local object that we'll return
    ret += rhs;             //  add in the contents of rhs
    return ret;             //  return ret by value
}
```

Code that uses the addition operator could then detect this error, write an appropriate error message, and continue:

```
//  use hypothetical bookstore exceptions
Sales_item item1, item2, sum;
while (cin >> item1 >> item2) {  //  read two transactions
    try {
        sum = item1 + item2;     //  calculate their sum
        //  use sum
    } catch (const isbn_mismatch &e) {
        cerr << e.what() << ": left isbn(" << e.left
            << ") right isbn(" << e.right << ")"
            << endl;
    }
}
```

17.1.8   Automatic Resource Deallocation

In Section 17.1.2 (p. 691) we saw that local objects are automatically destroyed when an exception occurs. The fact that destructors are run has important implication for the design of applications. It also is one (among many) reasons why we encourage the use of the standard library classes. Consider the following function:

```
void f()
{
    vector<string> v;                       // local vector
    string s;
    while (cin >> s)
        v.push_back(s);                     // populate the vector
    string *p = new string[v.size()];   // dynamic array
    // remaining processing
    // it is possible that an exception occurs in this code

    // function cleanup is bypassed if an exception occurs
    delete [] p;
}   // v destroyed automatically when the function exits
```

This function defines a local `vector` and dynamically allocates an array. Under normal execution, both the array and the `vector` are destroyed before the function exits. The array is freed by the last statement in the function, and the `vector` is automatically destroyed when the function ends.

However, if an exception occurs inside the function, then the `vector` will be destroyed but the array will not be freed. The problem is that the array is not freed automatically. An exception that occurs after the `new` but before the corresponding `delete` leaves the array undestroyed. No matter when an exception occurs, we are guaranteed that the `vector` destructor is run.

Using Classes to Manage Resource Allocation

The fact that destructors are run leads to an important programming technique that makes programs more **exception safe**. By exception safe, we mean that the programs operate correctly even if an exception occurs. In this case, the "safety" comes from ensuring that any resouce that is allocated is properly freed if an exception occurs.

We can guarantee that resources are properly freed by defining a class to encapsulate the acquisition and release of a resource. This technique is often referred to as "resource allocation is initialization," often abreviated as RAII.

The resource-managing class should be designed so that the constructor acquires the resource and the destructor frees it. When we want to allocate the resource, we define an object of that class type. If no exception occurs, then the resource will be freed when the object that acquired the resource goes out of scope. More importantly, if an exception occurs after the object is created but before it goes out of scope, then the compiler ensures that the object is destroyed as part of unwinding the scope in which the object was defined.

The following class is a prototypical example in which the constructor acquires a resource and the destructor releases it:

```
class Resource {
public:
    Resource(parms p): r(allocate(p)) { }
    ~Resource() { release(r); }
    // also need to define copy and assignment
private:
    resource_type *r;                    // resource managed by this type
    resource_type *allocate(parms p);   // allocate this resource
    void release(resource_type*);       // free this resource
};
```

The `Resource` class is a type that allocates and deallocates a resource. It holds data member(s) that represent that resource. The constructor for `Resource` allocates the resource, and the destructor frees it. When we use this class

```
void fcn()
{
    Resource res(args);    // allocates resource_type
    // code that might throw an exception
    // if exception occurs, destructor for res is run automatically
    // ...
}    // res goes out of scope and is destroyed automatically
```

the resource is automatically freed. If the function terminates normally, then the resource is freed when the `Resource` object goes out of scope. If the function is exited prematurely by an exception, the destructor for `Resource` is run by the compiler as part of the exception handling process.

Best Practices Programs in which exceptions are possible and that allocate resources should use classes to manage those resources. As described in this section, using classes to manage acquisition and deallocation ensures that resources are freed if an exception occurs.

EXERCISES SECTION 17.1.8

Exercise 17.6: Given the following function, explain what happens when the exception occurs.

```
void exercise(int *b, int *e)
{
    vector<int> v(b, e);
    int *p = new int[v.size()];
    ifstream in("ints");
    // exception occurs here
    // ...
}
```

Exercise 17.7: There are two ways to make the previous code exception-safe. Describe them and implement them.

17.1.9   The `auto_ptr` Class

The standard-library **`auto_ptr`** class is an example of the exception-safe "resource allocation is initialization" technique described in the previous subsection. The `auto_ptr` class is a template that takes a single type parameter. It provides exception safety for dynamically allocated objects. The `auto_ptr` class is defined in the memory header.

> `auto_ptr` can be used only to manage single objects returned from `new`. It does not manage dynamically allocated arrays.
>   As we'll see, `auto_ptr` has unusual behavior when copied or assigned. As a result, `auto_ptr`s may not be stored in the library container types.

An `auto_ptr` may hold only a pointer to an object and may not be used to point to a dynamically allocated array. Using an `auto_ptr` to point to a dynamically allocated array results in undefined run-time behavior.

Each `auto_ptr` is either unbound or it points to an object. When an `auto_ptr` points to an object, it can be said to "own" that object. When the `auto_ptr` goes out of scope or is otherwise destroyed, then the dynamically allocated object to which the `auto_ptr` points is automatically deallocated.

Using `auto_ptr` for Exception-Safe Memory Allocation

If memory is acquired through a normal pointer and an exception occurs before a `delete` is executed, then that memory won't be freed automatically:

```
void f()
{
    int *ip = new int(42);       //  dynamically allocate a new object
    //  code that throws an exception that is not caught inside f
    delete ip;                   //  return the memory before exiting
}
```

If an exception happens between the `new` and the `delete`, and if that exception is not caught locally, then the `delete` will not be executed. The memory will never be returned.

If we use an `auto_ptr` instead, the memory will be freed automatically, even if the block is exited prematurely:

```
void f()
{
    auto_ptr<int> ap(new int(42)); //  allocate a new object
    //  code that throws an exception that is not caught inside f
}            //  auto_ptr freed automatically when function ends
```

In this case, the compiler ensures that the destructor for `ap` is run before the stack is unwound past `f`.

Table 17.1: Class `auto_ptr`	
`auto_ptr<T> ap;`	Create an unbound `auto_ptr` named ap.
`auto_ptr<T> ap(p);`	Create an `auto_ptr` named ap that owns the object pointed to by the pointer p. This constructor is `explicit`.
`auto_ptr<T> ap1(ap2);`	Create an `auto_ptr` named ap1 that holds the pointer originally stored in ap2. Transfers ownership to ap1; ap2 becomes an unbound `auto_ptr`.
`ap1 = ap2`	Transfers ownership from ap2 to ap1. Deletes the object to which ap1 points and makes ap1 point to the object to which ap2 points, making ap2 unbound.
`~ap`	Destructor. Deletes the object to which ap points.
`*ap`	Returns a reference to the object to which ap is bound.
`ap->`	Returns the pointer that ap holds.
`ap.reset(p)`	If the pointer p is not the same value as ap holds, then it deletes the object to which ap points and binds ap to p.
`ap.release()`	Returns the pointer that ap had held and makes ap unbound.
`ap.get()`	Returns the pointer that ap holds.

`auto_ptr` Is a Template and Can Hold Pointers of Any Type

The `auto_ptr` class is a template taking a single type parameter. That type names the type of the object to which the `auto_ptr` may be bound. Thus, we can create `auto_ptr`s of any type:

```
auto_ptr<string> ap1(new string("Brontosaurus"));
```

Binding an `auto_ptr` to a Pointer

In the most common case, we initialize an `auto_ptr` to the address of an object returned by a new expression:

```
auto_ptr<int> pi(new int(1024));
```

This statement initializes pi to the address of the object created by the new expression. This new expression initializes that int to the value 1,024.

The constructor that takes a pointer is an `explicit` (Section 12.4.4, p. 462) constructor, so we must use the direct form of initialization to create an `auto_ptr`:

```
// error: constructor that takes a pointer is explicit and can't be used implicitly
auto_ptr<int> pi = new int(1024);
auto_ptr<int> pi(new int(1024)); // ok: uses direct initialization
```

The object created by the new expression to which pi refers is deleted automatically when pi goes out of scope. If pi is a local object, the object to which pi refers is deleted at the end of the block in which pi is defined. If an exception occurs, then pi also goes out of scope. The destructor for pi will be run automatically as part of handling the exception. If `pi` is a global object, the object to which `pi` refers is deleted at the end of the program.

Using an `auto_ptr`

Suppose we wish to access a `string` operation. With an ordinary `string` pointer, we'd do the following:

```
string *pstr_type = new string("Brontosaurus");
if (pstr_type->empty())
        // oops, something wrong
```

The `auto_ptr` class defines overloaded versions of the dereference (`*`) and arrow (`->`) operators (Section 14.6, p. 523). Because `auto_ptr` defines these operators, we can use an `auto_ptr` in some ways that are similar to using a built-in pointer:

```
// normal pointer operations for dereference and arrow
*ap1 = "TRex";     // assigns a new value to the object to which ap1 points

string s = *ap1;   // initializes s as a copy of the object to which ap1 points

if (ap1->empty()) // runs empty on the string to which ap1 points
```

The primary purpose of `auto_ptr` is to support ordinary pointerlike behavior while ensuring that the object to which an `auto_ptr` object refers is automatically deleted. As we'll see, the fact that objects are automatically deleted leads to significant differences between `auto_ptrs` and ordinary pointers with respect to how we copy and access their address value.

Copy and Assignment on `auto_ptr` Are *Destructive* Operations

There is a crucially important difference between how `auto_ptr` and built-in pointers treat copy and assignment. When we copy an `auto_ptr` or assign its value to another `auto_ptr`, ownership of the underlying object is transferred from the original to the copy. The original `auto_ptr` is reset to an unbound state.

Copying (or assigning) ordinary pointers copies (assigns) the address. After the copy (assignment), both pointers point to the same object. After copying (or assigning) `auto_ptrs`, the original points to no object and the new `auto_ptr` (left-hand `auto_ptr`) owns the underlying object:

```
auto_ptr<string> ap1(new string("Stegosaurus"));
// after the copy ap1 is unbound
auto_ptr<string> ap2(ap1);  // ownership transferred from ap1 to ap2
```

When we copy or assign an `auto_ptr`, the right-hand `auto_ptr` relinquishes all responsibility for the underlying object and is reset to be an unbound `auto_ptr`. In our example, it is `ap2` that deletes the `string` object, and not `ap1`. After the copy, `ap1` no longer refers to any object.

Unlike other copy or assignment operations, `auto_ptr` copy and assignment change the right-hand operand. As a result, both the left- and right-hand operands to assignment must be modifiable lvalues.

Assignment Deletes the Object Pointed To by the Left Operand

In addition to transferring ownership from the right-hand to the left-hand operand, assignment also deletes the object to which the left-hand operand originally referred—provided that the two objects are different. As usual, self-assignment has no effect.

```
auto_ptr<string> ap3(new string("Pterodactyl"));
// object pointed to by ap3 is deleted and ownership transferred from ap2 to ap3;
ap3 = ap2; // after the assignment, ap2 is unbound
```

After the assignment of ap2 to ap3,

- the object to which ap3 had pointed is deleted;

- ap3 is set to point to the object to which ap2 pointed; and

- ap2 is an unbound `auto_ptr`.

Because copy and assignment are destructive operations, `auto_ptrs` *cannot* be stored in the standard containers. The library container classes require that two objects be equal after a copy or assignment. This requirement is not met by `auto_ptr`. If we assign ap2 to ap1, then after the assignment ap1 != ap2. Similarly for copy.

The Default `auto_ptr` Constructor

If no initializer is given, the `auto_ptr` is *unbound*; it doesn't refer to an object:

```
auto_ptr<int> p_auto;  // p_auto doesn't refer to any object
```

By default, the internal pointer value of an `auto_ptr` is set to 0. Dereferencing an unbound `auto_ptr` has the same effect as dereferencing an unbound pointer—the program is in error and what happens is undefined:

```
*p_auto = 1024; // error: dereference auto_ptr that doesn't point to an object
```

Testing an `auto_ptr`

To check whether a pointer is unbound, we can test the pointer directly in a condition, which has the effect of determining whether the pointer is 0. In contrast, we cannot test an `auto_ptr` directly.

```
// error: cannot use an auto_ptr as a condition
if (p_auto)
    *p_auto = 1024;
```

The `auto_ptr` type does not define a conversion to a type that can be used as a condition. Instead, to test the `auto_ptr`, we must use its `get` member, which returns the underlying pointer contained in the `auto_ptr`:

```
//  revised test to guarantee p_auto refers to an object
if (p_auto.get())
    *p_auto = 1024;
```

To determine whether the `auto_ptr` object refers to an object, we can compare the return from `get` with 0.

get should be used only to interrogate an `auto_ptr` or to use the returned pointer value. get should not be used as an argument to create another `auto_ptr`.

Using `get` member to initialize another `auto_ptr` violates the class design principle that only one `auto_ptr` holds a given pointer at any one time. If two `auto_ptr`s hold the same pointer, then the pointer will be `deleted` twice.

The `reset` Operation

Another difference between `auto_ptr` and a built-in pointer is that we cannot assign an address (or other pointer) directly to an `auto_ptr`:

```
p_auto = new int(1024); //  error: cannot assign a pointer to an auto_ptr
```

Instead, we must call `reset` to change the pointer:

```
//  revised test to guarantee p_auto refers to an object
if (p_auto.get())
    *p_auto = 1024;
else
    //  reset p_auto to a new object
    p_auto.reset(new int(1024));
```

To unset the `auto_ptr` object, we could pass 0 to `reset`.

Calling reset on an `auto_ptr` deletes the object (if any) to which the `auto_ptr` refers before binding the `auto_ptr` to another object. However, just as self-assignment has no effect, if we call reset on the same pointer that the `auto_ptr` already holds, then there is no effect; the object is not deleted.

17.1.10   Exception Specifications

When looking at an ordinary function declaration, it is not possible to determine what exceptions the function might throw. However, it can be useful to know whether and which exceptions a function might throw in order to write appropriate `catch` clauses. An **exception specification** specifies that if the function throws an exception, the exception it throws will be one of the exceptions included in the specification, or it will be a type derived from one of the listed exceptions.

CAUTION: auto_ptr PITFALLS

The auto_ptr class template provides a measure of safety and convenience for handling dynamically allocated memory. To use auto_ptr correctly, we must adhere to the restrictions that the class imposes:

1. Do not use an auto_ptr to hold a pointer to a statically allocated object. Otherwise, when the auto_ptr itself is destroyed, it will attempt to delete a pointer to a nondynamically allocated object, resulting in undefined behavior.

2. Never use two auto_ptrs to refer to the same object. One obvious way to make this mistake is to use the same pointer to initialize or to reset two different auto_ptr objects. A more subtle way to make this mistake would be to use the result from get on one auto_ptr to initialize or reset another.

3. Do not use an auto_ptr to hold a pointer to a dynamically allocated array. When the auto_ptr is destroyed, it frees only a single object—it uses the plain delete operator, not the array delete [] operator.

4. Do not store an auto_ptr in a container. Containers require that the types they hold define copy and assignment to behave similarly to how those operations behave on the built-in types: After the copy (or assignment), the two objects must have the same value. auto_ptr does not meet this requirement.

EXERCISES SECTION 17.1.9

Exercise 17.8: Which of the following auto_ptr declarations are illegal or likely to result in subsequent program error? Explain what the problem is with each one.

```
int ix = 1024, *pi = &ix, *pi2 = new int(2048);
typedef auto_ptr<int> IntP;
```

(a) IntP p0(ix);	(b) IntP p1(pi);
(c) IntP p2(pi2);	(d) IntP p3(&ix);
(e) IntP p4(new int(2048));	(f) IntP p5(p2.get());

Exercise 17.9: Assuming ps is a pointer to string, what is the difference, if any, between the following two invocations of assign (Section 9.6.2, p. 339)? Which do you think is preferable? Why?

```
(a) ps.get()->assign("Danny");    (b) ps->assign("Danny");
```

Defining an Exception Specification

An exception specification follows the function parameter list. An exception specification is the keyword throw followed by a (possibly empty) list of exception types enclosed in parentheses:

```
void recoup(int) throw(runtime_error);
```

This declaration says that recoup is a function taking an int, and returning void. If recoup throws an exception, that exception will be a runtime_error or an exception of a type derived from runtime_error.

An empty specification list says that the function does not throw any exception:

```
void no_problem() throw();
```

An exception specification is part of the function's interface. The function definition and any declarations of the function must have the same specification.

 Note If a function declaration does not specify an exception specification, the function can throw exceptions of any type.

Violating the Exception Specification

Unfortunately, it is not possible to know at compile time whether or which exceptions a program will throw. Violations of a function's exception specification can be detected only at run time.

If a function throws an exception not listed in its specification, the library function **unexpected** is invoked. By default, unexpected calls terminate, which ordinarily aborts the program.

 Beware The compiler cannot and does not attempt to verify exception specifications at compile time.

Even if a casual reading of a function's code indicates that it *might* throw an exception missing from the specification, the compiler will not complain:

```
void f() throw()        // promise not to throw any exception
{
    throw exception();  // violates exception specification
}
```

Instead, the compiler generates code to ensure that unexpected is called if an exception violating the exception specification is thrown.

Specifying that the Function Does Not Throw

Because an exception specification cannot be checked at compile time, the practical utility of exception specifications is often limited.

 Best Practices One important case when an exception specification is useful is if a function can guarantee that it will not throw any exceptions.

Specifying that a function will not throw any exceptions can be helpful both to users of the function and to the compiler: Knowing that a function will not throw simplifies the task of writing exception-safe code that calls that function. We can know that we need not worry about exceptions when calling it. Moreover, if the compiler knows that no exceptions will be thrown, it can perform optimizations that are suppressed for code that might throw.

Exception Specifications and Member Functions

As with nonmember functions, an exception specification on a member function declaration follows the function parameter list. For example, the class bad_alloc from the C++ standard library is defined so that all its member functions have an empty exception specification. These members promise not to throw an exception:

```
//  ilustrative definition of library bad_alloc class
class bad_alloc : public exception {
public:
    bad_alloc() throw();
    bad_alloc(const bad_alloc &) throw();
    bad_alloc & operator=(const bad_alloc &) throw();
    virtual ~bad_alloc() throw();
    virtual const char* what() const throw();
};
```

Notice that the exception specification follows the const qualifier in const member function declarations.

Exception Specifications and Destructors

In Section 17.1.7 (p. 697) we showed two hypothetical bookstore application exception classes. The isbn_mismatch class defines its destructor as

```
class isbn_mismatch: public std::logic_error {
public:
    virtual ~isbn_mismatch() throw() { }
};
```

and said that we would explain this usage here.

The isbn_mismatch class inherits from logic_error, which is one of the standard exception classes. The destructors for the standard exception classes include an empty throw() specifier; they promise that they will not throw any exceptions. When we inherit from one of these classes, then our destructor must also promise not to throw any exceptions.

Our out_of_stock class had no members, and so its synthesized destructor does nothing that might throw an exception. Hence, the compiler can know that the synthesized destructor will abide by the promise not to throw.

The isbn_mismatch class has two members of class string, which means that the synthesized destructor for isbn_mismatch calls the string destructor. The C++ standard stipulates that string destructor, like any other library class destructor, will not throw an exception. However, the library destructors do not define exception specifications. In this case, we know, but the compiler doesn't, that the string destructor won't throw. We must define our own destructor to reinstate the promise that the destructor will not throw.

Exception Specifications and Virtual Functions

A virtual function in a base class may have an exception specification that differs from the exception specification of the corresponding virtual in a derived class.

However, the exception specification of a derived-class virtual function must be either equally or more restrictive than the exception specification of the corresponding base-class virtual function.

This restriction ensures that when a pointer to a base-class type is used to call a derived virtual function, the exception specification of the derived class adds no new exceptions to those that the base said could be thrown. For example,

```
class Base {
public:
    virtual double f1(double) throw ();
    virtual int f2(int) throw (std::logic_error);
    virtual std::string f3() throw
            (std::logic_error, std::runtime_error);
};
class Derived : public Base {
public:
    // error: exception specification is less restrictive than Base::f1's
    double f1(double) throw (std::underflow_error);

    // ok: same exception specification as Base::f2
    int f2(int) throw (std::logic_error);

    // ok: Derived f3 is more restrictive
    std::string f3() throw ();
};
```

The declaration of f1 in the derived class is an error because its exception specification adds an exception to those listed in the version of f1 in the base class. The reason that the derived class may not add to the specfication list is users of the hierarchy should be able to write code that depends on the specification list. If a call is made through a base pointer or reference, then only the exceptions specified in the base should be of concern to a user of these classes.

By restricting which exceptions the derived classes will throw to those listed by the base class, we can write our code knowing what exceptions we must handle. Our code can rely on the fact that the list of exceptions in the base class is a superset of the list of exceptions that a derived-class version of the virtual might throw. As an example, when calling f3, we know we need to handle only logic_error or runtime_error:

```
// guarantees not to throw exceptions
void compute(Base *pb) throw()
{
    try {
        // may throw exception of type std::logic_error
        // or std::runtime_error
        pb->f3();
    } catch (const logic_error &le)   { /* ... */ }
      catch (const runtime_error &re) { /* ... */ }
}
```

The function compute uses the specification in the base class in deciding what exceptions it might need to catch.

17.1.11 Function Pointer Exception Specifications

An exception specification is part of a function type. As such, exception specifications can be provided in the definition of a pointer to function:

```
void (*pf)(int) throw(runtime_error);
```

This declaration says that `pf` points to a function that takes an `int`, returns a `void`, and that can throw exceptions only of type `runtime_error`. If no specification is provided, then the pointer may point at a function with matching type that could throw any kind of exception.

When a pointer to function with an exception specification is initialized from (or assigned to) another pointer (or to the address of a function), the exception specifications of both pointers do not have to be identical. However, the specification of the source pointer must be at least as restrictive as the specification of the destination pointer

```
void recoup(int) throw(runtime_error);
// ok: recoup is as restrictive as pf1
void (*pf1)(int) throw(runtime_error) = recoup;
// ok: recoup is more restrictive than pf2
void (*pf2)(int) throw(runtime_error, logic_error) = recoup;
// error: recoup is less restrictive than pf3
void (*pf3)(int) throw() = recoup;
// ok: recoup is more restrictive than pf4
void (*pf4)(int) = recoup;
```

The third initialization is an error. The pointer declaration says that `pf3` points to a function that will not throw any exceptions. However, `recoup` says it can throw exceptions of type `runtime_error`. The `recoup` function throws exception types beyond those specified by `pf3`. The `recoup` function is not a valid initializer for `pf3`, and a compile-time error is issued.

EXERCISES SECTION 17.1.11

Exercise 17.10: What exceptions can a function throw if it has an exception specification of the form `throw()`? If it has no exception specification?

Exercise 17.11: Which, if either, of the following initializations is in error? Why?

```
void example() throw(string);
(a) void (*pf1)() = example;
(b) void (*pf2)() throw() = example;
```

Exercise 17.12: Which exceptions might the following functions throw?

```
(a) void operate() throw(logic_error);
(b) int op(int) throw(underflow_error, overflow_error);
(c) char manip(string) throw();
(d) void process();
```

17.2   Namespaces

Every name defined in a given scope must be unique within that scope. This requirement can be difficult to satisfy for large, complex applications. Such applications tend to have many names defined in the global scope. Complex programs composed of independently developed libraries are even more likely to encounter name collisions—the same name is used in our own code or (more often) in the code supplied to us by independent producers.

Libraries tend to define a large number of global names—primarily names of templates, types and functions. When writing an application using libraries from many different vendors, it is almost inevitable that some of these names will clash. This name-clashing problem is known as the **namespace pollution** problem.

Traditionally, programmers avoided namespace pollution by making names of global entities very long, often prefixing the names in their program with specific character sequences:

```
class cplusplus_primer_Query { ... };

ifstream&
cplusplus_primer_open_file(ifstream&, const string&);
```

This solution is far from ideal: It can be cumbersome for programmers to write and read programs that use such long names. **Namespaces** provide a much more controlled mechanism for preventing name collisions. Namespaces partition the global namespace, making it easier to use independently produced libraries. A namespace is a scope. By defining a library's names inside a namespace, library authors (and users) can avoid the limitations inherent in global names.

17.2.1   Namespace Definitions

A namespace definition begins with the keyword namespace followed by the namespace name.

```
namespace cplusplus_primer {
    class Sales_item { /* ... */};
    Sales_item operator+(const Sales_item&,
                         const Sales_item&);
    class Query {
    public:
        Query(const std::string&);
        std::ostream &display(std::ostream&) const;
        // ...
    };
    class Query_base { /* ... */};
}
```

This code defines a namespace named cplusplus_primer with four members: two classes, an overloaded + operator, and a function.

As with other names, the name of a namespace must be unique within the scope in which the namespace is defined. Namespaces may be defined at global scope or inside another namespace. They may not be defined inside a function or a class.

Following the namespace name is a block of declarations and definitions delimited by curly braces. Any declaration that can appear at global scope can be put into a namespace: classes, variables (with their initializations), functions (with their definitions), templates, and other namespaces.

 A namespace scope does not end with a semicolon.

Each Namespace Is a Scope

The entities defined in a namespace are called namespace members. Just as is the case for any scope, each name in a namespace must refer to a unique entity within that namespace. Because different namespaces introduce different scopes, different namespaces may have members with the same name.

Names defined in a namespace may be accessed directly by other members of the namespace. Code outside the namespace must indicate the namespace in which the name is defined:

```
cplusplus_primer::Query q =
                cplusplus_primer::Query("hello");
q.display(cout);
// ...
```

If another namespace (say, `AddisonWesley`) also provides a `TextQuery` class and we want to use that class instead of the one defined in `cplusplus_primer`, we can do so by modifying our code as follows:

```
AddisonWesley::Query q = AddisonWesley::Query("hello");
q.display(cout);
// ...
```

Using Namespace Members from Outside the Namespace

Of course, always referring to a namespace member using the qualified name

```
namespace_name::member_name
```

can be cumbersome. Just as we've been doing for names defined in the `std` namespace, we can write a `using` declaration (Section 3.1, p. 78) to obtain direct access to names we know we'll use frequently:

```
using cplusplus_primer::Query;
```

After this `using` declaration, our program can use the name `Query` directly without the `cplusplus_primer` qualifier. We'll see other ways to simplify access in Section 17.2.4 (p. 720).

Namespaces Can Be Discontiguous

Unlike other scopes, a namespace can be defined in several parts. A namespace is made up of the sum of its separately defined parts; a namespace is cumulative. The separate parts of a namespace can be spread over multiple files. Namespace definitions in different text files are also cumulative. Of course, the usual restriction continues to apply that names are visible only in the files in which they are declared. So, if one part of the namespace requires a name defined in another file, that name must still be declared.

Writing a namespace definition

```
namespace namespace_name {
// declarations
}
```

either defines a new namespace or adds to an existing one.

If the name *namespace_name* does not refer to a previously defined namespace, then a new namespace with that name is created. Otherwise, this definition opens an existing namespace and adds these new declarations to that namespace.

Separation of Interface and Implementation

The fact that namespace definitions can be discontiguous means that we can compose a namespace from separate interface and implementation files. Thus, a namespace can be organized in the same way that we manage our own class and function definitions:

1. Namespace members that define classes and declarations for the functions and objects that are part of the class interface can be put into header files. These headers can be included by files that use namespace members.

2. The definitions of namepsace members can be put in separate source files.

Organizing our namespaces this way also satisfies the requirement that various entities—non-inline functions, static data members, variables, and so forth—may be defined only once in a program. This requirement applies equally to names defined in a namespace. By separating the interface and implementation, we can ensure that the functions and other names we need are defined only once, but the same declaration will be seen whenever the entity is used.

 Best Practices Namespaces that define multiple, unrelated types should use separate files to represent each type that the namespace defines.

Defining the Primer Namespace

Using this strategy for separating interface and implementation, we might define the `cplusplus_primer` library in several separate files. The declarations for `Sales_item` and its related functions that we built in Part I (p. 31) would be placed in `Sales_item.h`, those for the `Query` classes of Chapter 15 (p. 557) in `Query.h`, and so on. The corresponding implementation files would be in files such as `Sales_item.cc` and `Query.cc`:

```
//  ---- Sales_item.h ----
namespace cplusplus_primer {
    class Sales_item { /* ... */};
    Sales_item operator+(const Sales_item&,
                         const Sales_item&);
    // declarations for remaining functions in the Sales_item interface
}
//  ---- Query.h ----
namespace cplusplus_primer {
    class Query {
    public:
        Query(const std::string&);
        std::ostream &display(std::ostream&) const;
        // ...
    };
    class Query_base { /* ... */};
}
//  ---- Sales_item.cc ----
#include "Sales_item.h"
namespace cplusplus_primer {
// definitions for Sales_item members and overloaded operators
}
//  ---- Query.cc ----
#include "Query.h"
namespace cplusplus_primer {
    // definitions for Query members and related functions
}
```

This program organization gives both the developers and users of our library the needed modularity. Each class is still organized into its own interface and implementation files. A user of one class need not compile names related to the others. We can hide the implementations from our users, while allowing the files Sales_item.cc and user.cc to be compiled and linked into one program without causing any compile-time or link-time error. Developers of the library can work independently on the implementation of each type.

A program using our library would include whichever headers it needed. The names in those headers are defined inside the cplusplus_primer namespace:

```
//  ---- user.cc ----
// defines the cplusplus_primer::Sales_item class
#include "Sales_item.h"
int main()
{
    // ...
    cplusplus_primer::Sales_item trans1, trans2;
    // ...
    return 0;
}
```

Defining Namespace Members

Functions defined inside a namespace may use the short form for names defined in the same namespace:

```
namespace cplusplus_primer {
// members defined inside the namespace may use unqualified names
std::istream&
operator>>(std::istream& in, Sales_item& s)
{
    // ...
}
}
```

It is also possible to define a namespace member outside its namespace definition. We do so in ways that are similar to defining class members outside a class: The namespace declaration of the name must be in scope, and the definition must specify the namespace to which the name belongs:

```
// namespace members defined outside the namespace must use qualified names
cplusplus_primer::Sales_item
cplusplus_primer::operator+(const Sales_item& lhs,
                            const Sales_item& rhs)
{
    Sales_item ret(lhs);
    // ...
}
```

This definition should look similar to class member functions defined outside a class. The return type and function name are qualified by the namespace name. Once the fully qualified function name is seen, we are in the scope of the namespace. Thus, references to namespace members in the parameter list and the function body can use unqualified names to reference `Sales_item`.

Members May Not Be Defined in Unrelated Namespaces

Although a namespace member can be defined outside its namespace definition, there are restrictions on where this definition can appear. Only namespaces enclosing the member declaration can contain its definition. For example, `operator+` could be defined in either the `cplusplus_primer` namespace or at global scope. It may not be defined in an unrelated namespace.

The Global Namespace

Names defined at global scope—names declared outside any class, function, or namespace—are defined inside the **global namespace**. The global namespace is implicitly declared and exists in every program. Each file that defines entities at global scope adds those names to the global namespace.

The scope operator can be used to refer to members of the global namespace. Because the global namespace is implicit, it does not have a name; the notation

```
::member_name
```

refers to a member of the global namespace.

Exercise 17.13: Define the bookstore exception classes described in Section 17.1.7 (p. 697) as members of namespace named `Bookstore`.

Exercise 17.14: Define `Sales_item` and its operators inside the `Bookstore` namespace. Define the addition operator to throw an exception.

Exercise 17.15: Write a program that uses the `Sales_item` addition operator and handles any exceptions. Make this program a member of another namespace named `MyApp`. This program should use the exception classes defined in the `Bookstore` namespace by the previous exercise.

17.2.2 Nested Namespaces

A nested namespace is a nested scope—its scope is nested within the namespace that contains it. Names in nested namespaces follow the normal rules: Names declared in an enclosing namespace are hidden by declarations of the same name in a nested namespace. Names defined inside a nested namespace are local to that namespace. Code in the outer parts of the enclosing namespace may refer to a name in a nested namespace only through its qualified name.

Nested namespaces can improve the organization of code in a library:

```cpp
namespace cplusplus_primer {
    //  first nested namespace:
    //  defines the Query portion of the library
    namespace QueryLib {
        class Query {  /* ... */  };
        Query operator&(const Query&, const Query&);
        // ...
    }
    //  second nested namespace:
    //  defines the Sales_item portion of the library
    namespace Bookstore {
        class Item_base { /* ... */ };
        class Bulk_item : public Item_base { /* ... */ };
        // ...
    }
}
```

The `cplusplus_primer` namespace now contains two nested namespaces: the namespaces named `QueryLib` and `Bookstore`.

Nested namespaces are useful when a library provider needs to prevent names in each part of a library from colliding with names in other parts of the library.

The name of a member in a nested namespace is formed from the names of the enclosing namespace(s) and the name of the nested namespace. For example, the name of the class declared in the nested namespace `QueryLib` is

```cpp
cplusplus_primer::QueryLib::Query
```

Exercise 17.16: Organize the programs you have written to answer the questions in each chapter into its own namespace. That is, namespace `chapterrefinheritance` would contain code for the `Query` programs and `chapterrefalgs` would contain the `TextQuery` code. Using this structure, compile the `Query` code examples.

Exercise 17.17: Over the course of this primer, we defined two different classes named `Sales_item`: the initial simple class defined and used in Part I, and the handle class defined in Section 15.8.1 that interfaced to the `Item_base` inheritance hierarchy. Define two namespaces nested inside the `cplusplus_primer` namespace that could be used to distinguish these two class definitions.

17.2.3 Unnamed Namespaces

A namespace may be unnamed. An **unnamed namespace** is a namespace that is defined without a name. An unnamed namespace begins with the keyword `namespace`. Following the `namespace` keyword is a block of declarations delimited by curly braces.

 Unnamed namespaces are not like other namespaces; the definition of an unnamed namespace is local to a particular file and never spans multiple text files.

An unnamed namespace may be discontiguous within a given file but does not span files. Each file has its own unnamed namespace.

Unnamed namespaces are used to declare entities that are local to a file. Variables defined in an unnamed namespace are created when the program is started and exist until the program ends.

Names defined in an unnamed namespace are used directly; after all, there is no namespace name with which to qualify them. It is not possible to use the scope operator to refer to members of unnamed namespaces.

Names defined in an unnamed namespace are visible only to the file containing the namespace. If another file contains an unnamed namespace, the namespaces are unrelated. Both unnamed namespaces could define the same name, and the definitions would refer to different entities.

Names defined in an unnamed namespace are found in the same scope as the scope at which the namespace is defined. If an unnamed namespace is defined at the outermost scope in the file, then names in the unnamed namespace must differ from names defined at global scope:

```
int i;    // global declaration for i
namespace {
    int i;
}
// error: ambiguous defined globally and in an unnested, unnamed namespace
i = 10;
```

An unnamed namespace, like any other namespace, may be nested inside another namespace. If the unnamed namespace is nested, then names in it are accessed in the normal way, using the enclosing namespace name(s):

```
namespace local {
    namespace {
        int i;
    }
}
    // ok: i defined in a nested unnamed namespace is distinct from global i
    local::i = 42;
```

> If a header defines an unnamed namespace then the names in that namespace will define different local entities in each file that includes the header.

In all other ways, the members of an unnamed namespace are normal program entities.

UNNAMED NAMESPACES REPLACE FILE STATICS

Prior to the introduction of namespaces in standard C++, programs had to declare names as `static` to make them local to a file. The use of file statics is inherited from C. In C, a global entity declared `static` is invisible outside the file in which it is declared.

> The use of file static declarations is *deprecated* by the C++ standard. A deprecated feature is one that may not be supported in future releases. File statics should be avoided and unnamed namespaces used instead.

EXERCISES SECTION 17.2.3

Exercise 17.18: Why would you define your own namespace in your programs? When might you use an unnamed namespace?

Exercise 17.19: Suppose we have the following declaration of the `operator*` that is a member of the nested namespace `cplusplus_primer::MatrixLib`:

```
namespace cplusplus_primer {
    namespace MatrixLib {
        class matrix {  /* ... */  };
        matrix operator*
                (const matrix &, const matrix &);
        // ...
    }
}
```

How would you define this operator in global scope? Provide only the prototype for the operator's definition.

17.2.4   Using Namespace Members

Referring to namespace members as `namespace_name::member_name` is admittedly cumbersome, especially if the namespace name is long. Fortunately, there are ways to make it easier to use namespace members. Our programs have used one of these ways, `using` declarations (Section 3.1, p. 78). The others, namespace aliases and `using` directives, will be described in this section.

Best Practices

> Header files should not contain `using` directives or `using` declarations except inside functions or other scopes. A header that includes a `using` directive or declaration at its top level scope has the effect of injecting that name into the file that includes the header. Headers should define only the names that are part of its interface, not names used in its own implementation.

`using` Declarations, a Recap

The programs in this book that use names from the standard library generally assume that an appropriate **using declaration** has been made:

```
map<string, vector< pair<size_t, size_t> > > word_map;
```

assumes that the following `using` declarations have been made:

```
using std::map;
using std::pair;
using std::size_t;
using std::string;
using std::vector;
```

A `using` declaration introduces only one namespace member at a time. It allows us to be very specific regarding which names are used in our programs.

Scope of a `using` Declaration

Names introduced in a `using` declaration obey normal scope rules. The name is visible from the point of the `using` declaration to the end of the scope in which the declaration is found. Entities with the same name defined in an outer scope are hidden.

The shorthand name may be used only within the scope in which it is declared and in scopes nested within that scope. Once the scope ends, the fully qualified name must be used.

A `using` declaration can appear in global, local, or namespace scope. A `using` declaration in class scope is limited to names defined in a base class of the class being defined.

Namespace Aliases

A **namespace alias** can be used to associate a shorter synonym with a namespace name. For example, a long namespace name such as

```
namespace cplusplus_primer     { /* ... */ };
```

can be associated with a shorter synonym as follows:

```
namespace primer = cplusplus_primer;
```

A namespace alias declaration begins with the keyword `namespace`, followed by the (shorter) name of the namespace alias, followed by the = sign, followed by the original namespace name and a semicolon. It is an error if the original namespace name has not already been defined as a namespace.

A namespace alias can also refer to a nested namespace. Rather than writing

```
cplusplus_primer::QueryLib::Query tq;
```

we could define and use an alias for `cplusplus_primer::QueryLib`:

```
namespace Qlib = cplusplus_primer::QueryLib;
Qlib::Query tq;
```

A namespace can have many synonyms, or aliases. All the aliases and the original namespace name can be used interchangeably.

using Directives

Like a `using` declaration, a **using directive** allows us to use the shorthand form of a namespace name. Unlike a `using` declaration, we retain no control over which names are made visible—they all are.

The Form of a using Directive

A `using` directive begins with the keyword `using`, followed by the keyword `namespace`, followed by a namespace name. It is an error if the name is not a previously defined namespace name.

A `using` directive makes all the names from a specific namespace visible without qualification. The short form names can be used from the point of the `using` directive to the end of the scope in which the `using` directive appears.

A `using` directive may appear in namespace, function, or block scope. It may not appear in a class scope.

It can be tempting to write programs with `using` directives, but doing so reintroduces all the problems inherent in name collisions when using multiple libraries.

using Directives and Scope

The scope of names introduced by a `using` directive is more complicated than those for `using` declarations. A `using` declaration puts the name directly in the same scope in which the `using` declaration itself appears. It is as if the `using` declaration is a local alias for the namespace member. Because the declaration is localized, the chance of collisions is minimized.

> A using directive does not declare local aliases for the namespace member names. Rather, it has the effect of lifting the namespace members into the nearest scope that contains both the namespace itself and the using directive.

In the simplest case, assume we have a namespace A and a function f, both defined at global scope. If f has a using directive for A, then in f it will be as if the names in A appeared in the global scope prior to the definition of f:

```
//  namespace A and function f are defined at global scope
namespace A {
    int i, j;
}
void f()
{
    using namespace A;       //  injects names from A into the global scope
    cout << i * j << endl; //  uses i and j from namespace A
    //  ...
}
```

> One place where using directives are useful is in the implementation files for the namespace itself.

using Directives Example

Let's look at an example:

```
namespace blip {
    int bi = 16, bj = 15, bk = 23;
    //  other declarations
}
int bj = 0;   //  ok: bj inside blip is hidden inside a namespace
void manip()
{
    //  using directive - names in blip "added" to global scope
    using namespace blip;
                              //  clash between ::bj and blip::bj
                              //  detected only if bj is used
    ++bi;                     //  sets blip::bi to 17
    ++bj;                     //  error: ambiguous
                              //  global bj or blip::bj?
    ++::bj;                   //  ok: sets global bj to 1
    ++blip::bj;               //  ok: sets blip::bj to 16
    int bk = 97;              //  local bk hides blip::bk
    ++bk;                     //  sets local bk to 98
}
```

The `using` directive in `manip` makes all the names in `blip` directly accessible to `manip`: The function can refer to the names of these members, using their short form.

The members of `blip` appear as if they were defined in the scope in which both `blip` and `manip` are defined. Given that `blip` is defined at global scope, then the members of `blip` appear as if they were declared in global scope. Because the names are in different scopes, local declarations within `manip` may hide some of the namespace member names. The local variable `bk` hides the namespace member `blip::bk`. Referring to `bk` within `manip` is not ambiguous; it refers to the local variable `bk`.

It is possible for names in the namespace to conflict with other names defined in the enclosing scope. For example, the `blip` member `bj` appears to `manip` as if it were declared at global scope. However, there is another object named `bj` in global scope. Such conflicts are permitted; but to use the name, we must explicitly indicate which version is wanted. Therefore, the use of `bj` within `manip` is ambiguous: The name refers both to the global variable and to the member of namespace `blip`.

To use a name such as `bj`, we must use the scope operator to indicate which name is wanted. We would write `::bj` to obtain the variable defined in global scope. To use the `bj` defined in `blip`, we must use its qualified name, `blip::bj`.

EXERCISES SECTION 17.2.4

Exercise 17.20: Explain the differences between `using` declarations and `using` directives.

Exercise 17.21: Consider the following code sample:

```
namespace Exercise {
    int ivar = 0;
    double dvar = 0;
    const int limit = 1000;
}
int ivar = 0;
// position 1
void manip() {
    // position 2
    double dvar = 3.1416;
    int iobj = limit + 1;
    ++ivar;
    ++::ivar;
}
```

What are the effects of the declarations and expressions in this code sample if `using` declarations for all the members of namespace `Exercise` are located at the location labeled *position 1*? At *position 2* instead? Now answer the same question but replace the `using` declarations with a `using` directive for namespace `Exercise`.

CAUTION: AVOID using DIRECTIVES

using directives, which inject all the names from a namespace, are deceptively simple to use: With only a single statement, all the member names of a namespace are suddenly visible. Although this approach may seem simple, it can introduce its own problems. If an application uses many libraries, and if the names within these libraries are made visible with using directives, then we are back to square one, and the global namespace pollution problem reappears.

Moreover, it is possible that a working program will fail to compile when a new version of the library is introduced. This problem can arise if a new version introduces a name that conflicts with a name that the application is using.

Another problem is that ambiguity errors caused by using directives are detected only at the point of use. This late detection means that conflicts can arise long after introducing a particular library. If the program begins using a new part of the library, previously undetected collisions may arise.

Rather than relying on a using directive, it is better to use a using declaration for each namespace name used in the program. Doing so reduces the number of names injected into the namespace. Ambiguity errors caused by using declarations are detected at the point of declaration, not use, and so are easier to find and fix.

17.2.5 Classes, Namespaces, and Scope

As we've noted, namespaces are scopes. As in any other scope, names are visible from the point of their declaration. Names remain visible through any nested scopes until the end of the block in which they were introduced.

Name lookup for names used inside a namespace follows the normal C++ lookup rules: When looking for a name, we look outward through the enclosing scopes. An enclosing scope for a name used inside a namespace might be one or more nested namespaces ending finally with the all-encompassing global namespace. Only names that have been declared before the point of use that are in blocks that are still open are considered:

```
namespace A {
    int i;
    namespace B {
        int i;          // hides A::i within B
        int j;
        int f1()
        {
            int j;      // j is local to f1 and hides A::B::j
            return i;   // returns B::i
        }
    }   // namespace B is closed and names in it are no longer visible
    int f2() {
        return j;       // error: j is not defined
    }
    int j = i;          // initialized from A::i
}
```

Names used in a class member definition are resolved in much the same way, with one important difference: If the name is not local to the member function, we first try to resolve the name to a class member before looking in the outer scopes.

As we saw in Section 12.3 (p. 444), members defined inside a class may use names that appear textually after the definition. For example, a constructor defined inside the class body may initialize the data members even if the declaration of those members appears after the constructor definition. When a name is used in a class scope, we look first in the member itself, then in the class, including any base classes. Only after exhausting the class(es) do we examine the enclosing scopes. When a class is wrapped in a namespace, the same lookup happens: Look first in the member, then the class (including base classes), then look in the enclosing scopes, one or more of which might be a namespace:

```
namespace A {
    int i;
    int k;
    class C1 {
    public:
        C1(): i(0), j(0) { }     // ok: initializes C1::i and C1::j
        int f1()
        {
            return k;            // returns A::k
        }
        int f2()
        {
            return h;            // error: h is not defined
        }
        int f3();
    private:
        int i;                   // hides A::i within C1
        int j;
    };
    int h = i;                   // initialized from A::i
}
// member f3 is defined outside class C1 and outside namespace A
int A::C1::f3()
{
    return h;                    // ok: returns A::h
}
```

With the exception of member definitions, scopes are always searched upward: A name must be declared before it can be used. Hence, the `return` in `f2` will not compile. It attempts to reference the name `h` from namespace `A`, but `h` has not yet been defined. Had that name been defined in `A` before the definition of `C1`, the use of `h` would be legal. Similarly, the use of `h` inside `f3` is okay, because `f3` is defined after `A::h` has been defined.

The order in which scopes are examined to find a name can be inferred from the qualified name of a function. The qualified name indicates, in reverse order, the scopes that are searched.

The qualifiers `A::C1::f3` indicate the reverse order in which the class scopes and namespace scopes are to be searched. The first scope searched is that of the function `f3`. Then the class scope of its enclosing class `C1` is searched. The scope of the namespace `A` is searched last before the scope containing the definition of `f3` is examined.

Argument-Dependent Lookup and Class Type Parameters

Consider the following simple program:

```
std::string s;
// ok: calls std::getline(std::istream&, const std::string&)
getline(std::cin, s);
```

The program uses the `std::string` type, yet it refers without qualification to the `getline` function. Why can we use this function without a specific `std::` qualifier or a `using` declaration?

It turns out that there is an important exception to the rule that namespace names are hidden.

 Functions, including overloaded operators, that take parameters of a class type (or pointer or reference to a class type), and that are defined in the same namespace as the class itself, are visible when an object of (or reference or pointer to) the class type is used as an argument.

When the compiler sees the use of the `getline` function

```
getline(std::cin, s);
```

it looks for a matching function in the current scope, the scopes enclosing the call to `getline`, *and in the namespace(s) in which the type of* `cin` *and the* `string` *type are defined*. Hence, it looks in the namespace `std` and finds the `getline` function defined by the `string` type.

The reason that functions are made visible if they have a parameter of the class type is to allow nonmember functions that are conceptually part of a class' interface to be used without requiring a separate `using` declaration. Being able to use nonmember operations is particularly useful for operator functions.

For example, consider the following simple program:

```
std::string s;
cin >> s;
```

In absence of this exception to the lookup rules, we would have to write either:

```
using std::operator>>;        //  need to allow cin >> s
std::operator>>(std::cin, s); //  ok: explicitly use std::>>
```

Either of these declarations is awkward and would make simple uses of `strings` and the IO library more complicated.

Implicit Friend Declarations and Namespaces

Recall that when a class declares a friend function (Section 12.5, p. 465), a declaration for the function need not be visible. If there isn't a declaration already visible, then the friend declaration has the effect of putting a declaration for that function or class into the surrounding scope. If a class is defined inside a namespace, then an otherwise undeclared friend function is declared in the same namespace:

```
namespace A {
    class C {
            friend void f(const C&);   // makes f a member of namespace A
    };
}
```

Because the friend takes an argument of a class type and is implicitly declared in the same namespace as the class, it can be used without using an explicit namespace qualifier:

```
// f2 defined at global scope
void f2()
{
    A::C cobj;
    f(cobj);   // calls A::f
}
```

17.2.6 Overloading and Namespaces

As we've seen, each namespace maintains its own scope. As a consequence, functions that are members of two distinct namespaces do not overload one another. However, a given namespace can contain a set of overloaded function members.

In general, function matching (Section 7.8.2, p. 269) within a namespace happens in the same manner as we've already seen:

1. Find the set of candidate functions. A function is a candidate if a declaration for it is visible at the time of the call and if it has the same name as the called function.

2. Select the viable functions from the set of candidates. A function is viable if it has the same number of parameters as the call has arguments and if each parameter could be matched by the corresponding argument.

3. Select the single best match from the viable set and generate code to call that function. If the viable set is empty, then the call is in error, having no match. If the viable set is nonempty and there is no best match, then the call is ambiguous.

Candidate Functions and Namespaces

Namespaces can have two impacts on function matching. One of these should be obvious: A using declaration or directive can add functions to the candidate set. The other is much more subtle.

As we saw in the previous section, name lookup for functions that have one or more class-type parameters includes the namespace in which each parameter's class is defined. This rule also impacts how we determine the candidate set. Each namespace that defines a class used as a parameter (and those that define its base class(es)) is searched for candidate functions. Any functions in those namespaces that have the same name as the called function are added to the candidate set. These functions are added *even though they otherwise are not visible at the point of the call.* Functions with the matching name in those namespaces are added to the candidate set:

```
namespace NS {
    class Item_base { /* ... */ };
    void display(const Item_base&) { }
}
//  Bulk_item's base class is declared in namespace NS
class Bulk_item : public NS::Item_base { };
int main() {
    Bulk_item book1;
    display(book1);
    return 0;
}
```

The argument, book1, to the display function has class type Bulk_item. The candidate functions for the call to display are not only the functions with declarations that are visible where the function display is called, but also the functions in the namespace where the class Bulk_item and its base class Item_base are declared. The function display(const Item_base&) declared in namespace NS is added to the set of candidate functions.

Overloading and using Declarations

A using declaration declares a name. As we saw in Section 15.5.3 (p. 592), there is no way to write a using declaration to refer to a specific function declaration:

```
using NS::print(int);    //  error: cannot specify parameter list
using NS::print;         //  ok: using declarations specify names only
```

If a function is overloaded within a namespace, then a using declaration for the name of that function declares *all* the functions with that name. If there are print functions for int and double in the namespace NS, then a using declaration for NS::print makes both functions visible in the current scope.

A using declaration incorporates all versions of an overloaded function to ensure that the interface of the namespace is not violated. The author of a library provided different functions for a reason. Allowing users to selectively ignore some but not all of the functions from a set of overloaded functions could lead to surprising program behavior.

The functions introduced by a using declaration overload any other declarations of the functions with the same name already present in the scope where the using declaration appears.

If the `using` declaration introduces a function in a scope that already has a function of the same name with the same parameter list, then the `using` declaration is in error. Otherwise, the `using` declaration defines additional overloaded instances of the given name. The effect is to increase the set of candidate functions.

Overloading and `using` Directives

A `using` directive lifts the namespace members into the enclosing scope. If a namespace function has the same name as a function declared in the scope at which the namespace is placed, then the namespace member is added to the overload set:

```cpp
namespace libs_R_us {
    extern void print(int);
    extern void print(double);
}
void print(const std::string &);
// using directive:
using namespace libs_R_us;
// using directive added names to the candidate set for calls to print:
//   print(int) from libs_R_us
//   print(double) from libs_R_us
//   print(const std::string &) declared explicitly
void fooBar(int ival)
{
    print("Value: ");  // calls global print(const string &)
    print(ival);       // calls libs_R_us::print(int)
}
```

Overloading across Multiple `using` Directives

If many `using` directives are present, then the names from each namespace become part of the candidate set:

```cpp
namespace AW {
    int print(int);
}
namespace Primer {
    double print(double);
}
// using directives:
// form an overload set of functions from different namespaces
using namespace AW;
using namespace Primer;

long double print(long double);

int main() {
    print(1);    // calls AW::print(int)
    print(3.1);  // calls Primer::print(double)
    return 0;
}
```

The overload set for the function `print` in global scope contains the functions `print(int)`, `print(double)`, and `print(long double)`. These functions are all part of the overload set considered for the function calls in `main`, even though these functions were originally declared in different namespace scopes.

EXERCISES SECTION 17.2.6

Exercise 17.22: Given the following code, determine which function, if any, matches the call to `compute`. List the candidate and viable functions. What type conversion sequence, if any, is applied to the argument to match the parameter in each viable function?

```
namespace primerLib {
    void compute();
    void compute(const void *);
}
using primerLib::compute;
void compute(int);
void compute(double, double = 3.4);
void compute(char*, char* = 0);

int main()
{
    compute(0);
    return 0;
}
```

What would happen if the `using` declaration were located in `main` before the call to `compute`? Answer the same questions as before.

17.2.7 Namespaces and Templates

Declaring a template within a namespace impacts how template specializations (Section 16.6, p. 671) are declared: An explicit specialization of a template must be declared in the namespace in which the generic template is defined. Otherwise, the specialization would have a different name than the template it specialized.

There are two ways to define a specialization: One is to reopen the namespace and add the definition of the specialization, which we can do because namespace definitions are discontiguous, Alternatively, we could define the specialization in the same way that we can define any namespace member outside its namespace definition: by defining the specialization using the template name qualified by the name of the namespace.

To provide our own specializations of templates defined in a namespace, we must ensure that the specialization definition is defined as being in the namespace containing the original template definition.

17.3 Multiple and Virtual Inheritance

Most C++ applications use `public` inheritance from a single base class. In some cases, however, single inheritance is inadequate, either because it fails to model the problem domain or the model it imposes is unnecessarily complex.

In these cases, **multiple inheritance** may model the application more directly. Multiple inheritance is the ability to derive a class from more than one immediate base class. A multiply derived class inherits the properties of all its parents. Although simple in concept, the details of intertwining multiple base classes can present tricky design-level and implementation-level problems.

17.3.1 Multiple Inheritance

This section uses a pedagogical example of a zoo animal hierarchy. Our zoo animals exist at different levels of abstraction. There are the individual animals, distinguished by their names, such as `Ling-ling`, `Mowgli`, and `Balou`. Each animal belongs to a species; Ling-Ling, for example, is a giant panda. Species, in turn, are members of families. A giant panda is a member of the bear family. Each family, in turn, is a member of the animal kingdom—in this case, the more limited kingdom of a particular zoo.

Each level of abstraction contains data and operations that support a wider category of users. We'll define an abstract `ZooAnimal` class to hold information that is common to all the zoo animals and provides the public interface. The `Bear` class will contain information that is unique to the `Bear` family, and so on.

In addition to the actual zoo-animal classes, there are auxiliary classes that encapsulate various abstractions such as endangered animals. In our implementation of a `Panda` class, for example, a `Panda` is multiply derived from `Bear` and `Endangered`.

Defining Multiple Classes

To support multiple inheritance, the derivation list

```
class Bear : public ZooAnimal {
};
```

is extended to support a comma-separated list of base classes:

```
class Panda : public Bear, public Endangered {
};
```

The derived class specifies (either explicitly or implicitly) the access level—`public`, `protected`, or `private`—for each of its base classes. As with single inheritance, a class may be used as a base class under multiple inheritance only after it has been defined. There is no language-imposed limit on the number of base classes from which a class can be derived. A base class may appear only once in a given derivation list.

Multiply Derived Classes Inherit State from Each Base Class

Under multiple inheritance, objects of a derived class contain a base-class subobject (Section 15.2.3, p. 565) for each of its base classes. When we write

```
Panda ying_yang("ying_yang");
```

the object ying_yang is composed of a Bear class subobject (which itself contains a ZooAnimal base-class subobject), an Endangered class subobject, and the nonstatic data members, if any, declared within the Panda class (see Figure 17.2).

Figure 17.2: Multiple Inheritance Panda Hierarchy

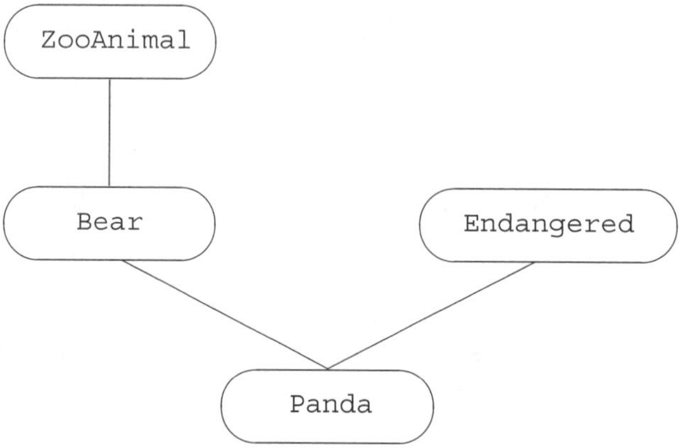

Derived Constructors Initialize All Base Classes

Constructing an object of derived type involves constructing and initializing all its base subobjects. As is the case for inheriting from a single base class (Section 15.4.1, p. 580), derived constructors may pass values to zero or more of their base classes in the constructor initializer:

```
// explicitly initialize both base classes
Panda::Panda(std::string name, bool onExhibit)
      : Bear(name, onExhibit, "Panda"),
        Endangered(Endangered::critical) { }
// implicitly use Bear default constructor to initialize the Bear subobject
Panda::Panda()
      : Endangered(Endangered::critical) { }
```

Order of Construction

The constructor initializer controls only the values that are used to initialize the base classes, not the order in which the base classes are constructed. The base-class constructors are invoked in the order in which they appear in the class derivation list. For `Panda`, the order of base-class initialization is:

1. `ZooAnimal`, the ultimate base class up the hierarchy from `Panda`'s immediate base class `Bear`

2. `Bear`, the first immediate base class

3. `Endangered`, the second immediate base, which itself has no base class

4. `Panda`; the members of `Panda` itself are initialized, and then the body of its constructor is run.

> The order of constructor invocation is not affected by whether the base class appears in the constructor initializer list or the order in which base classes appear within that list.

For example, in `Panda`'s default constructor, the `Bear` default constructor is invoked implicitly; it does not appear in the constructor initializer list. Even so, `Bear`'s default constructor is invoked prior to the explicitly listed constructor of `Endangered`.

Order of Destruction

Destructors are always invoked in the reverse order from which the constructors are run. In our example, the order in which the destructors are called is `~Panda`, `~Endangered`, `~Bear`, `~ZooAnimal`.

EXERCISES SECTION 17.3.1

Exercise 17.23: Which, if any, of the following declarations are in error. Explain why.

```
(a) class CADVehicle : public CAD, Vehicle { ... };
(b) class DoublyLinkedList:
        public List, public List { ... };
(c) class iostream: public istream, public ostream { ... };
```

Exercise 17.24: Given the following class hierarchy, in which each class defines a default constructor,

```
class A { ... };
class B : public A { ... };
class C : public B { ... };
class X { ... };
class Y { ... };
class Z : public X, public Y { ... };
class MI : public C, public Z { ... };
```

what is the order of constructor execution for the following definition?

```
MI mi;
```

17.3.2 Conversions and Multiple Base Classes

Under single inheritance, a pointer or a reference to a derived class can be converted automatically to a pointer or a reference to a base class. The same holds true with multiple inheritance. A pointer or reference to a derived class can be converted to a pointer or reference to any of its base classes. For example, a `Panda` pointer or reference could be converted to a pointer or a reference to `ZooAnimal`, `Bear`, or `Endangered`:

```
//  operations that take references to base classes of type Panda
void print(const Bear&);
void highlight(const Endangered&);
ostream& operator<<(ostream&, const ZooAnimal&);

Panda ying_yang("ying_yang");    //  create a Panda object

print(ying_yang);        //  passes Panda as reference to Bear
highlight(ying_yang);  //  passes Panda as reference to Endangered
cout << ying_yang << endl; //  passes Panda as reference to ZooAnimal
```

Under multiple inheritance, there is a greater possibility of encountering an ambiguous conversion. The compiler makes no attempt to distinguish between base classes in terms of a derived-class conversion. Converting to each base class is equally good. For example, if there was an overloaded version of `print`

```
void print(const Bear&);
void print(const Endangered&);
```

an unqualified invocation of `print` with a `Panda` object

```
Panda ying_yang("ying_yang");
print(ying_yang);                        //  error: ambiguous
```

results in a compile-time error that the call is ambiguous.

EXERCISES SECTION 17.3.2

Exercise 17.25: Given the following class hierarchy, in which each class defines a default constructor,

```
class X { ... };
class A { ... };
class B : public A { ... };
class C : private B { ... };
class D : public X, public C { ... };
```

which, if any, of the following conversions are not permitted?

```
D *pd = new D;
(a) X *px = pd;   (c) B *pb = pd;
(b) A *pa = pd;   (d) C *pc = pd;
```

Virtual Functions under Multiple Inheritance

To see how the virtual function mechanism is affected by multiple inheritance, let's assume that our classes define the virtual members listed in Table 17.2.

Function	Class Defining Own Version
	Table 17.2: Virtual Function in the ZooAnimal/Endangered Classes
`print`	`ZooAnimal::ZooAnimal`
	`Bear::Bear`
	`Endangered::Endangered`
	`Panda::Panda`
`highlight`	`Endangered::Endangered`
	`Panda::Panda`
`toes`	`Bear::Bear`
	`Panda::Panda`
`cuddle`	`Panda::Panda`
destructor	`ZooAnimal::ZooAnimal`
	`Endangered::Endangered`

Lookup Based on Type of Pointer or Reference

As with single inheritance, a pointer or reference to a base class can be used to access only members defined (or inherited) in the base. It cannot access members introduced in the derived class.

When a class inherits from multiple base classes, there is no implied relationship between those base classes. Using a pointer to one base does not allow access to members of another base.

As an example, we could use a pointer or reference to a `Bear`, `ZooAnimal`, `Endangered`, or `Panda` to access a `Panda` object. The type of the pointer we use determines which operations are accessible. If we use a `ZooAnimal` pointer, only the operations defined in that class are usable. The `Bear`-specific, `Panda`-specific, and `Endangered` portions of the `Panda` interface are inaccessible. Similarly, a `Bear` pointer or reference knows only about the `Bear` and `ZooAnimal` members; an `Endangered` pointer or reference is limited to the `Endangered` members:

```
Bear *pb = new Panda("ying_yang");
pb->print(cout);     // ok: Panda::print(ostream&)
pb->cuddle();        // error: not part of Bear interface
pb->highlight();     // error: not part of Bear interface
delete pb;           // ok: Panda::~Panda()
```

If the `Panda` object had been assigned to a `ZooAnimal` pointer, this set of calls would resolve exactly the same way.

When a `Panda` is used via an `Endangered` pointer or reference, the `Panda`-specific and `Bear` portions of the `Panda` interface are inaccessible:

```
Endangered *pe = new Panda("ying_yang");
pe->print(cout);  // ok: Panda::print(ostream&)
pe->toes();       // error: not part of Endangered interface
pe->cuddle();     // error: not part of Endangered interface
pe->highlight();  // ok: Endangered::highlight()
delete pe;        // ok: Panda::~Panda()
```

Determining Which Virtual Destructor to Use

Assuming all the root base classes properly define their destructors as virtual, then the handling of the virtual destructor is consistent regardless of the pointer type through which we delete the object:

```
// each pointer points to a Panda
delete pz; // pz is a ZooAnimal*
delete pb; // pb is a Bear*
delete pp; // pp is a Panda*
delete pe; // pe is a Endangered*
```

Assuming each of these pointers points to a `Panda` object, the exact same order of destructor invocations occurs in each case. The order of destructor invocations is the reverse of the constructor order: The `Panda` destructor is invoked through the virtual mechanism. Following execution of the `Panda` destructor, the `Endangered`, `Bear`, then `ZooAnimal` destructors are invoked in turn.

EXERCISES SECTION 17.3.2

Exercise 17.26: On page 735 we presented a series of calls made through a `Bear` pointer that pointed to a `Panda` object. We noted that if the pointer had been a `ZooAnimal` pointer the calls would resolve the same way. Explain why.

Exercise 17.27: Assume we have two base classes, `Base1` and `Base2`, each of which defines a virtual member named `print` and a virtual destructor. From these base classes we derive the following classes each of which redefines the `print` function:

```
class D1 : public Base1 { /* ... */ };
class D2 : public Base2 { /* ... */ };
class MI : public D1, public D2 { /* ... */ };
```
Using the following pointers determine which function is used in each call:
```
Base1 *pb1 = new MI; Base2 *pb2 = new MI;
D1 *pd1 = new MI; D2 *pd2 = new MI;

(a) pb1->print();   (b) pd1->print();   (c) pd2->print();
(d) delete pb2;     (e) delete pd1;     (f) delete pd2;
```

Exercise 17.28: Write the class definitions that correspond to Table 17.2 (p. 735).

17.3.3 Copy Control for Multiply Derived Classes

The memberwise initialization, assignment and destruction (Chapter 13) of a multiply derived class behaves in the same way as under single inheritance. Each base class is implicitly constructed, assigned or destroyed, using that base class' own copy constructor, assignment operator or destructor.

Let's assume that `Panda` uses the default copy control members. Using the default copy constructor, the initialization of `ling_ling`

```
Panda ying_yang("ying_yang");   // create a Panda object
Panda ling_ling = ying_yang;    // uses copy constructor
```

invokes the `Bear` copy constructor, which in turn runs the `ZooAnimal` copy constructor prior to executing the `Bear` copy constructor. Once the `Bear` portion of `ling_ling` is constructed, the `Endangered` copy constructor is run to create that part of the object. Finally, the `Panda` copy constructor is run.

The synthesized assignment operator behaves similarly to the copy constructor. It assigns the `Bear` (and through `Bear`, the `ZooAnimal`) parts of the object first. Next, it assigns the `Endangered` part, and finally the `Panda` part.

The synthesized destructor destroys each member of the `Panda` object and calls the destructors for the base class parts, in reverse order from construction.

As is the case for single inheritance (Section 15.4.3, p. 584), if a class with multiple bases defines its own destructor, that destructor is responsible only for cleaning up the derived class. If the derived class defines its own copy constructor or assignment operator, then the class is responsible for copying (assigning) all the base class subparts. The base parts are automatically copied or assigned only if the derived class uses the synthesized versions of these members.

17.3.4 Class Scope under Multiple Inheritance

Class scope (Section 15.5, p. 590) is more complicated in multiple inheritance because a derived scope may be enclosed by multiple base class scopes. As usual, name lookup for a name used in a member function starts in the function itself. If the name is not found locally, then lookup continues in the member's class and then searches each base class in turn. Under multiple inheritance, the search simultaneously examines all the base-class inheritance subtrees—in our example, both the `Endangered` and the `Bear`/`ZooAnimal` subtrees are examined in parallel. If the name is found in more than one subtree, then the use of that name must explicitly specify which base class to use. Otherwise, the use of the name is ambiguous.

When a class has multiple base classes, name lookup happens simultaneously through all the immediate base classes. It is possible for a multiply derived class to inherit a member with the same name from two or more base classes. Unqualified uses of that name are ambiguous.

Multiple Base Classes Can Lead to Ambiguities

Assume both `Bear` and `Endangered` define a member named `print`. If `Panda` does not define that member, then a statement such as the following

```
ying_yang.print(cout);
```

results in a compile-time error.

The derivation of `Panda`, which results in Panda having two members named `print`, is perfectly legal. The derivation results in only a *potential* ambiguity. That ambiguity is avoided if no `Panda` object ever calls `print`. The error would also be avoided if each call to `print` specifically indicated which version of `print` was wanted—`Bear::print` or `Endangered::print`. An error is issued only if there is an ambiguous attempt to use the member.

If a declaration is found only in one base-class subtree, then the identifier is resolved and the lookup algorithm concludes. For example, class `Endangered` might have an operation to return the given estimated population of its object. If so, the following call

```
ying_yang.population();
```

would compile without complaint. The name `population` would be found in the `Endangered` base class and does not appear in `Bear` or any of its base classes.

Name Lookup Happens First

Although the ambiguity of the two inherited `print` members is reasonably obvious, it might be more surprising to learn that an error would be generated even if the two inherited functions had different parameter lists. Similarly, it would be an error even if the `print` function were private in one class and public or protected in the other. Finally, if `print` were defined in `ZooAnimal` and not `Bear`, the call would still be in error.

As always, name lookup happens in two steps (Section 7.8.1, p. 268): First the compiler finds a matching declaration (or, in this case, two matching declarations, which causes the ambiguity). Only then does the compiler decide whether the declaration it found is legal.

Avoiding User-Level Ambiguities

We could resolve the `print` ambiguity by specifying which class to use:

```
ying_yang.Endangered::print(cout);
```

The best way to avoid potential ambiguities is to define a version of the function in the derived class that resolves the ambiguity. For example, we should give our `Panda` class a `print` function that chooses which version of `print` to use:

```
std::ostream& Panda::print(std::ostream &os) const
{
    Bear::print(os);           //  print the Bear part
    Endangered::print(os);     //  print the Endangered part
    return os;
}
```

CODE FOR EXERCISES TO SECTION 17.3.4

```
struct Base1 {
    void print(int) const;
protected:
    int    ival;
    double dval;
    char   cval;
private:
    int    *id;
};
struct Base2 {
    void print(double) const;
protected:
    double  fval;
private:
    double  dval;
};
struct Derived : public Base1 {
    void print(std::string) const;
protected:
    std::string sval;
    double      dval;
};
struct MI : public Derived, public Base2 {
    void print(std::vector<double>);
protected:
    int                 *ival;
    std::vector<double>  dvec;
};
```

EXERCISES SECTION 17.3.4

Exercise 17.29: Given the class hierarchy in the box on this page and the following `MI::foo` member function skeleton,

```
int ival;
double dval;
void MI::foo(double dval) { int id; /* ... */ }
```

(a) identify the member names visible from within `MI`. Are there any names visible from more than one base class?

(b) identify the set of members visible from within `MI::foo`.

Exercise 17.30: Given the hierarchy in the box on page 739, why is this call to `print` an error?

```
MI mi;
mi.print(42);
```

Revise MI to allow this call to `print` to compile and execute correctly.

Exercise 17.31: Using the class hierarchy in the box on page 739, identify which of the following assignments, if any, are in error:

```
void MI::bar() {
    int sval;
    // exercise questions occur here ...
}
(a) dval = 3.14159;   (d) fval = 0;
(b) cval = 'a';       (e) sval = *ival; (c) id = 1;
```

Exercise 17.32: Using the class hierarchy defined in the box on page 739 and the following skeleton of the MI::foobar member function

```
void MI::foobar(double cval)
{
    int dval;
    // exercise questions occur here ...
}
```

(a) assign to the local instance of `dval` the sum of the `dval` member of `Base1` and the `dval` member of `Derived`.

(b) assign the value of the last element in `MI::dvec` to `Base2::fval`.

(c) assign `cval` from `Base1` to the first character in `sval` from `Derived`.

17.3.5 Virtual Inheritance

Under multiple inheritance, a base class can occur multiple times in the derivation hierarchy. In fact, our programs have already used a class that inherits from the same base class more than once through its inheritance hierarchy.

Each of the IO library classes inherits from a common abstract base class. That abstract class manages the condition state of the stream and holds the buffer that the stream reads or writes. The `istream` and `ostream` classes inherit directly from this common base class. The library defines another class, named `iostream`, that inherits from both `istream` and `ostream`. The `iostream` class can both read and write a stream. A simplified version of the IO inheritance hierarchy is illustrated in Figure 17.3 on the facing page.

As we know, a multiply inherited class inherits state and action from each of its parents. If the IO types used normal inheritance, then each `iostream` object would contain two `ios` subobjects: one instance contained within its `istream` subobject and the other within its `ostream` subobject. From a design perspective, this implementation is just wrong: The `iostream` class wants to read to and write

Figure 17.3: Virtual Inheritance `iostream` Hierarchy (Simplified)

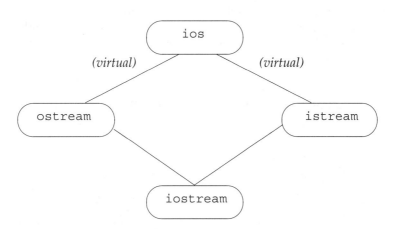

from a single buffer; it wants the condition state to be shared across input and output operations. If there are two separate `ios` objects, this sharing is not possible.

In C++ we solve this kind of problem by using **virtual inheritance**. Virtual inheritance is a mechanism whereby a class specifies that it is willing to share the state of its virtual base class. Under virtual inheritance, only one, shared base-class subobject is inherited for a given virtual base regardless of how many times the class occurs as a virtual base within the derivation hierarchy. The shared base-class subobject is called a **virtual base class**.

The `istream` and `ostream` classes inherit virtually from their base class. By making their base class virtual, `istream` and `ostream` specify that if some other class, such as `iostream`, inherits from both of them, then only one copy of their common base class will be present in the derived class. We make a base class virtual by including the keyword `virtual` in the derivation list:

```
class istream : public virtual ios { ... };
class ostream : virtual public ios { ... };

// iostream inherits only one copy of its ios base class
class iostream: public istream, public ostream { ... };
```

A Different `Panda` Class

For the purposes of illustrating virtual inheritance, we'll continue to use the `Panda` class as a pedagogical example. Within zoological circles, for more than 100 years there has been an occasionally fierce debate as to whether the `Panda` belongs to the `Raccoon` or the `Bear` family. Because software design is primarily a service industry, our most practical solution is to derive `Panda` from both:

```
class Panda : public Bear,
              public Raccoon, public Endangered {
};
```

Our virtual inheritance `Panda` hierarchy is pictured in Figure 17.4. If we examine that hierarchy, we notice a nonintuitive aspect of virtual inheritance: The virtual derivation (in our case, of `Bear` and `Raccoon`) has to be made prior to any actual need for it to be present. Virtual inheritance becomes necessary only with the declaration of `Panda`, but if `Bear` and `Raccoon` are not already virtually derived, the designer of the `Panda` class is out of luck.

Figure 17.4: Virtual Inheritance `Panda` Hierarchy

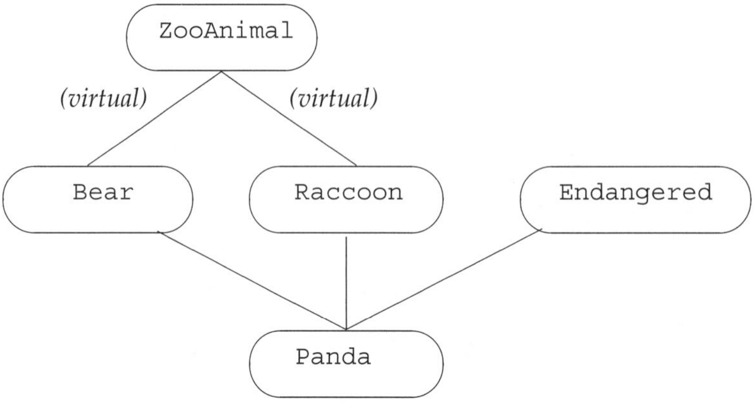

In practice, the requirement that an intermediate base class specify its inheritance as virtual rarely causes any problems. Ordinarily, a class hierarchy that uses virtual inheritance is designed at one time by either one individual or a project design group. It is exceedingly rare for a class to be developed independently that needs a virtual base in one of its base classes and in which the developer of the new base class cannot change the existing hierarchy.

17.3.6   Virtual Base Class Declaration

A base class is specified as being derived through virtual inheritance by modifying its declaration with the keyword `virtual`. For example, the following declarations make `ZooAnimal` a virtual base class of both `Bear` and `Raccoon`:

```
// the order of the keywords public and virtual is not significant
class Raccoon : public virtual ZooAnimal { /* ... */ };
class Bear : virtual public ZooAnimal { /* ... */ };
```

Specifying virtual derivation has an impact only in classes derived from the class that specifies a virtual base. Rather than affecting objects of the derived class' own type, it is a statement about the derived class' relationship to its own, future derived class.

The `virtual` specifier states a willingness to share a single instance of the named base class within a subsequently derived class.

Any class that can be specified as a base class also could be specified as a virtual base class. A virtual base may contain any class element normally supported by a nonvirtual base class.

Normal Conversions to Base Are Supported

An object of the derived class can be manipulated as usual through a pointer or a reference to a base-class type even though the base class is virtual. For example, all of the following `Panda` base class conversions execute correctly even though `Panda` inherits its `ZooAnimal` part as a virtual base:

```
void dance(const Bear*);
void rummage(const Raccoon*);
ostream& operator<<(ostream&, const ZooAnimal&);
Panda ying_yang;

dance(&ying_yang);      // ok: converts address to pointer to Bear
rummage(&ying_yang);    // ok: converts address to pointer to Raccoon
cout << ying_yang;      // ok: passes ying_yang as a ZooAnimal
```

Visibility of Virtual Base-Class Members

Multiple-inheritance hierarchies using virtual bases pose fewer ambiguity problems than do those without virtual inheritance.

Members in the shared virtual base can be accessed unambiguously and directly. Similarly, if a member from the virtual base is redefined along only one derivation path, then that redefined member can be accessed directly. Under a nonvirtual derivation, both kinds of access would be ambiguous.

Assume a member named X is inherited through more than one derivation path. There are three possibilities:

1. If in each path X represents the same virtual base class member, then there is no ambiguity because a single instance of the member is shared.

2. If in one path X is a member of the virtual base class member and in another path X is a member of a subsequently derived class, there is also no ambiguity—the specialized derived class instance is given precedence over the shared virtual base class instance.

3. If along each inheritance path X represents a different member of a subsequently derived class, then the direct access of the member is ambiguous.

As in a nonvirtual multiple inheritance hierarchy, ambiguities of this sort are best resolved by the class providing an overriding instance in the derived class.

Exercise 17.33: Given the following class hierarchy, which inherited members can be accessed without qualification from within the `VMI` class? Which require qualification? Explain your reasoning.

```cpp
class Base {
public:
    bar(int);
protected:
    int ival;
};
class Derived1 : virtual public Base {
public:
    bar(char);
    foo(char);
protected:
    char cval;
};
class Derived2 : virtual public Base {
public:
    foo(int);
protected:
    int  ival;
    char cval;
};
class VMI : public Derived1, public Derived2 { };
```

17.3.7 Special Initialization Semantics

Ordinarily each class initializes only its own direct base class(es). This initialization strategy fails when applied to a virtual base class. If the normal rules were used, then the virtual base might be initialized multiple times. The class would be initialized along each inheritance path that contains the virtual base. In our `ZooAnimal` example, using normal initialization rules would result in both `Bear` and `Raccoon` attempting to initialize the `ZooAnimal` part of a `Panda` object.

To solve this duplicate-initialization problem, classes that inherit from a class that has a virtual base have special handling for initialization. In a virtual derivation, the virtual base is initialized by the *most derived constructor*. In our example, when we create a `Panda` object, the `Panda` constructor alone controls how the `ZooAnimal` base class is initialized.

Although the virtual base is initialized by the most derived class, any classes that inherit immediately or indirectly from the virtual base usually also have to provide their own initializers for that base. As long as we can create independent objects of a type derived from a virtual base, that class must initialize its virtual base. These initializers are used only when we create objects of the intermediate type.

In our hierarchy, we could have objects of type `Bear`, `Raccoon`, or `Panda`. When a `Panda` is created, it is the most derived type and controls initialization of the shared `ZooAnimal` base. When a `Bear` (or a `Raccoon`) is created, there is no further derived type involved. In this case, the `Bear` (or `Raccoon`) constructors directly initialize their `ZooAnimal` base as usual:

```
Bear::Bear(std::string name, bool onExhibit):
        ZooAnimal(name, onExhibit, "Bear") { }
Raccoon::Raccoon(std::string name, bool onExhibit)
        : ZooAnimal(name, onExhibit, "Raccoon") { }
```

The `Panda` constructor also initializes the `ZooAnimal` base, even though it is not an immediate base class:

```
Panda::Panda(std::string name, bool onExhibit)
    : ZooAnimal(name, onExhibit, "Panda"),
      Bear(name, onExhibit),
      Raccoon(name, onExhibit),
      Endangered(Endangered::critical),
      sleeping_flag(false)   { }
```

When a `Panda` is created, it is this constructor that initializes the `ZooAnimal` part of the `Panda` object.

How a Virtually Inherited Object Is Constructed

Let's look at how objects under virtual inheritance are constructed.

```
Bear winnie("pooh");      // Bear constructor initializes ZooAnimal
Raccoon meeko("meeko");   // Raccoon constructor initializes ZooAnimal
Panda yolo("yolo");       // Panda constructor initializes ZooAnimal
```

When a `Panda` object is created,

1. The `ZooAnimal` part is constructed first, using the initializers specified in the `Panda` constructor initializer list.

2. Next, the `Bear` part is constructed. The initializers for `ZooAnimal` `Bear`'s constructor initializer list are ignored.

3. Then the `Raccoon` part is constructed, again ignoring the `ZooAnimal` initializers.

4. Finally, the `Panda` part is constructed.

If the `Panda` constructor does not explicitly initialize the `ZooAnimal` base class, then the `ZooAnimal` default constructor is used. If `ZooAnimal` doesn't have a default constructor, then the code is in error. The compiler will issue an error message when the definition of `Panda`'s constructor is compiled.

Constructor and Destructor Order

 Virtual base classes are always constructed prior to nonvirtual base classes regardless of where they appear in the inheritance hierarchy.

For example, in the following whimsical `TeddyBear` derivation, there are two virtual base classes: the `ToyAnimal` base class and the indirect `ZooAnimal` base class from which `Bear` is derived:

```
class Character { /* ... */ };
class BookCharacter : public Character { /* ... */ };
class ToyAnimal { /* ... */ };
class TeddyBear : public BookCharacter,
                  public Bear, public virtual ToyAnimal
                  { /* ... */ };
```

Figure 17.5: Virtual Inheritance `TeddyBear` Hierarchy

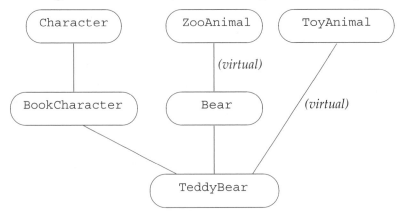

The immediate base classes are examined in declaration order to determine whether there are any virtual base classes. In our example, the inheritance subtree of `BookCharacter` is examined first, then that of `Bear`, and finally that of `ToyAnimal`. Each subtree is examined starting at the root class down to the most derived class.

The order in which the virtual base classes are constructed for `TeddyBear` is `ZooAnimal` followed by `ToyAnimal`. Once the virtual base classes are constructed, the nonvirtual base-class constructors are invoked in declaration order: `BookCharacter`, which causes the `Character` constructor to be invoked, and then `Bear`. Thus, to create a `TeddyBear`, the constructors are invoked in the following order:

```
ZooAnimal();        // Bear's virtual base class
ToyAnimal();        // immediate virtual base class
```

```
Character();          // BookCharacter's nonvirtual base class
BookCharacter();      // immediate nonvirtual base class
Bear();               // immediate nonvirtual base class
TeddyBear();          // most derived class
```

where the initializers used for ZooAnimal and ToyAnimal are specified by the most derived class—TeddyBear.

The same construction order is used in the synthesized copy constructor; the base classes also are assigned in this order in the synthesized assignment operator. The order of base-class destructor calls is guaranteed to be the reverse order of constructor invocation.

EXERCISES SECTION 17.3.7

Exercise 17.34: There is one case in which a derived class need not supply initializers for its virtual base class(es). What is this case?

Exercise 17.35: Given the following class hierarchy,

```
class Class { ... };
class Base : public Class { ... };
class Derived1 : virtual public Base { ... };
class Derived2 : virtual public Base { ... };
class MI : public Derived1,
           public Derived2 { ... };
class Final : public MI, public Class { ... };
```

(a) What is the order of constructor and destructor for the definition of a Final object?
(b) How many Base subobjects are in a Final object? How many Class subobjects?
(c) Which of the following assignments is a compile-time error?

```
Base    *pb;      Class    *pc;
MI      *pmi;     Derived2 *pd2;

(a) pb = new Class;       (c) pmi = pb;
(b) pc = new Final;       (d) pd2 = pmi;
```

Exercise 17.36: Given the previous hierarchy, and assuming that Base defines the following three constructors, define the classes that inherit from Base, giving each class the same three constructors. Each constructor should use its argument to initialize its Base part.

```
struct Base {
    Base();
    Base(std::string);
    Base(const Base&);
protected:
    std::string name;
};
```

CHAPTER SUMMARY

Most of C++ is applicable to a wide range of problems—from those solvable in a few hour's time to those that take years of development by large teams. Some features in C++ are most applicable in the context of large-scale problems: exception handling, namespaces, and multiple or virtual inheritance.

Exception handling lets us separate the error-detection part of the program from the error-handling part. Section 6.13 (p. 215) introduced exception handling and this chapter completes our coverage of exceptions. When an exception is thrown, the current executing function is suspended and a search is started to find the nearest `catch` clause. Local variables defined inside functions that are exited while searching for a `catch` clause are destroyed as part of handling the exception. The fact that objects are destroyed gives rise to an important programming technique known as "resource allocation is initialization" (RAII).

Namespaces are a mechanism for managing large complex applications built from code produced by independent suppliers. A namespace is a scope in which objects, types, functions, template, and other namespaces may be defined. The standard library is defined inside the namespace named `std`.

Names in a namespace may be made available to the current scope one at a time via a `using` declaration. Alternatively, but much less safely, all the names in a namespace may be brought into the current scope via a `using` directive.

Conceptually, multiple inheritance is a simple notion: A derived class may inherit from more than one direct base class. The derived object consists of the derived part and a base part contributed by each of its base classes. Although conceptually simple, the details can be more complicated. In particular, inheriting from multiple base classes introduces new possiblities for name collisions and resulting ambiguous references to names from the base part of an object.

When a class inherits from more than one immediate base class, it is possible that those classes may themselves share another base class. In cases such as this, the intermediate classes can opt to make their inheritance virtual, which states a willingness to share its virtual base class with other classes in the hierarchy that inherit virtually from that same base class. In this way there is only one copy of the shared virtual base in a subsequently derived class.

DEFINED TERMS

abort Library function that abnormally terminates a program's execution. Ordinarily, `abort` is called by `terminate`. Programs may also call `abort` directly. It is defined in the `cstdlib` header.

auto_ptr Library class template that provides exception-safe access to dynamically allocated objects. An `auto_ptr` cannot be bound to an array or a pointer to a variable. Copying and assigning an `auto_ptr` is a destructive operation: Ownership of the object is transferred from the right-hand operand to the left. Assigning to an `auto_ptr` deletes the object in the left-hand operand. As a result, `auto_ptrs` may not be stored in containers.

catch-all A catch clause in which the exception specifier is `(...)`. A catch-all clause catches an exception of any type. It is typically used to catch an exception that is detected locally in order to do local cleanup. The exception is then rethrown to another part of the program to deal with the underlying cause of the problem.

catch clause The part of the program that handles an exception. A catch clause consists of the keyword `catch` followed by an exception specifier and a block of statements. The code inside a `catch` does whatever is necessary to handle an exception of the type defined in its exception specifier.

constructor order Ordinarily, base classes are constructed in the order in which they are named in the class derivation list. A derived constructor should explicitly initialize each base class through the constructor initializer list. The order in which base classes are named in the constructor initializer list does not affect the order in which the base classes are constructed. In a virtual inheritance, the virtual base class(es) are constructed before any other bases. They are constructed in the order in which they appear (directly or indirectly) in the derivation list of the derived type. Only the most derived type may initialize a virtual base; constructor initializers for that base that appear in the intermediate base classes are ignored.

destructor order Derived objects are destroyed in the reverse order from which they were constructed—the derived part is destroyed first, then the classes named in the class derivation list are destroyed, starting with the last base class. Classes that serve as base classes in a multiple-inheritance hierarchy ordinarily should define their destructors to be virtual.

exception handler Another way to refer to a catch clause.

exception handling Language-level support for managing run-time anomalies. One independently developed section of code can detect and "raise" an exception that another independently developed part of the program can "handle." The error-detecting part of the program `throws` an exception; the error-handling part handles the exception in a `catch` clause of a `try` block.

exception object Object used to communicate between the `throw` and `catch` sides of an exception. The object is created at the point of the throw and is a copy of the thrown expression. The exception object exists until the last handler for the exception completes. The type of the object is the type of the thrown expression.

exception safe Term used to describe programs that behave correctly when exceptions are thrown.

exception specification Used on a function declaration to indicate what (if any) exception types a function throws. Exception types are named in a parenthesized, comma-separated list following the keyword `throw`, which appears after a function's parameter list. An empty list means that the function throws no exceptions. A function that has no exception specification may throw any exception.

exception specifier Specifies the types of exceptions that a given catch clause will handle. An exception specifier acts like a parameter list, whose single parameter is initialized by the exception object. Like parameter passing, if the exception specifier is a nonreference type, then the exception object is copied to the `catch`.

file static Name local to a file that is declared with the `static` keyword. In C and pre-Standard versions of C++, file statics were used to declare objects that could be used in a single file only. File statics are deprecated in C++, having been replaced by the use of unnamed namespaces.

function try block A `try` block that is a function body. The keyword `try` occurs before the opening curly of the function body and closes with catch clause(s) that appear after the close curly of the function body. Function try blocks are used most often to wrap constructor definitions in order to catch exceptions thrown by constructor initializers.

global namespace The (implicit) namespace in each program that holds all global definitions.

multiple inheritance Inheritance in which a class has more than one immediate base class. The derived class inherits the members of all its base classes. Multiple base classes are defined by naming more than one base class in the class derivation list. A separate access label is required for each base class.

namespace Mechanism for gathering all the names defined by a library or other collection of programs into a single scope. Unlike other scopes in C++, a namespace scope may be defined in several parts. The namepsace may be opened and closed and reopened again in disparate parts of the program.

namespace alias Mechanism for defining a synonym for a given namespace:

```
namespace N1 = N;
```

defines `N1` as another name for the namespace named `N`. A namespace can have multiple aliases, and the namespace name or one of its aliases may be used interchangeably.

namespace pollution Term used to describe what happens when all the names of classes and functions are placed in the global namespace. Large programs that use code written by multiple independent parties often encounter collisions among names if these names are global.

raise Often used as a synonym for throw. C++ programmers speak of "throwing" or "raising" an exception interchangably.

rethrow An empty `throw`—a `throw` that does not specify an expression. A rethrow is valid only from inside a catch clause, or in a function called directly or indirectly from a `catch`. Its effect is to rethrow the exception object that it received.

scope operator Operator used to access names from a namespace or a class.

stack unwinding Term used to describe the process whereby the functions leading to a thown exception are exited in the search for a `catch`. Local objects constructed before the exception are destroyed before entering the corresponding `catch`.

terminate Library function that is called if an exception is not caught or if an exception occurs while a handler is in process. Usually calls `abort` to end the program.

throw e Expression that interrupts the current execution path. Each `throw` transfers control to the nearest enclosing `catch` clause that can handle the type of exception that is thrown. The expression e is copied into the exception object.

try block A block of statements enclosed by the keyword `try` and one or more catch clauses. If the code inside the try block raises an exception and one of the catch clauses matches the type of the exception, then the exception is handled by that catch. Otherwise, the exception is passed out of the `try` to a catch further up the call chain.

unexpected Library function that is called if an exception is thrown that violates the exception specification of a function.

unnamed namespace A namespace that is defined without a name. Names defined in an unnamed namespace may be accessed directly without use of the scope operator. Each file has its own unique unnamed namespace. Names in the file are not visible outside that file.

using declaration Mechanism to inject a single name from a namespace into the current scope:

```
using std::cout;
```

makes the name `cout` from the namespace `std` available in the current scope. The name `cout` can be used without the `std::` qualifier.

using directive Mechanism for making *all* the names in a namespace available in the nearest scope containing both the using directive and the namespace itself.

virtual base class A base class that was inherited using the `virtual` keyword. A virtual base part occurs only once in a derived object even if the same class appears as a virtual base more than once in the hierarchy. In nonvirtual inheritance a constructor may only initialize its immediate base class(es). When a class is inherited virtually, that class is initialized by the most derived class, which therefore should include an initializer for all of its virtual parent(s).

virtual inheritance Form of multiple inheritance in which derived classes share a single copy of a base that is included in the hierarchy more than once.

C H A P T E R $\quad$ **18**

SPECIALIZED TOOLS AND TECHNIQUES

CONTENTS

The first four parts of this book discussed how to use those parts of
C++ that are generally useful. Those features are likely to be used at
some point by almost all C++ programmers. In addition, C++ defines
some features that are more specialized. Many programmers will
never (or only rarely) need to use these features presented in this
chapter.

18.1   Optimizing Memory Allocation

Memory allocation in C++ is a typed operation: new (Section 5.11, p. 174) allocates memory for a specified type and constructs an object of that type in the newly allocated memory. A new expression automatically runs the appropriate constructor to initialize each dynamically allocated object of class type.

The fact that new allocates memory on a per-object basis can impose unacceptable run-time overhead on some classes. Such classes might need to make user-level allocation of objects of the class type faster. A common strategy such classes use is to preallocate memory to be used when new objects are created, constructing each new object in preallocated memory as needed.

Other classes want to minimize allocations needed for their own data members. For example, the library vector class preallocates (Section 9.4, p. 330) extra memory to hold additional elements if and when they are added. New elements are added in this reserved capacity. Preallocating elements allows vector to efficiently add elements while keeping the elements in contiguous memory.

In each of these cases—preallocating memory to hold user-level objects or to hold the internal data for a class—there is the need to decouple memory allocation from object construction. The obvious reason to decouple allocation and construction is that constructing objects in preallocated memory is wasteful. Objects may be created that are never used. Those objects that are used must be reassigned new values when the preallocated object is actually used. More subtly, some classes could not use preallocated memory if it had to be constructed. As an example, consider vector, which uses a preallocation strategy. If objects in preallocated memory had to be constructed, then it would not be possible to have vectors of types that do not have a default constructor—there would be no way for vector to know how to construct these objects.

> The techniques presented in this section are not guaranteed to make all programs faster. Even when they do improve performance, they may carry other costs such as space usage or difficulty of debugging. It is always best to defer optimization until the program is known to work and when run-time measurements indicate that improving memory allocation will solve known performance problems.

18.1.1   Memory Allocation in C++

In C++ memory allocation and object construction are closely intertwined, as are object destruction and memory deallocation. When we use a new expression, memory is allocated, and an object is constructed in that memory. When we use a delete expression, a destructor is called to destroy the object and the memory used by the object is returned to the system.

When we take over memory allocation, we must deal with both these tasks. When we allocate raw memory, we must construct object(s) in that memory. Before freeing that memory, we must ensure that the objects are properly destroyed.

Assigning to an object in unconstructed memory rather than initializing it is undefined. For many classes, doing so causes a crash at run time. Assignment involves obliterating the existing object. If there is no existing object, then the actions in the assignment operator can have disastrous effects.

C++ provides two ways to allocate and free unconstructed, raw memory:

1. The **allocator class**, which provides type-aware memory allocation. This class supports an abstract interface to allocating memory and subsequently using that memory to hold objects.

2. The library `operator new` and `operator delete` functions, which allocate and free raw, untyped memory of a requested size.

C++ also provides various ways to construct and destroy objects in raw memory:

1. The `allocator` class defines members named `construct` and `destroy`, which operate as their names suggest. The `construct` member initializes objects in unconstructed memory; the `destroy` member runs the appropriate destructor on objects.

2. The placement `new` expression takes a pointer to unconstructed memory and initializes an object or an array in that space.

3. We can directly call an object's destructor to destroy the object. Running the destructor does not free the memory in which the object resides.

4. The algorithms `uninitialized_fill` and `uninitialized_copy` execute like the `fill` and `copy` algorithms except that they construct objects in their destination rather than assigning to them.

Modern C++ programs ordinarily ought to use the `allocator` class to allocate memory. It is safer and more flexible. However, when constructing objects, the placement `new` expression is more flexible than the `allocator::construct` member. There are some cases where placement `new` must be used.

18.1.2 The `allocator` Class

The `allocator` class is a template that provides typed memory allocation and object construction and destruction. Table 18.1 on the following page outlines the operations that `allocator` supports.

The `allocator` class separates allocation and object construction. When an `allocator` object allocates memory, it allocates space that is appropriately sized and aligned to hold objects of the given type. However, the memory it allocates is unconstructed. Users of `allocator` must separately `construct` and `destroy` objects placed in the memory it allocates.

Table 18.1: Standard `allocator` Class and Customized Algorithms	
`allocator<T> a;`	Defines an `allocator` object named a that can allocate memory or construct objects of type `T`.
`a.allocate(n)`	Allocates raw, unconstructed memory to hold n objects of type `T`.
`a.deallocate(p, n)`	Deallocates memory that held n objects of type `T` starting at address contained in the `T*` pointer named p. It is the user's responsibility to run `destroy` on any objects that were constructed in this memory before calling `deallocate`.
`a.construct(p, t)`	Constructs a new element in the memory pointed to by the `T*` pointer p. The copy constructor of type `T` is run to initialize the object from `t`.
`a.destroy(p)`	Runs the destructor on the object pointed to by the `T*` pointer p.
`uninitialized_copy(b, e, b2)`	Copies elements from the input range denoted by iterators b and e into unconstructed, raw memory beginning at iterator b2. The function constructs elements in the destination, rather than assigning them. The destination denoted by b2 is assumed large enough to hold a copy of the elements in the input range.
`uninitialized_fill(b, e, t)`	Initializes objects in the range denoted by iterators b and e as a copy of `t`. The range is assumed to be unconstructed, raw memory. The objects are constructed using the copy constructor.
`uninitialized_fill_n(b, e, t, n)`	Initializes at most an integral number n objects in the range denoted by iterators b and e as a copy of `t`. The range is assumed to be at least n elements in size. The objects are constructed using the copy constructor.

Using `allocator` to Manage Class Member Data

To understand how we might use a preallocation strategy and the `allocator` class to manage the internal data needs of a class, let's think a bit more about how memory allocation in the `vector` class might work.

Recall that the `vector` class stores its elements in contiguous storage. To obtain acceptable performance, `vector` preallocates more elements than are needed (Section 9.4, p. 330). Each `vector` member that adds elements to the container checks whether there is space available for another element. If so, then the member initializes an object in the next available spot in preallocated memory. If there isn't a free element, then the `vector` is reallocated: The `vector` obtains new space, copies the existing elements into that space, adds the new element, and frees the old space.

The storage that `vector` uses starts out as unconstructed memory; it does not yet hold any objects. When the elements are copied to or added in this preallocated space, they must be constructed using the `construct` member of `allocator`.

To illustrate these concepts we'll implement a small portion of vector. We'll name our class Vector to distinguish it from the standard vector class:

```
//  pseudo-implementation of memory allocation strategy for a vector-like class
template <class T> class Vector {
public:
    Vector(): elements(0), first_free(0), end(0) { }
    void push_back(const T&);
    //  ...
private:
    static std::allocator<T> alloc; //  object to get raw memory
    void reallocate(); //  get more space and copy existing elements
    T* elements;        //  pointer to first element in the array
    T* first_free;      //  pointer to first free element in the array
    T* end;             //  pointer to one past the end of the array
    //  ...
};
```

Each Vector<T> type defines a static data member of type allocator<T> to allocate and construct the elements in Vectors of the given type. Each Vector object keeps its elements in a built-in array of the indicated type and maintains three pointers into that array:

- elements, which points to the first element in the array

- first_free, which points just after the last actual element

- end, which points just after the end of the array itself

Figure 18.1 illustrates the meaning of these pointers.

Figure 18.1: Vector Memory Allocation Strategy

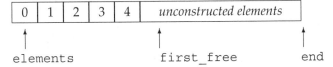

We can use these pointers to determine the size and capacity of the Vector:

- The size of a Vector (the number of elements actually in use) is equal to first_free − elements.

- The capacity of a Vector (the total number of elements that could be defined before the Vector has to be reallocated) is equal to end − elements.

- The free capacity (the number of elements that can be added before a reallocation is necessary) is end − first_free.

Using `construct`

The `push_back` member uses these pointers to add a new element to the end of
the `Vector`:

```
template <class T>
void Vector<T>::push_back(const T& t)
{
    //   are we out of space?
    if (first_free == end)
      reallocate();  //  gets more space and copies existing elements to it
    alloc.construct(first_free, t);
    ++first_free;
}
```

The `push_back` function starts by determining whether there is space available. If
not, it calls `reallocate`. That member allocates new space and copies the existing
elements. It resets the pointers to point to the newly allocated space.

Once `push_back` knows that there is room for the new element, it asks the
`allocator` object to `construct` a new last element. The `construct` function
uses the copy constructor for type `T` to copy the value `t` into the element denoted
by `first_free`. It then increments `first_free` to indicate that one more element
is in use.

Reallocating and Copying Elements

The `reallocate` function has the most work to do:

```
template <class T> void Vector<T>::reallocate()
{
    //   compute size of current array and allocate space for twice as many elements
    std::ptrdiff_t size = first_free - elements;
    std::ptrdiff_t newcapacity = 2 * max(size, 1);
    //   allocate space to hold newcapacity number of elements of type T
    T* newelements = alloc.allocate(newcapacity);

    //   construct copies of the existing elements in the new space
    uninitialized_copy(elements, first_free, newelements);
    //   destroy the old elements in reverse order
    for (T *p = first_free; p != elements; /* empty */ )
        alloc.destroy(--p);

    //   deallocate cannot be called on a 0 pointer
    if (elements)
        //   return the memory that held the elements
        alloc.deallocate(elements, end - elements);
    //   make our data structure point to the new elements
    elements = newelements;
    first_free = elements + size;
    end = elements + newcapacity;
}
```

We use a simple but surprisingly effective strategy of allocating twice as much memory each time we reallocate. The function starts by calculating the current number of elements in use, doubling that number, and asking the `allocator` object to obtain the desired amount of space. If the `Vector` is empty, we allocate two elements.

If `Vector` holds `ints`, the call to `allocate` allocates space for `newcapacity` number of `ints`. If it holds `strings`, then it allocates that space for the given number of `strings`.

The call to `uninitialized_copy` uses a specialized version of the standard `copy` algorithm. This version expects its destination to be raw, unconstructed memory. Rather than assigning elements from the input range to the destination, it copy-constructs each element in the destination. The copy constructor for `T` is used to copy each element from the input range to the destination.

The `for` loop calls the `allocator` member `destroy` on each object in the old array. It destroys the elements in reverse order, starting with the last element in the array and finishing with the first. The `destroy` function runs the destructor for type `T` to free any resources used by the old elements.

Once the elements have been copied and destroyed, we free the space used by the original array. We must check that `elements` actually pointed to an array before calling `deallocate`.

 `deallocate` expects a pointer that points to space that was allocated by `allocate`. It is not legal to pass `deallocate` a zero pointer.

Finally, we have to reset the pointers to address the newly allocated and initialized array. The `first_free` and `end` pointers are set to denote one past the last constructed element and one past the end of the allocated space, respectively.

EXERCISES SECTION 18.1.2

Exercise 18.1: Implement your own version of the `Vector` class including versions of the `vector` members `reserve` (Section 9.4, p. 330), `resize` (Section 9.3.5, p. 323), and the `const` and nonconst subscript operators (Section 14.5, p. 522).

Exercise 18.2: Define a typedef that uses the corresponding pointer type as the `iterator` for your `Vector`.

Exercise 18.3: To test your `Vector` class, reimplement earlier programs you wrote using `vector` to use `Vector` instead.

18.1.3 `operator new` and `operator delete` Functions

The previous subsection used the `vector` class to show how we could use the `allocator` class to manage a pool of memory for a class' internal data storage. In the next three subsections we'll look at how we might implement the same strategy using the more primitive library facilities.

First, we need to understand a bit more about how new and delete expressions work. When we use a new expression

```
// new expression
string * sp = new string("initialized");
```

three steps actually take place. First, the expression calls a library function named **operator new** to allocate raw, untyped memory large enough to hold an object of the specified type. Next, a constructor for the type is run to construct the object from the specified initializers. Finally, a pointer to the newly allocated and constructed object is returned.

When we use a delete expression to delete a dynamically allocated object:

```
delete sp;
```

two steps happen. First, the appropriate destructor is run on the object to which sp points. Then, the memory used by the object is freed by calling a library function named **operator delete**.

TERMINOLOGY: NEW EXPRESSION VERSUS OPERATOR NEW FUNCTION

The library functions operator new and operator delete are misleadingly named. Unlike other operator functions, such as operator=, these functions do not overload the new or delete expressions. In fact, we cannot redefine the behavior of the new and delete expressions.

A new expression executes by calling an operator new function to obtain memory and then constructs an object in that memory. A delete expression executes by destroying an object and then calls an operator delete function to free the memory used by the object.

Because the new (or delete) expressions and the underlying library functions have the same name, it is easy to confuse the two.

The operator new and operator delete Interface

There are two overloaded versions of operator new and operator delete functions. Each version supports the related new and delete expression:

```
void *operator new(size_t);        // allocate an object
void *operator new[](size_t);      // allocate an array

void *operator delete(void*);      // free an object
void *operator delete[](void*);    // free an array
```

Using the Allocation Operator Functions

Although the operator new and operator delete functions are intended to be used by new expressions, they are generally available functions in the library.

We can use them to obtain unconstructed memory. They are somewhat analogous to the `allocate` and `deallocate` members of the `allocator` class. For example, instead of using an `allocator`, we could have used the `operator new` and `operator delete` functions in our `Vector` class. When we allocated new space we wrote

```
// allocate space to hold newcapacity number of elements of type T
T* newelements = alloc.allocate(newcapacity);
```

which could be rewritten as

```
// allocate unconstructed memory to hold newcapacity elements of type T
T* newelements = static_cast<T*>
                (operator new[](newcapacity * sizeof(T)));
```

Similarly, when we deallocated the old space pointed to be the `Vector` member `elements` we wrote

```
// return the memory that held the elements
alloc.deallocate(elements, end - elements);
```

which could be rewritten as

```
// deallocate the memory that they occupied
operator delete[](elements);
```

These functions behave similarly to the `allocate` and `deallocate` members of the `allocator` class. However, they differ in one important respect: They operate on `void*` pointers rather than typed pointers.

> *Best Practices* In general, it is more type-safe to use an `allocator` rather than using the `operator new` and `operator delete` functions directly.

The `allocate` member allocates typed memory, so programs that use it can avoid the necessity of calculating the byte-count amount of memory needed. They also can avoid casting (Section 5.12.4, p. 183) the return from `operator new`. Similarly, `deallocate` frees memory of a specific type, again avoiding the necessity for converting to `void*`.

18.1.4 Placement new Expressions

The library functions `operator new` and `operator delete` are lower-level versions of the `allocator` members `allocate` and `deallocate`. Each allocates but does not initialize memory.

There are also lower-level alternatives to the `allocator` members `construct` and `destroy`. These members initialize and destroy objects in space allocated by an `allocator` object.

Analogous to the `construct` member, there is a third kind of new expression, referred to as **placement new**. The placement new expression initializes an object in raw memory that was already allocated. It differs from other versions of new in that it does not allocate memory. Instead, it takes a pointer to allocated but unconstructed memory and initializes an object in that memory. In effect, placement new allows us to construct an object at a specific, preallocated memory address.

The form of a placement new expression is:

```
new (place_address) type
new (place_address) type (initializer-list)
```

where place_address must be a pointer and the *initializer-list* provides (a possibly empty) list of initializers to use when constructing the newly allocated object.

We could use a placement new expression to replace the call to construct in our Vector implementation. The original code

```
//  construct a copy t in the element to which first_free points
alloc.construct(first_free, t);
```

would be replaced by the equivalent placement new expression

```
//  copy t into element addressed by first_free
new (first_free) T(t);
```

Placement new expressions are more flexible than the construct member of class allocator. When placement new initializes an object, it can use any constructor, and builds the object directly. The construct function always uses the copy constructor.

For example, we could initialize an allocated but unconstructed string from a pair of iterators in either of these two ways:

```
allocator<string> alloc;
string *sp = alloc.allocate(2);  //  allocate space to hold 2 strings
//  two ways to construct a string from a pair of iterators
new (sp) string(b, e);                       //  construct directly in place
alloc.construct(sp + 1, string(b, e));  //  build and copy a temporary
```

The placement new expression uses the string constructor that takes a pair of iterators to construct the string directly in the space to which sp points. When we call construct, we must first construct the string from the iterators to get a string object to pass to construct. That function then uses the string copy constructor to copy that unnamed, temporary string into the object to which sp points.

Often the difference is irrelevant: For valuelike classes, there is no observable difference between constructing the object directly in place and constructing a temporary and copying it. And the performance difference is rarely meaningful. But for some classes, using the copy constructor is either impossible (because the copy constructor is private) or should be avoided. In these cases, use of placement new may be necessary.

18.1.5 Explicit Destructor Invocation

Just as placement new is a lower-level alternative to using the allocate member of the allocator class, we can use an explicit call to a destructor as the lower-level alternative to calling destroy.

EXERCISES SECTION 18.1.4

Exercise 18.4: Why do you think `construct` is limited to using only the copy constructor for the element type?

Exercise 18.5: Why can placement new expressions be more flexible?

In the version of `Vector` that used an `allocator`, we clean up each element by calling `destroy`:

```
//  destroy the old elements in reverse order
for (T *p = first_free; p != elements; /* empty */ )
    alloc.destroy(--p);
```

For programs that use a placement new expression to construct the object, we call the destructor explicitly:

```
for (T *p = first_free; p != elements; /* empty */ )
    p->~T();   //  call the destructor
```

Here we invoke a destructor directly. The arrow operator dereferences the iterator p to obtain the object to which p points. We then call the destructor, which is the name of the type preceded by a tilde (~).

The effect of calling the destructor explicitly is that the object itself is properly cleaned up. However, the memory in which the object resided is not freed. We can reuse the space if desired.

Note Calling the `operator delete` function does not run the destructor; it only frees the indicated memory.

EXERCISES SECTION 18.1.5

Exercise 18.6: Reimplement your `Vector` class to use `operator new`, `operator delete`, placement new, and direct calls to the destructor.

Exercise 18.7: Test your new version by running the same programs that you ran against your initial `Vector` implementation.

Exercise 18.8: Which version do you think is better, and why?

18.1.6 Class Specific new and delete

The previous subsections looked at how a class can take over memory management for its own internal data structure. Another way to optimize memory allocation involves optimizing the behavior of new expressions. As an example, consider the Queue class from Chapter 16. That class doesn't hold its elements directly. Instead, it uses new expressions to allocate objects of type QueueItem.

It might be possible to improve the performance of Queue by preallocating a block of raw memory to hold QueueItem objects. When a new QueueItem object is created, it could be constructed in this preallocated space. When QueueItem objects are freed, we'd put them back in the block of preallocated objects rather than actually returning memory to the system.

The difference between this problem and our Vector implementation is that in this case, we want to optimize the behavior of new and delete expressions when applied to objects of a particular type. By default, new expressions allocate memory by calling the version of operator new that is defined by the library. A class may manage the memory used for objects of its type by defining its own members named operator new and operator delete.

When the compiler sees a new or delete expression for a class type, it looks to see if the class has a member operator new or operator delete. If the class defines (or inherits) its own member new and delete functions, then those functions are used to allocate and free the memory for the object. Otherwise, the standard library versions of these functions are called.

When we optimize the behavior of new and delete, we need only define new versions of the operator new and operator delete. The new and delete expressions themselves take care of constructing and destroying the objects.

Member new and delete Functions

 If a class defines either of these members, it should define both of them.

A class member operator new function must have a return type of void* and take a parameter of type size_t. The function's size_t parameter is initialized by the new expression with the size, in bytes, of the amount of memory to allocate.

A class member operator delete function must have a void return type. It can be defined to take a single parameter of type void* or to take two parameters, a void* and a size_t. The void* parameter is initialized by the delete expression with the pointer that was deleted. That pointer might be a null pointer. If present, the size_t parameter is initialized automatically by the compiler with the size in bytes of the object addressed by the first parameter.

The size_t parameter is unnecessary unless the class is part of an inheritance hierarchy. When we delete a pointer to a type in an inheritance hierarchy, the pointer might point to a base-class object or an object of a derived class. In general, the size of a derived-type object is larger than the size of a base-class object. If the base class has a virtual destructor (Section 15.4.4, p. 587), then the size passed to operator delete will vary depending on the dynamic type of the object to which the deleted pointer points. If the base class does not have a virtual destructor, then, as usual, the behavior of deleting a pointer to a derived object through a base-class pointer is undefined.

These functions are implicitly static members (Section 12.6.1, p. 469). There is no need to declare them `static` explicitly, although it is legal to do so. The member `new` and `delete` functions must be static because they are used either before the object is constructed (`operator new`) or after it has been destroyed (`operator delete`). There are, therefore, no member data for these functions to manipulate. As with any other static member function, `new` and `delete` may access only static members of their class directly.

Array Operator `new[]` and Operator `delete[]`

We can also define member `operator new[]` and `operator delete[]` to manage arrays of the class type. If these `operator` functions exist, the compiler uses them in place of the global versions.

A class member `operator new[]` must have a return type of `void*` and take a first parameter of type `size_t`. The operator's `size_t` parameter is initialized automatically with a value that represents the number of bytes required to store an array of the given number of elements of the specified type.

The member operator `delete[]` must have a `void` return type and a first parameter of type `void*`. The operator's `void*` parameter is initialized automatically with a value that represents the beginning of the storage in which the array is stored.

The operator `delete[]` for a class may also have two parameters instead of one, the second parameter being a `size_t`. If present, the additional parameter is initialized automatically by the compiler with the size in bytes of the storage required to store the array.

Overriding Class-Specific Memory Allocation

A user of a class that defines its own member `new` and `delete` can force a `new` or `delete` expression to use the global library functions through the use of the global scope resolution operator. If the user writes

```
Type *p = ::new Type; // uses global operator new
::delete p;           // uses global operator delete
```

then `new` invokes the global `operator new` even if class `Type` defines its own class-specific `operator new`; similarly for `delete`.

If storage was allocated with a `new` expression invoking the global `operator new` function, then the `delete` expression should also invoke the global `operator delete` function.

EXERCISES SECTION 18.1.6

Exercise 18.9: Declare members `new` and `delete` for the `QueueItem` class.

18.1.7 A Memory-Allocator Base Class

Like the generic handle class (Section 16.5, p. 666) this example represents a fairly sophisticated use of C++. Understanding this example requires (and demonstrates) a good grasp of both inheritance and templates. It may be useful to delay studying this example until you are comfortable with these features.

Having seen how to declare class-specific member `new` and `delete`, we might next implement those members for `QueueItem`. Before doing so, we need to decide how we'll improve over the built-in library `new` and `delete` functions. One common strategy is to preallocate a block of raw memory to hold unconstructed objects. When new elements are created, they could be constructed in one of these preallocated objects. When elements are freed, we'd put them back in the block of preallocated objects rather than actually returning memory to the system. This kind of strategy is often known as maintaining a **freelist**. The freelist might be implemented as a linked list of objects that have been allocated but not constructed.

Rather than implementing a freelist-based allocation strategy for `QueueItem`, we'll observe that `QueueItem` is not unique in wanting to optimize allocation of objects of its type. Many classes might have the same need. Because this behavior might be generally useful, we'll define a new class that we'll name `CachedObj` to handle the freelist. A class, such as `QueueItem`, that wants to opimize allocation of objects of its type could use the `CachedObj` class rather than implementing its own `new` and `delete` members directly.

The `CachedObj` class will have a simple interface: Its only job is to allocate and manage a freelist of allocated but unconstructed objects. This class will define a member `operator new` that will return the next element from the freelist, removing it from the freelist. The `operator new` will allocate new raw memory whenever the freelist becomes empty. The class will also define `operator delete` to put an element back on the freelist when an object is destroyed.

Classes that wish to use a freelist allocation strategy for their own types will *inherit* from `CachedObj`. Through inheritance, these classes can use the `CachedObj` definition of `operator new` and `operator delete` along with the data members needed to represent the freelist. Because the `CachedObj` class is intended as a base class, we'll give it a `public` virtual destructor.

As we'll see, `CachedObj` may be used only for types that are not involved in an inheritance hierarchy. Unlike the member `new` and `delete` operations, `CachedObj` has no way to allocate different sized objects depending on the actual type of the object: Its freelist holds objects of a single size. Hence, it may be used only for classes, such as `QueueItem`, that do not serve as base classes.

The data members defined by the `CachedObj` class, and inherited by its derived classes, are:

- A `static` pointer to the head of the freelist
- A member named `next` that points from one `CachedObj` to the next

The `next` pointer chains the elements together onto the freelist. Each type that we derive from `CachedObj` will contain its own type-specific data plus a single pointer inherited from the `CachedObj` base class. Each object has an extra pointer used by the memory allocator but not by the inherited type itself. When the object is in use, this pointer is meaningless and not used. When the object is available for use and is on the freelist, then the `next` pointer is used to point to the next available object.

If we used `CachedObj` to optimize allocation of our `Screen` class, objects of type `Screen` (conceptually) would look like the illustration in Figure 18.2.

Figure 18.2: Illustration of a `CachedObj` Derived Class

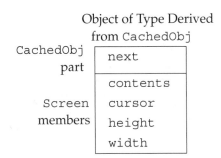

The `CachedObj` Class

The only remaining question is what types to use for the pointers in `CachedObj`. We'd like to use the freelist approach for any type, so the class will be a template. The pointers will point to an object of the template type:

```
/*  memory allocation class: Pre-allocates objects and
 *  maintains a freelist of objects that are unused
 *  When an object is freed, it is put back on the freelist
 *  The memory is only returned when the program exits
 */
template <class T> class CachedObj {
public:
    void *operator new(std::size_t);
    void operator delete(void *, std::size_t);
    virtual ~CachedObj() { }
protected:
    T *next;
private:
    static void add_to_freelist(T*);
    static std::allocator<T> alloc_mem;
    static T *freeStore;
    static const std::size_t chunk;
};
```

The class is quite simple. It provides only three public members: `operator new`, `operator delete`, and a virtual destructor. The `new` and `delete` members take objects off and return objects to the freelist.

The `static` members manage the freelist. These members are declared as `static` because there is only one freelist maintained for all the objects of a given type. The `freeStore` pointer points to the head of the freelist. The member named `chunk` specifies the number of objects that will be allocated each time the freelist is empty. Finally, `add_to_freelist` puts objects on the freelist. This function is used by `operator new` to put newly allocated objects onto the freelist. It is also used by `operator delete` to put an object back on the freelist when an object is deleted.

Using `CachedObj`

The only really tricky part in using `CachedObj` is understanding the template parameter: When we inherit from `CachedObj`, the template type we use to instantiate `CachedObj` will be the derived type itself. We inherit from `CachedObj` in order to reuse its freelist management. However, `CachedObj` holds a pointer to the object type it manages. The type of that pointer is pointer to a type derived from `CachedObj`.

For example, to optimize memory management for our `Screen` class we would declare `Screen` as

```
class Screen: public CachedObj<Screen> {
    //  interface and implementation members of class Screen are unchanged
};
```

This declaration gives `Screen` a new base class, the instance of `CachedObj` that is parameterized by type `Screen`. Each `Screen` now includes an additional inherited member named `next` in addition to its other members defined inside the `Screen` class.

Because `QueueItem` is a template type, deriving it from `CachedObj` is a bit complicated:

```
template <class Type>
class QueueItem: public CachedObj< QueueItem<Type> > {
    //  remainder of class declaration and all member definitions unchanged
};
```

This declaration says that `QueueItem` is a class template that is derived from the instantiation of `CachedObj` that holds objects of type `QueueItem<Type>`. For example, if we define a `Queue` of `int`s, then the `QueueItem<int>` class is derived from `CachedObj< QueueItem<int> >`.

No other changes are needed in our class. `QueueItem` now has automatic memory allocation that uses a freelist to reduce the number of allocations required when creating new `Queue` elements.

How Allocation Works

Because we derived `QueueItem` from `CachedObj`, any allocation using a `new` expression, such as the call from `Queue::push`:

```
//   allocate a new QueueItem object
QueueItem<Type> *pt =
    new QueueItem<Type>(val);
```

allocates and constructs a new `QueueItem`. Each `new` expression:

1. Uses the `QueueItem<T>::operator new` function to allocate an object from the freelist

2. Uses the element type copy constructor for type `T` to construct an object in that storage

Similarly, when we `delete` a `QueueItem` pointer such as

```
delete pt;
```

the `QueueItem` destructor is run to clean up the object to which `pt` points and the class `operator delete` is called. That operator puts the memory the element used back on the freelist.

Defining `operator new`

The `operator new` member returns an object from the freelist. If the freelist is empty, new must first allocate a new chunk of memory:

```
template <class T>
void *CachedObj<T>::operator new(size_t sz)
{
    //   new should only be asked to build a T, not an object
    //   derived from T; check that right size is requested
    if (sz != sizeof(T))
        throw std::runtime_error
          ("CachedObj: wrong size object in operator new");
    if (!freeStore) {
        //   the list is empty: grab a new chunk of memory
        //   allocate allocates chunk number of objects of type T
        T * array = alloc_mem.allocate(chunk);

        //   now set the next pointers in each object in the allocated memory
        for (size_t i = 0; i != chunk; ++i)
                add_to_freelist(&array[i]);
    }
    T *p = freeStore;
    freeStore = freeStore->CachedObj<T>::next;
    return p;     //   constructor of T will construct the T part of the object
}
```

The function begins by verifying that it is being asked to allocate the right amount of space.

This check enforces our design intent that CachedObj should be used only for classes that are not base classes. The fact that CachedObj allocates objects on its freelist that have a fixed size means that it cannot be used to handle memory allocation for classes in an inheritance hierarchy. Classes related by inheritance almost always define objects of different sizes. A single allocator would have to be much more sophisticated than the one we implement here to handle such classes.

The operator new function next checks whether there are any objects on the freelist. If not, it asks the allocator member to allocate chunk new, unconstructed objects. It then iterates through the newly allocated objects, setting the next pointer. After the call to add_to_freelist, each object on the freelist will be unconstructed, except for its next pointer, which will hold the address of the next available object. The freelist looks something like the picture in Figure 18.3.

Figure 18.3: Illustration CachedObj Freelist

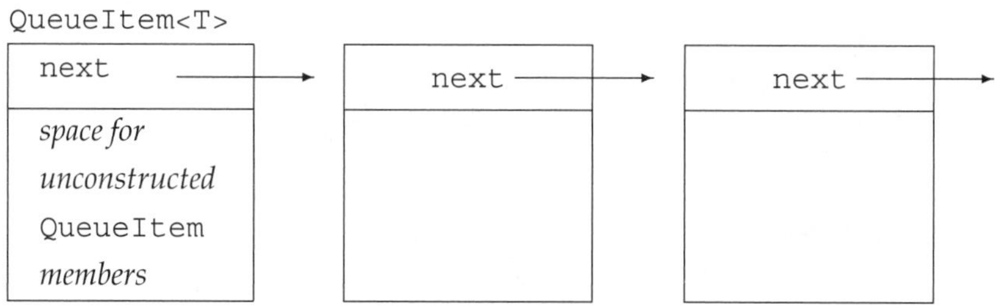

Having ensured that there are available objects to allocate, operator new returns the address of the first object on the freelist, resetting the freeStore pointer to address the next element on the freelist. The object returned is unconstructed. Because operator new is called from a new expression, the new expression will take care of constructing the object.

Defining operator delete

The member operator delete is responsible only for managing the memory. The object itself was already cleaned up in the destructor, which the delete expression calls before calling operator delete. The operator delete member is trivial:

```
template <class T>
void CachedObj<T>::operator delete(void *p, size_t)
{
    if (p != 0)
        // put the "deleted" object back at head of freelist
        add_to_freelist(static_cast<T*>(p));
}
```

It calls add_to_freelist to put the deleted object back onto the freelist.

The interesting part is the cast (Section 5.12.4, p. 183). `operator delete` is called when a dynamically allocated object of the class type is `deleted`. The compiler passes the address of that object to `operator delete`. However, the parameter type for the pointer must be `void*`. Before calling `add_to_freelist`, we have to cast the pointer from `void*` back to its actual type. In this case, that type is pointer to `T`, which in turn is a pointer to an object of a type derived from `CachedObj`.

The `add_to_freelist` Member

The job of this member is to set the `next` pointer and update the `freeStore` pointer when an object is added to the freelist:

```
//   puts object at head of the freelist
template <class T>
void CachedObj<T>::add_to_freelist(T *p)
{
    p->CachedObj<T>::next = freeStore;
    freeStore = p;
}
```

The only tricky part is the use of the `next` member. Recall that `CachedObj` is intended to be used as a base class. The objects that are allocated aren't of type `CachedObj`. Instead, those objects are of a type derived from `CachedObj`. The type of `T`, therefore, will be the derived type. The pointer `p` is a pointer to `T`, not a pointer to `CachedObj`. If the derived class has its own member named `next`, then writing

```
p->next
```

would fetch the `next` member of the derived class! But we want to set the `next` in the base, `CachedObj` class.

 To avoid any possible collision with a member defined in the derived class, we explicitly specify that we are assigning to the base class member `next`.

Defining the Static Data Members

What remains is to define the static data members:

```
template <class T> allocator< T > CachedObj< T >::alloc_mem;
template <class T> T *CachedObj< T >::freeStore = 0;
template <class T> const size_t CachedObj< T >::chunk = 24;
```

As usual, with static members of a class template there is a different static member for each type used to instantiate `CachedObj`. We initialize `chunk` to an arbitrary value—in this case, 24. We initialize the `freeStore` pointer to 0, indicating that the freelist starts out empty. There is no initialization required for the `alloc_mem` member, but we do have to remember to define it.

EXERCISES SECTION 18.1.7

Exercise 18.10: Explain each of the following initializations. Indicate if any are errors, and if so, why.

```
class iStack {
public:
    iStack(int capacity): stack(capacity), top(0) { }
private:
    int top;
    vector<int> stack;
};
(a) iStack *ps = new iStack(20);
(b) iStack *ps2 = new const iStack(15);
(c) iStack *ps3 = new iStack[ 100 ];
```

Exercise 18.11: Explain what happens in the following new and delete expressions:

```
struct Exercise {
    Exercise();
    ~Exercise();
};
Exercise *pe = new Exercise[20];
delete[] pe;
```

Exercise 18.12: Implement a class-specific memory allocator for Queue or another class of your choice. Measure the change in performace to see how much it helps, if at all.

18.2   Run-Time Type Identification

Run-time Type Identification (RTTI) allows programs that use pointers or references to base classes to retrieve the actual derived types of the objects to which these pointers or references refer.

RTTI is provided through two operators:

1. The typeid operator, which returns the actual type of the object referred to by a pointer or a reference

2. The dynamic_cast operator, which safely converts from a pointer or reference to a base type to a pointer or reference to a derived type

> These operators return dynamic type information only for classes with one or more virtual functions. For all other types, information for the static (i.e., compile-time) type is returned.

The RTTI operators execute at run time for classes with virtual functions, but are evaluated at compile time for all other types.

Dynamic casts are needed when we have a reference or pointer to a base class but need to perform operations from the derived class that are not part of the base class. Ordinarily, the best way to get derived behavior from a pointer to base is to do so through a virtual function. When we use virtual functions, the compiler automatically selects the right function according to the actual type of the object.

In some situations however, the use of virtual functions is not possible. In these cases, RTTI offers an alternate mechanism. However, this mechanism is more error-prone than using virtual member functions: The programmer must *know* to which type the object should be cast and must check that the cast was performed successfully.

 Dynamic casts should be used with caution. Whenever possible, it is much better to define and use a virtual function rather than to take over managing the types directly.

18.2.1 The `dynamic_cast` Operator

The **`dynamic_cast` operator** can be used to convert a reference or pointer to an object of base type to a reference or pointer to another type in the same hierarchy. The pointer used with a `dynamic_cast` must be valid—it must either be 0 or point to an object.

Unlike other casts, a `dynamic_cast` involves a run-time type check. If the object bound to the reference or pointer is not an object of the target type, then the `dynamic_cast` fails. If a `dynamic_cast` to a pointer type fails, the result of the `dynamic_cast` is the value 0. If a `dynamic_cast` to a reference type fails, then an exception of type `bad_cast` is thrown.

The `dynamic_cast` operator therefore performs two operations at once. It begins by verifying that the requested cast is valid. Only if the cast is valid does the operator actually do the cast. In general, the type of the object to which the reference or pointer is bound isn't known at compile-time. A pointer to base can be assigned to point to a derived object. Similarly, a reference to base can be initialized by a derived object. As a result, the verification that the `dynamic_cast` operator performs must be done at run time.

Using the `dynamic_cast` Operator

As a simple example, assume that `Base` is a class with at least one virtual function and that class `Derived` is derived from `Base`. If we have a pointer to `Base` named `basePtr`, we can cast it at run time to a pointer to `Derived` as follows:

```
if (Derived *derivedPtr = dynamic_cast<Derived*>(basePtr))
{
    // use the Derived object to which derivedPtr points
} else {   // BasePtr points at a Base object
    // use the Base object to which basePtr points
}
```

At run time, if `basePtr` actually points to a `Derived` object, then the cast will be successful, and `derivedPtr` will be initialized to point to the `Derived` object to which `basePtr` points. Otherwise, the result of the cast is 0, meaning that `derivedPtr` is set to 0, and the condition in the `if` fails.

 We can apply a `dynamic_cast` to a pointer whose value is 0. The result of doing so is 0.

By checking the value of `derivedPtr`, the code inside the `if` knows that it is operating on a `Derived` object. It is safe for that code to use `Derived` operations. If the `dynamic_cast` fails because `basePtr` refers to a `Base` object, then the `else` clause does processing appropriate to `Base` instead. The other advantage of doing the check inside the `if` condition is that it is not possible to insert code between the `dynamic_cast` and testing the result of the cast. It is, therefore, not possible to use the `derivedPtr` inadvertently before testing that the cast was successful. A third advantage is that the pointer is not accessible outside the `if`. If the cast fails, then the unbound pointer is not available for use in later cases where the test might be forgotten.

 Performing a `dynamic_cast` in a condition ensures that the cast and test of its result are done in a single expression.

Using a `dynamic_cast` and Reference Types

In the previous example, we used a `dynamic_cast` to convert a pointer to base to a pointer to derived. A `dynamic_cast` can also be used to convert a reference to base to a reference to derived. The form for this a `dynamic_cast` operation is the following,

```
dynamic_cast< Type& >(val)
```

where `Type` is the target type of the conversion, and `val` is an object of base class type.

The `dynamic_cast` operation converts the operand `val` to the desired type `Type&` only if `val` actually refers to an object of the type `Type` or is an object of a type derived from `Type`.

Because there is no such thing as a null reference, it is not possible to use the same checking strategy for references that is used for pointer casts. Instead, when a cast fails, it throws a `std::bad_cast` exception. This exception is defined in the `typeinfo` library header.

We might rewrite the previous example to use references as follows:

```
void f(const Base &b)
{
    try {
        const Derived &d = dynamic_cast<const Derived&>(b);
    // use the Derived object to which b referred
    } catch (bad_cast) {
        // handle the fact that the cast failed
    }
}
```

EXERCISES SECTION 18.2.1

Exercise 18.13: Given the following class hierarchy in which each class defines a `public` default constructor and virtual destructor,

```
class A { /* ... */ };
class B : public A { /* ... */ };
class C : public B { /* ... */ };
class D : public B, public A { /* ... */ };
```

which, if any, of the following `dynamic_casts` fail?

```
(a)  A *pa = new C;
     B *pb = dynamic_cast< B* >(pa);
(b)  B *pb = new B;
     C *pc = dynamic_cast< C* >(pb);
(c)  A *pa = new D;
     B *pb = dynamic_cast< B* >(pa);
```

Exercise 18.14: What would happen in the last conversion in the previous exercise if both `D` and `B` inherited from `A` as a virtual base class?

Exercise 18.15: Using the class hierarchy defined in the previous exercise, rewrite the following piece of code to perform a reference `dynamic_cast` to convert the expression `*pa` to the type `C&`:

```
if (C *pc = dynamic_cast< C* >(pa)) {
    // use C's members
} else {
    // use A's members
}
```

Exercise 18.16: Explain when you would use `dynamic_cast` instead of a virtual function.

18.2.2 The `typeid` Operator

The second operator provided for RTTI is the **typeid operator**. The `typeid` operator allows a program to ask of an expression: What type are you?

A `typeid` expression has the form

```
typeid(e)
```

where `e` is any expression or a type name.

If the type of the expression is a class type and that class contains one or more virtual functions, then the dynamic type of the expression may differ from its static compile-time type. For example, if the expression dereferences a pointer to a base class, then the static compile-time type of that expression is the base type. However, if the pointer actually addresses a derived object, then the `typeid` operator will say that the type of the expression is the derived type.

The `typeid` operator can be used with expressions of any type. Expressions of built-in type as well as constants can be used as operands for the `typeid` operator.

When the operand is not of class type or is a class without virtual functions, then the `typeid` operator indicates the static type of the operand. When the operand has a class-type that defines at least one virtual function, then the type is evaluated at run time.

The result of a `typeid` operation is a reference to an object of a library type named `type_info`. Section 18.2.4 (p. 779) covers this type in more detail. To use the `type_info` class, the library header `typeinfo` must be included.

Using the `typeid` Operator

The most common use of `typeid` is to compare the types of two expressions or to compare the type of an expression to a specified type:

```
Base *bp;
Derived *dp;
//   compare type at run time of two objects
if (typeid(*bp) == typeid(*dp)) {
    //   bp and dp point to objects of the same type
}
//   test whether run time type is a specific type
if (typeid(*bp) == typeid(Derived)) {
    //   bp actually points to a Derived
}
```

In the first `if`, we compare the actual types of the objects to which bp and dp point. If they both point to the same type, then the test succeeds. Similarly, the second `if` succeeds if bp currently points to a `Derived` object.

Note that the operands to the `typeid` are expressions that are objects—we tested `*bp`, not bp:

```
//   test always fails: The type of bp is pointer to Base
if (typeid(bp) == typeid(Derived)) {
    //   code never executed
}
```

This test compares the type `Base*` to type `Derived`. These types are unequal, so this test will always fail *regardless of the type of the object to which* bp *points*.

Dynamic type information is returned only if the operand to `typeid` is an object of a class type with virtual functions. Testing a pointer (as opposed to the object to which the pointer points) returns the static, compile-time type of the pointer.

If the value of a pointer p is 0, then `typeid(*p)` throws a `bad_typeid` exception if the type of p is a type with virtual functions. If the type of p does not define any virtuals, then the value of p is irrelevant. As when evaluating a `sizeof` expression (Section 5.8, p. 167) the compiler does not evaluate `*p`. It uses the static type of p, which does not require that p itself be a valid pointer.

18.2.3 Using RTTI

As an example of when RTTI might be useful, consider a class hierarchy for which we'd like to implement the equality operator. Two objects are equal if they have the same value for a given set of their data members. Each derived type may add its own data, which we will want to include when testing for equality.

Because the values considered in determining equality for a derived type might differ from those considered for the base type, we'll (potentially) need a different equality operator for each pair of types in the hierarchy. Moreover, we'd like to be able to use a given type as either the left-hand or right-hand operand, so we'll actually need two operators for each pair of types.

If our hierarchy has only two types, we need four functions:

```
bool operator==(const Base&, const Base&)
bool operator==(const Derived&, const Derived&)
bool operator==(const Derived&, const Base&);
bool operator==(const Base&, const Derived&);
```

But if our hierarchy has several types, the number of operators we must define expands rapidly—for only 3 types we'd need 9 operators. If the hierarchy has 4 types, we'd need 16, and so on.

We might think we could solve this problem by defining a set of virtual functions that would perform the equality test at each level in the hierarchy. Given those virtuals, we could define a single equality operator that operates on references to the base type. That operator could delegate its work to a virtual `equal` operation that would do the real work.

Unfortunately, virtual functions are not a good match to this problem. The trouble is deciding on the type for the parameter to the `equal` operation. Virtual functions must have the same parameter type(s) in both the base and derived classes. That implies that a virtual `equal` operation must have a parameter that is a reference to the base class.

However, when we compare two derived objects, we want to compare data members that might be particular to that derived class. If the parameter is a reference to base, we can use only members that are present in the base class. We cannot access members that are in the derived class but not in the base.

Thinking about the problem in this detail, we see that we want to return false if we attempt to compare objects of different types. Given this observation, we can now use RTTI to solve our problem.

We'll define a single equality operator. Each class will define a virtual `equal` function that first casts its operand to the right type. If the cast succeeds, then the real comparison will be performed. If the cast fails, then the `equal` operation will return `false`.

The Class Hierarchy

To make the concept a bit more concrete, let's assume that our classes look something like:

```
class Base {
    friend bool operator==(const Base&, const Base&);
public:
    //  interface members for Base
protected:
    virtual bool equal(const Base&) const;
    //  data and other implementation members of Base
};
class Derived: public Base {
    friend bool operator==(const Base&, const Base&);
public:
    //  other interface members for Derived
private:
    bool equal(const Base&) const;
    //  data and other implementation members of Derived
};
```

A Type-Sensitive Equality Operator

Next let's look at how we might define the overall equality operator:

```
bool operator==(const Base &lhs, const Base &rhs)
{
    //  returns false if typeids are different otherwise
    //  returns lhs.equal(rhs)
    return typeid(lhs) == typeid(rhs) && lhs.equal(rhs);
}
```

This operator returns false if the operands are different types. If they are the same type, then it delegates the real work of comparing the operands to the appropriate virtual `equal` function. If the operands are `Base` objects, then `Base::equal` will be called. If they are `Derived` objects, `Derived::equal` is called.

The Virtual `equal` Functions

Each class in the hierarchy must define its own version of `equal`. The functions in the derived classes will all start the same way: They'll cast their argument to the type of the class itself:

```
bool Derived::equal(const Base &rhs) const
{
    if (const Derived *dp
                = dynamic_cast<const Derived*>(&rhs)) {
        //  do work to compare two Derived objects and return result
    } else
        return false;
}
```

The cast should always succeed—after all, the function is called from the equality operator only after testing that the two operands are the same type. However, the cast is necessary so that the function can access the derived members of the right-hand operand. The operand is a Base&, so if we want to access members of the Derived, we must first do the cast.

The Base-Class `equal` Function

This operation is a bit simpler than the others:

```
bool Base::equal(const Base &rhs) const
{
    //  do whatever is required to compare to Base objects
}
```

There is no need to cast the parameter before using it. Both *this and the parameter are Base objects, so all the operations available for this object are also defined for the parameter type.

18.2.4   The `type_info` Class

The exact definition of the type_info class varies by compiler, but the standard guarantees that all implementations will provide at least the operations listed in Table 18.2

The class also provides a public virtual destructor, because it is intended to serve as a base class. If the compiler wants to provide additional type information, it should do so in a class derived from type_info.

Table 18.2: Operations on `type_info`	
t1 == t2	Returns true if the two type_info objects t1 and t2 refer to the same type; false otherwise.
t1 != t2	Returns true if the two type_info objects t1 and t2 refer to different types; false otherwise.
t.name()	Returns a C-style character string that is a printable version of the type name. Type names are generated in a system-dependent way.
t1.before(t2)	Returns a bool that indicates whether t1 comes before t2. The ordering imposed by before is compiler-dependent.

The default and copy constructors and the assignment operator are all defined as `private`, so we cannot define or copy objects of type `type_info`. The only way to create `type_info` objects in a program is to use the `typeid` operator.

The `name` function returns a C-style character string for the name of the type represented by the `type_info` object. The value used for a given type depends on the compiler and in particular is not required to match the type names as used in a program. The only guarantee we have about the return from `name` is that it returns a unique string for each type. Nonetheless, the `name` member can be used to print the name of a `type_info` object:

```
int iobj;
cout << typeid(iobj).name() << endl
     << typeid(8.16).name() << endl
     << typeid(std::string).name() << endl
     << typeid(Base).name() << endl
     << typeid(Derived).name() << endl;
```

The format and value returned by `name` varies by compiler. This program, when executed on our machine, generates the following output:

```
i
d
Ss
4Base
7Derived
```

> The `type_info` class varies by compiler. Some compilers provide additional member functions that provide additional information about types used in a program. You should consult the reference manual for your compiler to understand the exact `type_info` support provided.

18.3   Pointer to Class Member

We know that, given a pointer to an object, we can fetch a given member from that object using the arrow (`->`) operator. Sometimes it is useful to start from the member. That is, we may want to obtain a pointer to a specific member and then fetch that member from one or another object.

We can do so by using a special kind of pointer known as a **pointer to member**. A pointer to member embodies the type of the class as well as the type of the member. This fact impacts how pointers to member are defined, how they are bound to a function or data member, and how they are used.

Pointers to member apply only to nonstatic members of a class. `static` class members are not part of any object, so no special syntax is needed to point to a `static` member. Pointers to `static` members are ordinary pointers.

Exercise 18.20: Given the following class hierarchy in which each class defines a `public` default constructor and virtual destructor, which type name do the following statements print?

```
class A { /* ... */ };
class B : public A { /* ... */ };
class C : public B { /* ... */ };

(a)  A *pa = new C;
     cout << typeid(pa).name() << endl;

(b)  C cobj;
     A& ra = cobj;
     cout << typeid(&ra).name() << endl;

(c)  B *px = new B;
     A& ra = *px;
     cout << typeid(ra).name() << endl;
```

18.3.1 Declaring a Pointer to Member

In exploring pointers to members, we'll use a simplified version of the `Screen` class from Chapter 12.

```
class Screen {
public:
    typedef std::string::size_type index;
    char get() const;
    char get(index ht, index wd) const;
private:
    std::string contents;
    index cursor;
    index height, width;
};
```

Defining a Pointer to Data Member

The `contents` member of `Screen` has type `std::string`. The complete type of `contents` is "member of class `Screen`, whose type is `std::string`." Consequently, the complete type of a pointer that could point to `contents` is "pointer to member of class `Screen` of type `std::string`." This type is written as

```
string Screen::*
```

We can define a pointer to a `string` member of class `Screen` as

```
string Screen::*ps_Screen;
```

`ps_Screen` could be initialized with the address of `contents` by writing

```
string Screen::*ps_Screen = &Screen::contents;
```

We could also define a pointer that might address the `height`, `width`, or `cursor` members as

```
Screen::index Screen::*pindex;
```

which says that `pindex` is a pointer to a member of class `Screen` with type `Screen::index`. We could assign the address of `width` to this pointer as follows:

```
pindex = &Screen::width;
```

The pointer `pindex` can be set to any of `width`, `height`, or `cursor` because all three are `Screen` class data members of type `index`.

Defining a Pointer to Member Function

A pointer to a member function must match the type of the function to which it points, in three ways:

1. The type and number of the function parameters, including whether the member is `const`

2. The return type

3. The class type of which it is a member

A pointer to member function is defined by specifying the function return type, parameter list, and a class. For example, a pointer to a `Screen` member function capable of referring to the version of `get` that takes no parameters has the following type:

```
char (Screen::*)() const
```

This type specifies a pointer to a `const` member function of class `Screen`, taking no parameters and returning a value of type `char`. A pointer to this version of `get` can be defined and initialized as follows:

```
// pmf points to the Screen get member that takes no arguments
char (Screen::*pmf)() const = &Screen::get;
```

We might also define a pointer to the two-parameter version of `get` as

```
char (Screen::*pmf2)(Screen::index, Screen::index) const;
pmf2 = &Screen::get;
```

The precedence of the call operator is higher than that of the pointer-to-member operators. Therefore, the parentheses around `Screen::*` are essential. Without them, the compiler treats the following as an (invalid) function declaration:

```
// error: non-member function p cannot have const qualifier
char Screen::*p() const;
```

Using Typedefs for Member Pointers

Typedefs can make pointers to members easier to read. For example, the following typedef defines `Action` to be an alternative name for the type of the two-parameter version of `get`:

```
// Action is a type name
typedef
char (Screen::*Action)(Screen::index, Screen::index) const;
```

`Action` is the name of the type "pointer to a `const` member function of class `Screen` taking two parameters of type `index` and returning `char`." Using the typedef, we can simplify the definition of a pointer to `get` as follows:

```
Action get = &Screen::get;
```

A pointer-to-member function type may be used to declare function parameters and function return types:

```
// action takes a reference to a Screen and a pointer to Screen member function
Screen& action(Screen&, Action = &Screen::get);
```

This function is declared as taking two parameters: a reference to a `Screen` object and a pointer to a member function of class `Screen` taking two `index` parameters and returning a `char`. We could call `action` either by passing it a pointer or the address of an appropriate member function in `Screen`:

```
Screen myScreen;
// equivalent calls:
action(myScreen);        // uses the default argument
action(myScreen, get);   // uses the variable get that we previously defined
action(myScreen, &Screen::get);   // pass address explicitly
```

EXERCISES SECTION 18.3.1

Exercise 18.21: What is the difference between an ordinary data or function pointer and a pointer to data or function member?

Exercise 18.22: Define the type that could represent a pointer to the `isbn` member of the `Sales_item` class.

Exercise 18.23: Define a pointer that could point to the `same_isbn` member.

Exercise 18.24: Write a typedef that is a synonym for a pointer that could point to the `avg_price` member of `Sales_item`.

18.3.2 Using a Pointer to Class Member

Analogous to the member access operators, operators `.` and `->`, are two new operators, `.*` and `.->`, that let us bind a pointer to member to an actual object. The left-hand operand of these operators must be an object of or pointer to the class type, respectively. The right-hand operand is a pointer to a member of that type:

- The pointer-to-member dereference operator (.*) fetches the member from an object or reference.

- The pointer-to-member arrow operator (->*) fetches the member through a pointer to an object.

Using a Pointer to Member Function

Using a pointer to member, we could call the version of get that takes no parameters as follows:

```
//  pmf points to the Screen get member that takes no arguments
char (Screen::*pmf)() const = &Screen::get;
Screen myScreen;
char c1 = myScreen.get();        // call get on myScreen
char c2 = (myScreen.*pmf)();     // equivalent call to get
Screen *pScreen  = &myScreen;
c1 = pScreen->get();             // call get on object to which pScreen points
c2 = (pScreen->*pmf)();          // equivalent call to get
```

> The calls (myScreen.*pmf)() and (pScreen->*pmf)() require the parentheses because the precedence of the call operator— ()—is higher than the precedence of the pointer to member operators.

Without the parentheses,

```
myScreen.*pmf()
```

would be interpreted to mean

```
myScreen.*(pmf())
```

This code says to call the function named pmf and bind its return value to the pointer to member object operator (.*). Of course, the type of pmf does not support such a use, and a compile-time error would be generated.

As with any other function call, we can also pass arguments in a call made through a pointer to member function:

```
char (Screen::*pmf2)(Screen::index, Screen::index) const;
pmf2 = &Screen::get;
Screen myScreen;
char c1 = myScreen.get(0,0);       // call two-parameter version of get
char c2 = (myScreen.*pmf2)(0,0);   // equivalent call to get
```

Using a Pointer to Data Member

The same pointer-to-member operators are used to access data members:

```
Screen::index Screen::*pindex = &Screen::width;

Screen myScreen;
// equivalent ways to fetch width member of myScreen
Screen::index ind1 = myScreen.width;    // directly
Screen::index ind2 = myScreen.*pindex; // dereference to get width

Screen *pScreen;
// equivalent ways to fetch width member of *pScreen
ind1 = pScreen->width;     // directly
ind2 = pScreen->*pindex;   // dereference pindex to get width
```

Pointer-to-Member Function Tables

One common use for function pointers and for pointers to member functions is to store them in a function table. A function table is a collection of function pointers from which a given call is selected at run time.

For a class that has several members of the same type, such a table can be used to select one from the set of these members. Let's assume that our `Screen` class is extended to contain several member functions, each of which moves the cursor in a particular direction:

```
class Screen {
public:
    // other interface and implementation members as before
    Screen& home();        // cursor movement functions
    Screen& forward();
    Screen& back();
    Screen& up();
    Screen& down();
};
```

Each of these new functions takes no parameters and returns a reference to the `Screen` on which it was invoked.

Using the Function-Pointer Table

We might want to define a `move` function that could call any one of these functions and perform the indicated action. To support this new function, we'll add a `static` member to `Screen` that will be an array of pointers to the cursor movement functions:

```
class Screen {
public:
    // other interface and implementation members as before
    // Action is pointer that can be assigned any of the cursor movement members
    typedef Screen& (Screen::*Action)();
    static Action Menu[];      // function table
public:
    // specify which direction to move
    enum Directions { HOME, FORWARD, BACK, UP, DOWN };
    Screen& move(Directions);
};
```

The array named Menu will hold pointers to each of the cursor movement functions. Those functions will be stored at the offsets corresponding to the enumerators in Directions. The move function takes an enumerator and calls the appropriate function:

```
Screen& Screen::move(Directions cm)
{
    //  fetch the element in Menu indexed by cm
    //  run that member on behalf of this object
    (this->*Menu[cm])();
    return *this;
}
```

The call inside move is evaluated as follows: The Menu element indexed by cm is fetched. That element is a pointer to a member function of the Screen class. We call the member function to which that element points on behalf of the object to which this points.

When we call move, we pass it an enumerator that indicates which direction to move the cursor:

```
Screen myScreen;

myScreen.move(Screen::HOME);    //  invokes myScreen.home
myScreen.move(Screen::DOWN);    //  invokes myScreen.down
```

Defining a Table of Member Function Pointers

What's left is to define and initialize the table itself:

```
Screen::Action Screen::Menu[] = { &Screen::home,
                                  &Screen::forward,
                                  &Screen::back,
                                  &Screen::up,
                                  &Screen::down,
                                };
```

18.4   Nested Classes

A class can be defined within another class. Such a class is a **nested class**, also referred to as a **nested type**. Nested classes are most often used to define implementation classes, such as the QueueItem class from Chapter 16.

Nested classes are independent classes and are largely unrelated to their enclosing class. Objects of the enclosing and nested classes are, therefore, independent from one another. An object of the nested type does not have members defined by the enclosing class. Similarly, an object of the enclosing class does not have members defined by the nested class.

The name of a nested class is visible in its enclosing class scope but not in other class scopes or in the scope in which the enclosing class is defined. The name of a nested class will not collide with the same name declared in another scope.

A nested class can have the same kinds of members as a nonnested class. Just like any other class, a nested class controls access to its own members using access labels. Members may be declared `public`, `private`, or `protected`. The enclosing class has no special access to the members of a nested class and the nested class has no special access to members of its enclosing class.

A nested class defines a type member in its enclosing class. As with any other member, the enclosing class determines access to this type. A nested class defined in the `public` part of the enclosing class defines a type that may be used anywhere. A nested class defined in the `protected` section defines a type that is accessible only by the enclosing class, its friends, or its derived classes. A `private` nested class defines a type that is accessible only to the members of the enclosing class or its friends.

18.4.1 A Nested-Class Implementation

The `Queue` class that we implemented in Chapter 16 defined a companion implementation class named `QueueItem`. That class was a private class—it had only `private` members—but it was defined at the global scope. General user code cannot use objects of class `QueueItem`: All its members, including constructors, are `private`. However, the name `QueueItem` is visible globally. We cannot define our own type or other entity named `QueueItem`.

A better design would be to make the `QueueItem` class a `private` member of class `Queue`. That way, the `Queue` class (and its friends) could use `QueueItem`, but the `QueueItem` class type would not be visible to general user code. Once the class itself is `private`, we can make its members `public`—only `Queue` or the friends of `Queue` can access the `QueueItem` type, so there is no need to protect its members from general program access. We make the members `public` by defining `QueueItem` using the keyword `struct`.

Our new design looks like:

```
template <class Type> class Queue {
    // interface functions to Queue are unchanged
private:
    // public members are ok: QueueItem is a private member of Queue
    // only Queue and its friends may access the members of QueueItem
    struct QueueItem {
        QueueItem(const Type &);
        Type item;              // value stored in this element
        QueueItem *next;        // pointer to next element in the Queue
    };
    QueueItem *head;    // pointer to first element in Queue
    QueueItem *tail;    // pointer to last element in Queue
};
```

Because the class is a `private` member, only members and friends of the `Queue` class can use the `QueueItem` type. Having made the class a `private` member, we can make the `QueueItem` members `public`. Doing so lets us eliminate the friend declarations in `QueueItem`.

Classes Nested Inside a Class Template Are Templates

Because `Queue` is a template, its members are implicitly templates as well. In particular, the nested class `QueueItem` is implicitly a class template. Again, like any other member in `Queue`, the template parameter for `QueueItem` is the same as the template parameter of its enclosing class: class `Queue`.

Each instantiation of `Queue` generates its own `QueueItem` class with the appropriate template argument for `Type`. The mapping between an instantiation for the QueueItem class template and an instantiation of the enclosing Queue class template is one to one.

Defining the Members of a Nested Class

In this version of `QueueItem`, we chose not to define the `QueueItem` constructor inside the class. Instead, we'll define it separately. The only trick is where to define it and how to name it.

 A nested-class member defined outside its own class must be defined in the same scope as the scope in which the enclosing class is defined. A member of a nested class defined outside its own class may not be defined inside the enclosing class itself. A member of a nested class is not a member of the enclosing class.

The constructor for `QueueItem` is not a member of class `Queue`. Therefore, it cannot be defined elsewhere in the body of class `Queue`. It must be defined at the same scope as the `Queue` class but outside that class. To define a member outside the nested-class body, we must remember that its name is not visible outside the class. To define the constructor, we must indicate that `QueueItem` is a nested class within the scope of class `Queue`. We do so by qualifying the class name `QueueItem` with the name of its enclosing class `Queue`:

```
//  defines the QueueItem constructor
//  for class QueueItem nested inside class Queue<Type>
template <class Type>
Queue<Type>::QueueItem::QueueItem(const Type &t):
                            item(t), next(0) { }
```

Of course, both `Queue` and `QueueItem` are class templates. The constructor, therefore, is also a template.

This code defines a function template, parameterized by a single type parameter named `Type`. Reading the name of the function from right to left, this function is the constructor for class `QueueItem`, which is a nested in the scope of class `Queue<Type>`.

Defining the Nested Class Outside the Enclosing Class

Nested classes often support implementation details for the enclosing class. We might want to prevent users of the enclosing class from seeing the code that implements the nested class.

For example, we might want to put the definition of class `QueueItem` in its own file, which we would include in those files containing the implementation of the `Queue` class and its members. Just as we can define the members of a nested class outside the class body, we can define the entire class outside the body of the enclosing class:

```
template <class Type> class Queue {
    //  interface functions to Queue are unchanged
private:
    struct QueueItem;    //  forward declaration of nested type QueueItem
    QueueItem *head;     //  pointer to first element in Queue
    QueueItem *tail;     //  pointer to last element in Queue
};
template <class Type>
struct Queue<Type>::QueueItem {
    QueueItem(const Type &t): item(t), next(0) { }
    Type item;           //  value stored in this element
    QueueItem *next;     //  pointer to next element in the Queue
};
```

To define the class body outside its enclosing class, we must qualify the name of the nested class by the name of its enclosing class. Note that we must still *declare* `QueueItem` in the body of class `Queue`.

A nested class also can be declared and then later defined in the body of the enclosing class. As with other forward declarations, a forward declaration of a nested class allows for nested classes that have members that refer to one another.

Until the actual definition of a nested class that is defined outside the
class body is seen, that class is an incomplete type (Section 12.1.4, p. 437).
All the normal retrictions on using an incomplete type apply.

Nested-Class Static Member Definitions

If `QueueItem` had declared a static member, its definition would also need to be
defined in the outer scope. Assuming `QueueItem` had a static member, its definition would look somthing like:

```
//   defines an int static member of QueueItem,
//   which is a type nested inside Queue<Type>
template <class Type>
int Queue<Type>::QueueItem::static_mem = 1024;
```

Using Members of the Enclosing Class

There is no connection between the objects of an enclosing scope and
objects of its nested type(s).

Nonstatic functions in the nested class have an implicit `this` pointer that points
to an object of the nested type. A nested-type object contains only the members
of the nested type. The `this` pointer may not be used to fetch members of the
enclosing class. Similarly, the nonstatic member functions in the enclosing class
have a `this` pointer that points to an object of the enclosing type. That object has
only the members defined in the enclosing class.

Any use of a nonstatic data or function member of the enclosing class requires
that it be done through a pointer, reference, or object of the enclosing class. The
pop function in class `Queue` may not use `item` or `next` directly:

```
template <class Type>
void Queue<Type>::pop()
{
    //   pop is unchecked: popping off an empty Queue is undefined
    QueueItem* p = head;       //   keep pointer to head so can delete it
    head = head->next;         //   head now points to next element
    delete p;                  //   delete old head element
}
```

Objects of type `Queue` do not have members named `item` or `next`. Function
members of `Queue` can use the `head` and `tail` members, which are pointers to
`QueueItem` objects, to fetch those `QueueItem` members.

Using Static or Other Type Members

A nested class may refer to the static members, type names, and enumerators (Section 2.7, p. 62) of the enclosing class directly. Of course, referring to a type name or
static member outside the scope of the enclosing class requires the scope-resolution
operator.

Instantiation for Nested Templates

A nested class of a class template is not instantiated automatically when the enclosing class template is instantiated. Like any member function, the nested class is instantiated only if it is itself used in a context that requires a complete class type. For example, a definition such as

```
Queue<int> qi;   // instantiates Queue<int> but not QueueItem<int>
```

instantiates the template `Queue` with type `int` but does not yet instantiate the type `QueueItem<int>`. The `Queue` members `head` and `tail` are pointers to `QueueItem<int>`. There is no need to instantiate `QueueItem<int>` to define pointers to that class.

Making `QueueItem` a nested class of the class template `Queue` does not change the instantiation of `QueueItem`. The `QueueItem<int>` class will be instantiated only when `QueueItem` is used—in this case, only when `head` or `tail` is dereferenced from a member function of class `Queue<int>`.

18.4.2 Name Lookup in Nested Class Scope

Name lookup (Section 12.3.1, p. 447) for names used in a nested class proceeds in the same manner as for a normal class, the only difference being that now there may be one or more enclosing class scopes to search.

 When processing the declarations of the class members, any name used must appear prior to its use. When processing definitions, the entire nested and enclosing class(es) are in scope.

As an example of name lookup in a nested class, consider the following class declarations:

```
class Outer {
public:
    struct Inner {
        //  ok: reference to incomplete class
        void process(const Outer&);
        Inner2 val; // error: Outer::Inner2 not in scope
    };
    class Inner2 {
    public:
        //  ok: Inner2::val used in definition
        Inner2(int i = 0): val(i) { }
        //  ok: definition of process compiled after enclosing class is complete
        void process(const Outer &out) { out.handle(); }
    private:
        int val;
    };
    void handle() const;    // member of class Outer
};
```

The compiler first processes the declarations of the members of classes `Outer`, `Outer::Inner`, and `Outer::Inner2`.

The use of the name `Outer` as a parameter to `Inner::process` is bound to the enclosing class. That class is still incomplete when the declaration of `process` is seen, but the parameter is a reference, so this usage is okay.

The declaration of the data member `Inner::val` is an error. The type `Inner2` has not yet been seen.

The declarations in `Inner2` pose no problems—mostly they just use the built-in type `int`. The only exception is the `process` member function. Its parameter resolves to the incomplete type `Outer`. Because the parameter is a reference, the fact that `Outer` is an incomplete type doesn't matter.

The definitions of the constructor and `process` member are not processed by the compiler until the remaining declarations in the enclosing class have been seen. Completing the declarations of class `Outer` puts the declaration of the function `handle` in scope.

When the compiler looks up the names used in the definitions in class `Inner2`, all the names in class `Inner2` and class `Outer` are in scope. The use of `val`, which appears before the declaration of `val`, is okay: That reference is bound to the data member in class `Inner2`. Similarly, the use of `handle` from class `Outer` in the body of the `Inner2::process` member is okay. The entire `Outer` class is in scope when the members of class `Inner2` are compiled.

Using the Scope Operator to Control Name Lookup

The global version of `handle` can be accessed using the scope operator:

```
class Inner2 {
public:
    // ...
    //  ok: programmer explicitly specifies which handle to call
    void process(const Outer &out) { ::handle(out); }
};
```

EXERCISES SECTION 18.4.2

Exercise 18.32: Reimplement the `Queue` and `QueueItem` classes from Chapter 16 making `QueueItem` a nested class inside `Queue`.

Exercise 18.33: Explain the pros and cons of the original and the nested-class version of the `Queue` design.

18.5 Union: A Space-Saving Class

A **union** is a special kind of class. A `union` may have multiple data members, but at any point in time, only one of the members may have a value. When a value is assigned to one member of the `union`, all other members become undefined.

The amount of storage allocated for a union is at least as much as the amount necessary to contain its largest data member. Like any class, a union defines a new type.

Defining a Union

Unions offer a convenient way to represent a set of mutually exclusive values that may have different types. As an example, we might have a process that handles different kinds of numeric or character data. That process might define a union to hold these values:

```
//   objects of type TokenValue have a single member,
//   which could be of any of the listed types
union TokenValue {
    char    cval;
    int     ival;
    double dval;
};
```

A union is defined starting with the keyword union, followed by an (optional) name for the union and a set of member declarations enclosed in curly braces. This code defines a union named TokenValue that can hold a value that is either a char, an int, a pointer to char, or a double. Section 18.5 (p. 795) will look at what it means to omit the union name.

Like any class, a union type defines how much storage is associated with objects of its type. The size of each union object is fixed at compile time: It is at least as large as the size of the union's largest data member.

No Static, Reference, or Class Data Members

Some, but not all, class features apply equally to unions. For example, like any class, a union can specify protection labels to make members public, private, or protected. By default, unions behave like structs: Unless otherwise specified, the members of a union are public.

A union may also define member functions, including constructors and destructors. However, a union may not serve as a base class, so a member function may not be virtual.

A union cannot have a static data member or a member that is a reference. Moreover, unions cannot have a member of a class type that defines a constructor, destructor, or assignment operator:

```
union illegal_members {
    Screen s;        //  error: has constructor
    static int is;   //  error: static member
    int &rfi;         //  error: reference member
    Screen *ps;      //  ok: ordinary built-in pointer type
};
```

This restriction includes classes with members that have a constructor, destructor, or assignment operator.

Using a Union Type

The name of a union is a type name:

```
TokenValue first_token = {'a'};  // initialized TokenValue
TokenValue last_token;           // uninitialized TokenValue object
TokenValue *pt = new TokenValue; // pointer to a TokenValue object
```

Like other built-in types, by default unions are uninitialized. We can explicitly initialize a union in the same way that we can explicitly initialize (Section 12.4.5, p. 464) simple classes. However, we can provide an initializer only for the first member. The initializer must be enclosed in a pair of curly braces. The initialization of first_token gives a value to its cval member.

Using Members of a Union

The members of an object of union type are accessed using the normal member access operators (. and ->):

```
last_token.cval = 'z';
pt->ival = 42;
```

Giving a value to a data member of a union object makes the other data members undefined. When using a union, we must always *know* what type of value is currently stored in the union. Retrieving the value stored in the union through the wrong data member can lead to a crash or other incorrect program behavior.

> **Best Practices**
> The best way to avoid accessing the union value through the wrong member is to define a separate object that keeps track of what value is stored in the union. This additional object is referred to as the **discriminant** of the union.

Nested Unions

Most often unions are used as nested types, where the discriminant is a member of the enclosing class:

```
class Token {
public:
    // indicates which kind of value is in val
    enum TokenKind {INT, CHAR, DBL};
    TokenKind tok;
    union {              // unnamed union
        char   cval;
        int    ival;
        double dval;
    } val;               // member val is a union of the 3 listed types
};
```

In this class, the enumeration object tok serves to indicate which kind of value is stored in the val member. That member is an (unnamed) union that holds either a char, int, or double.

We often use a switch statement (Section 6.6, p. 199) to test the discriminant and then do processing dependent on which value is currently stored in the union:

```
Token token;
switch (token.tok) {
case Token::INT:
    token.val.ival = 42; break;
case Token::CHAR:
    token.val.cval = 'a'; break;
case Token::DBL:
    token.val.dval = 3.14; break;
}
```

Anonymous Unions

An unnamed union that is not used to define an object is referred to as an **anonymous union**. The names of the members of an anonymous union appear in the enclosing scope. For example, here is our Token class rewritten to use an anonymous union:

```
class Token {
public:
    //  indicates which kind of token value is in val
    enum TokenKind {INT, CHAR, DBL};
    TokenKind tok;
    union {                     //  anonymous union
        char    cval;
        int     ival;
        double dval;
    };
};
```

Because an anonymous union provides no way to access its members, the members are directly accessible as part of the scope where the anonymous union is defined. Rewriting our previous switch to use the anonymous-union version of our class would look like:

```
Token token;
switch (token.tok) {
case Token::INT:
    token.ival = 42; break;
case Token::CHAR:
    token.cval = 'a'; break;
case Token::DBL:
    token.dval = 3.14; break;
}
```

 An anonymous union cannot have private or protected members, nor can an anonymous union define member functions.

18.6   Local Classes

A class can be defined inside a function body. Such a class is called a **local class**. A local class defines a type that is visible only in the local scope in which it is defined. Unlike nested classes, the members of a local class are severely restricted.

 All members, including functions, of a local class must be completely defined inside the class body. As a result, local classes are much less useful than nested classes.

In practice, the requirement that members be fully defined within the class limits the complexity of the member functions of a local class. Functions in local classes are rarely more than a few lines of code. Beyond that, the code becomes difficult for the reader to understand.

Similarly, a local class is not permitted to declare `static` data members, there being no way to define them.

Local Classes May Not Use Variables from the Function's Scope

The names from the enclosing scope that a local class can access are limited. A local class can access only type names, `static` variables (Section 7.5.2, p. 255), and enumerators defined within the enclosing local scopes. A local class may not use the ordinary local variables of the function in which the class is defined:

```
int a, val;
void foo(int val)
{
    static int si;
    enum Loc { a = 1024, b };
    // Bar is local to foo
    class Bar {
    public:
        Loc locVal; //  ok: uses local type name
        int barVal;
        void fooBar(Loc l = a)    //  ok: default argument is Loc::a
        {
            barVal = val;      //  error: val is local to foo
            barVal = ::val;    //  ok: uses global object
            barVal = si;       //  ok: uses static local object
            locVal = b;        //  ok: uses enumerator
        }
    };
    // ...
}
```

Normal Protection Rules Apply to Local Classes

The enclosing function has no special access privileges to the private members of the local class. Of course, the local class could make the enclosing function a friend.

Best Practices In practice, `private` members are hardly ever necessary in a local class. Often all members of a local class are `public`.

The portion of a program that can access a local class is very limited. A local class is encapsulated within its local scope. Further encapsulation through information hiding is often overkill.

Name Lookup within a Local Class

Name lookup within the body of a local class happens in the same manner as for other classes. Names used in the declarations of the members of the class must be in scope before the use of the name. Names used in definitions of the members can appear anywhere in the scope of the local class. Names not resolved to class members are searched first in the enclosing local scope and then out to the scope enclosing the function itself.

Nested Local Classes

It is possible to nest a class inside a local class. In this case, the nested class definition can appear outside the local-class body. However, the nested class must be defined in the same local scope as that in which the local class is defined. As usual, the name of the nested class must be qualified by the name of the enclosing class and a declaration of the nested class must appear in the definition of the local class:

```
void foo()
{
    class Bar {
    public:
        // ...
        class Nested;      // declares class Nested
    };
    // definition of Nested
    class Bar::Nested {
        // ...
    };
}
```

A class nested in a local class is itself a local class, with all the attendant restrictions. All members of the nested class must be defined inside the body of the nested class itself.

18.7 Inherently Nonportable Features

One of the hallmarks of the C programming language is the ability to write low-level programs that can be readily moved from one machine to another. The process of moving a program to a new machine is referred to as "porting," so C programs are said to be **portable**.

To support low-level programming, C defines some features that are inherently nonportable. The fact that the size of the arithmetic types vary across machines

(Section 2.1, p. 34) is one such nonportable feature that we have already encountered. In this section we'll cover two additional nonportable features that C++ inherits from C: bit-fields and the `volatile` qualifier. These features make it easier to interface directly to hardware.

C++ adds another nonportable feature to those that it inherits from C: linkage directives, which make it possible to link to programs written in other languages.

18.7.1   Bit-fields

A special class data member, referred to as a **bit-field**, can be declared to hold a specified number of bits. Bit-fields are normally used when a program needs to pass binary data to another program or hardware device.

 The layout in memory of a bit-field is machine-dependent.

A bit-field must be an integral data type. It can be either `signed` or `unsigned`. We indicate that a member is a bit-field by following the member name with a colon and a constant expression specifying the number of bits:

```
typedef unsigned int Bit;

class File {
    Bit mode: 2;
    Bit modified: 1;
    Bit prot_owner: 3;
    Bit prot_group: 3;
    Bit prot_world: 3;
    // ...
};
```

The `mode` bit-field has two bits, `modified` only one, and the other members each have three bits. Bit-fields defined in consecutive order within the class body are, if possible, packed within adjacent bits of the same integer, thereby providing for storage compaction. For example, in the preceding declaration, the five bit-fields will be stored in the single `unsigned int` first associated with the bit-field `mode`. Whether and how the bits are packed into the integer is machine-dependent.

 Ordinarily it is best to make a bit-field an `unsigned` type. The behavior of bit-fields stored in a `signed` type is implementation-defined.

Using Bit-fields

A bit-field is accessed in much the same manner as the other data members of a class. For example, a bit-field that is a `private` member of its class can be accessed only from within the definitions of the member functions and friends of its class:

```
void File::write()
{
    modified = 1;
    // ...
}

void File::close()
{
    if (modified)
        // ... save contents
}
```

Bit-fields with more than one bit are usually manipulated using the built-in bitwise operators (Section 5.3, p. 154):

```
enum { READ = 01, WRITE = 02 }; // File modes

int main() {
    File myFile;

    myFile.mode |= READ;   // set the READ bit
    if (myFile.mode & READ) // if the READ bit is on
        cout << "myFile.mode READ is set\n";
}
```

Classes that define bit-field members also usually define a set of inline member functions to test and set the value of the bit-field. For example, the class `File` might define the members `isRead` and `isWrite`:

```
inline int File::isRead() { return mode & READ; }
inline int File::isWrite() { return mode & WRITE; }

if (myFile.isRead()) /* ... */
```

With these member functions, the bit-fields can now be declared as private members of class `File`.

The address-of operator (&) cannot be applied to a bit-field, so there can be no pointers referring to class bit-fields. Nor can a bit-field be a static member of its class.

18.7.2   `volatile` Qualifier

The precise meaning of `volatile` is inherently machine-dependent and can be understood only by reading the compiler documentation. Programs that use `volatile` usually must be changed when they are moved to new machines or compilers.

Programs that deal directly with hardware often have data elements whose value is controlled by processes outside the direct control of the program itself. For example, a program might contain a variable updated by the system clock.

An object should be declared **volatile** when its value might be changed in ways outside either the control or detection of the compiler. The volatile keyword is a directive to the compiler that it should not perform optimizations on such objects.

The volatile qualifier is used in much the same way as is the const qualifier. It is an additional modifier to a type:

```
volatile int display_register;
volatile Task *curr_task;
volatile int ixa[max_size];
volatile Screen bitmap_buf;
```

display_register is a volatile object of type int. curr_task is a pointer to a volatile Task object. ixa is a volatile array of integers. Each element of the array is considered to be volatile. bitmap_buf is a volatile Screen object. Each of its data members is considered to be volatile.

In the same way that a class may define const member functions, it can also define member functions as volatile. Only volatile member functions may be called on volatile objects.

Section 4.2.5 (p. 126) described the interactions between the const qualifier and pointers. The same interactions exist between the volatile qualifier and pointers. We can declare pointers that are volatile, pointers to volatile objects, and pointers that are volatile that point to volatile objects:

```
volatile int v;       //  v is a volatile int
int *volatile vip;    //  vip is a volatile pointer to int
volatile int *ivp;    //  ivp is a pointer to volatile int
//  vivp is a volatile pointer to volatile int
volatile int *volatile vivp;

int *ip = &v;    //  error: must use pointer to volatile
*ivp = &v;       //  ok: ivp is pointer to volatile
vivp = &v;       //  ok: vivp is volatile pointer to volatile
```

As with const, we may assign the address of a volatile object (or copy a pointer to a volatile type) only to a pointer to volatile. We may use a volatile object to initialize a reference only if the reference is volatile.

Synthesized Copy Control Does Not Apply to Volatile Objects

One important difference between the treatment of const and volatile is that the synthesized copy and assignment operators cannot be used to initialize or assign from a volatile object. The synthesized copy-control members take parameters that are const references to the class type. However, a volatile object cannot be passed to a plain or const reference.

If a class wants to allow volatile objects to be copied or to allow assignment from or to a volatile operand, it must define its own versions of the copy constructor and/or assignment operator:

```
class Foo {
public:
    Foo(const volatile Foo&);  // copy from a volatile object
```

```
    //  assign from a volatile object to a nonvolatile objet
    Foo& operator=(volatile const Foo&);
    //  assign from a volatile object to a volatile object
    Foo& operator=(volatile const Foo&) volatile;
    //  remainder of class Foo
};
```

By defining the parameter to the copy-control members as a const volatile reference, we can copy or assign from any kind of Foo: a plain Foo, a const Foo, a volatile Foo, or a const volatile Foo.

 Although we can define the copy-control members to handle volatile objects, a deeper question is whether it makes any sense to copy a volatile object. The answer to that question depends intimately on the reason for using volatile in any particular program.

18.7.3 Linkage Directives: extern "C"

C++ programs sometimes need to call functions written in another programming language. Most often, that other language is C. Like any name, the name of a function written in another language must be declared. That declaration must specify the return type and parameter list. The compiler checks calls to external-language functions in the same way that it handles ordinary C++ functions. However, the compiler typically must generate different code to call functions written in other languages. C++ uses **linkage directives** to indicate the language used for any non-C++ function.

Declaring a Non-C++ Function

A linkage directive can have one of two forms: single or compound. Linkage directives may not appear inside a class or function definition. The linkage directive must appear on the first declaration of a function.

As an example, let's look at some of the C functions declared in the cstdlib header. Declarations in that header might look something like

```
//  illustrative linkage directives that might appear in the C++ header <cstring>
//  single statement linkage directive
extern "C" size_t strlen(const char *);
//  compound statement linkage directive
extern "C" {
    int strcmp(const char*, const char*);
    char *strcat(char*, const char*);
}
```

The first form consists of the extern keyword followed by a string literal, followed by an "ordinary" function declaration. The string literal indicates the language in which the function is written.

We can give the same linkage to several functions at once by enclosing their declarations inside curly braces following the linkage directive. These braces serve to group the declarations to which the linkage directive applies. The braces are otherwise ignored, and the names of functions declared within the braces are visible as if the functions were declared outside the braces.

Linkage Directives and Header Files

The multiple-declaration form can be applied to an entire header file. For example, the C++ `cstring` header might look like

```
//  compound statement linkage directive
extern "C" {
#include <string.h>          //  C functions that manipulate C-style strings
}
```

When a `#include` directive is enclosed in the braces of a compound linkage directive, all ordinary function declarations in the header file are assumed to be functions written in the language of the linkage directive. Linkage directives can be nested, so if the header contained a function with a linkage directive the linkage of that function is unaffected.

The functions that C++ inherits from the C library are permitted to be defined as C functions but are not required to be C functions—it's up to each C++ implementation to decide whether to implement the C library functions in C or C++.

Exporting Our C++ Functions to Other Langauges

By using the linkage directive on a function definition, we can make a C++ function available to a program written in another language:

```
//  the calc function can be called from C programs
extern "C" double calc(double dparm) { /* ... */ }
```

When the compiler generates code for this function, it will generate code appropriate to the indicated language.

Every declaration of a function defined with a linkage directive must use the same linkage directive.

Languages Supported by Linkage Directives

A compiler is required to support linkage directives for C. A compiler may provide linkage specifications for other languages. For example, `extern "Ada"`, `extern "FORTRAN"`, and so on.

What languages are supported varies by compiler. You must consult the user's guide for further information on any non-C linkage specifications it may provide.

It can be useful sometimes to compile the same source file in both C or C++. The preprocessor name `__cplusplus` (two underscores) is automatically defined when compiling C++, so we can conditionally include code based on whether we are compiling C++.

```
#ifdef __cplusplus
// ok: we're compiling C++
extern "C"
#endif
int strcmp(const char*, const char*);
```

Overloaded Functions and Linkage Directives

The interaction between linkage directives and function overloading depends on the target language. If the language supports overloaded functions, then it is likely that a compiler that implements linkage directives for that language would also support overloading of these functions from C++.

The only language guaranteed to be supported by C++ is C. The C language does not support function overloading, so it should not be a surprise that a linkage directive can be specified only for one C function in a set of overloaded functions. It is an error to declare more than one function with C linkage with a given name:

```
// error: two extern "C" functions in set of overloaded functions
extern "C" void print(const char*);
extern "C" void print(int);
```

In C++ programs, it is fairly common to overload C functions. However, the other functions in the overload set must all be C++ functions:

```
class SmallInt { /* ... */ };
class BigNum { /* ... */ };
// the C function can be called from C and C++ programs
// the C++ functions overload that function and are callable from C++
extern "C" double calc(double);
extern SmallInt calc(const SmallInt&);
extern BigNum calc(const BigNum&);
```

The C version of `calc` can be called from C programs and from C++ programs. The additional functions are C++ functions with class parameters that can be called only from C++ programs. The order of the declarations is not significant.

Pointers to `extern "C"` Functions

The language in which a function is written is part of its type. To declare a pointer to a function written in another programming language, we must use a linkage directive:

```
// pf points to a C function returning void taking an int
extern "C" void (*pf)(int);
```

When `pf` is used to call a function, the function call is compiled assuming that the call is to a C function.

> A pointer to a C function does not have the same type as a pointer to a C++ function. A pointer to a C function cannot be initialized or be assigned to point to a C++ function (and vice versa).

When there is such a mismatch, a compile-time error message is issued:

```
void (*pf1)(int);                    // points to a C++ function
extern "C" void (*pf2)(int);   // points to a C function
pf1 = pf2; //  error: pf1 and pf2 have different types
```

> Some C++ compilers may accept the preceding assignment as a language extension, even though, strictly speaking, it is illegal.

Linkage Directives Apply to the Entire Declaration

When we use a linkage directive, it applies to the function and any function pointers used as the return type or as a parameter type:

```
//  f1 is a C function; its parameter is a pointer to a C function
extern "C" void f1(void(*)(int));
```

This declaration says that `f1` is a C function that doesn't return a value. It has one parameter, which is a pointer to a function that returns nothing and takes a single `int` parameter. The linkage directive applies to the function pointer as well as to `f1`. When we call `f1`, we must pass it the name of a C function or a pointer to a C function.

Because a linkage directive applies to all the functions in a declaration, we must use a typedef to pass a pointer to a C function to a C++ function:

```
//  FC is a pointer to C function
extern "C" typedef void FC(int);
//  f2 is a C++ function with a parameter that is a pointer to a C function
void f2(FC *);
```

EXERCISES SECTION 18.7.3

Exercise 18.34: Explain these declarations and indicate whether they are legal:

```
extern "C" int compute(int *, int);
extern "C" double compute(double *, double);
```

CHAPTER SUMMARY

C++ provides several specialized facilities that are tailored to particular kinds of problems.

Customized memory management is used by classes in two ways: A class may need to define its own internal memory allocation that allows it to streamline allocation of its own data members. A class might want to define its own, class-specific `operator new` and `operator delete` functions that will be used whenever new objects of the class type are allocated.

Some programs need to directly interrogate the dynamic type of an object at run time. Run-time type identification (RTTI) provides language level support for this kind of programming. RTTI applies only to classes that define virtual functions; type information for types that do not define virtual functions is available but reflects the static type.

Pointers to ordinary objects are typed. When we define a pointer to a class member, the pointer type must also encapsulate the type of the class to which the pointer points. A pointer to member may be bound to any member of the class that has the same type. When we dereference a pointer to member, an object from which to fetch the member must be specified.

C++ defines several additional aggregate types:

- Nested classes, which are classes defined in the scope of another class. Such classes are often defined as implementation classes of its enclosing class.

- Unions are a special kind of class that may contain only simple data members. An object of a `union` type may define a value for only one of its data members at any one time. Unions are most often nested inside another class type.

- Local classes, which are very simple classes defined local to a function. All members of a local class must be defined in the class body. There are no static data members of a local class.

C++ also supports several inherently nonportable features including bit-fields and `volatile`, which make it easier to interface to hardware, and linkage directives, which make it easier to interface to programs written in other langauges.

DEFINED TERMS

allocator class Standard library class that supports type-specific allocation of raw, unconstructed memory. The `allocator` class is a class template that defines member functions to `allocate`, `deallocate`, `construct`, and `destroy` objects of the allocator's template parameter type.

anonymous union Unnamed union that is not used to define an object. Members of the anonymous union are referred to directly. These unions may not have member functions and may not have private or protected members.

bit-field Class member with an signed or unsigned integral type that specifies the number of bits to allocate to the member. Bit-fields defined in consecutive order in the class are, if possible, compacted into a common integral value.

delete expression A `delete` expression destroys a dynamically allocated object of a specified type and frees the memory used by that object. A `delete[]` expression destroys the elements of a dynamically allocated array of a specified type and frees the memory used by the array. These expressions use the corresponding version of the library or class-specific `operator delete` functions to free raw memory that held the object or array.

discriminant Programming technique that uses an object to determine which actual type is held in a union at any given time.

dynamic_cast Operator that performs a checked cast from a base type to a derived type. The base type must define at least one `virtual` function. The operator checks the dynamic type of the object to which the reference or pointer is bound. If the object type is the same as the type of the cast (or a type derived from that type), then the cast is done. Otherwise, a zero pointer is returned for a pointer cast, or an exception is thrown for a cast of a reference.

freelist Memory management technique that involves preallocating unconstructed memory to hold objects that will be created as needed. When objects are freed, their memory is put back on the free list rather than being returned to the system.

linkage directive Mechanism used to allow functions written in a different language to be called from a C++ program. All compilers must support calling C and C++ functions. It is compiler-dependent whether any other languages are supported.

local class Class defined inside a function. A local class is visible only inside the function in which it is defined. All members of the class must be defined inside the class body. There can be no static members of a local class. Local class members may not

access the local variables defined in the enclosing function. They may use type names, static variables, or enumerators defined in the enclosing function.

member operators new and delete Class member functions that override the default memory allocation performed by the global library `operator new` and `operator delete` functions. Both object (`new`) and array (`new[]`) forms of these functions may be defined. The member `new` and `delete` functions are implicitly declared as `static`. These operators allocate (deallocate) memory. They are used automatically by `new` (`delete`) expressions, which handle object initialization and destruction.

nested class Class defined inside another class. A nested class is defined inside its enclosing scope: Nested-class names must be unique within the class scope in which they are defined but can be reused in scopes outside the enclosing class. Access to the nested class outside the enclosing class requires use of the scope operator to specify the scope(s) in which the class is nested.

nested type Synonym for nested class.

new expression A `new` expression allocates and constructs an object of a specified type. A `new[]` expression allocates and constructs an array of objects. These expressions use the corresponding version of the library `operator new` functions to allocate raw memory in which the expression constructs an object or array of the specified type.

operator delete A library function that frees untyped, unconstructed memory allocated by `operator new`. The library `operator delete[]` frees memory used to hold an array that was allocated by `operator new[]`.

operator new A library function that allocates untyped, unconstructed memory of a given size. The library function `operator new[]` allocates raw memory for arrays. These library functions provide a more primitive allocation mechanism than the library `allocator` class. Modern C++ programs should use the `allocator` classes rather than these library functions.

placement new expression The form of `new` that constructs its object in specified memory. It does no allocation; instead, it takes an argument that specifies where the object should be constructed. It is a lower-level analog of the behavior provided by the `construct` member of the `allocator` class.

pointer to member Pointer that encapsulates the class type as well as the member type to which the pointer points. The definition of a pointer to member must specify the class name as well as the type of the member(s) to which the pointer may point:

```
T C::*pmem = &C::member;
```

This statement defines `pmem` as a pointer that can point to members of the class named *C* that have type *T* and initializes it to point to the member in *C* named *member*. When the pointer is dereferenced, it must be bound to an object of or pointer to type *C*:

```
classobj.*pmem;
classptr->*pmem;
```

fetches *member* from the object *classobj* of the object pointed to by *classptr*.

portable Term used to describe a program that can be moved to a new machine with relatively little effort.

run-time type identification Term used to describe the language and library facilities that allow the dynamic type of a reference or pointer to be obtained at run time. The RTTI operators, `typeid` and `dynamic_cast`, provide the dynamic type only for references or pointers to class types with virtual functions. When applied to other types, the type returned is the static type of the reference or pointer.

typeid Unary operator that takes an expression and returns a reference to an object of the library type named `type_info` that describes the type of the expression. When the expression is an object of a type that has virtual functions, then the dynamic type of the expression is returned. If the type is a reference, pointer, or other type that does not define virtual functions, then the type returned is the static type of the reference, pointer, or object.

type_info Library type that describes a type. The `type_info` class is inherently machine-dependent, but any library must define `type_info` with members listed in Table 18.2 (p. 779). `type_info` objects may not be copied.

union Classlike aggregate type that may define multiple data members, only one of which can have a value at any one point. Members of a union must be simple types: They can be a built-in or compound type or a class type that does not define a constructor, destructor, or the assignment operator. Unions may have member functions, including constructors and destructors. A union may not serve as a base class.

volatile Type qualifier that signifies to the compiler that a variable might be changed outside the direct control of the program. It is a signal to the compiler that it may not perform certain optimizations.

APPENDIX A

THE LIBRARY

This appendix presents additional useful details about the library. We'll start by collecting in one place the names we used from the standard library. Table A.1 on the next page lists each name and the header that defines that name.

Chapter 11 covered the library algorithms. That chapter illustrated how some of the more common algorithms are used, and described the architecture that underlies the algorithms library. In this Appendix, we list all the algorithms, organized by the kinds of operations they perform.

We close by examining some additional IO library capabilities: format control, unformatted IO, and random access on files. Each IO type defines a collection of format states and associated functions to control those states. These format states give us finer control over how input and output works. The IO we've done has all been formatted—the input and output routines know about the types we use and format the data on input or output accordingly. There are also unformatted IO functions that deal with the stream at the char level, doing no interpretation of the data. In Chapter 8 we saw that the fstream type can read and write the same file. In this Appendix, we'll see how to do so.

A.1   Library Names and Headers

Our programs mostly did not show the actual #include directives needed to compile the program. As a convenience to our readers, Table A.1 lists the library names our programs used and the header in which they may be found.

Table A.1: Standard Library Names and Headers

Name	Header	Name	Header
abort	<cstdlib>	ios_base	<ios_base>
accumulate	<numeric>	isalpha	<cctype>
allocator	<memory>	islower	<cctype>
auto_ptr	<memory>	ispunct	<cctype>
back_inserter	<iterator>	isspace	<cctype>
bad_alloc	<new>	istream	<iostream>
bad_cast	<typeinfo>	istream_iterator	<iterator>
bind2nd	<functional>	istringstream	<sstream>
bitset	<bitset>	isupper	<cctype>
boolalpha	<iostream>	left	<iostream>
cerr	<iostream>	less_equal	<functional>
cin	<iostream>	list	<list>
copy	<algorithm>	logic_error	<stdexcept>
count	<algorithm>	lower_bound	<algorithm>
count_if	<algorithm>	make_pair	<utility>
cout	<iostream>	map	<map>
dec	<iostream>	max	<algorithm>
deque	<deque>	min	<algorithm>
endl	<iostream>	multimap	<map>
ends	<iostream>	multiset	<set>
equal_range	<algorithm>	negate	<functional>
exception	<exception>	noboolalpha	<iostream>
fill	<algorithm>	noshowbase	<iostream>
fill_n	<algorithm>	noshowpoint	<iostream>
find	<algorithm>	noskipws	<iostream>
find_end	<algorithm>	not1	<functional>
find_first_of	<algorithm>	nounitbuf	<iostream>
fixed	<iostream>	nouppercase	<iostream>
flush	<iostream>	nth_element	<algorithm>
for_each	<algorithm>	oct	<iostream>
front_inserter	<iterator>	ofstream	<fstream>
fstream	<fstream>	ostream	<iostream>
getline	<string>	ostream_iterator	<iterator>
hex	<iostream>	ostringstream	<sstream>
ifstream	<fstream>	out_of_range	<stdexcept>
inner_product	<numeric>	pair	<utility>
inserter	<iterator>	partial_sort	<algorithm>
internal	<iostream>	plus	<functional>

Table A.1: Standard Library Names and Headers (continued)

Name	Header	Name	Header
priority_queue	<queue>	sqrt	<cmath>
ptrdiff_t	<cstddef>	stable_sort	<algorithm>
queue	<queue>	stack	<stack>
range_error	<stdexcept>	strcmp	<cstring>
replace	<algorithm>	strcpy	<cstring>
replace_copy	<algorithm>	string	<string>
reverse_iterator	<iterator>	stringstream	<sstream>
right	<iostream>	strlen	<cstring>
runtime_error	<stdexcept>	strncpy	<cstring>
scientific	<iostream>	terminate	<exception>
set	<set>	tolower	<cctype>
set_difference	<algorithm>	toupper	<cctype>
set_intersection	<algorithm>	type_info	<typeinfo>
set_union	<algorithm>	unexpected	<exception>
setfill	<iomanip>	uninitialized_copy	<memory>
setprecision	<iomanip>	unitbuf	<iostream>
setw	<iomanip>	unique	<algorithm>
showbase	<iostream>	unique_copy	<algorithm>
showpoint	<iostream>	upper_bound	<algorithm>
size_t	<cstddef>	uppercase	<iostream>
skipws	<iostream>	vector	<vector>
sort	<algorithm>		

A.2   A Brief Tour of the Algorithms

Chapter 11 introduced the generic algorithms and outlined their underlying architecture. The library defines more than 100 algorithms. Learning to use them requires understanding their structure rather than memorizing the details of each algorithm. In this section we describe each of the algorithms. In it, we organize the algorithms by the type of action the algorithm performs.

A.2.1   Algorithms to Find an Object

The find and count algorithms search the input range for a specific value. find returns an iterator to an element; count returns the number of matching elements.

Simple Find Algorithms

These algorithms require input iterators. The find and count algorithms look for specific elements. The find algorithms return an iterator referring to the first matching element. The count algorithms return a count of how many times the element occurs in the input sequence.

`find(beg, end, val)`
`count(beg, end, val)`
Looks for element(s) in input range equal to `val`. Uses the equality (`==`) operator of the underlying type. `find` returns an iterator to the first matching element or end if no such element exists. `count` returns a count of how many times `val` occurs.

`find_if(beg, end, unaryPred)`
`count_if(beg, end, unaryPred)`
Looks for element(s) in input range for which `unaryPred` is true. The predicate must take a single parameter of the `value_type` of the input range and return a type that can be used as a condition.

f find returns an iterator to first element for which `unaryPred` is true, or end if no such element exists. `count` applies `unaryPred` to each element and returns the number of elements for which `unaryPred` was true.

Algorithms to Find One of Many Values

These algorithms require two pairs of forward iterators. They search for the first (or last) element in the first range that is equal to any element in the second range. The types of `beg1` and `end1` must match exactly, as must the types of `beg2` and `end2`.

There is no requirement that the types of `beg1` and `beg2` match exactly. However, it must be possible to compare the element types of the two sequences. So, for example, if the first sequence is a `list<string>`, then the second could be a `vector<char*>`.

Each algorithm is overloaded. By default, elements are tested using the `==` operator for the element type. Alternatively, we can specify a predicate that takes two parameters and returns a `bool` indicating whether the test between these two elements succeeds or fails.

`find_first_of(beg1, end1, beg2, end2)`
Returns an iterator to the first occurrence in the first range of any element from the second range. Returns `end1` if no match found.

`find_first_of(beg1, end1, beg2, end2, binaryPred)`
Uses `binaryPred` to compare elements from each sequence. Returns an iterator to the first element in the first range for which the `binaryPred` is true when applied to that element and an element from the second sequence. Returns `end1` if no such element exits.

`find_end(beg1, end1, beg2, end2)`
`find_end(beg1, end1, beg2, end2, binaryPred)`
Operates like `find_first_of`, except that it searches for the last occurrence of any element from the second sequence.

As an example, if the first sequence is 0,1,1,2,2,4,0,1 and the second sequence is 1,3,5,7,9, then `find_end` would return an iterator denoting the last element in the input range, and `find_first_of` would return an iterator to the second element—in this example, it returns the first 1 in the input sequence.

Algorithms to Find a Subsequence

These algorithms require forward iterators. They look for a subsequence rather than a single element. If the subsequence is found, an iterator is returned to the first element in the subsequence. If no subsequence is found, the `end` iterator from the input range is returned.

Each function is overloaded. By default, the equality (`==`) operator is used to compare elements; the second version allows the programmer to supply a predicate to test instead.

```
adjacent_find(beg, end)
adjacent_find(beg, end, binaryPred)
```
Returns an iterator to the first adjacent pair of duplicate elements. Returns `end` if there are no adjacent duplicate elements. In the first case, duplicates are found by using `==`. In the second, duplicates are those for which the `binaryPred` is true.

```
search(beg1, end1, beg2, end2)
search(beg1, end1, beg2, end2, binaryPred)
```
Returns an iterator to the first position in the input range at which the second range occurs as a subsequence. Returns `end1` if the subsequence is not found. The types of `beg1` and `beg2` may differ but must be compatible: It must be possible to compare elements in the two sequences.

```
search_n(beg, end, count, val)
search_n(beg, end, count, val, binaryPred)
```
Returns an iterator to the beginning of a subsequence of `count` equal elements. Returns `end` if no such subsequence exists. The first version looks for `count` occurrences of the given `value`; the second version `count` occurrences for which the `binaryPred` is true.

A.2.2 Other Read-Only Algorithms

These algorithms require input iterators for their first two arguments. The `equal` and `mismatch` algorithms also take an additional input iterator that denotes a second range. There must be at least as many elements in the second sequence as there are in the first. If there are more elements in the second, they are ignored. If there are fewer, it is an error and results in undefined run-time behavior.

As usual, the types of the iterators denoting the input range must match exactly. The type of `beg2` must be compatible with the type of `beg1`. That is, it must be possible to compare elements in both sequences.

The `equal` and `mismatch` functions are overloaded: One version uses the element equality operator (`==`) to test pairs of elements; the other uses a predicate.

```
for_each(beg, end, f)
```
Applies the function (or function object (Section 14.8, p. 530)) `f` to each element in its input range. The return value, if any, from `f` is ignored. The iterators are input iterators, so the elements may not be written by `f`. Typically, `for_each` is used with a function that has side effects. For example, `f` might print the values in the range.

```
mismatch(beg1, end1, beg2)
mismatch(beg1, end1, beg2, binaryPred)
```
Compares the elements in two sequences. Returns a pair of iterators denoting the first elements that do not match. If all the elements match, then the `pair` returned is end1, and an iterator into beg2 offset by the size of the first sequence.

```
equal(beg1, end1, beg2)
equal(beg1, end1, beg2, binaryPred)
```
Determines whether two sequences are equal. Returns `true` if each element in the input range equals the corresponding element in the sequence that begins at beg2.

For example, given the sequences meet and meat, a call to `mismatch` would return a `pair` containing iterators referring to the second e in the first sequence and to the element a in the second sequence. If, instead, the second sequence were meeting, and we called `equal`, then the `pair` returned would be end1 and an iterator denoting the element i in the second range.

A.2.3   Binary-Search Algorithms

Although these algorithms may be used with forward iterators, they offer specialized versions that are much faster when used with random-access iterators.

These algorithms perform a binary search, which means that the input sequence must be sorted. These algorithms behave similarly to the associative container members of the same name (Section 10.5.2, p. 377). The equal_range, lower_bound, and upper_bound algorithms return an iterator that refers to the positions in the container at which the given element could be inserted while still preserving the container's ordering. If the element is larger than any other in the container, then the iterator that is returned might be the off-the-end iterator.

Each algorithm provides two versions: The first uses the element type's less-than operator (<) to test elements; the second uses the specified comparison.

```
lower_bound(beg, end, val)
lower_bound(beg, end, val, comp)
```
Returns an iterator to the first position in which val can be inserted while preserving the ordering.

```
upper_bound(beg, end, val)
upper_bound(beg, end, val, comp)
```
Returns an iterator to the last position in which val can be inserted while preserving the ordering.

```
equal_range(beg, end, val)
equal_range(beg, end, val, comp)
```
Returns an iterator pair indicating the subrange in which val could be inserted while preserving the ordering.

```
binary_search(beg, end, val)
binary_search(beg, end, val, comp)
```
Returns a `bool` indicating whether the sequence contains an element that is equal to val. Two values x and y are considered equal if x < y and y < x both yield false.

A.2.4   Algorithms that Write Container Elements

Many algorithms write container elements. These algorithms can be distinguished both by the kinds of iterators on which they operate and by whether they write elements in the input range or write to a specified destination.

The simplest algorithms read elements in sequence, requiring only input iterators. Those that write back to the input sequence require forward iterators. Some read the sequence backward, thus requiring bidirectional iterators. Algorithms that write to a separate destination, as usual, assume the destination is large enough to hold the output.

Algorithms that Write but do Not Read Elements

These algorithms require an output iterator that denotes a destination. They take a second argument that specifies a count and write that number of elements to the destination.

```
fill_n(dest, cnt, val)
generate_n(dest, cnt, Gen)
```
Write cnt values to dest. The fill_n function writes cnt copies of the value val; generate_n evaluates the generator Gen() cnt times. A generator is a function (or function object (Section 14.8, p. 530)) that is expected to produce a different return value each time it is called.

Algorithms that Write Elements Using Input Iterators

Each of these operations reads an input sequence and writes to an output sequence denoted by dest. They require dest to be an output iterator, and the iterators denoting the input range must be input iterators. The caller is responsible for ensuring that dest can hold as many elements as necessary given the input sequence. These algorithms return dest incremented to denote one past the last element written.

```
copy(beg, end, dest)
```
Copies the input range to the sequence beginning at iterator dest.

```
transform(beg, end, dest, unaryOp)
transform(beg, end, beg2, dest, binaryOp)
```
Applies the specified operation to each element in the input range, writing the result to dest. The first version applies a unary operation to each element in the input range. The second applies a binary operation to pairs of elements. It takes the first argument to the binary operation from the sequence denoted by beg and end and takes the second argument from the sequence beginning at beg2. The programmer must ensure that the sequence beginning at beg2 has at least as many elements as are in the first sequence.

```
replace_copy(beg, end, dest, old_val, new_val)
replace_copy_if(beg, end, dest, unaryPred, new_val)
```
Copies each element to dest, replacing specified elements by the new_val. The first version replaces those elements that are == to old_val. The second version replaces those elements for which unaryPred is true.

```
merge(beg1, end1, beg2, end2, dest)
merge(beg1, end1, beg2, end2, dest, comp)
```
Both input sequences must be sorted. Writes a merged sequence to dest. The first
version compares elements using the < operator; the second version uses the given
comparison.

Algorithms that Write Elements Using Forward Iterators

These algorithms require forward iterators because they write elements in their
input sequence.

```
swap(elem1, elem2)
iter_swap(iter1, iter2)
```
Parameters to these functions are references, so the arguments must be writable.
Swaps the specified element or elements denoted by the given iterators.

```
swap_ranges(beg1, end1, beg2)
```
Swaps the elements in the input range with those in the second sequence beginning
at beg2. The ranges must not overlap. The programmer must ensure that the
sequence starting at beg2 is at least as large as the input sequence. Returns beg2
incremented to denote the element just after the last one swapped.

```
fill(beg, end, val)
generate(beg, end, Gen)
```
Assigns a new value to each element in the input sequence. fill assigns the value
val; generate executes Gen() to create new values.

```
replace(beg, end, old_val, new_val)
replace_if(beg, end, unaryPred, new_val)
```
Replace each matching element by new_val. The first version uses == to compare elements with old_val; the second version executes unaryPred on each
element, replacing those for which unaryPred is true.

Algorithms that Write Elements Using Bidirectional Iterators

These algorithms require the ability to go backward in the sequence, and so they
require bidirectional iterators.

```
copy_backward(beg, end, dest)
```
Copies elements in reverse order to the output iterator dest. Returns dest incremented to denote one past the last element copied.

```
inplace_merge(beg, mid, end)
inplace_merge(beg, mid, end, comp)
```
Merges two adjacent subsequences from the same sequence into a single, ordered
sequence: The subsequences from beg to mid and from mid to end are merged
into beg to end. First version uses < to compare elements; second version uses a
specified comparison. Returns void.

A.2.5   Partitioning and Sorting Algorithms

The sorting and partitioning algorithms provide various strategies for ordering the elements of a container.

A `partition` divides elements in the input range into two groups. The first group consists of those elements that satisfy the specified predicate; the second, those that do not. For example, we can partition elements in a container based on whether the elements are odd, or on whether a word begins with a capital letter, and so forth.

Each of the sorting and partitioning algorithms provides stable and unstable versions. A stable algorithm maintains the relative order of equal elements. For example, given the sequence

```
{ "pshew", "Honey", "tigger", "Pooh" }
```

a stable partition based on whether a word begins with a capital letter generates the sequence in which the relative order of the two word categories is maintained:

```
{ "Honey", "Pooh", "pshew", "tigger" }
```

The stable algorithms do more work and so may run more slowly and use more memory than the unstable counterparts.

Partitioning Algorithms

These algorithms require bidirectional iterators.

`stable_partition(beg, end, unaryPred)`
`partition(beg, end, unaryPred)`
Uses `unaryPred` to partition the input sequence. Elements for which `unaryPred` is true are put at the beginning of the sequence; those for which the predicate is false are at the end. Returns an iterator just past the last element for which `unaryPred` is true.

Sorting Algorithms

These algorithms require random-access iterators. Each of the sorting algorithms provides two overloaded versions. One version uses element operator < to compare elements; the other takes an extra parameter that specifies the comparison. These algorithms require random-access iterators. With one exception, these algorithms return `void`; `partial_sort_copy` returns an itertor into the destination.

The `partial_sort` and `nth_element` algorithms do only part of the job of sorting the sequence. They are often used to solve problems that might otherwise be handled by sorting the entire sequence. Because these operations do less work, they typically are faster than sorting the entire input range.

`sort(beg, end)`
`stable_sort(beg, end)`
`sort(beg, end, comp)`
`stable_sort(beg, end, comp)`
Sorts the entire range.

```
partial_sort(beg, mid, end)
partial_sort(beg, mid, end, comp)
```

Sorts a number of elements equal to mid - beg. That is, if mid - beg is equal to 42, then this function puts the lowest-valued elements in sorted order in the first 42 positions in the sequence. After `partial_sort` completes, the elements in the range from beg up to but not including mid are sorted. No element in the sorted range is larger than any element in the range after mid. The order among the unsorted elements is unspecified.

As an example, we might have a collection of race scores and want to know what the first-, second- and third-place scores are but don't care about the order of the other times. We might sort such a sequence as follows:

```
partial_sort(scores.begin(),
            scores.begin() + 3, scores.end());
```

```
partial_sort_copy(beg, end, destBeg, destEnd)
partial_sort_copy(beg, end, destBeg, destEnd, comp)
```

Sorts elements from the input range and puts as much of the sorted sequence as fits into the sequence denoted by the iterators `destBeg` and `destEnd`. If the destination range is the same size or has more elements than the input range, then the entire input range is sorted and stored starting at `destBeg`. If the destination size is smaller, then only as many sorted elements as will fit are copied.

Returns an iterator into the destination that refers just after the last element that was sorted. The returned iterator will be `destEnd` if that destination sequence is smaller or equal in size to the input range.

```
nth_element(beg, nth, end)
nth_element(beg, nth, end, comp)
```

The argument nth must be an iterator positioned on an element in the input sequence. After `nth_element`, the element denoted by that iterator has the value that would be there if the entire sequence were sorted. The elements in the container are also partitioned around nth: Those before nth are all smaller than or equal to the value denoted by nth, and the ones after it are greater than or equal to it. We might use `nth_element` to find the value closest to the median:

```
nth_element(scores.begin(),
        scores.begin() + scores.size()/2, scores.end());
```

A.2.6 General Reordering Operations

Several algorithms reorder the elements in a specified way. The first two, `remove` and `unique`, reorder the container so that the elements in the first part of the sequence meet some criteria. They return an iterator marking the end of this subsequence. Others, such as `reverse`, `rotate`, and `random_shuffle` rearrange the entire sequence.

These algorithms operate "in place;" they rearrange the elements in the input sequence itself. Three of the reordering algorithms offer "copying" versions. These algorithms, `remove_copy`, `rotate_copy`, and `unique_copy`, write the reordered sequence to a destination rather than rearranging elements directly.

Reordering Algorithms Using Forward Iterators

These algorithms reorder the input sequence. They require that the iterators be at least forward iterators.

`remove(beg, end, val)`
`remove_if(beg, end, unaryPred)`
"Removes" elements from the sequence by overwriting them with elements that are to be kept. The removed elements are those that are `==` to `val` or for which `unaryPred` is true. Returns an iterator just past the last element that was not removed.

For example, if the input sequence is `hello world` and `val` is `o`, then a call to `remove` will overwrite the two elements that are the letter `'o'` by shifting the sequence to the left twice. The new sequence will be `hell wrldld`. The returned iterator will denote the element after the first `d`.

`unique(beg, end)`
`unique(beg, end, binaryPred)`
"Removes" all but the first of each consecutive group of matching elements. Returns an iterator just past the last unique element. First version uses `==` to determine whether two elements are the same; second version uses the predicate to test adjacent elements.

For example, if the input sequence is `boohiss`, then after the call to `unique`, the first sequence will contain `bohiss`. The iterator returned will point to the element after the first `s`. The value of the remaining two elements in the sequence is unspecified.

`rotate(beg, mid, end)`
Rotates the elements around the element denoted by `mid`. The element at `mid` becomes the first element; those from `mid + 1` through `end` come next, followed by the range from `beg` to `mid`. Returns `void`.

For example, given the input sequence `hissboo`, if `mid` denotes the character `b`, then `rotate` would reorder the sequence as `boohiss`.

Reordering Algorithms Using Bidirectional Iterators

Because these algorithms process the input sequence backward, they requre bidirectional iterators.

`reverse(beg, end)`
`reverse_copy(beg, end, dest)`
Reverses the elements in the sequence. `reverse` operates in place; it writes the rearranged elements back into the input sequence. `reverse_copy` copies the elements in reverse order to the output iterator `dest`. As usual, the programmer must ensure that `dest` can be used safely. `reverse` returns `void`; `reverse_copy` returns an iterator just past the last element copied into the destination.

Reordering Algorithms Writing to Output Iterators

These algorithms require forward iterators for the input sequence and an output iterator for the destination.

Each of the preceding general reordering algorithms has an _copy version. These _copy versions perform the same reordering but write the reordered elements to a specified destination sequence rather than changing the input sequence. Except for `rotate_copy`, which requires forward iterators, the input range is specified by input iterators. The `dest` iterator must be an output iterator and, as usual, the programmer must guarantee that the destination can be written safely. The algorithms return the `dest` iterator incremented to denote one past the last element copied.

```
remove_copy(beg, end, dest, val)
remove_copy_if(beg, end, dest, unaryPred)
```
Copies elements except those matching `val` or for which `unaryPred` return true into `dest`.

```
unique_copy(beg, end, dest)
unique_copy(beg, end, dest, binaryPred)
```
Copies unique elements to `dest`.

```
rotate_copy(beg, mid, end, dest)
```
Like rotate except that it leaves its input sequence unchanged and writes the rotated sequence to `dest`. Returns `void`.

Reordering Algorithms Using Random-Access Iterators

Because these algorithms rearrange the elements in a random order, they require random-access iterators.

```
random_shuffle(beg, end)
random_shuffle(beg, end, rand)
```
Shuffles the elements in the input sequence. The second version takes a random-number generator. That function must take and return a value of the iterator's `difference_type`. Both versions return `void`.

A.2.7 Permutation Algorithms

Consider the following sequence of three characters: abc. There are six possible permutations on this sequence: abc, acb, bac, bca, cab, and cba. These permutations are listed in lexicographical order based on the less-than operator. That is, abc is the first permutation because its first element is less than or equal to the first element in every other permutation, and its second element is smaller than any permutation sharing the same first element. Similarly, acb is the next permutation because it begins with a, which is smaller than the first element in any remaining permutation. Those permutations that begin with b come before those that begin with c.

For any given permutation, we can say which permutation comes before it and which after it. Given the permutation bca, we can say that its previous permutation is bac and that its next permutation is cab. There is no previous permutation of the sequence abc, nor is there a next permutation of cba.

The library provides two permutation algorithms that generate the permutations of a sequence in lexicographical order. These algorithms reorder the sequence to hold the (lexicographically) next or previous permutation of the given sequence. They return a `bool` that indicates whether there was a next or previous permutation.

The algorithms each have two versions: One uses the element type < operator, and the other takes an extra argument that specifies a comparison to use to compare the elements. These algorithms assume that the elements in the sequence are unique. That is, the algorithms assume that no two elements in the sequence have the same value.

Permutation Algorithms Require Bidirectional Iterators

To produce the permutation, the sequence must be processed both forward and backward, thus requiring bidirectional iterators.

```
next_permutation(beg, end)
next_permutation(beg, end, comp)
```
If the sequence is already in the last permutation, then `next_permutation` reorders the sequence to be the lowest permutation and returns `false`. Otherwise, it transforms the input sequence into the next permutation, which is the lexicographically next ordered sequence and returns `true`. The first version uses the element < operator to compare elements; the second version uses specified comparison.

```
prev_permutation(beg, end)
prev_permutation(beg, end, comp)
```
Like `next_permutation`, but transforms the sequence to form the previous permutation. If this is the smallest permutation, then it reorders the sequence to be the largest permutation and returns `false`.

A.2.8   Set Algorithms for Sorted Sequences

The set algorithms implement general set operations on a sequence that is in sorted order.

These algorithms are distinct from the library `set` container and should not be confused with operations on `set`s. Instead, these algorithms provide setlike behavior on an ordinary sequential container (`vector`, `list`, etc.) or other sequence, such as an input stream.

With the exception of `includes`, they also take an output iterator. As usual, the programmer must ensure that the destination is large enough to hold the generated sequence. These algorithms return their `dest` iterator incremented to denote the element just after the last one that was written to `dest`.

Each algorithm provides two forms: The first uses the < operator for the element type to compare elements in the two input sequences. The second takes a comparison, which is used to compare the elements.

Set Algorithms Require Input Iterators

These algorithms process elements sequentially, requiring input iterators.

```
includes(beg, end, beg2, end2)
includes(beg, end, beg2, end2, comp)
```
Returns `true` if every element in the second sequence is contained in the input sequence. Returns `false` otherwise.

```
set_union(beg, end, beg2, end2, dest)
set_union(beg, end, beg2, end2, dest, comp)
```
Creates a sorted sequence of the elements that are in either sequence. Elements that are in both sequences occur in the output sequence only once. Stores the sequence in `dest`.

```
set_intersection(beg, end, beg2, end2, dest)
set_intersection(beg, end, beg2, end2, dest, comp)
```
Creates a sorted sequence of elements present in both sequences. Stores the sequence in `dest`.

```
set_difference(beg, end, beg2, end2, dest)
set_difference(beg, end, beg2, end2, dest, comp)
```
Creates a sorted sequence of elements present in the first container but not in the second.

```
set_symmetric_difference(beg, end, beg2, end2, dest)
set_symmetric_difference(beg, end, beg2, end2, dest, comp)
```
Creates a sorted sequence of elements present in either container but not in both.

A.2.9 Minimum and Maximum Values

The first group of these algorithms are unique in the library in that they operate on values rather than sequences. The second set takes a sequence that is denoted by input iterators.

```
min(val1, val2)
min(val1, val2, comp)
max(val1, val2)
max(val1, val2, comp)
```
Returns the minimum/maximum of `val1` and `val2`. The arguments must have exactly the same type as each other. Uses either < operator for the element type or the specified comparison. Arguments and the return type are both `const` references, meaning that objects are not copied.

```
min_element(beg, end)
min_element(beg, end, comp)
max_element(beg, end)
max_element(beg, end, comp)
```
Returns an iterator referring to the smallest/largest element in the input sequence. Uses either < operator for the element type or the specified comparison.

Lexicographical Comparison

Lexicographical comparison examines corresponding elements in two sequences and determines the comparison based on the first unequal pair of elements. Because the algorithms process elements sequentially, they require input iterators. If one sequence is shorter than the other and all its elements match the corresponding elements in the longer sequence, then the shorter sequence is lexicographically smaller. If the sequences are the same size and the corresponding elements match, then neither is lexicographically less than the other.

```
lexicographical_compare(beg1, end1, beg2, end2)
lexicographical_compare(beg1, end1, beg2, end2, comp)
```
Does an element by element comparison of the elements in the two sequences. Returns `true` if the first sequence is lexicographically less than the second sequence. Otherwise, returns `false`. Uses either < operator for the element type or the specified comparison.

A.2.10 Numeric Algorithms

Numeric algorithms require input iterators; if the algorithm writes output, it uses an output iterator for the destination

These functions perform simple arithmetic manipulations of their input sequence. To use the numeric algorithms, the `numeric` header must be included.

```
accumulate(beg, end, init)
accumulate(beg, end, init, BinaryOp)
```
Returns the sum of all the values in the input range. The summation starts with the initial value specified by `init`. The return type is the same type as the type of `init`.

Given the sequence `1,1,2,3,5,8` and an initial value of 0, the result is 20. The first version applies the + operator for the element type; second version applies the specified binary operation.

```
inner_product(beg1, end1, beg2, init)
inner_product(beg1, end1, beg2, init, BinOp1, BinOp2)
```
Returns the sum of the elements generated as the product of two sequences. The two sequences are examined in step, and the elements from each sequence are multiplied. The product of that multiplication is summed. The initial value of the sum is specified by `init`. The second sequence beginning at `beg2` is assumed to have at least as many elements as are in the first sequence; any elements in the second sequence beyond the size of the first sequence are ignored. The type of `init` determines the return type.

The first version uses the element's multiplication (*) and addition (+) operators: Given the two sequences `2,3,5,8` and `1,2,3,4,5,6,7`, the result is the sum of the initial value plus the following product pairs:

```
initial_value + (2 * 1) + (3 * 2) + (5 * 3) + (8 * 4)
```

If we provide an initial value of 0, then the result is 55.

The second version applies the specified binary operations, using the first operation in place of addition and the second in place of multiplication. As an example, we might use `inner_product` to produce a list of parenthesized name–value pairs of elements, where the name is taken from the first input sequence and the corresponding value is in the second:

```
//  combine elements into a parenthesized, comma-separated pair
string combine(string x, string y)
{
    return "(" + x + ", " + y + ")";
}
//  add two strings, each separated by a comma
string concatenate(string x, string y)
{
    if (x.empty())
        return y;
    return x + ", " + y;
}

    cout << inner_product(names.begin(), names.end(),
                          values.begin(), string(),
                          concatenate, combine);
```

If the first sequence contains `if`, `string`, and `sort`, and the second contains `keyword`, `library type`, and `algorithm`, then the output would be

    (if, keyword), (string, library type), (sort, algorithm)

partial_sum(beg, end, dest)
partial_sum(beg, end, dest, BinaryOp)

Writes a new sequence to `dest` in which the value of each new element represents the sum of all the previous elements up to and including its position within the input range. The first version uses the + operator for the element type; the second version applies the specified binary operation. The programmer must ensure that `dest` is at least as large as the input sequence. Returns the `dest` iterator incremented to refer just after the last element written.

Given the input sequence 0,1,1,2,3,5,8, the destination sequence will be 0,1,2,4,7,12,20. The fourth element, for example, is the partial sum of the three previous values (0,1,1) plus its own (2), yielding a value of 4.

adjacent_difference(beg, end, dest)
adjacent_difference(beg, end, dest, BinaryOp)

Writes a new sequence to `dest` in which the value of each new element other than the first represents the difference of the current and previous element. The first version uses the element type's - operation; the second version applies the specified binary operation. The programmer must ensure that `dest` is at least as large as the input sequence.

Given the sequence 0,1,1,2,3,5,8, the first element of the new sequence is a copy of the first element of the original sequence: 0. The second element is the difference between the first two elements: 1. The third element is the difference between the second and third element, which is 0, and so on. The new sequence is 0,1,0,1,1,2,3.

A.3   The IO Library Revisited

In Chapter 8 we introduced the basic architecture and most commonly used parts of the IO library. This Appendix completes our coverage of the IO library.

A.3.1   Format State

In addition to a condition state (Section 8.2, p. 287), each `iostream` object also maintains a format state that controls the details of how IO is formatted. The format state controls aspects of formatting such as the notational base for an integral value, the precision of a floating-point value, the width of an output element, and so on. The library also defines a set of manipulators (listed in Tables A.2 (p. 829) and A.3 (p. 833) for modifying the format state of an object. Simply speaking, a manipulator is a function or object that can be used as an operand to an input or output operator. A manipulator returns the stream object to which it is applied, so we can output multiple manipulators and data in a single statement.

When we read or write a manipulator, no data are read or written. Instead, an action is taken. Our programs have already used one manipulator, `endl`, which we "write" to an output stream as if it were a value. But `endl` isn't a value; instead, it performs an operation: It writes a newline and flushes the buffer.

A.3.2   Many Manipulators Change the Format State

Many manipulators change the format state of the stream. They change the format of how floating-pointer numbers are printed or whether a `bool` is displayed as a numeric value or using the `bool` literals, `true` or `false`, and so forth.

> Manipulators that change the format state of the stream usually leave the format state changed for all subsequent IO.

Most of the manipulators that change the format state provide set/unset pairs; one manipulator sets the format state to a new value and the other unsets it, restoring the normal default formatting.

The fact that a manipulator makes a persistent change to the format state can be useful when we have a set of IO operations that want to use the same formatting. Indeed, some programs take advantage of this aspect of manipulators to reset the behavior of one or more formatting rules for all its input or output. In such cases, the fact that a manipulator changes the stream is a desirable property.

However, many programs (and, more importantly, programmers) expect the state of the stream to match the normal library defaults. In these cases, leaving the state of the stream in a nonstandard state can lead to errors.

> It is usually best to undo any state change made by a manipulator. Ordinarily, a stream should be in its ordinary, default state after every IO operation.

Using `flags` Operation to Restore the Format State

An even better approach to managing changes to format state uses the `flags` operations. The `flags` operations are similar to the `rdstate` and `setstate` operations that manage the condition state of the stream. In this case, the library defines a pair of `flags` functions:

- `flags()` with no arguments returns the stream's current format state. The value returned is a library defined type named `fmtflags`.

- `flags(arg)` takes a `fmtflags` argument and sets the stream's format as indicated by the argument.

We can use these functions to remember and restore the format state of either an input or output stream:

```
void display(ostream& os)
{
    //  remember the current format state
    ostream::fmtflags curr_fmt = os.flags();
    //  do output that uses manipulators that change the format state of os
    os.flags(curr_fmt);     //  restore the original format state of os
}
```

A.3.3   Controlling Output Formats

Many of the manipulators allow us to change the appearance of our output. There are two broad categories of output control: controlling the presentation of numeric values and controlling the amount and placment of padding.

Controlling the Format of Boolean Values

One example of a manipulator that changes the formatting state of its object is the `boolalpha` manipulator. By default, `bool` values print as 1 or 0. A `true` value is written as the integer 1 and a `false` value as 0. We can override this formatting by applying the `boolalpha` manipulator to the stream:

```
cout << "default bool values: "
     << true << " " << false
     << "\nalpha bool values: "
     << boolalpha
     << true << " " << false
     << endl;
```

When executed, the program generates the following:

```
default bool values: 1 0
alpha bool values: true false
```

Once we "write" `boolalpha` on `cout`, we've changed how `cout` will print `bool` values from this point on. Subsequent operations that print `bool`s will print them as either `true` or `false`.

To undo the format state change to cout, we must apply noboolalpha:

```
bool bool_val;
cout << boolalpha      // sets internal state of cout
     << bool_val
     << noboolalpha; // resets internal state to default formatting
```

Now we change the formatting of bool values only to print of bool_val and immediately reset the stream back to its initial state.

Specifying the Base for Integral Values

By default, integral values are written and read in decimal notation. The programmer can change the notational base to octal or hexadecimal or back to decimal (the representation of floating-point values is unaffected) by using the manipulators hex, oct, and dec:

```
const int ival = 15, jval = 1024;  // const, so values never change
cout << "default: ival = " << ival
     << " jval = " << jval << endl;
cout << "printed in octal: ival = " << oct << ival
     << " jval = " << jval << endl;
cout << "printed in hexadecimal: ival = " << hex << ival
     << " jval = " << jval << endl;
cout << "printed in decimal: ival = " << dec << ival
     << " jval = " << jval << endl;
```

When compiled and executed, the program generates the following output:

```
default: ival = 15 jval = 1024
printed in octal: ival = 17 jval = 2000
printed in hexadecimal: ival = f jval = 400
printed in decimal: ival = 15 jval = 1024
```

Notice that like boolalpha, these manipulators change the format state. They affect the immediately following output, and all subsequent integral output, until the format is reset by invoking another manipulator.

Indicating Base on the Output

By default, when we print numbers, there is no visual cue as to what notational base was used. Is 20, for example, really 20, or an octal representation of 16? When printing numbers in decimal mode, the number is printed as we expect. If we need to print octal or hexadecimal values, it is likely that we should also use the showbase manipulator. The showbase manipulator causes the output stream to use the same conventions as used for specifying the base of an integral constant:

- A leading 0x indicates hexadecimal

- A leading 0 indicates octal

- The absence of either indicates decimal

Here is the program revised to use `showbase`:

```
const int ival = 15, jval = 1024;   // const so values never change
cout << showbase;     // show base when printing integral values
cout << "default: ival = " << ival
     << " jval = " << jval << endl;
cout << "printed in octal: ival = " << oct << ival
     << " jval = " << jval << endl;
cout << "printed in hexadecimal: ival = " << hex << ival
     << " jval = " << jval << endl;
cout << "printed in decimal: ival = " << dec << ival
     << " jval = " << jval << endl;
cout << noshowbase;   // reset state of the stream
```

The revised output makes it clear what the underlying value really is:

```
default: ival = 15 jval = 1024
printed in octal: ival = 017 jval = 02000
printed in hexadecimal: ival = 0xf jval = 0x400
printed in decimal: ival = 15 jval = 1024
```

The `noshowbase` manipulator resets `cout` so that it no longer displays the notational base of integral values.

By default, hexadecimal values are printed in lowercase with a lowercase x. We could display the X and the hex digits a—f as uppercase by applying the `uppercase` manipulator.

```
cout << uppercase << showbase << hex
     << "printed in hexadecimal: ival = " << ival
     << " jval = " << jval << endl
     << nouppercase << endl;
```

The preceding program generates the following output:

```
printed in hexadecimal: ival = 0XF jval = 0X400
```

To revert back to the lowercase x, we apply the `nouppercase` manipulator.

Controlling the Format of Floating-Point Values

There are three aspects of formatting floating-point values that we can control:

- Precision: how many digits are printed

- Notation: whether to print in decimal or scientific notation

- Handling of the decimal point for floating-point values that are whole numbers

By default, floating-point values are printed using six digits of precision. If the value has no fractional part, then the decimal point is omitted. Whether the number is printed using decimal or scientific notation depends on the value of the floating-point number being printed. The library chooses a format that enhances readability of the number. Very large and very small values are printed using scientific notation. Other values use fixed decimal.

Specifying How Much Precision to Print

By default, precision controls the total number of digits that are printed. When printed, floating-point values are rounded, not truncated, to the current precision. Thus, if the current precision is four, then 3.14159 becomes 3.142; if the precision is three, then it is printed as 3.14.

We can change the precision through a member function named precision or by using the setprecision manipulator. The precision member is overloaded (Section 7.8, p. 265): One version takes an int value and sets the precision to that new value. It returns the *previous* precision value. The other version takes no arguments and returns the current precision value. The setprecision manipulator takes an argument, which it uses to set the precision.

Table A.2: Manipulators Defined in iostream		
	boolalpha	Display true and false as strings
x	noboolalpha	Display true and false as 0, 1
	showbase	Generate prefix indicating numeric base
x	noshowbase	Do not generate notational base prefix
	showpoint	Always display decimal point
x	noshowpoint	Only display decimal point if fraction
	showpos	Display + in nonnegative numbers
x	noshowpos	Do not display + in nonnegative numbers
	uppercase	Print 0X in hexadecimal, E in scientific
x	nouppercase	Print 0x in hexadecimal, e in scientific
x	dec	Display in decimal numeric base
	hex	Display in hexadecimal numeric base
	oct	Display in octal numeric base
	left	Add fill characters to right of value
	right	Add fill characters to left of value
	internal	Add fill characters between sign and value
	fixed	Display floating-point in decimal notation
	scientific	Display floating-point in scientific notation
	flush	Flush ostream buffer
	ends	Insert null, then flush ostream buffer
	endl	Insert newline, then flush ostream buffer
	unitbuf	Flush buffers after every output operation
x	nounitbuf	Restore normal buffer flushing
x	skipws	Skip whitespace with input operators
	noskipws	Do not skip whitespace with input operators
	ws	"Eat" whitespace

x *indicates default stream state*

The following program illustrates the different ways we can control the precision use when printing floating point values:

```
//  cout.precision reports current precision value
cout  << "Precision: " << cout.precision()
      << ", Value: "   << sqrt(2.0) << endl;
//  cout.precision(12) asks that 12 digits of precision to be printed
cout.precision(12);
cout << "Precision: " << cout.precision()
     << ", Value: "   << sqrt(2.0) << endl;
//  alternative way to set precision using setprecision manipulator
cout << setprecision(3);
cout << "Precision: " << cout.precision()
     << ", Value: "   << sqrt(2.0) << endl;
```

When compiled and executed, the program generates the following output:

```
Precision: 6, Value: 1.41421
Precision: 12, Value: 1.41421356237
Precision: 3, Value: 1.41
```

This program calls the library `sqrt` function, which is found in the `cmath` header. The `sqrt` function is overloaded and can be called on either a `float`, `double`, or `long double` argument. It returns the square root of its argument.

The `setprecision` manipulators and other manipulators that take arguments are defined in the `iomanip` header.

Controlling the Notation

By default, the notation used to print floating-point values depends on the size of the number: If the number is either very large or very small, it will be printed in scientific notation; otherwise, fixed decimal is used. The library chooses the notation that makes the number easiest to read.

When printing a floating-point number as a plain number (as opposed to printing money, or a percentage, where we want to control the appearance of the value), it is usually best to let the library choose the notation to use. The one time to force either scientific or fixed decimal is when printing a table in which the decimal points should line up.

If we want to force either scientific or fixed notation, we can do so by using the appropriate manipulator: The `scientific` manipulator changes the stream to use scientific notation. As with printing the x on hexadecimal integral values, we can also control the case of the e in scientific mode through the `uppercase` manipulator. The `fixed` manipulator changes the stream to use fixed decimal.

These manipulators change the default meaning of the precision for the stream. After executing either `scientific` or `fixed`, the precision value controls the

number of digits after the decimal point. By default, precision specifies the total number of digits—both before and after the decimal point. Using `fixed` or
`scientific` lets us print numbers lined up in columns. This strategy ensures
that the decimal point is always in a fixed position relative to the fractional part
being printed.

Reverting to Default Notation for Floating-Point Values

Unlike the other manipulators, there is no manipulator to return the stream to
its default state in which it chooses a notation based on the value being printed.
Instead, we must call the `unsetf` member to undo the change made by either
`scientific` or `fixed`. To return the stream to default handling of float values
we pass `unsetf` function a library-defined value named `floatfield`:

```
//   reset to default handling for notation
cout.unsetf(ostream::floatfield);
```

Except for undoing their effect, using these manipulators is like using any other
manipulator:

```
cout << sqrt(2.0) << '\n' << endl;
cout << "scientific: " << scientific << sqrt(2.0) << '\n'
     << "fixed decimal: " << fixed << sqrt(2.0) << "\n\n";
cout << uppercase
     << "scientific: " << scientific << sqrt(2.0) << '\n'
     << "fixed decimal: " << fixed << sqrt(2.0) << endl
     << nouppercase;
//   reset to default handling for notation
cout.unsetf(ostream::floatfield);
cout << '\n' << sqrt(2.0) << endl;
```

produces the following output:

```
1.41421

scientific: 1.414214e+00
fixed decimal: 1.414214

scientific: 1.414214E+00
fixed decimal: 1.414214

1.41421
```

Printing the Decimal Point

By default, when the fractional part of a floating-point value is 0, the decimal
point is not displayed. The `showpoint` manipulator forces the decimal point to
be printed:

```
cout << 10.0 << endl;            // prints 10
cout << showpoint << 10.0        // prints 10.0000
     << noshowpoint << endl;     // revert to default handling of decimal point
```

The `noshowpoint` manipulator reinstates the default behavior. The next output expression will have the default behavior, which is to suppress the decimal point if the floating-point value has a 0 fractional part.

Padding the Output

When printing data in columns, we often want fairly fine control over how the data are formatted. The library provides several manipulators to help us accomplish the control we might need:

- `setw` to specify the minimum space for the *next* numeric or string value.

- `left` to left-justify the output.

- `right` to right-justfiy the output. Output is right-justified by default.

- `internal` controls placement of the sign on negative values. `internal` left-justifies the sign and right-justifies the value, padding any intervening space with blanks.

- `setfill` lets us specify an alternative character to use when padding the output. By default, the value is a space.

> `setw`, like `endl`, does not change the internal state of the output stream. It determines the size of only the *next* output.

The following program illustrates these manipulators

```
int i = -16;
double d = 3.14159;
//  pad first column to use minimum of 12 positions in the output
cout << "i: " << setw(12) << i << "next col" << '\n'
     << "d: " << setw(12) << d << "next col" << '\n';
//  pad first column and left-justify all columns
cout << left
     << "i: " << setw(12) << i << "next col" << '\n'
     << "d: " << setw(12) << d << "next col" << '\n'
     << right;                // restore normal justification
//  pad first column and right-justify all columns
cout << right
     << "i: " << setw(12) << i << "next col" << '\n'
     << "d: " << setw(12) << d << "next col" << '\n';
//  pad first column but put the padding internal to the field
cout << internal
     << "i: " << setw(12) << i << "next col" << '\n'
     << "d: " << setw(12) << d << "next col" << '\n';
//  pad first column, using # as the pad character
cout << setfill('#')
     << "i: " << setw(12) << i << "next col" << '\n'
     << "d: " << setw(12) << d << "next col" << '\n'
     << setfill(' ');     // restore normal pad character
```

When executed, this program generates

```
i:            -16next col
d:        3.14159next col
i: -16           next col
d: 3.14159       next col
i:            -16next col
d:        3.14159next col
i: -             16next col
d:        3.14159next col
i: -#########16next col
d: #####3.14159next col
```

Table A.3: Manipulators Defined in `iomanip`	
`setfill(ch)`	Fill whitespace with `ch`
`setprecision(n)`	Set floating-point precision to n
`setw(w)`	Read or write value to w characters
`setbase(b)`	Output integers in base b

A.3.4 Controlling Input Formatting

By default, the input operators ignore whitespace (blank, tab, newline, formfeed, and carriage return). The following loop

```
while (cin >> ch)
    cout << ch;
```

given the input sequence

```
a b    c
d
```

executes four times to read the characters a through d, skipping the intervening blanks, possible tabs, and newline characters. The output from this program is

```
abcd
```

The `noskipws` manipulator causes the input operator to read, rather than skip, whitespace. To return to the default behavior, we apply `skipws` manipulator:

```
cin >> noskipws;        // set cin so that it reads whitespace
while (cin >> ch)
        cout << ch;
cin >> skipws;          // reset cin to default state so that it discards whitespace
```

Given the same input as before, this loop makes seven iterations, reading whitespace as well as the characters in the input. This loop generates

```
a b    c
d
```

A.3.5 Unformatted Input/Output Operations

So far, our programs have used only formatted IO operations. The input and output operators (<< and >>) format the data they read or write according to the data type being handled. The input operators ignore whitespace; the output operators apply padding, precision, and so on.

The library also provides a rich set of low-level operations that support unformatted IO. These operations let us deal with a stream as a sequence of uninterpreted bytes rather than as a sequence of data types, such as char, int, string, and so on.

A.3.6 Single-Byte Operations

Several of the unformatted operations deal with a stream one byte at a time. They read rather than ignore whitespace. For example, we could use the unformatted IO operations get and put to read the characters one at a time:

```
char ch;
while (cin.get(ch))
        cout.put(ch);
```

This program preserves the whitespace in the input. Its output is identical to the input. Given the same input as read by the previous program that used noskipws, this program generates the same output:

```
a b    c
d
```

Table A.4: Single-Byte Low-Level IO Operations	
is.get(ch)	Puts next byte from the istream is in character ch. Returns is.
os.put(ch)	Puts character ch onto the ostream os. Returns os.
is.get()	Returns next byte from is as an int.
is.putback(ch)	Puts character ch back on is; returns is.
is.unget()	Moves is back one byte; returns is.
is.peek()	Returns the next byte as an int but doesn't remove it.

Putting Back onto an Input Stream

Sometimes we need to read a character in order to know that we aren't ready for it yet. In such cases, we'd like to put the character back onto the stream. The library gives us three ways to do so, each of which has subtle differences from the others:

- peek returns a copy of the next character on the input stream but does not change the stream. The value returned by peek stays on the stream and will be the next one retrieved.

- unget backs up the input stream so that whatever value was last returned is still on the stream. We can call unget even if we do not know what value was last taken from the stream.

- putback is a more specialized version of unget: It returns the last value read from the stream but takes an argument that must be the same as the one that was last read. Few programs use putback because the simpler unget does the same job with fewer constraints.

In general, we are guaranteed to be able to put back at most one value before the next read. That is, we are not guaranteed to be able to call putback or unget successively without an intervening read operation.

int Return Values from Input Operations

The version of get that takes no argument and the peek function return a character from the input stream as an int. This fact can be surprising; it might seem more natural to have these functions return a char.

The reason that these functions return an int is to allow them to return an end-of-file marker. A given character set is allowed to use every value in the char range to represent an actual character. Thus, there is no extra value in that range to use to represent end-of-file.

Instead, these functions convert the character to unsigned char and then promote that value to int. As a result, even if the character set has characters that map to negative values, the int returned from these operations will be a positive value (Section 2.1.1, p. 36). By returning end-of-file as a negative value, the library guarantees that end-of-file will be distinct from any legitimate character value. Rather than requiring us to know the actual value returned, the iostream header defines a const named EOF that we can use to test if the value returned from get is end-of-file. It is essential that we use an int to hold the return from these functions:

```
int ch;      //  NOTE: int, not char!!!!
//   loop to read and write all the data in the input
while ((ch = cin.get()) != EOF)
          cout.put(ch);
```

This program operates identically to one on page 834, the only difference being the version of get that is used to read the input.

A.3.7 Multi-Byte Operations

Other unformatted IO operations deal with chunks of data at a time. These operations can be important if speed is an issue, but like other low-level operations they are error-prone. In particular, these operations require us to allocate and manage the character arrays (Section 4.3.1, p. 134) used to store and retrieve data.

The multi-byte operations are listed in Table A.5 (p. 837). It is worth noting that the get member is overloaded; there is a third version that reads a sequence of characters.

CAUTION: LOW-LEVEL ROUTINES ARE ERROR-PRONE

In general, we advocate using the higher-level abstractions provided by the library. The IO operations that return `int` are a good example of why.

It is a common programming error to assign the return from `get` or one of the other `int` returning functions to a `char` rather than an `int`. Doing so is an error but an error the compiler will not detect. Instead, what happens depends on the machine and on the input data. For example, on a machine in which `char`s are implemented as `unsigned char`s, this loop will run forever:

```
char ch;        // Using a char here invites disaster!
// return from cin.get is converted from int to char and then compared to an int
while ((ch = cin.get()) != EOF)
        cout.put(ch);
```

The problem is that when `get` returns `EOF`, that value will be converted to an `unsigned char` value. That converted value is no longer equal to the integral value of `EOF`, and the loop will continue forever.

At least that error is likely to be caught in testing. On machines for which `char`s are implemented as `signed char`s, we can't say with confidence what the behavior of the loop might be. What happens when an out-of-bounds value is assigned to a `signed` value is up to the compiler. On many machines, this loop will appear to work, unless a character in the input matches the EOF value. While such characters are unlikely in ordinary data, presumably low-level IO is necessary only when reading binary values that do not map directly to ordinary characters and numeric values. For example, on our machine, if the input contains a character whose value is `'\377'` then the loop terminates prematurely. `'\377'` is the value on our machine to which -1 converts when used as a `signed char`. If the input has this value, then it will be treated as the (premature) end-of-file indicator.

Such bugs do not happen when reading and writing typed values. If you can use the more type-safe, higher-level operations supported by the library, do so.

The `get` and `getline` functions take the same parameters, and their actions are similar but not identical. In each case, `sink` is a `char` array into which the data are placed. The functions read until one of the following conditions occurs:

- `size - 1` characters are read
- End-of-file is encountered
- The delimiter character is encountered

Following any of these conditions, a null character is put in the next open position in the array. The difference between these functions is the treatment of the delimiter. `get` leaves the delimiter as the next character of the `istream`. `getline` reads and discards the delimiter. In either case, the delimiter is *not* stored in `sink`.

It is a common error to intend to remove the delimiter from the stream but to forget to do so.

Table A.5: Multi-Byte Low-Level IO Operations
`is.get(sink, size, delim)`
Reads up to `size` bytes from `is` and stores them in the character array pointed to by `sink`. Reads until encountering the `delim` character or until it has read `size` bytes or encounters end-of-file. If the `delim` is present, it is left on the input stream and not read into `sink`.
`is.getline(sink, size, delim)`
Same behavior as three-argument version of `get` but reads and discards `delim`.
`is.read(sink, size)`
Reads up to `size` bytes into the character array `sink`. Returns `is`.
`is.gcount()` Returns number of bytes read from the stream `is` by last call to an unformatted read operation.
`os.write(source, size)`
Writes `size` bytes from the character array `source` to `os`. Returns `os`.
`is.ignore(size, delim)`
Reads and ignores at most `size` characters up to but not including `delim`. By default, `size` is 1 and `delim` is end-of-file.

Determining How Many Characters Were Read

Several of the read operations read an unknown number of bytes from the input. We can call `gcount` to determine how many characters the last unformatted input operation read. It is esssential to call `gcount` before any intervening unformatted input operation. In particular, the single-character operations that put characters back on the stream are also unformatted input operations. If `peek`, `unget`, or `putback` are called before calling `gcount`, then the return value will be 0!

A.3.8 Random Access to a Stream

The various stream types generally support random access to the data in their associated stream. We can reposition the stream so that it skips around, reading first the last line, then the first, and so on. The library provides a pair of functions to *seek* to a given location and to *tell* the current location in the associated stream.

Random IO is an inherently system-dependent. To understand how to use these features, you must consult your system's documentation.

Seek and Tell Functions

To support random access, the IO types maintain a marker that determines where the next read or write will happen. They also provide two functions: One repositions the marker by *seek*ing to a given position; the second *tell*s us the current position of the marker. The library actually defines two pairs of *seek* and *tell* functions, which are described in Table A.6. One pair is used by input streams, the other by output streams. The input and output versions are distinguished by a suffix that is either a g or a p. The g versions indicate that we are "getting" (reading) data, and the p functions indicate that we are "putting" (writing) data.

Table A.6: Seek and Tell Functions	
seekg	Reposition the marker in an input stream
tellg	Return the current position of the marker in an input stream
seekp	Reposition the marker for an output stream
tellp	Return the current position of the marker in an output stream

Logically enough, we can use only the g versions on an istream or its derived types ifstream, or istringstream, and we can use only the p versions on an ostream or its derived types ofstream, and ostringstream. An iostream, fstream, or stringstream can both read and write the associated stream; we can use either the g or p versions on objects of these types.

There Is Only One Marker

The fact that the library distinguishes between the "putting" and "getting" versions of the seek and tell functions can be misleading. Even though the library makes this distinction, it maintains only a single marker in the file—there is *not* a distinct read marker and write marker.

When we're dealing with an input-only or output-only stream, the distinction isn't even apparent. We can use only the g or only the p versions on such streams. If we attempt to call tellp on an ifstream, the compiler will complain. Similarly, it will not let us call seekg on an ostringstream.

When using the fstream and stringstream types that can both read and write, there is a single buffer that holds data to be read and written and a single marker denoting the current position in the buffer. The library maps both the g and p positions to this single marker.

 Because there is only a single marker, we *must* do a seek to reposition the marker whenever we switch between reading and writing.

Plain iostreams Usually Do Not Allow Random Access

The seek and tell functions are defined for all the stream types. Whether they do anything useful depends on the kind of object to which the stream is bound. On most systems, the streams bound to cin, cout, cerr and clog do *not* support random access—after all, what would it mean to jump ten places back when writing directly to cout? We can call the seek and tell functions, but these functions will fail at run time, leaving the stream in an invalid state.

Because the `istream` and `ostream` types usually do not support random access, the remainder of this section should be considered as applicable to only the `fstream` and `sstream` types.

Repositioning the Marker

The `seekg` and `seekp` functions are used to change the read and write positions in a file or a `string`. After a call to `seekg`, the read position in the stream is changed; a call to `seekp` sets the position at which the next write will take place.

There are two versions of the seek functions: One moves to an "absolute" address within the file; the other moves to a byte offset from a given position:

```
// set the indicated marker a fixed position within a file or string
seekg(new_position);    // set read marker
seekp(new_position);    // set write marker

// offset some distance from the indicated position
seekg(offset, dir);     // set read marker
seekp(offset, dir);     // set write marker
```

The first version sets the current position to a given location. The second takes an offset and an indicator of where to offset from. The possible values for the offset are listed in Table A.7.

Table A.7: Offset From Argument to `seek`	
`beg`	The beginning of the stream
`cur`	The current position of the stream
`end`	The end of the stream

The argument and return types for these functions are machine-dependent types defined in both `istream` or `ostream`. The types, named `pos_type` and `off_type`, represent a file position and an offset from that position, respectively. A value of type `off_type` can be positive or negative; we can `seek` forward or backward in the file.

Accessing the Marker

The current position is returned by either `tellg` or `tellp`, depending on whether we're looking for the read or write position. As before, the `p` indicates putting (writing) and the `g` indicates getting (reading). The `tell` functions are usually used to remember a location so that we can subsequently `seek` back to it:

```
// remember current write position in mark
ostringstream writeStr;   // output stringstream
ostringstream::pos_type mark = writeStr.tellp();
```

```
// ...
if (cancelEntry)
        // return to marked position
        writeStr.seekp(mark);
```

The `tell` functions return a value that indicates the position in the associated stream. As with the `size_type` of a `string` or `vector`, we do not know the actual type of the object returned from `tellg` or `tellp`. Instead, we use the `pos_type` member of the appropriate stream class.

A.3.9 Reading and Writing to the Same File

Let's look at a programming example. Assume we are given a file to read. We are to write a new line at the end of the file that contains the relative position at which each line begins. For example, given the following file,

```
abcd
efg
hi
j
```

the program should produce the following modified file:

```
abcd
efg
hi
j
5 9 12 14
```

Note that our program need not write the offset for the first line—it always occurs at position 0. It should print the offset that corresponds to the end of the data portion of the file. That is, it should record the position after the end of the input so that we'll know where the original data ends and where our output begins.

We can write this program by writing a loop that reads a line at a time:

```
int main()
{
        // open for input and output and pre-position file pointers to end of file
        fstream inOut("copyOut",
                        fstream::ate | fstream::in | fstream::out);
        if (!inOut) {
            cerr << "Unable to open file!" << endl;
            return EXIT_FAILURE;
        }
        // inOut is opened in ate mode, so it starts out positioned at the end,
        // which we must remember as it is the original end-of-file position
        ifstream::pos_type end_mark = inOut.tellg();
        inOut.seekg(0, fstream::beg);  // reposition to start of the file
        int cnt = 0;                   // accumulator for byte count
        string line;                   // hold each line of input
```

```
    //  while we haven't hit an error and are still reading the original data
    //  and successfully read another line from the file
    while (inOut && inOut.tellg() != end_mark
                && getline(inOut, line))
    {
        cnt += line.size() + 1;     //  add 1 to account for the newline
    //  remember current read marker
    ifstream::pos_type mark = inOut.tellg();
        inOut.seekp(0, fstream::end);//  set write marker to end
        inOut << cnt;                //  write the accumulated length
        //  print separator if this is not the last line
        if (mark != end_mark) inOut << " ";
        inOut.seekg(mark);           //  restore read position
    }
    inOut.clear();                   //  clear flags in case we hit an error
    inOut.seekp(0, fstream::end);    //  seek to end
    inOut << "\n";                   //  write a newline at end of file

    return 0;
}
```

This program opens the fstream using the in, out, and ate modes. The first two modes indicate that we intend to both read and write to the same file. By also opening it in ate mode, the file starts out positioned at the end. As usual, we check that the open succeeded, and exit if it did not.

Initial Setup

The core of our program will loop through the file a line at a time, recording the relative position of each line as it does so. Our loop should read the contents of the file up to but not including the line that we are adding to hold the line offsets. Because we will be writing to the file, we can't just stop the loop when it encounters end-of-file. Instead, the loop should end when it reaches the point at which the original input ended. To do so, we must first remember the original end-of-file position.

We opened the file in ate mode, so it is already positioned at the end. We store the initial end position in end_mark. Of course, having remembered the end position, we must reposition the read marker at the beginning of the file before we attempt to read any data.

Main Processing Loop

Our while loop has a three-part condition.

We first check that the stream is valid. Assuming the first test on inOut succeeds, we then check whether we've exhausted our original input. We do this check by comparing the current read position returned from tellg with the position we remembered in end_mark. Finally, assuming that both tests succeeded, we call getline to read the next line of input. If getline succeeds, we perform the body of the loop.

The job that the while does is to increment the counter to determine the offset at which the next line starts and write that marker at the end of the file. Notice that the end of the file advances on each trip through the loop.

We start by remembering the current position in `mark`. We need to keep that value because we have to reposition the file in order to write the next relative offset. The `seekp` call does this repositioning, resetting the file pointer to the end of the file. We write the counter value and then restore the file position to the value we remembered in `mark`. The effect is that we return the marker to the same place it was after the last read. Having restored the marker, we're ready to repeat the condition in the `while`.

Completing the File

Once we exit the loop, we have read each line and calculated all the starting offsets. All that remains is to print the offset of the last line. As with the other writes, we call `seekp` to position the file at the end and write the value of `cnt`. The only tricky part is remembering to `clear` the stream. We might exit the loop due to an end-of-file or other input error. If so, `inOut` would be in an error state, and both the `seekp` and the output expression would fail.

Index

Bold face numbers refer to the page on which the term was first defined.
Numbers in *italic* refer to the "Defined Terms" section in which the term is defined.

Q

R

U

Additional C++ Books from Addison-Wesley

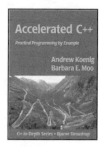

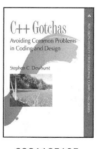